THE CATHOLIC ELEMENTARY SCHOOL PRINCIPAL

To My Mother and Father

THE CATHOLIC ELEMENTARY SCHOOL PRINCIPAL

SISTER M. JEROME CORCORAN, O.S.U., PH.D.

URSULINE SISTERS, YOUNGSTOWN, OHIO

DIOCESAN SUPERVISOR, DIOCESE OF YOUNGSTOWN

SPECIAL CHAPTERS BY

LEO WARD, C.S.C.; W. W. THEISEN, PH.D.; JOHN P. TREACY, PH.D.

THE BRUCE PUBLISHING COMPANY

MILWAUKEE

Nihil obstat:

✠ JAMES W. MALONE, D.D.
Auxiliary Bishop of Youngstown
Censor deputatus

Imprimatur:

✠ EMMET M. WALSH, D.D.
Bishop of Youngstown
January 5, 1961

Library of Congress Catalog Card Number: 61–11246

© 1961 The Bruce Publishing Company

Made in the United States of America

CONTENTS

CONTENTS

ACKNOWLEDGMENT

THE writer wishes to express her appreciation to the many persons who have contributed directly and indirectly to the writing of this book.

For encouragement and co-operation through the various phases of the work, the writer wishes to express her appreciation to her General Superiors, Mother M. Blanche, O.S.U., and Mother Edna Marie, O.S.U. For assistance in the tedious details of indexing and proofreading, special thanks are due to Sister Agnes Marie, O.S.U., and Sister Francis de Sales, O.S.U. For their suggestions and constructive criticisms, the author is deeply grateful to the Sisters of her own community and of the many other communities with whom she has been associated.

For providing professional materials and clerical services in preparation of the manuscript, the writer is grateful to The Most Reverend James W. Malone, D.D., Ph.D., Auxiliary Bishop of Youngstown and Diocesan Superintendent of Schools.

For their practical and timely approach to the topics of their chapters, the writer wishes to express appreciation to Reverend Leo R. Ward, C.S.C., Dr. John P. Treacy, Ph.D., and Dr. W. W. Theisen, Ph.D. Their command of their subjects makes their contributions valuable indeed.

For his generous and creative work in illustrating several ideas in the text, the writer is grateful to Paul Smith, Youngstown, commercial artist. For his expert rendering of the parish map in Chapter XI the writer wishes to thank Nicholas Horney, industrial arts teacher in Struthers High School, Struthers, Ohio.

For permission to reprint from their publications, the writer expresses her appreciation to the publishers of various books and magazines. Specific acknowledgment of authorship is given with each quotation.

Finally, the writer wishes to express her thanks for all that she has learned from the Sister Principals whom she has known, and who, she hopes, may get some little help or inspiration from this book written especially for them.

THE AUTHOR

vii

THE CATHOLIC ELEMENTARY SCHOOL PRINCIPAL

CHAPTER I

INTRODUCTION: THE ROLE AND STATUS OF THE CATHOLIC ELEMENTARY PRINCIPAL

John P. Treacy, Ph.D.*

> Progress in any aspect of education is influenced greatly by the leadership provided. One source of leadership in Catholic elementary schools is the Sister Principal. In general, does she exert the leadership that should be expected? How can the Sister Principal exert still more effective leadership?

THE REAL PROBLEM OF CATHOLIC EDUCATION

IN ANALYZING the many urgent problems facing Catholic education we are likely to lose perspective as to what really is most important. We may be justifiably concerned about the condition of our buildings, or of our equipment, or of our playground. We may question whether or not the curriculum is what it should be. We may note with some apprehension the increasing enrollments, and the shortage of teachers to instruct this expanding elementary school population.

These problems, and others, should be the concern of every Catholic educator. But they should not distract him from what is most important to the schooling of any child, namely, *good teaching in the classroom.*

Providing good teaching in every classroom is no simple matter. It involves, among other things, effective recruitment and selection of teaching candidates; it requires effective pre-service teacher education; it demands sacrifices on the part of parents in providing the conditions necessary for good teaching; and finally, it requires administrative and supervisory leadership which will help each teacher to develop and use all of her potential teaching ability.

Leadership for Catholic elementary schools is found in various personnel, such as principals, diocesan superintendents, supervisors, and pastors. The

* Professor of Education, Marquette University.

3

present book by Sister Mary Jerome, O.S.U., is concerned primarily with helping the Catholic elementary school principal carry out effectively her role as an educational leader — in all of her activities, but particularly in improving the quality of classroom teaching in her school.

THE CATHOLIC ELEMENTARY PRINCIPAL AS EDUCATIONAL LEADER

Leadership in the improvement of classroom teaching suggests to some educators only such activities as classroom visitation, conferences, supervisory visits, teachers' meetings, and other traditional procedures. Good elementary principals use some of these approaches; but real leadership is more comprehensive, more basic, often more subtle.

A Catholic elementary principal who has a broad and deep concept of educational leadership helps her teachers to develop a sound concept of what Catholic education should be; to understand human nature in general, and each pupil in particular; to appreciate the dignity and worth of each pupil; to study the unique forces in the community, and to adjust teaching accordingly; to realize the importance of co-operating with persons and agencies outside of the school; to differentiate between classroom mechanics and the real requisites of good teaching; to see teaching as the art of co-operating "with Divine Grace in forming Christ in those regenerated in Baptism" (Pius XI); so to perfect themselves that much "wordless teaching" will take place; and to evaluate children in terms of all the objectives of their teaching, and not just those which can be objectively measured. In general, an effective elementary principal will help her teachers to see education and teaching in their broader perspectives, and to guide their pupils accordingly.

In performing her role as educational leader, the ideal Catholic elementary principal will be on the alert for unique talents in her teachers, and will provide opportunities for the release and development of these latent forces. She will utilize the traditional approaches to supervision; but she will use other means, some of which are highly individualized.

PRESENT STATUS OF THE CATHOLIC ELEMENTARY PRINCIPALSHIP

To what extent do our Catholic elementary principals conform to this high standard of leadership? There is much that is encouraging in Catholic elementary administration. Many principals are fully trained for their work, with sufficient time free from teaching to give the professional leadership needed. Almost always one finds acting as principal a devoted Sister, making the most of conditions and facilities, and a staff that is responsive to the leadership provided.

But, there are weaknesses as well as strengths in the administration of some elementary schools, public and non-public. Some principals have little or no time free from teaching; some principals have little or no specific preparation in administration or supervision; some were chosen more for their experience, or for their success in discipline than for their interest or ability in administration. Because of these conditions, some elementary schools are not organized or administered as well as they should be — and instruction suffers accordingly.

WHY PRESENT WEAKNESSES?

Why do we have these weaknesses in elementary administration? Various reasons may be given for these conditions:

1. The shortage of teachers is so great that it is sometimes difficult to free a principal from teaching duties for administrative and supervisory leadership. In some situations the duties ordinarily associated with the principalship are performed by individuals other than the principal. In the absence of secretarial help, principals often must give much time to clerical duties. Occasionally, some authorities are not convinced that administrative and supervisory leadership is needed for effective work in the classroom.

2. Real administrative preparation involves graduate training and this, in turn, involves talent, time, and money. Then, too, the shortage of adequately trained teachers has brought about an emphasis on *teacher* preparation, rather than on *principal* preparation. Actually, attention to the principalship would help to make the most of the teachers who are available.

3. There are too few professional courses specifically designed for principals of elementary schools.

4. Professional literature on the problems of Catholic elementary principals is far from adequate. For example, at the present time there is not a single recent book on the problems of the Catholic elementary principalship to which a Mother Superior might refer a Sister newly appointed to such a position. It is true that there are some recent books for public school principals, and there are many common elements in public and Catholic administration. But there are enough problems peculiar to Catholic schools to warrant specific literature in this field.

5. Another possible explanation of weaknesses in the elementary principalship is that *too little thought and effort have been given to elementary administration as a profession*. If educational leaders of the past one hundred years had fully appreciated the relationship between capable administrative

leadership and the success of a given elementary school, they probably would have shown more concern about providing this leadership.

ROOTS OF THE CATHOLIC ELEMENTARY PRINCIPALSHIP

Of course, there are some good explanations of why early Catholic educators did not give attention to administrative leadership:

1. While there were some parochial schools from early colonial days, there was little evidence of anything resembling a *system* of Catholic elementary schools until comparatively recent times. No really positive legislation was enacted until 1884, when the Plenary Council of Baltimore issued the decree, still in force, which required, among other things, that within two years a parochial school be erected near each church, if such a school did not already exist. This Council stated that "all Catholic parents are bound to send their children to the parochial schools, unless either at home or in other Catholic schools they may sufficiently and evidently provide for the Christian education of their children, or unless it be lawful to send them to other schools on account of a sufficient cause, approved by the bishop, and with opportune cautions and remedies."[1]

2. Administration (and supervision) as a distinct profession is relatively recent, in all types of schools. See the bibliographies in pioneer books in the field as evidence of this.[2]

3. Large elementary schools, requiring detailed and efficient planning and administration, are comparatively recent. As late as 1920 the average number of teachers per Catholic elementary school was less than seven.

4. According to Browne, there was at one time a plan to make pastors, trained in pedagogy in the seminary, responsible for the administration of parish schools. However, the elementary principal soon was coming into her own:

> Directly at the head of the parish school was the principal who taught classes herself while striving to improve instruction throughout the school along with meeting parents, salesmen, and other representatives of the public. In the face of this the pastor who exercised a brand of benign and indirect supervision was soon looked upon as closer to the ideal than either the one who was always in the school or the one who never concerned himself.[3]

The increased complexity of the parish school, the continued professional-

---

[1] See *A History of Catholic Education in the United States* by J. A. Burns and Bernard J. Kohlbrenner (New York: Benziger Bros., 1937), for a detailed account of this topic.

[2] For example: W. H. Burton, *Supervision and Improvement of Teaching* (New York: D. Appleton and Company, 1923), and E. P. Cubberley, *The Principal and His School* (New York: Houghton Mifflin Co., 1923).

[3] Rev. Henry J. Browne, "The American Parish School in the Last Half Century," National Catholic Education Association, *Proceedings*, Vol. 50, August, 1953, p. 327.

ization of administration and supervision, and other demands on the pastor have resulted in his giving less attention to the immediate administration of the parish school. Browne noted in the article referred to above that:

> The trend in pastoral overseeing through the years has been toward diminution. By 1916 the pastor was being urged to take an interest in the school and ten years later the hope was being expressed that he might be of service in diocesan supervision. Four years after that it was devoutly desired that the parochial clergyman take a systematic part in the religious instruction of the school. He was reminded in 1940 that a course in theology did not automatically make him a good catechist.[4]

When we consider the recency of a real system of Catholic education, the recency of elementary administration as a profession, and the typical size of early Catholic elementary schools, it becomes evident why there has not been much emphasis on the Catholic elementary school principalship as a profession until quite recently.

EVIDENCE OF INTEREST INCREASING

On July 9, 1954, Very Rev. Monsignor William E. McManus addressed the annual convention of Serra International on the topic, "Ten Points for Catholic Education."[5] In this penetrating analysis of what is needed in Catholic education we find these key statements:

1. Dedicate the whole Catholic school enterprise — everything from fund raising to teacher training — to the honor and glory of God.
2. Conduct an intensive crusade of prayer for vocations to the religious life.
3. Recruit competent lay teachers, give them status as full-fledged members of the faculty; guarantee them security and tenure; pay them a living wage.
4. Maintain high professional standards.
5. Develop a reasonable procedure to select the students to be admitted to available accommodations.
6. Utilize Catholic schools to provide systematic religious instruction and extra-curricular activities for Catholic public school pupils.
7. Plan now for expanded high school facilities to accommodate by 1965 at least twice the number of students now enrolled in our Catholic high schools.
8. Economize on both building and operating costs by eliminating expensive frills.
9. Equalize the burden of financing Catholic schools by requesting all Catholic wage-earners — not only parents — to contribute a fixed yearly sum based on their annual income with due allowance for dependents and other standard deductions as permitted under our Federal income-tax laws.
10. Every parish school ought to have a home and school association.

---

[4] *Ibid.*, p. 327.
[5] Reprinted in *The Catholic Mind*, 52:710–717, Dec., 1954.

No. 4 above, "Maintain high professional standards," surely applies to the elementary principalship as well as to teachers.

There have been reported some discussions on the work of the Catholic elementary school principal at the annual conventions of the National Catholic Education Association. In the *Index* to articles appearing in the *Bulletin* of this organization from 1934–1948, one article pertaining to the elementary principal was listed under "Supervision." Recent issues of the *Bulletin* reflect more interest in this topic.[6] It is true, too, that some of the articles in the *Bulletins* can be adapted to the needs of the elementary principal.

The *Sister Formation Bulletin* is shot through with references to the need for capable classroom teachers, and to ways of developing such teachers. Much of this attention has been given to the *pre-service* aspect of teacher education. Three articles in recent issues of the *Sister Formation Bulletin* suggest that in-service education may receive more attention in the future: "A Community In-Service Program" (Sister Elizabeth Ann, I.H.M., December, 1955, pp. 21–22); "The In-Service Sister and the Problem of Time" (Winter, 1959, pp. 10–19); and, "The Education of Religious in Extension Courses" (Sister M. Thomas Aquinas, R.S.M., Spring, 1959, pp. 4–9).

An examination of recent articles in two other Catholic educational magazines — the *Catholic Educational Review* and the *Catholic School Journal* — showed that increased attention is being given to the specific problems of the Catholic elementary principal. Some articles in the *Catholic Management Journal* can be adapted to the needs of the elementary school.

Fortunately, the Catholic elementary school principalship as a profession probably has advanced further than the literature would seem to indicate. Some of this progress can be explained through a high degree of personal initiative among present principals of Catholic elementary schools.

SOME EFFECTS OF ADMINISTRATIVE LEADERSHIP

What are the effects of administrative leadership? In so far as any school lacks adequate administrative leadership, that school is likely to suffer. There may be a lack of comprehensive planning, of co-ordination, of self-evaluation. There may be limited teacher growth because of inadequate professional inspiration and guidance. There may be inefficiency in pupil welfare services, in pupil records, in plant management. There may be only "good" achievement where there are possibilities for excellence. There may be, and probably will be, a caliber of service to pupils and parents which falls short of what education should be.

---

[6] See, for example, "The Responsibility of the Principal to the Classroom Teacher," by Sister Aloyse Marie, S.N.D. de Namur in the 1958 *Proceedings*, pp. 253–259.

Improvement of administrative leadership in Catholic elementary schools will require a conviction among educators that the principalship is a profession which requires a competent and trained personnel; and that the time and effort given to professional administrative leadership will pay excellent dividends in teaching and learning, and consequently, in parental co-operation and support for all education.

THE SCOPE OF THIS BOOK

In the chapters which follow are found much helpful information and many stimulating thoughts for the alert Catholic elementary school principal. Chapter II reviews educational principles which should be basic to all Catholic elementary education. Chapter III shows the relationship of the Catholic elementary principal to other personnel: the bishop, the mother superior, the pastor, and the like. Chapter IV provides an analysis of the principal's main functions — planning, organizing, directing, and evaluating. Chapter V analyzes one of a principal's major problems, the distribution of her time. Chapter VI contains suggestions for meeting the problems growing out of the increasing proportion of lay teachers. Chapter VII recognizes the problem of providing good working conditions in the school. Chapter VIII raises and answers the perennial question, What is good teaching? Chapters IX and X are devoted to the most important aspect of administration and supervision: the in-service growth of teachers. Chapter XI relates the work of the school to other forces in the community. Chapter XII recognizes the importance of public relations in elementary education, and offers some concrete suggestions for the principal. Chapter XIII reviews principles of evaluation in education, and points out the principal's function in this area. This discussion leads naturally to grades, records, and reports — discussed in Chapter XIV. Chapter XV, "Special Services for Children," exemplifies the recent trend among principals to regard education as going beyond the work done in the classroom, through pupil guidance, health programs, food service, and the like. Chapter XVI, on clerical service, points out one means of finding time for the really professional duties of the principal. Chapter XVII provides the basic information which principals and pastors should know about the school plant. The last chapter provides a framework by which a principal may evaluate her own progress as an administrator and supervisor.

Earlier in this chapter it was stated that adequate attention probably has not been given to the elementary school principalship as a profession. The present work by Sister Mary Jerome, O.S.U., is an excellent contribution to this field and will help to meet a growing need.

CHAPTER II

PRINCIPLES FOR PRINCIPALS

Leo R. Ward, C.S.C.*

> Whether or not a teacher knows it, she always exemplifies in her teaching some philosophy of education. The ideal principal is aware of basic educational issues and principles, and strives to alert her staff members to them. Certain of these fundamentals are discussed in the pages which follow.

TOGETHER with the teachers, the principal of a Catholic school is dedicated, and the whole work of the school is seen as a sacred work, co-creative with the total work of God in the world. Faith and fractions are almost as if out of the same book. The reason is simple. Just as we reject the principle of divorcing faith and works, so we reject the principle and the practice of divorcing the life of faith and the life of study.

Being a principal, running a school, teaching a class — this is a kind of divine work. Take some parallels. The Christian physician has a great work to do for God and man, and so has the Sister in charge of a hospital. The Sister who is a principal has a work that is even greater because it is more directly spiritual.

Dignity of the Child. A first principle with teachers and administrators in schools is that the child is a being of dignity and importance. We can express this by saying that a person's body and soul are sacred and that the child is the child of God as well as the child of man.

All Catholics, and in fact all Christians, accept the principle just stated. At least they go with it in theory. To accept it in fact may at times be difficult, because such accidents as color or national origin may get in the way. Our task is to learn to bypass these accidents. Really accepting the principle means respecting every child's dignity and every child's freedom. It

---

* Professor of Philosophy, University of Notre Dame.

also means respecting him as an individual and as just this child in his mysterious identity.

Father James Keller has said this in simple words. "Treat every child as an individual. God gives slightly different talents and personalities to every child He sends into the world."

This child is a child like any other. And yet he is really and truly different. In the whole of time and the whole of the human race, this child is unique and unrepeatable. "Be it ever so homely, there's no face like your own." God and nature never before made a child just like this one and will never again exactly match him. As teachers and principals we are called to reverence him, first, as a child, second, as this individual child, and third, as this child of God. That, of course, is the way our principals and teachers do see the child. But here and throughout this chapter our aim is to clarify basic principles.

Children Are Persons. The child is to be respected as a person and as precisely this person. Being a person means being blessed in a special way by God and nature. A person is a being endowed from the first with freedom. Even from the start the child has initial and fundamental freedom. This initial freedom enables the quite young child to make some choices. The world is in many ways wished on him, and he might well say, "World I never made." Yet choice soon begins to be within his reach.

Using that first and initial freedom, the child is going to make or break himself, though of course both heredity and environment are big factors, along with his initial freedom, helping the child either to develop as a person or to handicap himself as a person.

The Catholic principal will want to understand a second freedom. This is a developed and won freedom — the child does not start with it. Using his initial freedom, the child can progressively free himself. He thereby has a new freedom, which is a won freedom. He can become great in the control and management of his own spiritual powers and in capitalizing on divine aids. He can become a wise, learned, and prudent man, and can give himself generously to the service of mankind.

It is true that, using his initial freedom, he can enslave himself and wreck himself. Hence the importance of the Catholic school, in which the child has the opportunity to learn reverence for all things, including freedom itself.

We all see that freedom in any one of us has those two distinct meanings. One is *initial* freedom and the other is *won* freedom. Education, rightly understood, recognizes and respects the first, and is engaged in helping the child to use that first so as to gain the second. The first has no degrees, the second is found in the most various degrees.

We stand in awe before the child because he has that first freedom, and because he can use it so as to become more and more completely free. In that way, man is truly free and truly man. In him, being free becomes at last a state or condition, as St. Paul says. It is a state of his being. It is what the philosopher Jacques Maritain calls a vital spiritual energy. The common word for that energy or state of being is "habit."

Every little child has within him this immense power of freedom to develop and to be developed. We in the schools want to help him. Of course, thinking about any such power is beyond the child. But with the aid of doctrines and liturgy and sacraments, the child can be guided along lines that will enable him to begin to develop the power.

Built-in Habits. In this regard the child is, above all, learning to be generous and self-sacrificial. And he is learning at the same time to understand something. He is learning to understand both *how to be good* and *that being good and doing good is itself a good thing.* He does two great things at once — he develops a built-in habit of doing good, and he more and more understands good.

Once we get "well set" in this built-in habit of acquired freedom, or again in the built-in habit of intellectual virtue, we can readily do the works corresponding to the habit. The good habit becomes like nature to us, and that is what pagans as well as Christians have always said. Habit is "second nature." Once we have the habit well established, we can do its proper works almost as simply as the bird flies or the bee makes honey: it is then our "nature."

Schools are maintained at much cost, in order to help children gain this remarkable command over their own powers and their own life of reason and love. If this is true of all schools, it is doubly true of Catholic schools, with their dedicated faculties and their dedicated Catholic public. We pay for these schools and work in them because of profound belief in the spiritual good and the total good of the child. At a time when the public is clamoring for spiritual and moral values in the life of society, and above all in the lives of youths, principals in Catholic schools can proceed in the confidence that their schools are established and operated for the sake of those values.

The job of helping youths to shed and to avoid an overemphasized self-seeking is a major task of those who tutor children, in school or out of school. What can principals and teachers do about it? Besides leading them to learn great meaningful formulas such as "Unless the grain of seed falling into the ground die" and "He who loses his life shall find it," we can help them by example and encouragement to learn to give time and effort and attention to serving others.

We said that the child has at the start a great dignity and importance. As he grows up in his life of understanding and love, he has a greater dignity and importance. Often a child has real beauty. But it seems to us that, as he develops the capabilities given him by God and nature, he has greater beauty.

Born for Infinite Truth. The child is born for the heights. Once I taught a little girl who was already so generous that her father said, "That child would give you the bite out of her mouth." She had learned to be and act like that. Step by step, others can become masters of good things. As Aristotle and St. Thomas Aquinas say, the child is born for virtues, for both intellectual and moral virtues. He is born for excellence and perfection. Each of those philosophers says that any little child has quasi infinite powers for good and for truth.

If that is so, the teacher and principal and pastor must avoid humiliating and discouraging the child. The child can do immense things, and we in the schools have the vocation of providing the opportunity and every encouragement to him.

One way to see that the child is possessed of a sort of infinite power for good and truth is to see that the child, left to himself, tends to draw no color or credal or national line. The child readily takes to the human race — notice how quickly he can get immersed in world missions. The color, or nationality, or the former state of religion, is as if nothing to him. He likes every child as a child and playmate, and as a brother.

This ready interest suggests three things. It suggests the child's tendency to romance, his openness to the heroic, and his willingness to go at one leap far beyond our acquired prejudices and selfish and local interests. "Go, teach all nations" makes an immediate sense to him. He wants to belong to the community of mankind, the whole world of man and God. Notably since 1917, the popes have been inviting all Catholics to be like the child and to team up in important ways with the whole of humanity. The normal child is almost ahead of the popes. And what the popes have been asking, world conditions today demand. The child can easily understand this, and it is a lesson that can be unobtrusively worked into his lessons on geography and outer space and the stars, and his first steps in modern science. It all goes together. To teach and learn in this way is far better than to study religious lessons in a sort of vacuum, as if God and religion had little to do with the realities of human experience. We must bring the things of God and the things of time and man together in our thinking and living. So too we must keep bringing them together in our studies.

Good teachers and principals will also take care to see with children how hard a lesson it was for St. Peter to learn that all the things of all men, and the things they live by, are to be brought together in our life of faith (see Acts of the Apostles, c. 10, 9–30).

That, then, is one grand principle of educational philosophy — that any man has great dignity and importance and ought to be honored. The child ought to be honored. The foreigner or "DP" ought to be honored, and the poor man, and the ignorant. It is hard for us, of course, to honor the peddler of dope, but we must learn to do it. All men ought to be honored — no holds barred. One of the glories of the Church in America, and particularly of Catholic schools, is that, even in the South (e.g., in North Carolina) we have been leaders in applying this principle.

The Child's Nature Is Good. In the matters of learning and of right living, which are the basic things in human life, we must learn to go with the good nature of the child. Man is made to know and love and serve God, and also to know and love and serve man. The pope has the wonderful title, "Servant of the servants of God," and of course the principal and teacher and student are learning to take and deserve a like title: "Servant of the servants of God and of man."

Practical Learning Requires a Doing. The kind of practical learning just mentioned is always needed in any society and is more needed today because of world conditions, international and interplanetary. The famous young American medical doctor, Thomas A. Dooley, by generously serving the Vietnamese, helped himself and all of us to understand the rightness of unselfish and sacrificial love. Book learning will help, but by itself it is far from enough. This learning requires a doing.

Aristotle puts this truth in the following way. He says: Suppose a young man has acquired all the book learning that the best medical schools have. Is the young man therefore a good surgeon? The reply is that he might in fact be a butcher. Of course, this practical learning of the good in loving our neighbors is begun before we go to school, and does not develop only or mainly in school. Its first and greatest teacher is the home.

With the help of book learning, and most of all with the help of example and of a liturgical and a sacramental life, Catholic schools do an immense lot to help carry forward a work already begun at home and continued through the home and the Church.

The School's First Work. The school, private or public, has a yet more proper work than any good moral work. What it is called to do, and nothing else has this high mission, is to make the life the child's intellect good, even to make it excellent. Here we must keep our flags waving high. Intellectual life is what schools have always been set up for, and that is what we need them for now. Catholic schools have the advantage of including God and the truths of faith as objects to be known.

The school's main work is to assist and encourage and direct in intellectual matters. This is its primary and proper function. It is to teach and lead children to be good and avid readers, to be sharp and exact in arithmetic, to spell correctly, to master a clear and precise introduction to geography and history. Good little children who are lagging behind the national average in learning are of course far from the Catholic ideal.

The school might be helping Johnny to be a good and pious boy and to be well on his way to heaven, and this would be a wonderful thing to do. But if one Johnny after another can't read, there is something seriously wrong with the school. As the famous teacher Etienne Gilson has said, piety is good, but it may not be substituted for mastery of subject matter and command of methods of school work.

Father McGucken's Words. This decisive point was so well and simply made by the late Father McGucken that we are happy to repeat his statement of it.[1] He said that though the school aids the family and the Church in functions which are common to it and them, the school itself is set up to do a work that it alone can do. What is that work? Father McGucken replied:

> Surely it is conceivable that virtues can be developed by young people who never went to high school. . . . But if the school does not attend to intellectual training at all, is not concerned with the fact that its students are not mastering grammar or reading or whatever . . . then it is not merely a poor school; it forfeits the right to be called a school at all, even though it may be successful in developing the virtues of a Christian character.

Confusion Is No Merit. In that case, it does other people's work well, but neglects its own. Of course, if a school were really harming virtue and character, we would have to close it at once, just as in case a shoe factory or a library interfered with virtue, it would have to be closed. Still, the shoe factory's business is not to make people good, but to make shoes and to make good shoes. We have other setups for making people good, but no other for making shoes. Making shoes justifies the existence of the shoe factory. If the shoe factory got confused and set out to write poetry or to make people good — which really are better things to do — it would be no good in its own line. Let the shoemaker stick to his last.

The same holds for the school. It has a magnificent work to do for the child, and thereby for society. Let it mind its most important business. Let it do its principal work. If it set out to convert mankind or to save the world for democracy — fine goals, both of them — it would be confused, and would be neglecting its proper function.

Public schools are often blamed for trying to do everything except the one thing that schools are supposed to do. We may hope that parochial schools do not imitate them in this regard. Neither pastors nor patrons have the right to get in the way of vigorous intellectual achievement, and this is true whatever the level of the school.

---

[1] William J. McGucken, S.J., "Intelligence and Character," *National Catholic Educational Bulletin*, xxxvi (1940), pp. 10–12.

That is a point that should scarcely have to be made. In the famous Oregon school case (1925) the federal Supreme Court said that schools are beneficent institutions. But what is their particular good? They are good because they help the child to begin to know and understand in a systematic way. They are nurseries of the mind's life. An old man's hand can hardly grasp anything — things keep falling out of his hand. Minds which lack training are like that. Things drop through them. Such minds are like sieves.

The Child's Short Steps. Schools certainly do help us to develop other goods such as good citizenship. But in schools such good ends are secondary. The child is there in school to try to get acquainted with the world of God and nature and man. It is a big assignment and we are well advised in making every effort to avoid things that would get in its way. It sounds frightening when we say that the child is groomed by God to know everything in heaven and on earth. Not all at once, of course! He begins by short easy steps. He knows the thing X and then the thing Y and then the relation between them. Rome was not built in a day, but it was built, all the same. Easy does it. Little by little. One thing at a time.

The maturer person goes faster and takes in bigger things. A few great minds do finally take in all being. There are, however, only a dozen or so really great minds in the history of the Western world, minds like Aristotle's and Dante's and Einstein's. We do not expect the child to become one of them, though he might do it.

Mind of the Primitive. The Catholic scholar, Christopher Dawson, says that even the mind of the primitive man already grasps pure being. Look at these words by Dawson:[2]

It may seem paradoxical to suggest that the starting point of human progress is to be found in the highest type of knowledge — the intuition of pure being, but it must be remembered that intellectually, at least, man's development is not so much from the lower to the higher as from the confused to the distinct. Art and literature, for example, do not advance in the same continuous line of development as we find in material culture. A "low" culture can produce an art which is in its kind perfect and incapable of improvement. In the same way even the backward peoples possess a highly developed religious sense which at times expresses itself with an almost mystical intensity. The ultimate foundation of primitive religion is not a belief in ghosts or mythical beings, but an obscure and confused intuition of transcendent being.

Why cite these words of Dawson? Because they show that in even the humblest and most downtrodden child or family or group we may find a divine spark of intelligence. A particular child may come along slowly, and, kept under difficult circumstances, many may make little progress. But we

---

[2] Christopher Dawson, *Progress and Religion* (New York, London and Toronto: Longmans, Green, 1929), pp. 89–90.

need to see the other side of the coin. This tells us that any child can know, and that we may not set advance or arbitrary limits to the height and depth of his knowing.

First Steps Are Big Steps. The little pre-school child, even in his earliest years, learns things that are astounding. For one thing, he learns to talk. This means that he does far more than learn a foreign language — he learns language: words, grammar, meanings. He grasps a highly complex set of symbols. We know how wonderful it is that the deaf and dumb can express their ideas to each other. To do this they have to master a set of symbols, and very odd symbols at that, and learn to understand things and to say things. Which means that they must first have acquaintance with things or reality, and translate from things to a world of ideas in their own minds; then they must form signs or symbols that will transfer those ideas to other persons who can pick them up and who can relay other related ideas, expressive of things, back to the first deaf and dumb person. Quite a feat!

The little child, hardly past the infant stage, is doing even more. He has to go to reality, too, and translate it into ideas in his mind, and he has to grasp the whole world of signs and symbols absolutely from scratch and begin to fit it to ideas and things, and to "communicate," as we say, with other persons who are already equipped with that strange world of signs and symbols.

The child lives by sense, even in prenatal life. But it is a long step from that to intellectual life, and to be able to communicate with adults. The life of sense, just by itself, is animal life. Then almost in jig time the child learns to surpass any and all animals. In an incomparable article well called "Human Education,"[3] Dr. C. Gattegno expresses the child's intellectual power better than we can. He says that any normal child is ready for amazing growth. The statement is simple, yet resounding:

> The work of the intellect is an attribute of every functioning mind. It is only necessary to think of educating the intellectual powers of each individual through the means of exercises that extend the range of those powers in their normal, spontaneous state. This should be the aim and the method . . . Children use, at a very early age, analytic powers to distinguish likes from unlikes; they experience the apprenticeship of a whole language with complex structures and appropriate symbols. The symbolic games and spontaneous drawings which they create at the age of five to seven are of such complex structure that no school work, including mathematics, can ever compare with them.

Dr. Gattegno goes on to say that of course we want to prolong that remarkable and really wonderful life of spontaneous growth in the child.

[3] C. Gattegno, "Human Education," *Main Currents in Modern Thought*, v (Mar., 1959), p. 83.

God and Nature Are With the Child. God and nature want the child's mind to grow, and to grow is the natural tendency of the mind. It naturally wants to know things and to be filled with realities. St. Thomas says the human mind has "an affinity to reality." It would be wrong, because against nature and God, to balk this innate demand to know. It would be wrong to stall it by an inept curriculum, by progressivist distractions, or by doing other good things which nevertheless do not belong in the school.

"I came that you should have life and have it more abundantly." Nature existing and expressing itself in the child's mind says almost the same thing. Fullness of life is what the child's mind is demanding.

The child wants to know. That is why he asks so many questions and is so full of curiosity. Nature and God are speaking through him.

At first the child's mind fails to get a firm hold on things. The child does not yet know things as they are. As if to make up for his present deficiency, he keeps asking. Also his imagination runs riot and is not yet much checked (at least as adults see things) by fact or reality. When a little boy asks whether an angel flies on his back or his tummy, the question seems funny to us. It is perfectly serious to the boy. He really wants to know. When a child, hearing the word *nine*, asks what "nine" is, and is told it is three times three, he naturally wants to know what "three" is, and what "one" is.

Questions such as these seem as if planted in the child's mind. The truth is that the child's mind is made to know. His questions are the working out of a divine plan.

As St. Thomas sees the matter, what is happening when the child plagues us with questions is that God and nature are prodding him. The child did not start this — God did. The chick just has to come pecking at the egg shell and breaking out. That is the way with a child's mind — it is breaking out all over.

Knowing Is Being for the Mind. The mind of child or man naturally wants to be, and the only way it can be is by knowing. That is the only way it can come into its proper inheritance. This desire of the mind is part of a universal desire present in nature. St. Thomas puts the whole thing in a nutshell. He says that everything wants to be, and of course to be in its own type of being. That is the over-all goal of nature and of desire present in nature. Man wants to be, and the particular man Smith or Brown wants to be. Each group such as a family or a nation naturally wants to be. This demand "to be" runs also through such things as rabbits and oaks and oxygen. It is a universal natural desire.

So, it is no surprise to find the desire "to be" operating so strongly in a child's mind. The mind wants to be, and of course to be in its own type of being. It wants to know, and knowing, even in the smallest degree, is an installment on the mind's being.

Even that is only half the story. St. Augustine says that the end for man is that he should fully be. That is true also for the mind. No halfway measures will do for mind. It wants fully to be. That, then, is the magnificent work of the school and the principal and the teacher — helping this divinely implanted desire to come to fruition.

Intellect — an "Infinity Well." That is what schools are for and what they are good for — to help do this human-divine job. They help minds to come to be and fully to be. That is the role in which they make a fundamental sense. God is letting schools and principals and teachers help forward the creative process.

Interesting and encouraging also is the view of Aristotle and St. Thomas that the human mind has a kind of infinite quality. God knows all things, and in this as in other matters, man wants to be like God. That is the way he is made. Hence such a grand intellectual and spiritual development as modern science, seen in its proper light, is within the divine plan, as indeed Pope Pius XII often said.

Man is made to know all things. The goal is far, far off; but he is made for it. Men digging oil wells sometimes hit what they call an "infinity well." This is a well which, pumped for twenty-four hours, shows no signs of lowering: the oil is still right there at the top. Man's mind is an infinity well. If all the wisdom and science of all the richest and deepest minds were present together in one mind, even that mind would not have exhausted man's possibilities to know. Nor can we exhaust the height and depth of things to be known.

The Child Is the Principal Agent. How does the child's mind grow? Much as his body does. By nourishment and exercise. By stretching itself, by reaching up, by work.

The principal agent in this exercise and growth is the child. Learning is a job that occurs principally from the inside. The teacher cannot grow for the child. The teacher, though far more than a referee of play, is first and last a secondary agent. The mind needs good and real food. It also needs vision, heroes, scientists, saints to show it what it can do.

Philosopher's Meaning of "School." The school is the formal organization set up by knowledge-hungry humanity so that the child can have the best chance to get good intellectual food, good intellectual exercise, and real intellectual growth. The school gives the child a chance to know as God and nature want the child to know.

There is no other organization to do this job. The home has another work to do, and so has the Church. Without the school, the child in our society would remain intellectually a child. He would lack the arts and sciences, of course. But he would also lack introductory things like spelling. We do not want any children to remain even close to the lowest rung on the ladder. As Cardinal Newman said, we do not want any to remain intellectually infantile all their lives.

Hence the good and justification of schools. These aid children to begin to see things as they are and to have at least a minimal command over their power to know. This seems little enough, but it presupposes learning how to use the basic tools.

Adequate Basic Instruction. That distinguished promoter of intellectual learning, the Council for Basic Education, in its statement of purpose puts these matters in unforgettable terms. We quote two of the Council's aims:

> That all students without exception receive adequate instruction in the basic intellectual disciplines, especially English, mathematics, science, history, and foreign languages.
>
> That school administrators are encouraged and supported in resisting pressures to divert school time to activities of minor educational significance, to curricula overemphasizing social adjustment at the expense of intellectual discipline, and to programs that call upon the school to assume responsibilities belonging to the home, to religious bodies, and to other agencies.

The Council is speaking of public high schools. Can anyone see any reason why these two aims do not apply also to parochial schools and to education on all levels, and especially to students who have the necessary mental ability?

We may not fool away our time in any school. We are there to work. We teachers, principals, and pastors helping with schools may not lightly divert school time to activities of minor intellectual worth or to action programs at the expense of intellectual values. We are there to work. In these matters, good principals will be extremely careful to see that novelties do not sweep the child's time and interest out of line. As the Council for Basic Education says, the child is in school to learn. He is there to study such necessary things as arithmetic, spelling, grammar, and science. Certainly the child enjoys play and needs play, and it is a good thing for teachers to play, too. Many children will come to us more or less spoiled and will not like to work. That is unfortunate. But we have the job of assisting children to master the basic elements and tools and skills without which the child will go through life handicapped. For instance, a girl tried out as a secretary, but could not spell, and therefore could not take dictation directly or from a dictaphone, and could not file things. Another girl had to be released from the information bureau of an air line because both her spelling and geography were inadequate.

The poorly taught in grade school become problems in high school, and may remain problems. If children are deficient in school, the home and Church and nation are sure to suffer.

An Adequate Educational Program. With a work so important for both the child and the parish, we need the co-operation of all concerned. A pastor is lapsing if he says or implies, "Oh, well, they're good kids. Suppose they don't get their lessons — they're saving their souls." A pastor is doing wrong to the child, the parish, community, and the Church itself if he frequently disrupts the plan of the principal and the work of students and teachers. He may not justifiably break into the middle of the forenoon and lift children out of school. The scientific achievements of Russian Communists have given Americans quite a jar. From this lesson we should learn that a solid grasp of rudimentary learning takes time, and discipline, and hard work. That is why we have used the words, "We may not fool around" in school.

Principals have many exacting tasks, among them the task of working out an adequate educational program. Then there is the task of seeing that this adequate program is adequately achieved. We have to go through with it. To do all this requires the co-operation of principals and teachers and any priests who in any way work with schools.

Play, of course, and the worship of God, of course. But the child is in school, public or private, to study and learn. To disrupt the school program is a serious thing. A complaint often made by teachers in public schools on all levels is that the teacher is overloaded with extracurricular jobs. They are — so some of them say — distracted from their proper work. The result is that they do not have a fair chance to help children get their lessons.

Just that kind of thing could happen also in private and parochial schools. The writer knows a pastor who for some years had the seventh and eighth grade students sing the seven canonical hours five days a week. Something might be said for the procedure. All the same, the pastor was imposing on the children, the principal, the teachers, and the community. He was making it impossible to get topnotch intellectual results from those children. The good man handicapped everybody.

"An adequate program adequately carried out." This formula must be taken seriously and must be allowed to mean in practice just what it says.

Our Responsibility. Mothers and fathers are given a high responsibility when they are given children. At school, the child is put into our hands. For these school hours and for this work we teachers and principals and pastors stand in the place of the parents. We stand responsible to them, and to the Church and parish and nation and to God. That is why the words must be repeated: "An adequate program adequately carried out." Our primary reason for existence as a school is intellectual accomplishment, from the first grade right on up through college. That is our principal work — intellectual work, and helping the child's mind to grow up. In the school, other ends, no matter how good and holy, have to play second fiddle.

In and With the Whole Society. Another important principle is this: In our nation, the child comes out of a society that is mixed and heterogeneous, and that is the kind of society in which we will always live. We are not called to train him to be a hermit or to live in a monastery. As Cardinal Newman said, we are educating youths to live in the world.

We in the schools should learn to do our part to assist in preparing him to live in that type of society. It is a "mixed" society — mixed in the several types of economy by which it lives, mixed in its religious faiths, mixed in its political parties, mixed in its types of education. That is how American society exists and operates.

What difference does that make to the principal of a parochial school? Very much difference! First of all, we have to learn to work with many and various agencies and groups. That is good for us. It is a good thing, too, that the State makes definite minimal requirements on all schools. If it did not, the vast majority of public and private schools would soon sink to a low level. It is a good thing that the State sees to upgrading, and demands it. In the name of God and the community, the good principal will be happy to honor such requirements.

All schools profit by the observance of building laws and seating and fire-hazard laws. We who love God and man should be the first to demand these things. Principals and pastors should take the lead in going with such laws. These laws are for the good of the child and the good of society. Honoring all men and especially loving the child, zealous for Church and nation, the good pastor or the good principal will on occasion help to frame basic educational laws.

Another aspect of the same principle lies in the fact that originally our nation was one made out of many: e pluribus unum. That is what it still is. Our society is very much mixed. It is one made out of many, and if some Catholics or Jews or Protestants dislike its being that way, that nevertheless is the way it is and the way it is going to remain.

The whole society is mixed or "pluralistic." Catholic schools, and indeed any others, must take due account of this fact. It would be a shame if some children were given the impression in school that there are no other good schools but theirs, no good people but themselves. As Cardinal Cushing has said of such a view, "It could only lead to bigotry and intolerance." To begin with, it is a false view and could only lead to evil results.

Whether children in Catholic schools do superior work in reading or arithmetic or geography is a complicated question, and it cannot be justly settled by assertion and self-complacency. Pastors and principals and teachers should be careful to avoid giving the impression that we Catholics alone are eligible for the kingdom of heaven. Perhaps St. Peter still has some room for Baptists and Jehovah Witnesses. It is a right thing to know and maintain and promote our own position. It is another thing to be narrow and intolerant and unsympathetic.

God allows us to be part of a great nation which in its schools as in several other basic matters is one made up of many.

The Catholic school system is indeed remarkable and is obviously a major achievement of modern American life. But it has to be humble and acknowledge that it is neither the whole nor able to receive anything like all the Catholic children. It lacks the money and equipment and man power to do the total job that needs to be done for Catholics. With these bulky facts staring us in the face we have special reason to bless every good effort of public as well as private schools.

SELECTED REFERENCES

Ashley, Benedict, O.P., *The Arts of Learning and Communication* (Dubuque, Iowa: Priory Press, 1958).

Brubacher, John S., *Modern Philosophies of Education* (New York: McGraw-Hill, 2nd ed., 1950).

Christian Education of Youth, Encyclical by Pius XI, 1929, National Catholic Welfare Council. (This is also brought out by others, e.g., America Press, Paulist Press, and the Catholic Truth Society of London.)

Cunningham, William F., C.S.C., *The Pivotal Problems of Education* (New York: Macmillan, 1940), Ch. 17, "The Philosophy of Catholic Education."

McGucken, William J., S.J., *The Catholic Way in Education* (Milwaukee: Bruce, 1937).

—— *The Philosophy of Catholic Education* (New York: America Press, 1942).

Maritain, Jacques, *Education at the Crossroads* (Yale University Press, 1943).

O'Brien, Kevin J., C.Ss.R., *The Proximate Aim of Education* (Milwaukee: Bruce, 1958).

Power, Edward J., S.J., *Education for American Democracy* (New York: McGraw-Hill, 1958).

Redden, John, and Ryan, Francis A., *A Catholic Philosophy of Education* (Milwaukee: Bruce, 3rd printing, 1946); rev. ed., 1956, Ch. 1, "The Position of Philosophy in Education."

Report of the Everett Curriculum Workshop (Seattle: Heiden's Mailing Bureau, 1956).

Smith, Vincent E., *The School Examined* (Milwaukee: The Bruce Publishing Company, 1960).

Ward, Leo R., C.S.C., *New Life in Catholic Schools* (St. Louis: Herder, 1958).

Yzermans, Vincent A., *Pope Pius XII and Catholic Education* (St. Meinrad, Ind.: Grail Publications, 1957).

CHAPTER III

THE PRINCIPAL AND DIOCESAN SCHOOL ORGANIZATION*

Various personnel have responsibilities toward the education of the elementary school child. The bishop, the diocesan superintendent, the mother superior, the pastor, the sister principal, the diocesan school board, the supervisory staff, all of these, and others, are confronted with questions and problems regarding elementary education. This fact raises important questions for the sister principal: What is the function of each of these individuals or groups? What is my relationship to each? What difficulties may arise in the interrelationships of these personnel? How may I best meet these situations?

IT MAY be hard to convince her, but the fact remains — the Sister Principal is a central figure in the diocesan school organization. Trained in humility from novitiate days, Sister Principals will demur. "We work hard, yes, and we try to carry the spirit of Christ into our schools and our classrooms. But central figure? How could that be?"

There are definite trends that make this so. Of these, two trends are particularly noteworthy — the growth of the parish school and the preparation of the principal herself. Changing conditions are actually forcing the Sister Principal into a central position, as a discussion of these trends will show.

THE SPECIAL FUNCTION OF PARISH SCHOOLS

The principal's reluctance to accept herself as a "central figure" is easy to understand. Part of the reason lies in the way parochial schools have developed in this country; a principal didn't even figure in the early planning. Parochial schools were first established to preserve Catholic children from the Protestant religious teaching found in many early public schools.

---

* Chapters III through XVI by Sister M. Jerome.

To safeguard the Faith of the children, Bishops urged each parish to conduct its own school. The subjects of the public school curriculum were taught, but in an atmosphere which would strengthen the religious beliefs of the Catholic children. Special impetus was given to the establishment of parochial schools by the mandate of the Third Plenary Council of Baltimore in 1884.

Since religious teachers were few at the time, many early parish schools were staffed entirely by lay people, chosen for their practical Catholicity as well as for their teaching competence. As religious communities became more numerous, teaching Sisters and Brothers gradually took over the parish schools. The primary emphasis was on religious instruction. Naturally, the nuns regarded themselves as missionaries rather than as administrators. In those early one- and two-teacher schools, there was little thought of educational leadership as a profession.

Today's Sister Principals have been brought up in this tradition. "Saving souls" has been, and still is, a fundamental reason for Catholic schools. However, there is another agency whose chief concern is this *spiritual* function; that agency is the Church. Today's parochial school has as its special function the *intellectual* development of its pupils, as Father Ward has so ably pointed out. To be a good school, it must achieve its own unique purposes. These purposes are established in its curricular objectives — to develop physically fit, socially and economically competent, intellectually mature, *and* morally responsible American citizens. This last purpose, moral and spiritual development, is only one of the functions of the parochial school, and a function for which the Church, not the school, is primarily responsible. The Sister Principal, conscious of the long-range objectives of the parochial school, hardly considers her own role to be of central importance. She is likely to be very humble about her own contribution to the broad objectives of the school.

The growth of the Catholic school system, however, is focusing more attention upon the Sister Principal. In numbers alone, there has been remarkable growth. In 1961, there were well over four million children in Catholic elementary schools throughout the nation. Buildings, too, have grown. From one- and two-room schools, many parochial schools have become extensive plants, which include an auditorium, a cafeteria, offices, a library, a clinic, a music room, and other special-purpose rooms. The curriculum has broadened, at the exhortation of the popes, and now the parochial school offers a program equal to that of the public school, in addition to a firm foundation in faith and morals. All of these factors have caused a growth in the size of the faculty. Many parochial schools have staffs of over twenty teachers. With the expanding enrollments of parochial schools, a sufficient number of Sisters to staff the schools was not available. Hence, lay teachers have been introduced in increasing numbers. On every count, parochial schools have witnessed a steady, cumulative growth over the past half century.

For the Sister Principal, this has meant added responsibilities, and a newly defined role. That all of the educational resources may be used to greatest advantage, a trained professional leader is needed. These facilities must, of course, be not merely administered; they must be organized so that they contribute to the purposes of Catholic education. A daily religion period is not enough to place the stamp of approval on a parish school; the entire curriculum, teachers, texts, and materials, must be permeated with the Christian spirit. This is a tremendous order; such a responsibility cannot be left to chance. To accomplish these lofty and difficult purposes, the Sister Principal emerges in a role of educational leadership.

THE PREPARATION OF THE SISTER PRINCIPAL

At first glance, the principal as a central figure may seem contradictory because of her background. Her preparation is opposed to a "career" concept of the principalship. In the religious community, the Mother Superior directs the spiritual formation of the Sisters, assigns them to schools, and in general structures the educational work of the community. Very often the Sister hears, "We are all useful, but not necessary"; "Christ must increase, but I must decrease." There is no emphasis on "job opportunities," so widespread in the public school system and in other fields. No Sister thinks of working herself up toward the principalship. In fact, the principalship isn't viewed as "up"; it is an appointment which, like any other appointment, is the means of working out one's sanctification.

Another factor that inclines the Sister Principal to minimize her own importance is her feeling of inadequacy as the local religious superior. Most religious communities feel it is desirable to appoint the same Sister in charge of both the convent and the school.[1] This arrangement certainly contributes to good order and simplified administration, both for the Mother General and for the local convent. However, the office of local superior carries with it a multitude of duties, many of them time-consuming. With pressures at school to administer the school well, and pressures at home to be an exemplary religious and efficient superior, the Sister Principal has no illusions about doing a perfect job. She looks upon herself as upon the other principals in her religious community — as a hard-working and well-meaning principal and superior, interested in both convent and school, but pressed for time to discharge both duties well.

---

[1] The principal's duties as religious superior are beyond the scope of this book. A helpful source for principal-superiors is Paul Hoffer, *Guide for Religious Administrators* (Milwaukee: The Bruce Publishing Company, 1958).

Of late, the Mother Superiors have taken steps to strengthen the principal's position. Forward-looking religious communities send the principals to annual conferences for religious superiors. Here, the Sisters receive guidance and practical solutions to the problems of their important office. Mother Superiors are also stressing the professional preparation of their principals; more and more principals are doing specialized work in educational administration and supervision. This training provides insight into school problems, and develops a professional outlook as well as competence. Though the principalship will never become a "career" as in the public schools, Sister Principals are becoming more conscious of their specific responsibilities, and are better prepared to meet them.

The expansion of Catholic schools, then, is calling for trained educational leadership. The Sister Principal is becoming ever better prepared to administer the program of the parochial school. At this stage, there is an obvious need for a clear statement of policies. A difficulty in the way of such a statement is the varying viewpoints of Catholic school personnel on the roles which the principal and others should play in the school organization. An ever present difficulty, too, is the complexity of the problems of expansion, and the little time there is to "sit down and think."

The Sister Principal has no neat little *vade mecum* which gives recipes for successful administration. Diocesan handbooks, to be sure, offer some direction, in that they sketch the relationships existing among the various personnel in the schools. Yet every principal knows how little of operational policy there is in diocesan handbooks! The principal, as well as the pastor and teachers, would be immensely helped by a clearer statement of policy. Such a statement can perhaps be arrived at in two ways: first, by showing the position of the principal in the typical diocesan organization; and second, by presenting the functional roles of the principal in everyday operation. These two approaches will be used here. The statement thus developed can help principals and pastors to work out the specifics of a harmonious and effective relationship for their own school.

THE PRINCIPAL IN DIOCESAN SCHOOL ORGANIZATION

Since there are many differences in school organization from diocese to diocese, it may be most helpful to discuss a typical diocesan organization in which there is a diocesan superintendent. Figure 1 below shows the Sister Principal at the mid-point of a typical diocesan organizational chart.

The Sister Principal certainly seems to be central in the organizational chart (Fig. 1). Directly above her in the diocesan setup are the superintendent and the Bishop, and below her are the staff and pupils. In somewhat parallel relationships above her are her Mother Superior and her pastor.

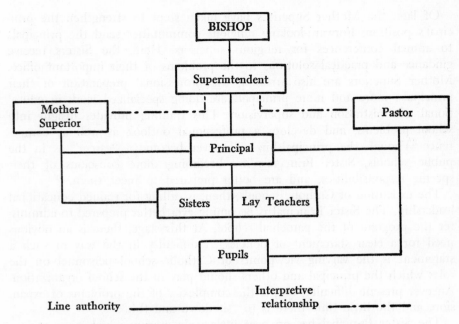

Figure 1.   The Flow of Educational Authority in a
Diocesan School System

Pictorially, the Sister Principal's position is clearly a central one.

In practice, the principal's position can be central, as the chart indicates. But just how significant her work is depends upon a great many factors. The following discussion will take up the matter of authority in the diocese, and will show the principal's role within this framework. The line officers in the system, those who have administrative authority over those below them in the organizational chart, will be considered first.

LINE OFFICERS IN THE DIOCESAN SCHOOL SYSTEM

The teaching authority of the diocesan school system flows down from the Bishop through the superintendent, who interprets the Bishop's directives to the Mother Superiors having schools in the diocese, and to pastors having schools. From these three sources — the superintendent, the religious superior, and the pastor — the Sister Principal receives directives for administering the school. Now each of these three line officers has varying degrees of authority over the principal, and each is in a certain sense absolute. At first glance, this triple source of authority seems to refute the general rule that a person should be responsible to only one superior officer. The flow of authority in the parochial school system is indeed not easy to grasp. The pattern works, however, as one can judge from the successful growth of the system in recent years.

Perhaps it might be helpful to explore a little the role of each person in the diocesan school system, as charted in Figure 1. Later there will be a discussion of other personnel, those who have advisory rather than administrative functions.

THE BISHOP

The Sister Principal probably studied the role of the Bishop in her courses in Catholic theology. From time to time, it is well for her to reorient her thinking about the Bishop and the apostolic mission of the Church. It is to her a source of strength and inspiration to be a part of the teaching body of the Church; dwelling upon the divine commission of her Bishop renews her spirit of dedication and lifts her sights, as it were.

In practice, the Sister Principal rarely has occasion to deal personally with the Bishop. Still, in analyzing the educational structure of the diocese, she must begin with the Bishop as the official head of the school system. It is a primary responsibility of the Bishop both to preach the Faith and to safeguard the Faith and morals of his people. To do this, he must either teach personally or provide for the instruction of his people; he must also supervise instruction and instructional materials, or provide for such instruction. In his official capacity, the Bishop is the teacher of his diocese.[2]

Obviously, to discharge his duty as teacher, the Bishop must delegate various responsibilities. He appoints pastors to care for the spiritual welfare of the people of a specified area, or of a particular nationality group. All parishes, ideally, build parish schools, in keeping with the mandate of the Third Plenary Council of Baltimore. To direct and co-ordinate the program of these schools, the Bishop selects a diocesan superintendent. Thus through delegation the Bishop shares his divinely ordained commission to teach the faithful.

Far more than most people realize, the Bishop continues to fulfill his teaching mission in various ways, both personally and through other delegates. He exercises vigilant censorship of religious materials published and used in the diocese; he appoints priests to teach religion; he keeps in contact with the school program through the reports of the superintendent and pastors; and he preaches to the faithful on numerous occasions such as Confirmation and dedications of churches and schools.

The far-reaching influence of the Bishop on education in the diocese can

[2] Sister M. Ruth Albert Ward, O.P., *Patterns of Administration in Diocesan School Systems*, Ph.D. dissertation (Washington, D. C.: The Catholic University of America Press, 1957), passim. This thesis summarizes a questionnaire study of authority exercised by the personnel of the diocesan school system.

be seen in his promoting of school building programs and of programs to upgrade the teaching staffs. Still more, perhaps, is the Bishop's influence extended to education by his ample delegation of authority to his diocesan superintendent. The executive authority in the diocese is ultimately that of the Bishop; therefore, only those directives which the Bishop supports find their way into practice. No diocese can progress educationally beyond the capacity of the Bishop to envision progress and to delegate educational authority commensurate with responsibility.

THE DIOCESAN SUPERINTENDENT

The office of the diocesan superintendent can be most clearly viewed when a section of Figure 1 is isolated for study. By reason of his appointment by the Bishop, the diocesan superintendent shares in the teaching authority of the Bishop. The superintendent is responsible directly to the Bishop (or the Archbishop, in the case of an archdiocese). The superintendent receives directives from his Bishop and reports back to him. The line of authority is clear and direct (Fig. 2).

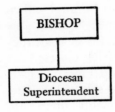

Figure 2.   The Bishop and the Diocesan Superintendent — Flow of Authority

The amount of authority which the Bishop delegates to his superintendent varies from diocese to diocese, and from time to time. Canon Law does not define the role of the superintendent; hence, he has as broad or as limited powers as the Bishop deems necessary for the situation. Smaller and far-flung dioceses may not have a superintendent at all; the Bishop himself or his Chancellor may undertake the direction of such parochial schools as exist. Larger and more highly developed dioceses and archdioceses may have one or more assistant superintendents; in such situations the assistant in charge of elementary education, for example, would be in line relationship to the chief superintendent, who in turn, is in line relationship to the Bishop. Again, the amount of authority invested in the assistant superintendent depends upon the latitude of the chief superintendent's powers, and the type of responsibilities assigned to the assistant.

Duties of the Superintendent

Because of these differing conditions from diocese to diocese, superintendents may differ greatly in the activities which they carry on. However, their typical duties can usually be grouped under these headings:

A. Representing the Bishop and reporting to him
B. Administering the diocesan school system
C. Interpreting state school law
D. Promoting in-service growth
E. Promoting good public relations

A. The Diocesan Superintendent Represents the Bishop. The first function, representing the Bishop and reporting to him, brings out the essential role of the superintendent as an extension of the Bishop's teaching authority. The superintendent represents the Bishop in the conduct of school affairs. Particularly is this apparent when the superintendent represents the Bishop's interests before state authorities, accrediting agencies, public school personnel, and civic and social groups. The reports which the superintendent makes to the Bishop underlines the superintendent's role as a representative of the Bishop, rather than as an executive authority in his own right.

One very real purpose of the superintendent's detailed and frequent reports to the Bishop is to keep his superior informed of school conditions. Another equally important purpose is providing professional counsel to the Bishop within the area of the superintendent's special competence. An example of this counsel would be in the superintendent's role as executive secretary of the Diocesan School Advisory Board (discussed later in this chapter). In this role, the superintendent provides statistical reports and interpretation to guide the board in reaching sound decisions on school policy. Still another purpose served by reports is to provide for the implementing of diocesan school policies. The superintendent may furnish leadership which disposes diocesan personnel favorably toward educational directives, but the superintendent is not empowered to enforce regulations personally. In reports to the Bishop, serious deficiencies are discussed, and where necessary, the Bishop as executive head of the diocese orders that deficiencies be corrected. Such instances would be rare, of course, but they indicate the flow of authority within the diocese.

B. The Diocesan Superintendent Administers the Diocesan School System. In carrying out this responsibility, the superintendent typically performs certain activities. Not every activity takes place in all dioceses, but the following list indicates the usual administrative duties of the superintendent. These duties are as follows:

1. To clarify the aims of Catholic education
2. To provide a curriculum in keeping with the aims of Catholic education
3. To develop school policies
4. To prepare a school calendar in accord with state standards

5. To organize a system-wide testing program
6. To establish a uniform system of pupil accounting
7. To maintain adequate teacher records
8. To evaluate the progress of the schools
9. To prepare statistical reports, as of enrollment and teacher status
10. To co-ordinate the work of the religious communities
11. To co-ordinate the work of pastors, principals, and teachers

C. The Diocesan Superintendent Interprets State School Law. In many states, there are school laws mandatory on parochial schools.[3] It is the diocesan superintendent's duty to see that these state laws are implemented in all schools of the diocese. In practice, this means keeping the schools informed of state regulations such as those concerning teacher certification, accreditation, compulsory attendance, and curriculum. At the local level, there may be safety and health laws binding on parochial schools. In certain states, parochial schools also make reports to local public schools and to state officials. The superintendent makes all necessary information available to the schools, and provides for the implementation of directives where necessary. The superintendent likewise is the executive head of the diocesan school system. Through him state requirements reach the schools, and school reports are submitted by him to the state.

D. The Diocesan Superintendent Promotes In-Service Growth. To provide for the professional growth of principals and teachers is one of the chief functions of the diocesan superintendent. Typical activities through which superintendents promote on-the-job improvement are:

1. Visiting the schools and observing teaching
2. Sponsoring teacher institutes and meetings devoted to professional topics
3. Arranging for demonstration teaching and interclass visitation
4. Providing for the orientation of new teachers
5. Assisting principals in improving their own supervisory activities
6. Working with committees on curricular problems
7. Assisting committees in selecting textbooks
8. Issuing professional growth guides
9. Developing criteria for evaluating teaching
10. Providing the schools with the services of trained supervisory personnel

E. The Diocesan Superintendent Promotes Good Public Relations. The final role of the diocesan superintendent is so essential that he is often thought of as a liaison person for the Catholic school system. In promoting good public relations, the superintendent goes further than in Role A — that of representing the Bishop. The superintendent carries on a comprehensive program by which he actively promotes mutual co-operation

---

[3] Fred F. Beach and Robert F. Will, *The State and Nonpublic Schools*, Misc. No. 28, U. S. Department of Health, Education, and Welfare (Washington, D. C.: Government Printing Office, 1958). Contains detailed information on state regulations affecting parochial schools.

between outside groups and the diocesan schools. Chief among his public relations duties are the following:

1. To interpret Catholic school policy and programs to civic, social, and educational groups
2. To assist the schools in promoting better home-school relations
3. To provide leadership for the diocesan Home and School Association
4. To issue interpretative reports on school statistics and programs
5. To keep significant school news before the public through the media of radio, television, and the press
6. To issue informative bulletins to diocesan schools
7. To maintain personal contact with religious superiors, pastors, supervisors, principals, teachers
8. To show a personal interest in all that concerns the diocesan schools

The foregoing duties of the diocesan superintendent are those performed typically. In larger dioceses, especially those with assistant superintendents and large supervisory staffs, many other activities are added. In smaller dioceses, some of the above activities may be curtailed or omitted altogether. The amount and kind of service rendered depend to a great extent upon the time and personnel available.

A Difficult Feature of the Diocesan Superintendent's Office

Before concluding the discussion of the diocesan superintendent, one should note a feature of his office which sometimes baffles outsiders. The public school superintendent directs personnel whom he himself has selected — with the approval of the local school board. The diocesan superintendent, on the other hand, has no voice at all in selecting school personnel. Even his assistant superintendents and supervisors are not appointed by him, but by the Bishop and the Mother Superior, and the lay teachers are usually hired by the pastor after some consultation with the principal. Only occasionally does the diocesan superintendent even suggest lay teachers for parish schools.

The diocesan superintendent's task is a gigantic one — to make a working unit out of personnel none of whom he has appointed himself. One convert to the Faith said of this anomalous situation: "Fortunately, all individuals involved in the conduct of Catholic parochial schools are motivated by the same desire to carry on Christian education. . . . Only through fervent dedication of self could such a condition of divided authority function without constant and serious friction."[4] This statement is all the more noteworthy because it was made by a former public school superintendent who entered the Church and then studied diocesan organization from the inside.

---

[4] Russell L. C. Butsch, "Administrative Organization of the Diocesan School System," *The Catholic School Journal*, XXXI (June, 1931), p. 201.

Perhaps the Sister Principal, analyzing the diocesan superintendency in this light, may gain insight into her own important role in the diocesan system. Practically every activity of the superintendent requires some co-operation on the part of the Sister Principal. To mention only two such activities, there are (1) the principals' reports to the Diocesan School Office; and (2) principals' reports utilized by the superintendent for statistical summaries made to the Diocesan School Board and the Bishop, to the local and diocesan newspapers, to the state department, to the National Catholic Welfare Conference, and even to the Pope. The system-wide efficiency of the schools is really an accumulation of the things which the alert individual principal tries to do every day in her own school: to provide an adequate school teaching day, to maintain a complete pupil and teacher record system, to supply the recommended textbooks and other instructional materials, and to stimulate better teaching on the part of all the staff. The superintendent must, it is true, possess definite qualities of leadership and must work consistently toward improving the schools. But faithful and competent Sister Principals are always needed to make a potentially good educator a successful diocesan superintendent.

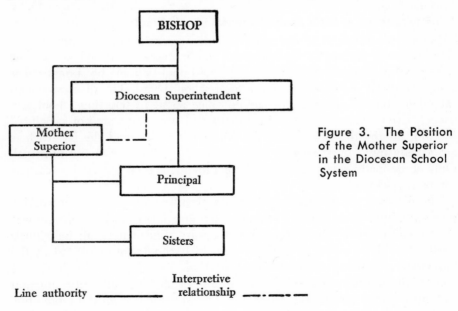

Figure 3. The Position of the Mother Superior in the Diocesan School System

THE MOTHER SUPERIOR

In the diocesan organizational chart (Fig. 3), the Mother Superior is shown in relationship to the Bishop (or Archbishop), the diocesan superintendent, and to her Sisters staffing schools in the diocese. The Bishop's line relationships to the Mother Superior pertains typically only to the school policies of the diocese. The superintendent maintains an interpretive relationship to the Mother Superior; that is, he interprets to her the school directives of the Bishop. The diocesan superintendent and the Mother Superior are both in line relationship to the Sisters whom the Mother Superior appoints to the diocese. The role of the Mother Superior and her relationships with the Bishop, the superintendent, and her Sisters in the diocese warrant further discussion here.

The Mother Superior's Relationship to the Bishop

The Bishop, as the canonically appointed teacher of the diocese, is responsible for the entire educational program of the diocesan school system. It is the Bishop who signs the contract permitting a religious community to establish a school within the diocese, and to terminate contract and withdraw from a school. The salaries of the Sisters is likewise stipulated by the Bishop. In the case of a religious community that is diocesan, or under the direction of the Bishop, it is the Bishop who may approve the allocation of Sisters to schools, give permission to establish schools outside of the diocese, and the like. In the case of pontifical religious communities, those under the direction of the Holy See, the Bishop has no jurisdiction over these larger issues. However, the Bishop does maintain the authority to implement diocesan school directives through his superintendent in the case of both pontifical and diocesan religious communities. In a spirit of Faith and zeal, the Mother Superior accords the Bishop, through his superintendent, the co-operation which school directives entail.

The Mother Superior's Relationship to the Superintendent

As mentioned earlier, the diocesan superintendent maintains an interpretive relationship with the Mother Superior. That is, he communicates to her the diocesan school directives, interprets them as needed, and thus helps her to co-operate with the plans of the Bishop for the schools.

Depending upon circumstances, the Mother Superior may have frequent contacts with the superintendent. For example, the superintendent clears with the Mother Superior all requests for participation of her Sisters in in-service work on a diocesan scale. The Mother Superior makes assignments of her Sisters to demonstration teaching, committee work, direction of lay teachers on the advisory program, and similar work. Likewise, most dioceses have routine reports made by the Mother Superior to the School Office. For example, in August the Mother Superior submits to the superintendent the proposed appointments for her schools in the diocese. The process is usually routine, though in the case of a Sister appointed without meeting state certification requirements or another diocesan standard, the superintendent would be empowered to request that a substitution be made. The Mother Superior is usually on the regular diocesan mailing list, so she is kept conversant with the activities of the schools. When contacts between the Mother Superior and the superintendent are frequent, their directions to the Sisters will be co-ordinated, and smooth working order will be ensured.

It seems almost too obvious to mention that the superintendent has no jurisdiction over the religious observances of the Sisters or other conventual matters. The relationship charted in Figure 1 refers only to such policies as the Bishop authorizes the superintendent to promulgate for the schools of the diocese.

Contribution of the Mother Superior

It is no exaggeration to say that the diocesan system can be only as strong as the Mother Superiors make it. That is to say, an efficient diocesan school system requires trained personnel, and the personnel are supplied, for the most part, by the religious community. The teaching in the diocese cannot be superior teaching unless the Mother Superiors assign to diocesan schools Sisters who are trained to do superior teaching. The same is true of administration; leadership can be provided by Sister Principals only if they have received adequate professional training through their religious community. A definite contribution of the Mother Superior is, then, to assign Sisters who have been, in the words of Pius X, "thoroughly prepared and well grounded in the matter they are going to teach." The diocese can and should provide additional in-service growth activities through professional meetings, demonstrations, and the like; but the Mother Superior's appointments determine just how effective an in-service program can be.

Problems of the Mother Superior

In the case of pontifical institutes, the religious community may staff schools in several dioceses, states, and even continents. Thus, diocesan directives might quite understandably conflict with general religious community policy. Or, more frequently, the Sisters who transfer from diocese to diocese may require time to absorb the new regulations. Somewhat the same difficulty is experienced by public school teachers who transfer across school district or state lines. It takes time and real concentration to make the new district's standards a part of one's mind set. It can be done, of course, as many have demonstrated.

The Mother General, therefore, has the problem of seeing that her Sisters offer ready co-operation with the regulations of their respective dioceses. This means, first of all, the superior's familiarity with the diocesan regulations, personally or through her supervisor. It means also her readiness to broaden her own viewpoint with regard to an adequate school program. And, further, it entails active indoctrination of the Sisters with regard to the need for identifying themselves with diocesan directives. Religious community customs and educational practices need to be maintained, wherever possible; these give the Sisterhood its peculiar atmosphere and personality. It requires no little art for the Superior General to maintain religious community traditions, while at the same time promoting diocesan policies.

In making these adjustments, the Sister Principal is the key figure. Part of her competence consists in being well informed of the duties of her position, and in orienting her staff to their duties. The Mother General, and of course the diocesan superintendent, are assisted when the Sister Principal is alert to the specifics of diocesan policy. The better disposed the principal is, and the better trained, the more effectively will diocesan school policy be carried out in her school. This is true whether she has taught in only one diocese, or in several. It is part of her job to operate within the framework of policy established for her present situation. In this matter, the central significance of the principal's position is again brought to the front.

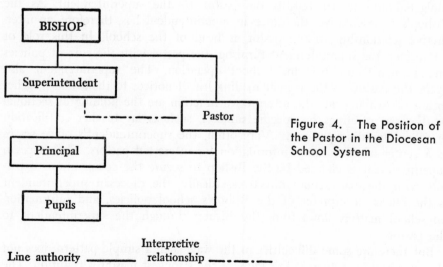

Figure 4. The Position of the Pastor in the Diocesan School System

Line authority _____   Interpretive relationship ___.__.__

THE PASTOR

Figure 4 shows the intermediate position of the pastor in the flow of educational authority in the diocese. The chart can best be understood through a discussion of the pastor's relationships with the Bishop, the diocesan superintendent, and parish school personnel.

The Pastor's Relationship to the Bishop

The Bishop, official teacher of the diocese, has delegated to the pastor the "cura animarum" of a specified geographical area, or of a particular nationality group. As a result of this delegation, the pastor is responsible for the spiritual welfare of all souls in the parish. To safeguard adequately the Faith and morals of the children, the pastor establishes a parochial school. The pastor is head of the school, for it is part of his pastoral responsibility.

As head of the parish school, the pastor has authority over the school. This authority is indicated in the chart by a line leading from the pastor to the principal. However, the pastor does not have sole authority over the school, for the school is under the jurisdiction of the Bishop. Thus, as regards the parish school, the pastor is in an intermediate position; he is subordinate to the Bishop and he is in authority over the principal and the pupils of the school.

The Pastor's Relationship to the Superintendent

The Bishop has delegated to the superintendent the responsibility for directing the diocesan school system. Hence, the Bishop's policies are promulgated and interpreted to the pastor by the superintendent. As the Bishop's representative, the diocesan superintendent has, therefore, an interpretive relationship to the pastor as head of the school. In this role of interpreter, the superintendent furnishes the pastor with the current policies and standards for parochial school operation. The superintendent also keeps the pastor on the regular mailing list of notices to the schools. Other means of carrying out the interpretive function are the holding of sectional or diocesan meetings on specific subjects, such as lay teacher certification or school building programs. Very often, the superintendent's office serves as a center of educational information for interested pastors. The diocesan superintendent is charged by the Bishop to secure the co-operation of pastors with diocesan school directives. Ideally, the diocesan superintendent is the official interpreter of the Bishop's school policies, and information on school matters flows from the Bishop through the superintendent to the pastors.

But there are some difficulties in the way; such a simple pattern does not always exist in practice. Why? Perhaps the strongest reason is tradition. The diocesan superintendency is of rather recent origin; the first diocesan superintendent was named (for New York City) only seventy years ago.[5] Smaller dioceses, and those formed later, naturally were slow in naming a priest to

---

[5] Bernard J. Kohlbrenner, A History of Catholic Education in the United States (New York: Benziger Brothers, 1937), p. 190.

co-ordinate the parish schools of the episcopal see. Therefore, the pastoral attitude has not been one of dependence upon a central authority for school directives. Most pastors, or at least many pastors, have had to rely on their own ingenuity and on their own studies to organize their schools. When a diocesan superintendent is named, it takes time for the position to assume importance in the minds of pastors.

There are still other reasons why the interpretive relationship between superintendent and pastor may be obscured in practice. In smaller dioceses, the superintendent may have other heavy duties, such as acting as the Bishop's chancellor or the pastor of a large parish. Or the superintendent may be handicapped by inadequate professional training, or his office may be understaffed with supervisory assistance. Thus, pastors may not be getting enough real leadership; diocesan policies may not be clearly formulated, and services may be limited.

Also, perhaps as a result of the pastor's obligation to contact his Bishop on certain matters, the pastor may have formed the habit of going directly to his Bishop on school matters as well. And, finally, the Bishop is the executive authority of the diocese. Canon Law does not direct the superintendent to enforce school regulations with regard to pastors. To a great extent, the pastor's attitude depends upon the superintendent's ability to enlist co-operation. Of late, many pastors have had more frequent contacts with the diocesan superintendent concerning the hiring of lay teachers. This is especially true in states having mandatory teacher certification. A central office can supply information more readily than an individual, and pastors have had recourse to data prepared by the superintendent's office. As pastors see the value of the superintendent's office to their schools, and as Bishops establish the superintendency more firmly, the interpretive relationship between superintendent and pastor in school matters becomes more effective.

The Pastor's Relationship to the School

As head of the school, the pastor has a variety of duties which can be grouped under three headings: duties in administration, in spiritual direction, and in public relations. In carrying out these duties, the pastor utilizes his line relationship to both principal and pupils.

The Pastor's Administrative Duties. The parish school is the administrative responsibility of the pastor. It is his duty to see that the school is up to standard, efficiently run, and achieving the objectives of Catholic education. Now it stands to reason that the pastor could not, with all his other duties, attend personally to the many details of school administration. So he delegates to a trained professional person, the principal, charge of the instructional program and direction of the teaching staff. In the diagram which introduces this section on pastoral duties, the line of authority goes from the pastor to the principal; but there is no line from the pastor to the teaching staff. This shows that the pastor acts through the principal in directing the school; the teaching staff works under the direction of the principal. In a smoothly operating program, suggestions and recommendations from pastor to the teachers, and from teachers to the pastor, go through the principal.

The more important administrative duties of the pastor may be divided into two groups: those concerned with school policy and those concerned with finance. The following list gives these duties briefly:

A. The Pastor's Duties in School Policy

1. To develop parish school policies within the framework of diocesan regulations
2. To co-operate with the superintendent by seeing that diocesan directives are carried out in the school
3. To comply with state and local regulations pertaining to Catholic schools
4. To delegate to the principal the direction of the instructional program and the details of school administration, and to keep in touch with school administration through frequent conferences with the principal, periodic reports of the principal, and visits to the classrooms
5. To deal with the teaching staff through the principal
6. To maintain co-operative relations with the Mother Superior and community supervisor of the Sisterhood staffing his school

B. The Pastor's Duties in School Finance

1. To arrange for adequate staffing of the school. This includes hiring qualified lay teachers to supplement the Sisters assigned.
2. To pay the salary of Sisters, lay teachers, and substitute teachers according to diocesan regulations
3. To provide a safe, clean, well-equipped, and healthful school building
4. To supply adequate clerical and custodial service
5. To supply textbooks and other instructional materials of the amount and kind needed, to arrange with the principal the rental or purchase fees for pupil materials
6. To provide a suitable convent, furnishings, and utilities, and to arrange for their maintenance and repair
7. To provide for adequate repair and replacement of school equipment and facilities
8. To plan ahead for timely expansion and enlargement of buildings, facilities, and staff

The Pastor's Spiritual Duties. In Figure 4, the line from pastor to pupils implies pastoral responsibility for the pupils of the parish school, as well as authority over them. This is particularly a spiritual responsibility, though in a sense everything the pastor does for the school contributes to the spiritual welfare of the children. The fact that the pastor has provided a Catholic school in itself helps the children to develop spiritually.

There are three specific duties which bring out the spiritual responsibility of the pastor for the pupils. The most important of these is to review catechism teaching in the parish school each week.[6] When possible, the pastor is to teach religion in the school, but he may discharge this duty by assigning an assistant priest to teach religion weekly to each group of pupils. Since one of the purposes of the Catholic school is moral and spiritual development, the duty to teach religion is a grave responsibility for the pastor.

It is also the pastor's prerogative to decide which children shall attend the parish school. Within the framework of diocesan and state regulations, the pastor has the authority to admit children to the parish school, and to exclude children for just cause. The ideal, of course, is "Every Catholic child in a Catholic school." It is the pastor's responsibility, in so far as possible, to provide a Catholic education for every child of the parish. Extraordinary cases of discipline must be brought to the pastor's attention, for it is his responsibility to decide whether a "problem" child should be retained in the school or excluded because of danger to other children. Usually, a diocesan directive obliges the pastor to inform the superintendent of the disciplinary action taken, but the responsibility for expulsion is the pastor's, as spiritual head of the parish school.

The pastor further discharges his spiritual duty by administering the sacraments and by providing spiritual direction to the students. Some pastors have arranged for frequent individual conferences with each seventh and eighth grade student, to give the children a chance to discuss whatever problems are confronting them. A further extension of the pastor's spiritual influence is in his informal contacts with the children, in their classrooms, on the playground, and in parish activities. The Catholic's opinion of the Church is usually one which he formed early in childhood through contact with the clergy. The pastor's association with the children through the sacraments and through church-related activities should strengthen the ties which bind them to the Church.

The Pastor's Duties in Public Relations. "Public relations" has a somewhat artificial ring; it may seem a little like advertising the school to the public. Public relations rightly understood, however, is nothing of the sort. It means that the pastor maintains good working relations with all those who are associated with him in educating his pupils. A later chapter elaborates on the role of the pastor in public relations, but at this point it may be helpful to list briefly the pastor's specific duties in this area:

---

[6] III Baltimore Council, VI, 1, 2, 201.

1. To provide good working conditions for the staff
2. To provide adequate physical facilities for a well-rounded education
3. To assist in policy formation and to keep in touch with the school program
4. To confer frequently with the principal on school matters
5. To show an interest in pupil progress
6. To provide leadership for the Home and School Association
7. To maintain pleasant, businesslike relations with parents
8. To promote cordial relations with civic, social, and school groups in the community, as well as with the local newspaper

Parish schools are an important part of the total educational system of our country. Effective working relations of the pastor with interested persons enable Catholic schools to take their rightful place in the community.

In summarizing the pastor's duties, it may be said that the pastor provides the policy, the physical conditions, the spiritual leadership, and the warm personal relations needed for a good school program. He delegates to a trained professional person, the principal, the direction of the program.

In his relationship to the diocesan superintendent, the pastor defers to the technical competence of the superintendent and implements diocesan policies. The pastor exerts his authority over the pupils in the manner described above. The many effective parochial schools today bear witness to the pastor's realistic acceptance of his role, and his sincere efforts to achieve the aims of Catholic education in his own school.

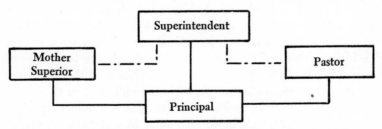

Figure 5.   Three Sources of the Principal's Authority in the Diocesan School System

THE SISTER PRINCIPAL

As shown in Figure 5, the Sister Principal has three persons in authority over her: her Mother Superior, her pastor, and her diocesan superintendent. Not shown on the chart are the persons below the principal in the diocesan framework: the staff members and the pupils. The discussion will deal first with the persons providing direction to the principal.

The Principal's Duties to the Diocesan Superintendent

Within each diocese, the superintendent sets the pattern of school policy. All diocesan handbooks emphasize the duty of the principal to carry out diocesan policies in her own school. This is much easier for the principal when her other two superiors — her Mother Superior and her pastor — also give precedence to diocesan policy. It goes without saying that the superintendent aids the principal in the performance of her duties when diocesan policies are clearly and consistently stated.

The specific duties of the principal to the diocesan superintendent are the following:

1. To acquaint the staff of diocesan policies, and to make available to the staff all diocesan bulletins and handbooks
2. To carry out diocesan policies in the school. This includes observing the school calendar, holding school the required number of hours each day, following the diocesan course of study, using required instructional materials, maintaining pupil and teacher personnel records, and conducting teacher orientation programs.
3. To submit reports to the diocesan office as required
4. To co-operate with the superintendent and diocesan supervisors in the supervisory program of the diocese

Quite apart from the above being duties, they strengthen the position of the principal within the school. The performance of these duties stamps the principal as the educational leader of the school, and establishes the necessary conditions for a wholesome teaching-learning situation.

The Principal's Duties to the Pastor

A second superior officer is the principal's pastor. As mentioned earlier, the pastor's duties to the school are of three kinds: administrative (policy and finance), spiritual, and public relations. In the effective performance of her duties, the principal's work is complementary to the pastor's and under his direction.

The principal's duties to the pastor may be summarized under four headings:

1. To ascertain the pastor's wishes concerning the school. This includes having conferences with the pastor before the opening of the school year, and frequently during the year, to plan school policy, financial arrangements, a program of public relations, the direction of custodial workers, the religious education of the pupils, and other important aspects of administration.
2. To keep the pastor informed, to bring to his attention all extraordinary disciplinary cases, to report regularly on the physical needs of the school and administration problems, to acquaint him with all matters of major importance, and to familiarize him with diocesan regulations
3. To carry out the pastor's policies in a spirit of loyal, gracious co-operation
4. To utilize all the resources of the school for a complete Catholic education for all the children

All of these four duties are undertaken, of course, within the broad framework of diocesan and state school regulations. Some handbooks simplify the relationship of the principal by stating that in *educational* matters the principal is directly responsible to the diocesan superintendent, and that in *all other school matters* the principal is responsible to the pastor. The spirit of her relationship with the pastor is outlined in the four points given above.

The Principal's Duties to the Mother Superior

The other two lines of authority leading to the principal — those from the superintendent and the pastor — indicate professional relationships almost entirely. True, the human element enters into all activity, but for the most part the duties are professional in nature. With the Mother Superior, however, the situation is different. The principal is bound to her superior first as a religious subject, and only second as a professional person. The first of these bonds is a strong one. The nun's vow of obedience predisposes her to say "Yes" to the superior under practically all circumstances. The nun, and thus the principal, is strongly disposed toward what the Mother Superior wants and what seems best for the community.

Ordinarily, Sisters do not feel for the diocese or the parish the same loyalty they have for their own religious community. This is natural, for the religious community nurtures and trains them, and receives them back in illness and old age. Superintendents and pastors should expect this religious community spirit, and should show their wisdom by deferring to it.

The principal's duties to her Mother Superior are of two kinds: the duties of a religious subject and the duties of a professional representative of the community. The first relationship is beyond analysis here; the second relationship can be very briefly summarized. Within the framework of state and diocesan school regulations, the Sister Principal performs these essential duties toward her Mother Superior and her religious community:

1. To work co-operatively with the staff assigned
2. To preserve the religious community's traditions
3. To utilize the in-service helps provided by the community
4. To keep the records and to make the reports required
5. To represent the religious community's viewpoint to superintendent and pastor, and their viewpoints to the religious community

In summary, then, having three persons in authority over her makes the principal's role complex indeed. It is a help to know the duties which the three individuals have toward her, and her reciprocal duties to them. Certainly, the Sister Principal can perform more effectively when she knows the limits of her own authority, the extent of authority which others have over her, and the functional relationships she has with all concerned.

The Principal's Duties Toward the Staff

Besides being subject to authority, the principal has authority over others, namely her staff and the pupils of the school. Though conditions vary from school to school, the following are some of the basic duties of principals to their staff:

1. To provide conditions for good teaching. This includes providing adequate physical facilities, good housekeeping, adequate instructional equipment, approved textbooks, orderly routines, a reasonable work load, and pleasant personal relations.
2. To supply teachers with definite information regarding their duties and school policy
3. To provide for the orientation and in-service growth of the staff
4. To develop staff potential through judicious delegation of responsibility
5. To safeguard the professional reputation of the staff
6. To show appreciation for the co-operation and service rendered
7. To convey the staff's problems and viewpoints to the pastor, Mother Superior, and diocesan superintendent
8. To assist the staff and individual teachers in achieving more fully the goals of Catholic education
9. To establish reasonable standards of staff performance, and to enforce these standards

It is here at the local level that the importance of the principal's position is seen. The three persons in power over the principal ideally provide her with the authority and conditions for effective administration. The principal, in turn, ideally provides her staff with the authority and conditions which they need for successful teaching. In other words, it is the principal who most directly affects how children learn.

What has been said here regarding the directing of the staff applies in general to the school clerk and to the janitor. The principal has certain duties to these nonprofessional workers because of their importance in maintaining a good teaching-learning situation. Also, almost parenthetically, it should be added that the principal performs the activities listed above through co-ordinating staff members she herself has not selected. The magnitude of this task underlines the major role of the principal in parochial school education.

Up to this point, the discussion has centered upon the line officers in the diocesan educational structure. The role of these line officers toward the Sister Principal has been developed somewhat in detail. The principal's corresponding duties to her superiors and to her staff have also been presented. Although the specifics of the principal's administrative duties have only been touched upon, the discussion attempted to sketch at least the broad features of her essential relationships.

The role of the Sister Principal is certainly not autonomous; she has definite duties to three superior officers in the diocesan organization. Still, the principal's role is not merely subservient. When one watches a competent principal in action, one is impressed with her creativity. Within her designated framework, she can make a new educational world for teachers and pupils alike. To a great extent, the Sister Principal, from her position of vantage, will be responsible for the ever-improving quality of Catholic elementary education.

ADVISORY PERSONNEL IN THE DIOCESAN SCHOOL SYSTEM

The preceding section has outlined the principal's relations with line officers in the diocesan school system. These officers show the flow of authority in educational matters from Bishop, through the superintendent to the Mother Superior and the pastor, and down to the principal and the staff.

Another kind of personnel has become very important in the diocesan school structure. These are the so-called advisory, or staff, or consultative personnel. Their positions are indicated with broken lines in Figure 6.

The principal advisory personnel of the diocesan school system are the members of the Diocesan School Advisory Board, the religious community supervisors, and the diocesan supervisors. These three types of advisory personnel will be discussed here.

THE DIOCESAN SCHOOL ADVISORY BOARD

Although this group is often called simply the Diocesan School Board, the term Diocesan School Advisory Board is used in this discussion. "Diocesan School Board" means to most teachers the office of the diocesan superintendent; so, too, "School Board" in the public school system can mean the office of the public school superintendent. Although this diocesan advisory group may be called the Board of Education, the School Committee, or the Parish School Board, the most common name is the School Board, diocesan or archdiocesan. The term "advisory" is inserted in this discussion merely to distinguish it from the diocesan school office itself.

It should be said at the outset that not every diocese has a Diocesan School Advisory Board. In fact, this group seems to be functional only in the West, South, and North Central regions of the country.[7] Many of the larger dioceses have no board; and most of the smaller dioceses operate without one. The first diocesan board was created in Fort Wayne, Indiana, in 1879,[8] as a kind of inspectional body, resembling the early public school

---

[7] Ward, op. cit., p. 89.

[8] Kohlbrenner, op. cit., p. 185.

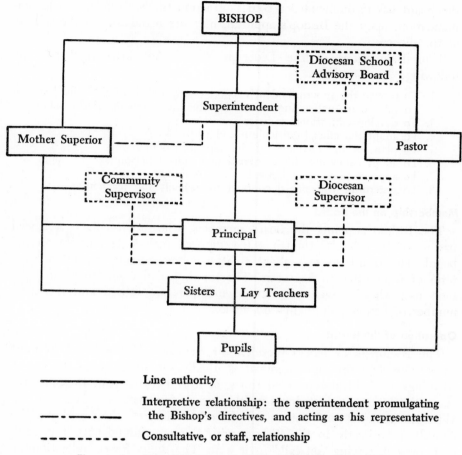

Figure 6.   Line Officers and Advisory Personnel in the
Diocesan School System

Board of Visitors. Since that time, advisory boards with varying responsibilities have developed, but chiefly, as indicated above, in the newer dioceses and in specified areas.

Functions of the Board

The Diocesan School Advisory Board is a policy-making group which serves in an advisory capacity to the Bishop on school matters. Since the Bishop is canonically responsible for education in the diocese, all other persons necessarily relate to him in advisory capacity only. The pooled wisdom and practical experience of the board members provide the Bishop with background for making mature decisions concerning the schools. When the board has recommended a course of action to the Bishop, this recommendation, upon the Bishop's approval, becomes mandatory in the schools of the diocese.

Typical functions of the Diocesan School Advisory Board are the following:

1. To receive the superintendent's report on the status of the school system
2. To offer constructive suggestions for the improvement of the schools
3. To develop educational policies
4. To adopt the official curriculum and textbooks
5. To plan for the financing of the superintendent's work
6. To adopt regulations for certification of school personnel
7. To approve plans for proposed school buildings
8. To determine the official contract for schools and teachers

Membership on the Board

The Bishop appoints the board members, who are usually experienced pastors of the diocese, though a few dioceses include lay people on the board. The boards average about eight members, usually appointed for a term of from three to five years. The rotating plan seems to be in common use, whereby each year several members are retired and the same number of new appointments are made.

Operation of the Board

The Bishop is ex officio president or chairman of the board in most cases. The diocesan superintendent is usually the secretary to the board. Meetings are held at scheduled times, at least twice a year. In some dioceses, the superintendent draws up the agenda for board meetings and provides the material to be discussed. In other dioceses, the board may be consultative directly to the Bishop, with the superintendent not present, or if present, serving "on call," as it were. The topics for consideration are discussed, motions passed if desired, and the recommendations are promulgated, over the Bishop's signature, as binding in the diocese. It is easy to see that the superintendent can effectively assist this policy-making group through his professional competence.

Relations of the Board to Other Personnel

In Figure 6, the Diocesan School Advisory Board is shown just below the Bishop and just above the superintendent. There is a line of authority, a straight line, from the Bishop to the board; this indicates the board's direct responsibility to the Bishop. The broken line from the advisory board to the superintendent indicates a consultative relationship; the superintendent does not direct the board, nor does the board direct the superintendent. In fact, in many cases, the superintendent is a member of the board and deliberates with the members on school matters.

The Diocesan School Advisory Board has no further relationship to any other personnel of the diocese, except informally, as any individual might. The Sister Principal knows of the board only through the issuance of school policy. The pastors do not deal with the board as such, but receive diocesan school directives through the superintendent's office. The Diocesan School Advisory Board is an advisory body in the strict sense of the term. They are an influential group, of course. They are sounding boards on school proposals; they provide acute insight into school problems; they recommend policies which they deem good and necessary; they usually operate schools themselves, and hence serve as examples of ideal pastoral relationship to the personnel in the school system. "He's a member of the Diocesan School Board" carries with it a definite prestige.

THE DIOCESAN SUPERVISOR

The second type of advisory personnel is the diocesan supervisor, appointed by her Mother Superior to work through the superintendent's office. Not all dioceses have diocesan supervisors, but the pattern seems to be gaining in popularity, especially in the newer dioceses. Usually, the diocesan supervisor works with all the teachers of the diocese, and not merely with the Sisters of her own community. Superintendents having diocesan supervision feel that the diocesan program is co-ordinated and strengthened by this more generalized kind of supervisory assistance.[9]

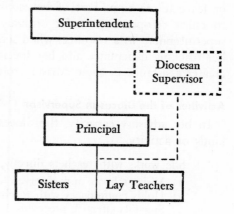

Figure 7. The Role of the
Diocesan Supervisor

The Role of the Diocesan Supervisor

In Figure 7, there is a line of authority from the superintendent to the diocesan supervisor, who acts as a staff member of his office. The

[9] Sister M. Patrice McNamara, O.S.F., *Supervision and Supervisors in the Catholic Elementary School Systems of the United States,* unpublished Ph.D. thesis (New York Fordham University, 1949). Contains interesting data on community and diocesan supervisors, and the so-called "Mixed" type (supervisors combining both functions).

diocesan supervisor receives her directions from the superintendent and reports back directly to him. The diocesan supervisor has no assigned relation to anyone else in the system, except to principals and teachers. Toward pastors, for example, the diocesan supervisor usually has no specific duties, though a few dioceses require a routine report of school visitation.

Broken lines in the above chart indicate the advisory capacity of the supervisor to principals and teachers. In best practice, the supervisor is really advisory; that is, her role is one of counseling, assisting, and recommending. She is ideally concerned with instructional improvement, and is not in any sense a lesser administrator. Although some diocesan handbooks speak of her as an assistant superintendent, in practice superintendents rarely delegate to a supervisor the authority which the Bishop has vested in them. The diocesan supervisor does not share in the superintendent's authority. She cannot, for example, dispense a school from a diocesan regulation. This is an administrative decision, and one which she wisely refers to the superintendent.

This insistence on the *advisory* role of the supervisor is in keeping with a definite trend away from the authoritarian type of school inspection formerly known as supervision.[10] Today, in many school systems throughout the country, the term supervisor is being replaced by such titles as "consultant, adviser, helping teacher, and curriculum director." This does not mean, of course, that the supervisor makes recommendations in a "take it or leave it" fashion. Part of her competence should consist in the ability to enlist co-operation under ordinary circumstances. There is always the superintendent as a resource, when serious deficiencies are noted. Because of her teaching experience and her special training, the supervisor can provide greater assistance in these advisory roles than she could as an administrator.

Activities of the Diocesan Supervisor

In her advisory capacity, the diocesan supervisor engages in three major kinds of activity.

1. She works with teachers directly, when she
    a) Visits schools and observes teaching in progress
    b) Holds conferences with teachers and principals
    c) Suggests effective procedures, suitable materials, and remedial measures
    d) Assists with the interpretation and use of test results

---

[10] Two references which are typical of current emphasis on supervision as an advisory service are the following:

Kimball Wiles, *Supervision for Better Schools* (Englewood Cliffs, N. J.: Prentice-Hall, Inc., 1955), pp. 3–9.

William H. Burton and Leo J. Brueckner, *Supervision: A Social Process* (New York: Appleton-Century-Crofts, Inc., 1955), pp. 70–89.

2. She provides instructional leadership, when she
   a) Works with committees to improve the curriculum, to revise reporting practices, to select textbooks and other instructional materials, and to prepare handbooks of diocesan school policy
   b) Arranges for demonstration teaching and interschool visitation
   c) Prepares bulletins on instructional topics
   d) Assists principals in improving their supervisory practices

3. She assists the superintendent in school-related activities, when she
   a) Prepares interpretive reports of school achievement
   b) Constructs diocesan tests
   c) Directs the program of in-service college work for lay teachers
   d) Directs the keeping of teacher and pupil personnel records
   e) Plans in-service growth programs for teachers and principals
   f) Conducts research on school matters
   g) Recommends ways of co-ordinating school policies and procedures throughout the diocese

By means of these activities, the diocesan supervisor works to unify and improve teaching in the diocese. Her efforts help to make diocesan school policy better known and more consistently observed.

Relationship of the Diocesan Supervisor to the Principal

Ideally, it seems that a primary purpose of diocesan supervision should be to strengthen the role of the Sister Principal. That makes good sense, for at the most the supervisor can make one or two visits to a school each year, whereas the principal is on the job every day. The stronger the principal, the better the school program will be. The principal could well expect from the diocesan supervisor an explanation of her procedures in classroom observation; or better still, the principal might accompany the supervisor during classroom visits and teacher conferences. This should give the principal some new ideas about observation and conferences; still more, it enables the principal and supervisor to emphasize the same points in working toward the improvement of teaching. Both principal and supervisor are interested in the same objective: a better education for every child. By working along with the diocesan supervisor, the principal can provide the supervisor with useful background information, and in return can get helpful suggestions for her own supervisory work.

THE RELIGIOUS COMMUNITY SUPERVISOR

The third kind of advisory personnel in the diocesan school system is the Sister Supervisor for the individual religious community. In most sisterhoods, particularly the larger ones, the Mother Superior appoints a Sister to visit schools and help teachers in their work. The religious community

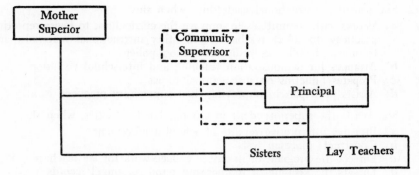

Figure 8.   The Role of the Religious Community Supervisor

supervisor, even when she is convinced of this, has a real problem. Sometimes she cannot be simply an advisory person. (See Figure 8.)

Her problem is this. As representative of the Mother Superior, the religious community supervisor visits all the schools and classes, and therefore knows intimately both the teachers and the way they teach. The Mother Superior herself, in most orders, makes an annual visitation of convents, and sometimes even a visitation of each classroom while teaching is in progress. The Mother Superior of course learns a great deal about her subjects while on visitation, but as superior, she is deeply concerned about their spirituality as well as their professional competence. So, the superior is likely to be more taken up with the spiritual progress of the nuns rather than with the proficiency of both nuns and lay teachers. It is the religious community supervisor who can supply the Mother Superior with the minute details of classroom performance.

Hence, the religious community supervisor very often assists the Mother Superior in making appointments, in removing teachers from work in which they were unsuccessful, and in assigning Sisters to special studies. In other words, the religious community supervisor works in an advisory capacity while helping teachers in the classroom, but at the same time, she is in somewhat of an administrative role in her influence on appointments. The religious community supervisor is evaluating teachers as she works with them; her evaluations almost inevitably reach the Mother Superior.

Also, because supervisory help is so limited, the religious community supervisor becomes somewhat of a representative of the Mother Superior in telling principals and teachers what is to be done. There would have to be many more supervisors in each Sisterhood, if co-operative procedures were to be used generally. And, there would have to be several assistant superiors, who would have the administrative authority to implement the General Superior's directives.

The personality of the religious community supervisor is all-important. To assist both teachers and the Mother Superior, the religious community supervisor needs practically the whole gamut of spiritual and professional qualities. To say that she has a "dual role" is underestimating the difficulties of her job.

Religious Community Versus Diocesan Supervision

The religious community supervisor and the diocesan supervisor may be performing practically the same kinds of activities. The three general headings given for the activities of the diocesan supervisor apply in general to the religious community supervisor, except one would substitute "Mother Superior" for "diocesan superintendent" in the last category. The difference, then, would not be in the kinds of services rendered.

In point of time, religious community supervisors came first. In fact, diocesan supervision was built around successful supervisory programs of religious communities. And, certainly, because of her unique value to the Sisterhood, the religious community supervisor will not be supplanted by the diocesan supervisor. Even in dioceses having both kinds of supervision, there is still much more work than can be done to everyone's satisfaction.

Perhaps the two kinds of supervision can best be distinguished in this way: religious community supervisors emphasize working directly with the individual teacher; diocesan supervisors place more emphasis on co-ordination of teaching procedures. Some dioceses have the benefit of a strong religious community supervision which attends to the details of classroom instruction. Diocesan supervision in these cases, then, can emphasize broader aspects of professional development, such as orientation programs for new teachers, lay teacher training, and systemwide curriculum committees. Without consistent religious community supervision, the diocese could not successfully carry on these co-ordinated professional activities. It would really be building on sand.

The dichotomy "religious community *versus* diocesan" supervision is not a good one. Rather, "religious community *plus* diocesan" comes closer to an ideal arrangement. And, when the co-operation between religious community supervisors and diocesan supervisors is active and cordial, the Sister Principal's work is greatly simplified. Community and diocesan supervisors can do much to strengthen the principal's position, and at the same time assist her in her own supervision.

THE FUNCTIONAL ROLE OF THE SISTER PRINCIPAL

Up to this point, the work of the Sister Principal may have looked rather insignificant. She occupies a central spot in the diocesan organizational chart, it is true. But there are so many persons over her that she may seem like a marionette rather than an administrator in her own right.

Actually, in practice, the Sister Principal is not circumscribed by the hierarchy of officers above her. She knows the limits of her authority, her privileges, and her duties; and knowing these, she is free to function on-the-job as illustrated in Figure 9.

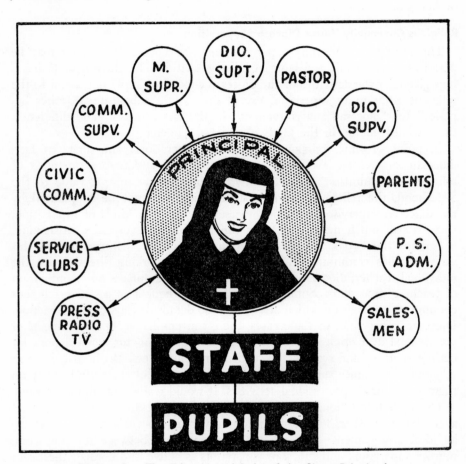

Figure 9.   The Educational Role of the Sister Principal

Figure 9 is quite a contrast to the static diocesan school organization charted earlier. At the local level, the Sister Principal is the center of operations. She is the liaison person for all outside agencies and interests; she co-ordinates the resources and personnel of her school within the framework of operating policy; she leads the staff in achieving the aims of Catholic education.

An entire book could be written to develop the implications of Figure 9.

In fact, the present book is an attempt in that direction.[11] Certainly, a thesis of the present book is plainly stated in the opening chapter: the Sister Principal is the functional leader of the Catholic elementary school. As time goes on, her position is being more clearly stated and her importance is becoming more evident. To increase her effectiveness in working with all of the persons and groups charted in Figure 9, the material in this book has been developed.

After reading a section dealing with parents, for example, the Sister Principal can evaluate her success in achieving good school-parent relations. The principal's relations with the pastor are discussed in a number of places throughout the book. By gathering these notes together, the principal can see how closely she has approached to ideal principal-pastor operational policies. The same is true of each person and group in Figure 9. All are discussed in the light of their relations to the Sister Principal as functional leader of the parochial school.

---

[11] Joseph H. Fichter, S.J., *Parochial School: A Sociological Study* (Notre Dame, Ind.: University of Notre Dame Press, 1958), passim. A readable analysis of inter-relationships of personnel in a parochial school.

FOR THE PRINCIPAL'S PROFESSIONAL LIBRARY

Committee on the Status and Functions of the Diocesan Superintendency of Schools, NCEA, *The Catholic School Superintendent, U.S.A.* (Washington, D. C.: National Catholic Welfare Conference, Department of Education, 1960), 11 pp., 25 cents.

Sister M. Richardine, B.V.M., *Catholic Elementary Schools, U.S.A.* (Washington, D. C.: National Catholic Welfare Conference, Department of Education, 1960), 16 pp., 25 cents.

CHAPTER IV

GUIDELINES FOR EFFECTIVE
ADMINISTRATION AND SUPERVISION

A principal should see her work in terms of sound educational objectives, and of the broad functions of administration and supervision. She should not regard her work as a conglomeration of unrelated day-to-day jobs to be done. What are the major functions of the principal? How is knowledge of these guidelines helpful in the day-to-day work of a principal?

IN YEARS gone by, the principalship could easily be "played by ear." There really wasn't a great deal to it — just some bookkeeping, ordering supplies, and disciplining big boys. The "head teacher" of the two-or-three room school of the past was a practitioner who operated according to tested rule-of-thumb procedures. School administration years ago was a relatively simple matter, in both public and parochial schools.

Changes in the past half-century, however, have made the principalship a very different kind of job. The preceding chapters have mentioned such changes as an increased emphasis on the objectives of Catholic education, an expanded curriculum, a growing school enrollment, improved facilities, and of course a larger and more highly trained staff. The Sister Principal attempting to administer a modern school plant and program needs much more than a "knack" for getting along with children and a way of keeping order. She needs to be an informed and well-prepared professional person. Before undertaking to direct others, and even while doing so, the principal must study the theory of administration.

THEORY OR PRACTICE?

The statement has just been made that the principal needs to know the theory of administration. Some people tend to shy away from theory; they say they are interested in what "works," not what looks good on paper. "How can those college professors tell me what will work in my school?"

THEORY AND PRACTICE DO NOT CONFLICT

With the increasing professionalization of teachers and principals, there is now much less resistance to "book learning" as opposed to on-the-job experience. As better trained principals work in their own schools, it becomes obvious that there is really no theory-practice conflict.[1] Theory, if it is good theory, can be tested in practice; practice, if it is intelligent practice, can implement theory and provide data for further theorizing. The person who relies purely on her "practical experience" is a day laborer whose attention is focused only on the job at hand. The person who consults professional literature for principles to guide her practice is an intelligent worker who can understand, interpret, and control educational situations.

A principal might experiment over the years to try to do a better job; sincere effort would no doubt improve her effectiveness. But, the principal who draws upon the literature takes a short cut. What makes for good home-school relations? What helps timid teachers? What strengthens staff morale? What promotes maturity in children? Experience supplies only limited answers to these questions. Theory provides a comprehensive framework and many "practical" solutions. Again, there is really no theory-practice conflict, when analyzed in this way. Using the literature to improve practice gives greater assurance of success, and also greater personal satisfaction.

THEORY PROVIDES A FRAME OF REFERENCE

However, there is still another cogent reason for utilizing theory in school administration. Common sense "hunches" may solve some problems; but "hunches" cannot be made part of an intelligent frame of reference. The guess may have worked in the past; but since it was not based on planned policy and procedure, administration was merely a series of random guesses, without professional insight. Administration in which common sense rather than theoretical guides predominate is likely to be administration of emergencies, a hand-to-mouth existence, a constant putting out of fires. When administration is based on basic professional study, the principal can state explicitly the reasons for the "hunches" or hypotheses selected.

The principal who is guided by sound administrative theory can propose a solution which is not a random guess, but rather is based on a knowledge of administrative principles, of child development, and of the curriculum. Put in another way, the principal can defend the actions which she proposes. Only by proceeding in this intelligent, objective manner can the principal make each experience a part of a frame of reference for improving her school.

---

[1] The theory *versus* practice problem is more fully discussed in Arthur P. Coladarci and Jacob W. Getzels, *The Use of Theory in Educational Administration,* "Stanford University School of Education Publications: Educational Administration, Monograph No. 5" (Stanford, Calif.: Stanford University Press, 1955).

Using theory selectively, and adapting practice intelligently, the principal does more than solve a single problem; she adds to a frame of reference for solving many other problems of her school in an intelligent, defensible way.

THEORY PROVIDES STANDARDS FOR JUDGING SUCCESS

Moreover, by using sound educational theory to guide practice, the principal can state with assurance just how much progress is being made. Theory supplies information for developing sound criteria for measuring the effectiveness of the school. Without criteria, no one can say whether or not a situation is improved. For example, a faculty may want to improve home-school relations, and hope that by trying several devices the relationships will improve. They will have no way of knowing whether they have been successful unless they have standards for measuring success. Theory will supply data for defining good home-school relationships, and will also suggest procedures likely to be effective. And, in retrospect, the criteria developed through theorizing will enable the faculty to determine how close to their goal they have arrived. Without criteria, there is no assurance of progress. "Book learning" is needed to formulate criteria which will be comprehensive, logical, and "practical."

The present chapter is planned as an orientation toward the functions of administration.[2] This sounds very abstract; actually, this theory can be thought of as a series of steps which a principal takes in carrying out her duties intelligently. The steps are essential to each of her duties. In a homely way, the principal should not "put the cart before the horse." There is a logical sequence in the phases of any activity. The discussion of these guidelines is intended to help the principal develop skill in the way she performs her various duties. By improving her *method* of work, the principal will necessarily improve the *quality* of her work.

FIRST, A LOOK AT OBJECTIVES

Father Ward, in Chapter II, expressed quite directly the reason why schools exist. Without any embellishments, this reason is — schools are for learning. Many other people have said this, and are saying it, but it is well to underline the idea here. So many and such various purposes are ascribed to the elementary school, and hence to elementary school administration, that it is well to set down a simple and clear statement of the real function of the school. The purpose of the school is to teach; therefore, it follows that everything connected with the school should further this

---

[2] Further discussion of the functions of administration may be found in Roald F. Campbell and Russell T. Gregg (eds.), *Administrative Behavior in Education* (New York: Harper and Brothers, Publishers, 1957), pp. 273–317.

single purpose. All activities of the school, and particularly the activities of the principal, should contribute to more effective teaching, and consequently, to more effective learning.

Catholic schools have this aim in common with other schools, but as Father Ward has pointed out, there are specific aims which the Catholic school must accomplish if it is to fulfill its purpose. The principal needs to be imbued with the spirit of Catholic educational philosophy in order to fulfill her role as leader of a Catholic school.

The Sister Principal must keep in mind that her chief objective is to "improve instruction." All that she does should, reasonably, help to improve instruction in the school. There is not a perfectly apt expression for this primary duty of the principal, so the term *supervision* continues to be used for this responsibility. "Supervision," used in its best sense, means all that the principal does to improve instruction in her school. If schools are for learning, and they most certainly are, then "supervision" in its best sense is the chief duty of the principal.

SUPERVISION AND THE PURPOSE OF THE SCHOOL

The principal's chief concern must be to insure ever better learning on the part of the pupils. Even teaching principals, to be effective, must assist teachers in upgrading their performance. To do this, principals engage in so-called supervisory activities. Some of the typical techniques in this area are providing instructional leadership through faculty meetings and committee work, arranging for demonstration teaching and intervisitation, supplying a balanced and attractive professional library, observing teaching in the classrooms, assisting teachers in lesson planning, and conferring with teachers on educational problems. All of these activities go straight to the heart of the matter; schools are for learning. Catholic schools in particular are committed to a complete education of the child; hence, in Catholic schools supervision of instruction is all the more imperative. In very simple terms, this fact can be stated for principals: "Children must learn effectively; therefore, I must supervise."

The typical teaching principal is hard pressed to provide adequate supervision for her school. The trend is, fortunately, toward more time free from teaching so that principals can do more supervision. However, even in the case of the teaching principal, and there are many, the purpose of the school remains the same. And supervision, even if somewhat limited, is necessary if children are to learn what the schools should teach them.

ADMINISTRATION AND THE PURPOSE OF THE SCHOOL

It stands to reason that the principal cannot simply supervise. She must do so as part of an operational pattern. Only in a smoothly operating school can the principal take time for supervisory activities. Another way of saying this is that the principal needs to be an efficient administrator if she is to supervise effectively. She first organizes, and then executes her plans for instructional improvement.

One phase of administration is organization — planning the framework for effective teaching and learning. Organization is the groundwork, the structure, the blueprint. A little later, the principal's role in organizing will be discussed as one of the guidelines for effective administration. Organization is basic to good administration, and is mentioned here because of the confusion that sometimes exists between the terms "administration" and "organization."[3]

Organization is only a beginning phase of administration. Another phase is the direction, control, and management of people and materials so that effective learning can take place within this operational framework. In these days of democratic administration, the words *direct, control*, and *manage* may seem harsh, but they indicate what the principal does in insuring a sound educational program for children. The tremendous resources of the parochial school could be frittered away by principals who did not administer the school intelligently and firmly. Democratic processes can be utilized, of course, in administering a school; but whatever the means used, it is the principal's ultimate responsibility to insure the best possible teaching, and hence, learning, in her school.

Later chapters in this book will deal with specific aspects of administration, such as teacher personnel policies, work load of teachers, office management, and plant maintenance. It is important to stress here that these and other aspects of administration provide the conditions in which effective learning can take place. Any of these administrative duties might usurp the place which pupil learning should occupy; maintaining an attractive building, for example, could well infringe upon the time needed for supervision. Administration is not an end in itself; it exists only for the purpose of promoting pupil learning. Good administration first works out a systematic and sound plan and then goes on to surround the teaching activity with conditions conducive to success. In this context, the principal can then employ her professional competence to work directly in improving instruction.

THE GUIDELINES IN PREVIEW

The preceding discussion has been presented in order to place the guidelines in their proper perspective. A guideline could become a fetish, if it

---

[3] The distinctions between "organization" and "administration" are clearly drawn in Will French, J. Dan Hull, B. L. Dodds, *American High School Administration* (New York: Rinehart and Company, Inc., 1957), pp. 5–17.

were not well grounded in the objectives of sound educational philosophy.

The guidelines proposed here for the Sister Principal's guidance are the following:

1. The principal must plan.
2. The principal must organize.
3. The principal must direct.
4. The principal must arrange for communication.
5. The principal must evaluate.

These five guidelines normally occur in sequence. Planning, for example, usually occurs before organizing and directing. But at times, several of the guidelines are operative at once. Planning ideally occurs at the beginning of an undertaking; but as the work progresses, old plans must be altered and new plans made. Evaluating, too, occurs throughout a project; achievement is analyzed critically, or organization, or direction, and the necessary adjustments are made. Although there may be some overlapping, it will be good for the principal to see how these five guidelines enter into efficient administration. By studying these guidelines, the principal can develop a more intelligent procedure for administering her school. This procedure can then be applied to whatever activity the principal is pursuing at the time.

GUIDELINE ONE — THE PRINCIPAL MUST PLAN

Some principals have a fear of being "caught" at their office desk. There are so many things to do that they feel they should keep in motion doing them. Then, too, sitting at a desk looks rather officious. The principal wants to feel competent to do her work, but she doesn't want to look as if she is neglecting the urgent demands of the moment.

As a matter of fact, planning is a prime essential for any worthwhile undertaking. Occasionally, a good idea flashes upon one unannounced, but usually good ideas aren't "brainstorms"; good ideas are developed through careful planning. It takes time to plan, and a certain amount of solitude. Some desk work is essential to planning. In fact, when the good results of planning become apparent to the faculty, they will be proud of the principal's desk work. For a teaching principal the need for careful planning is all the more urgent, for she has only limited time free from teaching to take care of the many duties of her office. These nonteaching hours are precious, and hence warrant judicious planning. The principal has decided that she must plan. But, where to start?

Basis of Good Planning

In order to provide competent leadership for her staff, the principal must first make long-range plans covering the entire year. A working knowledge of Catholic philosophy comes in handy here. Every Sister Principal needs to ask herself, "What am I doing this year to help our school become more Catholic?" "Which objectives of Catholic education need emphasis now?"[4] The principal need not apologize for emphasizing moral and spiritual values; many a public school principal wishes he had the Sister Principal's opportunities for promoting the moral and spiritual development of children.

At the same time, there are subject-matter objectives to be stressed. A particular school, or grade, may be weak in arithmetic, for example, as shown on standardized achievement tests. Or, public relations objectives may seem to be in need of additional emphasis; parents and teachers may seem indifferent to the many mutual interests they have. Or, the principal may use in her planning a checklist for good administration as presented in Chapter Five. All of these approaches furnish content for the long-range planning which a competent principal does.

Some of the more glaring needs will appear at a glance. However, in order to be sure of her footing, the principal might profitably study the diocesan handbook, the school handbook, the course of study, school records, and the professional literature. The more glaring deficiencies may be only surface ones; perhaps more fundamental needs should be stressed. Weakness in arithmetic may be due to a number of factors — a short school day, frequent class interruptions, unprepared teachers, or inadequate materials. Before deciding upon a plan, the principal should analyze the school situation carefully.

In addition to the long-range plans for the year, there will be smaller plans, made from time to time as the need arises. These plans, too, should be based upon careful study. The principal conscious of the need for planning knows that good plans are basic to progress. Good plans are needed in order to achieve the purpose of the school program — the best possible learning for children.

The Parts of a Good Plan

Planning is really problem solving, and it includes the same steps:

1. Know the purpose to be achieved
2. Gather the pertinent facts
3. Study the facts
4. Decide how to work for improvement
5. Choose the way which seems most likely to succeed

---

[4] Catholic University of America, Department of Education, *Criteria for the Evaluation of Catholic Elementary Schools*, "Realization of the Objectives of Catholic Education," pp. 96–102 (Washington, D. C.: The Catholic University of America Press, 1949). This discussion outlines the five objectives of Catholic elementary schools succinctly and clearly.

In practice, the Sister Principal plans her supervisory program for the year using the five steps given above. She has a feeling that the children do not know as much arithmetic as they should. She wants to plan for improved learning of arithmetic content during the coming year. This is her purpose (Step One). In her classroom observations, there seemed to be a lack of sureness about fundamental processes. Also, the standardized achievement tests taken in grades three and six showed a lack of mastery for the grade. These are the facts that bear out her own assumption (Steps Two and Three). How might she go about improving the mastery of arithmetic? Faculty discussions, demonstrations, committee work on devices for securing interest, an outside speaker on arithmetic — all of these are possibilities (Step Four). Knowing her faculty group well, the Sister Principal decides that demonstrations would be effective; so would having the consultant from the arithmetic text publisher speak to the faculty group on improved arithmetic teaching (Step Five). Whenever the principal plans well, even in very simple planning, she goes through these steps, at least mentally.

When the steps have been completed, the procedure decided upon should be put into writing. Written plans can be more surely carried out, and they are also likely to be more realistic. Can we accomplish this much? Will these methods be possible? A written plan makes one very self-conscious about the commitments being made. Another reason for written plans is that they chart the school's proposed progress through the year. Written plans show what the principal, the staff, and the pupils have attempted and what measure of success they have enjoyed.

Kinds of Planning

The Sister Principal who is a real educational leader makes definite plans for improving her own efficiency and that of her staff. However, the principal need not do this planning entirely on her own; other people can help materially in formulating good plans. It is important that persons who will be affected by changes be notified before the changes take place. It is still more important that the people who will be affected actually take part in making the plans. The plans themselves will be more practical, and the participants will be better disposed to implement them. The wise principal will do some planning with other individuals and with groups as she works to improve the school program.

Planning With Individuals. Within the framework of her all-over planning, there is ample room for planning with the individuals most interested in the school. With the pastor, the competent principal plans periodically throughout the year. Since the pastor is the spiritual head of the school as well as the provider of the necessary finances, the pastor and principal need to plan their sharing of responsibility in several areas, such as finance, discipline, religious training of pupils, and janitorial service. With supervisors, whenever opportunity presents, the principal can plan for more helpful supervisory service. With individual teachers, the principal plans for professional growth. Also with the nonteaching staff, the competent principal plans regularly; the secretary, the janitor, the nurse, and sometimes even bus drivers need to be taken into planning.

Planning With Groups. More and more, progressive principals are making use of a committee of teachers to help make plans for the school. Sometimes the members are voted into the Planning Committee by the faculty group; sometimes they are appointed by the principal and faculty together. This small group meets regularly with the principal to make recommendations, to suggest improvements, and to give the faculty's attitudes toward the ongoing program. An advisory council of this kind is invaluable; principals who have made use of it feel that their plans have been greatly improved. The principal also plans with the entire faculty at times, when their opinions would be more helpful than those of the advisory council alone. In connection with the Home and School Association, the principal should welcome the opportunity to plan with the pastor and parents for better home-school policies. Planning of the kind here discussed is essential to good administration.

Pitfalls in Planning

A cautionary note should be introduced. The principal needs to make a distinction between policies that can be developed through planning, and policies that are beyond the discussion of the group. The principal and faculty must accept as authoritative those policies established by the pastor and by the Diocesan School Office. Though suggestions might be made for modifying these policies, the faculty is not empowered to change the regulations. The faculty and others can be involved, however, in planning policies which adapt broader regulations to the local situation.

Another distinction which should be made is between planning and executing policy. It is certainly advisable to include the staff and parents in developing plans which immediately concern them. Those who work with the principal and the pastor in planning, however, serve in an advisory capacity. Members may suggest and recommend; but the principal does not merely count hands and act on group consensus. The principal may do so, of course, when she feels that the group's decision reflects the best course of action. Still, the principal, and not the group, has the administrative responsibility for the plans that are developed. The principal executes the policy, as the responsible administrative head of the school. At no time does group consensus tie the hands of the principal.

GUIDELINE TWO — THE PRINCIPAL MUST ORGANIZE

Once a plan has been decided upon, the principal systematically co-ordinates her staff so that this goal can be reached. "Organization" implies a co-operative and planned effort to achieve a common goal. Organization means also the framework within which the principal carries out her plans. So, organization means both the physical arrangement of people and things and also the co-ordination of activities.

The line and staff arrangement outlined in Chapter III shows the formal organization of parochial schools. Everyone knows that there are features of good organization not included on this line-and-staff plan. Those who people this chart, who make it live, are the real flesh-and-blood organization. And as with all other human relationships, organization depends upon the influence of people, no matter where they appear on the formal chart. It is well known that a janitor may wield greater influence on organization than a teacher; or, a secretary may outplay a principal in school strategy. So both the organization-on-paper and the organization-in-motion need to be studied.

The Purpose of Organization. Why organize? Obviously, to get things done quicker and better. When the principal plans carefully who will do what, and when, school routines can be taken care of with dispatch. There is an atmosphere of calm, efficiency, and productivity in a school that is well organized. Yet there is another and equally important reason for organizing. It is a reason which seems to be lost sight of in many cases; organization should satisfy the needs of all individuals concerned. Research in human relations has shown that when the individuals find an organization personally satisfying, they work harder and better to achieve the goals of the organization.

So, the Sister Principal organizes to achieve two purposes: to discharge the duties which the staff must share, and to satisfy the reasonable personal needs of the staff. The second kind of organization requires more attention and more skill than the first kind, but the wise principal accepts this responsibility along with the others.

What are the staff's needs? Good working conditions would be a basic minimum: a clean, attractive, well-equipped, well-ordered school and classroom. With lay teachers, a living wage and Social Security would also be minimal. Also, interpersonal relations with the principal contribute to personal satisfaction. The principal needs to plan so that each staff member sees the importance of the work she is doing, has a chance to develop creativity, gets recognition for good work, and feels a part of the great cause of Catholic education.

Because of the great variety among staff members in any parochial school today, this is a big order. But it is part of the principal's work in organization. Firmness is necessary, of course, to see that the staff members carry out their responsibilities; but co-operation can be better insured if the members identify themselves with goals of the school. This co-operation must be planned, for it is part of the principal's work as an organizer.

Organization, then, has two purposes: to get work done efficiently, and to contribute to the personal satisfaction of the members. Organization for the sake of organization is empty; organization for the sake of better instruction should be the goal. When teachers are happy in their work, children learn better. When teachers take an interest in trying new techniques, children learn better. When teachers want to do a "little extra" for the smooth operation of the school, children learn better. Artistry in organization achieves both the personal satisfaction of the staff and the realization of the goals of the school. To achieve these goals, the principal uses both the formal and the informal organization of staff members.

The Formal Organization. The structure of the formal school organization is the usual line-and-staff one. Authority flows from principal, to teachers, to pupils, and from the principal to the nonteaching staff. In matters directly subject to the pastor's jurisdiction, as the spiritual direction of the pupils, authority may flow from the pastor to the principal to the pupils, or from the pastor directly to the pupils. Within this formal organization, the Sister Principal plans to carry out her educational objectives. So that the principal can allot the necessary time to supervision, she delegates various administrative duties to the staff. The teachers themselves have good ideas about delegating these responsibilities. Through careful planning with the staff, the Sister Principal can work out an acceptable schedule for performing such duties. The principal needs to see that there is no overlapping of responsibility and no overloading of willing teachers. The formal organization of the staff helps to get these routine, but important, duties taken care of efficiently. It is a good idea to make a chart showing the extra-class responsibilities of the staff, and to post this chart so that all the teachers can examine it, work within the framework, and suggest improvements.

The Informal Organization. A formal chart shows just the hierarchy of roles, and who is assigned each responsibility. The formal chart shows nothing of the interesting interplay of human personalities. Formally, any two teachers are equal in rank; both are teachers, subject to the principal and superior to the pupils. However, no two teachers are actually equal in influence in staff relationships. Experience, personality, "drive" — all cause natural leaders to emerge in the group. Cliques are formed, and friendships. Some staff members align themselves with, and some more or less against, the administration. Some vacillate between loyalty to the school and self-interest.

Staff members have frequent contacts with one another, especially at lunch, and when engaged in the same kind of work such as playground supervision, and in the teachers' lounge. Out of these contacts develop common attitudes, viewpoints, and ways of acting. No kind of formal pattern of organization can prevent this; in fact, none should try to do so. The principal should recognize, though, the influence of the informal organization. It is difficult, but necessary, to plan so that the informal contacts of staff members contribute to the all-over effectiveness of the school. The principal must be a capable, informed, and strong individual to lead the diverse personalities of the school in pursuit of common objectives.

Capitalizing on "Get-Togethers." As mentioned in the purposes of organization, the principal will want to meet the reasonable personal needs of the staff members as individuals. This does not mean giving in to whim, or granting every request, or ignoring insubordination. Rather, the basic human needs of the staff can be met through such activities as planned "get-togethers." For example, teachers like to meet and talk things over. The wise principal arranges throughout the year satisfying occasions when teachers can talk among themselves. Examples of such occasions are a beautifully prepared luncheon to open the school year; a Christmas party with good food and well-selected gifts; an attractive convention or professional meeting to which delegates may be sent on the basis of experience or special interest; coffee and fancy cookies before a faculty meeting; a comfortable lounge arranged for conversation; provision for a coffee break during recess. The principal should be present frequently for such informal faculty gatherings. It should not create a stir when the principal drops into the lounge for a few minutes, or takes a cup of coffee with the faculty at recess. The goals of the school are advanced when staff members have organized opportunities to meet together informally, with the principal present from time to time.

Keeping People Informed. It is also important to keep everyone informed. Teachers are upset when notified at the last minute that they can't use the projector they have set up because their pupils are to be inoculated. Teachers like to know of coming events, of changes in routine. With lay teachers, it is good to have a published salary scale. Salaries should be no secret, and neither should most other things in the school. The informal organization can best serve the purposes of the school when the staff is kept informed, and when the staff has a feeling of personal worth and belongingness. The informal organization can be just as effective as the formal line-and-staff organization in achieving the goals of the school.

GUIDELINE THREE — THE PRINCIPAL MUST DIRECT

The third phase of good administration is direction. Earlier in the chapter, administration was defined as "directing, controlling, and managing." These actions are not the whole of administration, though they strike the dominant note. In popular opinion, to administer means to tell people what is to be done and then see that they do it. However, administration does not mean merely giving directions, though directions are needed to keep a school operating smoothly. Ideally, direction involves *leadership*, which points the way to good educational practice and provides the necessary conditions, *control*, which implements the policies needed for a good educational program, and *delegation*, which shares administrative responsibility with other competent people. Skillful direction is probably the most intricate competency which a good principal develops.[5]

Direction as Leadership. Direction implies that the principal accept her role as educational leader in the school, and that this role be recognized. As part of leadership, the principal sees that school policies are clearly stated: diocesan-wide policies, those issued by the pastor, and policies developed in the individual school — preferably through co-operative staff discussion. In addition to stating policies, the principal must be sure that staff members know exactly what is expected of them.

Direction as leadership also requires that the principal keep focused before her the aims of the school program, and effective means of achieving these aims. In this aspect of direction, the principal establishes standards co-operatively when possible, and provides the equipment, materials, and personal assistance needed to meet these standards. Direction, in carrying out this duty, need not be authoritarian at all; direction is expected and welcome, when the standards set are in keeping with the situation, and adequate means are provided for achieving the standards. On the other hand, a laissez-faire attitude is not leadership at all, but rather weakness. Positive and stimulating direction is needed if teachers are to work consistently to provide a better educational program for children.

Wise direction involves a broad background of information, skill in human relations, courage in carrying out one's plans, and at the same time, deep humility. For example, in working with a faculty group, the principal's direction may consist in conducting group discussions, supplying needed materials, arranging for clerical help, recognizing the contribution

---

[5] The difficult art of directing others is given, from the religious point of view, in Paul Hoffer, S.M., *Guide for Religious Administrators* (Milwaukee: The Bruce Publishing Company, 1958).

The human relations' points of view are presented well in Les Giblin, *How to Have Confidence and Power in Dealing with People* (Englewood Cliffs, N. J.: Prentice-Hall, Inc., 1956).

of each group member, and keeping in mind both the long-range objectives of the school and the immediate objectives of the group in progress. Of this kind of direction, the teachers are likely to say, "We did it ourselves." And this is good; the best kind of direction is least obvious.

Direction as Control. Ordinarily, the staff that is engaged in a stimulating, all-over school program will rarely need the exercise of control. However, as administrative head of the school, the principal is responsible for seeing that policies are carried out and that standards are met. When necessary, the principal must use her authority and exercise control in achieving these purposes.

The wise principal uses indirect control consistently, by keeping in touch with all aspects of the school program. In a later chapter, this kind of indirect control is illustrated in the principal's schedule for building and classroom supervision. Indirect control is also maintained by careful planning, organizing, communicating, and evaluating. Preventing difficulties is easier and wiser than trying to correct them after they have developed. Indirect control has this for its ultimate purpose.

On occasion, direct control is also necessary. The criterion here is this: Does this situation keep children from learning as they should? If so, then the principal must use direct control to prevent the situation from continuing. For example, the principal would need to exercise direct control if classes were unorganized when returning from recess, and as a result children were losing time from class instruction. Or, teachers anxious to get to the university for late-afternoon classes, were leaving the building with their ranks; and as a consequence, their rooms were left in imperfect order, and children waiting for buses were unsupervised. In the case of staff negligence, and some negligence can be expected, the principal must use direction as needed to remedy the deficiencies. The direct control exercised here cannot be justly resented when the principal has supplied adequate leadership.

The principal needs to keep her perspective in the disciplinary aspects of directing; nagging is disagreeable and ineffective. Nonconformity should not be viewed as a personal thing, but rather as a breach of school policy. An essential part of the principal's job is securing conformity with school policies and standards. The principal is expected to exercise such control as needed to provide a good teaching-learning situation.

Direction Through Delegation. Since it is not possible, or even good, to try to do everything one's self, the principal wisely delegates some administrative responsibility to her staff. Ordinarily, except for a few routine tasks, such as playground supervision, most principals don't delegate work to their staff. Why? Some principals just don't think of delegation as one of their responsibilities. Some principals are so busy themselves that they don't look around to see that their teachers are not too busy to take responsibility for some project. Or, principals may feel that it would be unworthy of them to pass on their jobs to someone else. Other principals have managed; they will manage somehow. However, today, delegation does not consist in merely passing out miscellaneous jobs to staff members; there is a whole new philosophy of delegation.

Principals should look over the duties they perform in a day, or a week, and organize these jobs into three categories or levels:

1. Jobs which a school clerk or janitor could do equally well
2. Jobs which a teacher could do, or could be trained to do
3. Jobs which administrators must do themselves

Level One — the most mechanical or routine type — could be done by a nonprofessional person. Counting money collections is in this category; so are passing out supplies, answering the telephone, typing letters, dusting shelves, and unpacking cartons. Some principals have confessed that they actually spend one third of their time on such picayune tasks. Most schools could arrange for at least a part-time secretary, even if only on a volunteer basis. Better janitorial service could also be arranged in most places. Jobs of a clerical or janitorial nature should be delegated to nonprofessional workers, and should not be done by a trained school administrator. A $4-an-hour person should not waste her time on $1.50-an-hour jobs. The principal's time is worth at least $4 an hour, as studies of public school salaries will show (see discussion later in this chapter).

Level Two — jobs which a teacher could do — requires some professional background, but teachers have enough training, or could be trained, to carry them out. For example, orienting new teachers could be taken over by an experienced teacher acting as an adviser. Preparing for home and school association meetings might be largely delegated to staff members working under the direction of the principal. Ordering, distributing, and inventorying supplies could be done by a clerk, under the direction of a staff member. Directing practice for First Holy Communion, preparing assembly programs, conducting the testing program — all of these responsibilities might be shared with faculty members acting under the principal's leadership.

Level Three — jobs which the principal must reserve to herself — involves responsibilities which the principal must discharge personally as responsible head of the school. One of these duties is directing the program of in-service growth. Another is acting as liaison person with outside individuals and groups such as the pastor, the diocesan superintendent, public school officials, and health agencies. Another of her administrative responsibilities is to formulate school policy and to see that policies are carried out. The final responsibility for the educational program of the school is of course the principal's. All that is strong, and weak, in the school program reflects not on an individual staff member, but on the principal as the responsible head of the school. Final responsibility is always hers.

Planning for Staff Development. Having seen that some of her work can be effectively done by others, the principal has only begun to study delegation. The next step is to consider delegation positively — as a means of developing the potential of her staff. Many teachers now have professional training equal to that of the principal: such teachers cannot be satisfied with the narrow limits of their classroom. They need the satisfaction that comes from broadened contacts and higher-level activity.

Really to develop people, the principal should delegate not only routine duties, but also work of a creative and responsible sort. Preparing faculty meetings can be a creative experience, as can committee work in formulating school policy. An effective principal also develops in her staff some of the competencies of the principalship; in her absence any one of several teachers should be able to take over and do a commendable job. If the work delegated is to give the teacher a feeling of accomplishment and growth, then the teacher must be given adequate responsibility and authority to carry out the assignment. The principalship should not be viewed as one expert directing amateurs; the principalship today should be a "constellation of experts." Teachers are improving steadily in professional competency; it is the principal's role to develop them into the experts needed for today's democratic schools.

Cautions When Delegating. First of all, the principal should be sure that the delegated work is important and needs to be done. It may seem almost too obvious to say that delegated work must never be mere busy work, masquerading as democratic procedures. Nothing kills interest and initiative more surely than the realization that the project isn't necessary and won't be used.

Also, the teacher's work load should be taken into consideration. The teacher's first duty is to her class: semi-administrative duties are in second place. If teachers are to devote themselves to both class work and delegated duties with energy and originality, their work load must be reasonable.

Further, the principal should make clear just what the limits of authority and responsibility are. The teacher, or clerk, should know exactly what is expected of her, how much authority she has, and how her work is to be co-ordinated with the work of the entire staff. Once the teacher has begun the project, the principal should assist as needed, but should not hover about as if she doubted the teacher's ability to carry out the assignment. Recognition should of course be given for delegated work well done.

Reaping the Fruits of Delegation. What are the rewards for delegating duties wisely? Most importantly, the principal has time to be what her title indicates — an educational leader. She can keep her attention resolutely fixed on the improvement of instruction. Also, through wise delegation, the principal has the satisfaction of developing the potential talent of her staff. Particularly in religious communities, this is a noteworthy contribution, for the talent thus developed is channeled into community projects. Wise delegation develops staff potential, while at the same time it permits present leaders to perform competently.

Direction, as discussed above, establishes the principal as the responsible head of the school, using her authority to direct in three ways: through leadership, through control, and through delegation. Through adequate direction, the principal utilizes her own talents and those of her staff members in the fullest degree.

GUIDELINE FOUR — THE PRINCIPAL MUST ARRANGE FOR COMMUNICATION

Communicating is a technical term meaning to keep informed, to "keep in touch," to establish rapport, to keep channels open. The principal who plans for adequate communication in her school uses a variety of devices. Handbooks, diocesan and school, provide information on routines. The bulletin board displays the principal's posted schedule of conferences and observations, and also the agenda for the coming faculty meeting. The faculty lounge is arranged for conversation and for coffee breaks. There is a suggestion box for use of the faculty. Teachers and principal exchange a friendly word on their way through the halls. Good communication is just the opposite of everyone's retiring to her own shell and "letting the rest of the world go by."

Good communication, one can readily see, promotes the interests of the school. Policies are understood, ideas are exchanged, and smooth operation is assured. Good communication also promotes the interests of the individuals in the organization; the principal, being human, wants to be accepted by the staff, and the staff, in turn, want to know the principal and their associates, on a friendly basis. When ideas can be exchanged freely, a spirit of group solidarity is fostered, and the group "feels good" about themselves and the school. In an atmosphere of friendliness, the group tends to work co-operatively toward the goals of the school. All is not "sweetness and light," but friction is kept to a minimum. Such communication doesn't happen by chance; it must be planned for; it is one of the important responsibilities of the Sister Principal. It is well for her to consider in her planning the three kinds of communication which she should promote.

Downward Communication. This kind of communication is from the higher officer to the subordinate, or in the school, from the pastor and principal to the teacher. Downward communication includes principal's bulletins, written statements of policy, messages from the principal or higher official, and various other means of keeping the staff informed. Downward communication is psychologically good; it makes the staff feel that they are important enough to share pertinent information. Downward communication is also good in that an informed staff can be a self-impelling staff, not dependent upon the principal for continual directives. In the examples given earlier, efficient downward communication is shown in the handbooks of policy, the posted supervisory schedules, and co-operatively planned faculty meeting agenda. Frequent face-to-face contacts, as well as written statements, are needed in downward communication.

Upward Communication. Equally essential is upward communication, a flow of information and opinion from the staff up to the principal. The principal must sincerely want to know how the staff feel, if upward communication is to be effective. Through upward communication, the principal learns how the staff is reacting to administrative practices and policies, and can prevent minor difficulties from becoming major. By sympathetic and unbiased listening, the principal can get valuable suggestions for operating the school. Upward communication will continue, however, only if valid suggestions are acted upon. A "listening" principal is a good one in the eyes of the staff, but only if necessary action follows listening. When a subordinate's complaints are unreasonable, sometimes just having the opportunity to talk the matter over releases tension. For the more timid staff members, a suggestion box helps to solicit ideas to guide administration. As a part of upward communication, the principal should arrange for frequent conferences with each staff member, teaching and nonteaching. It is a sad indictment when teachers say, "Our principal is so busy we hate to bother her with questions." Bother? Not at all. It is part of the principal's job to provide time for the staff to present their problems. Face-to-face discussion can iron out almost any difficulty. A principal who takes time to let teachers ask questions is helping the teacher and at the same time helping the school.

Horizontal Communication. It may at first seem unnecessary to plan for communication among staff members. Teachers seem to meet and talk as they go about their work. However, when the principal provides opportunities for the faculty to meet together informally, faculty morale is boosted. Faculty meetings conducted by the staff, orientation luncheons, coffee breaks, Christmas parties for the staff, small group staff work on projects of interest, grade level discussions — these provide a natural framework for interchange of ideas on topics of educational and personal interest.

The psychological effect of such face-to-face contacts is helpful in building a group feeling, and in ironing out petty difficulties.

Occasionally, of course, this planned-for horizontal communication may break down. The principal may learn from a staff member that the topic of conversation during a coffee break was the clumsy way the principal handled the play practice the day before. The principal's first reaction might be, "After all I've done to provide opportunities for them to relax and enjoy their recess period . . ." Though the principal may sincerely want constructive criticism, she naturally is irked by their "biting the hand that feeds them." At times, such criticism of the principal is introduced by a staff member who is undesirable for a number of reasons; criticism of the principal may be only one aspect of the general low quality of her performance. No matter what the caliber of the critic, however, the better the principal administers the school the less likely is she to be criticized, though some criticism is inevitable. Perhaps the principal *did* handle the practice clumsily. . . . By constructive, stimulating leadership, and control wisely exercised, the principal or pastor will not come in for undue censure during informal faculty get-togethers. In fact, the occasional presence of pastor and principal at an informal gathering shows their human side and makes for better acceptance.

Studies show that schools having good communication have high morale. Promoting the three kinds of communication should be part of the principal's objectives for the year.

GUIDELINE FIVE — THE PRINCIPAL MUST EVALUATE

If a principal were asked, "Have you a program of evaluation?," her answer would probably refer to the school's testing program. Certainly, tests are one of the most common kinds of evaluation. As an administrator and supervisor, the principal has, however, a broader responsibility than the term *tests* includes. "Testing" refers to measurement which gives a *quantitative* score, such as, a number, a percentile, or a grade placement. Such quantitative scores are obtained for example, on tests of intelligence, aptitude, achievement, hearing, and vision. "Evaluation" is a much broader term than "testing," for it includes testing, and much more. Evaluation includes the foregoing objective measures and also subjective or personal estimates, such as can be obtained through the use of such techniques as observation, case history, biography, interview, questionnaire, check list, and rating scale. Everyone knows from experience that we place a great deal of confidence in our own observations and impressions. Evaluation, then, draws upon these impressions as well as on test scores. Evaluation uses both tests and subjective techniques, integrates the data, interprets them, makes a diagnosis, and prescribes action to be taken.

Reasons for Evaluation

Evaluation in this broad sense tends to be neglected. The principal is so busy administering, and perhaps also teaching, that she does not take time to back off and scrutinize the school program and her own role in it. There is a natural tendency, when one is very busy, to lose sight of the end in attending to the means. The effective principal, however, plans specifically for evaluation for three very definite reasons.

Public Criticism of Education. The American public, and even educators themselves, have been highly critical of the work of the schools. Proof has been demanded that the billions of dollars spent on education is not being wasted. The fact that parochial schools are voluntarily supported by Catholics does not exempt them from a share of this criticism. In a sense, the shock of this criticism has been good, for it has caused education to re-examine its philosophy, aims, methods, and outcomes. The question which school people must answer with facts is this: How has your educational program been of positive benefit to children? How are you using the results of experience and research to improve your school program so that greater good will be done for children?

Many lectures, articles, even whole books have been written to defend present educational programs. Yet, these defenses are not fully convincing. Perhaps right after reading a stirring apologia, the Sister Principal has felt impelled to study more critically the results of teaching in her own school. Parochial school principals, and in fact most principals, feel sincerely that their own school program is producing good results. Yet, current criticism of education must cause some disturbing thoughts. To answer criticism of education to their own satisfaction and to the satisfaction of all interested persons, the parochial school principal should re-examine and perhaps broaden her program of evaluation.

Staff Interest in Evaluation. A more pressing reason, perhaps, for evaluation is the interest of the local staff. Teachers consistently want to know how well they are succeeding, and it is the responsibility of the principal to help the staff find satisfactory answers to this question. Sometimes these inquiries concern subject matter: How can I tell if my class is getting along all right in reading, or spelling, or arithmetic? Or, the teacher may ask a question on religious development: Are children of this age usually disposed to frequent reception of the sacraments? Or, the question may deal with physical, or social or emotional development. When teachers ask questions like these, they are interested in measuring the outcomes of their teaching. They are trying to evaluate their own effectiveness in the light of pupil progress. In providing opportunity to find answers to these questions, the principal is in an admirable position to offer effective leadership.

The principal need not be a specialist in measurement. She should, however, acquire enough background and experience in this area to provide satisfactory answers to questions on pupil and teacher evaluation.

The Administrator's Responsibility. The most urgent reason for evaluation is the administrator's responsibility for the effectiveness of the whole school program. The principal has the duty to see that the school accomplishes the purposes for which it exists. This duty can be fulfilled only when the principal maintains a continuous evaluation of the results of teaching in the light of the school's objectives.

This may be very true; but how can the teaching principal be responsible for evaluating pupil progress in her school when her own day is filled with teaching obligations? Although one may sympathize sincerely with the teaching principal, one would detract from her administrative status by inferring that she does not have this obligation. The teaching principal, as well as the supervising principal, has as one of her major responsibilities appraising the educational status of her school and planning for needed remedial measures. How can the teaching principal discharge this obligation in a schedule that is all too crowded now? There is no panacea for the crowdedness of the teaching principal's life, but there is hope in the ways alert teaching principals have attacked the problem of "no time." For the present, the fact must be re-emphasized that evaluation of the school's effectiveness is an important obligation of both supervising and teaching principals. The parochial school principal shares with the public school principal the duty of evaluating the school's program for the staff, parents, state authorities, and the public in general. The parochial school principal also has responsibilities for evaluation to the pastor, religious superior, and diocesan superintendent. The kind of evaluation made to each of these persons or groups varies from time to time, but the obligation to evaluate is continuous. For the cogent reasons mentioned above, the parochial school principal accepts evaluation as a duty of her office.

Characteristics of a Good Evaluation

Evaluation is a duty that pervades each activity of the principal, so evaluation is basic to successful performance. The present discussion will show how the principal can improve her evaluation, and hence her performance, by stressing the four C's of evaluation: criteria, comprehensiveness, co-operation, and continuity.

Evaluation Should Be Based on Valid Criteria. In order to judge how good her school is, the principal cannot rely on her own observations alone; she needs valid measuring rods, or criteria. What should a good school be like? What should a good school do for children? How can the principal know?

faith, love and spirit of sacrifice | which will inspire them to offer their children to God's service | and to rejoice when a child of theirs is called to the religious life. | Let Thy example and that of their Blessed Mother and St. Joseph | encourage both children and parents, | and let Thy grace sustain them. Amen.

O Mary, Queen of the clergy, pray for us; | obtain for us many and holy priests.—(An indulgence of 300 days.)

O Lord, grant unto Thy Church saintly priests and fervent religious. — (An indulgence of 300 days.)

Send forth, O Lord, laborers into Thy harvest. —(An indulgence of 500 days.) (Raccolta)

The Witness, February 26, 1953

VOCATION PRAYERS

O God | Whose will it is that all men be saved | and come to the knowledge of truth: | we beg You to send laborers into Your harvest | and grant them to speak Your word with confidence; | that Your word may spread and be glorified, | and that all people may know You, the only true God, | and Him Whom You have sent, | Jesus Christ Your Son, our Lord: | Who lives and reigns with You world without end. Amen.

O Divine Jesus, | Son of the Eternal Father and of Mary Immaculate, | grant to our youth generosity in following Thy call, | and bestow on them the grace to persevere | in overcoming all obstacles to their vocation. | Give to parents, likewise, | that

The principal can arrive at answers to these questions through professional reading, graduate courses, faculty discussion, observation of other schools, lectures of educators, and even from her own "hunches." No matter how the principal obtains her standards, if they are good ones, they must be directly related to the school's objectives. We cannot tell how well a school is doing unless we know what the school set out to do.

This is not as vague as it sounds. Father Ward's chapter refreshed the principal's background in the philosophy of Catholic education; she is now in a better position to state some of the criteria for judging the special objectives of a Catholic school. The present text presents criteria for evaluating effectiveness in various areas. Many state departments of education have developed standards for evaluating the schools within their jurisdiction.[6] Some state departments require the schools to have on file a statement of objectives and criteria for evaluation. These requirements make sense. To be effective, one must know what one is attempting to accomplish. A written statement of objectives and of criteria is fundamental to successful administration and supervision.

Evaluation Should Be Comprehensive. A good evaluation is broad in scope. It includes appraisal of each area of the principal's responsibility: building, schedule, equipment, policies, instructional materials, quality of teaching, pupil achievement, supervisory services, office routines, health and safety program, public relations. This list, though long, could be extended still further, for a good evaluation gives a comprehensive picture of all aspects of the school's program. The present text presents some helps for evaluating the school's program in many areas. For example, Chapters XIII and XIV present standards for evaluating pupil progress. Chapters VIII, IX, and X discuss criteria for judging teaching competence. Chapters IV, V, and X develop ways of appraising the principal's supervisory program. At least seven chapters help the principal measure her effectiveness as an administrator.

To provide a comprehensive evaluation, the principal must also use a variety of techniques and instruments. Pupil tests are in use in all schools, though some helpful tests are relatively untried. Check lists furnish ideas,

---

[6] Typical of the better criteria prepared by state departments of education are the following:

Colorado State Department of Education, *Self-Evaluation in Elementary Schools in Colorado, Evaluative Criteria for Use in Local Schools* (Boulder, Colo.: Colorado State Department of Education, 1956).

Connecticut State Department of Education, *How to Recognize a Good Elementary School: A Guide for Evaluation of Connecticut Elementary Schools.* Prepared by Bureau of School and Community Services, Bulletin No. 68 (Hartford: Connecticut State Department of Education, June, 1957).

Ohio State Board of Education, *Ohio Elementary School Standards* (Columbus, Ohio: Heer Printing Company, 1958).

as do rating scales, questionnaires, trained observation, interviews, pupil records, and just listening.

A comprehensive evaluation presupposes that the principal will develop a system for recording, interpreting, and using the data thus accumulated. A broad evaluation program can extend the horizons of principal, faculty, and parents, and yet important data for improving the school may lie buried and useless. One question on evaluation should not be neglected: "How do you file and use the data which your evaluation uncovers?" A truly comprehensive evaluation provides for wide use of the appraisals made.

Evaluation Should Be Co-operative. The principal must be an informed person, of course: she must be well read and experienced. However, to offer real instructional leadership the principal must know how to involve her staff in all phases of the school program. Certainly in evaluation co-operative work is necessary. Objectives and standards co-operatively developed by the staff are likely to be sound ones, and to enlist the all-out effort of the staff in their accomplishment.

In evaluation as in all other areas, the faculty cannot rise higher than the level the principal establishes. To achieve adequate evaluation of the school's program, the principal must develop in herself first, and then in her faculty as need be, basic understandings concerning the purposes and techniques of evaluation. The success of the principal in her work with evaluation lies in her tactful and informed handling of the particular type of faculty she has at the time. Co-operative evaluation by the staff may involve some criticism of the principal; where there is good communication, criticism should be welcomed and dealt with objectively.

Co-operative evaluation, rather than principal-dominated evaluation, develops in the staff a desire to improve "our" school, and to help "our" pupils more. Co-operative processes may be slower, but they have proved to be more effective.

Evaluation Should Be Continuous. A well-balanced program of evaluation is no end-of-the-year, or even beginning-of-the-year ordeal. Evaluation does not mean a check list or rating scale applied periodically with a comfortable respite in between. Evaluation is really a frame of mind. Capable professional workers develop a wholesomely critical attitude toward their own work. Expert teachers help their pupils to develop a habit of evaluating their own progress and that of the group. Professional staff members are accustomed to studying objectively the strong and weak points of the curriculum, the supervisory program, and their own teaching performance. Principals who are professionally alert keep their finger on the pulse of the whole school program as well as on personnel. Evaluation is going on constantly as the principal observes teaching in classrooms, pupils in the corridors, the clerk in the school office, the nurse in the clinic,

This does not mean that evaluation should be left to chance, that good people will evaluate despite themselves. The evaluation program should include definite tests, check lists, rating scales, and application of criteria at specified times. The results of these measures should be recorded, interpreted, and used. Over and above this, the principal and faculty need to develop the habit of being alert to signs of success and failure as they work for children. Only the staff can improve the teaching in the school; when the staff develops a healthy attitude toward self-evaluation, only then will teaching actually improve. A continuous evaluation implies the interested co-operation of sincere, interested, and capable professional people who want the best for their pupils.

In evaluating her own efficiency, the principal can review the five guidelines just presented.

1. Planning — Is she making sufficiently clear and detailed plans covering all of her duties?
2. Organizing — Is she scheduling her work systematically? Do her plans promote the reasonable personal needs of the staff?
3. Directing — Is she directing her staff competently, working co-operatively with them, and delegating wisely?
4. Communicating — How "open" are the channels of communication in the school — downward, upward, and horizontal?
5. Evaluating — If she wrote out her complete program of evaluation, how would she rate it for the four C's of evaluation — criteria, comprehensiveness, co-operativeness, and continuity?

FOR THE PRINCIPAL'S PROFESSIONAL LIBRARY

Pamphlets

A graphic description of good administration is given in a pamphlet from the U. S. Department of Health, Education, and Welfare, Office of Education, *Keystones of Good Internal Administration* by Ellsworth Tompkins and Galen Jones, Misc. No. 20, 1955, 24 pp., 20 cents.

Democracy in School Administration, published by the NEA Department of Classroom Teachers, 1953, 25 pp., 25 cents, gives a brief and readable account of the problems and techniques of the democratic administrator.

Principals who hesitate to delegate work will change their minds when they read Julius E. Eitington's *Don't Do It Yourself!* Personnel Leaflet No. 3, published by the Society for Personnel Administration, 5506 Connecticut Northwest, Washington 15, D. C., 5 pp., 10 cents.

Book

The principal will find helpful suggestions for administration in Paul Hoffer, S.M., *Guide for Religious Administrators*, published by The Bruce Publishing Company, Milwaukee, 1958, 171 pp., $4.50.

CHAPTER V

TIME FOR THE JOB

If a principal is to be effective as a principal, (1) she must have adequate time for the really professional aspects of her job; and (2) she must plan for the optimum use of this time. She must not allow the distribution of her time to be an accidental matter, dependent upon pressures of the moment. What is the optimum distribution of a principal's time among the various aspects of her job? How can she so plan her work that this optimum distribution of time will be achieved?

"TELL ME, Sister Principal, what did you do with your time today? What else did you hope to get done?" The answers to these two questions show pretty well how the principal views her job. Perhaps her aspirations — plans she *didn't* have time for that day — indicate most clearly what she thinks a good principal should do. Sister Principals aren't a complacent lot; they are impatient about the good that remains undone, even at the end of a long and arduous day. How often they sigh, "If only I had more time!"

Others, too, are concerned about what the principal does with her time. The Mother Superior, diocesan superintendent, pastor, parents, and teachers — each of these has very definite ideas about what the principal should accomplish. Each expects from the principalship certain abilities and results. Sometimes the expectations of these other informed people coincide perfectly with the principal's own expectations; sometimes there are wide divergences. Is there a way of determining just what the principal *can* be expected to achieve? Another way of asking the same thing is — What *should* the principal be doing with her time?

There seem to be three ways of approaching the problem.

1. Studying the distribution of principal's time. Are there norms to guide principals in distributing their time among their various duties? How are principals now distributing their time? Can they be expected to spend their time differently?

80

2. Making a job description of the principal's work. Such a description lists what the principal ideally does in the discharge of her many duties. How does this job description compare with what the principal is actually doing?

3. Preparing a schedule that would help the principal distribute her time better. This schedule would take into consideration an ideal distribution of time, and would at the same time specify the activities which a competent principal performs during a typical week.

These three ways of viewing the principalship will be discussed here. The discussion will show that the alert Sister Principal, even the teaching principal, can arrange to have "Time for the Job."

THE PRINCIPAL'S TIME DISTRIBUTION

In this discussion of the principal's time distribution, her *nonteaching* time is meant. Although many Sister Principals are full-time teachers, the discussion is concerned not with helping her teach better, but rather with helping her to be a better principal. Hence, the remarks will be limited to duties which are hers by reason of the principalship.

What are the duties of a principal? Many studies of the principal's work[1] group her essential activities into five categories. Since a study of the principal's time distribution depends upon *what* occupies her time, these five categories will be somewhat expanded upon here.

1. Supervision — improving instruction. Typical activities are the following:
   a) Working directly with teachers to improve learning and teaching
   b) Preparing materials that will help teachers teach better
   c) Preparing for conferences, for example, through specific professional reading and study of the classroom situation

2. Administration — providing the organization and conditions for good teaching. Typical activities are the following:
   a) Establishing effective school policies and routines
   b) Providing instructional materials and equipment
   c) Directing maintenance, bus and cafeteria service

3. School-community relations — interpreting the school to the community and the community to the school; also actively co-operating in worthy community projects. Typical activities are:
   a) Conferring with parents
   b) Participating in the Home and School Association
   c) Co-operating with health and welfare agencies

4. Clerical work — general office work. Typical activities are telephoning, typing, filing, record keeping, duplicating.

---

[1] National Education Association, Department of Elementary School Principals, *The Elementary-School Principalship — Today and Tomorrow*, Twenty-Seventh Yearbook (Washington, D. C.: National Education Association, 1948), p. 87.

5. Miscellaneous duties — duties which do not come under any of the above headings. Typical activities are school housekeeping, handling emergencies, directing church-related activities.

The above list of duties, though sketchy, will serve as an introduction to the following study of the principalship. The listing above shows that some of the principal's duties are clearly more important than others. Heading the list is *supervision*, the responsibility for improving instruction: helping teachers to teach better so that children may learn better. Her supervisory duties, then, are most important and should claim the greatest amount of time. In second place is her duty to provide conditions in which good teaching can be done. *Administration* provides the atmosphere, the routine, the materials, and the personnel which enable the principal to carry out her supervisory aims. Administration requires a considerable amount of time, but less time than supervision. A third duty is *school-community relations*, dealing with parents and others concerned with the school program. There is also the inevitable amount of *clerical work* — typing, filing, handling mail — which is done or at least directed by the Sister Principal. In the last place are *miscellaneous* duties, duties which do not seem to come under any of the above headings. Miscellaneous duties include handling interruptions and emergencies, and responsibilities such as choir practice, catechetical classes, acting as organist, doing sacristy work, directing church activities, school housekeeping and custodial work.

Using the above categories as a frame of reference, one can next see how the relative importance of each activity shows in a time distribution.

HOW SHOULD PRINCIPALS DISTRIBUTE THEIR TIME?

Professional educators and experienced principals have studied the many duties of the principalship, and have arrived at some practical standards

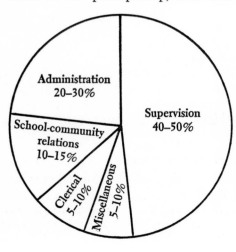

Figure 10.　How the Principal Should Distribute Her Time

for the principal's distribution of her nonteaching time.[2] Because of the hierarchy among her duties, the principal would ideally distribute her time as shown in Figure 10.

Supervision, the principal's first-ranking duty, should occupy almost half of her nonteaching time. Administration, which facilitates supervision, should take up about one fourth of her time, and the remaining duties would consume a little over one fourth of her time. This graph presents pictorially the emphasis which the competent principal gives to her duties in the order of their importance.

If a principal followed this recommended plan, how would she distribute her nonteaching time among her duties? First, one must consider how much time the Sister Principal spends on the duties of the principalship. A survey of parochial schools showed that the Sister Principal's average work week is fifty hours, not counting time spent in convent duties.[3] The supervising Sister Principal, then, or one who teaches only a few hours a week,[4] usually devotes fifty hours a week to the five categories listed earlier.

The teaching Sister Principal of course has much less time for these specific duties. Ordinarily, the teaching principal's teaching week is arranged as follows:

Teaches	25 hours a week
Prepares for class	5 hours a week
Total hours	30 hours a week in classroom duties

Since the teaching Sister Principal typically has a total week of fifty hours, she has only twenty hours weekly for the specific duties of the principalship. The discussion which follows, then, will assume a fifty-hour schedule for the supervising principal and a twenty-hour schedule for the teaching principal.

Using the percentages reported in Figure 10, the following table shows how Sister Principals would ideally distribute their nonteaching time among their various duties during a given week (Table I).

[2] Ibid., p. 90. Modifications for parochial schools can be based on an unpublished Ph.D. study by Reverend James W. Malone, Administration of the Teacher in the Parochial Elementary Schools of Ohio (Washington, D. C.: The Catholic University of America Press, 1957), p. 14.

[3] Reverend James W. Malone, op. cit., p. 99.

[4] In the National Education Association study cited above, a principal was considered "supervising" if he devoted at least 75 per cent of his time to the duties of the principalship. However, in the 1958 survey by the National Education Association (see the footnote to Figure 11), 50 per cent was used as the cutoff point: a principal was called "supervising" if 50 per cent or more of his time was free from regular teaching duties. In parochial schools, a principal is usually either a full-time teacher, or a full-time supervising principal. For convenience, then, in Table 1 and the tables which follow, the cutoff point arbitrarily chosen was five hours or less of regular teaching duties per week for the "supervising" principal. A Sister Principal who teaches regular class only one hour a day, or five hours a week, would be called a "supervising" principal.

TABLE I.　Hours Per Week Ideally Given to the Principal's Duties

Duty	Supervising* Principal	Teaching Principal
Supervision	23	8
Administration	13	6
School-Community Relations	5	2
Clerical Work	5	2
Miscellaneous	4	2
Total Hours Per Week	50	20

* "Supervising" principal — used here to mean a principal who teaches no more than five hours a week. "Teaching" principal is used here to mean a principal who is freed from classroom teaching no more than five hours a week.

The above allocation of time clearly indicates that first things come first; the principal's duty as instructional leader is obvious from the amount of time which she devotes to supervision. The supervising principal reserves at least twenty-three hours a week for her supervisory duties; the teaching principal reserves at least eight hours. Does this seem entirely too much time for supervision? Chapters IX and X will discuss the activities by which the principal carries out her program of instructional improvement. Upon examining this section, one will want even more time in order to use the effective techniques which are available.

Ideally, the supervising principal devotes thirteen hours a week to her administrative duties and the teaching principal, six hours. Five hours for the supervising principal and two hours for the teaching principal would be spent in school-community relations. Clerical work would claim five hours and two hours respectively, and miscellaneous duties would take up four hours of the supervising principal's time and two hours a week of the teaching principal's time. This ideal distribution of time shows the hierarchy among the principal's duties, with the most important duties taking up the most time.

Faithfulness to a good distribution of time requires real dedication, especially on the part of the teaching principal. All good teachers like to spend much more than thirty hours a week on their teaching; Sister Principals are no exception. However, when convinced of their role as instructional leader, teaching principals have shown that they can courageously follow such a schedule.

To do justice to their many responsibilities, this kind of time distribution is necessary. Let us examine the reports of the principals on the way they now spend their time.

HOW DO PRINCIPALS NOW DISTRIBUTE THEIR TIME?

Do Sister Principals now distribute their time as recommended in Table I? Or are there wide discrepancies? Figure 11 shows how principals in one study now spend their time, and how they would spend their time if they followed the pattern recommended in Figure 10 and in Table I.

Supervising Principals. Since supervising principals are in a good position to plan their own schedule, it is interesting to note how they distribute their time among their various duties. Figure 11 shows the contrast between the recommended time distribution and the way supervising principals report spending their time.

Upon examining Figure 11, one sees mostly discrepancies. Supervision now claims eleven hours a week instead of the recommended twenty-three hours. Administration is a little better, claiming nine hours instead of the ideal thirteen hours. School-community relations now receive only three hours a week, instead of five. The reasons for the discrepancies appear in an analysis of the time devoted to clerical work and to miscellaneous school duties. Clerical work takes up twelve hours a week of the supervising Sister Principal's time, more than twice as much as the recommended time allotment. Miscellaneous duties occupy thirteen hours a week, instead of the four hours recommended. One can see at a glance that the trouble

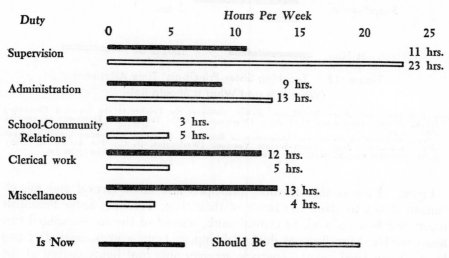

Figure 11. Supervising Sister Principals' Time Allotment
(What It Is and What It Should Be)

Source of Data: Rev. James W. Malone, *Administration of the Teacher* in the *Parochial Elementary Schools of Ohio*, unpublished Ph.D. thesis (Washington, D. C.: The Catholic University of America, 1957), p. 14.

National Education Association, Department of Elementary Principals, *Elementary School Principalship — A Research Study*, Thirty-Seventh Yearbook (Washington, D. C.: The Association, 1958), p. 98. The data were adapted, with permission, to apply to the parochial school principal.

with the supervising principal's work week is her overemphasis on clerical work and on miscellaneous duties. Figure 11 shows an unattractive picture for the supervising principal.

Teaching Principals. Do teaching principals manage to dole out their precious time more equitably? After subtracting thirty hours from their fifty-hour work week, teaching Sister Principals have twenty hours to devote to the duties of their office. Figure 12 shows how they distribute this time, and how they should distribute their time according to the ideal patterns presented here.

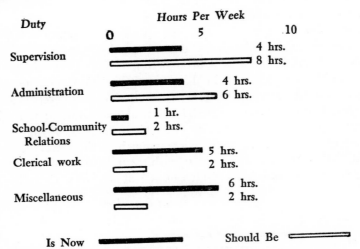

Figure 12. Teaching Sister Principals' Time Allotment
(What It Is and What It Should Be)

Source of Data: Rev. James W. Malone, *Administration of the Teacher* in the *Parochial Elementary Schools of Ohio*, unpublished Ph.D. thesis (Washington, D. C.: The Catholic University of America, 1957), p. 14.
  National Education Association, Department of Elementary Principals, *Elementary School prinicpal-ship — A Research Study*, Thirty-Seventh Yearbook (Washington, D. C.: The Association, 1958), p. 98. The data were adapted, with permission, to apply to the parochial school principal.

Figure 12 shows that teaching principals also allow clerical and miscellaneous duties to claim too much of their time. Teaching Sister Principals report five hours a week in clerical work, instead of the recommended two hours weekly. Miscellaneous duties take up six hours a week, instead of two hours. Supervision, on the contrary, receives only four hours instead of the recommended eight hours; administration receives four hours instead of six; and school-community relations are allotted only one hour instead of two. If the seven extra hours were taken from clerical and miscellaneous duties, the teaching Sister Principal could well devote more time to supervision, administration, and school-community relations.

Figures 11 and 12 show quite clearly that for the group studied both supervising and teaching Sister Principals are falling short of an ideal time distribution. The crux of the problem seems to be the time they are spending on clerical and miscellaneous duties.

HOW CAN PRINCIPALS DISTRIBUTE THEIR TIME BETTER?

An ugly monster raises its head. How can principals spend their time better, with school conditions as they are? Principals are so busy now they can't take on a single other duty. How can they spend more time in administration, supervision, and public relations?

There seem to be three factors entering into the "busyness" of principals. Perhaps a discussion of each may bring to light certain possible solutions to the problem of "no time" for the bigger issues of the school program.

Needed — More Clerical Help. Part of the difficulty certainly lies in the fact that parochial schools need more clerical help. Many parochial schools have no school clerks, and even some large schools have only part-time clerks. Therefore, the principal spends a good deal of time in such subprofessional tasks as opening mail, answering the telephone, and counting out supplies. Some principals resignedly spend several hours each week counting money for the school and the parish. A master's degree is not needed for such mechanical tasks! In fact, any average person could be trained to do the job as fast and as accurately.

This situation is not restricted to parochial schools alone. Public schools also decry the inadequacy of their secretarial help. In 1958, a National Education Association survey showed that one third of all public elementary schools had no paid clerical help. And, forty per cent of all public schools, even very large ones, had only one school clerk.[5] Ten years ago, the NEA made recommendations concerning clerical help for elementary principals.[6] Using these recommendations, one can draw up a table such as the following:

Guide for Hiring School Clerks

Pupil Enrollment	Number of Clerks
Below 200	¼ (10 hours a week)
200–400	½ (20 hours a week)
400–800	1 full time
Above 800	2 full time

[5] National Education Association, Department of Elementary School Principals, *The Elementary School Principalship — A Research Study*, Thirty-Seventh Yearbook (Washington, D. C.: National Education Association, 1958), p. 72.

[6] National Education Association, Department of Elementary School Principals, *The Elementary-School Principalship — Today and Tomorrow*, p. 67.

Ordinarily, to get efficient service, the salary must be in keeping with the rate for similar work in the vicinity. However, Teachers' Aides have proved effective in many parochial schools. Aides will be mentioned again in the discussion of school conditions in Chapter VII.

The question then arises: What could a school clerk do with all that time? The fortunate Sister Principals who have school secretaries know the answer. First of all, the clerk can relieve the principal of many routine tasks, such as making out office records and reports, typing, filing, requisitioning, and the like. Perhaps equally important, a school clerk can also relieve teachers of mechanical work, such as filling out pupil records, helping to score tests and to record the data, collecting and counting money. In fact, a school clerk should be viewed as one who helps both principal and teachers to do a better professional job. Only if teachers are relieved of some clerical work can they share adequately in administrative and supervisory responsibilities. The principal cannot delegate work to a staff that is already overburdened with routine chores. A clerk is an essential part of a sound plan for improving the school program.

Needed — More Custodial Help. The data in Figure 11 and Figure 12 showed that principals are spending a great deal of time on miscellaneous school duties. Included in miscellaneous duties are such things as taking care of school housekeeping, doing custodial work, and directing untrained custodial workers. Principals may regret the amount of time they spend each week on such work, but they are handicapped when janitorial service is poor.

It is true that women generally are more exacting of janitorial service than men are; but even allowing for this difference, some parochial schools obviously need better maintenance personnel, and more of them. All too often the same janitor is responsible for both the church and the school plant. Needless to say, an overworked custodian, or even one who thinks he is overworked, will not put forth his best effort. When cleaning and maintenance are unsatisfactory, the principal is likely to devote precious professional time to "tidying up."

Certainly, it seems minimal to have one full-time custodian for every 300 pupils. This would mean in a school of 600 pupils, two full-time custodians, and in a school of 1,000 pupils, three full-time workers. Such an allotment of custodial help would provide routine cleaning and repair work on a systematic long-range basis. Such a plan would save the pastor money in the long run; it would also enable the principal to direct custodial work with only a slight amount of her own or the teachers' time.

A clean, attractive, well-cared-for building is a strong incentive to high morale among both pupils and faculty. Adequate custodial service is a wise investment on the part of a pastor who is genuinely interested in providing a good education for the children of his parish. When principal and teachers use professional time for professional work, the school program is bound to be better.

Perhaps a little reasoning in dollars and cents might make the point clearer. The average public school principal makes a yearly salary of about $7,500, or $750 a month.[7] The public school principal's work week consists of 47 hours, at a rate of about $4 an hour. Because of her academic training, the Sister Principal's time can be viewed in terms of the money her services would realize if she were in a public school system. Why should she spend her precious professional time on jobs that a non-professional person can do for $1.50 an hour? While it is true that the Sister Principal's salary is about $90 a month (plus the use of parish convent facilities), still it is not the actual salary paid but the worth of her professional time that should be considered.

A principal who puts the equivalent of $4 an hour into work that can be done for $1.50 is obviously violating justice. The principal should feel obliged to devote her precious professional time to professional jobs exclusively. This cannot be considered a violation of humility, for it is the attitude of humility that is meritorious, not the lowliness of the task. In order to get a true picture of her role as supervisor, the principal needs first of all to place a proper valuation on her own time. After that, she will begin to devise ways of distributing her time wisely over her many duties.

Needed — More Delegation. Better secretarial and custodial help would certainly free the principal's time for professional duties. But a more fundamental need may be that the principal must learn how to delegate responsibilities. Sometimes principals pride themselves on the amount of production work they can do. They can cut a stencil and run 500 mimeograph copies in an hour. They can scrub and wax the office floor in much less time than it takes the cleaning woman. They can direct the choir and processions with finesse. They can take registration of first-grade pupils quickly and accurately. And so on. Of course, they can, and they can do a great many other routine jobs with dispatch.

But, the principal's job is not production work, but leadership. Time spent in production is time wasted, since lower level personnel can do production work. The point was made earlier that the principal's time is worth at least $4 an hour, perhaps more. So, her time is valuable simply from a pecuniary standpoint. Her time is valuable also because she alone

---

[7] National Education Association, Research Division, *Salaries and Salary Schedules of Urban School Employees, 1958–59*, Research Report, 1959–R16 (Washington, D. C.: National Education Association, 1959), p. 11. The average annual salary of public school principals, teaching and supervising, was given as $7,352.

can furnish her school with the educational leadership it needs. If the principal fails to furnish leadership, she fails completely. It is difficult to discipline one's self to keep away from production work and to concentrate one's efforts on leadership. To do so, the principal needs to learn how and why she must delegate responsibilities to her staff and to nonprofessional workers.

There may be difficult school situations, it is true. An extremely poor parish is hard pressed to provide adequate custodial and clerical help. Or staff members may be too young or too old, or ill, or too overburdened to take on additional work. However, the principal should know what constitutes an *ideal* distribution of her own time, and that of her teaching staff. She must do her utmost to delegate to her staff every duty for which they can be prepared, and she must delegate to nonprofessional workers duties of a nonprofessional sort. This will require real ingenuity at times. No matter what the difficulties, however, the ideal remains the same — save professional time for professional work. Delegation is necessary if the principal is to reserve her time for leadership rather than for clerical and miscellaneous jobs.

Religious communities can help their Sister Principals realize a better distribution of time by arranging for principals' planning groups. Diocesan superintendents can help by providing opportunities for principals to study their jobs objectively. Most help must come, however, at the local level, through co-operative planning between the pastor and the staff. If the principal is to lead, she must have time for leadership activities. Usually, it is her own ingenuity and vision that provide the means for realizing this leadership role.

A JOB ANALYSIS OF THE PRINCIPALSHIP[8]

It is all very well to say that the principal should spend a certain per cent of her nonteaching time in supervision. But what does supervision include? Classroom observations and conferences come to mind; but these would hardly take twenty-three hours a week on the part of the supervising principal. What else is included in supervision? What activities are involved in administration? What should the supervisory principal do during the thirteen hours a week which she devotes to administration? In order to say exactly what is meant by supervision, administration, public relations, and the rest, we need a job description of the principalship.

When the principal has a list of essential duties, she can analyze how she is succeeding as a principal. Without such a list, the principal plunges

---

[8] National Education Association, Department of Elementary School Principals, *The Elementary School Principalship — A Research Study*, p. 47.

in and does her best, but she has no assurance that she is stressing the important things. There have been many studies made of the principal's duties. Some studies have been time-and-motion studies, in which a record was kept of each thing the principal did over a period of a week or more.[9] Other studies have concentrated on the objectives of the elementary school, and what a principal must do in order to help children achieve these objectives. As mentioned earlier, many people have definite ideas about what the schools should accomplish, and how. Very often, these ideas are based on a sound philosophy of education and a knowledge of what can be achieved. By combining these two sources of information — time and motion studies and the opinions of informed persons — one can state specifically the essential duties of the principal.

THE TEACHING PRINCIPAL — A DILEMMA

Whether the principal is a full-time supervisor or teaching her own class, the duties of the principalship remain the same. However, the teaching principal necessarily achieves the objectives less adequately than does the principal who devotes all of her time to her office. We may sympathize with the frustration of the teaching principal, but we cannot subtract duties because of the pressures upon her. The duties remain to be done; the pity of it is that many Sister Principals are full-time classroom teachers. It is impossible to achieve the objectives of Catholic education unless there are trained personnel free to administer Catholic schools. It is false economy to put up a $200,000 building, and put another $30,000 into equipment and supplies, and then leave this tremendous investment without adequate direction. In the days of the one-room school, days long since past for most parishes, the "head" teacher could manage the few extra demands upon her time. Today, when schools have expanded ten and twenty times, a "head" teacher is an anachronism. No matter how intelligent and hard-working she is, the teaching principal simply cannot begin to meet her obligations as instructional leader. We cannot hope to achieve a high quality of education in our Catholic schools unless there is more time provided for leadership.

These parenthetical comments should dispel the idea that there are two distinct criteria for evaluating the principalship: one set of criteria for the teaching principal and a different set of criteria for the supervising principal. One cannot water down the requirements of the office because one sympathizes with the teaching principal. Religious superiors, superintend-

---

[9] Typical of these studies are the following: "The Principal Studies His Job," *The National Elementary Principal*, XXXIII (Oct., 1953); and the study by Robert E. Lucas and Howard Wakefield, *By Their Bootstraps: An Approach to Elementary School Leadership* (Columbus, Ohio: Ohio Education Association, 1955).

ents, and pastors with vision are insisting on time free for supervision and administration of our excellent parochial school facilities. Where the principal has insufficient time for all of her duties, she must concentrate on her most important duties. At least if she knows the "minimum essentials," as it were, she can organize her time efficiently to accomplish at least the essentials.

A job description, then, lists the basic activities of the principal. To be helpful, a job description is necessarily detailed. It gives a comprehensive picture of the principalship as an all-inclusive ideal. In an individual school, there would be some modification of this list: some duties would be expanded, and some duties may be curtailed. All of the items in the job description, however, are essential to the job.

A job description becomes more interesting when made into an instrument of evaluation. In the discussions which follow, each aspect of the principal's work is presented in check-list form.[10] The check lists will give the principal a quick appraisal of her present effectiveness. Later chapters will discuss each aspect of the principalship with a view toward presenting concrete suggestions for improvement.

THE PRINCIPAL'S JOB IN SUPERVISION

In Figure 10, the recommended allotment of time for supervision was given as forty to fifty per cent of the principal's nonteaching time. In practice, this means about twenty-three hours weekly for the supervising principal and eight hours weekly for the teaching principal (see Table I). Principals who are freed part time for supervision will have some intermediate number of hours per week for this important duty.

What activities should occupy the time allotted for supervision? How can the principal tell whether her supervisory program is adequate? The following check list will guide the principal in choosing supervisory activities and will also give her an idea of how she is doing right now. The principal should not be discouraged if her first rating is a little low. After all, she may only be beginning to study supervision scientifically! After she feels stronger, she may even want to have her faculty mark the check list with her, but that will probably come later.

In going through the above list, the Sister Principal may find that she is marking 1's for some activities, and perhaps 5's for others. A good supervising principal should aim at averaging at least 4 after a few years of

---

10 Many of the ideas for the check lists which follow were obtained from the following source: California Elementary School Administrators' Association, *C.E.S.A.A. Reviews Evaluation Procedures for the Elementary School Administrator* (San Francisco: The Association, 1958). The material has been used with permission of the California Elementary School Administrators' Association.

concentrated effort. A teaching principal may only be able to achieve a 3 average, even after great effort. The check list can be used over and over again as a stimulus to greater achievement.

One can lessen the pain of a low score by calling to mind that a job description, such as that presented above, is really an all-inclusive ideal. There probably isn't a principal living today who could blithely (and honestly) mark 4 and 5 for each item in the check list. The ideals presented here are guiding stars, so to speak, but not unattainable. Even teaching principals, by consistent effort, can advance their score from year to year.

Though it is an ideal, the job description of the principal as supervisor presents concrete activities which the principal should work toward. Reading over this check list, one can see that forty per cent of the nonteaching time will be all too short to realize all of the objectives. However, since improving instruction is her first responsibility, the conscientious Sister Principal will rigidly allocate at least this amount of time to supervision. Then she will find means of discharging her other duties in the time that remains. It cannot be said too often that Catholic schools should provide an education that is second to none in the country. Sister Principals then must provide unparalleled leadership.

THE PRINCIPAL'S JOB IN ADMINISTRATION

Second in importance is the principal's role as administrator. Put very simply, the principal's aim in administration is to make the school a place where children can learn to their fullest capacity. This means that the principal must *prevent* and correct harmful conditions and must also constructively plan for a well-rounded program for all children. In the check list which follows, the word *children* occurs very seldom, but in each activity, children's interests and needs are paramount.

In the discussion of supervision, children's needs were also emphasized. The difference here lies in this. As a *supervisor*, the principal works with teachers in helping children learn better. Supervisory assistance includes tests to determine the level of achievement with a view toward remedial work. Supervisory assistance also includes helping teachers by providing instructional materials, personal direction, observation, and the like. As an *administrator*, the principal is also furthering the interests for children, but less directly. Good administration provides a good school routine, a safe, healthful building and classrooms, adequate adult guidance on the playground, budgeting and bookkeeping necessary for just use of funds, records and reports needed for smooth operation of a school system, and the like. Administration provides the setting in which supervision can work directly with teachers and pupils to improve learning. At times, there will be some overlapping of these functions. However, for most purposes, the activities

A SELF-EVALUATION CHECK LIST FOR PRINCIPALS
Part I — Supervisory Duties*

Directions: Listed below are typical duties grouped under major headings. Following
each duty is a series of numbers from 1 to 5. Mark an X through the number
which you feel usually applies to you. Use this code for marking:

    1. I omit this altogether.
    2. I tend to neglect this.
    3. I am about fair in this.
    4. This is a strong area.
    5. This is one of my strongest areas.

Then connect the X's with a line. This will give you a profile showing strongest
and weakest areas, at least in your own judgment.

	Weak			Strong
A. Organization and planning					
1. Planning long-range supervisory objectives and procedures	1	2	3	4	5
2. Planning for group participation in the in-service program	1	2	3	4	5
3. Arranging a schedule of supervisory activities	1	2	3	4	5
4. Keeping records and reports of the supervisory program	1	2	3	4	5
5. Co-ordinating teaching methods in the school	1	2	3	4	5
6. Planning for more adequate instructional materials	1	2	3	4	5
7. Utilizing the services of community and diocesan supervisors	1	2	3	4	5
8. Orienting new teachers (also an administrative duty)	1	2	3	4	5
B. Helping teachers to instruct and guide children**	Weak			Strong	
1. Observing in classrooms	1	2	3	4	5
2. Holding individual and group conferences on instructional matters	1	2	3	4	5
3. Providing demonstration teaching	1	2	3	4	5
4. Helping teachers with pupil guidance	1	2	3	4	5
5. Assisting teachers in using instructional materials	1	2	3	4	5
6. Encouraging teachers to try new teaching techniques	1	2	3	4	5
7. Preparing bulletins to help teachers in the classroom	1	2	3	4	5
C. Helping teachers to develop as professional persons	Weak			Strong	
1. Co-operating with teachers in formulating supervisory objectives and procedures	1	2	3	4	5
2. Preparing and conducting supervisory faculty meetings	1	2	3	4	5
3. Leading teachers in a study of the curriculum	1	2	3	4	5
4. Stimulating professional reading among the staff	1	2	3	4	5

* For a discussion of each supervisory activity see Chapters VIII, IX, and X.
** B and C above — see discussion of teacher competences, Chapter VIII.

D. Evaluating outcomes	Weak				Strong
1. Planning, conducting, and interpreting the testing program	1	2	3	4	5
2. Studying pupil progress in order to improve teaching	1	2	3	4	5
3. Using various types of teacher evaluation procedures to improve teaching	1	2	3	4	5
4. Recognizing and praising effective teacher performance	1	2	3	4	5
5. Evaluating the effectiveness of the supervisory program.	1	2	3	4	5

listed in the preceding check list emphasize duties which are basically administrative.

The Sister Principal is not alone, of course, in administering the parochial school. She shares a number of responsibilities with the pastor, particularly in finance and maintenance. When the principal knows the standards for a good school program, she can greatly assist the pastor in making decisions in these areas. In the check list which follows, this sharing of responsibilities is indicated by (P), for pastor.

In marking this check list, the principal needs to keep in mind another matter of terminology. There may be some confusion as to when a duty is administrative and when clerical or custodial. For example, keeping pupil records might be either administrative or clerical. Likewise, maintaining a clean, safe, attractive building might be either administrative or custodial. Perhaps a simple distinction which helps here is this: a duty is administrative when the principal is *directing* the activity or "spot checking" an activity at spaced intervals. A duty is clerical or custodial when it is purely production work. "Keeping pupil records" is administrative when the principal is overseeing the process and keeping in touch with the accuracy and punctuality of routines. "Keeping pupil records" is purely clerical, when the principal types the records herself. A clerk or custodian rolls up his sleeves and goes to work. An administrator may work even harder, but the work is chiefly intellectual. The distinction between administrative and clerical or custodial is perhaps chiefly that of brain *versus* brawn.

As the principal works through the check list on administration, these points will be clarified. The check list will give her insight into the aspects of administration which she is now emphasizing, and perhaps aspects which are being slighted.

About one fourth of the principal's nonteaching time is ideally devoted to the above administrative duties. By working through the check list systematically, the Sister Principal can see just how thoroughly she is

A SELF-EVALUATING CHECK LIST FOR PRINCIPALS
Part 2 — Administrative Duties*
(See directions, page 94)

A. Organization	Weak				Strong
1. Organizing a program for opening and closing the school year	1	2	3	4	5
2. Preparing a master calendar of school events and activities	1	2	3	4	5
3. Posting schedules of principal and staff	1	2	3	4	5
4. Budgeting and bookkeeping	1	2	3	4	5
5. Making available adequate instructional materials and supplies	1	2	3	4	5
6. Establishing routines for requisitioning	1	2	3	4	5
7. Directing the ordering, storing and distributing, and inventorying of supplies	1	2	3	4	5
8. Conferring with secretary; directing her work	1	2	3	4	5
9. Preparing and submitting required administrative reports	1	2	3	4	5
10. Maintaining administrative records and filing system	1	2	3	4	5

B. Teacher Personnel	Weak				Strong
1. Recruiting, screening, and hiring lay personnel (P)**	1	2	3	4	5
2. Orienting new teachers (also a supervisory duty)	1	2	3	4	5
3. Developing staff through delegation of administrative responsibilities	1	2	3	4	5
4. Providing substitute teacher service	1	2	3	4	5
5. Interpreting Diocesan Office policy to staff	1	2	3	4	5
6. Preparing handbook of local personnel policies	1	2	3	4	5
7. Holding administrative meetings and conferences	1	2	3	4	5
8. Arranging distribution of duties for teachers	1	2	3	4	5
9. Providing good working conditions	1	2	3	4	5
10. Writing bulletins for smooth operation of school program	1	2	3	4	5
11. Enforcing teacher personnel policies	1	2	3	4	5

C. Pupil Personnel	Weak				Strong
1. Enrolling, transferring, and excluding pupils; establishing orderly procedure*	1	2	3	4	5
2. Assigning pupils to rooms, and assisting with special grouping, as needed	1	2	3	4	5
3. Checking attendance in school	1	2	3	4	5

* For a discussion of each area of administration, see Chapters III, VI, VII, XV, XVI.
** (P) means in co-operation with pastor.

4. Maintaining pupil record system for guidance use	1	2	3	4	5
5. Arranging for supervision of playground activities	1	2	3	4	5
6. Supervising movement of pupils through building	1	2	3	4	5
7. Maintaining discipline and order	1	2	3	4	5
8. Providing individual counseling and direction for pupils as needed	1	2	3	4	5
9. Maintaining a Catholic tone in character development and religious training (P)**	1	2	3	4	5

D. School Plant	Weak				Strong
1. Inspecting the building	1	2	3	4	5
2. Arranging with teachers for co-operation in maintaining an attractive building	1	2	3	4	5
3. Conferring with janitor; planning his schedule (P)*	1	2	3	4	5
4. Planning cleaning, upkeep, repair of school and facilities (P)**	1	2	3	4	5
5. Planning enlargement or replacement of school facilities (P)**	1	2	3	4	5

E. Special Services	Weak				Strong
1. Arranging for supervision of cafeteria service (P)**	1	2	3	4	5
2. Providing a school library, or equivalent library service	1	2	3	4	5
3. Establishing and carrying out bus schedule (P)**	1	2	3	4	5
4. Working with school physician, dentist, and nurse on problems of child health	1	2	3	4	5
5. Planning and conducting fire and air-raid drills	1	2	3	4	5
6. Maintaining a safe building and playground (P)**	1	2	3	4	5
7. Providing a policy and procedure for handling accidents on school grounds	1	2	3	4	5

preparing the groundwork for effective teaching. There are so many duties under *administration*, that the principal can discharge all of them only by delegating responsibilities wisely, and then seeing that delegated duties are responsibly carried out.

In general, the time required for supervision should be allocated first, and administrative duties taken care of only during the recommended time. However, the principal will need to vary this role at the beginning and the closing of the school year. Administrative duties are especially heavy at these periods, so supervision may have to be curtailed during the first two weeks of school in the fall and during the last two weeks of the school year. The extra time given then to administration should mean a heavier emphasis on supervision during the rest of the year. For example, during the first week of school the principal may allocate forty per cent of her time to administration, and only twenty per cent to supervision. By the third week of the fall term, the recommended time allotment should be followed.

As with supervision, the principal's role in administration is strengthened by adequate policies of her religious community and the diocese. Well-developed policies enhance the status of the Sister Principal and provide a framework within which local policies can be worked out. The pastor too can increase the prestige of the Sister Principal through co-operative development of policies in areas where the authority of the pastor and the principal may overlap. The need for clear-cut administrative procedures is especially urgent where there are many lay teachers, large schools, bus and cafeteria service, transients, and other factors making a complex situation. The Sister Principal needs to plan specifically for efficient administration, and to evaluate her progress frequently, so that pupil learning will be as excellent as school facilities.

SCHOOL-COMMUNITY RELATIONS

The third area of responsibility for the principal is the school's public relations program. Some principals shrink from the notion of advertising their school to the public. Even parents, some feel, should learn about the school's worth only by observing what the school does for children. A newer trend, and a more sound one, is to speak of "school-community relations," meaning school publicity plus many other things. Included in the term "school-community relations" are effective working relations with parents, businesslike school contacts with individuals and agencies interested in child welfare, interpreting the school program to parents and others outside the school, and using the resources of the community to enrich the school program. School-community relations, then, is not cheap publicity, but rather an obligation on the part of all schools, public and parochial alike.

Sister Principals will agree that relations with the community have not been the forte of the parochial school through the years. We have tended to go our own way, and let anyone misunderstand who would. As an integral part of the parish unit, and also of the civic community, the parochial school has the duty to take an active interest in both the parish community and the civic community.

In her time schedule, the competent Sister Principal will recognize the just demands of a good school-community program. The supervising Sister Principal will allot five hours a week to these activities, and the teaching

A SELF-EVALUATION CHECK LIST FOR PRINCIPALS
Part 3 — Duties in School-Community Relations*
(See directions, page 94)

	Weak				Strong
1. Leading the faculty in a study of the school community	1	2	3	4	5
2. Promoting the use of community resources in the classroom	1	2	3	4	5
3. Preparing a handbook and bulletins for parents	1	2	3	4	5
4. Conferring with parents about the guidance of pupils	1	2	3	4	5
5. Participating in the Home and School Association of the parish	1	2	3	4	5
6. Providing information to interested persons through open house activities, such as those preceding Home and School meetings	1	2	3	4	5
7. Participating in American Education Week	1	2	3	4	5
8. Working with public agencies, such as child welfare and juvenile court	1	2	3	4	5
9. Co-operating in approved "drives" and contests, such as Red Cross	1	2	3	4	5
10. Co-operating with the local public school system in such matters as pupil census	1	2	3	4	5
11. Providing newspapers, radio and television stations with school news	1	2	3	4	5

* For a discussion of school-community relations, see Chapters XI and XII.

principal two hours. The check list above shows the principal's chief obligations in this important area.

The Sister Principal will probably find in marking the check list that her ratings are not uniformly good. The unsatisfactory areas are likely to be points (1), (2), (3), (5), (10), and (11). In other words, the Sister Principal may tend to neglect about half of her duties in school-community relations.

The allocation of time to school-community relations should average five hours for the supervising principal and two hours for the teaching principal. How could one find enough ideas to fill that much time? Preparation for a Home and School Association meeting could well take up the entire week's allotment of time for school-community relations. Open House activities — such as demonstrations for parents, displays of pupils' work, or explanations of newer methods of teaching — would easily require several hours of work on the part of the principal. Another week, or for several successive weeks, the faculty might work on a handbook for parents. Still another time, there might be discussions of better parent-teacher conferences. When the activities of the check list are carefully analyzed, they make up a good guide to improved school community relations.

The teaching principal, it is true, is handicapped by time pressure. Her long-range plan for the year should, however, chart the progress she hopes to make in this important area. Because she cannot do everything recommended, the teaching principal should not despair of doing anything at all. Two hours a week can accomplish a great deal, when the time is carefully planned.

The NEA study of 1958[11] allocates considerably more time to school community duties than is here recommended for the Sister Principal. The reason is that the Sister Principal does not attend club meetings and luncheons, for example, of Kiwanis — and is seldom included in large-scale civic programs.

THE PRINCIPAL'S CLERICAL WORK

Clerical duties are really a part of administration. However, since these duties take up so much of the Sister Principal's time, it seems best to consider them apart from the usual administrative duties. As shown in Figures 11 and 12, a good distribution of time would give five hours a week to clerical work for supervising Sister Principals; but at present they are spending at least twelve hours in these mechanical routines. Teaching Sister Principals are giving five hours a week to clerical work, instead of the recommended two hours.

What are the duties which engage so much of the Sister Principal's time? Following is a check list of typical clerical duties performed by some principals. Since this work could be performed by a clerk or a staff member, a different kind of check list is used.

Is the principal's average for the check list near 5? Then Sister is spending too much time on these routine clerical tasks. Is the principal's average near 2? Then Sister is delegating or sharing these duties rather satisfactorily. Of course, one cannot judge, just from this check list, how wisely the Sister Principal has delegated work; one can judge only the fact that there has been delegation.

When the clerical tasks are merely listed, they look very subprofessional. Just offhand, one would say that a highly trained professional person simply would not be immersed in such chores. Yet, some Sister Principals who have filled out this check list admit they never looked at the tasks in this light. They simply kept on opening envelopes and putting the supplies on the

A SELF-EVALUATION CHECK LIST FOR PRINCIPALS

Part 4 — Clerical Work*

Directions: Listed below are clerical activities which some principals perform. Following each activity is a series of numbers from 1 to 5. Mark an X through the number which **usually** applies to you. The code is given above the columns to the right. Then connect the X's with a line to get your profile.

Activity	Delegated to Clerk	Staff	Shared With Clerk	Staff	Done by Principal
1. Answering the telephone	1	2	3	4	5
2. Receiving callers	1	2	3	4	5
3. Typing office records	1	2	3	4	5
4. Typing letters, notices, tests, and worksheets	1	2	3	4	5
5. Using the duplicating machine	1	2	3	4	5
6. Collecting and counting money	1	2	3	4	5
7. Making bank deposits	1	2	3	4	5
8. Writing checks	1	2	3	4	5
9. Filing	1	2	3	4	5
10. Placing orders for supplies and equipment	1	2	3	4	5
11. Distributing and inventory-ing supplies	1	2	3	4	5
12. Handling Lost and Found	1	2	3	4	5

* See Chapter XVI for a discussion of clerical assistance.

shelves. All of the activities on the check list could be done by persons of barely average intelligence and no college training at all. These clerical routines should, reasonably, be done by nonprofessional persons. If parish funds cannot provide paid clerical help, parish volunteers often serve usefully. With skillful direction, even volunteer help can save some of the principal's precious time for supervisory and administrative leadership.

THE PRINCIPAL'S MISCELLANEOUS DUTIES

Another problem is the amount of time which the Sister Principal typically spends in nonclassified jobs. The supervising principal uncritically spends thirteen hours a week in these activities, and the teaching principal six hours. (See Figures 11 and 12.) The check list on page 102 lists some of the miscellaneous activities which claim so much of the principal's time.

In Part 5 of the check list, the Sister Principal's average is again likely to be much closer to 5 than to 1. Sister Principals typically report spending an excessive amount of time in miscellaneous duties. An examination of the kinds of duties included may shed light on possible causes.

A SELF-EVALUATION CHECK LIST FOR PRINCIPALS

Part 5 — Miscellaneous Duties

Directions: Listed below are miscellaneous duties which some principals perform. Following each activity is a series of numbers from 1 to 5. Mark an X through the number which usually applies to you. The code is given above the columns to the right.

Activity	Delegated to Clerk	Delegated to Staff*	Shared With Clerk	Shared With Staff*	Done by Principal
1. Doing school housekeeping	1	2	3	4	5
2. Doing custodial work, or directing untrained workers	1	2	3	4	5
3. Handling emergencies and interruptions	1	2	3	4	5
4. Directing church activities, such as processions	1	2	3	4	5
5. Directing choir practice	1	2	3	4	5
6. Teaching catechetical classes	1	2	3	4	5
7. Acting as organist	1	2	3	4	5
8. Doing sacristy work	1	2	3	4	5
9. Supervising the cafeteria or lunchroom	1	2	3	4	5
10. Supervising the playground	1	2	3	4	5

* Includes custodial help.

Items (1) and (2) in the check list imply inadequate custodial service. Item (3) may show the need for better planning of the principal's daily schedule, and probably indicates also a lack of clerical help. The remaining activities — related to church activities and monitoring — go back to the old problem of lack of delegation. The principal should regularly take part in these last-named activities, but usually as directing them rather than doing the work herself. Again, staff members, or volunteer teacher aides, could be used to save the principal's time for her essential duties.

Perhaps it would not be amiss to re-emphasize the point made earlier — that the principal's time is worth money. Certainly if the principal were paying a carpenter to build bookshelves at a carpenter's rate, she would not think of using him to run errands. She would be very exact about saving him for his own — in her eyes — very costly work. The same attitude toward the value of time should apply also to the principal's time. Certainly her time is worth more than that of an expert carpenter; yet, very often the principal thoughtlessly dissipates her time in the nonprofessional tasks listed above. Leadership takes time; only the principal can supply the leadership. The principal should be miserly, actually, in using her fifty-hour work week for anything but strictly professional activities.

The preceding job analysis has broken down the principal's work into five main categories. The first three descriptions — of supervision, administration, and school-community relations — are presented as an ideal pattern, a model upon which the principal might base her own in-service growth. The check lists on clerical work and miscellaneous duties, on the other hand, are descriptions of practice, but of substandard practice. Many of the duties in these latter two sections can be delegated to teachers, school clerks, and custodial workers, and thus free principals from some of the production jobs claiming a disproportionate amount of their time. The principals themselves will profit from studying ways of delegating more responsibilities to their staff members. And, ideally, principal and faculty together can evaluate the principal's performance and suggest more effective utilization of her professional time.

THE PRINCIPAL'S SCHEDULE

A job description or analysis shows how complex and difficult the principal's work is, and also how challenging. Every Sister Principal wants to use her time to the best possible advantage. There arises the question then, of how to use her time most effectively. Should she make a formal schedule? If convinced that she should, how can she go about making a schedule? And, question of questions, how can one keep to a schedule? At the beginning of the chapter the principal was asked, "What did you do today? What else did you hope to get done?" A discussion of time schedules will help the principal answer these questions to her own satisfaction.

WHY A SCHEDULE?

Let us approach the matter first from a negative point of view. What happens when a principal does not have a time schedule of her own duties? For one thing, it is hard on teachers. Principals may be shocked, but teachers actually do not know what the principal does with her time. Apart from time spent in teaching, the principal's job is usually a mystery to the staff. Not knowing what the principal is doing with her time, the teachers wonder about things. The torn shade in the lounge, the supplies not delivered immediately, the last-minute request for enrollment figures, the cancelled choir practice — what is the reason? The principal is no doubt busy — the teachers themselves say she is busy — but, why is she not busy about something else?

Not having a time schedule is also hard on the principal. She is at the mercy of every emergency and interruption. She puts forth all her energy all day long, but she cannot see what she had accomplished. Being a principal seems to be a matter of patient endurance, almost drudgery. She is working hard; but, is she doing what she should be doing? Should she be doing something else?

When there is no schedule the pastor, parents, welfare workers, even the policeman are all inconvenienced. People are kept waiting, things are not ready, and there seems to be no hope of getting the lines of communication open.

Advantages of a Schedule. The above are just a few examples of a situation that may be all too familiar — the school where the principal has no time schedule. But what are the positive effects of having a schedule? The most obvious effect is a human relations one — everybody is happier when everybody is informed. The principal can only be as effective as her staff and her other co-workers will let her be. In order to increase their co-operativeness, the wise principal lets people know what she is doing, why, and when. At a certain time each day this coming week, the principal will be observing in classrooms. At a specified time, she will be holding conferences with specified teachers. At designated hours, the principal will be available for consultation. There is no reason for secrecy on the part of the principal; in fact, the principal is not trying to be secretive. She just had not looked at the matter as affecting her co-workers so directly. A schedule is a good human relations investment.

A schedule helps the principal to help the staff. Scheduled office hours for consultation are an important source of help. No one's time is wasted trying to see someone who is not free and who will not be free until much later. Teachers need help with such matters as supplies, instructional materials, test scoring, discipline problems, and a host of other important matters. If teachers do not know when the principal will be available, they will just let the problem go, or ask someone who is not qualified to help. Regularly scheduled conferences with each teacher give the teacher the opportunity to accumulate questions and suggestions.

A schedule also enables the principal to get help from her staff. No principal thinks she knows all there is to know about teaching methods, curriculum, pupil guidance, and the like. Classroom observations, conferences, faculty meetings, and other scheduled activities allow the principal to learn systematically from her own staff. The principal has an important duty in co-ordinating the teaching methods in the school. Through classroom observation the principal learns how to do this more effectively. The principal is probably a good teacher herself, but she can always learn from her faculty. The ideas she gets from them will enable her to influence other staff members.

Another strong reason for the principal's schedule is that it enables her to take care of her essential duties. The principal has more than enough work to fill every day, but she wants to make sure that first things come first. Is she doing the essential things, or is she just putting in time? A good schedule gives the principal the assurance that she is fulfilling her obligation. This is what she should be doing; this is the amount of success she has achieved; this is the way she must adapt her schedule to perform her duties more efficiently. Only when she is following a schedule does the principal have this satisfaction.

The staff and principal feel better, get more help, do a better job — when the principal schedules her time carefully. A schedule reflects the principal's aim in school administration — to promote the best interests of the children. The details of the schedule show how the principal puts this philosophy of administration to work. Once convinced of the need for a schedule, the Sister Principal will want some information about making a schedule. How can she go about this?

MAKING A SCHEDULE

Consulting Those Affected. A schedule is an aspect of administration, and administration is concerned with people. Though one can go through specific steps in constructing a schedule, they will be futile unless the schedule works with people. The approach to schedule-making, then, must be personal if it is to succeed. The principal should be in touch with everyone who will be affected by the schedule, and she should proceed only as fast as good human relations will permit. It is advisable to introduce one step at a time, and perhaps only part of the entire schedule can be introduced in a year.

Consulting the Pastor. Of all the people concerned with the parochial school, the pastor is most deeply concerned. A good schedule is impossible without the interested support of the pastor. In fact, a schedule is not a good schedule for a given school unless it has the pastor's interested support. To give only one example of the needed pastoral support, one may indicate the problem of a school clerk. In a school of any size today, some clerical help is needed. If the parish cannot afford clerical help, then the alternative is volunteer help from parishioners. In either case, the pastor's support is essential in order to maintain good relations. Another instance of needed pastoral support is the matter of substitutes for the teaching principal, occasionally during daily Mass and at least two hours during the school week. Every pastor wants the best possible education in his school; the requirements of a modern program must be adequately presented to the pastor before the needed assistance can be given. It is the role of the principal to interpret the school program to the pastor.

Consulting the Teachers. The teachers, too, need to be consulted about a proposed schedule. People fear what they do not know; teachers resist change as other people do, even when the change may be in their own interests. The principal should bring the teachers in on the planning of her schedule, as it gradually develops. Perhaps during the first semester, only the faculty meeting, an office hour, and conferences can be scheduled in advance. Classroom observations can perhaps be scheduled next, and a definite time for submitting requisition slips. Where the principal has customarily taken charge of routine playground supervision, for example, the teachers may resist her discontinuing this duty completely. Hence, gradual reduction in the time given to this type of work may be desirable. The school clerk, if fortunately there is one, and the janitor also will have to be inducted gradually into the idea of a set time for conferences.

It is better to introduce only a few features, and maintain them, than to introduce an entire schedule, and have it blocked. Bringing the teachers in on the planning will lessen their insecurity about the change. When they see that the schedule has real advantages, they will give it stronger support.

Beginning to Plan a Schedule. Though only a few aspects will be introduced at a time, the principal should plan her schedule as a whole. To do this, she will need to review the preceding sections, "A Job Analysis" and "The Principal's Time Distribution." To plan her weekly schedule, the principal will need the following information:

1. Time allotment for each area (see Table I)
2. Typical activities (see the foregoing check lists)
3. Daily schedule of the school, with recess and lunch periods, opening hour and dismissal time
4. Established events or appointments for the coming week, such as faculty meeting, Home and School Association meeting, inoculations and health inspections

Within this framework, the principal first makes up a preliminary schedule. This would be a listing of activities which might be performed at specified times during the day. This preliminary schedule is made out for each of the five areas: supervision, administration, school-community relations, clerical work, and miscellaneous school duties. It may be well at this stage to see how a supervising principal might proceed in making a preliminary schedule of supervisory activities for the coming week.

Table II shows how the supervising principal begins to plan her schedule of supervision for the week. Across from each hour of the school day, the principal enters the activity which might be carried out at that time. She notes also how often the activity will be performed during the week, and how many hours the activity will take up during the week. For example, teacher conferences are scheduled at 8:00 on two days and will occupy one hour through the week, or about thirty minutes each. Teacher conferences are also scheduled at 12:30 on two days, and at 3:30 on two days. A total

TABLE II.   Trial Schedule of Supervisory Activities for a Week
Supervising Principal (Time Allotment — 23 Hours)

Time of Day		Activity	How Often During Week	Total Hours During Week
A.M.	8:00	Teacher conferences	Two days	1 hour
	9:00	Classroom observation	Daily	4 hours
	10.00	. . . .	. . . .	. . . .
	11:00	Follow-up of supervisory visit (summarize notes on observation, locate materials suggested for teacher's use, study class records and test scores)	Daily	2 hours
P.M.	12:30	Teacher conferences	Two days	1 hour
	1:00	Conferences with pupils	As needed	1 hour
	2:00	Classroom observation	Daily	4 hours
	3:00	Follow-up of supervisory visit (as indicated for 11:00)	Daily	1 hour
	3:30	Teacher conferences	Two days	1 hour
	4:00	Preparation for faculty meeting	Two days	2 hours
		Faculty Meeting	One day	1 hour
Evenings		Planning for next day, preparing supervisory bulletins, instructional materials, new devices; checking lesson plans; evaluation	Four nights	4 hours
Saturdays		Review of week's work in supervision; schedule for next week's work	Saturday	1 hour
		Total hours scheduled for supervision		23 hours

of three hours for conferences is planned for the week. For another week, perhaps five hours of teacher conferences might be desirable.

Classroom observation is scheduled twice each day, at 9:00 and at 2:00. The total time to be devoted to classroom observation is eight hours for the week. Especially important is the scheduling of time to follow up supervisory visits. Twice a day, the principal has set aside time to summarize her notes and to provide the teacher observed with the materials or information needed.

The principal has planned to spend an hour each night on supervisory work, planning, preparing materials, checking lesson plans, and evaluating the progress of her work. During the week in question, the monthly faculty meeting will take place, so three hours that week will be devoted to preparing for and conducting the faculty meeting. Definite provision is being made to interview pupils who are having problems. On Saturdays, the supervisory work of the week will be reviewed and plans made for the next week.

From Table II it can be seen that twenty-three hours would be the minimum time that a supervising principal could hope to spend in improving instruction in the school. In fact, the principal would have to move quickly and systematically to accomplish all these aims during the time allotted. With this kind of emphasis on improving services to children, the school would certainly see a consistent improvement in all aspects of instruction.

As a further illustration, one might follow the principal in planning her schedule of administrative duties for the following week. The principal can profitably refer to the check list of administrative duties. It is these duties that the principal plans to discharge efficiently through her weekly schedule. Table III shows the supervisory principal's trial schedule of administrative duties for the coming week.

TABLE III.   Trial Schedule of Administrative Activites for a Week
Supervising Principal (Time Allotment — 13 Hours)

Time of Day		Activity	How Often During Week	Total Hours During Week
A.M.	8:00	Building inspection	Daily	½
		Pupil transfers	Daily	½
		Direction of clerk	Daily	1
		Yard duty	One day	¼
	9:00	. . . .	. . . .	. .
	10:00	Attendance check	Daily	½
		Recess hall traffic	Daily	½
		Recess yard duty	One day	¼
		Office hour	Two days	½
	11:00	Bookkeeping	Daily	1
		Dismissal traffic	Daily	½
		Direction of custodian	Two days	½
P.M.	12:30	Cafeteria duty	One day	½
		Office hour	Two days	1
	1:00	Hall traffic	Daily	¼
		Reports and records	Daily	1
		Band inspection	One day	¼
		Administrative bulletins	Daily	½
		Direction of clerk	Daily	1
	2:00	Recess hall traffic	Daily	½
	3:00	Traffic squad	Daily	¼
		Bus inspection	Two days	¼
		Yard duty	One day	½
	4:00	Plans for next day	Daily	1
		Total hours schedule for administration		13 hours

Administrative duties are harder to schedule because they usually take little time, but occur often during the week. For example, four times a day the principal is in the hall, observing the movement of pupils through the building. Checking attendance takes only a few minutes each day, but must of course be taken care of daily. It can readily be seen that a schedule such as Table III suggests would keep the principal in constant touch with all aspects of school operation.

In Table III, many of the administrative duties seem minor. However, some of the principal's major administrative responsibilities are also scheduled. For example, office hours are scheduled daily, at 10:15 and again at 12:30. One of the important functions of the principal is to listen to her staff and to give them the opportunity to discuss administrative matters with her. These office hours provide the principal with the opportunity to perform all of the functions of administration: to plan, to organize, to direct, to communicate, and to evaluate. Of course, the communication aspect is dominant during these informal conferences.

Another important duty of the principal is to maintain efficient records and to make accurate and punctual reports to the superintendent, to the state, and to others in authority. At 1:00 each day the principal examines her "To be done" file to see whether such records or reports require attention that day. During a typical week, after school is under way, these reports can usually be prepared in about an hour each week.

Of importance also is the preparation of administrative faculty bulletins. Many teachers have complained that getting frequent notes from the principal, especially while they are presenting a lesson, is very upsetting. Announcements made over the public-address system can be equally disturbing when they are not carefully pre-planned with teachers. Hence, the administrative bulletin is a wise measure. Usually, all messages for the week can be accumulated in advance and sent in a dittoed sheet to the staff at a scheduled time. At 1:00 daily, the principal works on this administrative staff bulletin.

Some of the urgent duties of administration do not appear in Table III. This is because not every duty occurs every week. Some weeks there will be much less attention to the movement of pupils through the building; there will be greater emphasis on safety, perhaps, or on scheduling the extra-class duties of teachers, or bookkeeping, or problems of child health, or requisitions. Table III shows how a supervising principal planned in a preliminary way for one week of her school year. Other weeks would be somewhat different, but through the year, the principal's planning would include all of her administrative duties.

The same steps are followed in making out a preliminary schedule for school-community relations, clerical work, and miscellaneous duties. When all five of these areas have been planned tentatively, the supervising principal is ready to put these partial schedules together. Table IV shows the supervising principal's schedule, but still in this formative stage. The breakdown into day-by-day scheduling follows after a study of Table IV.

TABLE IV.   Beginning to Plan a Schedule for the Supervising Principal (50-hour week)

Time	Supervision (23 hrs.)	Administration (13 hrs.)	School-Community (5 hrs.)	Clerical (5 hrs.)	Miscellaneous (4 hrs.)
8:00	Teacher conferences	Building inspection Pupil transfers Traffic squad Direction of clerk Yard duty (W)*		Supplies distributed	Mass (W)
9:00	Classroom observation				
10:00		Attendance check Recess hall traffic Recess yard duty (W) Office hour*		Correspondence Banking (W) Collecting and count-ing money	
11:00	Follow-up of supervisory visits with bulletins, in-structional materials, pro-fessional reading	Dismissal traffic Direction of custodian Bookkeeping	Health and welfare Civic contacts "Drives" Parent conferences		
Lunch 12:00					

12:30	Teacher conferences	Yard duty (W) Cafeteria duty (W) Office hour			
1:00	Pupil guidance	Hall traffic Reports and records Band inspection (W) Admin. bulletins Direction of clerk	Parent conferences Parent bulletins		
2:00	Classroom observation	Recess hall traffic			
3:00	Follow-up of supervisory visit Teacher conferences Faculty meeting (M)*	Traffic squad Bus inspection Observation on play-ground	Preparation for Home-School meeting	Office duties	Church-related duties (W)
4:00	Faculty meeting (M) Preparation for faculty meeting	Plans for next day	Parent conferences Preparation for Home-School meeting	Office duties	
Evenings (three hours)	Supervision — planning the program; preparing bulletins, instructional materials, new techniques; checking lesson plans; evaluation				
Saturdays (four hours)	Review of the week's work Schedule of next week's work			Office duties	School housekeeping Church-related duties

* W means weekly; M means monthly; all other duties are done daily or several times a week.
  Office hour means the principal is available for consultation.

Table IV, the preliminary schedule of a supervising principal, shows how the ground work is laid for a good weekly schedule. The principal has listed the five areas of her job — supervision, administration, school-community relations, clerical work, and miscellaneous school duties. She has also indicated the recommended time allotment for each area. Then, across from the hours of the day, the principal has written in the duties that could be taken care of at that time. It is important at this stage to schedule for a given hour only as many duties as can be discharged. At 8:00 in the morning, for example, all of the duties named should be taken care of from 8:00 to 9:00 each day, or a total of five working hours a week.

This beginning phase of schedule making is a necessary one. It is quite simple to say that one is going to allot five hours weekly to school-community relations, for example, but one must at the same time show that five hours are actually being used for this purpose. This beginning phase of schedule-making is a severe discipline, for the principal is forced to specify the purpose of the activity and at the same time to differentiate among supervisory and administrative and clerical activities. Once this ground work is laid, however, the principal can proceed with confidence to make specific plans for her own school for a given week. It could well be that the first few times the principal goes through this schedule-making process she will have very little time left for actual administrative duties. In the long run, however, scheduling time saves time.

Features of a Good Schedule.

1. **A good schedule includes the entire school plant and every phase of teacher and pupil activity.** For example, in Table IV the principal checks on hall traffic at each crucial period of the school day. Likewise, the principal is on the playground and in the cafeteria at stated times. For the week selected, the principal will observe in classrooms from 9:00 to 10:00, and again from 2:00 to 3:00. Thus, both afternoon and morning situations can be evaluated. It is the principal's responsibility to see that the entire school program is adequately directed at all times. By "spot checking" the principal can keep in touch with all aspects of the program. No week should pass without a visit by the principal to every area of the school and to every type of activity. Staff members and volunteers are reliable, it is true; but it is the principal's ultimate responsibility to see that children are safely and adequately cared for. A comprehensive schedule keeps the principal in touch with all the aspects of the school program.

2. **A good schedule is also realistic.** The activities scheduled must be possible at that time. Teacher conferences, for instance, are best scheduled before and after school hours, when children are not present. Parent conferences are scheduled at an hour convenient to parents. Direction of the

school clerk and the janitor are taken care of during slack times in their work, at the end of the school day. Urgent office duties are taken care of at 10:00, so that necessary contacts can be completed during the school day. Some free time is scheduled daily, so that unexpected events can be fitted in without upsetting the entire schedule. Scheduled free time also enables the principal to continue on activity longer than planned, and still keep within the schedule.

3. **A good schedule varies from week to week.** Duties are rotated from hour to hour, as much as possible. Supervision of the playground is good in the morning one week and in the afternoon the next week. Hall traffic and supervision of the cafeteria should also take in various groups and various periods. The principal should observe in classrooms at all times of the day, and for both long and short periods. A good schedule is flexible for it takes into consideration all aspects of the school program and personal variations as well.

A Schedule in Operation. The schedule given earlier was only the first step in schedule development. This generalized plan must be made specific. Table V presents a weekly schedule for a *teaching principal*, based on the recommended time distribution.

Table V shows how a teaching principal may schedule her time to meet the requirements in each of the major areas. To schedule eight hours for supervision, the principal arranges for five half-hour conferences, two forty-five minute observations, a faculty meeting, two office hours, and two evenings devoted to supervisory work. The principal's two hours for school-community relations are devoted to conferences with the safety director and parents, and planning for the Home and School meeting.

A teaching principal finds it difficult to keep in touch with all school activities, but Table V shows how an ingenious principal managed to do this. An office hour, for example, is scheduled each day, but at different times. Yard duty is spaced through the week, as is the inspection of hall traffic. By careful planning, at least the minimum attention can be given to each area of the school and to each activity.

It must be said again that a good schedule is possible only if clerical and custodial help can be obtained. After a little experimentation, a teaching principal can tell that it takes her much more than two hours a week to complete her own clerical work. When she secures the services of a school clerk, paid or volunteer, the principal can then manage clerical work in two hours weekly. The same is true of school housekeeping. Without adequate custodial service, the principal is forced to spend many hours a week trying to keep the building clean and attractive. With enough help, the principal need devote only an hour or so each week to directing custodial workers.

This fact points out again the important role of the pastor in promoting

TABLE V. Weekly Schedule, Teaching Principal (50-hour week)

(Desk Copy)

Time	Monday	Tuesday	Wednesday	Thursday	Friday
7:45	Building inspection Direction of clerk Office duties Traffic squad	Conference — Sr. Edith Yard duty	Office hour** Office duties Direction of clerk	Conference — Mrs. Q. Mass	Office hour Conference — Sr. Jude (planning for Home-School meeting)
9:00	Visit — Sr. Edith (Reading)	T*	Visit — Mrs. Q. (Arithmetic)	T	T
9:45	T	T	T	T	T
10:15			Yard duty		
10:30	T	T	T	T Dismissal traffic	T
12:00					
12:30		Office hour		Yard duty	Cafeteria duty
1:00	T	T	T	T	Hall traffic T
3:30	Dismissal traffic Observation on playground Office hour	Faculty meeting	Bus inspection — Officer B. (School Safety)	Conference — Mr. F. Planning for demonstration	Practice for procession
4:00	Conference — Miss G.	Faculty meeting	Mr., Mrs. Oexle (retarded child)	Office hour	
Evenings	Supervision — checking lesson plans, preparing for faculty meeting	Class preparation	Supervision — professional reading (helping teachers with test)	Class preparation	Class preparation
Saturday (four hours)	Review week's work Schedule next week's work	Class preparation	Direction of janitor and clerk School housekeeping	Reports and records Correspondence Requisitions	

* T means teaching; ** *Office hour* means principal is available for consultation.

a good school program. The principal's educational leadership is needed so that children may have the best possible education. This leadership is possible only if adequate clerical and custodial service is supplied. The pastor is a key figure in supplying these essential services.

KEEPING A SCHEDULE

When the schedule is made, the work is only begun. Keeping a schedule is a difficult and challenging task. In fact, only the most competent and dedicated persons will, week after week, try to improve on their own record of time distribution. Our schools will advance, we know, only as principals improve their leadership. Keeping to a sound time schedule is an effective way to insure constant improvement of leadership.

Writing Helps. Writing out the schedule has definite advantages. A written reminder is effective in pointing out our duties, and in reminding us of our failings. Since the schedule is to be made out each week, a number of copies of the skeletal outline can be dittoed at one time, and the items typed in each week. An ordinary typing sheet is a good size. Some space should be provided for comments at the bottom of the sheet. Each day, this written schedule should be consulted, followed, and evaluated. Shortcomings should be noted, as well as strong points. After several weeks of such experimentation, the principal will be able to arrange an effective and practical schedule.

Posting the Schedule Helps. One device to urge the principal on in this endeavor is to post her schedule for the staff to see. As mentioned before, the staff should be consulted beforehand about the most convenient arrangements possible. As mentioned previously, the schedule should be developed a little at a time, and gradually presented to those concerned. When these

TABLE VI. Posted Schedule of a Teaching Principal   Week of . . . .

Time	Monday	Tuesday	Wednesday	Thursday	Friday
7:45	Not free	Conference — Sr. Edith Yard duty	Office hour	Conference — Mrs. Quiole	Office hour Conference — Sr. Jude
9:00	Visit — Sr. Edith		Visit —Mrs. Quiole		
10:15			Yard duty		
12:30		Office hour		Yard duty	Cafeteria duty
3:30	Office hour	Faculty meeting	Not free	Conference — Mr. French	Practice for procession
4:00	Conference — Miss Meng	Faculty meeting	Not free	Office hour	Practice for procession

steps have been taken, and the idea of a schedule is well accepted by the group, then the principal should post the schedule on the faculty bulletin board. New Year's resolutions are more likely to be kept if they are written; how much better they would be kept if posted for the entire community to read! The same is true of the principal's schedule. The posted schedule will be a simplified form of the desk copy. The only items posted will be those directly affecting the staff members.

A posted schedule gives the staff the opportunity to consult with the principal during the stated office hours, and during the conferences assigned to them. The principal's share in playground and cafeteria supervision is also evident. The posting of the schedule is not meant to shock teachers by announcing a surprise observation by the principal. The information on the schedule should already have been told to the persons concerned. The posted schedule is only a reminder of what the staff already knows. A posted schedule also protects the principal from overly long conferences and observations, and from unanticipated demands upon her time. Having a schedule which is known to the staff, the principal is better able to portion out her time for necessary activities.

"Time for the Job," as presented in this chapter, assumes of course many essential ingredients of good administration. No principal will achieve perfection in each aspect presented here. But more and more, Sister Principals are striving to advance as professional leaders, and professional leadership demands planning and perseverance. The rigid scheduling described here has much to offer the interested principal who is eagerly looking for suggestions to improve her effectiveness in parochial school administration.

CHAPTER VI

THE PRINCIPAL AND LAY TEACHERS

Perhaps no recent trend in Catholic elementary education is more evident than the rapid increase in lay teachers. This trend will continue, at a more rapid tempo. This change has given rise to many questions and problems: Can an adequate supply of lay teachers be obtained? If so, how? How may lay teachers be retained on a staff? In dealing with lay teachers, what policies and procedures should govern salaries? Sick leave? Contracts and tenure? Retirement plans? Maintenance of morale?

RECENT National Catholic Educational Conventions devoted several sessions to discussing lay teachers in Catholic schools. These sessions were crowded with principals who had come to ask probing questions.

Catholic periodicals are carrying more and more articles on phases of the lay teacher program.

University courses in parochial school administration are stressing the role of the lay teacher, and diocesan school offices are probably spending more time in developing lay teacher policies than in any other area. Why this heightened interest in lay teachers?

TO SCHOOL TO THE SISTERS

In good Catholic families, children have gone to school to the Sisters whenever there was a parochial school that could possibly be reached. The Third Baltimore Council of 1884 re-emphasized the parents' duty to provide a complete education for their children. Hence, pastors and the laity exerted great efforts to build parochial schools, where religion as well as the other R's could be well taught. It was just taken for granted that the Sisters, because of their religious dedication, could do a good job of training children for all of their responsibilities, to God as well as to others. Parents often hoped that the "good Sisters" would be able to make up for many of the unwholesome effects of the environment.

The past ten years have seen radical changes in parochial schools. To name only a few areas of change, one could mention increased enrollment, school buses, cafeterias, buildings, and improved facilities. This expansion might have gone on serenely enough except for one factor — where were the Sisters for the new classrooms? At first, the Mother Superiors were saying to pastors, "Just for this year, do try to get a lay teacher for the extra classroom. Next fall, I certainly hope to send you another Sister." And principals were saying to the Sisters, "We're going to use Mrs. Jonas in the new third grade this year. Reverend Mother says we'll have a Sister for the room next year." And Mrs. Jonas came to "help out" during the emergency. But when the next September came still another classroom had been added to the school, and Reverend Mother was embarrassed that she didn't have even one more Sister to send, so the pastor added a second lay teacher. Mrs. Jonas and Miss Smith were nice parishioners, and they were treated as guests, not as employees, by the pastor and the Sisters. Miss Smith was Sister Estelle's cousin, so that made for even more cordial relations.

This pattern was repeated hundreds of times throughout the country. In fact, when a new parochial school was opened, there were usually lay teachers on the staff. As expansion continued, more lay teachers than Sisters seemed to be added. Parents were wondering each fall whether Junior would have a Sister or a lay teacher, for some staffs were just about equally divided between religious and lay. What was happening to the "Sisters' schools"?

BIRTH RATES AND RELIGIOUS VOCATIONS

Following World War II, birth rates in this country shot up in an unprecedented way. In the early 1950's, first grades were almost doubled, in public and parochial schools. Public schools were feeling the shortage of qualified teachers to meet the demands of expanded enrollments. The teaching Sisterhoods, too, were unable to staff the schools. The following graph shows how parochial school enrollments were outstripping vocations to the teaching orders (Fig. 13)

Parochial school enrollments were increasing at the rate of 6.6 per cent each year, while vocations to the teaching Sisterhoods were increasing only 1.8 per cent a year. This does not mean that there was a dropping off in religious vocations. Not at all. In fact, more young girls than formerly were dedicating themselves to religious life; but, these girls were from the low birth-rate families of the 1930's. Religious vocations were really increasing satisfactorily, except for the fact that enrollments were increasing more rapidly. Parents were clamoring for schools that would prepare their children for all of their responsibilities, spiritual as well as secular. And the demand

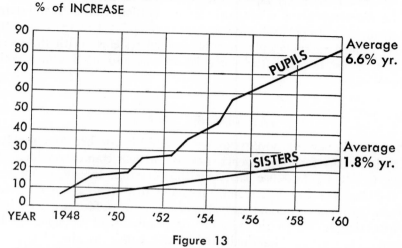

Figure 13

Source: Sister Mary Helene, C.H.M., "The Status of Community Expansion: Bearing on Sister Formation Policies," *Sister Formation Bulletin*, June, 1955. Used with permission.

for parochial school education was simply greater than the mother houses could meet. Even today, there is no discernible tapering off in the rising birth rates.

THE GROWING NEED FOR LAY TEACHERS

If parochial school training is to be made available to children whose parents wish it, Sisters alone cannot meet the need. Moreover, even present Catholic school facilities are not accommodating all of the Catholic children of school age. It is roughly estimated that only half of the Catholic children of the country are in parochial elementary schools. Even at that, lay teachers are clearly needed to serve the 50 per cent who are in Catholic schools. Lay teachers are urgently needed now, and this need will continue into the indefinite future. The lay teacher in the parochial school is here to stay.

This fact has obvious implications. Since the lay teacher is a necessary part of parochial school education, it stands to reason that she must be provided for. "She," the lay teacher is usually called, though some few men have also devoted themselves to work in the parish schools. It takes clear, bold, resourceful thinking to plan adequately for the lay teacher as an integral part of Catholic Education. This planning at first seems totally foreign to the Sister Principal's usual responsibilities. That may well be, but the Sister Principal as an administrator *must* focus her thinking on provisions for competent lay teaching personnel. These provisions cover a wide range. Of the many aspects which concern lay teachers, the following will be discussed here: salary, sick leave, transfer, contracts and tenure, retirement, recruitment, selection and orientation. A few years ago, these matters seemed to apply only to public school systems. With the increase in lay teachers, however, the parochial schools also need sound policies in these areas.

LAY TEACHER SALARY

The Sister's vow of poverty makes it difficult for her to estimate an appropriate salary for a lay teacher. Because of their community life, Sisters receive merely a subsistence salary for their services. In fact, many people call the Sisters' salary a "stipend," meaning that there is no relationship between the money paid and the value of the services. Sisters enter religious life expecting to forego the pleasure or possibility of a tidy little bank account. The Sisters' "hundredfold" usually comes in the afterlife, not here below. Hence, a lay teacher salary of $250 a month is ordinarily several times as large as the salary paid to the Mother Superior for the Sister's services. Consequently, $250 a month, or $2,500 a year, may seem at first glance to be a quite adequate lay teacher salary.

Another factor also makes it difficult for the Sister to set a just wage for lay teachers. To the Sister, and in fact to most parents, Catholic education represents a noble and apostolic work, one of high dedication. The people who take part in this noble mission of the Church should do so because of a dedicated love of children. It seems inconsistent to say on the one hand, "Catholic teachers are doing Christ's work," and then on the other hand say, "Lay teachers should be paid much more money." Are a sense of dedication and a discussion of salary incompatible? To some, they may seem so.

The matter could be discussed at some length, but perhaps the two most important points are these: Why do people decide to enter teaching? And, what is a living wage?

MOTIVES FOR BECOMING A TEACHER

Love of Teaching. It is nice to think that young people are attracted to teaching because they would "gladly learn and gladly teach." It is true, of course, that there have been in every age dedicated people who taught for the love of teaching and without regard for compensation. Religious teachers are one potent example of sheer dedication to the young. But is the typical teacher untouched by less noble motives?

There has been a good deal written about the so-called higher motives of teachers. "Serving children" and "benefiting mankind" are often given as major motivations for becoming a teacher. Questionnaires to teachers asking why they entered teaching play heavily on altruistic ideals such as these. Yet, can it be proved that teachers, more than other college graduates, are burning with a desire to serve humanity? It is really not belittling the teacher to ask these questions. To treat her fairly, one must attempt to satisfy her reasonable personal expectations. In Chapter IV, the discussion of the principal's role as organizer emphasized the need for satisfying the teacher in her job. What kind of job satisfactions does the typical teacher need?

Higher Status. Donald Super, who has studied the problem extensively, has said that teachers are strongly motivated toward higher social status. Educators haven't challenged Super's statement of the situation as quoted below.

> . . . teaching is essentially a poor man's profession. Like nursing, its training is inexpensive as professional training goes. As in the case of nursing, there is a high turnover rate due to the large number of women who marry and leave the profession after a few years of work. And, since the pay scale is lower than in most professions and in most business occupations requiring similar levels of ability and education, there is a constant need for new recruits to replenish the ranks. The end result is that teaching attracts a large percentage of its recruits from the middle, lower middle, and upper lower classes, to use Warner's classification. Many relatively unprivileged but not underprivileged persons see in teaching an inexpensive avenue to advancement, an avenue in which ability rather than contacts and capital opens the doors of opportunity.[1]

Chapter XI discusses the Warner classifications to which Super refers. In general, Super maintains that teaching means higher status for most young people aspiring to be teachers. Children whose fathers were blue collar workers aim to get a white collar job; teaching is a white-collar job for which the training is relatively inexpensive. Scholarships and part-time jobs remove financial obstacles for many teachers-in-training. Not only the writer quoted here, but many other writers, claim that when you look at a teacher you are ordinarily looking at a person who is trying to move upward on the social scale. There is nothing to prove that parochial school lay teachers are radically different from public school teachers in this regard. If one considers the background of lay teachers, the above statements will almost always apply.

Economic Motivations. But, the above indicates only that teachers want status. What has this to do with lay teacher salary? Here in America status has everything to do with salary. The higher social brackets make more

---

[1] Donald Super, *Psychology of Careers* (New York: Harper and Brothers, Inc., 1957), pp. 107–108. Used with permission.

money. When one has more money, one can associate with higher-status people. Prestige and money go hand in hand. Chapter XI elaborates further on the relationship between money and social class, but for the present purposes, the two are practically inseparable. Teachers are aspiring upward socially; a good salary check is needed in order to dress like a higher status person, drive a car, take a more expensive vacation, and have more of the "finer" things.

The above does not mean that teachers dislike children, and use them only as a means of getting ahead. Teachers very probably do love children, but this love of children does not make them indifferent to the economic and social rewards of teaching. The public elementary schools of the country, for example, are staffed largely by women, and yet these same schools are constantly agitating for higher salaries. A love of children does not seem to be enough to satisfy the elementary teacher. A higher salary seems to be a job satisfaction which the teacher requires.

The first pertinent question, then, is the motives that induce people to enter teaching. A love of children no doubt is one of the motives; but equally strong motives are a desire to rise socially and to receive a substantial pay check. As in other professions, there are mixed motives in the teacher trainee's mind. The Sister Principal and the pastor are being unrealistic if they overemphasize the desire to serve and neglect the other two equally strong motives.

A LIVING WAGE

Continued labor agitation for pay increases keeps the question of a living wage constantly before the public. Public school teachers are also pressuring for increased pay. Sometimes the parochial school administrator may feel that it is impossible to satisfy the worker's demands, so why bother? In order to have a well-qualified lay staff, the pastor and principal need to keep their thinking tuned to two stations: papal pronouncements on a living wage and salary patterns in local public schools.

The Popes' Recommendation. Many of the recent popes have made forthright statements on the worker's right to a living wage, Pope Leo XIII being one of the most outspoken. Pope Pius XII applied the principles of a just wage to the teaching situation in his address to Italian teachers:

> We are not ignorant of the fact that the salary of the greater part of teachers, far from assuring them the free time and the money necessary to round out their personal training and perfect their pedagogical methods, instead is barely enough for the daily needs of life, especially for those who have had the courage to take on the responsibility of a family.
> Besides, that salary cannot be considered to be on a par with your serious social responsibility. A society that is really interested in intellectual and moral values, a society that does not want to slip and slide toward that materialism

to which it is being drawn by the weight of the ever more mechanical life of technical civilization, must show the esteem that it has for the profession of the teacher, assuring him a return that corresponds to his social position. Let us not forget that the labor which produces spiritual values is real labor and even, in its kind, more than manual labor. This should be taken into account in calculating a just wage.[2]

Pope Pius XII's statement wisely takes into consideration the teacher's need to maintain higher social status. Certainly with regard to lay teacher salary, pastors and principals must be guided by the pope's directives. Parochial school administrators have an obligation in justice to pay a salary that enables the lay teacher to live at the level of her professional associates.

Public School Salaries. To get to the specifics of a living wage, one must consider what the lay teacher would get if she were teaching in the public schools. Perhaps some averages on a nationwide basis might be a good starting point for such a discussion. In 1960–1961, the average classroom teacher in the public elementary schools was receiving a salary of $5,034 a year.[3] This would be roughly $500 a month. And 50 per cent of all public school elementary teachers were making more than this amount.

Perhaps this comparison is not quite apt, since these public school salaries include teachers who have been in the system up to the point of retirement. Also, the public school average salary of $4,835 includes teachers with all variations in academic training, doctor's degrees as well as emergency teachers.

The Sister Principal and the pastor may be helped in their thinking about salaries by a breakdown of salaries for *beginning* public school teachers only. Since lay teachers are relatively recent in parochial schools, their salaries might be better compared with *beginning* public school teacher salaries. There are no exact figures available, but one can estimate rather closely from the averages reported by public school systems.

Cities above 100,000 in population reported that their average *beginning* salary for *degreed* teachers was $4,200[4] in 1960–61. Smaller cities and county systems would have somewhat lower salaries for teachers, and of course teachers *below* degree status would have lower salaries than those reported for degreed teachers. Considering all of these aspects, one can assume that the starting salary for public school teachers *with* degrees was at least $4,200 in most cities of the United States in 1960–61. This figure is practical for

---

[2] Pope Pius XII, "Aims of an Italian Teachers' Union," *The Pope Speaks* (First Quarter, 1954), pp. 11–12.

[3] National Education Association, Research Division, *Estimates of School Statistics, 1960–61*, Research Report 1960-R15 (Washington, D. C.: National Education Association, 1960), p. 5.

[4] National Education Association, Research Division, *Salary Schedules, Classroom Teachers, Urban Districts 100,000 and Over in Population, 1960–61*, Research Report 1960-R11 (Washington, D. C.: National Education Association, 1960), p. 9.

comparison with parochial schools, since most lay teachers are in the parochial schools located in cities.

These salaries may seem quite satisfactory for the public school teachers. However, they obviously are not so judged by public school teachers themselves. Public school authorities are complaining that they cannot attract and keep competent people when the salaries in industry and other status positions are drawing teachers away from the public schools; and that teaching is not attracting the most intelligent and most promising high school students. The public schools are giving up the notion that "dedication" or "serving humanity" will lure the right kind of talent into teaching; strong pressures are being exerted to raise salaries much higher in order to get and keep the very best in teaching talent.

A study of public school salaries will convince the pastor and the Sister Principal that most parochial school salaries have been inadequate. Definite plans need to be made for an adequate lay teacher salary. Valuable insight can be gained from the way public schools compute salaries. Using this experience as a background, parochial school administrators can develop more satisfactory salary patterns for their own schools.

SALARY SCALES IN PUBLIC SCHOOLS

There are two very important factors that can be measured objectively as regards teacher salaries: the amount of academic training and the years of teaching experience. These two factors can be used to determine how much money the teacher will receive. When training and experience alone establish the salary, the school system has what is called a "single salary scale." This means that the grade level has nothing to do with the amount paid, nor has one's sex, nor any other factor. "Equal pay for equal training and experience," has been the slogan in the public school circles for many years now. This plan has proved satisfactory for the most part, and is quite applicable to parochial schools. Table VII shows how a theoretical salary scale may look for a given public school district.

A beginning teacher in X Public Schools would be on Step 1 — no previous experience, or first year of experience. If this teacher has *two years of college* training she is in Class D and starts at the minimum salary of $3,400 for her first year. This beginning teacher can look forward to regular yearly increases, or increments, of $200 each, provided that her service is satisfactory. At the end of eight years, she will be in Step 9, and will be receiving her maximum salary of $5,000. She will continue at this top salary of $5,000 for the rest of her teaching career in X School System, until retirement or leaving the system for other reasons.

A beginning teacher with a *bachelor's degree* in X School System would

TABLE VII. Salary Scale for X Public School District[a]

| Step[b] (years of experience) | Classes According to Years of College Training | | | |
	Class D (two years of college)	Class C (three years of college)	Class B (bachelor's degree)	Class A (master's degree)
1	$3,400	$3,800	$4,200	$4,400
2	3,600	4,000	4,400	4,600
3	3,800	4,200	4,600	4,800
4	4,000	4,400	4,800	5,000
5	4,200	4,600	5,000	5,200
6	4,400	4,800	5,200	5,400
7	4,600	5,000	5,400	5,600
8	4,800	5,200	5,600	5,800
9	5,000	5,400	5,800	6,000
10		5,600	6,000	6,200
11		5,800	6,200	6,400
12			6,400	6,600
13				6,800
14				7,000

[a] Data generalized by the writer for the 1960–1961 school year.

[b] Step 1 means, for example, that the teacher has had no previous experience in the system; the teacher is on the first step, or is in her first year in the system.

be in Class B, and would receive a starting salary of $4,200. Master's degree people start at $4,400. The maximum salaries for the classes according to professional training vary greatly. The teacher described in the preceding paragraph would continue to earn $5,000 as long as she remained in the system. The teacher with three years of college would have a maximum salary of $5,800; bachelor's degree teachers' top salaries are $6,400; and teachers with master's degrees would earn $7,000 for each year they continued teaching beyond their fourteenth year of service. A teacher may cross over from a lower to a higher class, as when a teacher with two years of college finally gets a degree, and transfers to Class B. As a Class B teacher, she goes into a higher salary bracket and her maximum salary becomes higher.

The single type of salary scale described here has definite advantages over bargaining with individual teachers over salaries. When the scale is prepared, all can know the salary to be paid for a definite amount of college training and teaching experience. Teachers are rewarded financially for the money they have invested in their preparation, and also for continuing in teaching. A salary scale stimulates teachers to improve themselves professionally, and also to continue in the school system. Teachers can plan ahead with a view toward their expected income; and administrators can plan in terms of the cost of teachers' salaries in the total budget over a period of years.

SALARY SCALES IN PAROCHIAL SCHOOLS

The hypothetical salary scale presented in Table VII is typical of salaries in average-income cities in the United States, 1960–1961. Some lay teachers, however, would willingly work for a somewhat lower salary than that given in Table VII. In fact, some lay teachers have said that they would teach in parochial schools if the salary were "adequate." The following quotation by a lay teacher expresses the sentiments of many lay teachers:

> I think that most Catholic teachers would teach in a Catholic school on lesser pay, if they could possibly support themselves. The atmosphere is Christian, the children are better disciplined, and you work with people who love what they are doing. I would never consider a public school regardless of salary, if there was an opening in a Catholic school and the pay was adequate.[5]

A Proposed Salary Scale. What is an adequate lay teacher salary? Many lay teachers have said that 75 to 80 per cent of the local public school salary would permit them to live in reasonable security. Taking 80 per cent of typical public school salaries throughout the country (see Table VII), the Proposed Salary Scale for Parochial Schools was made up as given in Table VIII.

TABLE VIII. Proposed Parochial School Salary Scale

Step[a]	Classes According to Years of College Training		
	Class C (two years of college)	Class B (three years of college)	Class A (degree)
1	$2,720	$3,040	$3,360
2	2,880	3,200	3,520
3	3,040	3,360	3,680
4	3,200	3,520	3,840
5	3,360	3,680	4,000
6	3,520	3,840	4,160
7	3,680	4,000	4,320
8		4,160	4,480
9			4,640
10			4,800

[a] Step 1 means, for example, that the teacher has had no previous experience in the system; the teacher is on the *first* step, or is in her *first* year in the system.

The proposed salary scale in Table VIII is 80 per cent of the public school salaries given in Table VII. The increment each year is $160, or 80 per cent of the public school increment of $200 a year. The parochial school salary scale does not include as many steps or years of experience as does the

---
[5] Mary Zook, "Lay Teachers in Catholic Schools," *The Ave Maria*, Vol. 84, No. 17 (Oct. 27, 1956), p. 18. Used with permission.

public school scale. However, if finances permitted, the scale in Table VIII might be extended through additional years of experience.

A lay teacher beginning with only two years of college training would start at a minimum of $2,720. She would get annual increases of $160 for seven years, and her maximum salary would be $3,680 for the remainder of her service. However, such a lay teacher would be very likely to continue her college training and would therefore cross over to Class B, and finally to Class A.

Table VII and Table VIII presuppose that state standards permit a non-degreed teacher to fill in during an emergency. Some public school systems publish no salary figures for below-degree people, though in an emergency substandard teachers are hired. A sound approach to salary scheduling for parochial as well as public schools would include maintaining state standards with regard to teacher preparation.

To be realistic, the principal and pastor should base their actual salary scale on current local public school salary figures. The local public school district usually publishes these figures, or they can be obtained by asking. Each spring, the parochial school salary scale should be revised to equal 80 per cent of the public school district figures.

The Salary Scale and Parish Collections. What would happen to the parish budget if such a salary scale were put into effect in a parish school? Using Table IX, for a typical parish having three lay teachers, the following figures would result:

TABLE IX.   Introducing a Salary Scale for Lay Teachers

	Years of College	Years of Experience	Salary Table VIII	Salary Now	Difference
Lay Teacher X	2	First	$2,720	$2,500	$ 220
Lay Teacher Y	3	Fourth	3,520	3,000	520
Lay Teacher Z	BA	Eighth	4,480	3,000	1,480
			Total $10,720	$8,500	$2,220

Table IX shows how the parochial school salary scale would affect the lay teachers' salaries. Teacher X under the scale, would receive $220 more than she now receives, and Teacher Y would receive $520 more and Teacher Z $1,480 more. The scale would cost $2,220 more a year, but it would wisely recognize the superior value of the better trained teachers. How would the parish raise this $2,220? The money would logically come from the Sunday collections. Dividing $2,220 by 52 Sundays in the year, the pastor would need to take in just $40 extra each Sunday. There are usually four or five Masses a Sunday when the parish hires the above lay teaching staff, so the result would be just about $8 extra for each Sunday Mass throughout the year. The parishioners, who have already made great sacrifices to build and equip the school, would be quite ready to drop in a few extra coins each Sunday to increase the competence of the teaching staff.

The small amount of $2,220 a year would encourage the experienced teachers to stay longer in the parochial school. This fact alone would improve the school program. Salary schedules appear to be much more costly than they really are, when the all-over picture of competence and staff stability are taken into consideration.

SICK LEAVE POLICY

Another essential of good personnel policy is the provision for sick leave with pay. It is true that the teacher has agreed to be with her class daily for the entire school year. Yet there may be occasions when the teacher's absence would be warranted, or even desirable. If the teacher can be absent when ill, her sickness will probably be short-lived, and the class will not suffer from exposure to infection from the teacher or to "busy work." Sick leave policy should not be looked upon as a concession to too-delicate staff members. Sick leave policy is a plan to assure to children uniformly good teaching every day of the year.

PUBLIC SCHOOL POLICY

There is a trend in public schools toward a more generous sick leave policy. The larger systems are allowing teachers more days of sick leave, with pay, the average now being 12 days per year.[6] Many public school districts are also providing that unused days of sick leave may be accumulated over a period of years. A teacher may "save" the unused portion of her leave and put it into her sick leave reserve. For example, in a school system that allows 12 days' sick leave a year, a teacher may have been absent two days each year for three years. Then, at the beginning of her fourth year of service, she is hospitalized. The teacher would draw from her sick leave reserve; she would have accumulated ten days for each of the preceding three years, or a total of thirty days. The teacher would be paid her full salary during this extended illness, up to thirty school days, if required by her physician. Thirty school days is about six calendar weeks. This protection in time of serious illness adds to the security of the teacher and also strengthens her loyalty to the school system.

About 98 per cent of all city public school systems grant sick leave with full pay, for a specified number of days per year. About 94 per cent of the

---

6 American Association of School Administrators and Research Division of the National Education Association, *Leaves of Absence Regulations for Teachers, 1955–56*, Educational Research Service Circular No. 7 (Washington, D. C.: The National Education Association, 1956), p. 7.

city systems grant cumulative sick leave; 30 days is the average sick leave reserve which a teacher may accumulate.[7] Some public school systems, however, grant cumulative sick leave up to 100 days. The idea behind the provision is, of course, to safeguard children from exposure and to assure them good teaching. Sick leave is intended only indirectly to benefit the teachers themselves.

PREPARING A POLICY FOR PAROCHIAL SCHOOLS

There is frequently no written sick leave policy in parish schools. When a teacher is ill, a substitute is provided, but a teacher may insist on staying in school when ill because she doesn't want to inconvenience the principal. Then too, there is the "almost-never absent" record of Sisters. This tendency of Sisters to minimize their illnesses may make lay teacher absence seem excessive, when actually it is normal. With the increase in staff size, and the corresponding increase in lay teachers, it is necessary for the school to have a definite sick leave policy. The principal should be able to develop a good sick leave policy in co-operation with the pastor.

Keeping a Record of Absence. The principal could merely take over a sick leave policy used in a good public school district, but she would probably feel more satisfied if she worked out the plan herself. First, the principal should keep track of all teacher absence during a school year. Each teacher, religious and lay, should have an absence record in her folder, in the office file. Such a form as the following (Figure 14) might serve for the purpose.

Figure 14. TEACHER ABSENCE RECORD

Teacher ....   School year ....

Entered the school (date) ....   As of Sept. 1, 1961, teacher had accumulated .... days of sick-leave reserve.

Date	Day of Week	No. of Periods	Reason for Absence	Deductions[a]

[a] Indicate settlement of sick-leave allowance and deductions for lay teachers.

[7] Ibid.

On the above form, the principal, or preferably a school clerk, would enter each day's absence on the morning of absence. In this way, an accurate record can be kept of the absence of each teacher, and the absence for the staff as a whole. A summary of these records will show the principal what to expect by way of teacher absence. Tardiness would not appear on the record, unless the teacher misses half of the morning or afternoon session. Such extreme tardiness would be considered a half-day's absence.

Listing the Causes for Absence. Most teacher absence is caused by personal illness, hence, the name "sick leave policy." However, school systems have included under sick leave two separate groups of causes — personal illness and miscellaneous reasons. A sound sick leave policy might therefore cover:

a) Critical illness of a member of the immediate* family
b) Death in the immediate family
c) Attendance at a funeral of a member of the immediate family
d) Unforeseeable emergency beyond the employee's control

Absence for the above reasons might be included in the sick leave policy; that is, an employee absent for the above reasons might charge absence to his sick leave account. Absence would be chargeable, of course, only up to the specified number of days allowed in the school system. Absence for any other reason would not be chargeable to sick leave, and salary would be accordingly deducted.

A sound sick leave policy must be clear in stating exactly what kind of absence may be charged to sick leave. A written record of absence is essential to operating a just and consistent sick leave policy. All teacher absence, whether or not chargeable to sick leave, should be noted as it occurs.

Formulating the Plan. A study of teacher absence will usually show that ten days a year will be the maximum absence of the average teacher. For extended illnesses, as for surgery, a thirty-day cumulative period will ordinarily suffice. In writing up the sick leave policy for the school handbook, the wording might be as follows:

SICK LEAVE POLICY

The teacher is expected to be with her class except for grave reason. When a teacher must be absent, the sick leave policy operates as follows:

1. Absence for personal illness
   For personal illness, the school will grant one day of sick leave, with pay, for every month of service completed, up to ten days a year, and cumulative up to thirty days.

---

* See definition of "immediate" in the section following.

2. Absence for other reasons

Miscellaneous reasons included under sick leave are as follows:

a) Illness of a member of the immediate family (father, mother, brother, sister, spouse, grandmother, grandfather, or other relatives living in the same household)

b) Death in the immediate family

c) Attendance at the funeral of a member of the immediate family

d) Unforeseeable emergency beyond the employee's control

For any or all of the four reasons stated above, the teacher may charge to the unused portion of her sick leave account absence up to five days a year. Absence for miscellaneous reasons will be counted in the ten days of sick leave allowable during a year.

3. Deductions in salary

When sick leave pay has been used up, deductions in salary will be made for each day's absence, at the rate of the teacher's daily salary (original salary, minus deductions). Teacher absence for reasons other than those stated above will not be chargeable to the sick leave account.

The above sick leave plan seems just, in the light of public school policies in this area. The plan also provides the parochial school administrator with an orderly and consistent method of granting sick leave with pay, and also of making deductions in salary for excessive teacher absence, or for absence without due cause.

The Sick Leave Policy in Practice. Lay teachers following the above policy are paid their regular salary during absence caused by the reasons indicated. However, they are paid their regular salary only for days of sick leave pay owed to them. The following example will show how many days' salary is to be paid the lay teacher, and the point at which deductions begin.

EXAMPLE 1:

A lay teacher hired in September is absent for four days in October (cause — personal illness).

Applying sick leave policy: The lay teacher has completed the month of September, so she has one day of sick leave coming. In her salary check for October, *three days' pay should be deducted.*

EXAMPLE 2:

The same lay teacher is absent for two days in January (attending the funeral of a member of the immediate family).

Applying sick leave policy: The lay teacher has used up her sick leave for September. The month of October was not completed (four days' absence). November was completed and December. Therefore, the lay teacher is entitled to two days of sick leave with pay. There would be *no deductions* in her salary check for January.

EXAMPLE 3:

A lay teacher is absent for three days in April (husband is taking a trip for the company and she goes with him).

This absence is not chargeable to sick leave. In her salary check for April, these *three days' pay should be deducted.*

These deductions should be based on the daily salary. School systems use either of two methods for computing deductions. The simplest method is to divide the monthly take-home pay by 20 (20 school days in a month). A better method is to divide the yearly salary by the number of school days on the calendar, as for example dividing $3,040 (minus deductions) by 180 days. Each day's deduction would be consistent throughout the year for a given teacher. Deductions should always be based on the teacher's take-home salary.

Financing the Sick Leave Policy. The above policy is practical only if the means of financing it can be arranged. A good sick leave plan includes paying the salary of the teacher absent for specified causes, and also includes paying the salary of a competent substitute teacher. It is the salary of the substitutes that must be provided for if the sick leave policy is to prove effective. If a school tried to carry out the policy outlined above, what would it cost the parish? The following illustration of a typical case may be helpful.

> EXAMPLE: The parish school staff includes five Sisters and three lay teachers. From previous experience, the principal estimates that all of the Sisters together will not be absent more than ten days during the year. The three lay teachers will probably be absent a total of fifteen days during the year. The total absence expected, then, is twenty-five days for the whole staff. If the going rate for a competent substitute is $18 a day, the twenty-five days' absence would cost the parish $450 for the year.

Another way of viewing the cost is a percentage plan. In public school systems, from 2 to 3 per cent of the payroll is considered adequate to pay for substitute teachers needed. In the parochial school staff discussed in Table IX, there were three lay teachers who received a total yearly salary of $10,720. If the five Sisters receive a monthly stipend of $90 each, then the Sister's salary amounts to $4,500. Totaling the salaries for lay and religious, the amount is $15,220 a year. Two per cent of this amount is $304; three per cent is $456. The $450 estimated above comes very close to the percentage of the payroll which public schools allot to administering their sick leave plan.

Can the parish school afford paying for substitute teachers? The answer can only be in the affirmative. Unless good substitutes can be provided, children will suffer. It is true that some substitution can be arranged with volunteer workers from the parish. However, unless the volunteers are capable teachers themselves, the educational program is interrupted. In Chapter VII, there is a discussion of how to improve the services of substitute teachers. The quality of the substitute's work is all-important in administering a good sick leave policy.

Safeguarding the Plan From Abuse. Most lay teachers can be expected to co-operate with a sick leave policy. However, it is good practice to prevent abuse by taking the following precautions:

1. The conditions under which sick leave with pay will be granted should be clearly stated and understood by all. As the need arises, the policy should be further clarified, in writing.
2. Lay teachers should be asked each September to present a certificate showing a health examination recently passed.
3. Every effort should be made to provide healthful, hygienic working conditions.
4. Deductions in salary should be consistently and objectively made.
5. The principal should keep a record of all staff absence, with a statement of reasons. This record should also show which absences were deductible from sick leave reserve.
6. The principal should summarize at the end of the year the amount of staff absence, the reasons for absence, and the cost of paying substitute teachers. This summary will show the pastor and staff what it has cost to maintain a good educational program despite staff absence.
7. Teachers who are going to be absent should be required to telephone the principal by a stated hour, to provide within reason for the substitute teacher's day, and when possible to work with the substitute in case of an extended illness.

The above measures will, in most instances, enable the pastor to operate a good school through wisely providing for normal teacher absence.

CONTRACTS AND TENURE

In the early days of this country, teaching was looked upon as a job for a wandering teacher a few months during the year, perhaps when the children could not be engaged profitably in farm work. Some teachers "traveled with the crops," gathering children together at different seasons according to the harvest time in the district. Since those early days, there has been a great effort made on the part of the school district to make teaching a permanent position, one with status and respectable conditions of employment. To do this, the hiring board began to offer the teacher a promise of a continued position, a contract, in other words; the teacher, on his part (teachers were usually men), promised continued satisfactory service. Because of the benefits both to the employer and the teacher, teacher contracts have become common practice through the years. Today, practically all public school teachers are under contract.[8]

Teacher contracts are a means of encouraging good teachers to remain in the system. Tenure is so closely bound up with contracts that the two aspects of working conditions can best be considered together.

[8] National Education Association, Committee on Tenure and Academic Freedom, *Trends in Teacher Tenure thru Legislation and Court Decision* (Washington, D. C.: National Education Association, 1957), p. 7.

KINDS OF TEACHER CONTRACTS

Three major types of teacher contracts have been developed: annual, limited, and continuing. A brief discussion of these contracts may be helpful to the principal in developing a plan for her own school, in case a diocesan program is not in operation.

Annual Contracts. An annual contract is usually signed in the spring of the year and guarantees the teacher a position for the coming year only. The school board has no obligation to re-hire the teacher for any succeeding year, or even to explain why another contract was not offered to the teacher. Under the annual contract system, the teacher is "kept in the dark" about the length of time she will be kept in the system and about the reasons for discharge. The annual contract, though it has good features, is not entirely satisfactory for either teacher or employer. It is usually offered to a beginning teacher who is serving a probationary period in the system. After a series of annual contracts, the teacher may be admitted to the next higher class, or given a contract for more than a single year. In school systems which have this probationary period, teachers must prove satisfactory or they are not kept in the system after this trial period.

Limited Contract. The limited contract is usually signed for more than one year of service at a time. As mentioned above, the beginning teacher is usually expected to sign an annual contract for several years in succession. Then, if her service has been satisfactory and she wishes to continue in the system, she signs a *limited* contract. Under the terms of this contract, she is assured a position for a specified number of years, usually three years, and is, in her turn, expected to remain during the years specified. The limited contract is a sign that the teacher has successfully passed her probationary period and is judged adequate for continued service in the school system. The limited contract removes the uneasiness which a teacher may feel, wondering whether she will be asked to renew her contract for the fall. The contract also gives more assurance to the system that the teacher is interested in remaining in the schools.

Continuing Contract. After completing the term of the limited contract, the teacher in many systems is offered a continuing contract. This type of contract offers still more protection to the teacher and the hiring board than do the annual or limited types. When under continuing contract the teacher assumes she will be continued in the system. However, if her services will not be needed for the fall, she will be notified at an early date, usually by March 15. This is the typical kind of continuing contract, and is called "spring notification" type. In other words, the teacher assumes she will continue in the system unless she is notified in the spring that her services will not be needed. Ordinarily, the "spring notification" continuing contract means a promise of steady employment. However, the employing board need not give reasons, if the teacher's contract is not renewed in the spring.

TENURE

The three types of contracts described above offer the teacher and the hiring board a certain amount of security. However, the trend in the public school system is toward tenure. The term *tenure* has several interpretations. For example, tenure can mean the length of time a teacher has taught in a school system. Tenure can also mean the total time a teacher has been in the profession. However, with reference to contracts, tenure has a more complex meaning. The definition from the *Dictionary of Education* is as follows:

> *Tenure, indefinite* is a system of school employment in which the teacher or other employee, having served a probationary period of a certain number of years, retains his position indefinitely and is protected in his position either by statute or by rule of the school board; dismissal of employees having such protection must follow certain specified procedures.[9]

Advantages of Tenure. A public school teacher under tenure has more protection than under any of the contracts discussed above. A tenure law guarantees that a tenure teacher will not be dismissed at any time unless the following conditions are present:

1. Notice
2. Statement of reasons
3. A court hearing, with legal counsel and witnesses
4. The right of appealing to a higher court

Some tenure laws require that the notice of dismissal, with the statement of reasons, be sent to the teacher by registered mail. The length of time between receiving the notice and date of dismissal is also specified. If the teacher decides to request a hearing, time limits are also placed here.

On the part of the hiring board, tenure laws are desirable because they provide an orderly procedure for dismissing a teacher. However, the statement of reasons must be such as to include grounds for dismissal under the local school district regulations. In practice, many court cases develop because of a teacher's challenging his or her dismissal under the existing tenure laws.

As mentioned earlier, the trend in public school practice is toward indefinite tenure. About two thirds of all public school teachers were under tenure protection in 1956, 16 per cent of public school teachers were under continuing contract, and only 9 per cent of all public school teachers had

---

[9] Carter V. Good, Ed., *Dictionary of Education*, 2nd ed. (New York: McGraw-Hill Book Company, Inc., 1959), p. 556. Used with permission.

neither tenure nor annual contracts.[10] On a state-wide basis, thirty-six states have enacted tenure laws which apply to at least some of its teachers.

Disadvantages of Tenure. Some writers claim that teachers, if they are truly professionals, will not want or need tenure protection. A good person, these writers claim, can find and keep a good job. The hiring board often continues a poor teacher on the payroll because of the undesirable publicity resulting from a tenure trial. In fact, the critics of tenure continue, it is next to impossible for a board to fire a teacher except for a few flagrant violations of law and order. Tenure, they feel, takes away from the professional status of the teacher and handicaps the hiring board. Especially in these days of teacher shortage, indefinite tenure may seem unnecessary. Tenure laws do seem to have the shortcomings listed above. However, the laws also tend to lessen the likelihood of dismissal through caprice or injustice.

CONTRACTS AND TENURE IN PAROCHIAL SCHOOLS

Contracts for Sisters. In the case of Sisters, it is obvious that contracts and tenure do not apply as they do to lay people. If there is a contract made with Sisters, it is between the Mother Superior of the religious community and the Bishop of the diocese. This kind of contract is signed when the religious community agrees to staff a particular school in the diocese. Until conditions make a change necessary, the Mother Superior assigns Sisters to the school each year in specified numbers. When the Mother Superior wishes to withdraw her Sisters from a school, ordinarily she must notify the Bishop at least a year in advance. Thus, contracts do not affect the individual teaching Sister, but only the religious community as a group.

Contracts for Lay Teachers. In the case of lay teachers, contracts are an essential part of good working conditions. Informal verbal agreements between pastor and lay teacher have proved ineffective. However, many parochial schools do not have lay teachers sign contracts. Where there is no diocesan contract provided, the individual pastor may easily work out his own contract by studying contracts used in public school systems or in other diocesan schools. The annual contract used in the Diocese of Youngstown (Figure 15) may serve as a basis for developing a good contract for the individual parochial school.

---

[10] National Education Association, Committee on Tenure and Academic Freedom, *loc. cit.*

National Education Association, Research Division, *Estimates of School Statistics, 1959–60*, Research Report 1959–R23 (Washington, D. C.: National Education Association, 1959), p. 26.

Youngstown Diocesan Board of Education
Lay Teacher Contract

This Agreement,

entered into this .... day of ...., 19....,
by and between .... (teacher) and
........................Parish (or High School), provides as follows:

The teacher agrees to teach in the school designated above for the .... school term, or for such portion thereof as may remain after the beginning date of service, subject to the following conditions:

1. The school term shall be one hundred seventy-six days (176), the first school day for the term being September ...., 19....,
2. The teacher shall serve this school in the position and in the specific duties assigned by the principal. The teacher shall discharge this assignment to the satisfaction of the principal and the diocesan superintendent.
3. The teacher shall abide by all the rules and regulations of the parish school and those of the Youngstown Diocesan Board of Education as expressed in the diocesan handbook, which rules and regulations are incorporated herein by reference and made a part of this contract.
4. In case of absence covered by diocesan school policy, the pastor shall pay for one day's absence for each month of service completed, up to ten days' absence a year, and cumulative up to absence of ninety days. The pastor shall also pay the salary of the substitute teacher during such absence.

In consideration of such services, the Parish (or High School) agrees to pay the teacher a yearly salary of $.........., subject to deductions for Social Security, income tax, and local tax where operative. A day's salary shall be computed as 1/176 of the annual salary minus deductions. Salary payments shall be made as follows:.............................
....

Forward 4 copies to Diocese.   Pastor.........................
Copies will be returned for: (or Administrator)
Pastor (or administrator),   Superintendent......................
teacher, and school file.   Teacher...............................

This contract is valid upon receiving the Diocesan Superintendent's signature indicating that the teacher is approved for the position and is thereby permitted to teach.

For new teachers, the contract must be forwarded with **Diocesan Application for Teaching.**

Figure 15

This contract for the Diocese of Youngstown includes the essential elements of a good teaching contract.

1. It specifies the length of the school year and the opening date.
2. It states the salary for the year and for the month (before deductions).
3. It states the kind of service to be rendered and the name of the person who will direct this service.
4. It includes provisions for sick leave.
5. It has provisions for signatures.

The contract for the Diocese of Youngstown does *not* include certain *undesirable* features found in some contracts:

1. The specific teaching duties should not be named.
2. Causes of dismissal should not be listed.
3. There should not be a cancellation clause.

The cancellation clause, which entitles either party to terminate the contract upon a notice of, say thirty days, practically nullifies any value a signed contract may have. Naming the specific teaching duties weakens the contract, for conditions may change and other duties might be needed. The causes of dismissal are usually so few and so generalized that a listing of them is ineffective.

The individual pastor and principal may adapt this contract, or others, to the needs of their school, where a diocesan contract does not exist.

IMPROVING CONTRACTUAL ARRANGEMENTS IN PAROCHIAL SCHOOLS

Because of advantages both to the school and to the lay teacher, pastors would be wise to consider what they can do to improve contractual arrangements in their schools. The following plan is based on successful public school practice, and should be applicable in parochial schools. The plan includes the following steps:

Step I.   Probationary Period (three years)
Step II. Limited Contract Period (three years)
Step III. Continuing Contract Period (indefinite)

Step I. PROBATIONARY PERIOD (three years)

    A. The pastor's role

        1. Signs a one-year contract with the beginning lay teacher.
        2. The following spring, offers a satisfactory lay teacher a one-year contract for the next year; or in case of unsatisfactory services, withholds the contract. Repeats this in the spring of the second year.
        3. In the spring of the third year, either notifies the teacher that her services will not be needed in the fall, or admits her to the next level.

      B. The lay teacher's role
        1. Renders satisfactory service.
        2. Meets certification requirements.
        3. Gives evidence of required in-service improvement (perhaps in terms of added college credits).

Step II. THE LIMITED CONTRACT PERIOD (three years)
      A. The pastor's role
        1. At the end of the probationary period, offers the satisfactory lay teacher a three-year contract.
        2. In the spring of the second year, offers the satisfactory lay teacher a supplementary *salary* contract for the fall term. Withholds the contract of an unsatisfactory teacher. (Corresponds to Lay Teacher Advisory Program — see Chapter Ten).
        3. In the spring of the third year, either notifies the lay teacher that her services will not be needed in the fall, or admits her to the next level.
      B. The lay teacher's role
        Continues to fulfill obligations (1), (2), and (3) in 1-B, above.

Step III. CONTINUING CONTRACT PERIOD (indefinite)
      A. The pastor's role
        1. Offers a continuing contract to the lay teacher who has satisfactorily completed the Limited Contract period. This continuing contract assures the teacher of a position each fall, unless notified by April first that her services will not be needed in the fall.
        2. Each spring offers the lay teacher on a continuing contract a supplementary *salary* contract for the fall term.
        3. Enforces the age for retirement.
      B. The lay teacher's role
        1. Continues to fulfill obligations (1), (2), and (3) in 1-B, above.
        2. Retires at the age specified.

The three steps outlined above form the basis for contractual arrangements in public schools using the continuing contract. They are mentioned as steps, because each part of the plan can be introduced in sequence. If lay teachers hired in September, 1961, started with Step 1, they could complete the entire series and sign a continuing contract in the spring of 1967.

Objections to Continuing Contract for Parochial Schools. The idea of a continuing contract may cause some uneasiness on the part of pastors and principals. What if the lay teacher placed on a continuing contract is not needed because of reduced enrollment? To prevent this difficulty, the pastor can insert a clause in the contract to the effect that employment will be terminated if reduction in staff becomes necessary at some future date. Smaller enrollments in parochial schools are, however, not foreseeable in the near future. What if the lay teacher's services become unsatisfactory? In this case, the lay teacher may be notified by April first that she will not be needed for the fall term. The pastor is not required to give reasons, though he would probably do so as part of good administration.

The above plan for parochial schools is based on the "spring notification" type of continuing contract. As such, it does not afford the lay teacher the same protection as tenure laws. However, in parochial schools, the essential of tenure — the right to a court hearing — is incompatible with good administration. The continuing contract is probably the best type of contractual arrangement that can be made for parochial schools. A continuing contract would vastly improve the security of parochial school lay teachers, and would make lay teaching a more desirable career. Continuing contracts would also benefit the parish school, for greater stability and high morale help to improve classroom instruction. In these days of acute teacher shortage, pastors and principals would be wise to study the continuing contract as a means of improving their school staffing program.

PROVISION FOR OLD AGE

A necessary adjunct to longer service is provision for old and disabled teachers. School systems wish to encourage teachers to remain in the system for a long time, because turnover is harmful to the school program. In order to be fair to the teacher, therefore, the school should provide retirement benefits. A good retirement plan removes aged and disabled teachers from the classroom, and at the same time helps retired teachers to live decently without appealing to charity. Retirement benefits should be made available, not only to teachers, but to all staff members who serve the school. The retirement plan should include office workers, custodians, and other service workers. All of these, by their faithful performance of duty, enhance the value of the school program.

Social Security. The idea behind Social Security, or Old-Age and Survivors Insurance, is that during the working years both the employer and the employee pay taxes into a fund, and then when the employee retires, or is disabled, or dies, benefit payments are made from the fund to the employee or the beneficiaries. Social Security insurance is enjoyed by nine out of every ten working people in the United States. Since these benefits are now available to nonprofit organizations, most pastors have arranged for this routine protection for all lay employees.

A look at Social Security coverage may be helpful when thinking of providing more equitably for lay employees. In 1960, the Social Security tax was 3 per cent of the salary paid by the employer and 3 per cent paid by the employee.[11] Thus, if a single lay teacher with no dependents salary was

---

[11] This rate will gradually increase until 1969 and thereafter, the rate will be 4½ per cent paid by the employer and 4½ per cent paid by the employee.

For a fuller discussion see Your Social Security — Old-Age, Survivors, and Disability

$300 a month, the pastor deducted 3 per cent or $9, before giving her the pay check. The pastor matched this amount with 3 per cent, or $9, from parish funds, and sent a total of $18 each month to the District Director of Internal Revenue. These taxes were deposited in the Federal Old-Age and Survivors Insurance Trust Fund and were to be used exclusively to pay the benefits and expenses of operating the program.

If a single lay teacher with no dependents averaged a salary of $350 a month from 1951 on, then the lay teacher would receive from Social Security about $116 a month after her retirement at age 65. This amount is higher than benefits prior to the 1958 Social Security Amendments, though $116 would not enable her to live in complete security. Many lay teachers are not making $350 a month, however. Lay teachers receiving a lower salary contribute less to the Social Security fund, but they have less to look forward to in their old age. For example, a lay teacher averaging $250 a month from 1951 on could collect in Social Security benefits at age 65 or no more than $95 a month, or about $24 a week. With the present cost of living, $24 is indeed an inadequate income. It is evident from this that a lay teacher receiving a low salary is being penalized twice: right now her standard of living cannot be on a professional level, and at retirement she will barely be able to exist unless she has other sources of income. Lay teachers with dependents are further handicapped because of the high cost of living.

When one considers retirement benefits under Social Security, it is clear that many lay teachers need higher salaries in order to provide for their old age. In any parish where Social Security insurance is not offered to lay employees, the program should immediately be included.

RETIREMENT PLANS

Parochial schools have an obligation to provide a respectable living for lay employees who have served Catholic education faithfully over many years. In planning for a retirement program, the parochial schools cannot draw from state funds, as the public schools can. However, as higher salaries are possible through clear-sighted planning, so too retirement benefits for lay personnel can be arranged.

As mentioned in the preceding discussion, Social Security coverage does provide some protection for retired parochial school workers. However, Social Security benefits are not enough. Informed people feel that in retirement the worker's income should be about two thirds of the average income during active years. Social Security frequently provides less than half this

---

Insurance Benefits Under the Social Security Law, U. S. Government Printing Office, 1960. This pamphlet may be obtained from the Social Security Office, usually located in the local U. S. Post Office building in the town.

average income. For example, the teacher who averaged $3,500 a year should receive at least $2,300 a year, or $175 a month after retirement at 65. As pointed out in the example given earlier, Social Security benefits in this case would be not more than $116 a month, or considerably less than the $175 deemed adequate in retirement. In justice and charity, parochial schools should plan conscientiously to provide a dignified retirement period for their lay teachers, custodians, clerks, cafeteria workers, and any other lay employees in the service of the school.

Such planning almost always must be done on a large scale, usually diocesan-wide. The Archdiocese of Milwaukee and the Diocese of Peoria are two outstanding examples of progress in arranging retirement benefits for parochial school lay employees.[12] More recently, a plan has been developed by the American Province of the Xaverian Brothers for employees of the schools of their province. The following example shows how their plan will promote the old age security of their lay employees.

EXAMPLE OF A GOOD RETIREMENT PLAN

Take, for example, an employee who is hired in 1952 at age 25 and joins the plan on October 1, 1959 at age 32. His annual earnings at that time are $3,800, increase to $4,800 at age 48, and then remain unchanged until his normal retirement date. When he retires, his wife is also age 65. His retirement income can be estimated as follows:

Past Service Income	
5 years (age 27 to 32) × $3,800 × ½%	$ 95
Future Service Income	
10 years (age 32 to 42) × $3,800 × 1%	$ 380
23 years (age 42 to 65) × $4,800 × 1%	1,104
Total yearly retirement income from plan	$1,579
Estimated yearly Social Security primary amount	$1,452
His wife's Social Security (½ of his)	$ 726
Estimated yearly income after retirement	$3,757

Source: American Province of Xaverian Brothers, Inc., *Your Plan — Retirement Income and Group Life Insurance* (Hartford, Conn.: Connecticut General Life Insurance Co., 1959), p. 11. Used with permission. Employees are eligible to join after they have completed two years' service.

The plan outlined above shows that with careful planning helpful arrangements can be worked out to care for the retirement of lay employees. The above plan costs the employee just about 1 per cent of his annual income; the school pays a slightly higher percentage as its share. Together, the money invested provides a secure retirement period for lay employees of the Xaverian Brothers.

Another feature of the Xaverian Brothers' plan is voluntary group insurance. For the small monthly fee of 60 cents per $1,000 of insurance, the

12 Brother Leo V. Ryan, C.S.V., "The School Insurance Portfolio, Part III, Employee Insurance Programs," *The Catholic School Journal*, ILVI (Dec., 1956), pp. 305–307.

Brothers' lay employees can add substantially to their retirement income or arrange for payment to a beneficiary in case of death.

The individual pastor or principal cannot do much to provide this type of retirement benefit to the lay employees of the parish school. However, knowing about plans that are already operating, the pastor and principal may be able to do just a little more to discharge their duty in justice and charity. While looking forward to providing more adequate retirement benefits, the pastor can of course see that the lay employees are at least covered by Social Security. Pope John XXIII has led the way in providing greater economic security for the lay employees of the Vatican. The individual parish school must also exhibit the Church's concern for the economic welfare of her children.

IMPROVING LAY STAFFING OF PAROCHIAL SCHOOLS

In order to secure and retain a competent lay staff, the policies discussed above are essential:

1. A salary scale based on at least 80 per cent of the local public school district salary for equal training and experience
2. A sick leave policy of one day sick leave, with pay, for each month of service completed, cumulative up to thirty days
3. A contract plan which includes a probationary period, limited contract, and continuing contract
4. Retirement benefits including Social Security and, where possible, benefits of group insurance and retirement plan

As the diocese and the individual parish school work to provide more of the above desirable conditions, it becomes easier to achieve satisfactory lay staffing. When these conditions are established, then the pastor and principal are on a firm basis in their efforts to secure, screen, and induct lay teachers. These aspects of improved lay staffing will be discussed below.

SECURING COMPETENT LAY TEACHERS

Even when there is only one lay teacher needed, many harassed pastors and principals know how they must work to succeed in getting a lay teacher. Where there are fifteen or more lay teachers needed, the problems seem to be multiplied beyond measure. Parochial school administrators used to think that when they hired a lay teacher, they "had" one. Experience proved, however, that lay teachers do not remain long in the schools. Many factors enter into dropouts among lay teachers, as discussed in the next chapter. Whatever the causes, though, getting replacements seems to be more difficult each year.

Some individual pastors have really faced the problem of recruiting lay teachers for the parish school. Diocesan school offices have also tried to help. The day is gone when one can wishfully hope that somehow, somewhere, the needed lay teacher will be found. To have a good school, that is, one with a qualified staff, pastors and principals need to go out and actively recruit lay teachers. Recruitment cannot wait until near Labor Day, when Reverend Mother has said again and regretfully that there are simply no more Sisters available. Recruitment must be an on-going process in every parochial school which has lay teachers on the staff.

An effective recruitment program includes at least three aspects:

1. Informing the parishioners of the need and enlisting their support
2. Encouraging students to go into teaching
3. Paying from parish funds for training of future lay teachers for the parish school

Parish Support. Catholic schools are expanding because parents are fulfilling their obligation to give their children a complete education. Catholic schools are expanding also because of the parents' *demands* for a Catholic education. Parochial schools, though costly for parents, are becoming more and more desirable in the eyes of Catholic parents. Thus, it is only reasonable for the pastor to assume that everything that concerns the parish school will concern the parents. Lay staffing is one problem that should be fully explained to the parishioners. The chart introducing this chapter — showing the increase of pupils and Sisters — will convince the parishioners that action is needed if their school is to serve children well. When pastors faced with the prospect of curtailing parish school facilities have explained the situation to the laity, immediate help has been forthcoming.

The parishioners' action will take two forms: they will actively recruit trained teachers for the school, and they will provide the necessary funds to attract and keep competent lay teachers. It is rarely that the parish Sunday collections can entirely care for the upkeep of the parish school. When the parish is informed of the need, the resulting financial help will fill in the margin desired. Pulpit announcements, talks to parish groups, articles in the diocesan newspaper and even the daily paper, flyers at Sunday Mass, posters, financial reports — all of these means can keep the parish aware that the school is *their* school and needs *their* support.

Recruiting Students to Train for Lay Teaching. The parish needs to build up a supply of teachers from among the elementary and high school students of the parish. Seventh and eighth grade pupils are at a good age to decide their high school course with a view toward teacher training. Seventh and eighth graders are also making up their minds about their lifework. Recruitment, to be most effective, should begin in the grade school.

Particularly if there is a parish high school, a local unit of the Future

Teachers of America should be formed.[13] This organization has a well-developed program for interesting high school students in teaching. The FTA program provides students with a taste of teaching experience, and strengthens their desire to devote themselves to teaching. The parish sodality likewise has many young girls who could be interested in a career in lay teaching.

College students from the parish are also prospects for the parish school. The first two years of college are given to fundamental courses basic to many kinds of work. College students are an important resource for the parish school.

Subsidizing Lay Teacher Trainees. It very often happens that a promising young person cannot train for teaching because she lacks the money. The parish would be wise to give a certain number of scholarships each year to good lay teacher prospects for the parish school. The pastor can expect that about one out of every three lay teachers will leave in June, and perhaps more, depending upon the number in the "marriageable age" group. Therefore, the pastor will probably need to recruit and subsidize about one trainee for every three lay teachers on the staff. When working conditions are good in the parish school, the future teacher scholarships will be coveted by capable people, both students and older married women free to train.

These scholarships might well include a complete tuition scholarship for the entire program leading to state certification. Or, the scholarship might be arranged on a 50–50 basis, the student and the parish each paying half. Whatever the arrangement, all of the conditions should be put in writing. A contract should be signed specifying conditions, and the method of paying the money back in case the student withdraws from the program.

A number of dioceses have led the way in encouraging lay teacher trainees through scholarships. In Erie, Pennsylvania, at Mercyhurst College and Villa Maria College, worthwhile Cadet programs have been developed. In Buffalo, New York, at D'Youville College, a somewhat different but highly effective plan has been arranged. In the Diocese of Pittsburgh, young women are training at a local Catholic college for the schools of the diocese. In the Diocese of Youngstown, a successful program of recruitment and parish subsidy has been carried out. Interested pastors might study the details of these various plans in order to work out a good program of recruitment for their own schools. The Sister Principal is the key figure in recruitment, for she is familiar with teacher training programs and with qualities

---

[13] A number of Catholic high schools belong to the national and state organization called *Future Teachers of America*, sponsored by the National Education Association. The FTA Manual provides an outline for an effective teacher recruitment program at the junior and senior high school level.

Figure 16

APPLICATION FOR TEACHING POSITION

Diocese of Youngstown

Date.................

Personal History

Name... Phone......................... Sex: ...M ....F

Family Name / Christian Name

Street........................City............... Race: ....White ....Negro ....Oriental

Citizenship: ....American ....Naturalized

Place of Birth........................Date of Birth........... Marital Status: ....Single ....Widowed

....Married ....Divorced

Religion: specify denomination, if non-Catholic............... Ages of Children............................

Parish to which you belong..............City............ If married woman,

How Applicant Can Be Reached: Time:...........Phone:...... husband's first name......................

Address:................................ Maiden Name ....

Social Security Number....................

Educational Background

Level	Name of School	City and State	Dates Attended		Date of Graduation	Kind of Degree
			From	To		
Elementary						
Elementary						
High School						
High School						
College						
College						

Application Being Made For

If elementary school, list grades in order of preference:

1................. 2................. 3.................

If high school, list subjects you are qualified to teach:

1................. 2................. 3.................

Specify: ....Full-time teacher ....Substitute

School in which you are interested:.................

Teaching Experience

(*prior to this year*)

Public School, Grade 1–8 ....Years

Public School, Grade 9–12 ....Years

Catholic School, Grade 1–8 ....Years

Catholic School, Grade 9–12 ....Years

Total ....Years

(over)

Ohio Certificates*

Name of Ohio Teaching Certificates You Hold	Date Issued	Date of Expiration	Serial Number	Subjects or Grades Covered by Certificates

Work Experience

Place	Occupation (if non-teaching) Grade or Subjects (if teaching)	Dates	
		From	To

References

Full Name of Reference	Address	Position
		Your Pastor
		Your Employer (if employed)

PLEASE NOTE: *Application should be accompanied by Ohio teaching certificate. Request official transcripts of credit from all colleges you have attended. Have transcripts forwarded directly to:

> Diocese of Youngstown
> Department of Education
> 144 West Wood Street
> Youngstown 3, Ohio

requisite for good teaching. The Sister Principal is also good at keeping the necessary records. The collaboration of pastor and principal is needed for an effective recruitment and subsidy program.

SCREENING PROSPECTIVE LAY TEACHERS

With the current shortage of teachers, it may seem that there is no opportunity to be selective when a lay teacher is needed immediately to fill a vacancy or to staff an added classroom. However, when a parochial school has good personnel policies and high standards of operation, the principal will find that she does have an opportunity to be selective.

Securing Background Information. The first step in securing the services of an acceptable lay teacher is to make sure that enough information on her background is available. For this purpose, it is good to use an application blank. A form such as that provided by the Diocese of Youngstown (Figure 16) may be adapted to use in the individual school. If the teacher does join the staff, then the application blank can be used as her personal data record for filing in the principal's office.

When the applicant is a stranger to the pastor and the principal, it is well to contact the references listed on the application blank. A follow-up form may profitably be used to accumulate more data on the applicant. Although character references are sometimes of slight value, certainly every means should be taken to screen out undesirable persons.

An official transcript of credits should be forwarded by the college or colleges to the principal, and a copy of the teaching certificate should be obtained and filed. It would be wise also to request evidence of a recent physical examination successfully passed.

Evaluating the Data. When all of this information has been obtained, the principal evaluates the candidate's qualifications. The transcript of credit gives some clue to the ability of the teacher; D or even C grades give an unfavorable impression. The history of the applicant's schooling also gives insight into her desirability. An applicant with very little or no Catholic training is a poor prospect for a parochial elementary school, since most lay teachers are responsible for teaching religion to their own class.

When the principal has satisfied herself that the applicant has certain minimum essentials for good teaching, the principal can present a summary of the credentials to the pastor. Pastors ordinarily are interested in the over-all picture, not in minute details, so a summary of the candidate's background, references, college work, teaching experience, and certification will usually suffice.

The interview of the applicant with the pastor is an important part of the screening process. No matter how good a candidate looks on paper, the personal interview is needed to judge how well the applicant will fit into the local situation. Prior to the interview, the principal can have prepared, if the pastor so desires, a written statement of the lay teacher's duties, the school schedule, her salary and related benefits, and the lay teacher's role in the parish school. A diocesan and school handbook serve well for this interview. If the pastor considers the applicant satisfactory, the contract may be signed at the time. Four copies can be made if the diocese requires a copy; three copies are needed if only the lay teacher, the pastor, and the principal keep copies.

The hiring of lay teachers is of great importance to the parochial school program. If applicants are screened hastily and haphazardly, it will be impossible to develop the lay teacher through in-service devices. A certain amount of orientation must be given to new teachers; details of lay teacher orientation are given in Chapter VII and Chapter X. However, orientation can do only a little to improve teachers on the job; the applicant must be capable, or orientation techniques will be ineffectual. Screening is especially important when one considers how difficult it is to dismiss an unsatisfactory teacher, even at the end of the school year. The principal can perform a real service for the pastor in this regard by providing the necessary forms for applicants, by evaluating the applicants' credentials, and by preparing with her staff a helpful faculty handbook.

EMPHASIZING THE SPIRITUAL ELEMENT

In improving the lay staffing of parochial schools, the spiritual element needs to be kept constantly in mind. Lay teachers, despite all these arrangements for improving working conditions, must still be motivated by a desire to further the cause of Catholic education, or the purposes of parochial schools will not be achieved. The lay teacher's day of recollection should be arranged whenever possible. There should be in the teacher's lounge good books and magazines dealing with spiritual topics. The priests of the parish can give extra instruction to lay teachers whose religious training has been deficient. Working conditions are of course essential to good staffing; but within the framework of good conditions, every effort should be made to strengthen the spiritual motivation of the lay teacher.

MAKING THE LAY TEACHER AN INTEGRAL PART OF THE STAFF

Throughout this discussion, it has been assumed that the lay teacher is here to stay. The lay teacher is needed in Catholic education because there are not enough Sisters, but also for another equally important reason. The lay teacher can effectively show the pupils the "good Catholic" in action. Competent, interested, and zealous lay teachers strengthen the program in Catholic schools, because the children can immediately apply the lay teacher's example to their own lives. Sisters are expected to be pious, law-abiding, and studious; but when the lay teacher exemplifies these qualities, the children have a closer model to imitate.

The lay teacher, then, makes a definite contribution, and is rightly considered essential to an effective parochial school program today. The foregoing provisions for salary, sick leave, tenure, retirement plan, and spiritual helps indicate that the priests and Sisters want capable lay teachers in the parish school. The attitude toward lay teachers, however, must go beyond mere acceptance. Lay teachers are partners with Sisters, priests, and parents in the glorious work of Catholic education. Hence, lay teachers should be included in all phases of the program. Faculty meetings should see lay teachers present and actively participating. The Home and School Association should appreciate the role which lay teachers play in the school. There should be a lay teachers' lounge and library, and a lunchroom for lay teachers if the school has no cafeteria. Lay teachers should contribute positively to the program of in-service staff development; why not more lay teachers doing demonstration teaching for other lay teachers?

Expert administration requires that the potential of all staff members be utilized to the full, and that the responsibilities of all be clearly defined and followed through. One of the challenges to the parochial school principal is that she must assist the lay teacher to become a more active and effective member of the staff.

SELECTED REFERENCES

Books

There is no text in this area pertaining to parochial schools. The texts below are among the most useful references on public school personnel policy. The principal will probably prefer to borrow the books from the library rather than purchase them.

Chandler, B. J., and Petty, Paul V., *Personnel Management in School Administration* (New York: World Book Company, 1955), passim.

Huggett, Albert J., and Stinnett, T. M., *Professional Problems of Teachers* (New York: The Macmillan Company, 1956), passim.

Yeager, William A., *Administration and the Teacher* (New York: Harper and Brothers, Publishers, 1954), passim.

Pamphlets

National Education Association, Department of Classroom Teachers and Research Division, 1201 Sixteenth Street, N.W., Washington 6, D. C., publishes the following helpful pamphlets.

Salary Scheduling, Discussion Pamphlet No. 8, April, 1956, 24 pp., 15 cents.

Teacher Leaves of Absence, Discussion Pamphlet No. 7, November, 1952, 24 pp., 15 cents.

Teacher Retirement, Discussion Pamphlet No. 2, November, 1957, 23 pp., 25 cents.

Teacher Tenure, Discussion Pamphlet No. 1, July, 1954, 23 pp., 25 cents.

U. S. Department of Health, Education, and Welfare, Social Security Administration, U. S. Government Printing Office, Washington, D. C., publishes the following useful material:

How to Estimate Your Social Security Payments, Old-Age Survivors' Insurance Pamphlet No. 30, January, 1951. U. S. Government Printing Office, 14 pp., 15 cents. Can be obtained in most cities by contacting the United States Government Post Office.

Your Social Security, Old-Age, Survivors, and Disability Insurance Benefits Under the Social Security Law, OASI Pamphlet No. 35, U. S. Government Printing Office, September, 1960, 42 pp., 10 cents. Clear explanation of Social Security coverage, and includes a bibliography of government pamphlets on the subject.

CHAPTER VII

PROVIDING GOOD WORKING CONDITIONS

> *There are two aspects to effecting a strong teaching staff: hiring good teachers, and helping them to perform at their best after they have been hired. The latter approach is achieved in part by providing good working conditions. What are good working conditions? How may a principal bring about good working conditions?*

WHICH school has better working conditions for the staff — St. Peter's School in a deteriorating downtown area or St. Pius School in a sparkling new suburbia? One might be inclined to say immediately, "Why St. Pius, of course. The building is new; the location is ideal; the children are well cared for. St. Pius would be the teacher's dream." After more thought, one might qualify this statement somewhat. "Of course, the building doesn't make the school. So many other things enter into the picture. The teachers at St. Peter's seem happy, too. Maybe I should say — it all depends."

It does depend upon many factors, which are included under "working conditions." Good working conditions include a wide variety of factors. Some, it is true, are purely physical factors, such as the location, building, equipment, facilities, and maintenance. Other factors have to do with management — what kind of working order is there in the school? Still other factors have to do with interpersonal relations — how do the people get along? Still others relate to the kind of pupils enrolled — do the pupils make it more or less difficult for the teachers to get satisfaction from their work? Another aspect of importance is how much the teachers have to do — is the work load reasonable? For lay people, an essential factor in a good working situation is financial — is the salary attractive? And, finally, do the teachers have a chance to be creative, to share in formulating policy, to develop professionally? How worthwhile does the situation seem? Is it a school where one would "gladly teach"?

Where there are good working conditions, two people play essential roles — the pastor and the Sister Principal. The pastor provides the framework of operation; the principal supplies the professional leadership. In Chapters III and VI, the pastor's responsibilities in finance and policy formulation were outlined in some detail. Chapters III and IV considered the Sister Principal's duties as educational leader of the staff. The present chapter will discuss some of the specifics of good working conditions. Subsequent chapters in this book will relate at least indirectly to good working conditions, for everything about the school and the staff helps or hinders effective performance. "Good working conditions" might also be called a "good teaching-learning situation." As mentioned often in educational writings, everything in the school should contribute to better teaching and better learning. The conditions of service to be discussed here are important in determining just how well children will learn in the situation. Although all of the factors are interrelated, the following topics are selected for discussion: the teacher's work week, teacher turnover, substitute teacher service, teacher aids, school facilities, administrative policies, miscellaneous problems of teachers, personal relations, and evaluating working conditions.

THE TEACHER'S WORK WEEK

To insure good working conditions, the principal should analyze just what the teacher's duties are and how much time is required to discharge these duties adequately. Chapter VIII will discuss in some detail the various competencies which a good teacher should possess; these competencies will, in turn, indicate certain activities in which a good teacher engages. The present discussion will not go into the *quality* of the teacher's work, but will rather emphasize the *quantity* of her work.

How much time does a parochial school teacher spend on the job? What does she do with her time? How does this time distribution make her feel toward her job and toward the school? If there were an "average" parochial school teacher, the answers to these questions would be much simpler. The Sister's work week will differ from that of the lay teacher; the Sister's work satisfaction will also differ from that of the lay teacher. However, an analysis of working conditions in many parochial schools enables one to make a few generalizations concerning the work week of the teaching staff.

Studies of the teacher's work week show that public school teachers average from 47 hours a week down to 41 hours a week in their professional roles.[1] A work week of barely 40 hours cannot be wished for by

---

[1] California State Department of Education, *Teaching Load in California Public Schools* (Sacramento, Calif.: State Department of Education, 1955).

National Education Association, Research Division, "Teaching Load in 1950," *Research Bulletin*, XXIX (Feb., 1951), p. 17.

anyone calling herself professional, for the clock-puncher has much narrower objectives than the professional person has. And, to accomplish broader objectives simply takes more time. Averaging the work week of Sisters and lay teachers combined, one gets a typical work week of 45 hours in parochial schools.[2]

AN ANALYSIS OF THE TEACHER'S DUTIES

The teacher's time is devoted to three major kinds of work: classroom instruction, out-of-class professional duties, and miscellaneous or routine duties. Some of the usual activities of the teacher under each of these headings might include the following:

1. **Classroom instruction**
   Directing and guiding pupil learning during the school day
2. **Out-of-class professional duties**
   Lesson planning, preparing materials, helping individual pupils, professional reading, attending teachers' meetings, serving on staff committees, contacting parents, conferring with principal or supervisor on instructional problems
3. **Miscellaneous or routine duties**
   Monitoring the playground, cafeteria, and bus transportation; scoring tests and correcting papers; keeping records up to date, accounting for texts and other materials, collecting money and doing bookkeeping, "housekeeping," giving first aid, doing clerical work, and doing church related work, such as training altar boys and conducting choir practice

The above duties divide themselves rather definitely. "Classroom instruction" and "out-of-class professional duties" require specific training on the part of the teacher. The third category, "miscellaneous or routine duties," requires much less professional training, or perhaps none at all.

It is true that there may be some overlapping among the duties listed above. "Correcting papers," for example, can be considered a professional activity when correcting requires insight into the learning process. Correcting papers can, at other times, be a mechanical process of checking rights and wrongs and totaling. "Preparing materials" can also be a routine chore at times, as when the preparation consists in getting a projector ready, mending a film, sorting library books, and mounting pictures for the bulletin board. On the whole, however, the duties fit rather definitely into one of the three categories.

THE TEACHER'S TIME DISTRIBUTION

State Regulations. State regulations and good educational practice have

[2] Reverend James W. Malone, *Administration of the Teacher in the Parochial Elementary Schools of Ohio*, unpublished Ph.D. thesis (Washington, D. C.: Catholic University of America, 1957).

set standards that govern the teacher's time distribution to a certain extent. The number of hours which a school must be in session varies from state to state and from system to system, but the average public school day throughout the country is slightly more than five and one-half hours, or about 28 hours per week.[3] The trend is toward a longer school day, rather than a shorter one. This is reasonable, since many more subjects are being included in the curriculum, and teachers are now trained to serve children in more ways than formerly. Even in states where there are no regulations for the school day, parochial schools would do well to follow better practice in this regard.

School District Regulations. To analyze the teacher's work week, one must also know how many hours a day the teacher is required to be in the school building. Many public school districts have specified the daily schedule for teachers. Seven and one half hours seems to be the minimum required in many public schools; this would usually mean a working day that begins at 8:30 and ends at 4:00. Some school districts require that the teachers be in the building for eight hours a day, such as from 8:15 to 4:15.

In parochial schools, the Sisters are usually in the building almost nine hours daily. Regulations concerning the lay teacher's working day have been slow in developing. Certainly, a minimum for lay teachers would be the working day of the local public schools. This would probably mean seven and one half or eight hours daily scheduled for the lay teacher. In practice, the lay teacher would be required to be in the school building at least one half hour before and after the regular hours for the children.

If the teacher spends eight hours a day at school, and an hour each night on related professional duties, this totals a work week of 45 hours. Because there is so much to accomplish in Catholic education, 45 hours would really be the minimum time in which one could hope to do a satisfactory job. Good working conditions would require that all teachers conform to the daily schedule established for the building. The first requirement for a good teaching-learning situation would necessarily be to spend enough time on the job.

Per Cent of Time Devoted to Various Duties. How much time *should* a teacher devote to each of her three major duties? Using as a guide state standards on the length of the school day, and educational theory on desirable professional activity, one may arrive at the time distribution illustrated in Figure 17.

---

[3] American Association of School Administrators and Research Division, National Education Association, *Length of School Day and Class Periods in Urban School Districts, 1958–59*, Circular No. 7, 1960 (Washington, D. C.: National Education Association, November, 1960), p. 3.

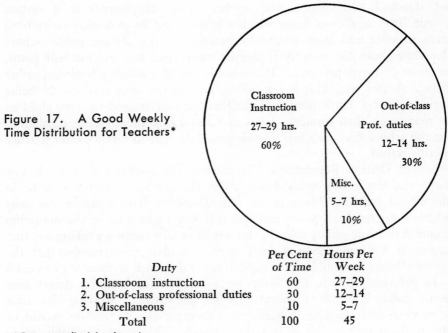

Figure 17. A Good Weekly
Time Distribution for Teachers*

Duty	Per Cent of Time	Hours Per Week
1. Classroom instruction	60	27–29
2. Out-of-class professional duties	30	12–14
3. Miscellaneous	10	5–7
Total	100	45

* Data generalized by the writer.

The time devoted to classroom instruction, 27–29 hours a week, would take up about 60 per cent of a 45-hour work week. Out-of-class professional duties would ideally take up between 12 and 14 hours a week, or 30 per cent of the teacher's working time. Miscellaneous duties should take up only 10 per cent, or about five hours each week. This distribution puts first things first; good working conditions provide the teacher with an opportunity to concentrate on her professional responsibilities.

In practice, what may happen? The teachers may be spending a disproportionate amount of time in miscellaneous tasks, rather than in professional activity. To illustrate, one may ask a few teachers to keep a chart of the time they spend each week doing school housekeeping, correcting papers, scoring tests, and monitoring pupils. The result would probably be shocking. In some schools, the teachers are spending almost ten hours weekly in these subprofessional tasks. In such situations, 30 per cent of their work week is devoted to miscellaneous chores requiring little or no academic training, while only 10 per cent of their time is devoted to out-of-class professional duties.

The cause of this imbalance? One cause might be inadequate custodial service. When teachers must be responsible for cleaning and dusting, their time is taken away from strictly professional work. Inadequate clerical help might also cause an improper distribution of time. Some teachers are required to do a great deal of clerical work such as typing, record keeping, and money counting. Another cause might easily be that the pastor and the principal have not given enough thought to a good time distribution for the teachers. When there is wise planning by the administrators, funds can usually be raised to provide custodial and clerical help of the kind and amount needed. Good working conditions require adequate custodial and clerical service. Teachers cannot be professional workers, cannot be creative, when they have no time for professional activities.

How does the teacher's work week make for good working conditions? Teachers know when their work is mechanical and repetitious. Though they may not complain, still they cannot be happy when working at a subprofessional level. In order to provide satisfactory working conditions, the principal should be sure that the teachers can distribute their time with an emphasis on professional activity. It is the principal's duty to provide adequate help and stimulating leadership, so that teachers can and will operate on a professional level. This condition is basic to personal satisfaction and professional growth.

TEACHER TURNOVER

"Turnover" was a word unknown in parochial schools before the introduction of lay teachers in large numbers. In the past, new Sisters were assigned to a mission, and others were transferred; for the most part, there was just an interchange of teachers. The Sisters were subject to transfer at any time the community's interests or the individual Sister's needs seemed to require a change. There was never a high percentage of Sisters discontinuing teaching for other kinds of work.

With the rapid increase in parochial school enrollment, however, lay teachers have been introduced to staff many new classrooms. And, with the coming of lay teachers, the parochial school has had to accept the fact that there will be a rather high percentage of new lay teachers in the school each fall. The new lay teachers will come both to staff added classrooms and to replace teachers who have dropped out of teaching or have gone to teach elsewhere. The rate of teacher turnover affects working conditions in the school, and perhaps also reveals something of the typical working conditions in the school. A discussion of causes of turnover and certain preventives may serve to show how necessary it is to plan for lay teacher turnover.

CAUSES OF TURNOVER

Why do teachers drop out of teaching? As mentioned earlier, Sisters are transferred by their religious superior, so Sisters cannot be included in a study of dropouts. Lay teachers, however, represent a less stable element in parochial school teaching staffs. Relatively few lay teachers tend to remain in the parochial schools. The reasons for dropouts among lay teachers are interesting to investigate.

The public schools of the country publish annually the number of teachers who left teaching during the year. The average of dropouts for the entire United States is about 7 per cent annually, or, about 7 in every 100 public school teachers discontinue teaching. For the country as a whole, this seems like a very low rate. However, many public school teachers leave their position and transfer to another school, and sometimes to another state. This percentage is bigger than that for dropouts only; about 9 per cent of all public school teachers either drop out of teaching completely or transfer to another teaching position. The individual states have a rather different story to tell, however. In some states, almost one fourth of all public school teachers either transfer to another teaching job outside the state, or drop out of teaching entirely. Given school systems vary greatly in their turnover rates. Some public school districts lose almost one third of their teachers annually, while other districts only lose 5 per cent or less. Teacher turnover is a problem that causes a great deal of concern in the public schools of the country.

The reasons for public school teacher turnover are given as follows. Of public school teachers who leave their position:

32%	leave for marriage or family reasons
22%	give miscellaneous reasons
20%	go to teaching in other states
14%	retire
12%	go to other kinds of work[4]

In the above list of reasons, one can see that teachers leave their jobs chiefly because of the *greater attractiveness of another situation.* Higher salary is often mentioned as a reason for leaving, or better staff relations, or better working conditions, or easier transportation. In both public schools and parochial schools, lay people can be expected to have pretty much these same motivations. Since this is so, the pastor and principal would be wise to study together their rate of lay teacher turnover so that substandard conditions can be remedied. Certainly it is easier on both principal and staff if lay teachers remain longer in the school. Hence, farsighted pastors and principals plan to provide lay teachers with the benefits described in Chapter VI — a salary scale, sick leave policy, retirement

---

[4] National Education Association, Research Division, *Estimates of School Statistics, 1958–59,* Research Report 1958–R6 (Washington, D. C.: National Education Association, 1958), p. 22.

benefits, and tenure. Good inducements such as these encourage lay teachers to remain longer in the school.

Another reason, and one which may not be emphasized enough, is this: *the high percentage of women teachers in both public and parochial schools in itself is a cause of turnover.*[5] In 1958–59, of all public school teachers leaving their jobs, 32 per cent left for marriage or family reasons. That is, one third of all dropouts were women who left to get married or to raise a family. Further, if one considers just the women who left teaching, and exclude the men, probably 80 per cent of all dropouts were caused by marriage or family reasons. This fact can be both the consolation and the despair, perhaps, of the parochial school administrator. In the public schools, there are about seven women to every man in the elementary schools.[6] In the parochial elementary schools, there are probably thirty or forty women to every man. Therefore, parochial schools can expect a high rate of turnover for marriage and family reasons.

EASING THE PROBLEMS OF TURNOVER

As mentioned above, a certain amount of lay teacher turnover is inevitable. But by working to improve salaries, "fringe benefits," and school conditions, the pastor and principal can reduce turnover considerably. However, there is still the problem of the new teacher and her adjustment to the school situation. In the interests of all concerned, the adjustment of the new teacher should be carefully planned for.

Teacher Orientation. In Chapter X, there is a discussion of lay teacher orientation, with special emphasis on supervisory services to the new teacher. In addition to these helps, the new teacher also needs to be oriented to the administrative aspects of her new situation. The principal will need to do some of this orienting herself, but much of the responsibility can be delegated to a Sister Adviser. This orientation should include a conference before school opens in the fall, a tour of the school plant, introduction of the staff personnel, and written information on school policies and the teacher's duties. The diocesan handbook provides helpful information; a faculty handbook is invaluable in orienting new teachers. Later in this chapter, there will be a discussion of the faculty handbook in its all-over administrative usefulness. For the new teacher, some additional information may be needed, but the handbook will solve many of her problems painlessly.

In the modern parochial school, teacher turnover is to be expected, and

---

[5] For a discussion of women in education, see Myron Lieberman, *Education as a Profession* (Englewood Cliffs, N. J.: Prentice-Hall, Inc., 1956), pp. 241–255.

[6] National Education Association, Research Division, *Estimates of School Statistics, 1958–59*, Research Report 1958–R6 (Washington, D. C.: National Education Association, 1958), p. 19.

should be planned for. This planning should include preventive measures —
efforts to make the teaching position more satisfying, and should also
include orienting new teachers systematically. Good working conditions
require that teachers function smoothly in their position; teacher turnover
poses a special problem in the smooth functioning of the staff.

Providing for Transfers to Other Parochial Schools. Another difficult
adjustment for the principal and pastor is the fact that lay teachers may
wish to transfer from one parochial school to another. Easier transportation is one reason for transfer; but higher salary, better working conditions, better staff relations are also reasons for transfer. When the pastor
has succeeded in hiring a satisfactory lay teacher, he would naturally like
her to remain in the school for some time. However, he should provide
a framework for requesting transfers to other parochial schools when
teachers feel them desirable. It is difficult to be completely objective about
the lay teacher's wanting to go to another school, but this is one of the
conditions that must be accepted.

Since transfers are to be expected, it is good to have a written policy
concerning transfers. Perhaps even a form can be provided for organizing
the information. The following request form can perhaps be adapted to
a school situation.

REQUEST FOR TRANSFER

Name of Teacher..

School...................... Grade and/or Subjects........................

I hereby request a transfer from my present assignment as follows:

   (1) Kind of assignment (or grade) I prefer (give first and second choices):

      1. ....

      2. ....

   (2) School I prefer (give first and second choices):

      1. ....

      2. ....

   (3) Reason for requesting transfer: ....

      ....

      ....

      ....

Background Information

1. Date of degree or total semester hours of college credit........................

2. Kind of teaching certificate held................................

3. Teaching experience: years in present school................................

                     years previous teaching................................

Date of this request................... Signed................................

                                             TEACHER

Such a form can be supplied by the principal, so that the pastor can be notified of the expected transfer. Usually it is wise for a pastor to arrange with the pastor of the school to which the lay teacher wishes to transfer. In this way, good relations can be maintained. Transfer, if possible, can then be carried out in a routine way, with a minimum of personal involvement. Requests for transfer should be made *before* contracts are signed in the spring. In this way, both the present school and the parochial school to which the teacher hopes to transfer can plan intelligently for fall staffing.

PROVISION FOR SUBSTITUTE TEACHERS

Chapter VI stated that a sound sick leave plan is a necessary part of teacher personnel policy. Good working conditions allow the teacher to be absent when ill or for other grave reasons, and at the same time the teacher is assured that her class will be taken care of adequately. It is the duty of the administration to see that no class remains untaught because of the unprovided-for absence of a regular teacher. Good administration insures an uninterrupted program of instruction for every child every day.

Like every other aspect of the school program, providing good substitute teacher service requires the co-operation of many people. The staff, the principal, the substitute teacher, and the pastor all can share in providing good instruction during the absence of the regular teacher. How can an effective program be worked out?

THE STAFF'S SUGGESTIONS

The staff can make good suggestions concerning substitute teachers. The regular teacher feels that during her absence the substitute should check or correct seatwork and homework, and leave the corrected papers for the regular teacher. The regular teacher also feels that the substitute should follow the lesson plan left for her, and should feel an obligation to teach, rather than just to "fill in." The regular teacher also feels strongly that the substitute should leave a written report of the work covered, anything unusual that happened, and should keep attendance and other records needed.

THE SUBSTITUTE TEACHER'S SUGGESTIONS

The substitute teacher also has some recommendations to make to improve the work she can do with children. A study of substitute teachers showed that they typically feel handicapped because the regular teacher or the principal doesn't plan adequately. The following obstacles were mentioned by many substitute teachers as interfering with their work.

TABLE X.   Obstacles for Substitute Teachers

Obstacle	Per Cent of Substitutes Naming the Obstacle
1. Lack of adequate lesson plans	54
2. Shortness of advance notice	31
3. Lack of information about pupils — seating charts, personal characteristics, etc.	29
4. Failure to acquaint substitute with special rules, routines, and schedules	21
5. Student behavior — disciplinary problems	20
6. Failure of regular teacher to prepare children to co-operate with substitute	15
7. Too little help from those in charge of substitutes	11

Source: "Substitute Teachers in the Public Schools, 1953–54," NEA Research Bulletin, Vol. XXXIII, No. 1 (February, 1955), p. 25. Used with permission.

Substitute teachers also mentioned that in some school systems the salaries are lower than those paid the regular teacher. The substitutes have special difficulty when teaching outside of their field of preparation and when they are not supplied with the materials needed, and keys to the classroom and cabinets.

THE PRINCIPAL'S SUGGESTIONS

The principal feels that both the regular teacher and the substitute might contribute a little more to the smooth operation of the substitute program. The regular teacher would eliminate many of the above complaints of substitutes by reporting expected absence as soon as possible, preferably the evening before; the absent teacher might also telephone the day before she plans to return to school. The regular teacher should make lesson plans in advance, and in sufficient detail to provide guidance for a substitute in case one might be needed. Ordinarily, when a teacher is absent, she doesn't have the opportunity to make a good deal of advance preparation. The regular teacher should keep textbooks, manuals, workbooks, lesson plan book, seating chart, attendance record, cumulative classroom records and keys, in the place specified by the principal. Thus, in case of absence the principal or adviser can readily locate the needed materials.

DEVELOPING A WORKING PLAN

The regular teacher, the substitute, and the principal all feel that certain requirements must be met if substitute service is to be most helpful. Every school should have a definite policy concerning substitute teachers. Part of this policy should be a sheet of directions to guide both the substitute and the person directing her. A study of the needs of both the school and the substitute shows that certain topics should be included in the directions given to the substitute teacher.

DIRECTION SHEET FOR SUBSTITUTE TEACHERS

Outline of Topics

1. Reporting to principal at beginning and end of assignment
2. School hours, for teachers and pupils
3. Out-of-class duties, if any
4. Adviser, if any, and her role
5. Materials needed for teaching
   a) Lesson plan book of regular teacher
   b) Seating plan
   c) Keys to desk, cabinets, and classroom
   d) Textbooks, workbooks, and supplies
   e) Requisitioning other materials needed
6. Records required and how to be kept
   a) Attendance
   b) New pupils and withdrawing pupils
   c) Money collected
   d) Work completed with class
   e) Corrected assignments and tests
7. Disciplining of pupils
8. Permitting children to leave the room or the grounds
9. Procedure for fire drills
10. Handling of money and valuables
11. Salary and method of payment

The above outline of topics includes most of the things which a substitute teacher needs, or needs to know, to discharge her assignment effectively. The outline might form the basis for the principal's or adviser's discussion with the incoming substitute. It would be a worthwhile in-service project for the entire staff to prepare the wording of the directions. This would enable the principal to prepare specific helps for the substitute and also to remind the regular teachers of their corresponding obligations to the school and to the substitute. Especially in the case of a teaching principal, a Sister Adviser in charge of substitute teachers can provide helpful assistance. The principal should keep an up-to-date list of substitutes available for service in her school. Either the principal or the adviser can draw on this list as needed, annotate it, and revise it through the year.

FINANCING SUBSTITUTE SERVICE

As pointed out in Chapter VI, in order to have competent lay teachers, the pastor must pay them a dignified wage. Eighty per cent of the local public school salary was named as a figure which would be somewhat attractive to the trained teacher. In paying substitute teachers, the pastor can use the regular lay teacher salary scale. The substitute teacher should receive for each day's service the amount she would get if employed as a regular staff member. For every day's service, the pastor would pay her $\frac{1}{180}$ of the yearly salary for a lay teacher with her training and experience, if the school year contains 180 days.[7] In Chapter VI, in the discussion of sick leave policy, it was mentioned that about 3 per cent of the total annual wages might be needed to provide adequate substitute service. In the case given there, the pastor would need to allocate about $450 a year to provide good substitute service for a staff of that size. Certainly this amount is well invested in providing continuously good teaching for all the children. No matter how well the principal and staff plan for substitute service, arrangements will be ineffective unless the substitute is a qualified, competent person. An adequate salary and a businesslike method of payment are necessary to procure the kind of substitute which the parochial schools need. In some parishes, volunteer teachers have worked out very well, though ordinarily the best administrative arrangement is to pay the teacher according to experience and training.

Through a good program of substitute teacher service, teachers are assured that they will have capable substitutes when they themselves are forced to be absent because of illness. This assurance contributes to high staff morale and promotes a good teaching-learning situation.

TEACHER AIDES

Teacher Aides have been an important resource in improving working conditions for the staff. In the discussion of the teacher's work week, routine or miscellaneous jobs were ideally assigned from five to seven hours weekly. In order to achieve this goal, the principal may be interested in investigating the possibilities in various Teacher Aide programs.

The Fund for the Advancement of Education has financed at least two Teacher Aide projects, with successful results.[8] Many schools have tried a modified Teacher's Aide plan, on a part-time or volunteer basis. Both types seem worthy of the principal's attention.

THE BAY CITY PLAN

Large classes and a shortage of both teachers and buildings resulted in

[7] In computing a day's salary, one should divide the annual salary (minus deductions) by the number of days in the school year. A school year of 180 to 182 days is typical. See, American Association of School Administrators and Research Division of the National Education Association, *Number of Days in School Year, 837 Urban School Districts over 2,500 in Population*, Circular No. 3, 1960 (Washington, D. C.: National Education Association, March, 1960), p. 2.

[8] Cooperative Study for the Better Utilization of Teacher Competencies, *A Description of Teacher Aide Experimentation*, A Second Report (Mount Pleasant, Michigan: Central Michigan College, 1955).

Central Michigan College, "The 'Why' and 'How' of the Teacher Aide Program" (Mt. Pleasant, Mich.: Central Michigan College, Department of Special Studies, 1958).

Sister M. Dominic, R.S.M., "Answering a Challenge with a Call to Action," *Catholic School Journal*, XLVI (June, 1956), pp. 178–179.

The Help That Schools Get From "Teacher Aides"

In Bay City, Mich.,
public schools have hired
"teacher aides" to help
teachers handle big classes.

AS A RESULT

A Typical Teacher Can Spend:

89% less time	correcting papers.
83% less time	monitoring written lessons.
76% less time	taking the roll.
61% less time	moving groups of pupils around.
36% less time	disciplining pupils.
25% less time	preparing reports.

A Typical Teacher Now Has:

105% more time	to prepare lessons.
57% more time	to hear recitations.
41% more time	to supervise activities such as art.
27% more time	to help pupils at their desks.
20% more time	to make lesson assignments.

Figure 18. Summary of Bay City, Michigan, Successful Program in
Utilizing Teacher Aides

some constructive thinking by the faculty of Central Michigan College and Bay City, Michigan, public school officials.[9] The plan they developed has in it many elements that might be applicable to parochial schools. The underlying idea was that a teacher with large classes cannot spend enough time "teaching"; instead she devotes from 21 to 69 per cent of her time to such tasks as correcting papers, moving groups of pupils, disciplining pupils, and making out records and reports. The officials reasoned thus: If a nonprofessional person at half-salary were given to each teacher with a crowded classroom, then the Aide could take care of many routine chores and free the teacher for teaching. In a class of 55 pupils on this plan, the officials continued, children should receive just as much of the teacher's time as in a class of 35 pupils. The school district would not save anything in salaries, but in the emergency shortage of personnel and buildings, the idea seemed worth trying. Applicants were carefully screened, and teachers wishing to work with Aides become part of a long-range and well-oriented program. The results were satisfying in Bay City, and other schools continued the experiment. Now after eight years and many adaptations, the officials feel that the Teacher Aide is a step forward. The program has helped the regular teacher, pupil progress seems to have been good, parents are pleased, and the superior teacher has been able to spread her influence further.

U. S. News and World Report published an interesting summary of the success of the Bay City plan (Fig. 18).

Certainly, such a listing of advantages deserves the serious attention of educators faced with the problem of crowded classrooms. The teacher with an Aide can concentrate on professional activities and can delegate to her assistant routines of a subprofessional nature. Officials in Bay City, parents, principals, and teachers who have used Aides are enthusiastic about the plan. There is of course another side to the picture. Some educators claim that anyone in close contact with pupils should be trained for her work; that it is impossible to separate a "professional" from a "subprofessional" activity because of the overlapping. The Bay City plan represents bold thinking about a critical situation. Some obvious benefits have resulted; it will take time to judge the long-range effectiveness of the program.

The chart on the Teacher Aide program has been presented so that the principal might see some of the ways in which an aide may be utilized. Most parochial schools will lack the funds for extensive experimentation with Teacher Aides, but the ideas behind the plan are provocative. To what extent can the Sister Principal use Teacher Aides in her own school to improve the working conditions for her staff?

---

[9] Cooperative Study for the Better Utilization of Teacher Competencies, op. cit.

TEACHER AIDES IN PAROCHIAL SCHOOLS

Teacher Aides have been used to a certain extent in some parochial schools. On a part-time salary basis, professionally trained Aides have been hired to teach reading to small groups of children. When a class is large, the teacher cannot give each reading group all the time the children need. The Aide takes selected groups to an unused room for their drill work in reading each day. Each month, the Aide works with a different group. Both regular teachers and parents have been pleased with the improvement in reading under this plan.

Aides have also assisted the teacher in many other ways. Mothers who had been librarians, secretaries, bookkeepers, and nurses have been delighted to come to school several hours a week to assist the teacher in their own line of work. Mothers without special training have volunteered for supervision of the children in the cafeteria, on the playground, in church, and on the bus. Of course, the principal needs to plan carefully in order to use volunteer workers profitably, but this can be done. Some of the needed measures would be careful selection of Aides, a salary scale that is attractive, orientation of the Aides with regard to school policies, professional ethics, duties to the co-operating teacher, to the children, and to the parents, and provision for in-service training of the Aide. A Teacher Aide might be assigned to a single classroom for the day, or might divide her time according to a definite plan between two or more classrooms. Whether with salary or on a volunteer basis, the use of the Teacher Aide seems to have definite possibilities for relieving teachers of routine chores and thus making school work more satisfying.

In the Diocese of Youngstown, voluntary service to schools and other charitable institutions has been made attractive by injecting a spiritual element. This was done by soliciting the help of the Ladies of Charity, a Catholic organization whose purpose is voluntary service wherever needed. One of the conditions of membership is a certain number of hours of service each month. The members wear an imprinted crucifix as a sign of their dedication. Meetings, spiritual talks, group reception of Holy Communion, and publication of the group's activities have enhanced the effectiveness of the association. The Sister Principal, in co-operation with the pastor and the staff, can develop a sound plan for utlizing and spiritualizing the vast resource of volunteer help available in the parish.

SCHOOL FACILITIES

Another factor that makes teaching easy or difficult is the kind of school facilities available. First of all, teachers need *attractive surroundings*. A little touch of beauty makes all the difference in the world. As far as possible, the pastor should try to see that the classrooms are of adequate size, delicately painted, well-heated and ventilated, with desks in good condition, and opportunity for homey touches here and there. Architects seem not to realize the extreme importance of adequate storage space for materials. Sometimes the principal can arrange additional storage space for teachers, and thus preserve the instructional materials better, and also improve teacher morale. Attractive rest rooms and teachers' lounges also add immeasurably to the teachers' feeling of dignity and relaxation. A telephone booth for the use of the staff has wisely been arranged in the larger schools. A mailbox for each teacher provides a quick and acceptable way of routing deliveries and messages. These details contribute to the teacher's feeling of well-being and to her sense of the value of the work she is doing.

Instructional equipment and materials also affect the teacher's job satisfaction. Good teaching presumes an adequate supply of required texts, supplementary texts, audio-visual materials, art materials, and library books for pupils and for teachers. The annual budget should include provision for replacements and additions in each of these important areas every year. Sometimes the principal may feel that the materials now on hand are not being fully used. If this is the case, then part of the in-service program for the year might be to develop procedures for the more effective use of equipment and supplies. A well-catalogued file of filmstrips facilitates teacher use of the material. Assistance in correlating the filmstrips with the course of study also causes the material to be used more extensively. The principal's work is not finished when she has purchased good equipment and supplies; her continuing work is to help teachers to use the material more widely and more effectively.

Providing the teachers with a variety of supplies in sufficient quantity means that the principal must set up a plan for requisitioning and distributing supplies. The money available can be apportioned among the staff and each teacher can know what materials she can obtain. Teachers will be unhappy unless they can get the materials they need for their classes. The wise principal endeavors to provide teachers with all facilities which the budget can cover, and lets the staff "in" on the budget limitations.

ADMINISTRATIVE POLICIES

Chapter IV discussed at some length the principal's essential activities as an administrator: her work in planning, organizing, directing, communicating, and evaluating. The principal's effectiveness as an administrator can be seen in the policies which govern the operation of the school. It is the principal's job to formulate good policies as needed. Working conditions are improved when the principal provides a good faculty handbook and regular faculty bulletins.

THE FACULTY HANDBOOK

A worthwhile in-service activity is to develop policies co-operatively with the staff and gather these policies together into a clear and attractive faculty handbook. The following topics might well be included in a faculty handbook.

Topics for the Faculty Handbook

A. SCHOOL POLICIES
    1. Calendars and schedules
      a. The school year
      b. The school day for pupils and teachers
      c. Calendar of coming events
    2. Attendance at Mass and the sacraments
    3. Diocesan handbook
    4. Staff relationships
      a. With school personnel
      b. With custodial and clerical workers
      c. With parents
    5. Supervisory program
      a. Lesson planning
      b. Observations and conferences
      c. Teachers' meetings
      d. Lay teacher advisory program
    6. Teacher absence
    7. Substitute teachers and Teacher Aides
    8. Out-of-class duties
    9. Requisitions
    10. Fees, collections, and bookkeeping
    11. Regulations for playground, building, bus, and cafeteria
    12. Disciplining pupils
    13. Excuses
    14. Accidents: reporting, and first aid
    15. Class parties
    16. Gifts
    17. Classroom housekeeping
    18. Fire drills

B. THE INSTRUCTIONAL PROGRAM
    1. The course of study and textbooks
    2. Supplementary instructional materials
    3. Daily schedule
    4. Music program, vocal and instrumental
    5. Health program
    6. Library service
    7. Safety program
    8. Homework

     9. Field trips
   10. Testing program
   11. Religious instruction

C. RECORDS AND REPORTS
    1. Pupil accounting system
       a. Permanent and cumulative records
       b. Pupil report cards
       c. Transfers and withdrawals
       d. Absence and tardiness
    2. Diocesan records
       a. Teacher Personnel Data
       b. Lay Teacher Advisory Reports
       c. Semester test medians
    3. Enrollment reports (September and June)
    4. Record of textbooks and supplies (June)
    5. Record of pupils promoted (June)

It is essential to good working order that all the staff know school policy and procedures in each of the areas indicated above. Each topic should be developed in such a way that the staff may use the handbook for ready reference. From time to time, the principal will need to hold administrative meetings to explain some policies more fully, or to provide for a change in policy. Part of good administration is keeping policies up to date.

Preparing a faculty handbook will enlist the interest of the entire staff. New teachers are in a good position to suggest ways of clarifying policy, while older teachers are familiar with school routines. The handbook can be developed a little at a time. It can be mimeographed or dittoed and placed in a loose-leaf binder. In this way, when policies change, a new sheet can be inserted and the old one removed. The staff may have an artistic member who can illustrate the handbook, or at least design a cover. Making copies for the pastor and the staff should not be an expensive project, and the good results of the handbook will far outweigh its cost. A well-prepared faculty handbook is an object of pride as well as of usefulness.

THE FACULTY BULLETIN

One of the chief causes of frustration among teachers is being interrupted frequently by a note from the principal, or by a public-address announcement in the midst of a lesson. A well-planned bulletin can eliminate this trouble spot almost entirely. Usually, a faculty bulletin is needed once a week for routine notices about a coming event, reports due, special precautions to take, and the like. A faculty bulletin is especially necessary on the opening day of school, when teachers' uncertainties are many.

To make the faculty bulletin serve well, the principal should work with the staff in deciding what the bulletin should contain, when it should be issued, and how the teachers are to co-operate with the announcements. Most schools have some teachers who are clever in wording and arranging notices; these staff members can serve as a committee to assist the principal in this important detail of administration. It is wise to number faculty bulletins, and to file them according to date issued. In this way, the principal has them for checking, and also for planning future bulletins. When filed from year to year, faculty bulletins can help the principal prepare similar bulletins, and also improve on content, style, and make-up.

The principal may be tempted to say, "Faculty bulletins? Why, the teachers don't *read* them! It's all right to say, 'Cut down on interruptions,' but how can I get the bulletins *read?*" The principal may broaden her perspective a little by asking herself, "How carefully do *I* read the superintendent's bulletins? Do *I* ever forget to hand in a report, or get mixed up in the directions or dates?" Everyone tends to emphasize the things that interest herself; teachers, then, are not as interested in the principal's directives as the principal is. However, well-planned bulletins in which the staff has a voice are likely to serve effectively in promoting good working order in the school. The better the bulletin, the better will be the response of teachers to it.

The faculty bulletin is usually one page long, is dittoed or mimeographed, is brief, simple, clear, and courteous. The bulletin should be perfectly typed and duplicated, and attractive in appearance. In the bibliography at the end of this chapter, there are some specific references on preparing effective faculty bulletins.

To illustrate the qualities of a good bulletin, the two excerpts below are included for the principal's examination. (See page 173 for second bulletin.)

Points All Teachers are to Observe Tuesday (Opening Day)

1. *Begin teaching the first day.* This year, *a full school day* will be observed throughout the school system.
2. *Distribute books and supplies.* The unfilled items of your requisition will be attended to as soon as the materials arrive.
3. *Admit only new pupils* who come to your room with an initialed tentative registration card.
4. *Before* collecting the enrollment cards, be sure that they have been filled out correctly and completely.
5. *Send to the office* any child *not admitted.* No one else can enroll him.
6. During the first hour, *hold a fire drill,* following the route indicated.
7. *At eleven o'clock* send to the office a list of the children who have not returned. Write briefly after each name any information you have obtained about the cause of each child's nonappearance.
8. *As early as possible,* send to Miss Evans any child who seems to have a cold. There has been an epidemic of measles the past two weeks. Otherwise the community is free of any communicable illness.
9. *At two o'clock* send to the office your enrollment sheet.

10. *Notice your scheduled routine duties.*   The first schedules are posted on the bulletin board.
11. *Please avoid requests.* Additional *supplies or books needed* may be obtained immediately after the school day ends. *Class adjustments* will be made Tuesday afternoon, if possible.

Source: George C. Kyte, *The Principal at Work*, rev. ed. (Chicago: Ginn and Company, 1952), pp. 111–112. Used with permission.

MISCELLANEOUS PROBLEMS OF TEACHERS

Teachers are bothered by a number of other problems in the school situation. In many cases, an understanding principal can reduce friction and difficulty and thereby promote a better teaching-learning situation. Some of the chief drawbacks to effective teaching will be discussed briefly here.

LARGE CLASSES

With the rapid expansion of elementary school enrollments, class size has increased in many schools. All too many public and parochial schools are on half-day sessions because of the shortage of buildings and teachers. Even where this drastic measure has not been used, class size has frequently grown too large. Catholic parents have become more aware of the need for religious training during the school day and have pleaded with the pastor and the principal to take "just one more" into an already crowded classroom. Some parochial schools have adopted a policy of registering pupils in the early spring, and then placing on a waiting list all those who cannot be reasonably accommodated in the school. This policy may not be a welcome one, but at least it holds the line on increasing class size beyond the point where pupils can be adequately taught. Other parochial schools have cut off the primary grades, and now begin with the fourth or fifth grade. In this way, class size can be kept down to a reasonable number, and all Catholic children can be accepted into the parish school.

Despite careful planning, however, there are large classes in too many places. And large classes, even of docile, studious, co-operative children — and how many such classes are there? — are a heavy strain on the teacher. Perhaps the only way to convey the difficulties of the crowded classroom would be to invite outsiders to go through several typical days in the crowded classroom. When visitors come just for a few minutes, they may be impressed with the orderliness, the work habits, and the cheerfulness of the group; but a few days spent in the classroom would open the eyes of outsiders. Teaching the reading groups, correcting seatwork, scoring tests, keeping pupil records — all of these are a heavy drain on the energy of the teacher. The teacher may be capable, and uncomplaining, and even

Check List for Closing School

Teacher_____

Room_____

By THURSDAY NIGHT:

( ) All supplementary books charged to you from our school library returned to it. (See posted schedule.)

( ) All pictures charged to you from our school library returned to it.

( ) All state textbooks charged to you returned to the storeroom. (See posted schedule.)

( ) All books from the public library, together with the list, tied in bundle and sent to the office. (The department truck is to return them. Be sure all books are returned, as requested by the librarian.)

( ) Individual record cards (yellow cards), with each child's record completed, returned to the office.

( ) Memorandum form regarding every pupil who knows he is to move out of our district during the summer vacation, filed in the office.

( ) Signed final report of nonpromotions (even though you may have no cases) filed in the office.

By FRIDAY NIGHT:

( ) Your inventory and requisition for first school month's supplies filed in the office.

( ) Your report on and request for state textbooks filed in the office.

( ) Your Tenth School Month Statistical Report checked and filed in the office.

( ) Your State Register together with your Statistical Summary completed, checked, and filed with Miss Hill by you in person. (See next item.)

( ) Both Register and Summary signed by you in Miss Hill's presence when you file them. (Your last month's warrant cannot be paid to you until these have been correctly balanced, signed by you, and filed.)

( ) Your summer address filed in the office.

( ) Report cards of and notices for absentees left with Miss Hill.

( ) All keys charged to you left with Miss Hill before you leave the building.

MEMORANDA: Teacher reports that:

( ) Every pupil's locker has been emptied by him.

( ) Every pupil's desk has been emptied by him.

( ) Teacher's desk is in good order. (Be sure the top is clear, so that it can be cleaned and varnished this summer.)

( ) Room supply closet is in good order.

( ) Potted plants and aquarium have been moved to Room 2.

_____has attended to every item listed_____

Clerk

Source: George C. Kyte, *The Principal at Work*, rev. ed. (Chicago: Ginn and Company, 1952), p. 252. Used with permission.

seemingly successful in the crowded classroom; but the effects of the large class will eventually tell on her health and efficiency.

What can the principal do about relieving crowded classrooms? The principal can first of all work with the pastor to establish policies with regard to class size. Early spring registration can supply information as to the number of classrooms and the teachers needed for the fall. Adhering to the policy established may be difficult, but consistency will be rewarded by a better teaching-learning situation. The principal can also work with the pastor in supplying help to teachers with crowded classes. Teacher Aides were mentioned earlier; they can be an immense help to the classroom teacher. Clerical help supplied by the office clerk, or volunteer workers, will also relieve the situation somewhat. Adequate custodial service will save teachers' time for their professional work. And finally, an understanding principal will constantly devise ways of making the best of a difficult situation that cannot be remedied immediately. The principal may herself be a teaching principal; but that should not lessen her sympathy for others in difficult situations. The principal's ingenuity can reduce to a certain extent the difficulties inherent in large classes.

CROWDED CURRICULUM

Many teachers feel overwhelmed by the number of subjects they are supposed to teach daily. Very often teachers complain that they simply "can't get it all in." New teachers are especially harassed by a crowded curriculum, but even experienced teachers find "covering the material" impossible at times.

Certainly, the case of the crowded curriculum needs to be investigated by the principal. One factor that contributes to pressure is a school day that is too short. When the subject matter has been planned for a 28-hour week, teachers will feel very pressed in trying to crowd the content into a 25-hour week or even less. With the many worthwhile activities of a modern curriculum, it is a pity to have teachers and pupils frustrated by lack of adequate time to carry these activities effectively. Another possible factor is the lack of correlation among the various subjects. A faculty committee studying correlation and integration would be sure to develop helpful suggestions. Still another factor is the teacher's trying to fit all pupils into a single mold, bright and dull alike. Some of the content will never be learned by the slower pupils; in fact, some of the material will be grasped only by the very bright. Another difficulty is trying to teach all the content to pupils in a combined grade, such as grades three and four taught in the same room. It is impossible to spend enough time with each group of pupils; hence, the regular content cannot be learned by all the pupils. Special adjustments of content are needed in combined grades.

It must be realized, of course, that the curriculum may be overcrowded. In such a case, the faculty should study together how the essential content can be taught, and how the less essential content can be introduced incidentally. In order to have satisfaction in their work, teachers must be able to achieve the objectives. Hence, the standards must be reasonable. In her in-service program, the principal can do much to set reasonable standards of achievement for teachers and pupils, and to assist teachers in attaining these standards.

NO FREE TIME DURING THE DAY

Very often, teachers are responsible for their group throughout the entire day. This means that the teachers meet the children before school begins, are with them during recess and lunch periods, and accompany them to the traffic intersection or to the bus after school. Although teachers no doubt love their pupils, it would help morale to allow the teacher some free time during the day. Some schools have arranged for volunteers to monitor the recess and noon play periods and the lunch hour. Volunteers have also served effectively as a bus committee, seeing that the children are cared for while waiting for the bus after school. Teachers will be fresher for their work if there are a few times during the day when they associate with adults rather than children.

LACK OF PREPARATION FOR GRADE

A real source of difficulty for teachers is their not being prepared for the grade they are teaching. A primary teacher may be needed in an upper grade, and agrees to work there. Or, an intermediate teacher may be drafted into a first-grade classroom. Having a teaching certificate and experience at one grade level does not mean that the teacher is equally well prepared for other grades. In so far as possible, the principal should try to assign teachers within their range of preparation. When teachers are working in grades for which they are not specifically trained, they need extra help in order to make the adjustment gracefully. The principal or religious superior may appoint a "buddy" teacher, or adviser, to new teachers, and even to experienced teachers working at a new grade level. Good working conditions require that teachers be helped to adjust to their present teaching situation.

DISTURBANCES

Many other factors create disturbances to the teacher and children during the school day. Noise is particularly annoying, whether from trains, buses, trucks, factories, or unnecessary bells. Odors make a teaching-learning situation difficult. Dampness, chilliness, stuffiness, glaring sunlight, dirt and smoke all tend to interfere with good learning. The matter of interruptions has been discussed under "faculty bulletins"; interruptions are particularly irritating to both teachers and pupils. Emotionally maladjusted children make teaching difficult; extreme behavior problems warrant the principal's attention.

All of these other factors, though seemingly trivial, lessen the good which teachers can do for children. The principal should be alert to these conditions and provide remedies as effectively as possible.

PERSONAL RELATIONS

Although the preceding factors are all significant in a good working situation, the most important factor by far is wholesome personal relations. "Morale," it is sometimes called, and "esprit de corps," but whatever the name, good personal relations make for an effective and happy teaching-learning situation. Without pleasant personal relations, nothing else can make for a good situation.

In Chapter IV, some aspects of personal relations were presented, chiefly those concerned with efficiency and communication among staff members. The principal must be a superior person, and an informed person, to get work done well in an atmosphere that is cordial, pleasant, and co-operative. Studies in the mental hygiene of teachers show that good personal relations are basic to personal adjustment. Since an extended discussion of mental health and school efficiency cannot be presented, it might be best to list some of the things which a principal can do to make the school a good place in which to work.

1. The principal must plan carefully for all details of the school program; but, she must not let detail and routines get too important. Regulations are needed, but should be kept to a minimum. Records and reports should not be made more important than working with children. Teachers suffer when emphasis is put on details, rather than on the larger objectives.

2. The principal must be flexible. When new problems arise, they must be considered as new problems; the "same old rules" may not apply. When the principal is willing to adapt, teachers feel that their problems have received fair hearing.

3. The principal must listen. Sometimes, when parents and teachers have had the chance to "talk it out," their problems are less formidable. A good listener helps to relieve pressure.

4. The principal must be objective. This means that she must be able to take criticism without being offended. She must also be able to see that when teachers complain, very often they need a scapegoat on which to pile their irritations. The principal should try to see that most criticisms are not directed to her personally, but rather to administration in general. The principal is wise to "let the teacher win sometimes."

5. The principal must be friendly. She must sincerely like the people she is working with. They have their faults, of course, but so has the principal. It is part of the principal's job to go at least three fourths of the way to

enlist the co-operation of the individual teacher or parent, and to help individuals function as valuable members of the group. "Coke and cookies" will help, as will many of the other devices to increase group communication. Basically, however, the real test is — does the principal genuinely like people? She must, if she is to work effectively with people.

6. The principal must respect the teacher's status. When there is a conflict with parents, the teacher needs the principal's support. The principal may not necessarily agree with the teacher's action, and must not agree if the teacher is in the wrong; but even when in error the teacher should feel that the principal respects and values her as a person. When corrections are needed, they should be made calmly and tactfully, and in private. The teachers' status with their peers requires that no one be corrected in public.

7. The principal must be realistic. Are the principal's demands reasonable? Could she herself have done better under the circumstances? What helps should the teacher be given in order to work more effectively in the future? Sometimes the principal sets the standards too high, either for the whole staff or for individual teachers. The principal's "level of aspiration" may make it impossible for the staff to work comfortably in the situation. It is not "my" school, but "our" school; the staff's comments and criticisms help the principal establish reasonable goals.

8. The principal must have, or try to develop, a sense of humor. "Smile and the world smiles with you; weep and you weep alone." Most of the mishaps in the school day are not tragedies; a smile will dispel many of them. The teachers need to feel that the principal can take a joke, even when the joke is on her. Seeing the "funny side," the staff learns to take their own reverses less seriously. From time to time, the principal should plan some entertainment for the staff, entertainment which will enable them to laugh and relax together.

The principal who excels in all these traits can be canonized tomorrow. The list certainly sounds like an impossible task, and yet many other traits could be added. No one is born with all these qualities; they need to be developed through consistent effort — through reading, through trial-and-error, and through the give-and-take of daily staff contacts. Certainly, the principal's Morning Offering can well include a prayer for an increase in the virtues needed for her office.

EVALUATING WORKING CONDITIONS

At the beginning of the chapter, the question was asked, "Which school has better working conditions for the staff — St. Peter's School in a deteriorating downtown area or St. Pius School in a sparkling new suburbia?" The preceding discussion has provided some criteria for answering the

SRA EDUCATORS OPINION DIRECTORY

Directions: Put a ✔ to the right of each statement, indicating whether you agree, do not know, or disagree.

	Agree	?	Disagree
1. I think my work load is about right for me......... 1.			
2. The condition of the building and grounds here makes this a pleasant place to work.............. 2.			
3. In general, I'm satisfied with the textbooks in our classes. .... 3.			
4. New curriculum materials tend to "sit on the shelf" instead of being used in the classroom............ 4.			
5. I am satisfied with the way salary matters are handled here................................ 5.			
7. Most of my fellow workers are quite friendly....... 7.			
8. My principal has usually been as fair as possible in her dealings with me........................... 8.			
9. My principal seldom gives us credit and praise for work well done................................. 9.			
10. The pastor and principal are not very interested in our welfare.................................. 10.			
12. The principal should rely more on the professional staff.. 12.			
13. My principal does her best to get us the professional help we need................................ 13.			
14. We have far too many classroom interruptions..... 14.			
15. The administration keeps us informed about school plans and developments........................ 15.			
16. The administration does a poor job of handling complaints and suggestions........................ 16.			
17. The parishioners are generally glad to give time and energy in order to help the school.............. 17.			
18. I am often bothered by unexpected extra assignments. 18.			
20. I'm convinced that my work is really worth while... 20.			
21. I have little opportunity to use my own judgment in my work.................................. 21.			
22. In general, the over-all curriculum in this school system is on the "right track."..................... 22.			
23. The longer you work for this school system the more you feel you belong............................ 23.			
25. There is plenty of opportunity for professional growth in this school system.................... 25.			

Source: *The SRA Educators Opinion Inventory* (Chicago: Science Research Associates, 1953), p. 1. Adapted, with permission, for use in parochial schools.

question. An analytical check list, *SRA Educators Opinion Inventory*, may be an interesting way to poll the faculty for their opinion of working conditions in the school. Page 1 of the inventory is reprinted on page 178.

The principal needs to know how the staff feels about working conditions in the school. By using this inventory, the principal can get insight into the way the staff feels about her administration. These suggestions can be used to remedy deficiencies and to develop strong areas more fully. By such an inventory, and also by listening, the principal can provide better working conditions for the staff.

FOR THE PRINCIPAL'S PROFESSIONAL LIBRARY

Books

American Association of School Administrators, National Education Association. *Staff Relations in School Administration*, Thirty-third Yearbook (Washington, D. C.: National Education Association, 1955), 460 pp., $5.

    This yearbook can perhaps be borrowed from the library. The principal will find two chapters particularly good on working conditions in the school:

        "Working Conditions and Staff Relations," pp. 133–151.

        "Improving the Economic and Community Status of Staff Members," pp. 153–173.

Hoffer, Paul, *Guide for Religious Administrators* (Milwaukee: The Bruce Publishing Company, 1958), 171 pp., $4.50.

Huggett, Albert J., and Stinnett, T. M., *Professional Problems of Teachers* (New York: The Macmillan Company, 1956). An interesting discussion of working conditions is given in Chapter Nine, "Professional Working Conditions for Teachers," pp. 199–252, $5.25.

Kyte, George C., *The Principal at Work*, rev. ed. (Chicago: Ginn and Company, 1952). Unfortunately, this book is out of print, but perhaps the principal can get a copy for the excellent discussions of faculty bulletins. Especially helpful are the following chapters:

    "Beginning the School Year," pp. 105–119.

    "Preparing for the Close of School," pp. 239–245.

    "The Principal's Bulletins," pp. 305–321.

Redl, Fritz, and Wattenberg, William W., *Mental Hygiene in Teaching* (New York: Harcourt, Brace and Company, 1951), 454 pp., $4.75.

    Readable account, from the teacher's viewpoint, of the factors in the mental health of pupils and teachers.

Wiles, Kimball, *Supervision for Better Schools* (Englewood Cliffs, N. J.: Prentice-Hall, Inc., 1955), 399 pp., $5.95.

    Staff morale is discussed in "How Can Staff Morale Be Built?" pp. 50–75.

Pamphlets

Central College, Michigan. The "How" and "Why" of the Teacher Aide Program (Mt. Pleasant, Mich.: Central Michigan College, Dept. of Special Studies, 1958), 8 pp., free. Other materials also available free of charge.

National Education Association, Department of Elementary School Principals, *Time for the Job.* Reprinted from *The National Elementary Principal* (Washington, D. C.: National Education Association, 1954), 96 pp., $1.25; presents good ideas on faculty handbooks and bulletins in:
"Effective Written Communication," pp. 54–73, faculty handbooks and bulletins.

Science Research Associates, *Confidential SRA Educators Opinion Inventory* (Chicago: Science Research Associates, Inc., 1953), 6 pp.

Tompkins, Ellsworth, and Jones, Galen, *Keystones of Good Internal Administration*, Misc. No. 20, U. S. Dept. of Health, Education, and Welfare (Washington, D. C.: U. S. Government Printing Office, 1956), 24 pp., 15 cents.

CHAPTER VIII

WHAT IS GOOD TEACHING?

Every teacher and principal is interested in good teaching. What is good teaching? Are teachers "born" or "made"? What are desirable personal qualities in teachers? What professional competencies should a good teacher have? How does a principal's concept of good teaching influence her supervision and administration?

SUPPOSE your Mother Superior said to you in June, "Next September you can have your pick of the Sisters for your new school. You'll have eight Sisters and four lay teachers. Just name the Sisters and you can have them." And suppose the Pastor said, "Money is no consideration at all. Get the four best lay teachers you can find. We'll pay whatever is necessary."

If you were able to survive both these shocks, you would at first be so excited you could not choose. Then you would try to calm yourself and think clearly. The chance of a lifetime — good teachers, all good teachers! What a school you would have in September! What a thrill next year would be!

It would be a little like a fairy tale, for you would know that you would have to give reasons for your choices. A fairy godmother was holding out a tempting offer, but at the same time, she was waiting for your answers. "You choose Sister Alma? Why?" "You want Mrs. Kerby? Why?" "This is your complete staff. How can you be sure that your school will have good teaching next year?" For a moment, you might feel that the game wasn't worth the candle. How could you justify your choices? How could you be sure you would have good teaching with the teachers you selected?

The fairy tale atmosphere would vanish once you began to analyze your own ideas about good teaching. You would select some people right away; but you would find that you could not make all twelve decisions so easily. You would have before you a task as difficult as that of the fairy tale in which the hero had to climb the glass mountain. Good teaching? In a sense, it is easy to define; but when you get right down to practical applications . . . How could you present reasons which would satisfy Reverend Mother, the pastor, and most of all, yourself?

Very probably, no Sister Principal living today will ever be faced with this dilemma. Yet, on a smaller scale, every principal is making such decisions continually. Good teaching — what it is, what helps it, what hinders it — the Sister Principal needs ready answers to these problems. The day will come, though not in the unreal setting given above, when the principal's convictions about good teaching will determine just how good the teaching in her building will be.

The Sister Principal is interested, then, in finding specific answers to the question: What is good teaching? She may approach the problem from two angles: the personal qualifications of a good teacher, and her professional competencies. Both approaches are needed for a well-rounded picture. For Catholic schools, there is fortunately an excellent source on the personal qualifications basic to good teaching — the papal encyclical, *The Christian Education of Youth*. For an analysis of professional competencies, the principal can draw upon studies which show the good teacher in action. Through these two approaches, the principal can develop a realistic and helpful view of what constitutes good teaching.

Though there are some who say that teaching is an art and cannot be defined, for practical purposes we know that we *must* define good teaching, at least operationally. If we cannot say what we mean by good teaching, we cannot claim to have good teaching in our schools. There is sufficient material available on the subject for the Sister Principal to develop a reasonable security when discussing good teaching. This does not mean that a single sentence, or a single page of writing, will end once and for all any differences of opinion on good teaching. Rather, the principal, having studied the problem, can state objectively the personal qualifications and the professional competencies essential to good teaching. Only then can the principal exert her leadership for the improvement of teaching.

WHAT ARE THE PERSONAL QUALIFICATIONS OF A GOOD TEACHER?

A good teacher is neat, it is true, and systematic, and happy, and co-operative, and alert, and many other fine things. But the fundamental qualities of a good teacher for Catholic schools go much deeper. *The Christian Education of Youth* points out that every teacher in a Catholic school should possess certain minimum essentials: professional preparation, intelligence, good character, a love of Christ's little ones, and an interest in the family and the nation. In other words, even before we say what a good teacher should *do*, we must know what she *is* as a person. No matter what techniques she has acquired, she cannot be a good teacher for Catholic schools unless she has first satisfied the above criteria.

The text of Pope Pius XI's statement is impressive. We should say it over so often that it becomes inseparable from our own thoughts on teaching:

> Perfect schools are the result not so much of good methods as of good teachers, teachers who are thoroughly prepared and well grounded in the matter they have to teach; who possess the intellectual and moral qualifications required by their important office; who cherish a pure and holy love for the youths confided to them, because they love Jesus Christ and His Church, of which these are the children of predilection; and who have therefore sincerely at heart the true good of family and country.[1]

Is Sister Alma a good teacher? Is Mrs. Kerby? They cannot be, unless they first measure up to these standards. Let us examine each of these four criteria somewhat in detail.

THE TEACHER'S PREPARATION

Pope Pius says that good teachers "are thoroughly prepared and well-grounded in the matter they have to teach." This means not less than a complete teacher training program, and it rules out the idea that just any nice person can teach. The harassed administrator might say, wishfully, "She may not have much formal training, but she is such a good person; she'll work out, I'm sure." This is hopeful, but unfounded, optimism. Studies made in teachers' colleges show that students often do not know even basic arithmetic content until they are given specific help with arithmetic. Other studies show that the same is true of English, science, and social studies. The content of the elementary curriculum must be taught to the teacher-in-training. Some school systems require that the teacher applicant take a comprehensive test over all the material she expects to teach. It is certainly not too much to require that the teacher know as much as the pupils will be expected to know. A teacher who is "thoroughly prepared and well-grounded" will have a firm grasp of the content she is expected to teach. In addition to content, the teacher needs to study the nature of children, and ways to help them develop. Proper preparation for teaching includes courses in content, psychology, and methodology. Native ability cannot compensate for deficiencies in these areas.

Sister Formation Program. Most principals will not have on their staff this year any young Sisters who have gone through the Sister Formation program. But the program has been so enthusiastically accepted by leading religious communities that principals will want to support it. The Sister Formation program is planned in the belief that the religious teacher should

---

[1] Pope Pius XI, The Christian Education of Youth (New York: The Paulist Press, 1944), p. 33.

be thoroughly prepared, academically and spiritually, before she is assigned to a classroom. Under the Sister Formation program, college work is systematically begun during postulancy. During the first year of novitiate, doctrine and liturgy are studied, and during the three years following, a comprehensive course in liberal arts and teacher education is pursued. Right along with this logically planned professional preparation, the Sister Formation program develops the young Sister spiritually, giving her a sound training in philosophy, religion, ethics, and the spirituality of her own religious institute. The Sister Formation program presents an intelligent approach to adequate pre-service training of religious teachers. The Everett Report[2] of proposed Sister-teacher-training curricula has been acclaimed by both Catholic and non-Catholic educators alike. Pre-service education such as this would reduce poor teaching to a minimum. Our Catholic schools would be second to none in the world if the Sister Formation program were universally adopted by teaching sisterhoods.

"But," some say, "there is a shortage of Sisters now, and young Sisters can't be kept out of the classroom long enough to complete this program!" There is indeed a shortage of teaching Sisters, and with the present rate of expansion in Catholic schools, this shortage will continue. The considered opinion of Catholic leaders — religious superiors, bishops, and directors of teacher training institutions — is that the shortage can best be met by thoroughly preparing the Sisters we have. Let us have well-trained teachers who are also fervent religious, they say, and the *quality* of these teachers will do more for Catholic education than will any *quantity* of untrained and spiritually unformed teachers.

In religious communities which have a four-year program leading to a degree at the pre-service level, at least nine out of every ten young Sisters finishing the program could become good teachers. In the hypothetical case given earlier, the Sister Principal could select some of her prospective staff members from the group of young Sisters just coming out for duty. When the Sister Formation program is really in operation, the young Sister beginning her teaching will be a well-prepared person, better prepared by far than those Sisters who have had to finish their training in summer school.

Should the young Sisters be so favored? Would it not be better to start with the older Sisters, and release them from teaching to study full time? Experienced religious superiors feel very strongly that the training program should begin with the postulants. Within a few years, all Sisters in the community will have degrees, and from that point on, all Sisters

---

[2] Sister Formation Conference of the National Catholic Education Association, *Report of the Everett Curriculum Workshop* (Seattle, Washington: Heiden's Mailing Bureau, 1956).

beginning to teach will have degrees. While regretting perhaps her own inadequate pre-service training, the Sister Principal will give wholehearted support to the Sister Formation program, which will upgrade the teaching in her school more than any other single factor.

Lay Teachers' Training. If the principal sincerely wants good teaching in her school, she will be adamant about lay teachers' college training. The Sister Principal who keeps up with Catholic education knows that lay teachers are no longer an emergency measure; they now make up a substantial part of our parochial school staffs throughout the country. When a pastor says, "Get the best lay teachers you can find; money will be no consideration at all," that schoool will have good teaching because it will have well-trained lay teachers. Sometimes the principal likes to let the pastor off easy, by keeping down the bills; but well-trained lay teachers cost money. Good teaching cannot be had without paying lay teachers a living wage, as discussed in Chapter VI.

On-the-Job Growth. Preparation includes both pre-service college education and in-service professional growth. No matter how complete her training, no teacher can be called a finished product when she gets her degree. The good teacher prepares thoroughly for her classes; she makes long-range plans covering a large block of time, and daily plans for immediate objectives. Further, the good teacher is not just a classroom technician; she functions effectively in the principal's all-over plan for the professional growth of the staff. These activities take time, of course. The eight o'clock to three o'clock teacher cannot be called a good teacher. The clock-punching person does not belong in a profession that requires a sense of dedication, and the Christian education of youth definitely requires that, of lay teachers as well as of religious.

All teachers, then, must continue to grow professionally on the job. To assist in their development, the principal must provide competent leadership. The amount of teacher growth depends heavily upon the principal's ability to develop people. Good teaching? When the staff is well educated, how broad the horizons for good teaching!

But suppose that some staff members are inadequately prepared. Because of expanding enrollments, the shortage of trained teachers is being acutely felt. What, then, of on-the-job growth? The principal is the key person in developing teachers who have inadequate pre-service training. Even in the ideal situation mentioned above — where the principal herself selects her own teachers — there may be some with incomplete training. In such cases, the principal must become a trainer on the job. Her efforts will not make poorly prepared persons into good teachers, but consistent directing will improve the general tone of teaching. However, the principal must keep her perspective in this; no amount of improvement in service reduces the need for pre-service education. The principal's appraisal of teacher preparation should be frank; she must hold the line on adequate training.

To have good teaching, then, the staff must have good pre-service education and adequate on-the-job professional growth. Only the "thoroughly prepared" teacher can do good teaching.

INTELLIGENCE AND CHARACTER

Good teachers, according to Pius XI, must possess the "intellectual and moral qualifications required by their important office." Perhaps an applicant has a college degree; does this guarantee good teaching? Not at all. Intellectual and moral requirements are also indispensable.

Intellectual Qualifications. How bright must a good teacher be? Or, need she be bright at all? Do persons of average IQ make better teachers than very bright people? Just as in the case of college degrees, the Sister Principal is not all-powerful in the matter of staff selection on the basis of IQ. However, the more informed the principal, the better choices she will make. And, where she is not free to choose, even there the informed principal can better utilize the intelligence which her staff possesses.

In the research on the intelligence of public school teachers, some disconcerting data have come to light.[3] Education majors in college ranked as a group considerably below the average for the other professions. The IQ of the average college graduate was found to be 121; the average IQ of the education graduate was 117, whereas engineering graduates averaged 124 IQ, and doctors and lawyers about the same. Also, about one fourth of the education majors had IQ's below 110. Are teachers throughout the nation as bright as engineers, doctors, lawyers? Obviously not, though in all occupations there is a range of intelligence quotients.

This leads to the next question: How bright should teachers be? Well, the IQ range of "average" persons is 90 to 109. For Sisters one can safely say that an IQ well above 100 would be needed to complete the Sister Formation program as planned. For lay teachers, adequate intelligence is also required, if full benefits of training are to be achieved. Some veteran teachers may protest that this is unreasonable. "Miss Aiken was anything but bright in school, and she's a dandy little teacher." "Girls who want to serve God in religion shouldn't be turned away because of their IQ."

Perhaps we can be jolted out of our complacency by looking at the harm done by a dull teacher, as described by the writer Pearl Buck:

> Dull teachers produce dull pupils. Heredity of the mind, through communication, is just as certain as heredity of the body, through birth, and more certain, for there is the unexpectedness of the genes in the flesh to

---

[3] Myron Lieberman, *Education as a Profession* (Englewood Cliffs, N. J.: Prentice-Hall, Inc., 1956), pp. 225–234.

bring surprise. But the dull and uninspired teacher can kill the mind at its source, for the beginning of all thinking and education is wonder. When a child's wonder and eagerness to know are discouraged and stifled by stupid routine, by arbitrary unnecessary rules, the techniques of the dull teacher, then a crime is committed against the child.[4]

The Sister Principal and religious superiors share the responsibility of preventing this indictment from being true of Catholic schools. The religious community should accept for teaching only those candidates who can successfully complete the college training needed for teaching. The Sister Principal can often screen out lay teachers with inadequate intelligence by examining an official transcript of credit before a contract is signed. Poor college students do not become overnight good students of the material they are to teach. An A college student might not necessarily make a better teacher than a B+ student; but certainly both of them have a better chance of doing good teaching than a D or even a C student has. Higher intellectual qualifications, other things being equal, enable one to teach better. Brighter teachers can grasp the content faster, and are then free to devote their time to improving their methods of presentation. It is not harshness, it is kindness, to direct to other types of work candidates who lack the necessary intelligence to do satisfactory work in college and in the classroom.

Moral Qualifications. A good teacher must have proper moral qualifications. In other words, a good teacher must be a person of good character and behavior, a person who conforms to high standards of ethical conduct. Moreover, the best teachers for Catholic schools are themselves exemplary Catholics. "No one can give what he does not have." A teacher who instructs children in the moral virtues without practicing these virtues herself will not affect the children's attitudes.

In justice to children, there should be careful screening of applicants for teaching communities and for teaching generally. To a certain extent, the principal can screen lay teacher applicants on the basis of moral character. The applicant's pastor is likely to know whether the candidate made her Easter duty, and is a parishioner in good standing. Religious communities have an even more serious responsibility as regards the moral character of applicants to the Sisterhood. Not only religious communities, but teacher education institutions generally have a grave duty to direct undesirable persons away from teaching. Both psychological and psychiatric testing have been included in the screening programs of forward-looking colleges and religious communities. The cost of such services is negligible when one considers that children are thereby saved from damage done by unstable and neurotic teachers.

---

[4] Frederick C. Gruber, Ed., *Teaching in America*, Forty-third Annual Schoolmen's Week Proceedings (Philadelphia: University of Pennsylvania Press, 1956), p. 18. Used with permission.

Screening to date has not been completely effective, however, as one can tell from observing some teachers. It is unpleasant, but necessary, to face the fact that teachers can be unjust, untruthful, explosive, weak-willed, and even cruel. In the interests of children, such teachers should be removed from teaching. Less severe cases require intelligent therapy. Ignoring the situation merely aggravates the condition and increases nervous strain on the part of the pupils. Definite in-service work offers some solution to "conduct" problems in teachers. A course in mental hygiene may give the deviant teacher better insight into her own motives and those of children. A psychiatrist addressing a faculty group, or speaking with an individual teacher, can help develop healthier mental attitudes. A priest trained in directing religious and lay Catholics can also provide invaluable assistance in teaching problems which may be basically personal problems.

As with teacher preparation, moral qualifications are not completely eliminated by a pre-service screening. On-the-job growth is essential, if the teacher is to develop fully. Good teaching must be based on a solidly moral foundation. Someone has said, "Education is not teaching people what they do not know; it is teaching people to act as they do not act." Certainly in Catholic schools, the character and behavior of teachers is of utmost importance, since improved moral conduct is one of our main objectives.

THE TEACHER'S LOVE OF CHILDREN

"Good teachers," says Pope Pius XI, "cherish a pure and holy love for the youths confided to them, because they love Jesus Christ and His Church, of which these are the children of predilection." How can one judge whether teachers love children in this way? One can only roughly gauge during an interview how an applicant feels toward children. On the job, however, the teacher's attitude is reflected in the class. Children are happy with a teacher who loves them; they want to come to school; they make good progress in their work. There is always something to interest them, to keep them enthusiastic.

These are signs of a teacher's love of children, but not necessarily of a supernatural love. In what way does a "pure and holy love" show itself? Perhaps the story of Jimmy might be used as an illustration.[5] Jimmy, the six-year-old son of a college professor, had been asked to leave three successive schools because of his behavior. In desperation, the non-Catholic father asked that Jimmy be admitted to another school. Sister graciously added Jimmy to her already heavy enrollment. Jimmy's awe of her garb gave way to interest, and then a sort of good will developed. After a month, when Jimmy was still on the roll, the relieved father wanted to know how Sister

---

[5] Walter B. Barbe, "I Love Jimmy," *Elementary English*, XXXIII (Dec., 1955), pp. 523–524. Used with permission.

had managed to win him over. Her answer was simply, "You see, I love Jimmy." The problem child had responded to a kind of love he had not known before.

A supernatural love is not, however, limited to such "conversions." It includes all the qualities which the professional worker must have to be effective with children: insight into their problems, sympathy for them, a willingness to help, and patience and skill in working with them when there is no guarantee of success. All effective work with children is based on this kind of love. Over and above all this, however, the Catholic teacher should see in each pupil a soul for whose destiny she is in part responsible, a soul dear to God and capable of achieving union with Him. Like other good teachers she respects the essential dignity of the human personality, but she also reverences the child because of the divine image, grace, within him.

This kind of love may be more fully realized in religious teachers, who have sublimated their natural loves through their vows. Once for all, the religious teacher has cut herself off from purely personal attachments and has vowed herself to the service of God's creatures. Instead of humanly loving just "persons," the nun dedicates herself to love "people," much as the gentle St. Francis did by his all-embracing love of mankind. This transmutation of love is divinely inspired, and it is divinely aided by the satisfactions that come from seeing the good it does for children.

In lay teachers, also, something of this "pure and holy love" is necessary in order to provide the kind of education which Pope Pius urges. Our Catholic schools have enjoyed the services of many dedicated lay persons, who love their children because of a personal love of God.

Good teaching requires a great expenditure of time and energy in any situation. However, good teaching in Catholic schools often involves intense personal sacrifice. This sacrifice is evident in the extra hours which Sisters devote to catechetical instruction, and to manual work in the church, school, and convent. Moreover, living conditions on some missions are especially difficult, and the daily schedule of the teaching Sister is usually rigorous. The cheerfulness and even gaiety with which Sisters go about their work are proof that they are motivated by a more than human love. Again, it may be said that many lay teachers have also shown this brave unconcern for the personal hardships involved in leading little ones to Christ.

The suprahuman character of this love is actually good for the development of children. Studies have shown that children react best to a teacher who does not try to center interest in herself, and that emotionalism in a teacher's love for her pupils is harmful rather than helpful. The teacher who has a truly dedicated love for her pupils has a good chance of being the mature, balanced, emotionally warm, and secure kind of adult who can work most effectively with the young.

This is the kind of teacher whom the principal and parents want in their school. It is partly in what the teacher says, but mostly in what she does, that her "pure and holy love" of children is shown.

THE TEACHER'S INTERESTS

Interests that go far beyond the classroom are Pope Pius' final prerequisite. The good teacher must have "sincerely at heart the true good of family and of country." In her work with children, she must strive to develop the qualities needed for strong home life and a healthy national life.

An Interest in the Home. "Know your pupils' homes" is one of the first rules for helping children. The good teacher has "in the head" not just "on the books" information on her pupils' background. The good teacher knows the tone of family relations in the home, financial conditions, the education of the parents, the religious spirit of the parents, and their attitude toward their children. The teacher acquires this information, first of all so that she may teach the child as an individual, and relate her teaching to his home. The teacher also uses this information in order to work with parents in the guidance of children.

Today's teacher has definite responsibilities toward developing a strong bond between the home and the school. More and more, parents need to know what is going on at school; they need to know what is being taught, how, and why. The teacher trained to be a leader of adults is admirably fitted to assume this role. The good teacher can conduct information sessions for parents, in groups or as individuals. The good teacher knows what to present, and how to present it so that parents can see the relationship between their work in the home and the teacher's work in the school. Home and school cannot ignore each other if children's best interests are to be served. If a real partnership is to be worked out, the trained, competent teacher will be the liaison person. In Chapter XI and XII, there are specific suggestions for developing this kind of bond between home and school.

An Interest in the Nation. "For God and for country" frequently heads a bulletin board display in parochial schools. "Render to Caesar the things that are Caesar's, and to God the things that are God's" — the rights of Church and State are an integral part of Catholic teaching. The parochial school curriculum includes training for citizenship as well as knowledge of American history and geography. However, it is only the good teacher who makes these routines come to life for the child. The good teacher prepares the child for adult citizenship by systematic training in the democratic processes: problem solving, reaching group consensus, sharing responsibilities, and using discussion techniques according to his needs and ability. In the interests of the nation as a whole, the good teacher also prepares youth for success in their lifework. This objective consists first of all in helping pupils learn the subject matter required. At higher levels, vocational training is given more specifically, based upon the groundwork laid in the elementary school. The good teacher teaches children how to take part in activities, worship, work, play, and self-development necessary to our American democracy. She also relates these activities to the thrilling realization, "I am an American. That I might enjoy the privileges of American democracy, men have given their lives. I must, as an American and as a Catholic, contribute the best that is in me that this way of life may endure."

It is true that the home and society at large influence children's attitudes. However, many have felt, with the philosopher, "Whatever we wish to see introduced into the life of a nation, we must first introduce into its schools." This is where the Catholic teacher in the Catholic school exercises her strongest influence — she bases instruction in citizenship and vocational competence upon a firm foundation in the moral law. The objectives of "good citizenship" and "success" are empty in themselves; how few people can be good just for the sake of goodness! The individual's obligations to his country and to his employer are made all the more real and imperative because he understands his duties as expressions of God's law, carrying with them the sanctions of God's law. The pupils of today are the adult citizens and parents of tomorrow. The good teacher views her pupils in this larger context.

This fourth characteristic of the good teacher concludes the encyclical discussion of the teacher's personal qualifications. The Sister Principal can confidently accept as *sine qua non* of good teaching the four criteria stressed by Pius XI; preparation, intelligence and character, love of children, and interest in the family and the nation. This listing of qualifications can help the principal solve the problem posed at the beginning of this chapter — that of deciding who would be good teachers for her staff. Personal qualifications are an important first index to good teaching.

Still another approach may be used to complement personal qualifications. In order to judge teaching, one should also ask: "How has this personally acceptable teacher developed her capabilities?" "How effective is this 'good person' in the classroom?" Or, to put it technically, what teaching competencies does she demonstrate? To round out our picture of the good teacher, we need to follow through these questions as well.

WHAT ARE THE PROFESSIONAL COMPETENCIES OF THE GOOD TEACHER?

THE "COMPETENCY" APPROACH

In judging good teaching, the principal may supplement the philosophical approach by studying the things that teachers *do*. How many times the principal has sighed, "I do wish the third-grade teacher wouldn't . . ." Or, "How capably the first-grade teacher handles a phonics lesson!" In both of these statements, the principal is saying in effect that a good teacher should *not* do certain things, but that she should do other things. This is essentially what is known as the competency approach in judging teaching.

The principal might develop her own criteria of teacher competence by listing the things which she feels a good teacher should do. This would be a time-consuming process, but it would certainly clarify her own ideas about good teaching. This list which she would draw up could be used as a check list of things which an effective teacher ideally does in the performance of her duty.

This same kind of thing has been done on a formal scale by educators interested in teacher evaluation. The recent trend in teacher evaluation has been toward things which can be *seen*, and hence judged more objectively. This approach has been a welcome one, for educators were getting uneasy and teachers impatient with the use of teacher traits as the chief means of judging a teacher's effectiveness. No one questions the value of such traits as punctuality, tolerance, and co-operation, but it is difficult to say just how these traits contribute to good teaching. A real advantage of the older approach was the ease and speed with which one could administer a check list of teacher traits. The competency approach does take more time and more training; but today's principal is a more professional person and ready for the challenge of evaluating teaching more objectively.

To do this, we try to take our eyes off the *person* of the teacher and turn our attention to what she is *doing*. Instead of rating the teacher's insight, for example, we instead look at the way she handles the slow learner, the kind of assignments she makes, and the rewards she offers for achievement. We find we can be less emotional when we talk about the things the teacher is *doing*, rather than the qualities which she needs to develop. This approach requires a radical change in our thinking, and it also presupposes better prepared teachers. With the steady upgrading of teacher training, especially through the Sister Formation movement, Catholic schools are ready, or just about ready, to undertake this newer kind of evaluation.

The research in this area is very extensive, and truthfully, rather frustrating.[6] Many of the writers seem to throw up their hands and say that one opinion is as good as another. The National Commission on Teacher Education and Professional Standards, however, has effectively opposed a negativistic attitude with this statement on teaching effectiveness:

[6] See, for example, the summaries of research in Arvil S. Barr, David E. Eustice, and Edward J. Noe, "The Measurement and Prediction of Teacher Efficiency," *Review of Educational Research*, XXV, No. 3 (June, 1955), pp. 261–269.

Arvil S. Barr and Robert E. Jones, "The Measurement and Prediction of Teacher Efficiency," *Review of Educational Research*, XXVIII, No. 3 (June, 1958), pp. 256–264.

Occasionally, we hear it stated that teaching competence is a subtle thing that cannot be objectively defined or that research has demonstrated the impossibility of any objective measure of teaching competence. If these things are true, then many of us are guilty of practicing under false pretenses. For in our profession there are many who must make crucial decisions on the basis of such a definition, just as there are several key processes in education that assume its existence. What good teaching is, and how to recognize a good teacher are questions that confront every administrator, supervisor, school board member, teacher educator, parent, pupil, and teacher.[7]

A promising approach to an objective analysis of teaching skill has been developed by the California Teachers Association, under the title *Teacher Competence: Its Nature and Scope*.[8] This study analyzes teaching effectiveness so clearly and realistically that it warrants the attention of all who are concerned with the question — What is good teaching? The check lists which follow have adapted to the parochial school situation the criteria presented in *Teacher Competence*.

Organizing the Approach

To study teacher competence, one must first decide what different roles a good teacher must assume. We know from the papal encyclical and from experience that the teacher is more than just a classroom instructor. And even as an instructor, the teacher has more than one function. Perhaps a practical outline of the essential roles of a good teacher today would include the following:

Role One: The teacher instructs pupils.
Role Two: The teacher counsels and guides pupils.
Role Three: The teacher interrelates the school with the home and the larger community.
Role Four: The teacher co-operates as a professional member of the school staff.

In order to be considered a good teacher, the individual should show some proficiency in each of these four roles. The school situation would require some adaptation in the teacher's approach, but by and large good teachers perform many activities in common wherever they teach. The discussion which follows will list typical activities in each of these four areas. The list will be detailed, since teaching is a complex process. Though

---

[7] National Commission on Teacher Education and Professional Standards, National Education Association of the United States. *Measures of Teacher Competences*, Report of Special Group D, Miami Beach Conference, June 24–27, 1953 (Washington, D. C.: National Education Association, 1953), p. 5. Used with permission.

[8] California Teachers Association, Commission on Teacher Education, *Teacher Competence: Its Nature and Scope* (San Francisco: California Teachers Association, 1957). With permission of the California Teachers Association, the areas defined in *Teacher Competence* were reorganized and modified for use in a checklist for parochial elementary schools.

the entire list may not be used with each teacher, this analytical approach to teaching has been found helpful by principals. An in-service growth program, to be effective, must be based on the specifics of good teaching, such as revealed by this kind of approach.

Before proceeding to the analysis of teaching competencies, however, it would be well to recall a basic principle of leadership. A good leader tries to develop the potential of each individual in the group. A little girl loves to place a doll pattern over folded paper and cut out a whole row of paper dolls exactly alike. She is thrilled that they all look the same. The educational leader, however, is working with human potential; her endeavor should be, not to mold her staff to her own preconceived model, but to help each individual develop her own personality and ability.

The check list which follows allows for the fact that teachers are really very different from one another and should remain different. In fact, a highly capable staff will evince greater variety in methods and materials than a mediocre staff will. And, when offered expert leadership, a capable staff will become increasingly different from one another. The following check list, then, is not as simple to use as those which enumerate specific items which a teacher must do. This check list will prove more helpful, however, for it is adaptable to all levels of teaching skill. The check list can thus be used over a long period of time. As the principal uses the check list, she will want to modify it somewhat and add to it as time goes on.

ROLE ONE — THE TEACHER INSTRUCTS PUPILS

"Instructing pupils" was the aspect of teaching which received most emphasis in the past. Even today, instructional skill is fundamental to good teaching. In fact, the picture we have in mind of "teacher" is an instructor at the chalkboard, demonstrating or directing a group of pupils. Certainly, competency in instructing groups of pupils is basic to successful teaching, for the teacher is not a clinician working with single individuals at a time. This skill is not merely the "know-how" of proved techniques, but involves wide knowledge and experience. The principal can judge instructional competence by observing how typically the teacher acts in the manner described.

There are five subtopics in the check list on instructional skill:

A. Does the teacher show a knowledge of child psychology and the principles of learning?
B. Does the teacher work to achieve the objectives of the school curriculum?
C. Does the teacher demonstrate skill in instructional procedures?
D. Does the teacher utilize adequate evaluation procedures?
E. Does the teacher maintain an effective balance between freedom and control in the classroom?

From the analysis of each subtopic, one gets a picture of the breadth and depth of the teacher's competence as an instructor. In a check list like this, one cannot of course get an average score; a mathematical averaging of widely different skills would defeat the purpose of the diagnosis. However, by drawing a line between the check marks on the list, one can get an idea of relative strengths and weaknesses.

ROLE ONE — THE TEACHER INSTRUCTS PUPILS

Competency*	Usually	Often	Seldom	Never	No Chance to Observe
A. Does the teacher show a knowledge of child psychology and the principles of learning?					
Does the teacher —					
1. Recognize differences in pupils and deal with pupils according to needs?					
2. Provide a classroom environment which promotes good learning?					
3. Make and use pupil records to determine needs, plan work, and guide learning?					
4. Develop co-operatively with pupils objectives for large units?					
5. Utilize a variety of classroom *activities* adapted to the purposes of the lesson?					
6. Utilize a variety of *materials* adapted to the purposes of the lesson?					
7. Provide opportunity for creative expression, both for individual pupils and for groups?					
8. Arrange differentiated assignments to meet individual needs and abilities?					
9. Use a variety of devices to keep pupils informed of their progress?					
10. Help pupils apply their learning to other situations?					
B. Does the teacher work to achieve the objectives of the school curriculum?					
Does the teacher —					
11. Give evidence of promoting the objectives of Catholic education? (See Chapter XII)					
12. Instill a respect for moral, spiritual, and supernatural virtue?					
13. Demonstrate adequate knowledge of the content to be taught?					
14. Make long-range plans which include all basic learnings of the grade?					
15. Make daily plans which are complete but flexible?					
16. Utilize procedures outlined in the teachers' manuals?					
17. Help children to achieve satisfactorily in all subjects of the curriculum?					
18. Help children to develop democratic ideals through experience in group work?					
19. Strengthen religious ideals by encouraging reading of religious books and magazines?					

Directions: 1. Place a check in the column to the right of each item. 2. Connect the check marks with a line. This will show relative strengths and weaknesses.

Competency	Usually	Often	Seldom	Never	No Chance to Observe
C. Does the teacher demonstrate skill in instructional procedures?					
Does the teacher —					
20. Conduct clear and practical demonstrations and explanations?					
21. Give directions clearly and thoroughly?					
22. Make purposeful assignments related to ongoing activities?					
23. Provide for wide pupil participation in class discussion?					
24. Provide for adequate and interesting drill?					
25. Use questioning in a logical, interesting, and purposeful way?					
26. Use materials skillfully to further the purposes of the lesson?					
D. Does the teacher utilize adequate evaluation procedures? (See Chapters XIII and XIV)					
Does the teacher —					
27. Base evaluation on the objectives of the unit?					
28. Use the results of evaluation as a basis for re-teaching as needed?					
29. Use a variety of devices and procedures for evaluation?					
30. Organize, summarize, and interpret evaluation meaningfully?					
31. Lead the learner to evaluate his own growth and development?					
E. Does the teacher maintain an effective balance between freedom and control in the classroom?					
Does the teacher —					
32. Show an honest liking and sincere regard for boys and girls?					
33. Help pupils work together in a co-operative and natural way?					
34. Help children develop good study and work habits?					
35. Develop pupil responsibility for managing classroom routines?					
36. Provide opportunity for pupils to be leaders as well as group members?					
37. Keep behavior problems to a minimum by developing habits of self-direction?					

When the principal first examines this list of instructional competencies, it may seem too comprehensive to be at all useful. Further study will show, however, that the complex act of instructing pupils well requires many individual skills. A comprehensive check list like the foregoing will help the principal to clarify her own ideas about instructional competence, and will at the same time prove a challenge to the highly capable teacher. It needs to be emphasized constantly that the competency approach looks at what the teacher is *doing,* and not merely at *qualities* which the teacher seems to possess. As mentioned earlier, the principal will want to adapt the above list to the needs of her own staff.

ROLE TWO — THE TEACHER COUNSELS AND GUIDES PUPILS

The second important role of the teacher is to counsel and guide pupils in both educational and personal matters. This role of the teacher may be somewhat misjudged on two scores. First, the term *guidance* may cause some confusion and uneasiness. Guidance is a technical name for some very limited services rendered to children, but the term connotes vague and mysterious powers, and perhaps a seeming superiority on the part of guidance personnel. Most elementary schools do not have a guidance director, but rather emphasize the role of the classroom teacher in guidance. However, at first, many teachers are likely to be in awe of the term. They should not be. Long before guidance specialists got their name, good teachers were effectively guiding and counseling children. Even today, when guidance has become rather specialized, the role of the classroom teacher in guidance is always stressed. As will be seen in the check list on page 198, the good teacher routinely helps children to prevent difficulties, and to iron out trouble spots. The "pure and holy love" which Pope Pius recommends is the basis for effective guidance. However, as a recent book puts it, "Love is not enough." Teachers need more information on how to guide children and how to provide classroom conditions conducive to good mental health. "Guidance" is not just an esoteric cult, though there is a considerable body of research in the area. The good teacher can and does effectively guide her pupils, as the check list on page 198 indicates.

The second difficulty with the role of the teacher in counseling and guiding pupils is this: "guidance" seems to imply spiritual guidance or spiritual direction. Nothing could be farther from the truth. Catholic teachers know that only a priest can direct spiritual formation. Only the priest has the needed background in moral and dogmatic theology, and only he has been ordained for this lofty work. So, "guidance" does not mean that the classroom teacher, even a religious of long experience and perhaps great virtue, takes over the difficult and delicate role of spiritual direction. The check list which follows indicates the activities understood as "guidance" by the classroom teacher. (In Chapter XV, the principal's own duties in guidance are outlined.)

The amount of guidance, in this limited sense, which the teacher can give depends to a certain extent upon the size of her class. In very large classes, individual guidance must necessarily be curtailed. However, the skillful teacher values personal counseling, and even in average and large classes manages to devote some time to it. The interested teacher will find that considerable guidance can be provided to small groups of pupils, or even to an entire class, at one time. Individual interviews, when possible, do of course provide the better setting for effective guidance.

There are four areas in which the good teacher shows skill in *counseling* and *guiding pupils:*

1. Does the teacher collect sufficient information about each pupil?
2. Does the teacher use diagnostic and remedial procedures effectively?
3. Does the teacher help the pupil to understand himself?
4. Does the teacher recognize the need for specialized services for exceptional children — the gifted, the retarded, the physically handicapped, the emotionally disturbed?

ROLE TWO — THE TEACHER COUNSELS AND GUIDES PUPILS*

Competency	Usually	Often	Seldom	Never	No Chance to Observe
A. Does the teacher collect sufficient information about each pupil?					
Does the teacher —					
1. Use informal devices, such as anecdotal records, interviews, and questionnaires?					
2. Use the results of standardized tests of IQ and achievement?					
3. Construct and use sociograms?					
4. Use pupil records as a background for interpreting tests?					
5. Use the sacramental record and data on religious practice in the home?					
B. Does the teacher use diagnostic and remedial procedures effectively?					
Does the teacher —					
6. Identify learning potential and learning difficulties through observation and testing?					
7. Use appropriate materials according to pupil needs?					
8. Work constructively with pupils in groups or individually according to all of their needs?					
9. Vary her procedures in working with gifted and slow children?					
C. Does the teacher help the pupil to understand himself?					
Does the teacher —					
10. Help the child to understand his own abilities and limitations?					
11. Guide the child in analyzing his own personal problems?					
12. Assist the child in setting realistic goals for himself?					
13. Direct the child to sources of information on vocational opportunities and careers, including priestly and religious vocations?					
14. Help the child to interpret his problems in the light of religious truths?					
D. Does the teacher recognize the need for specialized services?					
Does the teacher —					
15. Recognize when to supplement her own work with outside services, as in the case of the gifted, the retarded, the physically handicapped, the emotionally disturbed?					
16. Carry out suggestions made by specialists?					

* See Directions, p. 196.

In her role of counselor and guide, the good teacher typically demonstrates most of the competencies listed above. It is in this role particularly that the flexibility of the check list can be seen. For example, in Part B, Number 7, "Uses appropriate materials according to pupil needs," merely calls attention to whether the teacher does this. The *kind* of materials and the *methods* for using them are left to the teacher's resourcefulness. The same is also true of Part C, Number 11, for example, "Guide the child in analyzing his own personal problems." Library reading might be a method of helping children in this way, or role playing, or interviews. The good teacher does assist the child in analyzing and facing his personal problems. In doing so, she calls into play her professional preparation as well as her experience in dealing with children. Practically all of the items in the check list might be noted in a public school teacher. The Catholic school teacher should permeate her guidance with a realization of the child's role in the Mystical Body of Christ.

The good teacher performs many activities not mentioned in the check list. However, the items listed can be observed, discussed, and improved upon. The check list may be helpful as a starting point for faculty group work in improved guidance services for children.

ROLE THREE — THE TEACHER INTERRELATES THE SCHOOL WITH THE HOME, THE COMMUNITY, AND THE CHURCH

The two foregoing functions — instructing and counseling pupils — are more commonly thought of as "teaching." However, the good parochial school teacher today functions importantly as a link between the school, the home, the community, and the Church. Good teaching cannot be confined to children alone; it includes work with adults, and work that looks forward to adulthood. It is perhaps in this role of educational leader that one sees most clearly the need for the well-qualified person described in *The Christian Education of Youth.*

This third role of the teacher involves skills discussed in Chapters XI and XII. Since many of these skills involve complex areas of human relations, and moral and spiritual growth, they do not lend themselves readily to objective appraisal. The check list includes only the skills which can be somewhat objectively measured.

A. Does the teacher utilize the educational resources of the community?
B. Does the teacher work co-operatively with parents?
C. Does the teacher develop in her pupils a love of the American way of life?
D. Does the teacher develop in her pupils a love of the parish and the universal Church?

In this third role, the teacher is serving the pupil in three important ways: giving him a better understanding of the civic and the parish com-

ROLE THREE — THE TEACHER INTERRELATES THE SCHOOL WITH THE HOME, THE CHURCH, AND THE LARGER COMMUNITY*

Competency	Usually	Often	Seldom	Never	No Chance to Observe
A. Does the teacher utilize the educational resources of the community?					
Does the teacher —					
1. Enrich classroom teaching by inviting parents and other adults to share pertinent information with the pupils?					
2. Utilize well-chosen and carefully prepared field trips to broaden the children's knowledge of the community?					
3. Interpret the community to the pupils through pertinent materials and teacher presentation?					
B. Does the teacher work co-operatively with parents?					
Does the teacher —					
4. Enlist the co-operation of parents within the framework of school policy?					
5. Endeavor to know personally most of the pupils' parents through conferences, and home visits when possible?					
6. Prepare for parents' information cumulative records showing the child's abilities, interests, and achievement?					
7. Conduct individual and group parent conferences with increasing skill?					
C. Does the teacher develop in her pupils a love of the American way of life?					
Does the teacher —					
8. Use democratic techniques and processes in the classroom?					
9. Promote a knowledge and appreciation of America's achievements?					
10. Help the pupils acquire the values realized as the ideals of democracy?					
D. Does the teacher develop in her pupils a love of the parish and of the universal Church?					
Does the teacher —					
11. Help the pupils to take part more effectively in liturgical worship?					
12. Promote participation in parish activities, social and religious?					
13. Develop interest in the work of the Church, in the past and in the present?					
14. Cultivate in her pupils the Christian virtues, such as reverence, devotion, obedience, and prayerfulness?					

* See Directions, p. 196.

munity, increasing his appreciation of them, and preparing him for more effective participation in both the parish and the civic community. Viewed in a slightly different way, the teacher is transmitting the culture, arousing an appreciation for it, and, in so far as possible, improving the culture by raising the educational level of its citizens. It is difficult of course to note objective evidence of the teacher's activity in this sphere. The items listed are ones which lend themselves to concrete discussion by the principal and the teachers. Again, in marking the check list, a line connecting the check marks will show the teacher's all-over effectiveness in this critical area of teacher competence.

ROLE FOUR — THE TEACHER CO-OPERATES AS A PROFESSIONAL MEMBER OF THE SCHOOL STAFF

Because of improved pre-service training, teachers are tending more and more to regard themselves as co-workers in an important educational endeavor. The day is past when the principal alone knows the answers to school questions. Today, the wise principal relies upon the pooled wisdom of her staff. On the part of the teacher, there is a corresponding sense of responsibility for the operation of the school and for the improvement of instruction.

Concerning her role as professional staff member, three questions must be asked:

A. Does the teacher improve herself in service?
B. Does the teacher contribute to the smooth operation of the school?
C. Does the teacher promote good staff relations?

The check list on page 202 analyzes each of these responsibilities of the professionally minded teacher.

The check list description of Role Four may help the principal evaluate the competence of teachers, and may also supply her with data on the breadth of the in-service program. If a teacher is to perform well in the areas listed, then the principal must provide adequate supervisory and administrative services. The leadership of the principal is essential to the personal and professional development of the individual teacher and of the entire staff. Topic A, "planned professional reading" and "trying new techniques," for example, presuppose alert leadership. The principal must plan well if teachers are to "contribute to the smooth operation of the school." Democratic procedures and high faculty morale are necessary if teachers are really to "promote good staff relations."

Many other competencies might be expected of the professional teacher. However, the ones listed above are relatively objective evidences of the teacher's growth in service and her responsibility toward the staff and the school.

ROLE FOUR — THE TEACHER CO-OPERATES AS A PROFESSIONAL MEMBER OF THE SCHOOL STAFF*

Competency	Usually	Often	Seldom	Never	No Chance to Observe
A. Does the teacher improve herself in service?					
Does the teacher —					
1. Keep informed of trends and practices in education through planned professional reading?					
2. Try new techniques for improving her work?					
3. Participate adequately in the in-service growth program of the school?					
4. Utilize spiritual direction available, as the teachers' day of recollection and the staff religion library?					
B. Does the teacher contribute to the smooth operation of the school?					
Does the teacher —					
5. Carry a fair share of out-of-class responsibilities?					
6. Conform to school policies and the principal's requests?					
7. Co-ordinate her classroom program with the whole school program?					
C. Does the teacher promote good staff relations?					
Does the teacher —					
8. Contribute positively to formulating school policy?					
9. Accept decisions and directives, though not necessarily agreeing with them?					
10. Use discretion and consideration in speaking of the school and her colleagues?					
11. Work co-operatively with the principal, supervisors, and the pastor?					

* See Directions, p. 196.

    The above check lists develop the "competency approach" to teacher evaluation in four essential roles — instructing pupils, counseling pupils, interrelating the school with the larger community, and co-operating as a professional member of the school staff. The items listed tend to be objective evidences of abilities known to be basic to good teaching. Numerous other abilities could be added, and no doubt will be added by the principal and staff interested in promoting teacher competence.

    No teacher, even an out-and-out master teacher, can answer "Usually" to every competence listed. All good teachers, however, should possess at least average ability in each competence. In other words, a good teacher should be able to check at least "often" for each skill, and "usually" for many skills. As mentioned earlier, teachers will vary in their strengths.

Teacher A might be superior as a professional staff member, and only average in school-community relations. Teacher B might be exceptionally skilled in counseling and guiding pupils, and only average in her professional staff membership. Since there will be stronger and weaker areas in each teacher, the Sister Principal needs to have on her staff teachers who, taken as a group, possess well-balanced competence in each of the four areas. The figure of speech often used of educational leadership applies here: the Sister Principal must be able to orchestrate the abilities and interests of her staff and thus provide children with a balanced and effective educational program. In other words, the principal must develop and integrate these competencies so that there is good teaching in every classroom, and the school as a whole is characterized by good teaching.

The question — What is good teaching? — has been discussed from two points of view: the person as a teacher, and the teacher as a person. The criteria advanced by Pius XI and the check lists of teacher competencies provide the principal with a comprehensive background for her judgments concerning teachers and teaching. As someone has said, "A man's judgment is no better than his information." The better the principal's information concerning teaching, the surer will be her evaluation of teaching. At the beginning of this chapter, the principal was asked to select good teachers for her school and then to justify her choices. The foregoing discussion can assist the principal in making valid judgments.

It would be unwise to end this discussion without mentioning the rewards of teaching. Perhaps the words of William Lyon Phelps express the feelings of good teachers everywhere:

> I love to teach as a painter loves to paint, as a musician loves to play, as a singer loves to sing, as a strong man rejoices to run a race. Teaching is an art — an art so great and so difficult to master that a man or a woman can spend a long life at it, without realizing much more than his limitations and mistakes and his distance from the ideal.[9]

No matter how one analyzes teaching, there will be a spirit in good teaching that is above and beyond analysis. It is this spirit that the principal attempts to foster in her work of supervision. A principal must be in a sense a visionary, one who leads her teachers from check lists and discussions to a fuller dedication to the great cause they are promoting. St. John Chrysostom epitomizes the work of the Catholic teacher thus:

> There is no painter, there is no sculptor nor artist that can be compared to the man who knows how to form the minds and hearts of the young. To reproduce in souls the living image of Jesus Christ is a work far surpassing the finest creations of human art.

[9] William Lyon Phelps, "I Love to Teach," *Ohio Schools,* Vol. III (Oct., 1930), p. 319. Used with permission.

All good teachers seek to develop both the science and the art of teaching. Good teachers in a Catholic school do still more, for their ultimate objectives are concerned with eternal as well as temporal values.

FOR THE PRINCIPAL'S PROFESSIONAL LIBRARY

Pamphlets

Education — True or False? Simplified edition of Pope Pius XI's The Christian Education of Youth, prepared with study outlines by Reverend Gerald C. Treacy, S.J., and published by the Paulist Press, New York, 31 pp., 10 cents.

The principal will want to be thoroughly familiar with this papal encyclical on Christian education. Good teaching in Catholic schools must be oriented toward a sound philosophy of education.

California Teachers Association, Commission on Teacher Education, Teacher Competence: Its Nature and Scope (San Francisco: California Teachers Association, 1957), 48 pp., 50 cents.

The check list of traits in the second part of Chapter VIII is based on this pamphlet. The principal will find the whole pamphlet helpful in understanding good teaching and in improving teaching.

Books

Fitzgerald, James A., and Fitzgerald, Patricia G., Methods and Curricula in Elementary Education, "Teaching as a Profession," pp. 56–93, and "Knowing Children and Guiding Them," pp. 16–53 (Milwaukee: The Bruce Publishing Company, 1955), 591 pp., $5.50.

Valuable for a comprehensive and detailed treatment of the principles underlying good teaching, and the handling of specific subjects in the curriculum. Every principal can use this book over and over again in working with teachers.

Wiles, Kimball, Teaching for Better Schools, 2nd ed. (Englewood Cliffs, N. J.: Prentice-Hall, Inc., 1959), 341 pp., $5.95.

This book offers a fresh and interesting approach to good teaching. The principal will find it helpful in judging and promoting good teaching.

CHAPTER IX

THE IN-SERVICE GROWTH OF TEACHERS

No matter how well a teacher teaches, she can still do better. The principal has a responsibility to help all teachers — good and poor — to grow in teaching efficiency, and she should plan accordingly. What means should a principal use in bettering classroom teaching?

AS INDICATED in Chapter V, "Time for the Job," the principal's most important duty is to supervise, meaning by supervision to improve instruction in the school. Chapter VIII presented criteria for judging teaching effectiveness. Chapters IX and X will present the more commonly used techniques for helping teachers to improve on the job, to "grow in service," as this process is typically known.

In preparation for these chapters on supervision, the principal might well consider two important aspects of in-service growth: (1) "Must I *really* emphasize supervision to this extent? I am a teaching principal." (2) "Will I be a 'snoopervisor' if I do try to carry out these suggestions? The things I have said about supervisors!"

SUPERVISION, A DUTY

Repeatedly, the point has been made that Catholic schools operate in order to provide the best possible education for Catholic children. This means that the teaching in Catholic schools should be second to none, and that children should be learning in Catholic schools better than they would elsewhere. It follows, then, that we must, first of all, know what the teaching is actually like in our schools, and that, second, we must work to improve our teaching. The individual teacher, of course, examines her own teaching from time to time, but the *responsibility* for judging and improving teaching is the principal's. All of her activities must be oriented toward this goal. No matter how attactive or satisfying other duties may be, the improvement of instruction must be the all-embracing objective of the sincere principal.

Principals tend to shrink before the prospect of supervising. Convincing reasons can be advanced for this shyness. Many principals are teaching principals, and hence absorbed and weighed down by their own classroom duties. Some principals feel inadequate for supervision, because of lack of formal training in this area. Other principals think that, since all teachers are mature persons, they ought to be able to take care of their own classrooms. Still other principals insist on viewing the principalship as a job for a "head teacher," or one who orders supplies and writes checks. And some principals, it must be admitted, are more interested in management, that is, the smooth operation of the school. Certainly management is easier, more "showy," and more flattering. Highly polished floors and carefully chosen planters are easier to maintain than a conscientious supervisory program.

However, the Sister Principal is responsible for providing the highest kind of education for the pupils in her school, even if she is a teaching principal. So whatever the reasons to the contrary, she must accept the responsibility to improve instruction, and hence to promote better learning. The principal can do this only through a well-planned supervisory program, using the procedures now known to be effective for improving teaching. "I must supervise" should be the slogan of the principal. Facing this duty squarely, the principal must solve the problems inherent in her own school situation.

The time problem is of course the chief one. Chapter V, "Time for the Job," showed that all principals must allocate time each week for supervision, their most important responsibility. A practical rule-of-thumb presented was this: at least forty per cent of her nonteaching time should be devoted to improving instruction. For the supervising principal, this means at least twenty-three hours a week, and for the teaching principal, eight hours. (See Chapter V.) Twenty-three hours a week is all too short; the supervising principal must budget her time carefully to keep all aspects of the in-service program moving satisfactorily. In eight hours a week, the teaching principal will of course accomplish less, but she can improve the teaching-learning situation through a conscientious use of her time for the detailed weekly schedule. This time for supervision should be planned before any other activity. It should never be a question of how to "get in" supervisory duties; it should rather be a question of how all other duties might be delegated or subordinated so that ample time is given to the duty of primary importance — the duty of supervision.

SUPERVISION, THE MODERN CONCEPT

The chapters which follow outline the typical activities of the principal as supervisor. Chapter IX discusses faculty meetings, classroom observations, conferences, demonstration teaching, professional reading, and college courses. Chapter X discusses help with lesson planning, orienting new teachers, and evaluating teaching and the supervisory program. These are the things which principals do to help teachers teach better so that children may learn better. A good in-service growth program includes most of these activities.

However, the activity may or may not achieve its purpose, depending upon the situation. A faculty meeting, for example, may weary still further teachers who are weary after a long day's work. A classroom observation may have no effect at all on teaching. Professional reading may be unrelated to the teacher's own needs, and hence ineffectual in promoting her development. This not to belittle the techniques of supervision; it is rather to emphasize the importance of the *purposes* behind supervision.

Perhaps the simplest way to discuss the use of supervisory techniques is to examine the levels of supervisory activity as presented in Figure 19. This figure illustrates both the purposes of techniques and the history of supervision in this country.

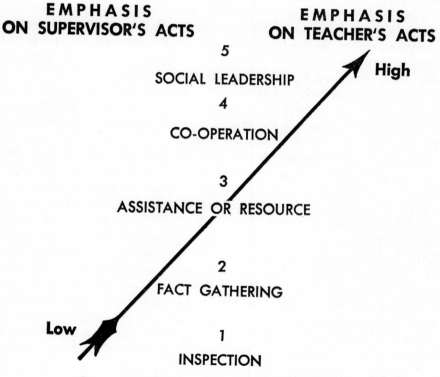

EMPHASIS ON SUPERVISOR'S ACTS **EMPHASIS ON TEACHER'S ACTS**

5

SOCIAL LEADERSHIP High

4

CO-OPERATION

3

ASSISTANCE OR RESOURCE

2

FACT GATHERING

Low 1

INSPECTION

Figure 19. The Levels of Supervisory Activity

Source: Harlan J. Hagman, *The Administration of American Public Schools* (New York: McGraw-Hill Book

In Figure 19, over the upper left-hand side, the heading is: "Emphasis on Supervisor's Acts." In the lower left, the arrow begins, and the area there is marked "Low." The arrow proceeds to the upper right-hand side of the figure where the heading is: "Emphasis on Teacher's Acts." The arrowhead reaches up into the area marked "High." In the center of the figure, the broken line reaches from the bottom of the page up to the top. Along this broken line are placed the levels of supervisory activity, the highest level at the top and the lowest level at the bottom. The levels of supervisory activity are given in descending order:[1]

Highest Level	(5)	Social Leadership
Next Level	(4)	Co-operation
Mid-point	(3)	Assistance or Resource
Lower Level	(2)	Fact Gathering
Lowest Level	(1)	Inspection

The general import of the drawing is that supervision is at a relatively low level when it emphasizes the supervisor's acts, acts such as inspecting and rating, and assembling data for administrative purposes. Supervision achieves a higher level of performance at the assistance or resource level, when the supervisor is equally concerned with her own or the system's objectives, and with the teacher's problems and interests. At the level of co-operation, the supervisor's concern is largely with teacher needs and the development of the individual teacher. At the highest level, social leadership, the supervisor aims to bring about the participation of all concerned — lay and professional people, the school and the community — in a study of ways in which the school can better serve society and achieve the objectives of Catholic education.

The levels of supervision presented in Figure 19 can help the Sister Principal in viewing the purpose of her own supervisory activities. In classroom observation, for example, at what level does the principal operate? Is she merely inspecting, or gathering information? Or is she coming to the class to offer assistance to the teacher? Is the visit a chance to work with a superior teacher, to be "an expert among experts"? At the very highest level, that of social leadership, is the classroom observation planned as part of a long-range study of educational improvement throughout the school or the entire system?

All supervisory techniques might be analyzed in a similar way. From such an analysis, it would be evident that it is the *purpose* which the supervisor has in mind that determines whether or not the activity will really improve the teaching-learning situation. Thus, one principal may conduct

---

[1] The brief description given here of levels of supervisory activity is amplified in Harlan J. Hagman, *The Administration of American Public Schools* (New York: McGraw-Hill Book Company, 1951), pp. 145–205, particularly pages 148–165.

a faculty meeting as a sheer administrative routine; the effects upon teaching would be negligible. Another principal might hold a faculty meeting in which teachers worked together in such a way as to stimulate use of new teaching procedures; the effects upon teaching would be pronounced.

And now to face the question which the principal asked earlier: Will I be a "snoopervisor" if I try to carry out these activities? The answer is clear: the activity is what the principal makes it. As part of the in-service growth program, the principal can visit classrooms and hold conferences at the level she chooses. If she chooses to be a mere inspector, she will be operating at Level 1, and will not be helping teachers at all. At Level 2, her classroom visit might not be resented quite as much, but the visit would hardly improve the teaching-learning situation. Only beginning with Level 3 does the principal avoid the implication that she is a "snoopervisor." At the levels of co-operation and social leadership, the principal obviously cannot be so regarded. When the principal provides an all-round supervisory program geared to the interests and needs of the staff, then she can operate at Levels 4 and 5 almost entirely. Social leadership, Level 5, will not be possible to the principal except in a limited way, as, for example, in the Home and School Association program.

The suggestions made in Chapter V, "Time for the Job," will help the principal and staff to get a true picture of the purposes and activities of a good in-service program. The tiptoeing inspector of earlier days has no place in a modern supervisory program. Neither has listening over the public-address system, or unplanned, "surprise" visits. Supervision, properly understood, has real dignity. It is working with trained people who are all interested in providing children with the best possible education. The picture of an "expert among experts" is the ideal concept of the principal as supervisor.

DIFFICULTIES IN THE WAY

Figure 19 has been used to illustrate the levels at which the principal can operate as supervisor. The figure can also be used to show how supervision developed in this country,[2] and at the same time, why the principal cannot always operate at the very highest levels in her own situation. History repeats itself, even in supervision.

First, a brief word about the changing concept of in-service growth over a period of years. In the very early days, teachers in America were woefully undertrained, and inspectors were assigned to correct some of these defi-

[2] The historical development of supervision is surveyed by Harold Spears, *Improving the Supervision of Instruction* (Englewood Cliffs, N. J.: Prentice-Hall, Inc., 1953), pp. 36–96.

ciencies in preparation. First there were the inspectors from outside, and as principals themselves improved in competence, the building-principal was assigned the task of upgrading teaching. "Growth" for these ill-prepared teachers really meant on-the-job methods courses. As one writer described supervision of the period: "It was necessary to tell her (the teacher) what to do, how to do it, and when to do it. It was useless to tell her why, because she would not have understood."[3] With the gradual improvement of pre-service training, teachers needed less indoctrination on the job. They knew more of content and methodology before beginning their teaching career. This upgrading of teaching has continued, with the result that in many states a degree is required for certification of elementary teachers.

The early concept of supervision was one of authoritarian control and direction of poorly prepared teachers. Today, because of improved teacher training, supervision has become "an expert technical service primarily aimed at studying and improving co-operatively all factors which affect child growth and development."[4] When teachers have had adequate preparation, in-service growth means developing new techniques, broadening informational background, and maturing as professional workers.

The parallel is clear between the history of supervision and variations in teacher preparation in schools today. When pre-service training has been poor, the principal must resort to some of the earlier authoritarian measures. No matter what the date, ill-prepared teachers need on-the-job training by the principal. In-service growth for these teachers will be vastly different from that undertaken by qualified teachers. In order to prevent inadequately trained teachers from harming pupils educationally, the principal needs to remedy at least the most glaring deficiencies. Authoritarian supervision is not in good repute these days, but poorly prepared teachers require strong, consistent direction as they learn on the job. The orientation program for teachers who have not completed their training will resemble somewhat a student-teaching process.

One of the chief difficulties, then, of the principal as supervisor is the inadequate preparation of some teachers on the staff. Another difficulty is the problem of adjusting the in-service program to the varying needs of the staff. Teachers who are especially capable, weak, colorless, resistant, or old require specific attention in the in-service program. Chapters IX and X will attempt to offer suggestions for a satisfactory in-service growth pro-

---

[3] Willard S. Elsbree and Edmund E. Reutter, Jr., *Staff Personnel in the Public Schools* (Englewood Cliffs, N. J.: Prentice-Hall, Inc., 1954), p. 231. Reprint from Alonzo Myers, *Cooperative Supervision in the Public Schools* (Englewood Cliffs, N. J.: Prentice-Hall, Inc., 1938). Used with permission.

[4] William H. Burton and Leo J. Brueckner, *Supervision, A Social Process*, 2nd ed. (New York: Appleton-Century-Crofts, Inc., 1955), p. 11. Used with permission.

gram for all parochial school teachers. The illustration of levels of supervisory activity can assist the principal in adapting her procedures to the varying capabilities of her staff.

There are many activities and devices which the Sister Principal can use to promote the in-service growth of her staff. The following will be discussed in the present chapter: faculty meetings, classroom observation, conferences, inter-visitation, college courses, and professional reading. Additional in-service growth activities will be discussed in Chapter X.

FACULTY MEETINGS

Properly used, faculty meetings are a most effective means of in-service growth. Well-planned faculty meetings provide for the all-over development of the teacher: as instructor, as counselor, as link with the community, and as staff member. Faculty meetings give teachers the opportunity to share in planning and to work together on problems of mutual interest. Particularly with teachers whose preparation has been somewhat adequate, faculty meetings develop leadership and skill in group processes.

But, we may as well admit it, faculty meetings are not loved by teachers! Judged by teachers' reactions — and who is better informed on the subject? — faculty meetings don't accomplish much. At best, faculty meetings are just tolerated in most schools. In case you doubt this, give yourself a shock treatment. Solicit the honest opinions of your staff, or of other teachers whom you know well. If your little survey is written, by all means have the papers unsigned. Or, if you don't want to ask questions directly, read Kenneth Benne's *Human Relations in Curriculum Change*,[5] particularly Chapter 10, "Complacency Shock and Retraining." You will see that teachers often resent and resist faculty meetings. Your first reaction will be a defensive one: "After how hard I've tried . . . They should *want* to improve!"

But this shock treatment will set you on the right path. For, you see, teachers don't think the same things important that you rate top priority. Just think back to the time when you weren't principal. Did you just love to attend faculty meetings? Did you volunteer enthusiastically for every new job? Did you welcome the chance to have your work criticized? Ask yourself a few penetrating questions, and you will see that your staff is not so very different from you after all. Your point of view has changed; theirs has not. In order to provide the kind of meetings your staff wants and needs, you must realize that faculty meetings can stand improvement. It is the principal's job as educational leader to arrange for better staff meet-

[5] Kenneth D. Benne and Bozidar Muntyan, *Human Relations in Curriculum Change* (New York: The Dryden Press, 1951).

ings and this requires effort and planning, of course. But have you ever watched a football coach plan with his team, going through the plays for the game just ahead? The planning is meticulous — each individual's strong points are put into focus, co-operative teamwork is arranged, obstacles are foreseen, and morale is kept at a high pitch. To be sure, the situations are different, but planning is basic to any kind of successful enterprise.

KINDS OF FACULTY MEETINGS

The first step in improving faculty meetings is to recognize that there are different kinds of meetings: administrative, supervisory, and social. When a meeting is scheduled, the principal and everyone else should know exactly what purpose the meeting is to serve. An *administrative* meeting may be called when the principal wishes to impart information to the staff, such as details of the medical examinations to be conducted in the school the following week. A *supervisory* meeting is intended to help teachers grow professionally, as in knowledge of certain curricular content, or in teaching skills. A *social* meeting — the purpose is obvious — a coffee hour, for example, at the beginning of the year, for staff members to get acquainted.

An entire faculty meeting may be devoted to one of these three purposes, or a meeting may be divided so that all three purposes enter in. The following agenda may illustrate this composite kind of faculty meeting:

Agenda

Opening prayer

Announcements by the principal

Teacher panel — "How Are We Helping the Gifted Child?"

Group questions and discussion from the floor

Refreshments

In this faculty meeting, the principal's announcements are of an *administrative* nature; they concern administrative policy and school organization. Typical items include routines in the cafeteria, events of the coming week, procedure for marking the new report cards, and other items of similar informational nature. Explanation of each item is given as needed by the group.

The *supervisory* part of the meeting is the panel discussion on helping the gifted child in the regular classroom. Four teachers have previously volunteered — or been assigned! — aspects of the topic and have read professional literature in preparation for the meeting. The question period which follows gives other staff members the chance to explore the topic further and to relate it to the local school situation. In applying the panelists' remarks to their own classrooms, teachers pave the way for better teaching.

The *social* aspect of the meeting comes with the coffee and doughnuts, or the tea and cookies. The staff relaxes in friendly and informal conversation. Some schools prefer to have refreshments before the meeting, especially when the meeting is held at the end of the school day; other schools prefer to socialize at the end of the meeting.

While a faculty meeting can be comfortably devoted to all three purposes — administrative, supervisory, and social — to be a good meeting the supervisory aspect should predominate, with staff participation in improving their own teaching. Also, there should be a distinct division of the meeting into parts; one should not have to guess what purpose is being served at any given time. Occasionally, an entire meeting can be administrative, as the orientation meeting for new teachers. Or, before a holiday, a completely social get-together is in order. The faculty meetings for the entire year should be so planned that there is variety, and at the same time adequate attention to in-service growth activities.

FEATURES OF A GOOD FACULTY MEETING

Time and Frequency for Holding Meetings. Meetings have been tried before school in the morning, during an extended lunch hour, after school, on Saturday, and beginning half an hour before afternoon dismissal. Each time has advantages and disadvantages. It seems that faculty meetings after school continue to be in the majority. Teachers seem to prefer meetings after school, rather than having to adjust to a special schedule.

How often should faculty meetings be held? Meetings involving the entire faculty seem best when held once a month. Planning meetings, in which groups of teachers prepare for the general faculty meetings, will need to be held oftener. Perhaps two or three small-group planning meetings may be held in preparation for a meeting in which teachers present a demonstration of teaching methods. Or, in larger schools, committees may meet to work on topics of special interest, such as materials for enriching the music program. Faculty meetings involving the whole staff should be scheduled in September, and the schedule posted, so that all teachers can arrange to attend the meetings. Ten general faculty meetings are the rule, one a month, with an orientation meeting for new teachers before the opening of school in the fall.

In deciding on the hour, the day, and the frequency of meetings, the principal would be wise to utilize the suggestions of her staff, so that the best co-operation can be achieved.

Place for Holding Meetings. In the newer buildings, there are conference rooms which are delightfully pleasant and well-arranged for staff meetings. In the older schools, very often a classroom is the only available place for a meeting. If so, every effort should be made to have the arrangements as comfortable and informal as possible. Particularly are comfortable chairs needed; pupil desks are cramping physically and intellectually. Chairs should be arranged so that all teachers can talk face-to-face, in a circle, or around a table. Ventilation, heat, and lighting should be good, and distracting noises and interruptions should be kept to a minimum. The time spent on the physical aspects of the meeting place will be more than repaid in the improved participation which will result. A chairman of arrangements can assume this responsibility, and leave the principal free for other matters.

Length of the Meeting. If you poll your teachers about faculty meetings, you are sure to find that long meetings are poor meetings. Particularly are long meetings boresome when the staff cannot estimate how long the meeting will continue. The very uncertainty of a poorly planned meeting adds to its bad effect upon morale. It is important that faculty meetings be carefully planned as to time, and that they begin and end at the time stated. The agenda given earlier can be used to illustrate the timing of a good meeting.

Agenda

Administrative:	Principal's announcements	(5 to 15 minutes)
Supervisory:	a) Panel of teachers	(30 to 40 minutes)
	b) Questions and discussion from the floor; applying material to the classroom situation	(10 minutes)
	c) Summary of discussion	(5 minutes)
Social:	Refreshments	(15 minutes)
	Total time	1¼ hours

For a good faculty meeting, one and a quarter hours seems quite adequate. As mentioned before, the meeting should begin and end on time. Further, each part of the meeting should take only the time allotted to it. A chairman usually keeps the meeting moving on schedule, but a timekeeper may be needed in some instances.

The Agenda. In the Latin, agenda means "things to be done." Applied to meetings, the agenda is a list of things to be done, or topics to be brought up for discussion. In a faculty meeting, ordinarily the agenda should be divided into the three parts already mentioned, with emphasis on the supervisory aspect. Decision-making does not play a prominent role in faculty meetings. Principals are advised not to ask the whole faculty to consider extensively a topic which they have no power to decide.

The agenda is indispensable for an effective faculty meeting. It is the road map of the meeting, the calendar of events, the timetable. During the early part of the year, the principal can propose possible topics for faculty meetings and enlist the help of a faculty advisory committee in choosing topics that will most interest and help the teachers. In selecting topics the principal should sample each of the four areas of teacher competence: instructional skill, guidance, school and community relations, and staff membership. In a large school, it may be good to have a few faculty meetings devoted to primary teachers, while upper grade teachers have their own meeting on topics of interest to them. Of the ten monthly meetings to be scheduled, perhaps seven can be definitely decided upon in September, with three meetings spaced through the year for important local topics that might develop. Another reason for leaving a few months with topics unscheduled is that occasionally the faculty might wish to pursue a topic further, and might arrange for another presentation of the material the following month. Topics should not be continued after the interest has waned, but some topics cannot be adequately handled in a single period.

The agenda should be dittoed and distributed to the faculty a few days before the meeting. Sometimes, a short reading list might be included, giving pertinent references available on the teachers' library shelf. Additional copies of the agenda should be passed out to the faculty just before the meeting begins.

Sharing Responsibility for Meetings. To encourage group participation in faculty meetings, it is a good idea to let the teachers choose the duties they wish to assume. An outline of meetings of the coming year may be passed out to the teachers, who may sign up as they wish. The following excerpt from a schedule of faculty meetings is illustrative.

Teamwork in Our Faculty Meetings for the Coming School Year

Month	Activity	Participants	Chairman of Arrangements	Secretary	Refreshment Hostess
September	Panel: "The Gifted Child" (4 participants needed)	1. . . . . . . 2. . . . . . . 3. . . . . . . 4.			
October	Group Discussion With Leader (see attached reading list and guide sheet) "Our Policy on Homework"	Principal as Leader			
November	Demonstration "Improving Oral Reading" (2 teachers needed)	1. . . . . . . 2.			

In a faculty of twelve, each teacher would have an opportunity to take part in almost every activity, from participant to hostess. Each teacher would be expected to work in one of the in-service activities, such as a panel or demonstration, or book review. Sharing responsibilities for meetings develops the teachers professionally, and also gives them a sense of achievement. The meetings can be no better than the staff makes them; this puts the responsibility for growth squarely where it belongs. Through her leadership, of course, the principal provides material which the teachers can use, and helps them develop needed skills.

Principal's Bulletins.   Usually, the principal opens each meeting with a prayer, followed by administrative announcements. It is best to have these announcements dittoed so that each member can have a copy. The principal comments on the notices which are especially important, or which might be misinterpreted. The wise principal does not read each announcement aloud to the staff. This bulletin keeps the announcements from being a monologue on the part of the principal. If possible, the announcements should cover routine administrative notices until the next faculty meeting. The principal's bulletin is an orderly way of getting information to the staff, without taking too much time from the supervisory aspects of the meeting. At times, the bulletin may list topics to be discussed with the staff, on which decisions must be reached.

Good Group Discussion.   The principal needs to read up on discussion techniques. The teachers may want to use an early faculty meeting to explain the different ways of handling group discussion. This would make a profitable meeting, not only for the development of discussants, but also for carry-over to the classroom situation. The same techniques which function well at the faculty meeting can be applied to children's discussions. References listed in the bibliography are inexpensive and helpful.

Granted that a teaching principal is pressed for time, she can read just a pamphlet or two, and put the ideas into practice. One idea that she must use is this: don't make a faculty meeting the occasion to pontificate. A meeting is not the place for orations. The principal should keep uppermost in her mind the question: What are faculty meetings for? Teacher growth. So, her whole attitude should be to encourage teachers to grow by means of these meetings. When teachers plan, share ideas, participate, the faculty meeting has served its purpose. To encourage good group discussion, the principal should keep the spotlight on the teachers. She should plan with them beforehand, supply them with materials, help them reach decisions. But, during the meetings, the discussion should be theirs, with direction from the chairman of arrangements, but not from the principal when at all possible.

It will help stimulate discussion if the principal prepares a guide and distributes it to the teachers a week or two before the meeting. Perhaps a panel of teachers will discuss the problem of the gifted child in the regular classroom. The guide might be somewhat like this:

HELPING THE GIFTED CHILD IN THE REGULAR CLASSROOM

1. What IQ must a child have to be called "gifted"? "superior"? "bright"?
2. What are the special characteristics of gifted children?
3. How can the teacher guide gifted pupils in the regular classroom?
4. What enrichment activities can be provided for gifted pupils in the regular classroom?
5. Why is it important that teachers identify and guide the gifted child?

REFERENCES

Birch, Jack W., and McWilliams, Earl M., *Challenging Gifted Children* (Bloomington, Ill.: Public School Publishing Company, 1955), 48 pp., $1.

California Elementary School Administrators' Association, *The Gifted Child: Another Look*, California Elementary School Administrators' Association, 693 Sutter Street, San Francisco 2, Calif. Monograph 10, 66 pp., $2.

Gallagher, James J., *The Gifted Child in the Elementary School*, "What Research Says to the Teacher, 17" (Washington, D. C.: Department of Classroom Teachers, National Education Association, 1959), 32 pp., 25 cents.

Ginn and Company Contributions in Reading, *Enrichment Activities for the Superior Child in the Reading Program*, Circular No. 22 (Columbus: Ginn and Company, n.d.), free.

Scheifele, Marian, *The Gifted Child in the Regular Classroom* (New York: Bureau of Publications, Columbia University, 1953), 84 pp., 95 cents.

Witty, Paul, *Helping the Gifted Child* (Chicago: Science Research Associates, 1951), 48 pp., 75 cents.

For a total cost of about $6, the principal can supply the above references for her faculty to read prior to the meeting devoted to this topic. The panelists will draw largely from these references. The other teachers will use the references. It is better to buy enough material for the faculty to read, than to ask them to go to the library. The time saved can be devoted to reading the material. In the interests of economy, perhaps several principals might group together, each purchase one set of references, and share the material for use at faculty meetings. If a meeting is challenging, the teachers will keep coming back to take another look at the pamphlets. The $6 invested is well spent in the interests of in-service growth.

GROUP EVALUATION OF THE MEETING

Every worthwhile project has three parts: planning, execution, and evaluation. We cannot know what to do next unless we first know how we are doing now. The principal and staff can tell fairly well how successful a faculty meeting was just by watching reactions. The success of a faculty meeting can also be measured by results in the classroom: How many more teachers are using the records and filmstrips to accompany the music series? There should be a follow-up of every faculty meeting, to re-emphasize the points made and also to evaluate the effectiveness of the meeting.

In addition to these informal evaluations, it is good at least occasionally to ask the group to fill out a check list on the way they felt about the meeting. The check lists should of course be unsigned. The following check list might prove helpful to use with your faculty.

HOW DID OUR MEETING GO?

1. When the meeting started, did we know exactly what we were going to do?   1. ....Yes ....No
2. Did we keep to our agenda?   2. ....Yes ....No
3. Did the group seem to profit by the meeting?   3. ....Yes ....No
4. Was the work so shared that no one had too much to do?   4. ....Yes ....No
5. Were you satisfied with the meeting?   5. ....Yes ....No
6. Did you have a chance to give your opinion?   6. ....Yes ....No
7. Did you help others take part in the discussion — by asking a question, or inviting someone to comment, etc.?   7. ....Yes ....No
8. How would you rate those in charge of the meeting —

	Excellent	Very Good	Good	Fair
chairman	......	......	......	......
secretary	......	......	......	......
hostess	......	......	......	......
speakers	......	......	......	......
leader	......	......	......	......

9. Please give some suggestions for improving future meetings.

(Please hand in to the secretary before you leave today. You need not sign your name.)

THANK YOU SO MUCH FOR YOUR HELP

In summary, principals can be sure that well-planned faculty meetings pay rich dividends in group spirit as well as in improved teaching. All that the principal knows of group processes can be utilized in preparing and conducting faculty meetings. In providing for the in-service growth of the staff, the faculty meeting is one of the best techniques.

CLASSROOM OBSERVATION

Three important people in education interact during a supervisory visit to the classroom: teacher, principal, and child. Therefore, classroom observation should be viewed as a co-operative endeavor of principal and teacher to help the child learn better. If an improved teaching-learning situation is to be provided for the child, then the principal as supervisor and administrator should utilize all the potential of the classroom visit to achieve this purpose.

Most principals will agree verbally with these truisms, but many will then proceed to object: "That is all well and good, but —." "For somebody else in some other school, maybe in another city, visits to the classrooms would be ideal, but —." This attitude on the part of principals is the chief reason why classroom observation is perhaps the least used and hence the least effective technique for the in-service growth of teachers.

DIFFICULTIES INVOLVED IN OBSERVATION

What are the principal's reasons for shying away from supervisory visits? The first reason is — no time. Teaching principals just throw up their hands; obviously there is no time. Why, they are in their own classrooms all day long. Even nonteaching principals complain of not having enough time. Supervising principals are assigned mainly to the larger schools, and the clerical work is very heavy in large schools. Besides having no time, principals are ill at ease about going into classrooms to supervise. The first-grade teacher certainly knows more about first-grade methods than the principal, who perhaps never taught in the primary grades. No principal can be an expert in all subjects; how can she make constructive suggestions in art, music, science, and all the other areas? Furthermore, the Sister Principals in her community usually don't go into classrooms. The staff would think her aggressive if she suddenly announced she was going to visit all classes. And, finally, there are so many other things she would rather do than observe in classrooms. The supply shelves need attention; the drapes in the office are getting faded; the janitor isn't sweeping the stairs; the pastor's jubilee program is just getting under way; and there are innumerable other little things that nobody else seems to think of. For all of these cogent reasons, the principal just does not observe in classrooms, or she does so very seldom.

NEED FOR VISITING CLASSES

A principal who has not been holding regular faculty meetings can be converted rather easily; but a principal who does not visit classes — it seems that this vice is cast out only with great difficulty. The principal needs first of all to be convinced that she is no longer in the days of the one-room school, where the principal did everything. The principal at that time was teacher, secretary, janitor, librarian, cook, nurse, and supply manager. Even in the two-room school, conditions had not changed much. The principal was only the head teacher, or the one consulted when there was a fight on the playground or coal to be bought.

Today's principal is not in the same category at all as the head teacher of the past century. Today's principal is the instructional leader of the school. Schools are now much larger, it is true, but the main difference is in the quality of leadership rather than in the size of the enrollment. As instructional leader, the principal must know firsthand what the instruction is like in her building. Only when she knows familiarly what each classroom situation is like can she attempt to improve instruction. And it follows that the principal must visit the classrooms while teaching is going on to know how classes are being conducted. This is not to make the principal an authoritarian taskmaster, dictating exactly how lessons are to be taught. The real purpose of classroom observation is to insure for each child the best possible education under the circumstances. The principal cannot lightly set aside this obligation under pretext of more urgent duties; no other duty is as urgent as providing a good education for the pupils entrusted to her care. A good principal observes classes and accepts her responsibility for heading the educational program of her school.

Principals should not think that observations will harm her good relations with the staff and the students. It is a fact that teachers want the principal to come into their classrooms. Studies of teachers' opinions have repeatedly shown that teachers need the security of having their principal discuss classroom matters with them. Teachers feel uneasy about having no instructional conferences with the principal. New teachers report this dissatisfaction most frequently, but even older teachers dislike being ignored. Teachers resent domination, of course, but a good supervisory visit is a far cry from domination. The children themselves, of course, love to have a visitor. Unfortunately, some pupils go through eight years without knowing the thrill of having a principal interested in their work. When classroom observations are well conducted, teachers profit by them and want them. Children also respond favorably. And the principal? The crux of the matter is that the principal needs to "learn by doing" that supervisory visits are indispensable to a good educational program.

To make classroom observations most profitable, the principal needs to plan carefully what she will do, before the visit, during the visit, and after the visit. This will mean in-service growth for her also, for this planning will keep her "on her toes" professionally.

PREPARING FOR THE SUPERVISORY VISIT

Before going into a classroom to observe, the Sister Principal has some preliminary work to do. She must first of all schedule the time for the visit, and if she is a teaching principal, this requires real ingenuity. The principal must also familiarize herself with the course of study and text-books, the teacher's lesson plans, the pupils' records, and notes on previous observations and conferences. A preliminary conference with the teacher is invaluable. The thoroughness of this preparation determines to a great extent just how helpful the classroom observation will be.

RESULTS OF CLASSROOM OBSERVATION

The principal may wonder how she can improve instruction by visiting classes. She can do this in two ways: first, by learning how the teachers are presenting the content and dealing with children, the principal is in a good position to co-ordinate the program of the school. Co-ordination is one of the chief reasons for visiting classrooms. It is true that the course of study should be followed by all teachers. But newer teachers, and even more experienced ones, omit certain basic learnings or overemphasize units which they like especially. Also, the kinds of homework assignments given and seatwork exercises need to be co-ordinated. Slow-moving pupils need special help in all the grades, a certain minimum of direction consistently given. Group work, for example, is needed at all levels. All too often upper-grade teachers keep the entire class together for all instruction. Gifted students need a longitudinal pattern of enrichment activities. And there are many other ways in which the principal can co-ordinate the learning going on in the school.

The principal also improves instruction by sharing good ideas among her staff. During classroom observations, the principal sees fine techniques and deft handling of instructional problems. Other teachers would never benefit by these excellent devices unless the principal were there to gather the honey, as it were, and spread it among the staff. Older teachers especially can be drawn upon to help newer teachers through this sharing process. Also, in a negative way, the principal improves instruction by sharing good ideas with teachers who are obviously ineffective. Though one dislikes mentioning it, there are teachers who do not prepare their classes, who waste time changing from one subject to another, who give unreasonable assign-ments, who teach according to caprice. Only if the principal visits classes consistently will such teachers be kept in line. In justice to children, visits to weak teachers are obligatory. But visits to weak teachers will be accepted only if all classes are visited.

After thinking over these reasons seriously, the principal should be convinced that she can improve instruction through supervisory visits. At first, the principal will feel inadequate and will be able to make only super-ficial comments. But after a time, the ideas she gets from the teachers themselves will enable her to function effectively in improving the teaching-learning situation in her school.

Scheduling the Visit. The principal's schedule presented in Chapter V shows that supervising principals should devote at least two hours a day to classroom observation, and a teaching principal at least two hours a week. Chapter V also presents suggestions for wise allocation of this time throughout a typical week.

There are certain aspects of scheduling visits that are common to both teaching and nonteaching principals. The first is the amount of time that should be devoted to any individual teacher. A rule of thumb might be to apportion the time available according to the years of experience of the staff member. A teaching principal responsible for seven teachers might allocate her two hours of observation weekly as follows.

Allotment of Time to Classroom Observation

Teacher	Years of Experience	Amount of Time Per Month		Schedule for Month of March			
		Hr.	Min.	1st wk.	2nd wk.	3rd wk.	4th wk.
A	0	2	20	30 min.	50 min.	30 min.	30 min.
B*	40		10	. .	. .	. .	10 min.
C	29		20	. .	20 min.	. .	. .
D	15		20	20 min.	. .	. .	. .
E	2	2	. .	30 min.	10 min.	50 min.	30 min.
F	5		50	10 min.	10 min.	30 min.	. .
G	1	2	. .	30 min.	30 min.	10 min.	50 min.
	Total	8 hours		2 hrs.	2 hrs.	2 hrs.	2 hrs.

* Observation may be only a visit to the classroom to note pupil papers, projects, or achievement charts.

A supervising principal could allocate her two hours of daily observation in a somewhat similar way. For the supervising principal, observations would be more frequent and typically longer per visit.

A division such as that given above is a mechanical one, and should be varied according to the individual needs of the teachers. Weaker teachers may require more of the principal's time early in the year, while stronger teachers may profitably experience supervisory visits of greater length later in the year, perhaps when preparing for inter-visitation. By following this schedule, a teaching principal would visit each of her seven teachers at least once a month, and would spend about two hours a month in the classrooms of newer teachers. In all, the teaching principal would be spending about eight hours a month in supervisory visits, and would make a total of eighteen visits per month. Certainly, this schedule would do much to establish the principal as an instructional leader in her school, and at the same time, improve her own knowledge of curriculum and methodology.

The length of the visit, then, depends partly upon experience and need, but also upon the kind of lesson to be observed. The supervising principal has greater flexibility in planning her visits, but the teaching principal may be limited to a lesson of no more than fifty minutes, because her own class is to be considered. Several shorter lessons, as, for example, drill lessons, might be observed during a fifty-minute period. The principal should schedule her visits so that most teachers are visited for both longer and shorter lessons. The principal should arrange to be in the classroom before the lesson begins and to remain there until it is finished.

Getting time for the visit is a major problem for the teaching principal. But it need not be an insurmountable obstacle, as inventive principals have shown. If the teaching principal is convinced of her duty to observe classes, then she will find a way. One principal suggested hiring a substitute teacher one morning a week to take over the principal's class. A teacher's aide, carefully screened and directed, might occasionally supervise the principal's room. Another principal has arranged with the pastor for scheduled religion classes each week. In this way, the teachers thus freed might assist in supervising the principal's class, and also accompany the principal on supervisory visits. In schools where there is a gymnasium, auditorium, or other large room, a teacher might show an instructional film to two classes, while the companion teacher assisted the principal. One particularly inspiring principal arranged to begin classes with her eighth grade at 8:00 daily, so that at 2:30 each day she could be free to supervise. Not an ideal time for observing, but at least supervision was not neglected.

It need hardly be mentioned, however, that the principal's own class should not suffer because of her duty to observe other teachers at work. The principal needs to maintain at all times good control of her own class in each subject, so that a substitute does not hinder their development. With careful arrangement and consistent watchfulness, the teaching principal can usually be absent from her own class two hours a week without detriment to the children.

The problem of whether to announce visits beforehand troubles many principals. In general, scheduled, announced visits are most beneficial to teachers and children. A posted schedule of visits for the coming week, or month, allows teachers to make adequate preparation for the visit. Principals are after all not trying to trap teachers, but to help them. Seeing teachers when they are prepared usually makes them more at ease, certainly when observations are frequent and routine. Even in the case of a teacher who is extremely timid or nervous, tension should disappear if observations are well planned. The principal is probably wise to adhere to her plan of scheduled, announced observations.

Developing Background for the Lesson. No good can come of an observation if the principal visits the classroom "cold." The principal owes it to the teacher and the pupils to be thoroughly acquainted with the work they have done and the work they are now doing. This means that before an arithmetic lesson, for example, the principal should consult the course of study to get an overview of the material for the grade, and particularly for the present unit. Also, the principal should read through the teacher's manual for the unit, study the textbook, and the workbook. The principal goes into a classroom to note pupils' development; intelligent observation presumes that the principal knows the content to be presented and how this content fits into the all-over program for the grade and the school.

It is helpful to examine also the *teacher's lesson plan book*, especially for the subject to be observed. In this way the principal can notice the kinds of lessons taught, the amount of progress made, the testing, and the reteaching that takes place. Many schools have the policy of submitting lesson plan books to the principal each week; in this case, the principal need only to study more carefully than usual the subject to be observed next.

The *pupils' records* furnish essential information. The principal will of course know some of the pupils from previous experience, but having the pupils' cumulative record provides information on intelligence, achievement, absence and tardiness, progress through school. Ideally, the principal studies the pupils' records before the classroom visit; but if not, then the records should be available to the principal to glance at as needed during the lesson. A seating plan, arranged for viewing from the back of the room, also helps the principal interpret the lesson.

Finally, before the lesson the principal should *review all notes* she has taken regarding previous work of the teacher to be observed. Especially, the principal should make sure that she has carried out any offer of assistance previously made. If possible, the principal should have a preliminary conference with the teacher to discuss her aims for the lesson. Either during the conference or at a faculty meeting, the principal can explain the points she notes during an observation. It is often helpful to examine with the faculty *The Ohio Teaching Record* and the list of teacher competencies given in Chapter VIII.

The beginning principal will develop assurance faster if she concentrates on *a single subject matter area at a time.* For example, during October, all visits during the first two weeks might be to arithmetic classes, during the third week to reading, and during the fourth week to arithmetic again.

When the principal feels that she has a rather sure grasp of a single subject, then she can proceed to another subject. It is wise to return several times to a subject already observed in order to maintain familiarity with the area and also to help the teachers maintain their own skill. The principal cannot improve instruction in all areas during a single year, so she would be wise to single out certain areas for emphasis. These areas could well be emphasized also in faculty meetings, so that the entire staff is working on the same general objectives at the same time.

Before each supervisory visit, then, the principal needs to make a general, long-range preparation, and also specific preparation. The better the principal knows the material, the pupils, and the teacher, the more effective will the visit be.

PROCEDURE DURING OBSERVATION

The most important thing about procedure is how people feel about what is being done. In classroom observation, everything the principal does should be motivated by interest, sincerity, kindliness, and professional purpose. If the principal's motives are not of the highest, no rules of procedure will help her to arouse a co-operative response in teacher and pupils. If her motives are genuinely good, then a little clumsiness now and then will not estrange those whom she proposes to help.

The principal should arrange to be in the classroom *before the lesson begins.* Teachers and pupils usually expect a smile and word of greeting, though a lengthy talk is out of place. The principal then goes to the back of the room, where she will not distract the pupils, and examines the lesson plan which the teacher has given her. The pupil records and a seating plan are also there, as well as the text and manual. The principal's attention should be focused upon what the pupils are doing and what the teacher is doing, and not upon any mannerisms or traits peculiar to the teacher. The principal should be alert to what is going on, since both teacher and children react favorably to a responsive observer. A passive observer is annoying, as is one who seems to be oblivious of everything that is going on about her.

During the class, the lesson plan can be used as a guide in following the presentation of the teacher and the text. Pupil records help in interpreting the pupils' answers and activities. It is usually best not to take any notes during the lesson, because note-taking seems to make most teachers uneasy. However, if the notes are shown to the teacher after the lesson and discussed with her, few teachers mind note-taking during observation. Mental notes are necessary, however, as guides to the conference following the lesson. Particularly one should notice how the teacher realizes the objectives of the lesson, and how the lesson leads on to the next day's work.

Should the principal "take over" when the lesson seems to be going badly? The teacher is making mistakes in presentation of factual information; or she is floundering and not able to get her presentation across; or pupils are noisy and inattentive, or merely listless. The principal may be tempted to take over the class, and show the teacher how it should be done. Except in extreme cases, this temptation should be resisted. If the teacher is unorganized during observation, she probably is at other times also, and intervening will not remedy the condition. More good will result in the long run by an analytical conference afterward, and perhaps a planned demonstration lesson. When a teacher is ineffective, the rule here is the same as for other problem situations: When in doubt, do the kindly thing. Exposing a teacher before her class will not improve her teaching; instead it will remove one prop she may have counted on — the principal's regard for her. An extremely weak teacher should be removed from service, but only after a consistent supervisory program has failed to develop her adequately. So, in visiting a classroom, the principal should consider herself an observer, a visitor, and should not have a mental set which says, "If she can't do better than that, she should be shown." By all means, in the conference following the lesson, the principal should be frank in her appraisal of weakness, and should make specific plans for helping the teacher.

Putting a lesson on tape may be a good idea if there is good rapport and visits have been frequent. Taping is an excellent way to keep the lesson alive. It is also a means of making the most of the principal's time, for forgetting causes suggestions to be weak and desultory. With a tape to play back as often as needed, very specific helps can be suggested. And in the case of a good teaching, the tape may be used as illustrative material with weaker teachers. A criticism of a lesson which has been recorded should of course include other aspects of the lesson, such as handling of materials, involving all pupils in discussion, and the like.

When the lesson is over, the principal again nods to the teacher, perhaps makes a single pleasant remark to the class, and leaves the room unobtrusively. If the lesson is running overtime, the principal should feel free to leave at the scheduled time, but without interrupting the class, if possible.

KEEPING A RECORD OF OBSERVATIONS

With so many details to keep in mind, the principal cannot hope to retain all the important aspects of lessons observed. If these important points are forgotten, then the supervisory visit is less effective. The practical principal arranges to keep a written record of classroom observations, so that she can best contribute to the in-service growth of the teacher.

A simple form such as the following might be kept in the teacher's folder or in a loose-leaf notebook devoted to supervisory reports. Each report should contain examples of teacher and pupil activity so that the conference can be specific and helpful.

REPORT ON OBSERVATION AND CONFERENCE

Teacher.............................. Grade...... Subject................

Observation (date)............. Time...... to...... Observer................

1. Type of lesson

2. Materials used

3. Activities

4. Purposes achieved

5. Notes for conference

CONFERENCE: Date........................ Time.......... to..........

6. Topics discussed (other than the above)

7. Comments and suggestions

        Principal

        Teacher

8. Proposed follow-up

A record of classroom observations is essential if the principal is to make good use of her time. When a teaching principal devotes two precious hours weekly to visiting classes, she should be able to show what she has accomplished. A record enables the principal to do this. First, the record shows the pattern of the observations — subjects observed, time of day, teachers visited most often, and follow-up recommendations. It is futile just to flit in and out of classrooms spreading good cheer. Observations should be carefully planned; a written record helps to show how this plan works out in practice.

Another good reason for keeping records of supervisory visits is for co-ordination purposes. Faculty meetings ordinarily stress points that can be carried over into classroom practice. The principal should make a point of unifying instruction by keeping teachers conscious of worthwhile conclusions made during faculty meetings. Also, during conferences following visits, teachers make sound comments on the present program in the school and what should be done to help children learn better. These suggestions are lost, hence cannot be implemented, without a written record. At the end of the year, in looking forward to the following September, the principal can summarize the records of her observations and plan helpful continuing work.

By keeping a simple record of observations, the principal will find that she works more efficiently and more satisfyingly. The principal, too, needs the assurance that she is doing a worthwhile job. Written records help to give her this assurance.

CONFERENCES

In her in-service work with teachers, the Sister Principal needs to develop various kinds of discussion skills. The principal will be chairman of staff meetings, will talk to parents about the school program, will lead faculty groups in reaching decisions on administrative policies, and will discuss with individual teachers plans for improving instruction. It is ordinarily difficult for the principal to develop ease in addressing groups of adults; very few Sister Principals eagerly anticipate their talks to the Home and School Association. Yet, difficult as "public appearances" are, skill in conducting conferences is usually still more difficult to develop. It is not easy to maintain the role of leader while at the same time promoting an atmosphere conducive to free group discussion.

Because of the advantages both to herself and to the school program generally, the Sister Principal will analyze and try to improve her conferences with staff members. Figure 20 shows the differences among the lecture, the question and answer period, and the conference.

SMALL GROUP CONFERENCES

Conferences may be held with a small group of teachers when the discussion centers on a problem of interest and concern to them as a group. There are certain basic principles underlying group conferences.

1. The conference deals with a definite topic, one which the conferees know well enough to discuss, and about which they can reach conclusions.
2. The conference is preplanned. The leader, the principal, sets the time and place, states the topic specifically, and gives the members background data — such as the reason for the conference, the contributions which the members can make, and the expected outcomes. The outcomes, however, are not preplanned; the leader will get from the group a consensus on action to be taken.
3. The leader starts the discussion, encourages each conferee to take part, keeps bringing the discussion back to the original problem, clarifies comments as needed, emphasizes a positive approach, and de-emphasizes fault finding and arguments.
4. The leader contributes to the discussion, as any other member would, not forcing his opinion on the group.

Lecture

Here, the principal talks; the teachers listen. The lecture illustrates a one-way flow of information.

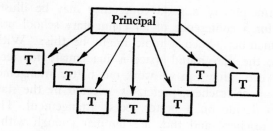

Lecture Followed by Questions or Comments

There is a little interchange of ideas; teachers direct questions or comments back to the principal for her answers.

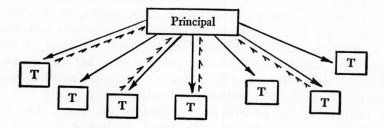

Group Conference

The group directs questions and comments to one another. The principal's role is to keep discussion flowing among the members until consensus is reached.

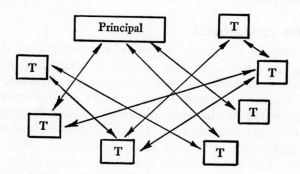

Fig. 20.   How the Conference Differs From the Lecture

5. When practical suggestions have been offered, the leader summarizes the discussion. The conclusions are clearly stated, and future action is outlined.
6. The conference is ended at the time scheduled.

The above principles of a good conference may be illustrated by proposing a topic for a conference of an elementary school principal with a group of staff members. Such a topic might be this: "With the increasing enrollments, the playground space is inadequate for recess periods as held in former years. How can we work out better arrangements for recess periods?" A group of teachers, preferably selected by the staff, meets with the principal to decide on a better recess arrangement. The topic is of concern to the teachers, and they are familiar enough with the situation to make practical suggestions. The principal's interest is to find a working solution, not to impose a preconceived plan, or she would merely publish the plan in a teachers' bulletin. When the group meets, the principal states the problem, keeps the discussion moving forward, sees that all the teachers have a chance to contribute, and summarizes the conclusions reached. The conclusions are put into a bulletin and distributed to the entire faculty. The action taken in such a case will be more acceptable to the teachers, because they have had a share in the decision. The action will also be better in itself, because the principal has utilized the ideas of several mature persons, rather than depending entirely upon her own judgment.

Conferences, then, have a specific objective — discussion resulting in decision and usually in action. Aimless conversation has no place in a conference; neither has the leader's manipulation of the group. The leader has faith in the group's ability to reach sound conclusions, and that faith is demonstrated in the courtesy and sincerity with which the meeting is conducted. A conference should end on a happy note, but time should not be wasted in pleasantries. A conference is a businesslike interchange of views among equals, but conducted by a professional leader according to accepted principles.

INDIVIDUAL CONFERENCES

The individual conference may differ somewhat from the above description of group conferences. The amount of democracy, or sharing of ideas, in the individual conference depends upon the situation. With a mature, qualified teacher, a principal can conduct a conference as with a coworker interested in the same objectives. It is refreshing for a principal to be able to say sincerely to a teacher, "Let us analyze together the work you are doing with your third group in reading." With almost complete objectivity (but never entirely complete!), the teacher will discuss the pupils' intelligence test scores and their reading achievement, the materials they are using at the time, and her plans for their future work. If the principal has noticed some expert teaching elsewhere in remedial reading, she may present the idea as a suggestion, but not one which she expects the teacher to use. With many teachers — we should like to think *most* teachers — the principal can conduct conferences in an entirely democratic way. In such instances, the criteria for group conferences apply completely.

With new teachers, however, and with weak teachers, such a show of democracy would be insincere. The conference would be a two-way process, in a sense, but it would be more of a learning situation for the teacher. The principal's approach would *not* be, "Here is a teaching technique which you may wish to use." Instead the principal's attitude would be, "To vary your presentation in arithmetic, I should like you to try this procedure. After my next visit to your class, we shall discuss together how effective you found it."

With beginning teachers especially, but with most teachers from time to time, the principal will conduct a post-visit conference that will be a learning situation for the teacher. Such conferences follow a definite pattern. The factors of time, place, and procedure are very important.

Time for Holding Individual Conferences. To be effective, a conference should be held shortly after classroom observation, but not before the principal has had time to prepare her notes for the conference. The record form given earlier provides most of the information which the principal needs to hold a profitable conference. Usually the conference lasts about half an hour, which is typically enough time for the principal and teacher to discuss the observed lesson. However, occasionally, because of the kind of lesson observed, or the needs of the teacher, a conference may last anywhere from ten minutes to an hour. The conference should not be rushed, but it should conform to the standards given earlier for a good conference. With teaching principals, the conference is held either after school or before school in the morning. As shown in the principal's schedule presented in Chapter V, conferences should also be scheduled in advance, and the time for conferences posted.

Place for Conferences. The teacher's classroom provides an informal atmosphere for a friendly conference, and also is convenient because the teacher's materials are readily available. However, usually the principal's office is the best place for conferences. There are fewer interruptions there, the tone is more formal, and the supervisor-teacher relationship is more clear. Especially when the conference is with a beginning or weak teacher should an instructional atmosphere be maintained. The principal is a busy person, and though she does not want to stress this fact, she must use her time efficiently in conducting conferences. The place of the conference has much to do with the effectiveness of her allotted time.

Procedure for Individual Conferences. The immediate pre-planning for the conference includes the principal's reviewing her conference record, both for the lesson just observed and for previous visits to the teacher. All materials needed for the discussion should be on hand; these materials include the course of study, textbooks and manuals, teacher's lesson plan book and lesson plan for the class observed, pupils' cumulative records, and any other data that seem pertinent.

The long-range planning for the conference includes a discussion with the teachers, both individually and in group meetings, of the particular criteria used to evaluate lessons. For example, the principal may wish to use *The Ohio Teaching Record* mentioned earlier and the standards developed in Chapter VIII. Also, faculty meetings may have been devoted to specific aspects of classroom procedures; these meeting notes may be utilized in evaluating the lesson observed. The principal should write down the particular points she intends to bring up during the conference. These should be carefully chosen, and few in number, probably not more than four or five.

In all previous contacts with the teacher and during the conference, the principal deals with the teacher in a friendly, interested, and professional way. Together, they are engaged in an important and serious work, yet a work which is at the same time interesting and challenging. The conference opens with some praise from the principal on the successful aspect of the lesson observed. Then the principal and teacher go over together the points selected for improvement. The principal's comments and suggestions must be specific and ones which the teacher is capable of carrying out. The conference continues with a joint evaluation by principal and teacher of other material, perhaps sections of Chapter VIII. The discussion must not wander; it should emphasize selected points, though the teacher should have an opportunity to comment and ask for assistance as needed. Follow-up suggestions are made by teacher and principal, and these suggestions are written down in the record of the conference. If it seems desirable, plans can be made for a demonstration lesson or particular help from the community or diocesan supervisor. It is good to have the teacher read over the record of the observation and the conference; some principals feel it clinches the experience if the teacher is given a copy of the record. The conference closes on a constructive and pleasant note.

THE INDIVIDUAL CONFERENCE

Teacher conferences fit into the principal's all-over supervisory objectives for the year. Her program includes the long-range objectives worked out through faculty meetings and small group work, as well as the day-today work in the individual classroom. Thus, in conducting individual conferences the principal should keep in mind that this conference is only one of many; each conference should be part of an ongoing plan to help the teacher improve her teaching. Therefore, the attitude of the principal and teacher toward the conference is of utmost importance. The teacher's active interest and effort to improve must be solicited, or there will be no improvement. As far as practical, the teacher should be helped to analyze her own teaching procedures, and suggest better ways of working. There should be a sequential development of the teacher from conference to conference. Suggestions that are just imposed upon the teacher remove the need for using her own judgment and implementing her own ideas. On the other hand, with teachers who are not adequately trained or who lack interest and drive, the principal will need to be firm about the minimum essentials in procedure. Good human relations must be maintained, and at the same time children must be assured a sound educational program. Individual teacher conferences give the principal the opportunity to work with each teacher in the way which will help her most. At the same time, through conferences the principal herself grows in professional competence. Principals learn from teachers during conferences how other teachers might be helped. Principals learn through conferences how to achieve the objectives of their supervisory program for the year, and how these objectives may need to be modified, enlarged, or extended.

DEMONSTRATION TEACHING AND INTERVISITATION

When asked what would help them most, teachers generally answer, "Watching a good teacher teach." Principals like to think that faculty meetings, professional reading, and conferences rate first place, but the teachers themselves universally favor demonstration lessons. The principal who observes classes regularly knows how much she herself learns. It stands to reason that other teachers would benefit from observing good teachers at work. Not that demonstration teaching overshadows all other methods for promoting the in-service growth of teachers. Rather, carefully planned demonstrations should be part of the principal's supervisory program for the year.

CHANGING ROLES OF DEMONSTRATIONS

The function of demonstration lessons has changed greatly over a period of years. Some time ago, demonstration lessons were needed to help poorly prepared teachers do their work. Very often, when the principal visited a class, the teacher would ask the principal to take over the group and show her how the lesson should be presented. Or, the principal or supervisor might present a typical procedure to a group of teachers, as at a Teachers' Institute. Thus, in the days of inadequate teacher training, a principal might have done demonstration teaching quite frequently for an individual teacher or for groups.

Gradually, however, it became evident that such demonstrations were not well advised. There were other urgent duties clamoring for the principal's time. Also, the principal was not always qualified to demonstrate techniques at all grade levels and in all subjects. And, since the level of teacher preparation was improving, the teachers themselves often did an outstanding job in their own classrooms. Thus, capable staff members began to assist in presenting good teaching techniques. Demonstration teaching passed largely out of the hands of the principal, and was taken on by teachers selected for superior work in special areas. When this happened, the auditorium was less used for demonstration lessons; instead, the demonstrating teacher played host to visiting teachers in her own classroom. Demonstration teaching came to be known as intervisitation, because classroom teachers had the opportunity to visit other classrooms. Demonstrations are effective during the student's training period, and also on the job. Intervisitation is no longer regarded only as a means of improving weak or new teachers; all teachers can profit from seeing superior teaching.

Because demonstrations are so effective in helping teachers, and are so well liked, the Sister Principal should consider carefully various ways of using this device to advantage.

WHEN TO USE DEMONSTRATIONS

Particularly with new teachers, or teachers returning to service, demonstration lessons are welcome. In this case, the demonstration, or intervisitation, should be given early in the year, and repeated as often as advisable to develop specific skills. Demonstrations are also helpful for experienced teachers in illustrating particular techniques, as, introducing a unit, using visual aids, and improving the art of questioning. In conferences and meetings, teachers often ask for help in making their work more effective. A well-chosen demonstration shows the teacher how to translate theory into satisfying everyday practice. Demonstrations are also enlightening to the entire faculty group, as demonstrations on the methods of teaching music at various grade levels. Parents report that their most enjoyable Home and School Meetings were those at which teachers showed how particular subjects were taught in the regular classroom. By instructing a reading group, for example, the teacher shows parents the methods used, and indirectly impresses parents with the good job the school is doing.

With beginning teachers, and those coming back into the classroom after a number of years, demonstration lessons are looked upon as a godsend.

Ordinarily, the principal needs only to plan carefully, and the teachers' receptiveness is assured. Having a Sister Adviser demonstrate techniques is genuinely appreciated by new teachers. However, with experienced teachers, even though they may not be strong teachers, the principal needs to wait for, or develop, a willingness to observe demonstration lessons. This is puzzling in a way. Experienced teachers want demonstrations, but usually from someone outside of their own faculty group. "No man is a prophet in his own country." The principal must be careful not to offend a teacher by implying that one of her peers does a much better job of teaching geography. Usually, the principal should not suggest that an experienced teacher observe in another classroom unless the teacher asks to do so. The principal's long-range supervisory program for the year might well include demonstration of techniques to the faculty as a group. Readiness for self-appraisal is necessary, however; the principal needs insight into her faculty before suggesting observations for experienced teachers.

HOW TO GET TIME FOR DEMONSTRATIONS

This is of course the crux of the matter. In the case of a teaching principal, a schedule of classroom observations might be worked out through careful planning. But to arrange that others leave their own classrooms to observe teaching — this is more difficult to plan. If the principal is convinced of the value of this device, certain plans will suggest themselves to her.

First, as mentioned earlier, *weekly religion periods taught by priests* do a double service for teachers. Children are better instructed in their Holy Faith, and teachers are released from the classroom one or two periods a week. These so-called "free" periods can be utilized to great advantage. Beginning teachers may observe in the classroom of a Sister Adviser, and the Sister Adviser may also visit the new teacher's room. Wherever possible, having several teachers observe at one time reduces the amount of preparation which the demonstrating teacher must make.

Teachers' Aides are also a fruitful source of help. When carefully selected and specifically trained, mothers may take over a classroom for a study period while a regular teacher is observing a lesson. In the more fortunate schools, a secretary's schedule can be arranged so that occasionally the secretary monitors a class during observation.

A device known as *"team teaching"* offers promise in this respect. The larger schools have two or more sections of the same grade. Perhaps once a month, two sections of upper grade pupils may be combined in a large room. The two teachers may take turns presenting a lesson, say in history or geography, in which various techniques may be used. Teacher A in the October "team teaching" period may use a panel of pupils discussing a problem currently studied in the text. Teacher B in the November "team teaching" period may develop certain difficult subject matter through the use of visual aids — flash cards, maps, models, pictures, and the like. The principal is a key figure in the effective use of "team teaching," for the participating teachers need careful guidance in choosing devices, planning the lessons to be presented, and evaluating results. The pupils should learn at least as much from these combined periods as during a normal period in their own classroom. The "team teachers," however, learn more than they would if working independently with their own classes.

Another device is to combine two or three classes to watch a pertinent educational film or filmstrip. Several groups of pupils may profitably watch a film on safety, on music appreciation, and on literature appreciation. As in "team teaching," one teacher might take charge of the period devoted to safety. This teacher would present the introduction to the film, and follow up the showing with a question or discussion period. The other teachers would be monitors, or assist as planned. Sometimes it has been possible to release one of the teachers whose group was present for this film, so that she can observe demonstration teaching in another classroom. When pupils are grouped together for instruction, however, discipline problems can negate any good results of the experiment. Important as it is for a teacher to observe demonstration teaching, it is never advisable to group pupils in situations in which they cannot learn well. Many factors need to be considered before combining classes for any purpose.

HOW TO USE DEMONSTRATIONS MOST EFFECTIVELY

It is a waste of time to release teachers to observe in classrooms unless the program has definite aims and expected outcomes. Teachers will not improve their teaching just by relaxing and examining the art display in someone else's classroom. The principal must plan well, if this activity really serves to improve teaching.

First, the principal should plan with the demonstrating teacher. Because the teacher is willing to spend a good deal of effort to help other teachers, the principal should try to foresee difficulties that might arise, and also to make the experience profitable for the teacher herself. Through her own observations and conferences, the principal knows what the teachers need and would like to see. This information, together with the teacher's own interest and skill, determines the type of lesson and the subject matter. Together the principal and teacher work out the lesson plan: the aims, content, and procedures. The lesson selected should be in correct sequence in the course of study, and the materials used should be typical. The lesson should cover only a limited amount of material; demonstrations are often spoiled because the teacher attempts too much. There should be no exhibitionism; the experience should be as normal as possible, prepared for but not rehearsed. Before a teacher gives a demonstration, the principal should see her present the same kind of lesson. In this way, the lesson will be made most beneficial to the visitors.

Besides the lesson itself, there are other aspects of teaching which observers will note: the attractiveness of the classroom, pupil papers, efforts at character development, such as courtesy, pupils' speaking in a clear voice, the teacher's deftness in moving from one part of the lesson to another, and the general tone of satisfaction and work which permeate the classroom. It is good to prepare an outline of points which the teacher should include in her preparation. Sometimes it is helpful to work out a guide for the discussion following the lesson — questions on the aspects mentioned above.

Second, the principal plans with the visiting teachers. At times, a demonstration may be given for a single observer; but wherever possible, more than one should be present to warrant the expenditure of the demonstrating teacher's time. Whatever the number, the principal holds a briefing session before the lesson. The principal and demonstrating teacher show how the lesson relates to the ongoing unit of work: the lessons that prepared the class for the day's work and the lessons that will follow. The lesson plan for the day is explained in some detail, and a copy of the plan given to the visitors. The visiting teachers are given pertinent facts about the class, and also a seating plan. The visitors may ask questions about the lesson and the class. The procedure for conducting the demonstration is next explained: how visitors are to enter and leave the room, how they are to observe but not interrupt the class.

After the lesson, the principal and demonstrating teacher hold a follow-up conference with the visitors. The purposes and activities of the lesson are reviewed; the visitors' questions are answered. Application is made between the lesson and the observers' work in their respective classrooms. In the case of beginning teachers, plans are made for follow-up observations of the techniques or procedures presented in the demonstration lesson. The visitors should take notes on the lesson observed, and file these notes as part of their professional growth record. The demonstration teacher should be prepared for some adverse criticism, or questions on other ways of achieving the aims of the lesson. Through experience in conducting conferences and in giving demonstrations, the teacher can learn to deal objectively with such questions.

A demonstration lesson should be prepared for and followed up in this manner. When so conducted, it is a time-consuming activity. Obviously, teachers who present demonstrations in this manner are bound to increase their professional stature. That is their reward. Those who come to observe will necessarily learn new techniques and procedures, and may also be rewarded by finding their own teaching similar to that observed. Properly conducted, demonstration lessons, or intervisitations, are a valuable in-service growth activity and not old-fashioned in the least.

IN-SERVICE COLLEGE COURSES

Ideally, all teachers have a degree in elementary education before they begin to teach. Practically, however, this is not always so. Many teachers continue to work toward a degree while engaged in full-time teaching. For such teachers, the principal should establish certain regulations. For one thing, first-year teachers should not be permitted to enroll in any college courses during their first semester of teaching, and then should take no more than three semester hours of credit during the second semester. Teachers of longer experience should be restricted to six hours of credit during a semester. This regulation is made first of all in fairness to the children, for children deserve the services of a teacher who has had adequate time for class preparation, and who also is refreshed at the beginning of the school day. In justice to the teacher, too, only a reasonable college load should be undertaken. Health, mental and physical, suffers from too heavy a college load.

"Credit chasing," a problem in some public school systems because added credits mean added pay, also affects parochial school lay teachers in systems having a salary scale. Teachers with more credits, other things being equal, are better teachers; hence, they deserve higher salary. However, the above regulations about college load should control the "credit chasing" to a certain extent.

On the other hand, there is a real value in the teacher's continuing to grow through professional study. At least every five years, a teacher should take a refresher course. This renews her contacts with research and professors, and provides association with other teachers. A college course in child psychology or mental hygiene can open up a whole new world of ideas. Both the teachers themselves and their pupils benefit by the course.

In-service college courses, taken during regular terms or in summer sessions, and particularly summer workshops, are effective means of continuing individual advancement.

PROFESSIONAL READING

We like to think of the Catholic school teacher as a well-read person. Many principals' offices and teachers' lounges display an attractive array of professional literature. Yet, the truth of the matter is, as teachers themselves confess, they don't read enough. In fact, the principal need only look back over her own reading habits to know that reading needs encouragement.

But — how encourage professional reading among teachers? In earlier times, there were the Reading Circles and Book Clubs, in which a teacher was required to read a certain number of books and magazines, write out a review, and receive a rating. That device probably encouraged some reading in the days of meager pre-service training; teachers woefully needed to read something. However, the plan had its defects, as all of us know who have ever tried to get children to make book reviews.

The inventive principal today doesn't abandon all hope of stimulating reading among her staff. Instead, she tries a variety of devices, and keeps on trying, for reading is essential to self-improvement. First and foremost, if teachers are to read, there must be a pleasant place, comfortably furnished and well lighted. Right along with this, there must be an array of interesting material. These books should be on various topics — reference books in the various subjects, particularly in religion, and fresh and interesting books on professional subjects. Professional magazines have a prominent role in the teachers' library, for they invite reading on budgeted time. A good encyclopedia is an asset, as are a dictionary, Bible, and atlas. It is practical to have there a complete set of the textbooks used in the school so that teachers may see how the work of their grade compares with work in earlier and later grades. Many parochial school principals have found fiction attractive to their teachers, as well as a good biography or two. The school library is not meant to supplant the local public library, but it is a well-known fact that a book at hand is more likely to be read than a book on the shelves of a distant library.

In addition to providing a pleasant library corner and selected books and magazines, the principal needs to invent devices for getting the material used by the staff. In preparation for faculty meetings, the principal assembles a kit of interesting and helpful pamphlets, articles, and books, all marked for easy consumption. A faculty committee can keep alive a bulletin board devoted to encouraging reading — clippings of articles and pertinent book reviews, all of which must be on the faculty bookshelf if they are to be helpful. During a teacher conference, the principal has occasion to suggest references but she must be sure that the material is simple, pertinent, and ready at hand. Lay teachers in one school had the commendable practice of buying one recommended book each semester. Then they exchanged books among themselves, so that they had a full year of the best reading for about $8 each. Then these devoted lay teachers donated the books to the faculty library. In another school, a teacher group undertook to make up a file of the best articles from the professional magazines to which the school subscribed. Articles which the teachers considered first-rate were clipped, filed in manila folders according to subject, and an alphabetical list of title and author was made for quick reference. During the year, about thirty articles were filed in this top-priority drawer. These were the most-used part of the teachers' library.

Principals have long used the device of marking an especially good article, and routing it among the teachers, or sending it to a teacher who might be especially interested. A guest speaker at the faculty meeting can do much to stimulate professional reading, particularly if he suggests specific books and articles.

Like any other device for self-improvement, professional reading needs to be motivated. The strongest of all motivations is the influence of a principal who reads. There is an irresistible force in being with a principal who has read the books and magazines herself, who knows them intimately, and who uses them. *The principal who reads is likely to have a faculty who reads.*

FOR THE PRINCIPAL'S PROFESSIONAL LIBRARY

The most helpful single reference on modern *supervision* is Wiles Kimball, *Supervision for Better Schools,* 2nd ed. rev. (Englewood Cliffs, N. J.: Prentice-Hall, Inc., 1955), 399 pp., $4. The principal will want to become familiar with this book. Although there are some techniques, the emphasis is on the philosophy underlying democratic supervision. The principal cannot be quite as "democratic" as the supervisor here presented, but there is real value in understanding what the good principal can accomplish.

Principals can improve their *meetings* by using the ideas suggested in: Strauss, Bert and Frances, *New Ways to Better Meetings* (New York: Viking Press, 1952), 240 pp., $2.95.

Hader, John, *Better Staff Meetings — And You,* Personal Leaflet No. 5, Society for Personnel Administration, 5506 Connecticut Avenue, N.W., Washington 15, D. C., 1957, 8 pp., 20 cents.

Oncken, William, Jr., *You Are a Better Speaker Than You Think,* Personnel Leaflet No. 4, Society for Personnel Administration, 5506 Connecticut Avenue, N.W., Washington 15, D. C., 1957, 13 pp., 20 cents.

How to encourage *discussion* during faculty meetings? There are several inexpensive pamphlets which help:

Adult Education Association of the United States. *How to Lead Discussions,* Leadership Pamphlet No. 1, 743 N. Wabash Avenue, Chicago 11, 48 pp., 60 cents.

Junior Town Meeting League, 356 Washington Street, Middleton, Conn. *Learning Through Group Discussion,* 1949, 31 pp., 10 cents.

Let's Have a Discussion, n.d., 4 pp., $1 per hundred.

Youth Discussion; Patterns and Techniques, 1953, 32 pp., 10 cents.

National Congress of Parents & Teachers, 700 N. Rush St., Chicago, Ill., *New Hope for Audiences,* 1954, 48 pp., 40 cents.

Conferences can be improved by following suggestions offered in Adams, Harold P., and Dickey, Frank G., *Basic Principles of Supervision,* pp. 125–167 (New York: American Book Company, 1953), 320 pp., $3.75.

CHAPTER X

PROMOTING THE IN-SERVICE GROWTH OF TEACHERS (Continued)

Anything worth doing should be planned. Why? How should lessons be planned? Can the same approach to lesson planning be used in all subjects? What are signs of a good lesson plan? What special problems confront a new teacher in a school? How can a principal help a new teacher to become oriented? Should teachers be evaluated? If so, why and how? What criteria should be used in evaluating teaching?

HELP WITH LESSON PLANNING

OCCASIONALLY, a provocative writer in education may seem to disparage daily lesson planning, but by and large, lesson planning is recognized as a key factor in successful teaching. Help with lesson planning, then, is an important service which principals can render.

Immediately, problems present themselves. Teacher A has been teaching over twenty years; she used to write out lesson plans, but now she knows the work so well she "just teaches," to use her own words. Teacher B is new, in her first year, but she is carrying college courses, and she just doesn't have time to write out daily lesson plans. Teacher C loves projects, but doesn't organize them well enough to manage a systematic scheduling of her time. Teacher D has just come from long experience in a campus laboratory school, where a great deal of emphasis was placed on lesson planning with student teachers. The principal may have on her staff at one time all these teachers, with widely different attitudes toward lesson planning. Can the principal give specific help in lesson planning?

REGULATIONS OF RELIGIOUS COMMUNITIES

When the religious community has a definite policy on lesson planning, the Sister Principal's way is paved for her. In some communities, Sisters make out detailed daily lesson plans for the first five years of teaching, and submit them to the principal weekly for suggestions. For the next ten years, a less detailed plan is made, but is given to the principal weekly as before. After fifteen years, the *kind* of plan becomes optional, but some kind of plan is made for each day's work; the plan book is made available to principal and supervisors during classroom observation. Where such a system is in effect, the principal can readily keep in touch with the procedures and materials being used by all the Sisters in the school. The lesson plan book serves as a guide to observations, conferences, and to in-service work generally.

Such a system makes it easy for the principal to improve planning. For one thing, the principal herself learns a great deal about planning through a study of the plans submitted to her. Also, plan books can be used as examples of particularly effective work at the various grade levels. New teachers have the opportunity to examine completed plan books in order to study techniques, the use of materials, and aspects of daily and long-range planning. The practice within the religious community has a strong influence on the quality of plans generally, and also upon the success of the principal's work with planning.

THE NEED FOR PLANNING

However, even if the community does not have an established routine for making and evaluating lesson plans, the principal as supervisor must emphasize planning as basic to good teaching. It would seem natural, for example, to pair off Teacher D, with her long campus school experience, as an adviser to Teacher B, who neglects daily planning in order to accumulate college credits. Older teachers would not engage the principal's direct attention; but indirectly, as through faculty meetings, even older teachers can be helped to improve their planning. Lesson planning is an essential to good teaching as an architect's sketch is to building. Understandingly, but perseveringly, the principal must work to improve the planning which teachers do.

Since the principal's time will be limited, her attention can best be focused on beginning teachers. Certainly, with the ever-growing number of lay teachers in Catholic schools, there will be beginning lay teachers on most school staffs. These new lay teachers, in addition to new religious, may form a considerable portion of the faculty. The principal's work with them can be very effective, both for their own professional development, and for the good of the children. Teachers with adequate pre-service training have completed their student teaching; but in these days of teacher shortage, many teachers are entering classrooms without student teaching. And, even in the case of certificated beginning teachers, the campus school situation was quite different from their present assignment. All beginning teachers need specific direction in lesson planning; some need more help than others, and some need help over a longer period. The principal need have no misgivings about emphasizing lesson planning with new teachers. She would be wise not to stifle initiative, of course, by too rigid regulations on planning. The highly capable and well-prepared beginning teacher should be allowed full scope for her talents, but within the school's policy on lesson planning.

BACKGROUND FOR THE DAILY LESSON PLAN

To construct a good daily lesson plan, the teacher needs a broad background of information. She needs, first of all, to become acquainted with the course of study, textbooks, and teachers' manuals for the grade. She needs to study the cumulative records of her pupils, and to consider materials and procedures adapted to individual differences. She needs, further, to plan an overview of the semester's work, and a more detailed outline of the units as they occur. Into every lesson plan, the good teacher puts the broad background she has developed through study, observation, and personal experience.

The Course of Study and the Textbooks. Some of the recent writers might object to beginning the discussion of planning with materials they consider incidental. The course of study and textbooks are used, in some situations, only as resources to be referred to as occasion demands. Beginning teachers, however, are not in a position to experiment broadly with the curriculum. Many experienced supervisors feel that the beginning teacher can be most helped by working within the course of study and the textbooks used in the system. An "experience" unit, for example a study of space ships quite apart from the regular course of study, can undermine order and bring frustration to a beginning teacher. Hence, supervisors advise beginners to undertake these "experience" units cautiously. Perhaps during the second semester, if the teacher has promoted good pupil self-control, one or two such "experience" units might be carried out. The beginner should not be too eager to "try her wings" with these more difficult teaching procedures until she has learned how to use the course of study and textbooks with assurance.

This decision implies, then, emphasis on subject matter. The new teacher needs to determine what the children of her grade should achieve in each subject during the year. Detailed objectives for each subject will be found in the course of study and the textbooks or manuals. The course of study might also show the emphasis which the particular school system places on certain learnings or activities. The teacher should also learn at least in a general way, how the objectives for her grade fit into the sequential pattern of development. What did the children learn in arithmetic last year? What will they be taught next year? How does the music outline for this year lay the groundwork for next year's work? To reason this through, the teacher will divide her work into a long-range semester outline and also a unit outline.

A Semester Overview. It is very useful to be able to see at a glance what the children will learn in each subject during a given semester. Such planning prevents the shock of discovering that one is far behind expected achievement or the equally painful shock of "finishing the book" in April. Beginning teachers who fail to make a semester outline have been known to go to both extremes. If the course of study does not do so, the new teacher should write down a semester overview for each subject. With the help of an experienced person, the teacher can apportion the material wisely, omitting or skimming the less important content, and selecting activities judiciously. It is not the pages covered, but the amount of learning that indicates the success of a teacher. However, a semester outline such as the following will help the new teacher to succeed in at least the essentials.

SUGGESTED SEMESTER OUTLINE

Chapter	Subject Matter	Manual	Workbook	Time
I pp. 1–43	Review addition, subtraction, multiplication, and division of whole numbers.	pp. 20–63	pp. 1–26	2 weeks
II pp. 44–95	Review division with 2-place divisors. Introduce 3-place divisors.	pp. 64–111	pp. 27–51	6 weeks
III pp. 96–129	Review and extend fraction meanings. Addition and subtraction of fractions and mixed numbers.	pp. 112–145	pp. 52–69	4 weeks
IV pp. 130–173	Introduce multiplication of fractions and mixed numbers. Scale drawing.	pp. 146–187	pp. 70–88	5 weeks

The teacher will want her pupils to achieve mastery in this basic content, to be sure, but she will also enrich her program with varied and interesting activities and materials. The more capable teachers will accomplish more; but all teachers must accomplish at least the above minimum.

The Unit Outline. The next step in remote preparation is the analysis of each unit of work. As mentioned earlier, subject-matter units are being emphasized here for the sake of the beginning teacher. Textbooks and courses of study are typically organized into subject-matter units. Though the beginner must proceed slowly, still her general approach to teaching should be based on the "unit" idea. Since suggestions for developing units are given in a number of excellent sources (see references at end of chapter), only a brief discussion will be included here for the principal's guidance of the new teacher. Each unit of every subject should ideally be so analyzed before the teacher begins the unit. Obviously, the suggestions which follow apply particularly to such subjects as the social studies, science, and religion. The other areas must be prepared somewhat differently, though the suggestions given here can help direct the new teacher to prepare more effective lesson plans in general.

Planning a Typical Ten-Day Unit in Content Subjects
Guide for Beginning Teachers

1. BEGINNING THE UNIT (two class periods)

    FIRST DAY — ORIENTATION

    The teacher arouses interest and provides background for the unit.
    The teacher lists possible devices, and then places a ✔ before those she will use.

    ✔ a. Exhibit or bulletin board display
       b. Filmstrip or movie
       c. Story
    ✔ d. Pupil discussion
       e. Books and magazines
    ✔ f. Pre-test of the material to be taught
    ✔ g. Overview of the material

    SECOND DAY — PLANNING AND ORGANIZING

    Teacher and pupils will suggest topics and questions to be studied and the ways of working. The teacher will have studied carefully the text and manual. The four aspects to be decided upon and clarified are these:

    a. Objectives — expected outcomes in information, skills, and personal-social traits (The teachers' manual usually provides help here.)
    b. Activities — the various ways in which they will achieve their objectives (for example, textbook study, reports, dramatizations)
    c. Sources of information — texts, maps, movies, field trips. The teacher will have prepared a list of materials and collected most of these beforehand. The pupils may supply additional materials as the unit progresses.
    d. Methods of work — planning and forming committees, stating rules of working together

2. BODY OF THE UNIT (six class periods)

    Using the text and manual, and suggestions made during the planning period, the new teacher decides to handle the class periods as follows:

Class Period	Pages in Text	Type of Lesson
Third	45–48	Explanatory
Fourth	48–49	Directed Group Reading of Text
Fifth	49–53	Guided Individual Reading of Text
Sixth	48–53	Discussion — "Panel of Experts"
Seventh	53–56	Explanatory
Eight	45–56	Drill — "Quiz Box" and "Matching Cards"

The type of lesson used will depend upon the nature and difficulty of the material. On the third and seventh days, the material requires teacher explanation. (In the next section, "Steps in the Daily Lesson Plan," the teacher receives suggestions for the individual class lesson outlined above.)

3. CONCLUDING THE UNIT (two class periods)

NINTH DAY — SHARING PERIOD

Pupils will share their information and experiences through one or more of the following activities. The activities checked are the ones tentatively decided upon by the teacher in her pre-planning.

   ✔ a. Reports of individuals and of committees
      b. Stories they have written or read
   ✔ c. Notebooks and scrapbooks
   ✔ d. Dramatizations and impersonations
      e. Drawings and paintings
      f. Songs learned

TENTH DAY — EVALUATION

Teachers and pupils will judge how much they have learned and how well they have worked during the unit. Their evaluation will include each objective set up during the planning period, the second day of the unit.

      a. Information — teacher test on material covered
      b. Skills — discussion of specific skills being stressed during the unit, as skill in locating information
      c. Social objectives — discussion of the class's measuring up to their standards and the teacher's in such areas as courtesy, work habits, co-operation, responsibility

When the teacher plans her work in advance, as indicated in the above preliminary unit planning, she can see how much material should be taught each day and what procedures would be best to use. Long-range planning, even of the simple kind illustrated above, will prevent many difficulties and discipline problems for the new teacher.

Teachers' Manuals. The newer teachers' manuals provide a wealth of suggestions for all teachers, but especially for beginning teachers. A well-planned manual would probably include such a long-range plan as that given above. The manuals, in addition, often include helpful pupil and teacher bibliographies, sources of free and inexpensive materials, and appropriate activities. Despite the careful workmanship of the typical teachers' manuals, teachers don't use them enough. This is especially true of beginning teachers, who feel that they have all they can do to master the material in the textbook. The principals will be performing a real service by showing the teacher the helpfulness of the manuals.

Manuals that accompany the reading series are particularly important. Each step of the lesson is worked out by experts, repetition of vocabulary is assured, and there is variety of presentation. By following her reading manual consistently, the teacher can be sure that her pupils will progress satisfactorily. Teachers' manuals are so essential to good teaching that there should be two available for each teacher: one set for home use and one set for school. The same applies to textbooks as well. Because of the importance of texts and manuals, the set for school use should be kept in the place assigned, so that it will be available at all times, such as for use by a substitute teacher, and for reference during conferences.

Pupil Records as a Background for Lesson Planning. All the effort that goes into teaching has only one purpose: that children may learn to the best of their ability. The preceding discussion introduced briefly the value of the course of study, textbooks, and manuals, the semester overview and the unit outline. These materials and devices can effectively promote pupil learning, but only if adapted to the needs of the pupils as a class and as individuals.

Careful and repeated study of pupil records is needed if the teacher is to adapt her instruction to the children she is teaching. Scores on standardized achievement tests furnish guides, as do also intelligence test scores. Data on home background and the child's progress through school also supply clues; notes and correspondence in the pupil's folder supplement the recorded information.

A study of this information gives insight into the child's work in school, his attitudes, and his achievement. When a teacher has "in the head" knowledge of each pupil, she can note danger signals immediately. Daydreaming, restlessness, careless work, absence, attention-getting mechanisms — are all signs that children need understanding and help. The new teacher, instead of being alert to these signs of trouble, tends to follow her lesson plan rigidly. Intelligent study of pupil records will guide the teacher in planning, and in modifying her plans so that children will receive optimal benefit. Her own observation should be used to supplement, and even correct, the information where needed.

Appropriate Materials. The principal and the new teacher may well plan together how to get the maximum use of the instructional materials available. Pictures, film strips, movies, exhibits, resource people, library books — all can be had in practically any school situation. The materials purchased by the school can be supplemented by materials from the library, museum, local public school board, and other sources. The new teacher needs to be shown how the materials can enrich her teaching, when the materials might best be used, how to obtain them, and how to care for them.

Through the teacher's ingenuity, her own file of appropriate materials can be built up. The bulletin boards in her classroom are one indication of her resourcefulness. Not all lessons require special instructional materials, but concrete and timely aids do add to both interest and retention. Perhaps, through class demonstration, the principal can show the new teacher the effectiveness of well-chosen and properly used instructional materials.

STEPS IN THE DAILY LESSON PLAN

Having developed the background indicated, the teacher is ready to concentrate on a plan for an individual class lesson. She first notes the daily and weekly time allotment for each subject, and plans within this framework. There is rather general agreement on the necessary steps in a good lesson plan. The outline given below can be used for a detailed lesson plan for a single class period.

Figure 21

PLAN FOR A CLASS PERIOD

Subject.................................. Time............ Date............

Subject Matter   Text pp. ...... Manual pp. ...... Workbook pp. ....

                      Topic for Today..

Type of Lesson   ....

Objectives   1..

                      2..

Materials to be used ....

                      ....

Procedure

    1. Approach

    2. Presentation

    3. Summary, checkup, application

        Assignment, if any

Reminders

Evaluation of plan

                    Teacher's Name..................................

The above "Plan for a Class Period" should be worked out in detail by a new teacher for several classes each week. It is good if a detailed plan like this is prepared for the class which the principal or adviser is to observe. It is easier to help a beginning teacher when one knows just what she is attempting to do.

The proposed form above follows the *S T O M P* pattern, used extensively at St. John College of Cleveland and elsewhere. The initials *S T O M P* stand for the major headings of the plan: subject matter, type, objectives, materials, and procedure. By using this form, all the necessary information is included. The teacher would not, of course, have time to work out such a detailed lesson plan for each class every day, but the beginning teacher would profit by preparing detailed plans frequently during each week.

The most important part of the plan is the procedure. Like any well-planned action, the procedure has a beginning, a middle, and an end. Brief consideration will be given to each of these parts.

The Approach. A carefully planned lesson begins with an approach, or a motivation to arouse interest. The teacher does not actually prepare the approach first; she works on the presentation until that has taken shape, and only then decides on an interest-getting device. However, as the logical first part, the approach is being discussed first.

The approach should be brief (not more than two or three minutes long), and easy to understand. To prepare a good approach, the teacher must know her class well, and also her material. What are some possible approaches?

1. An anecdote, humorous or sad, as need be, but interesting, is one of the most effective approaches. Well-known public speakers use the anecdote skillfully. Teachers should keep a file of anecdotes; a "just right" little story is priceless.
2. A pertinent item of local or national news
3. A question phrased to direct class thinking along certain lines
4. A well-chosen picture, cartoon, map, or object related to the lesson
5. An attractive bulletin board display, as for the beginning of a unit
6. A display of library books related to the topic under discussion

However, to find a good approach takes time, time which a busy classroom teacher cannot get every day. So, the teacher should not expect to captivate her class with an excellent approach for each lesson. Very often, the teacher presents one or two sentences summarizing the previous content, and then gives a simple introductory sentence linking previous material with the content for the day. Showmanship is an asset in teaching, but children do not expect, or need, continual high-pressured motivation. A word of warning should be given the new teacher about farfetched, artificial, and false motivations. An approach which arouses interest in itself rather than in the lesson detracts from the presentation. If the teacher promises "surprises," invariably the children are disappointed. The reward of learning should be the learning itself, not some extrinsic attraction.

The Presentation. By far the most important part of the lesson, and the longest, is the presentation, or the explanation, as it is sometimes called. The principal will want to show the teacher, and perhaps to demonstrate in a class situation, that there must be "body" or substance to each lesson. Each lesson should result in definite learning and should show progress in achieving the goals of the course.

In her presentation, the teacher will use a combination of the following methods:

1. Lecture, but briefly! The child's attention span is short.
2. Tell an illustrative story (again, brief and pointed)
3. Demonstrate at the chalkboard
4. Ask skillful questions

    There should never be a whole period of teacher questioning. Questions should lead developmentally from what the children know to the new material the teacher wishes to present.

5. Use the textbook with the class
    a) Directed reading of the text using a list of previously written-out questions prepared by the teacher. The class as a group locates and an individual child reads answers orally when textual material is difficult and requires explanation and interpretation.
    b) Independent reading of the text and related reference materials. This reading is to be guided by a list of questions or problems.

6. Have pupil discussion (previously prepared for)
    a) Following either directed or independent reading of the text. The study guide questions form the basis for the pupils' contributions.
    b) Devices such as the panel of experts, the round table, or the individual pupil reports furnish material to stimulate class discussion.
    c) Problem-solving situations. The class and the teacher propose a list of problems which the children answer from the content just studied. Reference to the class text and related material provides definite answers to the problem-situations. For example, in a study of the Third Commandment, a problem for the young child might be: "Martha felt sick on Sunday morning, and did not go to Mass. Should her mother let Martha go to the show in the afternoon?"

7. Use pupil committees

    Pupils in small groups may work together on a map, a play, a report, a notebook, a test, an experiment.

8. Use audio-visual aids, such as pictures, filmstrips, or objects
9. Provide varied and interesting drill devices at spaced intervals

    Games such as question box, matching flash cards, completing sentences, map locations, "Who am I?" Many of the games used on television can be adapted to the classroom situation. The new teacher should be cautioned to make the "game" subordinate to the practice in factual material.

10. Evaluate pupil progress

    Formal tests may be used, as well as check lists and pupil self-evaluation. The standards set up by the class for giving a report, for example, are a practical means of pupil evaluation.

Probably, a careful combination of several methods would be most effective. Variety is important in keeping the pupils' attention and helping them to learn, but the new teacher should not clutter her lesson with too many things. In the presentation, the new teacher should list in detail the steps she plans to take in achieving the objectives of the lesson. Nothing should be left to chance. "The secret to success is excess." The new teacher should actually overplan in order to be sure that pupils will be busy learning every minute of the class period.

The Summary, Checkup, Application. The third step in the procedure brings the lesson to a purposeful close. The summary allows the class, under teacher direction, to recall the main points of the lesson, and thus to fix them more firmly in mind. The beginning teacher needs to see how the summary relates to the objectives of the lesson: the objectives are developed in the presentation, and the summary now re-phrases and epitomizes these objectives. Like the approach, the summary should be brief and brisk.

The old recipe for a successful talk applies to a class lesson: "First tell them what you're going to tell them; then tell them; then tell them that you told them." The approach, presentation, and summary carry out this homely directive.

Instead of a summary, some lessons will have only an application of the content to the child's life; religion lessons especially require purposeful applications. Some lessons will have an assignment to provide further practice or enrichment. Ideally, the assignment is an outgrowth of the lesson and not "busy work." After using a plan, the teacher should evaluate it, see what modifications she had to make, and then file the plan for future reference. Though she will not use the plan again exactly as she did the first time, it will be a guide in presenting a future lesson.

A SIMPLIFIED DAILY PLAN

As noted above, a detailed lesson plan cannot be prepared for each class of the day, though detailed plans should be made out frequently. For the most part, the elementary teacher needs an outline form which can be filled in more quickly. Figure 22 (p. 252) is a form which can be dittoed for teacher use. This form contains the essential parts of a lesson plan, but requires less writing than that in Figure 21.

A CHECK LIST ON LESSON PLANNING

In discussing lesson planning, the principal will be helped by a check list which covers the major aspects of planning. The check list below may be useful in conducting a co-operative evaluation of a teacher's plans.

A. Semester overview of the course
    1. Is proper time allotted to each phase of the course?
    2. Is satisfactory progress being made in keeping to this outline?
B. Unit outline
    1. Is the unit outline in keeping with the time allotment given in the semester overview?

Figure 22

Day.............   DAILY LESSON PLAN   Date.............

	CONTENT	PROCEDURE
Subject	Objectives	
Time		
Text | W.B. | Manual P..... | P..... | P..... Topic for Class	Materials to be used	
Type of Lesson		Assignment
	CONTENT	PROCEDURE
Subject	Objectives	
Time		
Text | W.B. | Manual P..... | P..... | P..... Topic for Class	Materials to be used	
Type of Lesson		Assignment
	CONTENT	PROCEDURE
Subject	Objectives	
Time		
Text | W.B. | Manual P..... | P..... | P..... Topic for Class	Materials to be used	
Type of Lesson		Assignment
	CONTENT	PROCEDURE
Subject	Objectives	
Time		
Text | W.B. | Manual P..... | P..... | P..... Topic for Class	Materials to be used	
Type of Lesson		Assignment

2. Is there a realistic allotment of content to each class period?
3. Is there provision for a variety of teacher procedure and pupil activity during the unit?
4. Are the materials appropriate, varied, and interesting?
5. Do tests and observations show satisfactory pupil progress in attaining the goals of the unit?

C. Daily lesson plans
1. Do daily plans follow the recommended procedure?
2. Does the typical class lesson show clearly the three essential parts: motivation, explanation, and summary?
3. Do daily plans show the teacher's awareness of the needs of the class as a group and as individuals?
4. Are daily plans modified, when necessary, to meet pupil needs better?
5. Are daily plans related to the previous day's work and to the work of the following day?
6. Are the assignments an outgrowth of class work, and differentiated according to pupil needs?
7. Is there sufficient information given in plans for a substitute teacher to use readily?
8. In the lesson observed, was the lesson plan followed closely?

D. Lesson planning — general
1. Does the plan book show interested effort?
2. Are daily plans made out a week in advance?
3. Is the plan book submitted to the principal or adviser as required?
4. Is the plan book available to supervisors during classroom observation?
5. Do plans show that the teacher has profited by suggestions made on previous occasions?

The discussion on lesson planning has emphasized helping the new teachers. However, experienced teachers often want some fresh ideas on lesson planning. The lesson plan form in Figure 22 may be acceptable to older as well as younger teachers. On occasion, the faculty may welcome a talk by a guest on such a topic as "Fresh and Interesting Classroom Materials," or "How to Enliven Your Classes with Illustrations," or "Your Pupils Will Read More — If You Let Them." All of these, and similar topics, relate directly to lesson planning; all are aspects of good planning.

A direct frontal attack on the lesson planning of experienced teachers is probably unwise. The old adage, "You can lead a horse to water but you can't make him drink," is true, but one can also add, "No, but you can make him thirsty." Teachers are in teaching because they love teaching and want to be good teachers. In her work on planning, the principal can at least try to make her staff *thirsty* to improve pupil learning through better planning.

ORIENTATION OF NEW TEACHERS

"Orientation" includes all types of help given to new teachers to help them adjust to their position more rapidly and more successfully. Some kinds of orientation come under the heading of *administration*. For example, in order to help a new teacher fit into the school program smoothly from the start, the principal furnishes some orientation in matters of schedule, routines, and policies. Orientation is also concerned with helping new teachers to teach better. When new teachers are assisted with classroom methods, for example, this is a *supervisory* service. Since the present chapter is emphasizing the principal's role in improving instruction, the discussion of orientation will deal with supervisory aspects.

WHY ORIENTATION?

Just a few years ago, orientation was practically unknown in most schools. When a new teacher came, she was given some information about the school, but very little specific direction. She usually learned the "hard way," figuring out what she could, and asking questions only if she couldn't solve her problems alone. In this process of trial-and-error, a good deal of time and effort was lost; and as veteran teachers have testified, there were many unnecessary headaches and heartaches.

When schools weren't expanding so rapidly as they are now, this situation didn't seem critical. There might be a new teacher only once every few years. Particularly in parochial schools, the "new teacher" problem wasn't keenly felt, for the staff was made up largely of Sisters. Being members of the same religious community, the Sisters had a way of orienting one another to new situations, at least in the externals. With rapid school expansion, however, the situation has changed. For one thing, since there aren't enough Sisters, many new lay teachers are being added each year to take care of new classrooms opened. Right along with this, there is also a high rate of lay teachers leaving the parochial schools each year. "Turnover," the rate of teachers leaving the system, began to affect parochial schools seriously only with the introduction of a large percentage of lay teachers. It is well established that women teachers usually don't plan to make teaching their lifework. Hence, lay teachers tend to remain in parochial schools only a few years, on the average. Expansion and turnover are two reasons for the many new lay teachers in parochial schools each fall.

Particularly because of the many new lay teachers each year, parochial schools need to consider the problem of orientation. This is so, first, because new teachers need direction generally. More than that, new teachers in parochial schools need particular assistance because of the specific objectives of Catholic education. We need hardly deny the fact that parochial schools exist in order to give children the very best education possible. The parochial school program should include the offerings of the public school, and in addition, a religious education which will teach the child how to know, love, and serve God better. These objectives are so tremendous, and so difficult to attain, that nothing can be left to chance. Certainly, the program cannot be left in the hands of new teachers without specific guidance. The religious community staffing the school has taken on the responsibility to achieve the objectives of a Catholic education for all the pupils. The Sister Principal, then, and the religious staff members have a clear-cut duty with regard to teacher orientation. Beginning Sisters need special orientation, but lay teachers need this help even more. Only by a planned induction program can the school effectively provide a truly Catholic education for all the pupils.

THE TIME ELEMENT

To orient new teachers takes time. With many parochial school principals also responsible for their own classroom, orientation seems like an impossible burden. Two new Sisters and five new lay teachers this year? How can the principal, even a supervising principal, provide adequate induction helps for all these new teachers? The answer is — she can't. By herself, she simply cannot take on the added duty of directing new teachers as they would need to be directed if the aims of Catholic education are to be achieved by each of them. The principal might try to fit new teachers into her time scheduled for supervision, but the time would not be adequate.

Even before parochial schools were as large as they now typically are, this problem was faced by the religious community. For half a century at least, some religious communities have had a planned orientation program for their beginning Sisters. For every Sister going out to teach for the first time, a companion-Sister, or helping-teacher, was assigned. This helper was herself a successful teacher of considerable experience; one of her chief duties for the year was to see that the beginning Sister learned how to conduct a class, how to guide and direct children, and how to transmit the ideals of Catholic education as expressed in community traditions and rules. The principal, as head of the school, supplied direction to the Sister-helper, but the detail work was done by the Sister-helper personally. In many cases, this work occupied several hours a week and included all phases of classroom instruction.

Recent literature shows that this "helper" idea has also been found successful in public schools.[1] The "buddy" system, it is sometimes called. Many

---

[1] Research on teacher orientation includes of course many aspects of the program. The "buddy" system is mentioned in the following studies in some detail:

California Teachers Association, *Teacher Orientation in California Elementary Schools*, Bulletin No. 78 (Nov., 1954).

National Education Association, Research Division, "First-Year Teachers in 1954–55," *Research Bulletin*, XXXIV, No. 1 (Feb., 1956).

of the functions performed by the Sister-helper are also taken on by an older public school teacher who directs the orientation of a beginning teacher. Where this "buddy" system is well carried out, beginning teachers feel that their needs are adequately provided for. Principals, too, welcome the help given by a staff member, who actually may be better able than the principal to answer detailed questions on classroom procedures and materials.

In parochial schools, where the principal's time is at a premium, this companion-teacher idea is the answer to the question of time for orientation. The principal, as head of the school, remains in charge of all direction given; but the time-consuming aspects can be delegated to a competent, experienced staff member. This delegation of responsibility to a Sister Adviser enables the principal to concentrate on large supervisory objectives, while the face-to-face work in orientation is taken over by the principal's representative, the adviser.

TWO BASIC CONSIDERATIONS

Granted that there must be orientation, and that a companion-teacher is the answer to prayer, how can the principal judge the *amount* of orientation needed by the teacher? As with children, one could go to the extreme of saying, "Every teacher is different. Each must be treated individually." However, we know that despite individual differences children can be grouped for instruction. Teachers, too, can be classified according to objective criteria; college training and teaching experience are generally accepted as sound criteria for grouping teachers. In fact, public school salary scales single out these criteria when determining how much money a given teacher should be paid. The salary scale given in Chapter VI, for example, shows how the public school teacher's salary goes up each year by definite increments, according to her college credits and her teaching experience.

For purpose of orientation, academic preparation and experience can be used to estimate how much help the teacher should receive. These classifications are not perfect, of course; there can be wide differences in beginning teachers who have degrees. Likewise, teaching experience does not enable all teachers to develop comparable skill. But, other things being equal, college credits and experience give the principal two safe criteria for planning her orientation program.

These criteria are safe for a number of reasons. Parochial schools want and need well-trained teachers. It is only logical to regard a degreed teacher

National Education Association, Educational Research Service, *Teacher Orientation Programs in City School Systems*, Circular No. 8 (Washington, D. C.: The Association, 1952).

Evert C. Strickland, "Orientation Programs for New Teachers in Ohio Schools," *Educational Research Bulletin*, XXXV, No. 7 (Oct., 1956).

as superior to a less well-prepared person. It is also psychological to do so, for this recognition gives the degreed person a certain prestige; her years of work and expenditure of money for a college degree are in a sense being rewarded by this recognition. As far as teaching experience is concerned, somewhat the same is true. In most cases, added years of experience increase the teacher's effectiveness, and this added effectiveness should be recognized in the orientation program.

In practical application, this means that all teachers coming into a new school situation require a planned program of orientation. This is because each system has its own special characteristics, needs, and procedures, and incoming teachers require orientation for the particular system. Teaching experience in public schools, for example, does not provide familiarity with parochial school operation. In fact, it has been shown that experienced teachers returning to service, or transferring to another system, need orientation as definitely as do beginning teachers. As teachers acquire experience in the system, they gradually spend less time in orientation activities. The adviser, of course, adjusts her direction to the capabilities of the teacher.

Experimentation with new teachers has shown that an effective program, especially for lay teachers, should extend over three years. This three-year period corresponds to the probationary period discussion in Chapter VI.

THE ESSENTIALS OF A WORKING PROGRAM

A balanced orientation program can be planned around these five features: conferences, supervisory visits, help with lesson planning, help with pupils' work, and reports on progress made. Under the direction of the Sister Principal, the adviser works with the new teacher in carrying out these activities.

Conferences. An indispensable part of a good orientation program is the planned conference between adviser and new teacher. The discussion of conferences in Chapter IX offers basic information on conferences, information which can be adapted to use in the advisory program. There should be regularly scheduled conferences, more frequently at the beginning of the year, and less frequently as the year progresses. For an effective conference, definite preparation is needed. The new teacher should bring to the meeting her course of study, manuals, textbooks, worksheets, lesson plan book, and some written topics to be discussed. Each conference should deal with a specific purpose, should begin and end on time, and should have a definite follow-up. The lay teacher should keep notes on information received during conferences, to enable her to carry out the recommendations more fully. These notes, systematically kept, will be the basis of the routine progress report regularly submitted by the lay teacher. (See "Reports of Progress" later in this chapter.)

The Sister Adviser's role is to help the new teacher in a supervisory way. Suitable topics for supervisory conferences are the following: the goals of Catholic education, classroom routines, conduct and courtesy of the pupils, diocesan course of study for the grade, diocesan handbook, lesson planning, professional reading, testing and grading, records and reports, teaching procedures, and the lay teacher advisory program itself. Other instructional topics may be introduced according to the need of the individual teacher and the school situation.

The principal, as responsible head of the school program, holds administrative conferences with new teachers on matters of school policy. The principal retains authority over such matters as requisitions, extra-class duties, finance, and discipline problems. The Sister Adviser, through her conferences, does for the lay teacher in a supervisory way what the principal would do if she had the time. Administrative matters, however, remain in the hands of the principal.

Supervisory Visits. Beginning the first week of school, the new teacher is assisted by visits from the Sister Adviser. These brief visits early in the year are intended to help the new teacher with such routines as passing materials, saying prayers, assembling for reading groups, and other aspects of classroom management. The new teacher can get good ideas on organization by visiting the Sister Adviser's room for a few minutes occasionally in the early part of the year. The longer visits between new teacher and adviser have a specific purpose, and are most helpful when preceded and followed by a planned conference.

Exchange of classrooms between adviser and lay teacher has proved effective. The adviser can, for example, teach geography daily in the lay teacher's room, while the lay teacher is teaching English in the adviser's room. This exchange of classrooms has many beneficial effects. First of all, the daily contact with the adviser's pupils shows the lay teacher what to expect by way of study habits, courtesy, and written work. The adviser has the opportunity to assist the new lay teacher's pupils in developing habits of application. Also, parents like their children to have a Sister every day, even if only for a class period. When the adviser and the new teacher both know the pupils intimately, there is a much better basis for discussing pupil needs. This exchange of classrooms can be worked out so that the adviser teaches each subject successively in the new teacher's room, perhaps for a month at a time. Varying the time of the day also gives the adviser insight in the new teacher's problems. By using this exchange plan thoughtfully, the principal can be sure that pupil achievement is up to standard and that discipline and motivation are satisfactory.

When the principal and community and diocesan supervisors visit the new teacher, they should be aware of the directions previously given by the adviser. The principal has in her school file a progress report filled out by the new lay teacher, and the principal, using this record, can brief supervisors in the office before they visit the new lay teacher's classroom. Supervisors and principal may wish to broaden the scope of the adviser's observations, but there should be no conflicting recommendations made in the presence of the new teacher. The principal will need to keep in constant touch with the adviser to see how the program is going, and to make sure that the major objectives are being achieved. The adviser's effectiveness requires that she be supported by the principal's approval and the approval of visiting supervisors. Hence, there is a continuing need for co-ordination of suggestions made to the new teacher.

Help With Lesson Planning. The discussion of lesson planning earlier in this chapter refers particularly to assistance with lesson planning during an orientation program. After the Sister Adviser has worked for a time with the new teacher, lesson plans can be submitted to her a week in advance. The frequency of submitting plans varies with the training and parochial school experience of the teacher. At least in the beginning, it is good to have the new teacher submit her plans on Monday after school, so that the adviser can examine them that evening. The plan book can be returned to the new teacher early Tuesday morning, with written or oral comments. Occasionally, the principal can examine the plan book, and discuss the plans with the new lay teacher.

Help With Pupils' Papers. Pupils' papers show the instruction they have received, and the standards maintained by the teacher. To help the new teacher to upgrade the work which her pupils submit, the Adviser and teacher should analyze sets of pupils' papers regularly. This analysis includes such matters as the purpose of the assignment, provision for individual differences, quality of handwriting, completeness of the work, accuracy, spelling, English usage, neatness, and the way the teacher has corrected and graded the assignment.

A set of papers can be submitted to the adviser on Friday afternoon, the adviser and principal can look over them, and the papers can be returned to the lay teacher, with comments, on Monday. It is encouraging to both teacher and pupils if the principal stops in occasionally to compliment the class on an especially fine set of papers. Such contacts keep the principal conversant with the advisory program, while also conserving her time.

Reports of Progress. A summary is good both for retention of information, and also for morale. For these two reasons, the new teacher should make regular, written reports on the activities of the orientation program. A report form such as illustrated in Figure 23 can be used. The lay teacher should keep one copy for her own information, and the principal should retain a copy in the school file. If the program is organized on a diocesan

Figure 23. DIOCESE OF YOUNGSTOWN

LAY TEACHER ADVISORY REPORT

*Date..........

Group } below degree.. ....
(Check) } degree   ....

Experience: { in 1st year ....
(Check)   { in 2nd year ....
          { in 3rd year ....

.... Sister Adviser....................

School....................

City.................... Lay Teacher....................

CONFERENCES

*Date	Topics Discussed	Progress S	U
	Number required		

LESSON PLAN BOOK

Submitted Date	Comments	Progress S	U

SUPERVISORY VISITS

*Date	Subject Observed	By Whom	Progress S	U
	Number required			

PUPILS' PAPERS

Submitted Date	Subject	Progress S	U

* Write all dates 1961-9-27

Report to be filled out in duplicate by lay teacher according to requirements of program.

Figure 24.   IN-SERVICE PROGRAM FOR LAY TEACHERS

Group A — Degree

Activity	Before School Opens	First Week of School	Rest of First Quarter	Rest of Year
1. CONFERENCES	Meeting with principal and adviser to discuss lay teacher program. Time as needed in own classroom.	1st yr., 15 min. daily 2nd yr., 45 min. distributed 3rd yr., 45 min. distributed	1st yr., 45 min. weekly 2nd yr., 30 min. weekly 3rd yr., 30 min. monthly	1st yr., 45 min. monthly 2nd yr., 30 min. monthly 3rd yr., 30 min. monthly
2. SUPERVISORY VISITS	Details of supervisory program discussed.	*1st yr., several brief visits to lay teacher to help with routines.	*1st yr., two to adviser, two to teacher 2nd yr., one to adviser, two to teacher 3rd yr., one to teacher	1st yr., monthly 2nd yr., monthly 3rd year., monthly
3. LESSON PLANS	Recommended types explained, and routine for submitting.	1st yr., daily help as needed 2nd yr., discussed Friday 3rd yr., discussed Friday	1st yr., weekly 2nd yr., monthly 3rd yr., monthly	1st yr., monthly 2nd yr., monthly 3rd yr., monthly
4. PUPILS' PAPERS	Standards set up for content and form, and for teacher correction.	1st yr., several sets examined 2nd yr., one set discussed 3rd yr., one set discussed	1st yr., one set weekly 2nd yr., one set weekly 3rd yr., one set monthly	1st yr., one set weekly 2nd yr., one set monthly 3rd yr., one set monthly
5. REPORTS TO DIOCESE	Purposes and type discussed.		1st yr., monthly 2nd yr., quarterly 3rd yr., quarterly	1st yr., monthly 2nd yr., quarterly 3rd yr., quarterly

* Mostly brief visits, for help with passing seatwork, saying prayers, assembling for reading groups, etc.

Figure 25. IN-SERVICE PROGRAM FOR LAY TEACHERS

Group B — Less Than Degree

Activity	Before School Opens	First Week of School	Rest of First Quarter	Rest of Year
1. CONFERENCES	Meeting with principal and adviser to discuss lay teacher program. Three half days in own classroom, plus two hours with adviser.	1st yr., 30 min. daily 2nd yr., 20 min. daily 3rd yr., 15 min. daily	1st yr., 30 min. daily 2nd yr., 60 min. weekly 3rd yr., 30 min. weekly	1st yr., 45 min. weekly 2nd yr., 30 min. weekly 3rd yr., 30 min. monthly
2. SUPERVISORY VISITS	Details of supervisory program discussed.	*1st yr., several brief visits to lay teacher to help with routines.	*1st year, two to adviser, six to teacher 2nd yr., one to adviser, four to teacher 3rd yr., one to adviser, two to teacher	1st yr., three a month 2nd yr., two a month 3rd yr., two a month
3. LESSON PLANS	Recommended types explained, and routine for submitting.	1st yr., daily help as needed 2nd yr., daily help as needed 3rd yr., discussed Friday	1st yr., daily help as needed; submitted weekly 2nd yr., weekly 3rd yr., weekly	1st yr., weekly 2nd yr., weekly 3rd yr., monthly
4. PUPILS' PAPERS	Standards set up for content and form, and for teacher correction.	1st yr., one set examined daily 2nd yr., one set daily 3rd yr., one set discussed	1st yr., one set weekly 2nd yr., one set weekly 3rd yr., one set weekly	1st yr., one set weekly 2nd yr., one set weekly 3rd yr., one set monthly
5. REPORTS TO DIOCESE	Purposes and types discussed.		1st yr., monthly 2nd yr., monthly 3rd yr., monthly	1st yr., monthly 2nd yr., monthly 3rd yr., monthly

* Mostly brief visits, for help with passing seatwork, saying prayers, assembling for reading groups, etc.

basis, a copy of the report would be forwarded to the Diocesan Office. The report gives the lay teacher and the adviser a chance to summarize their work together, and also to note whether progress has been satisfactory. The frequency of reports will vary according to the teacher's experience in the system and her college training.

THE PROGRAM IN OUTLINE FORM

The preceding discussion has presented briefly the five aspects of a minimal orientation program: conferences, supervisory visits, lesson planning, pupils' papers, and progress reports. No doubt other worthwhile activities might also be included to enrich the program. As developed in the foregoing discussion, the orientation program has proved effective in the Youngstown Diocese for several years. After trial and adaptation, the program now operates as outlined in Figure 24 for lay teachers with a degree, and in Figure 25 for lay teachers below degree status.

In Figures 24 and 25, the five essential activities of the program are listed in the first column: conferences, supervisory visits, lesson planning, pupils' papers, and progress reports. The other four columns indicate time periods: before school opens, during the first week of school, for the next eight weeks of the first quarter, and for the remainder of the year. These time divisions seem to coincide with the varying needs of the new teacher. "Before school opens" is a time when teacher orientation is crucial. During the weeks prior to the fall term, the new teacher profits by meeting the principal and adviser, spending time in her own classroom, studying the advisory program, and preparing specifically for the first week.

"During the first week," the new teacher also requires considerable help in each aspect of the program. Relatively more time is given then to each activity than is allotted later on. "During the rest of the first quarter," the activities are spaced, and the first progress report is made. "During the rest of the year," orientation activities take up less time, since the most urgent needs of the new teacher have been met. However, activities continue systematically throughout the year, so that the teacher may steadily develop increasing maturity and skill.

This same figure shows the gradual reduction in time from the first, through the second and third years of orientation. In fact, the time spent in orientation for a third-year lay teacher is really the minimum that should be devoted to supervision under ordinary circumstances. The teacher is continued in the orientation program, however, so that the needs of the teacher and also the requirements of the school program can be adequately attended to.

It may seem at first glance that the time allotments are too frequent and too short. During the first week of school, for example, the degreed lay teacher has a conference with the Sister Adviser for about fifteen minutes each day. There are two reasons for this distribution of time. First, the new teacher welcomes the opportunity to ask questions every day during the opening week of school. There are many things to confuse a new person, even though there has been thorough preparation before the opening day. Fifteen minutes a day can clear up the usual difficulties.

The second reason for frequent and brief sessions is the Sister Adviser herself. The Sister Adviser has a class of her own to conduct, and she may not be able to afford more time. Also, the adviser is accustomed to keeping a schedule and does not find it a hardship to remember the appointments. It has been found that most difficulties can be cleared up in the time given in Figure 24 for degreed teachers. Scheduling a conference with a definite time limit also protects the interests of both adviser and advised; over-long meetings are not productive, though one enthusiastic member might wish to continue the meeting beyond scheduled time. However, if in the judgment of principal, adviser, and lay teacher more time is needed and can be given, then by all means additional time should be devoted to the program early in the year.

The advisory program, as outlined in Figure 25, recognizes the greater need of the teacher who is below degree status. In each of the five activities, the nondegreed teacher spends more time than the degreed teacher. Again, the program should be considered minimal; if the teacher requires more time, then when possible more time should be given.

Experimentation over several years has proved the effectiveness of the above program in the Diocese of Youngstown. Religious communities have given the program their interested co-operation and support. Supervisors, diocesan and community, have found that the program is good both for the school and for the lay teacher. Certainly teaching is better from the start, and the lay teacher is more satisfied. An important outcome of the program is the increased professional competence of the Sister Adviser. The orientation program is an excellent example of the good that results from authority wisely delegated to a capable staff member.

EVALUATION OF TEACHING

There has been a nervous tendency to dismiss the idea of teacher evaluation. Saying that Teacher X is better than Teacher Y seems undemocratic. Also, ideas are hazy about what constitutes good teaching. Further, if happy relations are to continue among the faculty, perhaps it is best just to go along as now, not doing anything about teacher evaluation. We may shrug our shoulders and say, "There have always been good teachers and poor teachers. Anything I do won't change that."

Chapter IV pointed out that evaluation is one of the essential functions of the principalship. Chapter V indicated that the primary purpose of the principalship is to improve teaching. Chapter VIII discussed the qualifications of the teacher as a person, and the person as a teacher. We cannot evaluate teaching fairly? We should not evaluate teaching? Hardly. All of the proof is on the other side. The principal can, and should, judge the quality of teaching in her school. As the preceding chapters have indicated, evaluation is not easy; it requires knowledge and effort and time. But evaluation of teaching is basic to any attempt to improve teaching in the school.

As a matter of fact, teaching is actually being judged all the time. The principal has definite ideas about who the good teachers are in her building. If a visitor comes to the school to observe a lesson, the principal is not likely to say, "Just go into any class at all. They're all about the same." The teachers on the staff also have decided who the better teachers are, and even pupils and parents are quick to approve or disapprove a given teacher's way of conducting class. Informally, judgments about teaching are going on all the time. As educational leader of the school, it is the principal's role to make more informed judgments about teaching and to enlist the help of others in judging teaching.

THE PRINCIPAL EVALUATES TEACHING

As a supervisor, the principal evaluates teaching primarily to improve teaching. A well-planned schedule, as outlined in Chapter V, provides time for teacher evaluation. When observing in classrooms, holding conferences and faculty meetings, checking lesson plans, testing pupil progress, the principal is accumulating data for evaluation. These data must be recorded, summarized, and interpreted in order to direct the in-service growth program of the school. This implies the need for formal evaluation of teaching, including written evaluation, so that the time spent in evaluating is worth while; the time will be worthwhile only if the data are used to promote better learning for children. The problem is not at all simple; but then, the matter of human development is never simple. Evaluation furnishes some insight into better ways of furthering this development.

Guides to Evaluation. The principal needs a solid background of information before beginning her program of evaluation. In fact, as she goes along, she would be wise to keep broadening and enriching her background in this challenging area. Chapter VIII, "What Is Good Teaching?" furnishes a good starting point for the program.[2] The four areas of teacher competence might well be reviewed at this point:

[2] Adapted from California Teachers Association, *Teacher Competence: Its Nature and Scope* (San Francisco: California Teachers Association, 1957).

1. The teacher instructs pupils.
2. The teacher guides and counsels pupils.
3. The teacher is a link between the school, home, and the larger community.
4. The teacher is a professional staff member.

In each of these four areas, the teacher should have at least a minimum of competence. The check list in Chapter VIII supplies objective standards for judging how competent the teacher is in each area, and where her weak points lie. In all her work with teachers, the principal should keep these four areas in mind, as well as the specific competences in each area. This will help her avoid an ironclad ruling on points of classroom management, for "many roads lead to Rome." Having objective criteria for judging teaching helps the principal to discuss good teaching impersonally. In addition to the check list of teacher competences, the bibliography lists other sound approaches to the problem of teacher evaluation. A knowledge of several approaches strengthens the principal's use of the particular procedure she decides will be best for her school.

Whom Shall the Principal Evaluate — All Teachers? The principal will be informally evaluating the effectiveness of all teachers in the regular round of her duties. Her *formal* evaluation will usually be limited to beginning teachers, or teachers in their first three years of service. Beginning teachers need and welcome constructive help from the principal for improving their work. On the other hand, the school system itself is benefited when new teachers are carefully supervised and evaluated. Community and diocesan supervisors cannot get the time to evaluate new teachers as thoroughly as would be desired. The Sister Principal is really the one who discharges this duty to the best interests of both the new teacher and the school system. As mentioned in the section on teacher orientation, the first three years of service correspond to a probationary period. During this period, the new teacher, under the advisory program, receives specific help, including formal evaluations. At the end of this period, the teacher should be able to function effectively without formal evaluation by the principal. Constant stimulus to self-improvement should of course be available to the teacher throughout her teaching career.

In judging the quality of work, the principal can use the teacher competences mentioned above. Another instrument of proved helpfulness is *The Ohio Teaching Record*.[3] This is an anecdotal observation form to be used co-operatively by the principal, or adviser, and the beginning teacher. The comprehensive scope of *The Ohio Teaching Record* is evident from a listing of the areas to be discussed:

---

[3] *Ohio Teaching Record.* Anecdotal Observation Form, 2nd ed. (Columbus: College of Education, The Ohio State University, 1945), p. 5. Used with permission.

1. Materials of instruction
2. Function of the subject matter
3. Methods of instruction
4. Effectiveness of materials and methods
5. Help with student personal problems
6. Good school-community relations
7. Democratic attitudes and relationships
8. Good human relationships

The authors of this evaluative instrument intend the form to be used with teachers. There is provision for evaluation by the teacher and the principal, or adviser, and after each of three detailed observations, the principal and the teacher summarize their impressions together. The Ohio Teaching Record is a valuable in-service growth technique, besides being helpful for evaluating new teachers.

Using such a diagnostic guide requires time. When the direction of new teachers is delegated to an experienced Sister Adviser, the principal's role is assisting the adviser and only occasionally working directly with the new teacher. This procedure saves the principal's time for the broader aspects of the supervisory program. The evaluations made of new teachers should be filed for better direction of the teacher and for use in improving the in-service program. Needless, to say, these records are confidential and should be available only to the principal and other supervisors.

How to Deal With Older Teachers. With more experienced teachers, evaluation presents a different problem. Teachers, like other workers, are inclined to think that after a few years they should be left alone to operate as they see fit. Added years seem to increase sensitivity and, when feelings are hurt, efficiency is lowered. Besides, principals are prone to forget how they themselves felt about evaluation before becoming principals. They didn't exactly relish submitting their lesson plan book for scrutiny and comments. However, a laissez-faire attitude toward veteran teachers, or "touchy" teachers, does not thereby become defensible. In evaluating more experienced teachers, the principal uses leadership techniques quite different from those used with beginning teachers. Principals are most successful when they can develop esprit de corps which motivates the staff to want a better school. Staff members will of course vary in their participation in such group efforts to improve teaching. A later discussion of group evaluation will give some specific suggestions for this type of evaluation.

Merit Rating. In parochial schools, the principal is not likely to be faced with the problem of Merit Rating. Merit Rating is a plan used in some public schools, whereby better teachers may receive additional increases in pay. The crux of the matter is how to decide who is a "better" teacher. The teacher competences listed earlier might of course be used, and very effectively used for in-service improvement. However, when the bankbook is involved, teachers become especially sensitive to formal evaluation by administrators. It seems as if some sort of Merit Rating may become necessary in public schools, in order to attract and retain qualified people. At the present time, Merit Rating seems rather remote for parochial schools. Evaluation in parochial schools will probably continue to be solely for the purpose of improving teaching.

Improving the Principal's Techniques. Many principals have expressed their feeling of inadequacy in the area of evaluation. Though they might sincerely wish to have better teaching, still they lack the know-how or the conviction to go ahead. Certainly, principals can learn by doing. They can use the material available and carry out teacher evaluation, at least in a modified form. Several principals working together can arrange specific helps to improve their evaluation. Religious communities, universities, and diocesan school offices can offer a real service to principals and to education in general by providing in-service training in this important area. However, since outside help may not be available, the principal's improvement in evaluation will depend largely upon her own inventiveness and perseverance.

PUPILS EVALUATE TEACHING

"Ask my pupils to criticize my teaching? Never! How would they know if I am a good teacher?" Many teachers, even experienced teachers, feel like this. They think children should be seen and not heard from, especially when criticism might be involved. Yet, as a matter of fact, children are constantly evaluating teaching, and who sees more of teaching than children do? Why not test pupils' opinions, just to see if they can be of assistance to us in judging teaching?

We would not think of having pupils fill out a report card for their teachers. Nor would we appreciate the principal's questioning children about what their teacher does in class. Such procedures would not be ethical, nor would they help children develop desirable character traits. Yet, teaching is a many-sided affair, and many people should share in evaluating it. Pupils should share in evaluation to round out the description of good teaching.

Soliciting Pupils' Opinions. A question of first importance is how we can get pupils' opinions without losing our prestige. This really can be done quite simply. One teacher of long experience invites pupil reactions at the end of each year. She merely asks her pupils to write down what they liked about the class that year, and what they would suggest that the teacher do differently with next year's class. The papers are unsigned, and the writing can even be disguised. Without fail, this Sister has received practical suggestions for improving her teaching.

If one is interested in formal testing, the scale prepared by Sister

Amatora[4] would be interesting. This scale for pupil evaluation of teaching is easy to administer, and has norms for interpretation. Selections from this scale are of interest. For example, the first area contains the following descriptions, to be marked *plus* if the statement is true of their teacher:

I. LIKING THE TEACHER

...... 1. Is the best teacher I ever had.
...... 2. Has a smile.
...... 3. Is very polite.
...... 4. Is good-looking.
...... 5. Does not keep things in the room neat.
...... 6. Has no sense of humor.

Area VII gives the pupils a chance to evaluate the way their teacher presents the lesson.

VII. LIKING FOR THE LESSONS

...... 43. Always makes the lessons full of "pep."
...... 44. Gives interesting lessons.
...... 45. Starts and stops the lessons on time.
...... 46. Gives everyone a chance to recite.
...... 47. Gives too many tests.
...... 48. Does not speak loud enough to be heard easily.
...... 49. Always makes the lessons very dry.

A scale such as the above affords the teacher an opportunity to see how the class feels about her teaching, and also to see what characteristics contribute to good teaching. When pupils need not sign their names, their answers are likely to be frank and informative.

With older children, evaluation can be somewhat more analytical. Some interesting results have come of asking students two questions: (1) Of all the teachers you have had, think of the teacher you *liked* best. Can you give some examples of why you *liked* this teacher best? (2) Think of the *best* teacher you ever had. Can you give examples of how this teacher taught you *better* than any other teacher? When children are assured that their opinions are wanted, and that no one will know who wrote the papers, their answers will be detailed and sincere.

Whatever method is used to solicit children's opinions of their teachers, the information should be received by the teacher herself, or by the research student. All such information should be kept in strictest confidence. The purpose of such surveys is to give the teacher greater insight into her own

---

[4] Sister Mary Amatora, O.S.F., *Diagnostic Teacher-Rating Scale* (Indianapolis: The Public School Publishing Co., Test Division of Bobbs-Merrill Co., Inc., 1952). Reproduced with permission.

teaching. Only if the teacher wishes, should she share the opinions with others.

Using Pupils' Opinions. Teachers who have solicited pupil opinion have been favorably impressed with its true-to-life quality. Children aren't guided by lists of desirable teacher traits; they react only to what they experience themselves. Therefore, there is an honesty and a directness in pupil opinion that one cannot get from sophisticated sources.

Specifically, however, studies of pupil opinion have shed light on both teacher traits and teacher competences. First, teachers and principals will be interested to know that pupils feel they learn most from teachers they like best. In certain research studies,[5] where children were questioned about the teacher they liked best, and the teacher who taught them best, almost invariably the child named the same teacher for both answers. Also, the reasons which children gave for liking a certain teacher and for feeling that she taught them best show real insight into the qualities of good teaching. Children mention most frequently the following good qualities in their favorite teacher (generalized from research studies):

1. Helpfulness: she really taught us clearly and thoroughly
2. Enthusiasm and cheerfulness: she made us like to learn
3. Patience, kindness, and understanding: she understood our problems and never gave up wanting to help us
4. Fairness, "no pets": she treated us all the same, in class and on report cards
5. Sense of humor: she could see a joke and take a joke
6. Friendliness and human-ness: we could see that she liked us and didn't consider herself too good for us
7. Respected our opinion: gave us credit whenever she could

From this list, a teacher can see whether her own teaching would make children feel this way about her. Pupils' opinions of teaching are a valuable supplement to the judgments of adults about teaching.

TEACHERS EVALUATE TEACHING

Since so much has been written lately about human relations, it seems strange that teachers are usually left out of the evaluation of teaching. A study of public school practice[6] showed that teachers very seldom took part in rating their own work, and that the most common type of rating form was a checklist marked by the principal without any discussion with the teacher concerned. We want competent teachers; we say we try to develop

---

[5] Paul A. Witty, "The Mental Health of the Teacher," in The National Society for the Study of Education, Fifty-fourth Yearbook, Part II, *Mental Health in Modern Education*, edited by Nelson B. Henry (Chicago: The University of Chicago Press, 1955), pp. 307–333.

[6] William V. Hicks, and Marshall G. Jameson, *The Elementary School Principal at Work* (Englewood Cliffs, N. J.: Prentice-Hall, Inc., 1957), p. 221.

good teachers; yet in practice teachers seem to be ignored in the very activity which would develop them most. Teachers improve their teaching primarily through their own analysis of their work and through studying their work along with their colleagues.

Self-Evaluation by Teachers. Interested teachers are constantly analyzing their teaching in an informal way. "That drill was good; it kept their attention. I must try it again." Or, of an unsuccessful attempt, the teacher might say, "I shouldn't have done so much talking. I must prepare better lead questions to keep the children interested." Without calling this process "evaluation," most teachers continually analyze their work in this constructive way. This is good, for self-criticism is more effective than criticism by others.

This tendency toward self-analysis can be utilized by the principal who is well informed and who has established good rapport with her staff. There are some good printed forms which teachers might use for their own improvement. However, no self-evaluation form is absolutely valid; there is a danger of the teacher's being misguided in her own opinions of her teaching. Self-evaluation questionnaires are more of a guide to good practice than a measure of teaching performance. With beginning teachers especially, self-analysis should be made in co-operation with the principal or adviser, so that sound criteria can be established. *The Ohio Teaching Record,* mentioned earlier, is an excellent form for co-operative use in this way. All teachers need to examine their work critically from time to time; the principal who provides a variety of self-evaluation helps is doing a real service for her teachers and indirectly for the children.

Group Evaluation by Teachers and Principal. The secret of success in group evaluation is to begin where the group is. A principal might want the group to go "all out" for the unit method of teaching social studies. But the staff might be concerned about children not knowing the "facts" in history. The wise principal files away for the time being her ideas on unit planning and agrees that children should know more history than they do. When interest is aroused, even though it cannot be called high interest, the principal can begin the process. She may ask for suggestions on how to decide pupil achievement in history, how to get children to retain basic information better, and how to evaluate the progress made at the end of the program. This is a beautifully clear plan of evaluation. In fact, the simpler the plan, the surer it is to succeed. If the principal moves ahead too rapidly, she will not bring her staff along with her. There is a readiness for professional growth just as surely as readiness for any other new phase of development. Evaluation of the kind here indicated is closely related to curriculum study.

There are three simple steps for the faculty to follow in answering the question, what must we do to improve our teaching? Or, how can we help our pupils learn better?

Steps in Evaluation

1. Objectives — what we are trying = Learn history facts better
   to achieve
2. Methods — how we shall teach = Drills, discussions, reviews
   and
   Materials — what we shall use = Flash cards, maps, workbooks, texts

3. Evaluation — how we can know = Tests, reports, attitude of children
   our success   toward the subject

It is a good idea to put down in writing the staff's objectives, the methods suggested, and the proposed evaluation. Definite time limits should be set, perhaps a month, or a semester. By means of a project such as this, the faculty can do a great deal of critical thinking. The principal has not said, "Our teaching is not as good as it should be; how can we improve it?" But the outcome will be improved teaching.

Another group of teachers might suggest that children should be more courteous or should have better handwriting. Courtesy and handwriting are also objectives of the curriculum; they form excellent topics for group work in evaluation. Usually, teachers will suggest topics concerned with pupil growth, rather than with their own personal growth. This is good, for the proof of our teaching is precisely in its effects upon pupils. Evaluating pupil progress in geography, in courtesy, in handwriting leads inevitably to better teaching.

The above suggestions are concerned only with one function of teaching — the teacher's role in instructing pupils. As discussed in Chapter VIII, there are three other essential roles: counselor, link with the community, and professional staff member. Improving these aspects of teaching can also be worthwhile projects. In the third role — link with the community, for example, one sign of good teaching is skillful handling of parent-teacher conferences. These conferences can become the subject of faculty study over a period of time. The result is that the teacher grows, and teaching itself is improved.

It is a healthy sign of good teaching when a faculty evaluates its progress as a group. After some such project as outlined above, the faculty might ask itself: "What devices have we successfully used this semester in helping our children learn geography better?" A question like this gives the more capable teachers an opportunity to suggest effective techniques, while the new teacher can for the time being be a less articulate member of the group, learning though perhaps not contributing much at this stage. Concrete examples of improvement, a résumé of new procedures, and evidence of pupil growth — and the evaluation project has been well worth while.

Group evaluation is the most effective kind of evaluation. It gives the faculty the feeling that "we did it ourselves." Of course, the principal must be a real leader, skilled in developing others, to achieve this kind of group spirit. Good teaching is bound to become better when co-operative evaluation is carried out in an atmosphere of high morale.

EVALUATION OF THE IN-SERVICE GROWTH PROGRAM

The professional principal has planned and carried out many of the activities discussed in the preceding pages. As she worked to improve instruction, she formed certain impressions of the effectiveness of the in-service activities. However, it is important to know what the teachers thought of the program. Did they like the faculty meetings, or was the principal alone in her enthusiasm? Did the teachers really find the conferences helpful, or were they just being polite? Did they feel that their teaching actually was improved because of the activities planned? The principal should not assume that everything is going well just because there are no open criticisms. It is sometimes surprising how differently the staff and the principal view the same things!

A written evaluation form can clear up many of these doubts. To follow along with the teacher competencies developed in Chapter VIII, a check list of matching in-service activities was developed. The check list is an inventory of the in-service activities and a questionnaire soliciting teachers' reactions. The Faculty Advisory Council of the school can prepare a direction sheet similar to the one given here. This co-operative aspect of the evaluation enlists staff participation more surely than a request made by the principal alone.

Letter to the Staff

Dear Faculty Member:

During the year, we have engaged in various activities to help us grow professionally in the four areas of teaching competence:

1. Instructing pupils
2. Counseling and guiding pupils
3. Interrelating the school with the home and the community
4. Co-operating as a professional staff member

In order to plan for next year, the Faculty Advisory Council would like you to fill in this evaluation sheet. Try to give your opinion of each item, but leave blank any point that does not apply. Please answer completely and frankly.

Procedure for Marking the Check List. Listed below in alphabetical order are the activities of the in-service program as carried out this year. Use these activities on the evaluation sheet to show which ones helped you to develop certain skills.

ACTIVITIES THIS YEAR

A. College course during the year
B. Committee work
C. Conference with adviser
D. Conference with principal
E. Conference with supervisor (community)
F. Conference with supervisor (diocesan)
G. Demonstration lesson
H. Evaluation (self)
I. Evaluation (group)
J. Evaluation (with principal)
K. Evaluation (with adviser)
L. Faculty meeting
M. Lesson planning (help with)
N. Observation by adviser
O. Observation by principal
P. Observation by supervisor (community)
Q. Observation by supervisor (diocesan)
R. Professional reading
S. Others

For example, in the first area — "instructing pupils," the first point on the check list is "Use new devices." Did any of the activities listed really help you to use new devices in your teaching? If so, *write in* the name of the activity *after* "Use new devices." On the check list, "faculty meetings" is written in to help you get started. Name each activity as often as you wish.

Number 5 under each heading reads — "Other" (. . . . .). In this blank, write in any other benefit received through the in-service program.

When you have finished the check list, turn over the sheet and tell us what you would like to have changed in the in-service program next year. Put the completed form back in the envelope and drop it in the suggestion box before Friday, June 1. You need not sign your name, but we do need a reply from all staff members.

Thank you for your co-operation. Your suggestions will be appreciated.

Your Faculty Advisory Council

The replies to the check list will enable the principal to see how her staff feels about the supervisory program. Have some activities been over-emphasized? Some omitted? Some beneficial, and some a waste of time? An evaluation such as this may be another "shock treatment," but the principal needs to know just how the staff feels. To expand and improve her supervision, the principal can draw upon the replies for specific direction.

CHECK LIST — EVALUATING THE IN-SERVICE PROGRAM

Area of Growth*	Growth Promoted by Means of These In-Service Activities
A. *Instructing pupils*	
I was helped to —	*Faculty Meetings*
1. Use new devices	_____
2. Use group work	_____
3. Give better explanations . . .	_____
4. Develop study habits	_____
5. Other ( ) .	_____
B. *Counseling and guiding pupils*	
I was helped to —	
1. Improve my knowledge of child development	_____
2. Increase my skill in guiding pupils .	_____
3. Work more effectively with exceptional children	_____
4. Learn how to give better classroom tests	_____
5. Other ( ) .	_____
C. *Interrelating the school, home, and community*	
I was helped to —	
1. Work co-operatively with parents .	_____
2. Use resource material in my classes .	_____
3. Understand the school community better	_____
4. Promote participation in Church worship	_____
5. Other ( ) .	_____
D. *Co-operating as a professional staff member*	
I was helped to —	
1. Know the curriculum better . .	_____
2. Work with teachers on problems of interest	_____
3. Develop my leadership in the faculty group	_____
4. Do more professional reading . .	_____
5. Other ( ) .	_____

* See pages 273–274 for code and directions.

FOR THE PRINCIPAL'S PROFESSIONAL LIBRARY

Help With Lesson Planning

Catholic University of America, Department of Education, *Criteria for the Evaluation of Catholic Elementary Schools*, "Teaching-Learning Activities," pp. 90–97 (Washington, D. C.: The Catholic University of America Press, 1949), 139 pp., $2.

Fitzgerald, James A., and Fitzgerald, Patricia G., *Methods and Curricula in Elementary Education,* "The Unit Technique," pp. 276–313 (Milwaukee: The Bruce Publishing Company, 1955), 591 pp., $5.50.

Hanna, Lavone A., Potter, Gladys L., and Hagaman, Neva, *Unit Teaching in the Elementary School* (New York: Rinehart and Co., Inc., 1955), 592 pp., $5.50.

O'Leary, Rt. Rev. Timothy F., Sister M. Veronica, S.P.B.V., Elwell, Rt. Rev. Clarence E., and Roche, Rev. Patrick J., *Land of Our Lady History Series* (Cincinnati: Benziger Brothers, Inc., 1955). The Teacher's Key and Manual for each grade contains an excellent explanation of the unit procedure, source units for the entire text, a sample teaching unit and selected lesson plans for each grade. The manual can be purchased by writing to the company.

Philadelphia Public Schools, *Choosing Appropriate Techniques* (Philadelphia: Curriculum Office, Public Schools, 1958), 20 pp., 50 cents. This is one of the best discussions of lesson planning available.

Preston, Ralph C., *Teaching Social Studies in the Elementary Schools,* rev. ed. (New York: Rinehart, 1958), 382 pp., $5.

Orientation of New Teachers

Diocese of Youngstown, *Lay Teacher Advisory Program, Elementary Schools* (Youngstown, Ohio: Diocese of Youngstown, Department of Education, 1959), 11 pp., 50 cents.

FOR THE PRINCIPAL'S PROFESSIONAL LIBRARY

Evaluation of Teaching

Teacher Competence: Its Nature and Scope, published by the California Teachers Association, San Francisco, 1957, 48 pp., 50 cents. Best and most concise information available on teacher evaluation. *Teacher Competence* was used as the basis for the check lists presented in Chapter VIII.

Vander Werf, Lester S., *How to Evaluate Teachers and Teaching* (New York: Rinehart and Company, 1958), 58 pp., $1. Helpful discussion.

Alexander, William M., *Are You a GOOD Teacher?* (New York: Rinehart and Company, Inc., 1959), 57 pp., $1. Emphasis on self-evaluation.

Merit Rating

National Education Association, Research Division, *Teacher Rating* (Washington, D. C.: The Association, 1954), 24 pp., 25 cents. Clear discussion of the controversial problem of merit rating.

Measuring Instruments

The Ohio Teaching Record Anecdotal Observation Form, 2nd rev. ed. (Columbus, Ohio: The Ohio State University, College of Education, 1945), 30 pp., 25 cents. This form is widely used and very effective in co-operative teacher evaluation.

Cincinnati Public Schools, *An Evaluation of Teaching Performance* (Cincinnati, Ohio: Cincinnati Public Schools, Pupil Personnel Service, 50 cents).

Catholic University of America, Department of Education, *Criteria for the Evaluation of Catholic Elementary Schools,* "Teaching-Learning Activities," pp. 89–105 and "Professional Efficiency of the Teacher," pp. 127–128 (Washington, D. C.: The Catholic University of America Press, 1949), 139 pp., $2.

CHAPTER XI

THE PARISH SCHOOL AND THE COMMUNITY

Not only should teaching be adjusted to each individual; it should also be adjusted to each community. What should a teacher know about the community? How can a principal help in obtaining needed information? How may the community be used in teaching?

MANY thousands of today's adult Catholics attended a parish school like downtown St. Peter's, with the noise of trains and trucks a common interruption. Many learned the fundamentals in a little rural school like St. Mary-of-the-Fields, after doing their farm chores each morning. There has been an exodus to smart new suburban schools like St. Pius, the pride of the "younger set" of Catholics. The Bishops in 1884 directed that every parish should have a parish school, but the kind of building and the type of program were not prescribed. Hence from one parish to another, and from one city to another, parochial schools differ widely. Some of these differences are consciously planned by Catholic school administrators; other differences, it seems, "just happen." Surely a principal should be aware of the factors or forces which make a given parish what it is.

Looking at the school buildings and the locale, one can know something about the people involved. St. Peter's is a three-story brick building of the 1920's, located in a deteriorating downtown district. St. Mary's is a modest little frame structure in a farm area which is gradually losing its people to city industries. St. Pius is a booming suburban plant, serving a rapidly expanding residential section. Knowing something of the locality, one can draw certain conclusions about the parishioners — their age, type of work, income, education, interests, and even their mortgages. It would be nice if there were three set descriptions for these parishes: Set One — St. Peter's, Set Two — St. Mary's, and Set Three — St. Pius. Then one could classify the parishioners, the children in the parish school, and the community. A certain emphasis could be recommended in each type of school, and a certain pattern of relationships with parents, and with civic and social leaders. However, the matter is not so simple as all that. Although a parish may serve predominantly one kind of income group, most parishes contain a cross section of income groups. The same is true of educational level, national origin, and racial make-up. Because the parish school usually represents a cross section of society, many variations are found in its pupils in all of these respects.

Teachers and principals could of course ignore all such differences and teach in St. Peter's School just as they do in St. Pius. Obviously this sometimes has been done. In fact, the same religious Sisterhood may conduct both of these schools, and the interchange of Sisters between the two schools may make adjusted teaching methods rather difficult. Yet, really good teaching, the kind we like to think characterizes our Catholic schools, is keyed to the children in the classes. There are basic similarities in all ten-year-olds, for example; but there are also differences among ten-year-olds. The fifth grade in St. Peter's should not be handled just like the fifth grade in St. Pius. But how can the principal and the staff know which differences are of major importance in their group this year?

Many of the differences among children are now known to be greatly influenced by their environment. Within rather recent years, certain aspects of the environment — called the "community" — have received considerable attention. Parochial school educators would do well to consider such "community" questions as these: What do we mean by "community"? How can we learn about the "community"? How do parishioners fit into the school-community picture? How can the parish school best serve the "community"? The present discussion will take up each of these questions in order, so that a better understanding of the parish school and the community will result.

WHAT DO WE MEAN BY "COMMUNITY"?

It is a little difficult to get a clear picture of what is meant by the term "community." The word was formerly used to mean a very close-knit group — close in both geographic boundaries and in personal relations. Of the "community" fifty years ago, it could be said: "The mark of a community is that one's life may be lived wholly within it, that all one's social relationships may be found within it."[1] This definition of community implies a small, integral, rural group. Communities of this sort were common some years ago here in America, and even more certainly in the homelands of our ancestors. However, the expansion of our cities has progressed so rapidly that relatively few such communities exist today. Rather, people in urban

---

[1] R. M. MacIver and Charles Hipage, *Society: An Introductory Analysis* (New York: Farrar and Rinehart, Inc., 1949), pp. 8–9. Used with permission.

society have gone far away from this close, familiar type of association; in fact they have gone so far in the direction of individualism that there seems to be no center or core of group living to which they can return. Social philosophers bemoan what they call the disintegration of our society; they feel that a return to some type of community living is necessary to restore balance to the nation.

The urban community of the modern day, then, cannot be the close, neighborly community of the past. But, on the other hand, "community" cannot mean just the world in general, or all of society outside of the school. Sociologists have set down certain criteria for describing a community today.[2]

A region can be called a community when —

1. It has a definite geographic boundary.
2. It has an historical past.
3. Its people share at least a few activities in common.
4. Its people are aware of some sort of unity.
5. Its people are capable of acting together for a common purpose.
6. It possesses certain basic institutions, such as schools, churches, and business establishments.

Using these six criteria, one can see that the parish itself can be called a sort of community. In fact, the parish unit may be the most closely-knit community which some Catholics belong to today. On the other hand, few parishes can keep their members united in spirit and activities. However, because a parish can exhibit many of the qualities of a bona fide community, it will be considered one in the present discussion. As will be indicated later, it is possible to strengthen the "community" spirit of the parish group.

Using the above criteria, one can identify many other communities in modern society, and a number of these communities are closely associated with the parish school. For example, parochial school pupils may belong to all of the following communities at the same time: neighborhood, block, ward, zone, parish, city, diocese, state, region, and country. Some of these communities are concentric: the smaller one is contained in the next larger one; as, the neighborhood is contained in the city, the state, and the region. Some communities have the same boundaries; for example, a parish and a city may have the same limits. Some of these communities overlap, as in the case of a diocese covering several cities, counties, or states.

---

[2] See, for example, the discussion of "The Nature of the Community" in Lloyd A. Cook and Elaine F. Cook, A Sociological Approach to Education (New York: McGraw-Hill Book Company, 1950), pp. 47–69. Also informative is Edward G. Olsen, Ed., School and Community, 2nd ed. (Englewood Cliffs, N. J.: Prentice-Hall, Inc., 1954), pp. 49–87. Additional information can be found in National Society for the Study of Education, The Community School, Fifty-second Yearbook, Part II, edited by Nelson B. Henry (Chicago: University of Chicago Press, 1953), pp. 15–30.

Some communities exert greater influence on the child than do other communities. For example, the child's learning may be more conditioned by its own neighborhood than by the city as a whole. Within the broad framework of diocesan regulations, a given parish may provide better educational facilities than another parish within the same section of the city. Certain dioceses greatly influence the educational program of the parish schools; local substandard conditions can be quickly remedied through diocesan mandate. Likewise, the country as a whole may exert such influence that the diocese and the parish cannot completely counteract this influence, as in the matter of entertainment, social class, and economic pressures. One could spend a whole lifetime studying the effect of the "community" on the way children learn and adjust.

Since the child is a definite member of several influential communities, the school can be seen as only one factor in the child's development, and not the major factor. In fact, when all of the child's communities are considered, perhaps the *parish* is the community which most directly influences the parochial school child. This does not mean the parish in the sense of religious service only, but the parish as the area served by the parish school. This is not to minimize the religious contribution of the parish church; it is rather to limit the field of study to a definite geographical unit. In studies of public schools, the attendance district is frequently the community studied. In the discussion which follows, then, the "community" will be *the parish area*. There will also be a recognition of the importance of the larger communities, such as the city, state, and nation, in the development of the parochial school child.

HOW CAN WE LEARN ABOUT THE COMMUNITY?

The community that most concerns the Sister Principal is the geographical area served by the parish school. However, because of the many important contacts outside the parish, the community of the parochial school may also be thought of as including the whole city, town, village, or state. In learning about the community, then, there should be special emphasis on the parish, but an awareness also of the larger political units.

How can one learn about the community which centers about St. Peter's School, or St. Mary's, or St. Pius? Teachers who have been stationed several years in a school can give some summary statements about the neighborhood, the nationality groups, the parents' work, and the like. However, pooling these informal judgments is not enough to furnish a sound basis for guiding children. Systematic study of the community is needed if principal and staff are to understand and serve the community better.

It is rare, even in large public school systems, to have an all-out community survey made. For most purposes, a great deal of interesting and helpful information can be gathered through faculty meetings devoted to community study. The topic may seem dull at first, but the ingenuity of the principal can arouse the necessary interest by well-directed questions and faculty assignments. Granted that interest is aroused, how can the staff proceed to study the community?

TOUR OF THE PARISH

This first suggestion may sound too obvious to mention, but experience shows that most teachers have never made a systematic tour of their own parish. A walking tour is most informative, for in this way teachers can see the neighborhood at close range. In the faculty discussion, the group can point out things to look for, such as the type of building, the kind of neighborhood (residential or business), the construction of the homes, the amount and kind of play space, the distance from school, and other factors which affect the children's welfare. With class lists in hand, teachers should note where their own pupils live, and get an idea of the kind of family life fostered in the homes.

A parish tour supplemented by home visits is still more effective. Some religious communities advocate that the Sisters and lay teachers visit all homes at least once a year. Although this sounds like an impossible task, there is no better way of getting to know pupils. Scheduled visits to at least a sampling of the homes would round out the parish tour as a means of gathering essential information. Teachers should also make a planned tour of their city or town, to compare their parish territory with the rest of the locality. Touring the parish, visiting the homes, and getting the feel of the entire city furnish preliminary data for a study of the community.

MAP OF THE PARISH AND THE CITY

With the many chores that face them each September, teachers are not likely to welcome the idea of drawing a map of their parish or city. However, co-operative work on such a project can be very rewarding. The local city planning commission or the Chamber of Commerce is usually glad to supply the skeleton of such a map. Teachers, parents, and perhaps selected pupils may fill in the details, such as the kinds of buildings, business places, dangerous areas, recreation centers, and the like. The "wrong side of the tracks" area would show up on such a map, as well as the "Hills and Dales" suburban community. Figure 26 shows what a parish map might look like.

The parish in the following map has boundaries which coincide roughly with the city boundaries. The city of Struthers has a population of 17,000; the parish has about 3000 families. The parochial school enrollment is 1600

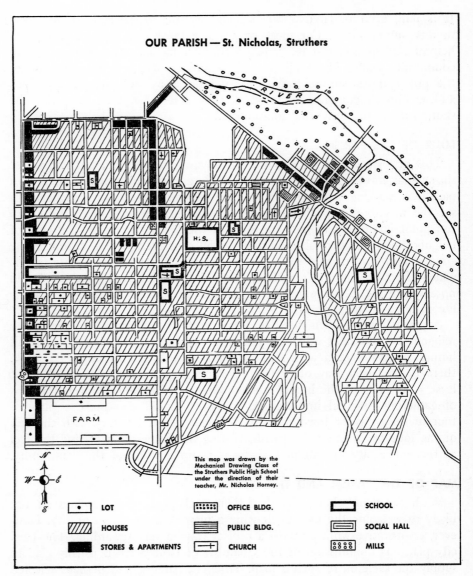

Figure 26.　Map of St. Nicholas Parish, Struthers, Ohio

in grades one through eight; the six local public schools enroll about 2000 pupils in grades one through eight.

How does the map of the parish help teachers understand something of the community? The code below the map indicates what is technically called "land use." The symbols show the types of buildings in the locality where the pupils live. For example, on the west side of the parish, there is a long line of stores and apartment buildings. Farther east, the area is predominantly residential. To the south and the extreme east of the city, there are large sections of land not developed. To the north, along the river is an industrial area, where the mills are located which furnish most of the jobs for parishioners.

Such a map supplies teachers with a wealth of information on their pupils. The socioeconomic level of the family is clearly indicated by the district. Children who come from homes over stores will usually have fewer cultural advantages than the children will have who live in the new split-level dwellings on the outskirts of the city. Children from the mill area will have problems not shared by children of the farm district.

Children at all grade levels have shown intense enthusiasm while making a map of their parish. The project readily lends itself to a mural and even to an industrial arts problem. The finished product will be an object of pride and a source of information, but of still greater importance is the growth of understanding that comes to both pupils and teachers through map study of their parish.[3]

Upper-grade pupils profit by this kind of study, thereby enlarging their own experience. Having the map on display greatly increases interest in the locality. Making a map of the parish and of the city is one effective means of studying the community — learning the framework within which most pupil activities center.

DATA FROM THE SCHOOL FILES

The principal's files contain a wealth of information not fully utilized. But how to get the faculty to use this information as a means of understanding the community better? And perhaps even a prior question — how can this information be used to further an understanding of the community?

Nationality of the Pupils' Fathers. Most teachers will agree that the birthplace of the parents, or their nationality, is an important influence in education. Teachers might also grant that the amount of formal schooling of parents is also important. The occupation of the father and the family income might not seem as relevant, but these, too, may be considered in a tentative way. Most of this information is on file in parochial schools and can be utilized in a study of the school community. Figure 27 shows how St. Peter's and St. Pius' schools compare as regards the birthplace, or nationality, of the pupils' fathers.

---

[3] If the teachers are interested in surveying their own community, they will find practical suggestions in George C. Kyte, *The Principal at Work*, rev. ed. (New York: Ginn and Company, 1952). Out of print. The two chapters dealing with community surveys are Chapter III, "Survey and Analysis of Community Conditions," pp. 37–58, and Chapter IV, "Survey and Analysis of School Conditions," pp. 59–85.

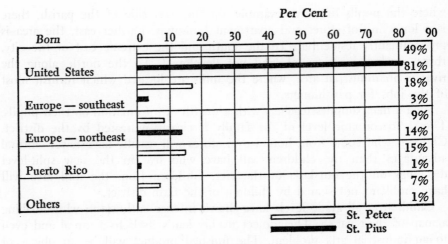

Figure 27.   The Birthplace of Fathers*

* These data have been generalized by the writer from the enrollments of two typical schools.

St. Peter's, the downtown parish, presents a very different picture of nationalities from that of St. Pius. St. Peter's has many southern Europeans and Puerto Ricans, while St. Pius has mostly American-born or north eastern Europeans. St. Peter's pupils would very likely hear a foreign language in the home, and many pupils would need to have difficult concepts interpreted to them. Although language is not so prominent a factor in the St. Pius homes, at least in some cases a foreign language and culture affect children deeply.

Formal Schooling of the Pupils' Fathers. During registration, some schools ask how much formal schooling the parents have had. Even if this information is not on file, it is usually easy to get an answer to the question: What was the last grade which your father finished in school?

The answer to this question provides significant information on the educational level of fathers in the two parishes.

TABLE XI.   Average Years of Schooling of Fathers[a]

St. Peter's Parish	9.8 years	(3% attended college at least one year)
St. Pius' Parish	12.3 years	(31% attended college at least one year)
Average, U. S.[b]	10.9 years	

[a] Data generalized by the writer.

[b] U. S. Bureau of the Census, *Statistical Abstract of the United States: 1960;* Eighty-first edition (Washington, D. C.: U. S. Government Printing Office, 1960), p. 108.

Many children in St. Peter's School have fathers who did not attend high school at all, whereas about a third of the fathers in St. Pius' parish went to college. The average years of schooling for St. Pius fathers seems high in contrast with the average for St. Peter's, though the figure is really just above average for all employed adults in the United States. Certainly, the formal education of parents has a great deal to do with the children's interest in academic subjects, their desire to get good grades, and their vocational plans. The educational level of the fathers will be important in studying the community, and what it expects and needs from the parish school.

The Fathers' Occupations. A third type of information usually found in the school file is the occupation of the father. Considering just an individual father here and there, occupation doesn't seem significant. However, when the occupations of all the fathers in the parish are graphed, some interesting results appear.

The U. S. Census Bureau reports occupations under ten headings. However, a recent NEA study groups the occupations somewhat more simply. In the table which follows, occupations are ranked from those in highest prestige to those in lowest prestige. The three major groups are "white-collar workers," "manual and service workers," and "farm workers." Under each of these headings are given a few typical workers in each category. For specific details see: U. S. Department of Commerce, Bureau of the Census, Current Population Reports: Series P-2, No. 91; Series P-20, No. 83; Series P-50, No. 78.

TABLE XII.   Percentage of Workers in Various Occupations, 1965*

OCCUPATION	Per cent of U. S. Workers
WHITE-COLLAR WORKERS	42.5
Professional, technical, and kindred workers	11.3
Managers, officials, proprietors	10.3
Clerical workers	14.4
Sales workers	6.5
MANUAL AND SERVICE WORKERS	49.9
Craftsmen, foremen	13.5
Operatives	19.6
Industrial laborers	5.0
Service workers	11.8
FARM WORKERS	7.6
Farmers and farm managers Farm laborers	7.6
Total	100
Numbers of workers	73,500,000

* "Occupational Trends," *National Educational Association Research Bulletin*, Vol. 37, No. 1 (February, 1959), p. 24. The NEA acknowledged as the source of data unpublished material compiled by the Bureau of Labor Statistics, September 12, 1958.

In Table XII, one can see that by 1965 approximately 43 per cent of all workers in the United States will be white-collar workers. Manual and service workers will be about 50 per cent of all workers, and farmers will make up only 7.6 per cent of the total workers. In general, white-collar workers make more money, enjoy higher status than do the other two groups. Many manual and service workers aspire to these higher-level jobs, and even among white-collar workers there is some striving upward.

Using the eight categories mentioned above, one can compare the occupational status of St. Peter's and St. Pius' parishes.

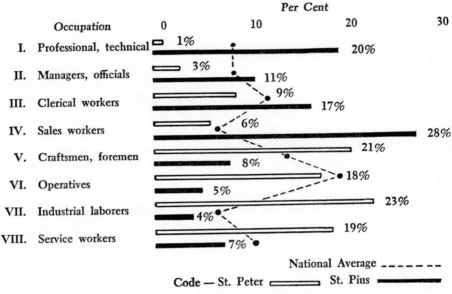

Figure 28. Occupation of the Fathers[a]

[a] Data generalized by the writer.

A study of the fathers' occupations shows great differences between the two parishes. The influx of immigrant workers is shown in the many St. Peter's parishioners in the three lowest occupational groups. Sixty per cent of St. Peter's fathers are in the three lowest-status groups, while only 16 per cent of St. Pius fathers have these kinds of jobs. In the highest group — the professional and technical workers — there are 20 per cent of the St. Pius fathers and only 1 per cent of St. Peter's fathers. In sales workers, the greatest differences appear. St. Pius' parish has 28 per cent of its fathers in the ranks of salesmen and clerks, while in St. Peter's parish only 6 per cent of the fathers do sales work. It is interesting to compare the national average for each occupation with the averages for the two parishes. St. Peter's is always *below* average in the prestige-bearing occupations; St. Pius is always *above* average. St. Peter's has more than its normal share of lower-status workers; St. Pius has fewer lower-status workers.

A study of the parish community might well emphasize the occupations of the fathers. The kind of work one does is a good index to the amount of money earned and also to social position.

The Fathers' Incomes. From the foregoing graph one can estimate, at least in a general way, the average income in the two parishes, for here in America occupation and income are closely associated. The average annual earnings of the fathers in the two parishes may be estimated as follows:

TABLE XIII. Annual Income of Fathers

St. Peter's	$3,900[a]
St. Pius	$7,300[a]
Average, U. S.	$4,200[b]

[a] Data generalized by the writer.
[b] Average U. S. Men taken from U. S. Bureau of the Census, *Statistical Abstract of the United States: 1960,* Eighty-first edition (Washington, D. C.: U. S. Government Printing Office, 1960), p. 323. This average is for men working in cities, 1958.

There is a difference of over $3,000 in the average annual income of the fathers in the two parishes. Although the fathers in St. Pius parish are not far above the national average in schooling, there are enough professional men to bring the average income up considerably beyond that for the United States as a whole. This extra $3,000 in St. Pius parish makes a great deal of difference in the books purchased for the home, the amount of sleeping and study space for each child, the play area and toys, and the food and medical care available. Income is an important index to the child's opportunity to make normal school progress.

A summary of the four aspects studied above shows interesting contrasts between the fathers in St. Peter's and St. Pius' parishes.

TABLE XIV. Summary of Data on Fathers

	St. Peter's	St. Pius
Birthplace	48% American-born	86% American-born
Education	9.8 grades completed	12.3 grades completed
Occupation	60% semiskilled and unskilled	16% semiskilled and unskilled
Income	$3,900 a year average	$7,300 a year average

Assembling these few statistics for the parish would take a little time. Very probably, it would be best to have each teacher tabulate her own data, and then the principal or a committee of teachers could combine the data for all the grades. However, gathering the data is only a first step. The important thing is interpretation. Here the professional preparation of the principal will be evident. The principal will need to enlarge her own background in this area, and also get her faculty interested in doing a little reading on their own. The interpretation of data for a given school may follow along some such lines as the following discussion.

INTERPRETING DATA FROM THE SCHOOL FILE

Studying Social Class. Many teachers have had a course in educational sociology in the process of their training. However, the content of sociology courses may seem remote from practice; perhaps this is inevitable with college students who have had little or no classroom experience. At any rate, the faculty needs a reorientation to the problem of social class and its effects in the classroom. Perhaps book reviews of *Elmtown's Youth*[4] and parts of *Yankee City*[5] would supply this reorientation at a faculty meeting. Staffs vary, of course, and the principal may prefer an outside speaker or a workshop approach. By whatever means, some background of information should be supplied.[6]

The main idea to develop is that of social class. Americans usually think of themselves as one large middle class, the *demos*, but as a matter of fact, there is a definite hierarchy of classes in American society. The chief determinant of a person's class, or status in the community, is economic — his wealth, or income, and closely related to his money as a criterion is his occupation. The community esteems men who drive longer cars, live in landscaped homes, and provide mink stoles for their wives. The people who are thus esteemed ordinarily have professional and technical jobs. Income and occupation go hand in hand. There are some exceptions to this general rule of community esteem, however. Two physicians, for example, may have approximately the same income, and the same success in practice, yet the community may rate one physician higher than the other in social status. In addition to money and occupation, then, there are two other factors that greatly affect social position in the community — one's behavior and one's associations. It is true that one must have a certain minimum income to be considered "high class" in a community; but one must also "act that way" and "go around with the right people." "Quality is as quality does" and "blood will tell." A university president may have a lower income than a local broker, but the university president may be assigned a higher social position because of his behavior and associations.

---

[4] August B. Hollingshead, *Elmtown's Youth* (New York: John Wiley and Sons, Inc., 1949).

[5] W. Lloyd Warner, and Paul S. Lunt, *The Social Life of a Modern Community* (New Haven: Yale University Press, 1941).

[6] A particularly good source of information on social class in American schools can be found in Robert J. Havighurst and Bernice L. Neugarten, *Society and Education* (Boston: Allyn and Bacon, Inc., 1957). Especially pertinent for faculty study are the following chapters: "Social Structure in America," pp. 1–34; "Mobility in the Social Structure," pp. 35–55; and "The School in the Social Structure," pp. 221–241.

Warner's Classification. No study of class can be at all complete without attention to Warner's classification[7] of status in Yankee City. Warner used as his criteria of social class these factors: income, occupation, education, family, friends, clubs, as well as manners, speech, general behavior, and place of residence. Warner arrived at the following strata or levels of social class in a typical New England city.

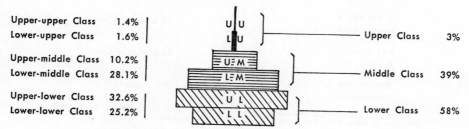

Upper-upper Class	1.4%			
Lower-upper Class	1.6%		Upper Class	3%
Upper-middle Class	10.2%			
Lower-middle Class	28.1%		Middle Class	39%
Upper-lower Class	32.6%			
Lower-lower Class	25.2%		Lower Class	58%

Figure 29.   Social Class in a New England City.

Source: W. Lloyd Warner and Paul S. Lunt, *The Social Life of a Modern Community* (New Haven, Conn.: The Yale University Press, 1941), p. 88. Adapted with permission.

In the Warner classification, the Upper-upper, or very highest class in Yankee City, contains only 1.4 per cent of the population. The Lower-upper group contains 1.6 per cent, making a total of only 3 per cent of all inhabitants as members of the Upper Class. The Middle Class is made up of 10.2 per cent in the Upper-middle and 28.1 per cent in the Lower-middle, or a total of 39 per cent of the population. The Lower Class comprises 58 per cent of the inhabitants — 32.6 per cent in the Upper-lower and 25.2 per cent in the Lower-lower Class.

The six classes in Yankee City are roughly equivalent to the six occupational levels, ranging from high professional status down to the low status of the nonskilled worker. A professional person from occupational level Number I may be assigned a social position equivalent to a store proprietor, or Level II; however, a professional person is quite unlikely ever to be accorded lowest class, e.g., "on a par with a caretaker." Conversely, a mill hand, Level VII, is likely to rise in social status no higher than Upper-lower Class. Some Lower Class men or women may move up the scale through the opportunity to associate with "higher class" people. Or, conversely "higher class" people may move downward, by marrying "beneath" them, by losing their money, or by unapproved conduct. Probably about one third of Middle and Lower Class people are moving up the social scale, but moving upward or downward is within a rather limited range. The Horatio Alger pattern is not being duplicated to any great extent today.

[7] W. Lloyd Warner, and Paul S. Lunt, *The Social Life of a Modern Community* (New Haven: Yale University Press, 1941), p. 88.

Other cities would of course have a pattern of social class structure different from that depicted by Warner. Father Fichter, for example, found the following structure in a typical southern parish.

TABLE XV.   Social Class in a Southern Parish School

Social Class	Per Cent of Pupils	
Upper-upper	6.1 ⎫	
Lower-upper	12.8 ⎭	19% Upper Class
Upper-middle	26.5 ⎫	
Lower-middle	19.6 ⎭	46% Middle Class
Upper-lower	26.0 ⎫	
Lower-lower	9.0 ⎭	35% Lower Class

Joseph H. Fichter, S.J., *Parochial School: A Sociological Study* (Notre Dame, Ind.: University of Notre Dame Press, 1958), p. 24. Used with permission.

The fathers in the school which Father Fichter analyzed are predominantly in the Middle Class, with about one-third in the Lower Class. The parish also has almost one fifth of its parents in the Upper Class. The above table illustrates again the wide scatter of social and income levels that may be found in a typical parish.

Even though other cities would vary from the Warner classification, the implications for teachers are clear. Teachers come predominantly from the Upper-lower Class or the Lower-middle Class, and teachers are known to favor Upper-middle Class values. Teachers tend to forget whence they themselves came, and look upward to values of the class to which they aspire. But, 50 per cent of the total population of most parishes will very likely occupy the lower half of the scale. If education is to serve the community, and community service is said to be one of the school's chief aims, then teachers should certainly accept the social class pattern of their own community.

Social Class and Marks.   As an illustration of effects of social class in the school, one may use report card marks for conduct, or citizenship, or co-operation. Who gets the A's? Why, of course, the better behaved children, the more co-operative ones. However, when we analyze the background of the pupils who get A's, some interesting and perhaps embarrassing facts emerge.

Let us compare the conduct marks with fathers' occupations in a certain sixth-grade class of 45 pupils (Table XVI).

Teachers may at first object to such a comparison, saying that they don't grade conduct by looking at the cumulative record to see what kind of work the child's father does. But upon consideration, teachers will admit that very often the children from the lowest economic classes do not behave

TABLE XVI.   School Grades and Fathers' Occupations

Grade in Conduct	Number Receiving Grade	Average Occupational Level of Fathers*
A (Excellent)	6	II
B (Very good)	22	III
C (Fair)	14	IV
D (Unsatisfactory)	3	V

* In figuring the average occupational level of the fathers, the eight levels of Figure 28 were used. For example, the three pupils who got D in conduct have fathers in occupational levels II, V, and VII, or an average level of V. Likewise, of the six pupils who got A in conduct, the occupational levels of their fathers were as follows: I, I, II, III, III, IV, or an average of II.

as well as children from the upper class homes. So, if children really do not behave, why grade them higher? Why give A to Eddie who fights with the children, will not do his work, talks all the time, is not respectful, and plays truant so often? Or a teacher may object, "But I always give an A in conduct to Betty. Her father has a very poor job, and the family is often on relief." Granted that teachers do try to grade conduct objectively, still the causes of good and poor conduct often lie in the home environment of the child. And home environment is strongly related to income and occupation.

Report card grades in "Effort" also show this tendency to favor higher-income children. Effort may be graded as such, or it may be in terms of "Makes an effort to improve," "Applies himself to class work," "Follows directions exactly," and the like. Who gets an A in Effort? Usually, those who get good marks in conduct also get good marks in Effort. But the same children who behave well also try hard in class! Granted that they do, still the problem remains: why do they? Research shows that children from the so-called "better" homes, that is, on a higher social and economic plane, are constantly motivated to do well in school. College entrance looms large on their horizon. Also, parental approval and the prestige that comes from getting good grades are strong motivations for the "better" type of child. In fact, research shows that from the primary grades up there is very little change in a child's effort. Or, in other words, higher class parents keep up the pressure throughout the child's school years. There are again some exceptions to this rule; but on the average, the report card grade for effort is the parents' grade, not the child's.

Social Class and Intelligence. What is true of marks for conduct and effort is also true of marks for the academic subjects. Reading, social studies, English, science, in fact, most subjects, depend heavily upon verbal ability, and verbal ability is closely related to socioeconomic status. The curriculum of the typical elementary school is largely made up of verbal tasks. Higher IQ children do these verbal tasks better than do the children of lower intelligence. Thus, a vicious circle is created. The children of "better" homes are of higher verbal ability; hence, they do well in their work, and are motivated to keep on trying. Children from the "lower" type homes have less verbal ability; hence they, on the other hand, do not do as well in school subjects, and are discouraged from putting forth continued effort.

Teachers may challenge the idea that IQ and money mean one and the same thing. Actually, the score on group intelligence tests is based largely on language ability. Children from the more privileged homes usually are higher in verbal ability because they typically associate with more highly educated adults, who in turn "use better English."

Also, there are more magazines, books of fiction and travel, dictionaries and encyclopedias in the more privileged homes, and hence the child is exposed to correct form in reading as well as in oral usage. These very factors enter heavily into the IQ tests as used in our schools. Most of these IQ tests are verbal; they are tests of knowledge of words and word relationships; they employ expressions and symbols familiar in the more privileged homes. Usually the correlation between a verbal IQ test and a reading test is somewhat better than .50. Obviously the reading test is testing some of the factors tested by the IQ test.

Teachers of course like pupils to succeed; successful students appeal to teachers, and, trying becomes easier for children who know they appeal to their teachers. Thus, school marks reflect not only ability and achievement, but the pupils' effect upon the teacher. This is not to say that school marks are invalid; it is merely to underscore some of the factors included in the A's awarded to the "better" class of children and the D's assigned to children from the "wrong side of the tracks."

Teachers' Reaction to Parents. This discussion can be carried to a further aspect of this same topic — teachers' reactions to parents of pupils who are brighter, who try harder, and who get better marks. When Sister wants someone to do a favor for her, who is approached? The need may be a centerpiece for the faculty dinner, or a car for the class picnic, or a Room Mother for clerical tasks. Whatever the need, Sister is likely to contact the parent of a child from a "better" home. By this is not implied that Sisters are mercenary; no Sister would be working for the salary she gets if she were truly mercenary. But, can we detect in parochial schools a tendency to cultivate the "better homes"?

It is alleged that public school teachers are upward mobile; that is, teachers themselves are not typically from the higher occupational homes, but are working their way up, that is, working upward on the social scale, and that teachers tend to favor the standards of the classes higher than themselves. The teacher's college degree can give her entree to a higher socioeconomic level than that of her parents. Is this drive for higher class status true of teachers in general, not just public school teachers? The charge has been made that parochial school teachers also tend to favor middle-class values — cleanliness, order, neatness, effort, good manners, study habits, citizenship. Should teachers *not* encourage these traits? Middle-class values are the best we know; most emphatically teachers should encourage them. However, in encouraging these values, teachers should be aware of the many underlying factors — parents' education, occupation, income, and social class, and the effect of these factors on school performance.

Teachers, like all other human beings, like to be appreciated. Most often this appreciation is shown in a tangible way, frequently through gifts. The upper-class home is adept in expressing appreciation of the work of the teacher. The lower-class mother may say in her heart, "I'm glad Tom's teacher is helping him with his reading," but the lower-class mother hasn't the money, or the time, or the "training" to make the kind of overt gesture that teachers like. Expressions of appreciation create a bond between teacher and parents, a bond which strengthens the emphasis on *middle-class* rather than *lower-class* values.

Implications for Teaching. Teachers like to think that teaching is a dedicated work. Critics of the public schools question the dedication of teachers, on the basis of their agitation for higher salary, better working conditions, greater security, and less work. These criticisms have been debated pro and con over many years. However, in the case of parochial schools, the situation is, or should be, quite different. Basically, parochial schools are established to insure a good all-round education for Catholic children, in an atmosphere that is religious. The all-round education is to include systematic instruction in the truths of the Catholic faith. The religious atmosphere includes, besides religious symbols, inculcation of attitudes and ideals which can be called Christlike. If the parochial school fails in this, it fails in everything.

This is the chief reason why a parochial school faculty should study the community and understand how community influences affect the parochial school. The subtle influence of social class on school adjustment, marks, and teachers' attitudes needs to be boldly analyzed by the staff. There are of course lay teachers as well as nuns in the parochial schools, hence, not quite the same type of dedication can be expected, though the underlying motivations can be similar.

It is more blessed to give than to receive, and nowhere is this more true than in teaching. Teachers "give" to their pupils when they serve them according to their needs, without seeking reward from pupils or their parents. Rewards come in the form of recognition by parents, expression of satisfaction with the work done, and even in the personal gratification aroused by the appearance, docility, alertness, and "co-operation" of the "nicer" children. A teacher can spend herself in helping lower socioeconomic pupils improve in reading and consequently in school adjustment, but she may never be thanked — by pupil, parents, other teachers, or the principal. Still more, the child who requires the most attention may seem not to improve, and may even drop out of school. However, to be true to her dedication, the parochial school teacher must continue to further the development of each child to the limits of his ability. Lower class homes typically lack motivation for school achievement and even for continuing in school. With lower class children, then, the teacher must develop the motivation needed if they are to utilize their potential more fully.

Souls will be saved to the Church, and educated citizens to the State, only when teachers make the best possible education available for all children, regardless of social class. Once the staff has recognized, as a group, the influence of social class in the school, they can readily devise specific techniques to combat the undesirable effects of class discrimination. It should be the pride of the parochial school staff that there is no class bias in their school. In the final evaluation, the excellence of the school plant will be secondary; the spirit of dedication will be of primary importance.

HOW IS RELIGIOUS PRACTICE A PART OF COMMUNITY INFLUENCE?

The preceding discussion of social class applies equally to public and parochial schools. Religious practice, however, is a subtle influence which most directly concerns the parochial school. Parochial school teachers meet such instances of remissness as the following: Kathy is consistently absent from Sunday Mass, Jimmy brings meat in his lunch on Friday, Eddie is missing when the Scouts have their Communion Sunday. . . . In a way, each is an individual problem: Jimmy, and Kathy, and Eddie have been in Catholic schools for several years, and know the meaning of these religious practices. Yet, in a sense, these deviations reflect an out-of-school influence. Devout parents usually have devout children; negligent parents usually have negligent children. Can the individual child's religious practice be studied in the context of interacting influences?

The parochial school of course stands for religion in education. An integration of religion and education is sought, not subordinating the three R's to religion, but by suffusing the entire program with Christian attitudes, ideals, and practices. Something rather comparable is attempted, for example, in the teaching of moral and spiritual values in the public schools. A science project may help children learn about electricity and at the same time help them develop democratic ways of solving problems. In the parochial school, one aim of the curriculum is to strengthen the faith and religious practice of the pupils. One outcome of a science project in a parochial school might be to strengthen the children's awareness of the beauty of God reflected in creation. Opportunities to form habits of fervent religious practice are also found in the regular and extracurricular program.

What influences counteract the effort of the parochial school to develop habits of religion? In an area so difficult to analyze, there have been very few studies, and these have produced only limited conclusions. However, the data available are well worth studying. Even Sisters and lay teachers who have been Catholics all their lives will find these studies enlightening. In analyzing these studies, the teacher will need to keep in mind that not all Catholics have attended parochial schools. In fact at the present time, just about 50 per cent of Catholic elementary children in the United States are in Catholic schools. Perhaps only one third of the Catholic adults in this country have attended parochial school. Still, a study of religious practice reveals "what is" in the everyday life of Catholics. The most complete study available analyzed a city parish which may be typical of urban parishes generally.[8] Comparisons among parishes can be profitably made, as will be shown in the following discussion.

CATHOLIC RELIGIOUS PRACTICES

There is a certain hierarchy in religious practices, ranging from those commanded by the Church down to those which are optional. "Making one's Easter duty" — that is, receiving the Sacrament of Holy Eucharist sometime during the Easter season — is a religious practice of first importance. Fulfilling this duty is necessary in order to continue as a Catholic in good standing. Another requisite is regular attendance at Sunday Mass. Neglecting either of these duties is, as every Catholic knows, a mortal sin. Hence, these two duties would seem to be minimum essentials of religious practice. Not mandatory, but strongly urged because of its beneficial effects, is frequent reception of Holy Communion. A person who goes to Holy Communion once a month shows a certain realization of the efficacy of this sacrament; a person who receives once a week exhibits a still stronger spirit of faith. These four examples of religious practice may then be taken as a measure of the religious spirit of Catholic adults: making one's Easter duty, attending Sunday Mass, receiving Holy Communion monthly, receiving Holy Communion weekly. Figure 30 shows the pattern of religious observance among the eight thousand parishioners studied by Father Fichter.

Of persons considered Catholic, in fact listed as parishioners, only 74 per cent had made their Easter duty that year. The same percentage had

[8] Joseph H. Fichter, S.J., *Social Relations in the Urban Parish* (Chicago: The University of Chicago Press, 1954).

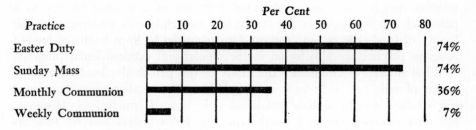

Figure 30.   Religious Practice of Adult Catholics

Source: Joseph H. Fichter, S.J., *Social Relations in an Urban Parish* (Chicago: University of Chicago Press, 1954), p. 85. Adopted with permission.

attended Sunday Mass regularly. Only 36 per cent went to Holy Communion once a month, and 7 per cent went to Holy Communion once a week. For each of these practices, the age group between 30 and 50 had the lowest percentage.

These figures will not apply exactly to another parish at another time. However, if one analyzes one's own impressions of religious practices, the above percentages may seem rather close. Particularly important are the figures for the two required practices — the Easter duty and Sunday Mass. Teachers in parochial schools tell children that good Catholics are faithful without exception to these two acts of worship. Yet, in the pupils' homes represented in Fichter's study, one out of every four Catholic adults does not observe these practices regularly. Likewise, frequent reception of Holy Communion is stressed in parochial schools. There is only fair carry-over of this teaching to the home, for about one third of the adult parishioners receive Holy Communion once a month, and weekly Communion is still more rare. With the Pope's recent modification of the laws of Eucharistic fast, reception of Holy Communion may become more frequent than it has been.

Children may not be getting even the good example which the above graph seems to indicate. The reason is this: the graph shows only the practice of *Catholics*, and does not include non-Catholic parents or other non-Catholic adults living in the home. There is today a rather high percentage of mixed marriages; the non-Catholic parent does not normally strengthen Catholic religious practice in the family. Thus, one must revise these figures downward for a truer picture of the parents' influence as regards religious practices. Instead of three fourths of the parents making their Easter duty and attending Sunday Mass regularly, there may be only one half. Instead of one third receiving Holy Communion monthly, there may be only one fifth.

The school's teaching, then, as regards religious practices, may not seem very important in the home. In some cases, of course, the child has been an agent of reform. Catholic men, in particular, have admitted that their own religious practices improved when their children entered parochial school. The parents' reception of Holy Communion on the day of their child's First Holy Communion has been the occasion of a renewal of fervor for many parents. Father-son and mother-daughter Communion breakfasts have had similar effects. The parochial school has had strong influence on the religious practices of parents, at least while the children were in the parochial school. It seems that the parochial school also strongly motivates the religious practices of the pupils themselves, for at no later time do they show greater fidelity to the sacraments. Furthermore, Catholics who have had parochial school training seem to be in general more regular in the practice of their religion than are Catholics with a public-school background.

CLASSIFYING PARISHIONERS

There is still another way of analyzing religious practices as part of community influence. That is, Catholics can be classified according to their religious and social closeness to their parish. Father Fichter has analyzed a city parish according to the degree of identification of parishioners with their parish. Figure 31 shows how this parochial spirit may be depicted.

Figure 31. Per Cent of Parishioners Who Are "Ideal,"
"Ordinary," and "Borderline"

Source: Joseph H. Fichter, S.J., *Social Relations in the Urban Parish* (Chicago: The University of Chicago Press, 1954), p. 62. Data adapted and put into graph form with permission.

This bar graph shows the relative percentage of parishioners who come under the three headings. There is a small group of "ideal" Catholics, about twice as many "borderline" Catholics, and a large group of "ordinary" or typical Catholics. Positions are of course not fixed. Persons in each group may be gravitating toward better observance or may be drifting farther away. It is rather startling, however, to see in graphic form this classification of parishioners.

The teacher can profitably study the types of Catholics because parents of school children will fall roughly into one or other group. Ideal Catholics, or those who are most fervent, the "leaders," seem to make up about 10 per cent of a typical city parish. Ideal parishioners, according to Father Fichter's definition, receive Holy Communion weekly or oftener and belong to a parish organization. Thus, they exhibit both a personal love of the Church by religious fidelity and a social love of their fellow Christians. The ideal Catholic applies Christian principles in every activity — civic, social, occupational, family, and religious. The "ideal" Catholic fits Pope Pius X's classic description of the true Christian — "the supernatural man who thinks, judges, and acts constantly and consistently in accordance with right reason illumined by the supernatural light of the example and teaching of Christ."

The large bulk of Catholics are "ordinary" Catholics, constituting about 70 per cent of the parish. Ordinary Catholics usually attend Mass on Sundays, though not always on holydays of obligation. They abstain from meat on Friday, send their children to the parish school, and are usually at least nominal members of a parish society. The ordinary parishioner is "the Church" to his non-Catholic neighbors and associates. His attitudes and practices are assumed to be those of the Church itself.

"Borderline" Catholics, 20 per cent of all parishioners, are in an uncomfortable position. They call themselves Catholics, but they seldom attend Mass or frequent the sacraments. Their children are not in the parochial school. Since they are so far removed from the nucleus or heart of the parish, they are forcibly pulled toward other standards — in politics, in business, in social life, and in marriage. They may resent and resist certain teachings of the Church for personal reasons, but they do "cut themselves off" from the Church.

"Fallen away" Catholics never attend church services or go to the sacraments, but they have not joined another church. They may or may not call themselves Catholics, though they were baptized and may have been married in the Church. "Fallen away" Catholics never "bother about the Church" sacramentally or socially; hence, they cannot be called parishioners. It is disturbing that an estimated one third of all babies baptized in the Church will probably "fall away," according to Father Fichter.

Application to Teaching. The above types of parishioners are interesting from a sociological point of view, but they are also important because of their influence on religious training in the parish school. Instruction on the duties of a Catholic can become more effective when presented with reference to the religious spirit of the family. Kathy misses Mass on Sunday, and Eddie doesn't go to Holy Communion. These may be individual phenomena; but they are more likely part of the family pattern of religious observance. Kathy and Eddie have free will and are responsible for a certain minimum of religious observance; but they are also influenced by their environment. This environment includes both their own families and the families of their friends. When children have borderline or "fallen away" parents, they seldom develop the robust kind of Catholicity that the children of fervent parents exhibit.

There are, happily, brilliant exceptions to this rule. There are the shining examples of Bernadette Soubirous, whose father was at best a borderline Catholic, and Lucy of Fatima, who received very little edification from her father. Yet both of these young girls developed a courageous love of religion. By contrast, Theresa Martin's home exhibited the ideal type of Catholicity, and Theresa's own spirituality was no doubt deepened by her parents' example. God's grace may supplant nature; there have been saints in unlikely circumstances. But a study of environmental influence is an asset to the teacher who would build solid habits of piety in her students.

IS PARISH LIFE CHANGING?

Since the parish is part of American society, changes in society directly affect the parish. During the present century the American parish has undergone fundamental changes, some of which will be discussed here.

"Old" and "New" Parishes. At Sunday Mass in downtown St. Peter's Church, the congregation is not like the one of thirty years ago. There is a predominance of older people and of poorly kept children. The pulpit announcements indicate that deaths outnumber marriages, and that there will be few parish activities in the coming week. Surrounding the church, rooming houses and hotels are interspersed with used-car lots, office buildings, and warehouses. Although much priestly zeal may be expended on the dwindling congregation, the area breathes of decadence.

At St. Pius Church in the suburbs, the situation is quite different. Young families predominate; well-groomed couples with children crowd the temporary church-auditorium for seven Masses each Sunday. Pulpit announcements indicate the progress of the building fund drive for the ten-classroom addition to the school. There is a bustle and a businesslike dispatch about the services, and, the Mass completed, and the parishioners drive off to trim, newly built homes.

St. Peter's and St. Pius' congregations are the result of many social and economic changes over the past few decades. The rush to the suburbs has taken off the cream of St. Peter's parish — meaning by the "cream" the more progressive, more intelligent, higher salaried, and socially mobile members. The industrialization of the downtown area is following the pattern of all large cities; within another decade, very probably the parish territory will be largely slums. Likewise, the rapid development of the outer metropolitan fringe attracts young families of better-than-average potential. St. Peter's and St. Pius represent opposite extremes on the social and economic scale. There are of course many intermediate stages. Some parishes include diverse socioeconomic levels almost equally, and hence cannot be so easily categorized. Depletion of downtown parishes, the gradual spread of business through residential districts, and the continual development of new districts farther and farther away from the heart of the city — this pattern continues with minor variations in most cities. Some changes in parishes are inevitable because of this one factor alone. The implications of these changes for the parochial school are obvious. As the community changes, so must the educational program.

Other changes in American society are somewhat more complex. Though they cannot be traced easily, their effects are evident in present-day culture. The change in kinds of *recreation* has had marked effect on the parish. The middle-aged Catholic can recall how social life once centered largely in the parish hall. The church calendar showed a succession of dinners, minstrels, festivals, smokers, card parties, and dances. The various sodalities stressed their weekly meetings and monthly Communion Sunday. Picnics and lawn fetes enlivened the summer months. Athletic contests absorbed much of the men's time and energies. The fact that social life centered in the parish gave the priests a strong hold on the loyalty of the parishioners.

Today the picture is quite different. Parishioners now have many opportunities for entertainment, and few center in the parish. Also, recreation has become passive, with radio, movies, television, and spectator sports predominating. Shorter work weeks and vacations with pay have given moderate-income workers the chance to travel in this country and abroad. Recreation has drawn individual Catholics away from the parish rather than toward it.

Secularization, or de-Christianization of society, has also weakened bonds with the parish church. Family life has become tainted with pagan ideals, and there is little dependence upon the clergy for personal direction, except in the confessional. The high percentage of mixed marriages has tended to develop an attitude of broad-mindedness verging on absence of religious standards. American culture seems to favor a "live and let live" philosophy, in matters of religious belief as well as in social and business life. The parochial school cannot prepare students adequately to meet the challenge of secularism; the students are too immature to understand the attractions of pagan philosophies.

Still other changes have occurred in the modern parish. *The rising level of education* and contacts with religiously indifferent persons have tended to foster a critical attitude toward some of the social and moral teachings of the Church. The parish school has come in for criticism both because of poor public relations and because of an educational program which is either not understood or not accepted. *Increase in specialization* has caused the growth of many agencies, besides the parish, to care for the multitude of parishioners' needs — financial, marital, occupational, social, and legal. Where once the pastor performed many of these services for his flock, diversified agencies are now available. The Catholic is free to choose who will assist him, and he uses this freedom. All of these developments have tended to draw parishioners away from the parish as a source of authority and assistance.

Supraparochial Organizations. One force that may be weakening parish bonds has not in general weakened the spirit of religion, however. Such a force is the trend toward supraparochial organizations. The horizon of the modern Catholic is broader than that of his parents, and this breadth of view is evident in the numerous broad organizations transcending parish boundaries. Pope Pius XII strongly urged trade unions, occupational guilds, group work for migrants, and various associations of an intellectual and cultural sort. The past few decades have witnessed the growth of the Cana Conference movement, the Diocesan Council of Catholic Men (and Women), collegiate clubs, associations of Catholics according to occupation (scientists, physicians, newspapermen, for example), diocesan and national Home and School Organizations, and even interparochial high schools. All of these movements have strengthened Catholicity and created a bond of solidarity among Catholics of similar interests. Yet these supraparochial societies and movements have to a certain extent reduced the individual Catholic's contacts with his own parish.

The influence of the teaching Sisters as a supraparochial group is pertinent here. Sisters are transferred from parish to parish, and from diocese to diocese, and thus develop a breadth of view concerning the interests of the Church as a whole. Mission-minded Sisters can, for example, make the ransom of pagan babies in Uganda as real to the pupils as Thanksgiving baskets for the poor. Because of their supraparochial character, Sisters might be thought of as lessening the students' loyalty to their parish.

On the contrary, the Sisters may be at times a stronger influence toward parish solidarity than even the parish priests. For one thing, children spend a great deal of time in the classroom, and their parents have a close feeling, usually, toward the Sister teaching their child this year. Any parish project is likely to enlist the Sister's and consequently the child's and the parents' wholehearted support. Preparation for First Holy Communion and Confirmation strengthens the parents' ties with the school, and it is usually the classroom teacher who is responsible for this training. Teaching Sisters, then, belong to a supraparochial organization and tend to develop in their pupils an appreciation of the "catholicity" of the Church. The Sisters, also, because they identify themselves with parish interests, strengthen the pupils' allegiance to the parish.

Parish Response to Current Trends. In the past, particularly in the national parishes, there was an intense loyalty to the parish, and at times a strong competition with other national parishes. There is the story told, however false, of the little Irish boy from St. Brigid's who felt he couldn't hear Mass at St. Anthony's Italian Church. National parishes are dying out, and people today move across parish boundaries so frequently that the feeling toward the parish is changing. Social and economic conditions discussed earlier have likewise tended to de-emphasize the parish as the fundamental point of reference for Catholics. The question arises as to whether these changes are good. Should an all-out campaign be inaugurated to restore the parish to its former status? Haven't Catholics suffered in losing the group spirit that characterized parish activities of the past? Can society substitute for the seeming disintegration of such groups?

Nostalgia for the "good old days" might incline one to wish for the simplicity of life a half or a quarter of a century ago. But the complexities of modern society cannot be removed just by wishing. The parish must change to accommodate itself to people who have changed. How can this be done? Since this discussion is concerned mainly with the school and not with the rectory, no sweeping generalizations can be made concerning the role of the clergy in the changing parish. However, because the pupils of today are the Catholic adults of tomorrow, teaching Sisters will want to orient their thinking toward proper solution of the problem.

In general, the solution lies in the *wider use of the laity* in promoting the spiritual goals of the parish. The recited Mass and even the sung Mass have "caught fire," as it were, where liturgy-minded priests have enlisted the co-operation of the faithful. The "togetherness" so lacking in modern society is appropriately and beautifully fostered by participation in the liturgy. Adult education programs have filled an urgent need, for the moral and personal problems of adult Catholics cannot be anticipated satisfactorily in the school. The school, however, can take an active part in adult education through an intelligently planned Home and School Association program.

Furthermore, the parish must go beyond "saving the saved," and enlist the help of the laity in reaching those who are not active members of the parish. The Confraternity of Christian Doctrine, begun centuries ago and reactivated by Pope Pius X, is an effective means of utilizing the laity in teaching Christian Doctrine to pupils not in Catholic schools. The Legion of Mary likewise has as one of its aims the reclaiming of "lost" Catholics. The clergy must continue, of course, as parish administrators, for such is the hierarchical organization of the Church; but in increasing numbers the laity are needed as contact people and as active participants. The informed leadership of the clergy can channel the energies and talents of the laity in spreading the Church's message to Catholics not now being reached.

Most urgently needed in today's parish is a positive effort to increase the spirit of brotherly love between classes and also between races in the parish. Centuries ago, the hallmark of the Christian was love of neighbor: "Behold how these Christians love one another!" Today, this is not always true. Parishioners tend to associate with others of their own social and economic level. In fact, the middle class Catholic has more contacts with middle class non-Catholics than he has with lower class Catholics of his own parish. The lawyer, the banker, the accountant, the teacher seldom mingle socially with parishioners whose jobs are of the less skilled type: factory workers, mill hands, bus drivers, and store clerks. How much less often the middle or lower class Catholics associate informally with Negroes and other minority groups.

It seems that only the small group of ideal Catholics try to cross class lines and race lines in the interests of brotherly love. In most northern parishes Negroes have been accepted in churches and schools, it is true. But caste lines are sharply drawn. "By this shall all men know that you are My disciples; that you have love one for another." A sophisticated shrug cannot dispose of the absoluteness of that statement.

Can the parish regain its former priority in the social life of Catholics? Probably not. Can the parish function effectively in ministering to the spiritual and social needs of Catholics? Certainly, when those spiritual and social needs are understood in the light of changing times. The Church has long been known for its adaptability. The ever ancient, ever new efficacy of the Church can meet the challenge of the parish in modern times.

WHAT OBLIGATION HAS THE PARISH SCHOOL
TOWARD THE COMMUNITY?

The faculty that engages in community study gathers a great deal of interesting information. Sociological facts invite experimentation. Teachers like to "try out" their findings in their own classrooms. Applying what has been learned through community study, the faculty can increase the effectiveness of their teaching and their own satisfaction as well. Such outcomes are highly desirable.

Should there be any other follow-up of community study? Have the principal and faculty any obligation to do more than apply sociological facts in the classroom? Persons studying the community are bound to learn that school and community are interrelated; that each has obligations to the other; that each helps the other to accomplish its purposes. One purpose of the parochial school is to transmit the learning, culture, and Faith of the past to the children of today, and thus to help children fulfill their human and divine destiny. In so doing, the parochial school directly improves the community, and hence, serves the community. The community in its turn is responsible for providing children with the best possible conditions in which to learn. Good learning conditions include adequate building facilities, materials and equipment, a good staff, and the opportunity for children to develop skills and abilities which the community needs.

In the parochial school, the community which furnishes financial support is the parish. However, larger communities, the city and the state, have valuable resources available for use in parochial schools. Thus, the parish supplies the essential conditions of good learning, while these larger communities supply resources for enriching the parochial school program. It is these larger communities which will later on provide a living for students now in Catholic schools. The interrelatedness of parochial schools and these larger communities is clear.

It is to the advantage of the parochial school to keep its various communities in mind. By intelligently serving these communities, the parochial school serves its own best interests.

Among the many ways in which the parish school can serve and improve the community, three have been selected as most important.

1. *The parochial school serves the community by good teaching.* It will profit little to graduate pupils who are weak in fundamentals because they have taken too many field trips and built too many projects. Nor will it profit, on the other hand, to force concentration on academic skills unrelated to either community needs or personal development. Good teaching endeavors to develop individual potential to the full, using content and

methods that have been proved effective. Good teaching is attuned to supernatural, spiritual, and moral development, and is sensitive to the environment as an influence in learning. Both religion and democracy are best served when schools place first priority on good teaching.

In some cities a pleasant working relationship between public and parochial schools has furthered good teaching by intervisitation of schools. On a holyday, parochial school personnel observe in the classrooms of the public schools. On another convenient day, the public school teachers return the visit. Discussions following these visits are stimulating. Both systems have provided good teaching. Both have benefited by the mutual interchange of ideas. And, ultimately, the renewed emphasis on good teaching tones up classroom instruction for many days to come. The community is particularly well served when the joint efforts of both systems emphasize good teaching.

2. *The parochial school serves the community by wise use of resources to broaden and improve the school program.* In the days of the small, close-knit community, people knew each other "face to face," and most adults were familiar with all the occupations and activities of the village. Children were inducted into the ways of the community in the course of their daily living. Today, specialization has multiplied occupations and activities, and many children know only their own neighborhood, or their own home. Learning through books is helpful to a certain extent. Broadened contacts through persons, films, exhibits, and tours crystallize learning about other people and other activities. Many outside agencies and individuals can provide pertinent information. The local library, museum, industries, business concerns, newspaper, health and welfare agencies, and private individuals can supply services which broaden and interpret the material studied in books. Careful selection and pre-planning are necessary in order to co-ordinate all materials in a meaningful whole. In using these resources, the parochial school serves the community. Greater understanding of the community results in informed participation by pupils and hence a greater interest in the community as a whole.

3. *The parochial school serves the community by providing sound educational leadership.* It is here that Sister Principals may want to draw the line. Of all aspects of administration "leadership in the community" probably appeals least to women in general and to Sisters in particular. The usual textbooks in administration have been written by men and for men, and stress activities that men value. The usual connotation of "leadership" implies large groups of people being directed by professional men who have ability and specific training. Some of the books on community leadership assume that the principal is able and willing to undertake large-scale improvement programs involving the civic community.

The leadership expected of the parochial school principal, however, is well within her power to achieve. The principal provides leadership to her staff in studying the community so that a better program will evolve. The principal provides leadership assistance to the pastor in studying the needs of the school as related to an ideal program. The principal provides leadership to adults outside the school usually through the Home and School Association. As a member of the Executive Committee, the principal uses her professional training to assist in program planning, to guide discussions of school policy, and to present to the committee and to the parents clear, practical talks on school matters. The better leaders know how to use democratic procedures. In discussing school policy and programs with parents, the principal leads best by involving parents in planning and discussion. This is not to say that parents dictate what the school will teach; rather it means that the principal wisely uses parents' experience in deciding issues of policy. Lay participation in the Church has been widely urged by the popes. By her leadership, the Sister Principal can involve the interests and talent of parents in improving what the school can do for children.

The parochial school, though not supported by public taxes, has as real an obligation to the community as the public school has. The parochial school should not "hide its light under a bushel," but rather take its place as one of the contributing institutions of the community. In some places, public school administrators have never been inside a Catholic school. In other cities administrators of the two systems have never spoken to one another. Conferences on professional topics, conducted for all interested school personnel, have been weakly represented by parochial school staffs. Those familiar with the training patterns of Sisters know that a good deal of professional work has been done. Yet, one mark of the professional person is to take her place in the community of professional persons. To date, Sisters have not done this adequately. The check list in Chapter V will enable the principal to get a clearer idea of her specific duties in school-community relations. With the increasing professionalization of the Sister Principal, her relationships with the community will become more frequent and more effective, to the good of both the school and the community.

FOR THE PRINCIPAL'S PROFESSIONAL LIBRARY

Books

Fichter, Joseph H., S.J., *Social Relations in the Urban Parish* (Chicago: The University of Chicago Press, 1954), 264 pp., $5.50.

Especially pertinent are the following chapters:

"Typology of Parishioners," pp. 9–82.

"Conceptualization of the Urban Parish," pp. 181–194.
"Major Issues in the Sociology of the Parish," pp. 195–217.
Greeley, Reverend Andrew M., *The Church and the Suburbs* (New York: Sheed and Ward, 1959), 206 pp., $3.50.

> Will "open the principal's eyes" to religion, family life, and education in suburban parishes. A well-written, factual, readable account by a thirty-three-year-old priest.

Havighurst, Robert J., and Neugarten, Bernice L., *Society and Education* (Boston: Allyn and Bacon, Inc., 1957), 465 pp., $6.25.

> If the principal can add a book in this area, the above text would be the most useful.

Nuesse, D. J., and Harte, Thomas J., C.Ss.R., *The Sociology of the Parish* (Milwaukee: The Bruce Publishing Company, 1950), 354 pp., $4.50.

> "The Social Structure of the Parish," pp. 75–99, by John D. Donovan, is pertinent.

Scheuer, Reverend Joseph F., C.PP.S., "This Metropolitan Parish Has Four Distinct Social Areas," *Catholic Management Journal*, Vol. 2, No. 2 (Spring, 1959), pp. 18–22.

PAMPHLETS

Kelly, Reverend George A., *American Parish: Changing Needs*, "Techniques for Convert-Makers," Monthly Release of the Paulist Fathers (New York: Paulist Fathers), 10 cents.
Lennon, Joseph L., O.P., *Sociological Study of the Urban Parish* (a review of the book by Father Fichter, listed above). "Techniques for Convert-Makers," Monthly Release of the Paulist Press (New York: Paulist Fathers), 10 cents.

CHAPTER XII

SCHOOL-COMMUNITY RELATIONS

> The parish school always creates an image, favorable or unfavorable, among parishioners. How? How may this image help or harm the work of the school? How may a principal show leadership in giving parents and others a fuller interpretation of the school?

AT FIRST glance, it seems that the parish school, built beside the parish church, stands for religion in education, but not especially for community influences in education. The tax-supported public school is logically bound up with various local organizations and activities, but the parish school seems more remote. The Sister Principal will tell you, however, that the parish school has many contacts with civic, social, and educational groups. Excerpts from the parochial school principal's calendar for a typical year will prove this.

Calendar

AUGUST	Federal Lunch Workshop for school lunchroom personnel
SEPTEMBER	School safety program — local police department meeting for school bus drivers; television program on rules for safe bicycle riding; inspection by fire department
OCTOBER	Home and School Association meeting
	Boy Scouts and Girl Scouts, organization meeting
	Medical and dental health program
	Red Cross, Community Chest, United Fund, UNICEF
NOVEMBER	American Education Week — open house
	Children's Civic Theater tryouts
DECEMBER	Favors for Red Cross distribution to hospitals
	"Keep Christ in Christmas" poster and essay contest — Chamber of Commerce
JANUARY	Telephone company — demonstration of telephone technique
FEBRUARY	Business-Education-Industry Day
MARCH	Easter Seal Campaign
APRIL	Registration of eighth-grade pupils for local public high school
	Local newspaper Spelling Bee
MAY	Symphony concert for elementary schools

Besides these scheduled events, there are many other contacts with the community. Some of these are: classroom observation by local university students, librarian's visits to the school and class visits to the library, the medical and dental program — tests, inoculations, and treatments, referrals to juvenile department, hearing, speech, guidance centers, and field trips to places of local interest.

There are also the contacts that don't get on the calendar at all. Parents come to see the teacher about their child's schoolwork. The secretary — in the more fortunate schools — answers inquiries made by the traffic department concerning the daily schedule. Mothers help in serving breakfast on First Friday. The attendance officer checks on pupil absence. Salesmen come — we hope, after dismissal — to display their educational materials. Local firms request an opportunity to exhibit their free source material for schools. The Knights of Columbus offers an award for citizenship. And the list is almost endless. The people and agencies who are in frequent contact with the parochial school are almost too numerous to name. This proves, if there is need of proof, that the parochial school is part and parcel of the activities of the local community. The public has an interest in the parochial school.

WHAT DOES THE PUBLIC THINK OF US?

We speak of the public and our schools, and of public opinion. But who is the public? A vague audience, something like the readership of the local newspaper? Or is the group very specific, say, just the parents and people who visit our school? What "public" should be kept in mind?

Actually there is no such thing as the school public. Sociologists have shown that people outside of the school do not form a single body, united in their reactions to school matters. The "public" is really made up of many publics, all of whom have different reasons for being interested in the school. These "publics" are dynamic, changing, loose-knit groups, many of them containing subgroups. For example, the Union Local may be one of the school's publics, and so are the parents' organization and the grocer across the street. The Altar Sodality may be one of the publics, and the Women's Symphony Concert Committee for elementary schools. The local public school board is definitely one of the more important "publics" of the parish school, as also is the editorial staff of the local newspaper.

No principal can weld these diverse publics into a single group united once-for-all in their opinion of the school. Understanding this fact of social composition, however, the principal can work out a program that will keep these various publics in view. Public relations is not a single campaign, enthusiastically sponsored and then forgotten. To keep all of the school's

publics informed, interested, and well-disposed requires a continuous interpretation of the school, and a variety of techniques. The school-public has
to be built, and kept built. This is one of the aims of a good public relations
program.

HOW DO WE FEEL TOWARD THE PUBLIC?

How do you, as principal, feel toward the many publics interested in your
school? Do you feel that you have an obligation to explain to parents and
others what the school is trying to accomplish? Do you work with your
faculty to increase their interest in community relations? What have you
done this year to improve home-school co-operation?

Perhaps you are about to say, "But I am a teaching principal. By the time
my papers are corrected, and my lessons planned, there is no time — ." It
is true that her class is an important consideration of the teaching principal,
but besides being a teacher, the Sister Principal is also an administrator. As
such, the Sister Principal has an obligation to consider the following questions seriously: Do you believe in Catholic education? Do you think that
Catholic schools are contributing something worthwhile to American society?
Do you accept parents as co-educators, with you, of their children? Do you
consider Catholic school personnel competent to work with lay adults to
improve education?

To each of these questions, the typical parochial school principal replies
in the affirmative. The principal rates Catholic schools high, and wants to
do everything in her power to advance the cause of Catholic education. The
experts say that one cannot have a good school today without keeping the
public in mind. The Sister Principal may hesitate to embark on a so-called
program of community relations, but in effect that is what she must do to
satisfy her obligations as administrator of a Catholic school.

WHAT DOES A COMMUNITY-RELATIONS PROGRAM DO?

Community relations, or public relations, does two things: it makes every
community contact count, and it arranges for the right kinds of contacts.
Both of these things require real leadership on the part of the principal.
The excerpts from the parochial school principal's calendar show that many
people and agencies come into the school regularly. Each of these can help
the school, and does, even without a public relations program. With such
a program, however, still greater help is given. A public relations program
sees all these contacts as part of the child's education and does not resist,
or merely tolerate, outside influences. By means of a planned program, the
school capitalizes upon everything the community has to offer to improve

the school's program. Shall safety, for example, be taught merely as part of the course of study, or can the local fire department help to make safety instruction meaningful? Shall the dry-as-dust study of the home state be enriched by the use of resource people and field trips? Good teaching and good administration see community interaction as part of the child's development. The efficient principal tries to use all community contacts so that children will benefit; a program of community relations helps her to do this most effectively.

A good program of community relations includes still more positive action than this; it means that the principal must go out and arrange for community contacts that will help children. For example, contacts with parents are inevitable, as, right after report cards are issued. Parents will certainly come to inquire, to complain, to resist. How much wiser it is to plan early in the year for the visits which parents will make. A school handbook, prepared by the faculty and parents, will cut in half misunderstandings about report cards. Bulletins to parents further explain the why's and wherefore's of the school grading systems. Home and School Association meetings can give parents a chance to ask questions and to give suggestions concerning report cards. Faculty meetings may be devoted to clearing up the teachers' ideas about grades and marks. It is not just to eliminate trouble that the wise principal plans in advance for report card grades or other school matters; good planning goes far beyond that. Everything that is done in the school should have one ultimate purpose: to help children. Children are greatly helped when their parents and their teachers see eye to eye, or very nearly so, in controversial areas. School personnel need professional training and good will in proper proportions to make parent-teacher contacts help children most effectively.

What is true of planned teacher-parent discussions is also true of the numerous other contacts of school and community. Patiently enduring community contacts is not virtue; it is myopia. The school directs the child's learning barely six hours a day; his out-of-school learning goes on during the remaining eighteen hours. Unless out-of-school learning is integrated to some extent with in-school learning, teachers are dissipating their efforts in the classroom.

Public relations is not merely propaganda which tries to "sell the school" to the public. Good public relations is a partnership affair; it is a sharing process in which the school is interpreted to the public, and the public shares in forming school policy. When the public understands the school's aims and has helped to form them, the necessary support will be forthcoming. This support will at times be financial; it would be foolish to belittle the importance of paying for the new cafeteria tables. Far more important than finances, however, are the understanding and co-operation which result when the school has adequately explained its program and its goals. Good public relations is alert to the need for support, but it also reciprocates by its service to the community.

DO WE HAVE TIME FOR PUBLIC RELATIONS?

Principals are busy, of course. They cannot spend as much time as they would like on every activity; they have only so many hours in the week to portion out among their various duties. Parochial school principals now spend some time in public relations — preparing handbooks and bulletins for adults outside the school, dealing with parents and other interested persons, working with the Home and School Association, taking part in community projects, and getting news to the press and perhaps radio and television, as well. Is there any measuring stick to compare the time now spent in these activities with the time that might well be devoted to them? Two studies of the elementary principalship show the following number of hours per week devoted to community relations.

TABLE XVII.   Time Spent in Public Relations Each Week

Group	Supervising Principals	Teaching Principals
Public School[a]	8 hours	5 hours
Parochial School[b]	3 hours	1 hour

[a] National Education Association, Department of Elementary Principals, *The Elementary School Principalship — A Research Study*, Thirty-seventh Yearbook (Washington, D. C.: National Education Association, 1958), p. 98. Used with permission.
[b] Reverend James W. Malone, *Administration of the Teacher in the Parochial Elementary Schools of Ohio*, unpublished Ph.D. thesis (Washington, D. C.: The Catholic University of America, 1957), p. 14.

The above table shows that public school principals spend much more time in community relations than parochial school principals do. It is true, of course, that the public school principal gets his bread and butter from the community and hence knows he must please the community. Out of his forty-seven-hour work week, the supervising public school principal gives eight hours, or about one sixth of his time, to outside persons and agencies. The teaching public school principal gives five hours, or about one ninth of his working time to public relations.[1]

The supervisory parochial school principal averages three hours a week of her fifty-hour work week in community-related activities.[2] The teaching parochial school principal averages only one hour a week in public relations.

[1] National Education Association, Department of Elementary School Principals, *The Elementary School Principalship — A Research Study*, Thirty-seventh Yearbook (Washington, D. C.: The National Education Association, 1958), p. 98 and p. 241.
[2] Reverend James W. Malone, *Administration of the Teacher in the Parochial Elementary Schools of Ohio*, unpublished Ph.D. thesis (Washington, D. C.: The Catholic University of America, 1957), p. 45.

What could one do in three hours a week with regard to public relations? One could talk with a few parents, deal with the school doctor and nurse, and perhaps prepare a bulletin to parents about the coming Home and School Association meeting. In an hour a week, one couldn't even "hold the line." One certainly could not carry on an adequate program of informing the public of the many worthwhile activities going on in the school. Nor could one consider parents' suggestions for modifying some aspects of school policy.

How much more time should principals devote to this important aspect of their work? Chapter V presented an ideal time distribution for the parochial school principal. Using these figures, the following table can be drawn up of the time recommended for school-community relations.

TABLE XVIII. Recommended Hours Per Week for Public Relations

Group	Supervising Principals	Teaching Principals
Public School[a]	9 hours	7 hours
Parochial School[b]	5 hours	2 hours

[a] National Education Association, Department of Elementary School Principals, *The Elementary School Principalship — A Research Study*, Thirty-seventh Yearbook (Washington, D. C.: The National Education Association, 1958), pp. 90 and 241. Used with permission.

[b] Reverend James W. Malone, *Administration of the Teacher in the Parochial Elementary Schools of Ohio*, unpublished Ph.D. thesis (Washington, D. C.: The Catholic University of America, 1957), p. 45.

According to the above recommendations, both public school and parochial school principals would spend more time in school-community relations than they now do. Public school supervising principals would add another hour to their present time allotment, and public school teaching principals would add two more hours. In the parochial schools, supervising principals would add two hours, and teaching principals would add one hour. All principals, then, feel that the public deserves more of their time.

What seems to stand in the way of a better distribution of time? Both public school and parochial school principals feel strongly that they now spend entirely too much time on non-professional tasks. Many schools have no secretary, and some have only a part-time secretary. Some schools have poor janitorial service. Thus, principals with degrees in educational administration are spending their time typing letters and passing out supplies, jobs which an average high school graduate could do quite as well. In a sense, it is easier to go on opening cartons and rearranging stockroom shelves than to revolutionize one's thinking and one's work by delegating these nonprofessional jobs to others. (See Chapter IV for a discussion of delegation.) Delegation of such chores would take real ingenuity, especially in schools having no paid secretarial help.

Women are known for their ingenuity, however, and the ingenious Sister

Principal can arrange time for duties deemed most important. The Sister Principal should write out the routine jobs which a nonprofessional person could take over for her, and then diligently set about securing at least a minimum of clerical help. At least for a start in her public relations work, the Sister Principal can take as a norm the amount of time which parochial school principals say they would *like* to devote to public relations activities — about five hours weekly, or about an hour a day. Using this guide, she can then plan desirable activities with her staff. Fulfilling their obligation to the public requires time on the part of school personnel. Arranging for the necessary time is one criterion of good administration.

IS EVERYTHING IN PUBLIC RELATIONS "PROGRAMED"?

So far the discussion has been of a comprehensive program of public relations involving the principal's leadership. Such a program is a definite need in every school. Are there, however, things that affect public opinion independently of any planned program?

Thinking it through, one finds that a good many "little things" influence the way parents and others regard the school. The way the secretary, or student officer, handles phone messages can make a caller feel welcome and satisfied. The custodian's thoroughness in cleaning gives visitors a favorable impression. The milkman likes it when the principal notifies him of vacation dates. The school physician appreciates having preliminary routines taken care of so that he can work more swiftly and efficiently. The Red Cross representative is pleased that the Christmas favors for the sanatorium are attractive and ready on time. Family ties with the school are strengthened because of the fruit basket sent to a hospitalized pupil.

It is through such individual contacts as these that the public learns about the school. A series of satisfactory contacts makes the outsider feel that the school is a good one. Many of the things which people appreciate are spontaneous acts of thoughtfulness; Christian courtesy and kindliness prompt innumerable such acts throughout the day. However, in the bustle of our many duties, one is likely to forget such courtesies, and they are too important to be left entirely to chance. The manner of handling contacts with the public should be planned by the staff, just as in the classroom, planned experiences are part of the teaching job. Good public relations, like good teaching, is made up of countless little things prearranged to produce a desired cumulative effect. When the principal and staff have planned, or programed, their public relations activities well, they will most certainly *look* better because they *are* better than they would otherwise be.

WHO ARE THE PEOPLE IN THE PUBLIC RELATIONS PROGRAM?

Progressive institutions nowadays hire a full-time expert to head their public relations program. This expert has the know-how — what to do, when and how to do it, whom to involve, and what to expect. In the parochial school, the Sister Principal must be the expert. Through her reading and her watchful attitude, she must develop the know-how for her own situation. Chiefly, the principal must develop a knowledge of human relations, for a paper program is worthless; good planning includes careful attention to the people who really make the program work. The Sister Principal can write out her objectives for the year, explain them to the staff, show them how to accomplish them, and it is still possible for the faculty to think, and feel, and act as before. The principal may have aroused their interest, and even perhaps disposed the group to her point of view, but action may not be forthcoming.

A public relations program is, then, a matter of both knowledge and motivation. It is like teaching in this. A teacher may have begun her lesson with an interesting "lead" story, and may have the class pleasingly alert. However, when the teacher wishes the class to go on enthusiastically from there, she may note that interest has waned. In other words, though she may have aroused the group's interest momentarily, she really did not "motivate" them. Motivation means that the group has accepted the leader's goals as its own; in fact, the group has so identified itself with the leader's goals that these goals are actually what the group wishes for itself. In a democratic situation, the leader has helped the group to evolve goals which are its own, though within the limits of choice set by the leader. Where self-direction has been developed in a class, the teacher's motivation provides the spark for meaningful pupil activity.

The same is true of a public relations program. Directives neatly typed out and handed down from above may fail utterly to motivate the faculty to change their ways of thinking and acting. When the principal knows the human beings with whom she deals — knows their likes and dislikes, their weak spots and strengths, their "readiness" for new ideas — her motivation will be the kind that will truly "motivate." The personnel of the parish school, as individual persons, must identify themselves with the principal's goals or no change will take place. Human relations is an area which principals need to study, if they wish people to want to change. A study of human relations will also help the principals to want to change themselves.

The people most closely associated with the parish school differ in many ways. It is the principal's work to stimulate and co-ordinate the efforts of diverse personalities. Let us consider the people who work with the principal in interpreting the parochial school to the public.

THE PASTOR

The key figure in public relations is the pastor, as discussed in Chapter III. In a sense, the pastor functions somewhat like the public school board of education; that is, he provides the funds and the framework within which the school program can be carried out. As outlined in Chapter III, the pastor constructs and furnishes the building, provides equipment and supplies, and pays salary checks. By these means, he largely determines just how effective his school can be. In other words, children will learn well, the faculty will be happy, the community will be professionally received — only in so far as the pastor has provided the conditions requisite.

School morale is highly affected by the pastor's provisions for his school. The amount of money which the pastor reserves from the Sunday collection for school needs is an index of how important he feels the school is. The initial investment in a parochial school plant is a large one: half a million dollars is not uncommon in rapidly expanding areas. The appearance of a well-constructed building tones up morale. Perhaps even more, the pastor affects morale by his regular investment of parish funds for cleaning, for repair and replacement of equipment, for beautifying the grounds, and for planned additions of books and supplementary materials. In most parochial schools, there is no set budget, and needless to say, there is no excess of money. However, the pastor's attitude toward school expenses affects the morale of both principal and staff. And the morale of the faculty directly affects public relations.

This is not to say that in poor parishes teacher morale is low. In a little national parish in a downtown district, with meager Sunday collection and an old school building, there is a faculty with high morale. The key to staff morale is the pastor, who provides the best conditions he can with his limited Sunday income. By careful planning, he manages to meet all state standards. There are sufficient facilities but nothing extra. However, and this is significant, Sisters love to be appointed to the school, and are loath to be withdrawn, because of the pastor's interest and consideration, far transcending the extra conveniences that can be purchased with money.

The pastor is also a key figure in public relations because he is the administrative head of the parish school. Parishioners, and the general public, know the parish school mostly through its policies. Since the pastor is the administrative head of his school, he issues school policy within the broad framework provided by state and diocesan regulations. The pastor may decide details of school policy himself, or he may develop policy in collaboration with the principal and staff, and perhaps also in conference with parents. Within recent years, more pastors are regularly present at faculty meetings and thus must work with the staff in shaping school policy. It is the principal's role to supply professional information to the pastor to guide his formulation of policy. It is also her role to co-ordinate the decisions of the pastor and the opinions of her staff.

Obviously, the first and most important person in the school's public relations program is the pastor, and with him the assistant priests in the parish. It is futile to try to dispose outsiders toward the school unless the principal harmoniously integrates the working relationships of those closest to the parish school.

THE TEACHERS

Informally, teachers are shaping public opinion all day long. What teacher says, and does, is told and re-told on buses, in stores, and in homes. Parents and other adults usually feel toward the school the way the child feels toward his teacher. No planned public relations program can offset the attitudes built up by day-to-day contacts of teachers with pupils.

Since this is so, public relations centers around the teacher. The principal may send home an occasional news bulletin on school events; every day the teacher sends home scores of "talking" bulletins — her pupils. It is true that here and there a parent is not interested in his child's schooling; but that is the rare parent. For the most part, parents are eager to hear of the day's happenings. They know what the lay teacher wore, how the boy next door behaved, who had the best writing papers, what kind of practice they had for Confirmation, which room was ahead in the mission drive, and — ultimately, how junior's teacher affected him that day. Pupils using public transportation have told the passengers the same vivid happenings. One bus driver, after listening for months to the after-school roundup, knew an entire faculty well enough to recognize their nicknames. The neighbors and relatives usually do not have to inquire how Junior likes school: unsolicited commentaries keep them informed. It would be easier for the teacher if children didn't talk so much, but they do, so the teacher can expect to have classroom scenes played back in the kitchen.

No harm would be done — in fact, good would be done, because of children's tendency to relay the day's experience, if the children liked their teachers. A younger child hearing about Sister Mary all year long, said, "Oh, I can't wait to get to Sister Mary's room; then I'll have fun too." Even at the elementary level, children long for, or dread, passing to a certain teacher's room. Parents say, "We're so relieved he's in Sister Ann's room this year; we had an awful time getting him to school last year, one excuse after another. This year, he even insists on re-copying his homework if it isn't neat."

Parents rarely say that Junior loves school because the principal is nice, or because the pastor had the yard black-topped, or because the eighth grade won in baseball. When a child loves school, it is because of the teacher. And he loves school only when his teacher loves him.

Teachers who *love children* are then the school's best assets, and indirectly the schools best public relations agents. Teachers in parochial schools have the highest possible motive for loving children, all children, the forward, the dirty, the stubborn, the flighty, the conceited, the dull. Mrs. Jones' third group beam when it is their turn for reading, though their progress is so slow. Sister Jean plans her classes in social studies so that everyone can have the thrill of achievement by contributing to the unit. Sister Ellen is patient with the disorderliness of the child whose parents have just been divorced. The love of the teacher for all of her pupils has a steadying effect on every individual pupil.

Yet, love is not enough, as a recent book puts it. To do her work adequately, and to have a happy classroom, the teacher needs knowledge and training, as outlined in Chapter VIII. First of all, she needs sufficient training to know both the content she is teaching and ways of imparting subject matter effectively. She needs to know how children learn and how they interact with one another. She should know how the parents of her pupils live, what kinds of work they do, what values they have, and how they feel about the school. She needs to know the facts of social class in America — the fate of the lower classes, even at the hands of teachers. She should know the story of immigrant groups in our country and the process of their adaptation. Only with a broad background in general and professional education can teachers be tolerant of differing cultural groups, and be at ease with both adults and children regardless of nationality, religion, social class, or personal qualities. Love disposes the teacher to accept the child; training gives the teacher insight into the proper handling of his individual needs.

To be happy in her work and thus to provide a happy classroom, the teacher needs *good mental health.* Religious communities have made considerable progress in screening out applicants who show signs of maladjustment; superiors have also provided courses in mental hygiene and the opportunity for counseling and therapy. As in other school systems, however, much remains to be done in the area of mental hygiene in parochial schools. Some of the bad public relations resulting from teacher's remarks and actions could be prevented by a more thoroughgoing program of personality analysis and direction.

Satisfactory contacts with other adults also help teachers develop good personal relations and, as a result, to have happier classrooms. Community contacts have a broadening effect; activities such as Business-Industry-Education Day and institutes sponsored by industrial, artistic, civic, and social groups familiarize teachers with important influences in children's lives. Taking part in educational conferences with parochial and public school personnel also contributes to the teacher's maturation. Then there are the social activities, such as clubs, which by frank conversation, remove some of the scales from the teachers' eyes. An effective teacher mingles easily and happily with other adults, is able to discuss her own views on education, but is also able to accept the viewpoints of others. More and more, the good teacher must be a good leader of adults. Her own maturity in adult personal relations contributes stability to her work in the classroom.

Are such teachers paragons and nowhere to be found? Such teachers should be typical of parochial schools. Such teachers are needed for the full and harmonious development of children. In their own self-improvement, the teachers develop a happier personality, a happier classroom, and better public relations.

THE SERVICE STAFF

Pastors and principals are becoming more aware of the public relations potential of the service staff — the secretary, the custodian, bus drivers, and cafeteria workers. It often happens that these nonprofessional employees give the public their only impression of the school. Hence, it is wise educationally to consider the service staff as full-fledged members of the public relations team.

Money figures in the kind of service staff a school has. With adequate salaries and fringe benefits (see Chapters VI and VII), a high caliber person can be obtained. The additional money for better qualified people is well spent, for good service personnel give an undeniable tone to the school. When competent service workers are part of the school team, they can take an active and informed part in formulating school policies which affect them. The nonteaching staff should be present at several faculty meetings each year and share in administrative decisions. Properly selected and directed, the service staff has a feeling of responsibility for their personal appearance, their speech, their attitude toward the children, the faculty, and the public, and a sense of pride in the competent handling of their respective jobs. The machinery of the school runs more smoothly when service personnel are happy in their work and appreciated by the faculty and the pastor. Good service workers free the principal and teachers for strictly professional activities, and as a result improve public relations.

THE PARENTS' ORGANIZATION

Parents are the most interested public which the school has. The public relations program of the school naturally places the parents' organization high on its list of people who count. It was not always so. There was a time when the parents' group was an appendage, something extra added on but not directly related to the work of the school. The mothers' club may have poured tea of an afternoon and smiled indulgently at the children's teachers. There may even have been a thoughtful gift for the faculty at Christmas. But the activities of the parents' group were unrelated to the educational program. It was hardly proper to bring up an educational topic in such utterly sweet situations. In fact, only the mothers of the sweetest children tended to come.

Today the modern parish school needs and wants an active, informed parents' organization, not just a mothers' club. Parents and teachers are coeducators of children; they both profit by planned meetings to discuss matters of an educational nature. Unhappy experiences with parents' groups in the past should not condition pastors and principals against such groups. Rather, by using a positive, constructive approach, the school will find the parents' organization its most satisfactory ally in reaching the objectives of Christian education.

Fortunately, there is a model plan which the parish school can adapt to its own specific needs. In the public school system, the national parents' organization is known as the Parent-Teachers Association. In the parochial schools, the Home and School Association is the P.T.A.'s national counterpart. The National Council of Catholic Women has drawn up an effective manual of operations for the Home and School Association, and issues monthly program leaflets to stimulate better meetings. The National Council of Catholic Men also issues helpful program suggestions. Whether or not the parish is affiliated with the national Home and School Association, the parish school program will benefit by using these suggestions.

Purposes of the Home and School Association. To those accustomed to the traditional parents' meetings, with their drawn-out sessions and money-raising campaigns, the Home and School program represents a radical change in thinking. The Home and School Association is not organized for any of the age-old purposes of raising money, getting together socially, or staging pupil entertainments. The association exists to develop a better mutual understanding between parents and teachers. The association aims to help parents achieve their high mission as coeducators of their children. At the same time, the association gives both parents and teachers the opportunity to discuss and explore aspects of child development essential to a better handling of children.

The Home and School Association has three stated objectives: spiritual formation, information, and action. Perhaps the typical Home and School agenda[3] may be used to illustrate the accomplishment of these three purposes.

---

[3] National Council of Catholic Women, *A Manual of Home and School Associations* (Washington, D. C.: National Council of Catholic Women, 1957), p. 12. Adapted with permission.

PARISH HOME AND SCHOOL ASSOCIATION MEETING
Agenda

1. Call to Order
2. Opening Prayer
3. Five-minute talk by Spiritual Adviser or another priest on family spirituality
4. PROGRAM

   This may be a lecture, panel, a discussion, or demonstration on an educational topic. Suggested time length — 45 minutes.
5. BUSINESS MEETING

   This part of the meeting should be conducted according to parliamentary procedure. Suggested time length — 30 minutes or less.

   Minutes of previous meeting
   Statement of Treasurer
   Report of Executive Committee by President
   Reports of Standing Committees —
       Discussion and action as needed
   Letters received by the association
   Old Business
   New Business
   Announcements
   Adjournment
6. SOCIAL HOUR

   Simple refreshments; opportunity for friendly conversation for those who wish to remain

In this outline for a parent-teacher meeting, *the spiritual formation* objective is reached through the opening prayer and the pastor's talk on family spirituality. This talk helps parents to know how to do a better job of rearing their children in their holy Faith. The pastor or the study committee may prepare a bookshelf of readable articles and booklets related to the topic for the evening. Parents need to be and want to be better informed in matters of spiritual guidance; the Home and School meeting provides for this need.

Imparting information is the second objective of the association. The agenda gives prominence to the program for the evening. The high spot of interest at each meeting is the forty-five minutes devoted to a specific aspect of the educational program. Topics may be suggested by parents and teachers, or they may be selected because of the general interest. For example, topics such as these are bound to be of interest and value to both parents and teachers: homework, television, sex education, vocational guidance, reading instruction, and school policies. During the summer, the programs can be planned ahead for the entire year, in order to insure variety and comprehensiveness. A qualified speaker may present the topic, or a panel of parents, or parents and teachers. On occasion, the entire program may be an explanation of some phase of the instructional program of the school, such as a demonstration of the way reading is taught in selected grades. The program is never to be entertainment. When children participate, as in reading groups to demonstrate methods of teaching reading, entertainment is incidental, not planned. At each meeting, the forty-five minutes devoted to educational information are the most important part of the evening. Parents should expect and should get something practical from each program.

The third objective of the Home and School Association is *action*. It is natural that parents will want to put into action the information and inspiration which they get from a well-organized home and school meeting. "Action" in this sense means implementation of suggestions made at the meetings; "action" does not mean money-raising activities. So often, one hears the question, "But what does the Home and School Association *do?*" The association strengthens understanding and co-operation between parents and teachers; it helps parents and teachers fulfill their God-given rights and duties in the education of children.

Organization of the Group. There may be four, or three, elected officers; the president, the vice-president, the secretary, and the treasurer, or one person as secretary-treasurer. It is recommended that a father be elected president, and that one of the other officers also be a man. The reason for this is that the other fathers will be encouraged to attend meetings if they know that a man will be conducting it. Men somehow do not relish watching women conduct a discussion. This may be due to a realization that men typically conduct meetings better than women do, or the feeling may be due to a natural resentment on the part of men to be dominated by women. The psychological bases for this feeling are interesting to study, but the important point to make here is that the association will have a better chance to succeed if fathers are among the officers.

Besides the officers, an essential feature is the *executive committee*. This group is made up of the elected officers, the pastor, and the principal. The executive committee really makes the association what it is. This committee has full responsibility for the association's business affairs, including review of the report of all committees, consideration of suggestions concerning school policy, the association's budget, and all other administrative matters. The work of the executive committee outside of regular meeting makes it possible to keep the business meeting down to twenty or at the most thirty minutes. The executive committee also prevents airing grievances against the school during the regular meeting. When parents wish to recommend an investigation of school policy, or some change, the president refers the matter to the consideration of the executive committee. The executive committee, in the period before the next regular meeting, considers the matter at length, and prepares a report which the president will present at the next meeting. The executive committee is well qualified to study school conditions objectively and thoroughly, and their report to the general membership can be unbiased and satisfying.

There are also the standing committees, as many as needed. The recommended standing committees are those which manage the year's program, publicity, hospitality, and reading materials. The chairmen of the standing committees report the work of their group to the executive board prior to regular meeting, so that the business meeting can proceed without too many detailed reports. It is good to have the executive committee mimeograph the reports of the standing committees before each meeting. The reports can then be placed on the chairs a few minutes before the meeting, and members can peruse the reports at their leisure.

Frequency of Meetings. Four or five meeting a year are sufficient. Well-planned educational programs for these meetings give a wealth of information and inspiration to parents. Parents will be more interested in coming when they know they will benefit from the meeting. Also, many more fathers come, for they know it is only four or five times a year and they can plan ahead for these meetings. Experience has shown that a few good meetings are better attended, and better liked, than nine or ten meetings.

The committees, however, meet more often. The executive committee, made up of the elected officers, the pastor and the principal, meets at least once before each general meeting to plan the business meeting. Other committees meet as often as their work requires group discussion. The general meetings can be shorter because of these in-between meetings by the committees.

Attendance at Meetings. Both fathers and mothers must attend the meetings, or there is no Home and School Association. In fact, the attendance should be about evenly divided between fathers and mothers. So the question arises: How can we get better attendance at meetings? First, make the meetings so interesting and useful that parents will not want to miss. Have parents share in the program planning during the summer months; especially get the fathers in on the planning. Let the parents evaluate the meetings, and tell how they could be improved. Study the techniques of group discussion, so that every parent feels he had his say and people listened to him. To get attendance, the meetings must become much better than they typically are.

Second, the time element can be worked on. Meetings should be held in the evening, when fathers can come. Meetings should begin right on time, and end on time. Do not let the secretary drone on with the minutes of the last meeting. And do not have endless reports by committee chairmen.

Highlight the program part of the meeting — forty-five minutes packed with interest. Then make sure that the remainder of the meeting lasts no longer than another forty-five minutes. When the program is good, and the business meeting is held to a minimum, attendance is bound to improve.

Third, reminders help. A parents' bulletin early in the year can carry the dates and program topics for the entire year. The parish Sunday bulletin can carry an interesting comment on the program and the time of the meeting. A mimeographed reminder taken home by children the day of the meeting also helps. The more interesting the reminder, the better response it evokes. A good percentage of absenteeism is caused by sheer forgetfulness.

Fourth, hold Open House in the classrooms prior to the meeting. It is good for teachers to be in their classrooms for an hour before the scheduled meeting time. Parents can visit the room, see their children's work, and talk with the teacher. Sisters sometimes prefer to hold Open House, then attend the program part of the meeting, and go to their convent before the business session. Having Open House prior to the meeting gives the parents a chance to talk with the Sisters. One interesting variation of Open House is to have room meetings with parents prior to the general meeting. In this way, the classroom teacher can present to the parents a single aspect of the work for the grade, as, teaching phonics. These room meetings give parents the opportunity to ask questions about their own child's everyday activities.

Fifth, avoid negative devices to increase attendance. Sometimes, teachers have contests to see which grade has the most parents present at the meeting. Or an individual class gives stars to the pupils whose parents are present. Or a banner is passed from grade to grade after each meeting, the grade with the highest parents' attendance winning the banner. All of these are extrinsic motivations, and try to threaten or cajole parents into coming. Seeing the high pressured methods sometimes used, one would think that the meetings must be very poor to warrant such extreme measures.

Last, study the kinds of parents who do *not* attend the meetings. Some forget, some are busy elsewhere, and some are ill. But the others — why did they not come? Teachers sometimes tend to overlook a very important fact with regard to attendance at home and school meetings. Parents from the lower classes, from the poorer homes, from the "fringe" of the group, are not comfortable when attending meetings and hence tend to stay away. There is no doubt that teachers favor parents from the higher socioeconomic levels. It would be splendid if this sad reflection on teachers' attitudes did not at all apply to parochial schools, but we have no assurance of this. The children who are cleaner, brighter, better dressed, and better behaved appeal to teachers. What kind of parents do these children have? Parents who rather enjoy dropping in at the school to talk with teacher, and express their appreciation of her work — parents typically from the "better" homes. They are usually the "white-collar" workers.

Teachers do not have to express their preference in words, but children and their parents can feel approval and disapproval. Parents who are poor, or even relatively poor with respect to the parish average, need the interest of teachers, especially religious teachers. It does not prove teachers to be righteous when they declare, "The parents I most want to see never show up at the home and school meeting." When teachers truly love the poor little ones, whether poor financially or poor socially or poor intellectually, the children know it. And so do their parents. The really Christian teacher, religious or lay, makes every effort to reach the parents, through the Home and School Association if possible, but if not, then through privately arranged conferences. Perhaps a good indication of whether teachers love the underprivileged can be gleaned by noting the type of parent who visits the school; many who stay away do so because they are not loved.

Working systematically at these six suggestions should increase attendance at Home and School Association meetings. When attendance has improved, then the people are there to benefit by the evening's program.

Role of the Principal in the Home and School Association. The principal, as a member of the Executive Committee, has an opportunity to work with the pastor and the elected officers frequently during the year. The principal, in this capacity, can bring to the committee the teachers' attitudes about the problems discussed. Further, the principal serves as a resource person for the Executive Committee, doing a great deal of "behind the scenes" preparation. The principal is qualified to suggest good program ideas, practical procedures for teacher demonstrations, and helpful suggestions for parents' reading. The principal also represents the pastor's point of view. Though the pastor is present at the committee meetings and the regular meetings, he may not wish to state baldly his reasons for supporting or rejecting a proposal. The principal can tactfully discover beforehand what would be to the best interests of the parish school, administratively speaking, and then at the meetings provide the background for the pastor's remarks. The principal is in this sense "filling in" details, and solidifying the work of the committee.

However, the principal should keep in mind that she is a resource person, and is not to dominate the group. The three purposes of the association should be uppermost in her mind: spiritual formation, information, and action. The Home and School organization should not be subordinated to the principal's interests, but should be assisted by her to realize its essential functions. The principal *directs* the school's program, in co-operation with the pastor, but she should merely *assist* the parents' organization to develop its own leadership.

The Home and School Association, to operate effectively, needs the active interest of the faculty. In fact, of all public relations activities, those connected with the parents' organization do most to promote the mutual interests of the staff and parents.

Other Groups. In addition to the Home and School Association, there are a number of other groups with which the school has frequent and valuable contacts. In some places, there may be considerable contact with the local public school board, for the services of the attendance officer, for transfer of pupils between the two systems, and for educational conferences. The local public library likewise furnishes assistance to the parochial school, by supplementing the school library and by rendering professional services, such as librarian's book talks to the individual classes and conducted tours of the library. The juvenile bureau, the fire department, and the health department provide necessary resources for a good school program. The community welfare agencies are a valuable asset in servicing needy children.

The parochial school principal should ascertain the type of co-operation required in her own situation, and should then proceed to work systematically and professionally with these various groups. Teaching principals especially need to co-ordinate their energies with regard to these out-of-school services, because of the amount of scheduling and clerical work involved. The opinion which these agencies have of Catholic schools and the extent of the services provided will be largely determined by the pleasantness and efficiency of the Sister Principal's contacts with them. The principal needs to be firm, of course, in opposing exploitation of pupils by any groups, whether through contests, campaigns, or projects. All proffered services should be evaluated as they contribute to the educational program.

WHAT ARE SOME PROMISING PUBLIC RELATIONS TECHNIQUES?

Whatever devices the principal uses to interpret the school to the public, results are best when the whole faculty has had a hand in the planning. The principal is really interpreting people (the staff) to people (the parents and other interested lay persons). Therefore, the more people involved in the interpretation the more likely it is to be effective.

HANDBOOKS FOR PARENTS

Parents like to know about their child's school, its policies, routines, and program. Explaining the school's objectives and procedures to parents is an excellent means of unifying the staff, and at the same time of informing the parents. Where there is a diocesan manual, the local school can use this as a basis for its own handbook. Some helpful ideas can be obtained from the parents' handbook of the local public school system. When the faculty have drawn up the points which they feel are essential, a staff member may be appointed as editor, and another in charge of format. A foreword by the pastor is read with appreciation by both faculty and parents. In preparing the first school handbook, it may not be practical to involve the help of parents because of the time element involved, but in subsequent revisions, the Home and School members can offer valuable suggestions. The handbook can be simple but should include essential points of policy. The time spent in working out a parents' handbook is more than repaid by the good public relations which it promotes.

BULLETINS TO PARENTS

Parents like to know what is going on at school. They like to be kept informed of important activities. Although children talk a great deal about school, they frequently forget things which parents need to know. A well-planned bulletin, regularly issued, attractively arranged, is welcome in the home. The bulletin can provide a calendar of coming events — such as inoculations, holidays, and report cards. The bulletin can also highlight educationally significant events which children are unaware of, such as faculty work with Puerto Rican children, school participation in the national safety program, the progress of the band, or the purchase of new audio-visual materials. The bulletin can also be a good-will ambassador, cheerful in its content and its appearance. Too few parochial schools have realized the full potential of the parents' bulletin. In fact, it seems that not more than one in every five parochial schools issue regular bulletins to parents. To the parents, the bulletin can be a very significant and most effective public relations technique.

OPEN HOUSE

Open House has been mentioned in the discussion of the Home and School Association meeting. Another especially good time for Open House is during American Education Week, when both public and parochial schools have activities emphasizing important features of their systems. Some schools have found it profitable to invite parents in for a half-day, or for a single class, while the children are in session. Whether children are in session or not, some helpful suggestions have been developed for handling Open House for parents and other interested adults.

Parents register as they enter the building, and are given large, clear name cards to wear. The faculty, too, wear name cards, and greet the parents on entering the building. Parents then receive a schedule of the activities, with the names of the teachers and their room numbers. Student guides may conduct the visitors to their assigned room. Large floor plans of the school, posted for easy visibility, give parents a sense of ease in the building. Signs indicating routes to take, and names of important rooms, also help. An information booth is always a boon to some lost parent, or a parent in need of a telephone. Refreshments add to the friendliness of the occasion.

Open House may begin with a general session in the auditorium or cafeteria, at which the pastor welcomes the guests, and the principal outlines the activities of the occasion. There may be a brief talk on the particular points to be noted — as, displays of pupil work, library books in the classrooms, or special facilities. Student guides may then conduct the visitors to the classrooms. Here, there may be a smaller meeting of the parents of children in the grade, again emphasizing certain aspects of the school program, perhaps manuscript and cursive writing in the primary grades. Then there will be the opportunity for parents to talk individually with the teachers about the pupils' work. A well-conducted Open House is a satisfying experience for both faculty and parents and one which promotes good human relations.

DEMONSTRATION LESSONS

Probably the activity of most interest to parents is a demonstration lesson in which a lifelike classroom atmosphere is simulated. Parents have repeatedly asked for demonstration lessons, and have been highly enthusiastic in comments on the lessons' helpfulness to them. In presenting demonstrations, the problems of space and acoustics are vital. A trial demonstration for the faculty could be used to iron out difficulties before actual presentation to parents. Both before the demonstration, and afterward, there should be discussion periods, led by the teacher herself or the principal, in which aims, materials, and procedures are explained. The demonstration lesson is welcomed as the program part of the Home and School Association meeting from time to time.

CONFERENCES WITH PARENTS

At Home and School meetings, during Open House and at many other times, teachers and parents talk together about children. Such discussions are usually very brief, for other parents are waiting. The discussions can be longer when they have been previously scheduled. Since parent-teacher conferences are a source of much satisfaction, they deserve the serious attention of the faculty.

First, a Good Conference is a Two-Way Process. Both parent and teacher come to the conference to learn; neither has all the answers, or the conference would not be necessary. A conference is not the perfect opportunity to "set the parents right" about their child, nor is it the time when parents should "trim teachers down to size." It is true that in her professional studies the teacher has learned a great deal about methods of teaching content and of helping child development. At the same time, it is also true that parents have acquired a fund of information about what schools should be accomplishing.

Since a good conference is a learning process, both parents and teacher may experience some embarrassment because learning of one's own mistakes can be painful. The teacher may learn that her method of pupil rewards is harming the more sensitive pupils. The parents may learn that their own pressure for good grades is having ill effects on their child's relations with his classmates. In the sharing of ideas during a conference, the teacher will probably come to realize the intelligence and common sense of the parents; the parents, in their turn, will come to appreciate the teacher's ability to teach. A good conference is a meeting of mature, adult minds, capable of facing a situation. It is a mutual interchange of ideas on what is best for an individual child.

A Good Conference Is Carefully Planned. Teachers are busy, it is true, but so are parents, and very often the parents have even greater difficulty in arranging time to talk over the child's needs. Hence, teachers should plan very carefully for the conference. Prior to the meeting, teachers need to examine the child's cumulative record — his intelligence and achievement test scores, his record of classwork, absence, and tardiness, and notes on his personal qualities. Actual scores on tests are usually not given to parents, but parents can be told whether the child is in the fast moving, average, or slow-moving group. The teacher should have a folder of typical samples of the pupil's papers, showing his achievement in the various subjects. It is also helpful to have samples of other pupils' papers for reference, in case parents wish to see how their child compares with others in the class. The identity of the other children should of course not be revealed. About the room there can be evidences of group activities; parents can be shown how their child took part in the various projects. The teacher should have clearly in mind just what she wishes to accomplish through the conference. An outline of her aims for the conference will help her guide the discussion, and a few notes written on this outline after the conference will help her in following up suggestions made by the parents and herself.

A Good Conference Is Motivated by a Loving Interest in the Child. Love of the child is basic to helping him. Truly professional love of children is unemotional; it is not upset at failure, and is inventive in devising new methods of helping children. When the teacher really loves the child and accepts him, parents will be disposed to work co-operatively with her. Parents too love the child; in fact their love of him is the teacher's strongest ally. The teacher's professional training should be the element of the conference which channels their mutual love of the child into ways of helping him most effectively.

Conferences such as these are bound to improve public relations because the interest of both parents and teachers is involved in a practical, satisfying way. The faculty will profit by preparing their own suggestions for better parent-teacher conferences. A committee might work out this material and mimeograph it so that all teachers will benefit, especially beginning teachers.

NEWSPAPER RELEASES

For the most part, parents think that their school is doing a good job. However, they feel more assured of this when they see accounts of their school's activities in the newspaper. Principals might be surprised to learn that both the local newspaper and the diocesan paper welcome contributions that are really "news." To be acceptable, write-ups should tell the *who, what, when, how* and *why* of the event, and preferably *before* the event takes place.

As with other good endeavors, planning newspaper publicity takes time. A committee of capable, interested teachers, or even a single good person, would facilitate adequate newspaper reporting by noting and writing up newsworthy items. Schools that have planned for regular information news releases have felt that the effort was well received by both parents and the general public. Planned reporting to radio and television stations can also be viewed by parochial schools as effective means of improving public relations.

WHAT ARE SOME "FIRST STEPS" IN IMPROVING SCHOOL-COMMUNITY RELATIONS?

As with every other project, it is not enough to bemoan the present situation. One must take positive steps toward improvement. In the area of school-community relations, the Sister Principal might well proceed as follows:

First, be convinced of the importance of "PR," public relations. The bibliography at the end of this chapter gives a selected list of readable articles on improved public relations. An hour or two of interested reading will convince the principal that much can be done to improve her own school situation.

Second, schedule time for public relations. In Chapter V, there is a suggested time schedule for supervising and teaching principals. Every week, the recommended time should be given to public relations — five hours for the supervising principal and two hours for the teaching principal. This amount of time should be inviolably scheduled for school-community relations only.

Third, invest some money in brief, readable selections on school public relations. Again, the bibliography at the end of the chapter furnishes some good starting points. It is good to get enough material for the faculty to have access to, for public relations involves the entire staff.

Fourth, devote one or two faculty meetings a year to improved public relations. Chapter IX discussed the supervisory faculty meeting at some length. This type of meeting enlists the co-operation of the staff through planning, taking part in meetings, and evaluation of outcomes.

Fifth, maintain a "public relations" point of view throughout the year. The faculty bulletin can carry timely displays of clippings, handbooks, "PR" suggestions. Public relations techniques can be worked on by the staff; conferences with parents, for example, can be discussed, held, and evaluated. A school handbook can be prepared; parent bulletins can take on new life. Newspaper, radio, and television can be utilized periodically; a staff publicity committee is invaluable here. The Home and School Organization can be brought into planning policies and preparing meetings. All of the techniques mentioned in this chapter need periodic attention if public relations is to improve.

The goals of Catholic education are sound and worthwhile. Parochial school personnel are convinced of this. But one of the greatest needs of the parochial school in American society is an improved program of interpreting the parochial school to the community and of inviting the community to share in planning for the school. The Sister Principal is a key figure in improved "PR" for Catholic schools.

FOR THE PRINCIPAL'S PROFESSIONAL LIBRARY

Books

Hymes, James J. Jr., *Effective Home-School Relations* (Englewood Cliffs, N. J.: Prentice-Hall, 1953), 263 pp., $4.
> Readable, common sense, and stimulating.

Pamphlets

Suggestions for Better Home and School Association *meetings:*
> *A Manual for Home and School Associations,* National Council of Catholic Women (Washington, D. C., 1958), $1.
> *The Lady and the Law,* National Council of Catholic Women (Washington, D. C., 1956), 75 cents.

Program Manual for Parish Meetings, National Council of Catholic Men (Washington, D. C., 1958), $2.

The NEA has a number of pamphlets on various aspects of better parent-teacher relations, all readable and practical.

National School Public Relations Association, *Action and Reaction: Public Relations for Educational Secretaries* (Washington, D. C.: National Education Association, 1959), 32 pp., $1.25.

National School Public Relations Association, *Person to Person* (Washington, D. C.: National Education Association, 1956), 48 pp., $1.50.

National School Public Relations Association, *Public Relations Gold Mine* (Washington, D. C.: National Education Association, 1957), 63 pp., $1.25. *Public Relations Gold Mine*, No. 2, 1959.

National School Public Relations Association, *Let's Go to Press* (Washington, D. C.: The National Education Association, 1954), 48 pp., $1.

National School Public Relations Association, *Print it Right*, 1953, 48 pp., $1.50.

Other pamphlets on Home and School Relations:

Ciodini, Rev. J. J., and Felknor, Rhea, *Your Parish School, A Handbook for Parents* (Notre Dame, Ind.: Ave Maria Press, 1959), 40 pp., 25 cents. An excellent booklet to help parents see some of the ways they can help the school to accomplish their mutual aims.

D'Evelyn, Katherine E., *Individual Parent-Teacher Conferences* (New York: Teachers College, Columbia University, 1946), 97 pp., $2.00.

Grant, Eva H., *Parents and Teachers as Partners* (Chicago, Ill.: Science Research Associates, Inc., 1952), 48 pp., 60 cents.

CHAPTER XIII

EVALUATING PUPIL PROGRESS

> *"We should first learn John and then teach him."*
> Explain: How may one "learn" John? Why do we
> evaluate the results of teaching? What are charac-
> teristics of a good measuring device? How may a
> principal use an evaluation program to further the
> objectives of the school? What are common criti-
> cisms of measurement in elementary education?

THE real test of a school's worth is how well the children progress by means of its offerings. The organization of the school plant, the excellence of the equipment, the activity in the classrooms — all of these are important only in so far as they contribute to pupil development. To judge the worthwhileness of the school program, the principal and staff must continually be aware of the effects upon pupil progress. The principal's duty to evaluate was discussed in some detail in Chapters IV and V; the teacher's duty to evaluate was presented in Chapter VIII, particularly in the discussion of her roles as instructor and guide of youth. Since very few elementary schools have a formal guidance program, the principal and staff have a joint responsibility for evaluating pupil progress. This evaluation, as will be shown in the discussion which follows, should be a comprehensive program which includes the usual pencil-and-paper tests, and also many other techniques and materials.

The present chapter will give an all-over view of pupil evaluation, and then will discuss testing intelligence and achievement, getting the most out of standardized tests, and measuring the more subtle aspects of pupil progress. The next chapter will be devoted to the important role of school grades, records, and reports in the program of pupil evaluation.

AN OVER-ALL VIEW OF PUPIL EVALUATION

CHARACTERISTICS OF A GOOD PROGRAM

First, a good evaluation program is based on sound criteria for evaluation. Every Catholic school exists for specific purposes. Although teachers are aware of these objectives in a general way, it helps to refresh their minds as they work together through the year. The criteria presented in *Guiding Growth in Christian Social Living* may be used as source material, or the objectives given in textbooks on the Catholic philosophy of education, or the summary statement prepared at The Catholic University of America.[1] Perhaps this last-named statement of aims may be helpful in guiding the discussion of a good evaluation program:

The Catholic school curriculum aims to develop in pupils:

1. Physical fitness
2. Economic competency
3. Social responsibility
4. Intellectual and cultural fineness
5. Moral and spiritual perfection

Since these are the aims of the curriculum, these should be the criteria also for judging how well pupils are progressing by means of the curriculum. Certainly a study of these aims dispels the idea that textbook learning is alone important in the school day, though certain basic skills are fundamental to a good program.

Having sound criteria also implies that the school will use valid measures of pupil progress toward the many objectives of the curriculum. The principal needs to select valid standardized tests and to help teachers improve their own tests. The principal also needs to help teachers develop satisfactory criteria for evaluating the objectives which cannot be measured by pencil-and-paper tests. Validity is all-important; are teachers using valid ways of determining pupil progress toward the valid objectives of Catholic education?

Second, a good evaluation program is comprehensive. This is in a sense

---

[1] The Catholic University of America, Department of Education, *Criteria for the Evaluation of Catholic Elementary Schools*, 2nd ed. (Washington, D. C.: The Catholic University of America Press, 1949), pp. 96–102.

Commission on American Citizenship, *Guiding Growth in Christian Social Living* (Washington, D. C.: The Catholic University of America Press, 1944), pp. 1–14.

Commission on American Citizenship, *Better Men for Better Times* (Washington, D. C.: The Catholic University of America Press, 1943), p. 114.

John D. Redden and Francis A. Ryan, "Educational Aims," *A Catholic Philosophy of Education*, rev. ed. (Milwaukee: The Bruce Publishing Company, 1956), pp. 99–144.

another way of saying that the evaluation must be based on all of the objectives of Catholic education, and not just the intellectual objectives, which are easiest to measure. The grade a child receives in spelling on his report card is one part of evaluation, but behind that grade should be a variety of evaluations over many aspects of his development. A comprehensive program includes many different techniques for judging pupil progress. Tests, though important, are only one kind of evaluation.

Third, a good evaluation program is continuous. Because there are so many objectives to achieve, and so many instruments to use, and so many people involved, a good program of evaluation goes on continuously. The principal evaluates for administrative and supervisory purposes; teachers evaluate to improve their teaching and to help children more effectively; pupils evaluate to develop their powers of judgment and to profit more from the school program. Many evaluative instruments are used, many records are kept, and there is a frequent interchange of ideas on the results obtained. Some evaluation is made at the beginning of the year or the beginning of a unit; other evaluation is a check on progress, with a view toward re-teaching. There is a spaced evaluation of pupil intelligence, for example, and of pupil achievement on standardized tests. Achievement and intelligence tests are used to interpret each other, and to show the need for further testing. There is no starting point and no finish in a continuous program of pupil evaluation.

Fourth, a good evaluation program is co-operative. In the past, evaluation was pretty much the teacher's own concern. If standardized tests were given, they were scored and interpreted and filed away by the teacher herself. Her own classroom tests were likewise an individual matter, to be used as she saw fit. In grading report cards, her judgments were usually final. The principal, being a classroom teacher herself, could spend very little time trying to improve pupil evaluation.

However, with increased professional preparation, and with a stronger realization of the need for better pupil guidance, the Sister Principal is in a position to explore and expand the program of pupil evaluation. An outstanding feature of an improved program is the co-operative activity of the staff, pupils, and even parents. The purpose of evaluation, in fact of the entire school program, is to help children develop better. It is reasonable, then, to involve all the people concerned in a co-operative effort to achieve this worthy aim. Co-operative evaluation makes teachers and principal more objective in their attitude toward the children; group activity of this sort also arouses the interest of teachers in self-evaluation. The next section will discuss in greater detail the co-operative nature of a good evaluation and the worthwhile effects upon faculty, student body, and parents.

AN IN-SERVICE PROJECT ILLUSTRATING THESE CHARACTERISTICS

Pupil evaluation is intrinsically interesting to teachers. They are constantly wondering how effective their teaching is, and what they can do to help children learn better. A stimulating in-service project for the whole faculty might include pupil evaluation as an important aspect. The following activity is only one of many which might be developed as a co-operative faculty project. It will be noted that the project has all the characteristics of a good evaluation program, though in the teachers' minds the project may be primarily one to improve reading. The activity is presented here because of its emphasis upon objectives as a starting point for evaluation.

Teachers usually feel that children do not read as well as they should. In small groups and at faculty meetings, reading improvement is often mentioned as one of the biggest needs of the school. The staff might verbalize that their teaching this year will aim especially to help children read better. In a democratic country, with its need for an informed citizenry, literacy is of course fundamental. As an objective, however, "helping children to read better" is too general to be evaluated satisfactorily.

At the point where interest has been aroused in improved reading, the principal might help the group to clarify their ideas by presenting the following chart (Fig. 33).

EVALUATION

Relates Outcomes to Objectives

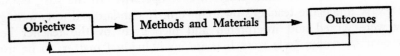

Objectives — the goals we are working toward

Methods and Materials — the means we will use

Outcomes — the results of our using these methods and materials

Evaluation — a judgment on the progress made in achieving objectives

Figure 32. The Elements of Evaluation

It seems logical to decide the objective one wishes to accomplish, suitable means to carry it out, and then at the end judge the success of the activity. Yet, in practice, a group might not always follow a logical outline. For example, in the faculty situation mentioned above, the objective proposed for the year was "helping children to read better." Would this objective stand analysis such as outlined in the chart above? The following diagram answers this question.

Figure 33.   Beginning to Plan for Improved Reading

Objective	Methods and Materials	Outcomes
Helping children to read better	**Methods** Grouping	?

	Materials
	  Readers, workbooks,
	  library books
		?

Teachers ask themselves, "How will we help children to read better?" There are some general suggestions offered: grouping the class and using certain reading materials. When the faculty tries to say how they will judge the success of their project, they really cannot. How will they know if they have succeeded? It will be obvious to them that their planning has been too general.

The principal can then go back to the earlier chart on evaluation, and encourage the group to be more specific about the objective decided upon for the year or the semester. Narrowed down, the objective might become "To increase children's reading of fiction" and "To improve children's enjoyment of fiction." With this limited objective, the faculty might then proceed to specify *what materials* and *what methods* they would use, and just *how* they would measure their success. The detailed outline in Figure 34 shows how the faculty might then plan to achieve their objective and to measure their success.

In this plan to help children read better, the faculty stated specific, attainable objectives. Definite materials and methods were decided upon. And the faculty knew from the beginning of the program how they were going to judge their success: the expected outcomes were stated in terms of a final evaluation. No doubt other desirable outcomes resulted from the staff's careful planning, such as better discipline because the children were interested in reading books when finished with their regular assignments. The formal evaluation would, however, concentrate on outcomes as related to stated objectives. One can well imagine the enthusiasm of the principal, staff, pupils, and parents. It is quite certain that the staff's concentration on specific outcomes increased pupil and faculty growth, and their personal satisfaction as well. When a faculty has had success in carrying out a project such as this, individual teachers carry the enthusiasm over into their own planning with children. Not every faculty would develop as specific a program as this, but when the principal has the ideal pattern in mind, she can guide the group in selecting worthwhile objectives, methods and materials, and techniques of evaluation.

An in-service project such as this is effective when working with objec-

Figure 34. Evaluation is a School-Wide Project to Improve Reading

Relates Outcomes to Objectives

Objectives	Methods and Materials	Evaluation of Outcomes
1. To increase children's reading of fiction	**Methods** a) Encourage pupils to read fiction after finishing class assignments. b) Have librarian talk to each class on interesting books of fiction. c) Have weekly "book sharing" period twenty minutes on Friday after lunch. **Materials** a) Classroom collection of about 50 books of fiction at various reading levels b) Additional $50 invested in new books of fiction for each room; many reading levels c) Commercial posters to advertise reading and individual books	Success of methods and materials will be judged by the following devices: a) Tabulation of circulation of classroom fiction library and comparison from month to month b) Pupil and teacher evaluation of how much of a book a pupil had read before presenting it to the class during "book sharing" period. Record of pages kept for each pupil.
2. To improve children's enjoyment of fiction	**Methods** a) Have several visits to public library so that pupils can select fiction of greatest interest. b) Allow for completely voluntary selection of books, both in classroom and at library. (Methods listed for Objective I also influence Objective II) **Materials** a) Posters, dioramas, displays to share best-liked books; these voluntarily prepared by pupils. Pleasure emphasized; artistic skill subordinated. b) Classroom library collection	a) Pupil enthusiasm and interest shown during "book sharing" periods; principal and librarian evaluate three spaced periods in each room. b) Home and School Assn. report on children's reading fiction at home; answers to two questions: Did child have to be urged to read the book brought from school? To what extent did child give up TV viewing to read fiction (without urging)? Tabulation of answers and summary report.

(Suggested time limit: one semester.)

tives that can be measured by noting what children *do*. Other outcomes can be measured by noting what the children *know*. In such cases, tests will probably enter into the evaluation. Oral and written tests evaluate the children's knowledge of certain content and information. "Understandings," "appreciations," and "attitudes" can be measured to some degree by school tests. Mastery of terms in geography and of selected language skills can also be measured thus. Even in the religious area, some factual information is needed, along with understandings, attitudes, and appreciations. In the evaluation of these outcomes of instruction, tests work out very well. While ideally teachers should try whenever possible to measure outcomes by what pupils *do*, rather than by what they say on a test, certain factual information is required for *doing* intelligently.

Seen in this light, "evaluating pupil progress" is far from a simple job. Much effort enters into an evaluation that has the four essentials of a good program: sound criteria for evaluation, comprehensiveness, continuity, and co-operativeness. The pages which follow will discuss specific ways in which pupil intelligence and progress can be satisfactorily evaluated in the parochial school.

TESTING INTELLIGENCE

The intelligence quotient, or the IQ, is so closely related to success in school that intelligence testing is one of the most important approaches to pupil evaluation. Intelligence tests are sometimes called tests of scholastic aptitude, because they measure the child's aptitude or capacity for schoolwork, particularly in the academic subjects. IQ tests have also been humorously called the child's "school-ability," quite an apt term.

The IQ has two important meanings for the principal and the teacher. First, as mentioned above, the IQ, or at least a series of IQ scores, can usually predict the child's ability to do schoolwork. Hence, it is important to use intelligence tests wisely in the school. Second, the IQ is not absolute and unchanging, but is rather subject to the influences of the environment. Excellent schools have been shown to affect IQ scores favorably; ideal foster homes have also caused IQ scores to go up for the fortunate children involved. And, by contrast, unfavorable environment, such as poor health standards, improper diet, family strain, and poor teaching have kept the child from performing at his true potential on intelligence tests.

THE NORMAL CURVE

In courses in educational psychology, teachers have studied the distribution of intelligence in a normal population. However, in practice, people often forget that the normal curve is normal. Parents and teachers would like all children to be rapid learners; teachers are sometimes resentful when they have to re-teach slow pupils, while the bright ones are speeding through their extra assignments. It is excellent in-service training, and also an examination of pedagogical conscience, to consider occasionally the normal curve pattern as given in Figure 35.

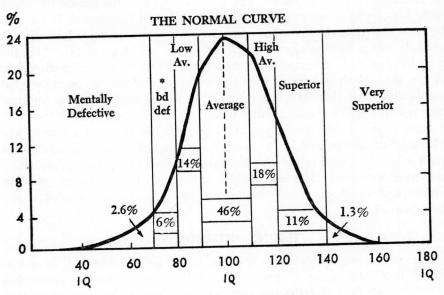

Figure 35.　The Normal Curve

* Borderline Defective

Source: Louis Terman and Maud Merrill, *The Stanford-Binet Intelligence Scale* (Boston: The Houghton Mifflin Company, 1960), p. 17. Used with permission.

Figure 35 shows that 46 per cent of all pupils, or almost half, are in the average group, with IQ's ranging between 90 and 110. About one third of all pupils are above 110 IQ, and about one fourth are below 90 IQ. However, these generalizations apply only to a large population, selected entirely by chance. Schools represent selected groups, not unselected, so the above percentages will not apply exactly to each classroom. For example, the typical classroom would not have so many pupils below 90 IQ, because the very lowest IQ's are in institutions, and some low IQ children do not continue in school.

Children from more privileged homes, because of their better environment, will tend to be higher on the scale; children from underprivileged homes will tend to be lower. Schools that draw chiefly from the professional class will have a higher average IQ; schools in the lower socioeconomic districts will have a lower average IQ.[2] However, the normal

_____

[2] See, for example: Robert J. Havighurst and Bernice L. Neugarten, *Society and Education* (Boston: Allyn and Bacon, Inc., 1957), pp. 221–224. For a more extended

curve pattern as presented in Figure 35 offers helpful insight into the way intelligence is distributed typically.

Another familiar interpretation of IQ distribution is given in Table XIX from the classic study by Terman and Merrill.

TABLE XIX.   Distribution of IQ's in a Normal Population

IQ	Per Cent	Classification
140 and above	1.3	Very superior
120–139	11.3	Superior
110–119	18.1	High average
90–109	46.5	Normal or average
80–89	14.5	Low average
70–79	5.6	Borderline defective
Below 69	2.6	Mentally defective

Source: Louis Terman and Maud Merrill, *The Stanford-Binet Intelligence Scale* (Boston: The Houghton Mifflin Company, 1960), p. 18. Used with permission. (Percentages regrouped by the writer.)

The above classifications correspond in general to the graphic presentation in Figure 35. The classifications are useful for educational purposes, though teachers should be careful about considering a pupil "mentally defective" on the basis of a group intelligence test. At both the high and the low end of the curve, individual intelligence tests are needed to be sure of the child's true rating. Group tests, though valid for ordinary purposes, do not discriminate sufficiently well at the extreme ends of the normal curve distribution. Table XIX supplements Figure 35 in giving a general idea of the way intelligence is distributed.

RECOMMENDED INTELLIGENCE TESTS

Intelligence, or scholastic aptitude, is measured by both group and individual intelligence tests. The Stanford-Binet Intelligence Test and the Wechsler-Bellevue Intelligence Scale are highly valid *individual* intelligence tests. Since these tests must be given by a trained examiner, and to only one person at a time, they are expensive and are used only when group test results seem questionable. Most pupils now in our schools have taken a number of group intelligence tests, which may be given to an entire class of pupils at one time. The group intelligence tests given on page 342 are reputable and are widely used in the parochial schools of the country.

Of these tests, the Otis, Pintner, and California are perhaps the easiest to administer and score. The Kuhlmann-Anderson Tests are said to resemble Stanford-Binet scores more closely than the other group tests do, but the Kuhlmann-Anderson Tests are harder to administer and score, and hence require better trained personnel. All of the above tests are practical

discussion, see: Kenneth Eells, Allison Davis, Robert J. Havighurst, Vergil E. Herrick, and Ralph W. Tyler, *Intelligence and Cultural Differences: A Study of Cultural Learning and Problem-Solving* (Chicago: University of Chicago Press, 1951).

SUGGESTED INTELLIGENCE TESTS*

NAME OF TEST	Available for Elementary Grades
California Short-Form Test of Mental Maturity	1–8
California Test of Mental Maturity	1–8
Henmon-Nelson Test of Mental Ability	3–8
Kuhlmann-Anderson Intelligence Tests	1–8
Lorge-Thorndike Intelligence Tests	1–8
Otis Quick-Scoring Mental Ability Tests	2–8
Otis Self-Administering Test of Mental Ability	4–8
Pintner General Ability Tests: Verbal Series	1–8
SRA Primary Mental Abilities Test	1–8
Terman-McNemar Test of Mental Ability	7–8

* This is a selected list of tests. There are other good tests not given here, though all of the above tests are recommended in Buros' *Mental Measurements Yearbooks*. Addresses of publishers are given at the end of chapter.

for use in parochial schools, as the reviews in Buros' *Mental Measurements Yearbooks*[3] will show. Principals should be cautious about buying new intelligence tests without checking carefully on their value. It is better to use a proved test, than to waste time and money on an untried test.

A MINIMUM PROGRAM

There is no one program of intelligence testing which is good for all schools and all pupils. More than one intelligence test seems desirable, and some educators urge three or four intelligence tests during elementary grades. A program which represents good practice, and is also economical, might be arranged as follows:

TABLE XX. Planning an Intelligence Testing Program

Plan A	Grade One	Readiness test*
	Grades 2, 4, and 7	Group intelligence test
Plan B	Grade One	Readiness test*
	Grades 1, 3, 6, and 8	Group intelligence test

* Readiness tests, though they do not yield IQ scores, are a measure of the child's ability to begin the important work of the first grade. Some schools use readiness test scores as a rough measure of intelligence during the first year of school. Among the better readiness tests are the Gates Readiness Tests, the Metropolitan Readiness Test, the Lee-Clark Readiness Test, and tests prepared for the basal reading series. Publishers' addresses are given at the end of the chapter.

[3] Most principals will not have the time or the opportunity to study these yearbooks, but they are listed here because of their unique value in test selection. When visiting a university library, the principal would be interested in pursuing the critical reviews of the tests she is now using in her school.

Oscar Krisen Buros, Ed., *The Third Mental Measurements Yearbook* (New Brunswick, N. J.: Rutgers University Press, 1949).

Oscar Krisen Buros, Ed., *The Fourth Mental Measurements Yearbook* (Highland Park, N. J.: Gryphon Press, 1953).

Oscar Krisen Buros, Ed., *The Fifth Mental Measurements Yearbook* (Highland Park, N. J.: Gryphon Press, 1959).

Plan A provides for three IQ scores through the eight grades, while Plan B provides four IQ scores. If the budget permits, and if teachers can devote sufficient time to administering and interpreting tests, four good intelligence tests are to be preferred. However, local conditions will determine the frequency of intelligence tests. Articulation of the elementary testing program with the high school test schedule eliminates duplication and provides for spaced IQ tests through the 12 years of school.

It is good to use the same intelligence test series for several years in succession, so that a given pupil's scores can be more readily compared. The intelligence tests listed earlier are all valid tests, yet IQ scores vary somewhat from test to test because of the different factors being measured. If a pupil's score varies greatly on a second administration of a test, re-testing with another form of the test is recommended. In cases of continued divergence, individual testing may be advisable. When pupils are absent for the testing program, or enter the school after intelligence tests have been taken by a given class, the principal should arrange to test these children privately. It is part of the administrative responsibility of the principal to provide spaced IQ scores for all pupils in the school.

The cost of the above program is not exorbitant. Plan A, which includes three intelligence tests and a readiness test, would cost about forty cents for the eight-year period. Plan B, which includes four intelligence tests, would cost about fifty cents. Where possible, paid clerical help should be utilized for some of the scoring process, and this item would increase somewhat the cost of testing. Some schools have their testing programs administered by the testing bureau of a nearby university or a professional testing service company. In this case, the cost of the minimal program might be $1 per child for an intelligence and achievement test combined. However, this testing service includes scoring the papers and sending back to the school a tabulation of individual scores and group averages. In dealing with a test service company, it is well for the principal to know clearly just what constitutes a minimal program. Tests over and beyond the minimum can be justified only if teachers will make extensive use of the test results to guide their work with children.

RECORDING IQ SCORES

Soon after an intelligence test is administered, the scores should be entered both on the office and classroom record cards, and in the teacher's roll book. In this way, the cost of testing in terms of both money and time is justified because available scores are likely to be used. Through the pupil's eight years in a parochial school, his record card should contain at least two or three intelligence test scores — identified as to date, name of test, level, and form — and his IQ, mental age and chronological age when the test was administered. Also, any especially significant information regarding the test should be entered, as, "John's score on this test may have been affected by his recent absence due to scarlet fever." The IQ score is the most important entry on the pupil's school record. Principals should endeavor to see that the IQ test scores are accurately entered on record cards, so that scores can be of real service.

INTERPRETING INTELLIGENCE SCORES

Class Distribution of IQ's. The normal curve presented earlier and the table from Terman and Merrill provide good reference points for test interpretation. It is wise always to relate a given IQ score to norms given in the test manual, and to the normal distribution of IQ's, with 100 IQ as the mid-point, and the range of 90 to 110 as the average group. It is particularly helpful to the principal to have the teachers prepare a distribution of the IQ's in their class immediately after an intelligence test has been administered. In this way, the principal and teachers get a picture of the relative brightness of the classes tested, and the position of given pupils in the class.

For example, when intelligence tests have been administered to the second, fourth, and seventh grades of a school, the distribution of IQ's might be somewhat as follows:

TABLE XXI. Distribution of IQ's in Three Classes

IQ	Grade 2	Grade 4	Grade 7	TOTAL Grades 2, 4, and 7
130– +	0	0	2	2
125–129	1	0	2	3
120–124	1	0	2	3
115–119	2	1	3	6
110–114	2	2	5	9
105–109	3	1	7	11
100–104	8	5	6	19
95– 99	5	9	3	17
90– 94	6	4	2	12
85– 89	4	6	3	13
80– 84	1	2	2	5
75– 79	1	1	0	2
70– 74	0	1	0	1
65– 69	0	1	0	1
Total Pupils	34	33	37	104
Median IQ	99.0	95.8	106.8	100.3

When scores for grades 2, 4, and 7 have been combined, the median IQ is 100.3, or just about average. Grade 7 is obviously the brightest of the three classes, having a median IQ of 106.8. Grade 2 is just about average, with an IQ of 99. Grade 4 is slightly below average, having a median IQ of 95.8. All three classes have an IQ range of about 50 points from lowest to highest pupils. Differentiated instruction is necessary in all three of the classes tested, to care for wide differences in intelligence.

A table such as this furnishes helpful information to the principal. Compiling these distributions should be part of the routine testing procedure. Over a period of several years, these distributions provide insight into needed changes in instructional procedures. Evaluation of the school program can be more efficiently carried on when graphic representations of intelligence quotients are used.

Reporting of IQ Scores to Parents. Reliable authors, test makers, psychologists, and administrators may disagree about reporting IQ's to parents. Although IQ is a term bandied about very lightly, even professional educators are hard put to explain the meaning of the IQ. It is true that the IQ is a ratio (usually), a score obtained when the mental age is divided by the chronological age and the answer multiplied by 100: MA/CA times $100 = IQ$. The IQ is a commonly used index of relative brightness; the IQ shows how a child compares in academic potential with others of his class. Still, an IQ of 119 will probably be meaningless to many parents. Furthermore, the IQ seems to be a matter of pride or of embarrassment. If the child has a high IQ, parents are elated. If the child has a low IQ, parents feel stigmatized. The IQ is a measure, as weight and height are measures, but parents are emotionally involved over IQ scores. Hence, in most cases, it may be best not to tell parents their child's IQ, though in some localities, informing parents of the child's IQ has proved to be very satisfactory. Usually, the teacher reports to parents in general terms regarding the child's IQ, and whether the child seems to be doing work in keeping with his ability. The teacher might ask parents to accept low marks if the child applies himself, and seems to be making an effort to work to his capacity. A teacher should base such comments upon several IQ and achievement test scores whenever possible. The principal would be wise at the beginning of each school year to establish a school policy on telling IQ's to parents, and there should be uniformity in carrying out the policy that is adopted.

TESTING ACHIEVEMENT

The informational objectives of the curriculum are usually measured through pencil-and-paper tests. In fact, it is so easy to measure some objectives in this way that tests may be used to excess. As one writer said recently, "There is a rash of testing all over the country." Emphasis on college entrance screening has been one cause for the great increase in testing; but even at the elementary level, more and more achievement testing is being done all the time.

These tests are of two kinds. The *formal* achievement tests are the so-called "standardized" tests, those prepared by test experts according to rigid standards of construction, tryout, and revision. The *informal* achievement tests are those made out by teachers, usually, for testing of classroom teaching. These *informal* tests, because of their frequency and importance, will be discussed first. The *formal* achievement tests will be discussed in the next section.

INFORMAL TESTS OF PUPIL ACHIEVEMENT

Informal tests are not commercially prepared for use on a nationwide basis; they are specially made out to fit the local course of study and textbooks. The tests which a teacher makes for her own class are informal tests, and so are the tests made up by teachers or supervisors for the diocesan semester tests. Informal tests, whether for a single group of children or for a whole diocese, are alike in that they are not standardized. Informal tests may be carefully constructed, but they lack the essential qualities of standardized tests.

Informal Classroom Tests. Though informal classroom tests seem unimportant, they actually are more important than standardized tests. For every standardized test a pupil takes, he may take twenty teacher-made tests. Teachers are constantly giving tests which they themselves have made out. Even in the primary grades, "tests" are given, though these may resemble seatwork exercises. Some teachers spend one class period each week in every subject to test the material taught during the preceding four days. This means that one fifth of the child's time is devoted to tests. Because of the time element involved, and for other reasons as well, informal tests warrant serious thought on the part of the principal.

Since so many informal tests are being made up and given every day, teacher-made tests should have reached a high degree of excellence. However, this is usually not the case, for two reasons: first, teachers seldom have had training in test construction; and second, teacher-made tests are usually hurry-up jobs and do not fit into a long-range testing program. Not many teachers save their tests and file them away for future reference. By studying informal tests, the Sister Principal can offer specific suggestions for improving them, and thereby indirectly improving the teaching-learning situation in the school.

Teacher-made Tests Are Aids to Learning. The chief value of teacher-made tests is that they can be used to improve instruction. By means of these tests, the teacher sees what success the pupils have achieved in reaching the proposed objectives of the course. In the light of pupil achievement, the teacher may modify objectives, re-teach parts that were poorly grasped, and for certain pupils, insist on better application. Good informal tests stimulate learning on the part of the pupil. Besides, good tests in themselves offer a learning activity. Teachers typically say that they want to test more than facts; they want to help pupils learn how to apply facts in new situations. Good teacher-made tests should give pupils the opportunity to relate facts to problem-solving situations. However, it is well known that pupils tend to learn that which will be tested. So, teacher-made tests determine to a considerable extent what pupils will study. Good informal tests are a strong stimulus to better teaching and learning.

Developing an Appreciation of Good Tests. A necessary first step in improving informal testing is developing an appreciation of good tests. In almost every school there will be one or two teachers who have developed some fairly good tests for their own use. In her supervisory visits, the principal can enhance the value of these tests in the eyes of the teacher by sincerely praising their good points. To improve tests still further, the principal can recommend a readable book on testmaking.[4] Just as an interest in art is catching, so too is an interest in tests. Other faculty members will want to use good tests made up by their peers, and inevitably will come around to contributing a test or two of their own. The faculty bulletin board provides an opportunity to display good teacher-made tests, as an encouragement to the teacher herself and as an incentive to other staff members. Religious communities have an advantage here, for tests constructed by their own Sisters can be filed in common and used wherever the members are assigned. Some communities have taken a real pride in their file of original tests, and have built up a collection in each subject, and at each grade level. When teachers see the values of tests, the principal will have done a great deal toward improving the use of tests in the school.

Diocesan Tests. Some dioceses provide their schools with tests which cover the content of the diocesan course of study. Diocesan tests are usually made up by a committee of teachers and supervisors who are familiar with the work of the grade. Diocesan tests are typically given as an end-of-the-semester check in the following subjects: Religion, English, arithmetic, social studies, science, and spelling. Because they test material covered during the semester just ended, diocesan tests are usually welcomed by teachers.

What has been said previously about good teacher-made tests applies to diocesan tests. If the diocese supplies well-constructed tests, the principal

---

[4] If the principal can spend some time in improving classroom tests, and if the staff is interested in test construction, there are several good books listed after Chapter Fourteen under "For the Principal's Professional Library."

and the teachers are stimulated to improve their own informal testing. Also, good diocesan tests stimulate intensive teaching of certain materials. Teachers are like students in that they will emphasize material they know will be tested. No matter what is in the course of study, the diocesan test may determine the content or skills that will be stressed. This, of course, can become dangerous.

A weakness of diocesan tests is that they have no national norms. It is true that the diocese may ask teachers to send in a tabulation of the results of the tests and give the median for the group on each test. In return, the diocese often publishes diocesan-wide medians. In this way, teachers can compare what their pupils did with the system-wide medians. However, the diocesan medians are not standards, but are only a summary of the reports which the schools sent in. A very good diocesan test, administered well throughout the diocese, can produce data which offer a fairly accurate picture of pupil achievement in the items selected for testing. But diocesan medians have definite limitations.

Some dioceses invite a testing agency to make up a test covering a course of study and administer the test to the individual schools, or at least to tabulate the returns from the schools. Tests like this, though prepared by an outside agency, probably come under the heading of informal tests. The "norms" which the company prepares are typically like the usual diocesan medians — a summary of reports on scores for the individual schools. As these testing agencies accumulate more scores from the schools, the relative achievement of individual schools can be known better.

To decide whether a given class should have done better on the diocesan semester examination, the principal and teacher would need to examine co-operatively at least the following data: the IQ scores of the class and of the individual pupil; the achievement of the class of the beginning of the semester; the scores on reading achievement tests; the kind of diocesan test administered; the amount of material sampled from the essential content of the course, and other related factors. Teachers should not feel stigmatized if their class does not reach the diocesan median. When used in connection with other tests, and when interpreted as indicated here, diocesan tests can be an effective part of an all-round testing program.

The informal test of pupil achievement — the classroom test and the diocesan test — figure so importantly in the minds of teachers and children that the principal's attention to this area is well warranted.

FORMAL TESTS OF PUPIL ACHIEVEMENT

Formal achievement tests, or the "standardized" tests, are an essential part of a good school testing program. Standardized tests differ from teacher-made tests in a number of ways:

First, standardized tests provide norms for comparing one's pupils with a large group of pupils on a nationwide basis. Standardized tests have been administered to large, representative groups through the country, under specified conditions, so that valid comparisons can be made between a given class and national norms for similar ages and grades.

Second, standardized tests are not based on any one course of study. When preparing standardized tests, experts study a wide sampling of courses of study and textbooks. Content which occurs very frequently, or is judged very important, is included in the test.

Third, standardized tests are meant to be administered exactly as directions indicate. This includes the timing for each part, the kind and amount of directions given to the pupils, and the way the tests are scored. A teacher cannot compare her group with the norms unless all directions are followed exactly.

Fourth, good standardized tests are reliable. That is, a child would score about the same if he took the test again at a slightly later date (but without coaching, of course). Or, another form of the same test would yield about the same score for the child. Standardized tests measure consistently, that is, without much variation in score, and without much element of chance in the scores obtained.

Fifth, good standardized tests are valid. That is, a valid test of reading indicates how well the child can read that kind of material. A valid test in arithmetic measures knowledge of arithmetic, and is not purely a reading test. Valid tests measure what the manual says they will measure, be it a knowledge of vocabulary, or fractions, or map symbols.

Recommended Achievement Batteries. The above characteristics apply, of course, only to a *good* standardized test. There are some achievement tests which are good in certain respects and weak in others. Because the principal cannot study standardized tests intensively, she can rely upon tests recommended in various *Mental Measurements Yearbooks* by Oscar Buros. The following selected achievement batteries are among those recommended for the elementary grades:

An achievement battery, as the chart on page 350 indicates, usually contains a test in reading, arithmetic, English, and spelling. Batteries above the primary level may also contain tests in social studies, science, and work-study skills. The batteries are planned to sample the content taught in most schools throughout the country.

Other commercially prepared tests of value to teachers are the separate subject matter tests available for most of the above batteries. The reading achievement tests accompanying the *Faith and Freedom Readers* and the *Cathedral Basic Readers* can profitably be administered after each book is completed. These latter tests, though not completely standardized, are

SUGGESTED ACHIEVEMENT BATTERIES*

Name of Test	Content	Available for Elementary Grades
California Achievement Test	Vocabulary, reading, arithmetic, language	1–8
Iowa Test of Basic Skills	Reading, arithmetic, language, work-study skills	3–8
Metropolitan Achievement Test	Reading, vocabulary, arithmetic (grades 1–3), language, social studies, science (added above grade 3)	1–8
Science Research Associates Achievement Series	Language perception, arithmetic, language arts, reading (grades 2–4) Reading, arithmetic, language arts, work-study skills (grades 4–8)	2–8
Sequential Tests of Educational Progress (STEP)	Reading, writing, mathematics, science, social studies, listening, and essay test	4–8
Stanford Achievement Test	Reading, arithmetic (grades 2–3), language, social studies, science, study skills (added above grade 3)	2–8

* The above list of tests is selective. There are other good tests which are not included in this list.

helpful in judging the child's progress in the reading series. The Scholastic Testing Service has prepared a recommended reading test for grades four through eight, especially for use in Catholic schools.

Principals can request the recent catalog of the companies publishing the recommended achievement batteries. Additional information on these tests, such as cost, timing, and particular helps available will assist the principal in arranging the testing program, or in carrying out a program that is required.

A Minimum Testing Program. Experienced educators feel that a good school testing program should include at least two standardized achievement batteries. These seem to be most needed at the end of two major periods of the elementary school: the primary period and the intermediate period. In other words, the principal should plan for an achievement battery in late third grade or early fourth, and again in late sixth grade or early seventh. In preparation for high school, another battery can profitably be given in the eighth grade.

It is usually recommended that pupils have at least two intelligence tests during the eight-year period, and preferably three. A standardized reading test is also recommended in the second grade. Combining these recommendations for intelligence and achievement testing, the following chart can be drawn up.

TABLE XXII.   Planning a Minimum Standardized Testing Program

Plan A		Plan B	
Grade	Test	Grade	Test
1	Readiness	1	Readiness
2	Intelligence	2	Intelligence
	Reading		Reading
3	Achievement Battery	3	. . . .
4	Intelligence	4	Achievement Battery
			Intelligence
5	. . . .	5	. . . .
6	Achievement Battery	6	. . . .
7	Intelligence	7	Achievement Battery
			Intelligence
8	Achievement Battery	8	. . . .

Supplementing the Minimum Program.   Additional standardized tests can and should be given as needed by individual classes or pupils. It would be ideal if schools could administer a good achievement battery in the fall of each year, and then in the spring repeat another form of any subtest which showed the need for remedial work. This would be particularly true of reading tests, which may be purchased separately and administered without a great expenditure of teacher time. Some teachers find diagnostic tests helpful in individualizing instruction; arithmetic diagnostic tests are particularly effective in this respect.

The principal's guide in deciding on additional tests should be this: "How will the test improve the teacher's guidance and instruction of individual pupils?" When the school can afford more tests, they should be bought, if the test results will actually be used. A great deal of teacher time can be spent in routine testing without sufficient use of test results to warrant the time and money spent. It is better to concentrate on utilizing the minimum testing program and supplement only when additional tests will be conscientiously used by teachers to improve the instruction of the pupils.

The Cost of the Minimum Program.   Plan A, consisting of a readiness test, a reading test, three intelligence tests and three achievement batteries, would cost about $1 for each child through the eight grades. Plan B, consisting of a readiness test, a reading test, three intelligence tests, and two achievement batteries, would cost about 80 cents per child. However, some achievement batteries are considerably more expensive than others, so the cost in a given school would vary according to the tests selected. Standardized testing is actually inexpensive when compared with other costs in the parochial school. However, the money invested in testing should be expected to show results in improved teaching.

GETTING THE MOST FROM STANDARDIZED TESTS

To get full benefit from a program of standardized tests, there must be careful planning of many details. Tests must be administered and scored as directed; there must be provision for a wide use of test results; and the program must be introduced according to the needs of the local situation.

ADMINISTERING THE TESTS

Who Should Give the Tests? Ideally, the teacher who will use the test results should administer standardized tests. The teacher knows her own group and can foresee certain reactions and difficulties which an outside examiner would not be prepared for. Also, giving a test is a good professional experience, and one which all teachers should be able to share. However, with the current rate of teacher turnover, it is understandable that many beginning teachers, substandard teachers, and teachers just coming back into service will have difficulty in administering a standardized test. Superintendents and principals have found that expensive testing programs can be worthless because of poor test administration. It is the principal's duty to make sure that standardized tests are properly administered. The principal should take such steps as are necessary to insure accuracy in reported test scores.

In a given school, the classroom teachers may be qualified and experienced in giving tests. By all means, then, these teachers should have the satisfaction of administering their own standardized tests. If, however, it has been the principal's experience that several faculty members have violated good test procedure, perhaps a briefing session shortly beforehand will prevent the recurrence of these errors. The principal can stress the use of the manual, giving directions, timing, going from one section of the test to another, and the manner of handling pupil questions. The principal should make it very clear, when necessary, that the test is good only if directions have been followed exactly as written.

In the case of inexperienced teachers, the principal or adviser may administer the test or assign this duty to another staff member. If this is done, the principal should endeavor to prepare the teacher for the test administration by an individual briefing session. Then the regular classroom teacher should observe the expert administration of the test, preparing for the time when she will administer a similar test herself.

The question of who is to administer standardized tests is a difficult one. Systems that have trained testing personnel to administer all tests feel that their results are highly valid. However, some authorities recommend that the in-service program of the school prepare teachers for test administration whenever possible. A good deal of in-service work may be needed to be sure that correct testing procedures will be followed.

When Should Tests Be Given? The first consideration here is *what grades to test*. There seems to be no difficulty about the program in first grade; a readiness test is generally recommended. Many principals and teachers have been dissatisfied with intelligence test results in first grade, so the intelligence test may be put off until second grade at the earliest.

Table XXII presented two proposed programs of standardized tests for all the grades. In choosing between these programs or some modification of them, the major factors are money and co-ordination with the high school testing program. Fewer tests are of course more economical; Plan B would be preferable for this reason. As for the high school testing program, the principal would be wise to inquire when the receiving school gives certain tests. This applies, of course, when the principal is free to choose the tests or to make recommendations concerning them. If the high school gives both intelligence and achievement tests to entering ninth graders, then it would hardly be worthwhile to give these tests in late eighth grade. If the high school postpones these tests until tenth grade or later, then the eighth grade of parochial school might profitably take one or both tests. Especially where there are Catholic high schools to receive parochial school eighth graders, there can be close co-ordination of the elementary and high school testing programs.

Another consideration is the *time of the year* that is best for testing. Generally, it seems best to administer intelligence tests in the early fall. In this way, the teacher who gives the test can use the results throughout the year. As for achievement tests, if given in grades three and six, then January might be the best month. If achievement tests are given in grades four and seven, early fall might be best. Standardized tests given in June are burdensome to teachers. In June, teachers are thinking of closing up their accounts for the year. They know that the work involved in the tests will be of no benefit to them, and perhaps the next teacher may not even use the test results. Psychologically and practically, standardized tests should be given when the teacher who works on them can use the results of her labors.

How Should Tests Be Given? Standardized tests, if the results are to be valid, should be given exactly as the manual directs. The teacher should prepare beforehand by studying the manual and having all necessary materials ready. Time allotments should be followed exactly; a stop clock or at least a watch with a second hand is indispensable for accurate timing. The principal should arrange so that the class being tested will be free from interruptions and outside noises. The atmosphere of the room should be businesslike and orderly, but not tense.

In larger schools, some principals have arranged to have several classrooms take a test at the same time. The directions are read aloud over the public-address system, and the classroom teacher acts as monitor, distributing materials and making sure directions are being followed. With practice, this system has much to recommend it.

As with the administration of the test, scoring must likewise follow the directions of the manual. The procedure should be followed exactly, and every fifth paper or so should be re-scored as a check on accuracy. When scores must be totaled, or transferred, or converted, each step should be checked. Even the final transferring of scores to a summary sheet or to the pupil records needs at least partial re-checking. Because of the importance of test scores in the guidance of pupils, every effort should be made to assure that test scores represent actual pupil performance unadulterated by scoring error.

USING TEST RESULTS

It happens only too often that the testing program ends much too soon. The tests are ordered, administered, scored, and recorded. With a sigh of relief after checking papers, teachers go back to their daily routines. Another duty is taken care of; the tests are over. Actually, only after this point do tests make any returns for the money and professional time invested in them. It would be easier, and better for teacher morale, not to give tests at all unless more time is spent on the tests *after* the results are filed away. It can easily take ten hours to complete the steps in administering an achievement battery to a group of pupils. Unless the teacher and the rest of the faculty get ten hours' use out of the test results, the expenditure of time and money can hardly be justified.

Recording Test Results for Use. Test results are intended primarily to help the teachers provide better instruction and guidance for every pupil. Therefore, the scores for each pupil, in every test, should be carefully analyzed with a view toward diagnostic and remedial teaching.

Test results for the individual pupil should be summarized on a single cumulative record for the entire eight years. This longitudinal record enables the teacher to note deviations from the usual performance of the pupil. Intelligence test scores should be expressed in a form which compares readily with achievement test scores: date administered, name of test, level and form used, raw score, grade and percentile norm (where applicable), and comments on anything unusual about the test results. For the class as a whole, there should be a single summary sheet showing the distribution of IQ's, with necessary identifying data about the tests. Likewise, the standardized achievement tests should be summarized for the class on a single sheet. A frequency distribution of both IQ and achievement test scores is very useful for interpretive purposes. Sometimes graphs help to show salient facts about classes and individuals.

The Teacher Uses the Test Results. When she first prepares the data, the teacher should carefully analyze each child's scores. Individual pupil achievement and intelligence test scores should be compared; the teacher should know whether a given pupil is achieving above, or below, or just equal to his measured intelligence. Likewise, for the class as a whole, similar comparisons should be made between intelligence test scores and achievement test scores in each subject. If in the judgment of the teacher a pupil, or several pupils, scored considerably above or below expectation, another form of the same test can be administered as a check.

From time to time, if pupils have difficulty with their schoolwork, these sheets can again be referred to with profit. Before assigning report card grades, the professional teacher will be sure that she knows the reasons why any report card grade deviates markedly from intelligence and achievement test scores. The teacher should follow the school's policy on reporting such scores to parents.

The Principal Uses the Test Results. A good standardized testing program provides the principal with data for viewing pupil progress in the school as a whole and in the individual classrooms. Where weaknesses or strong points show up in the entire school, or for a large number of children, this information can be discussed with the faculty as a whole. For the most part, however, the results of standardized tests are useful in working with individual teachers.

It is true that test scores should not be used to evaluate a teacher's efficiency. However, teachers have a responsibility for keeping their class up to normal expectations. When the principal notes that in a given class the achievement scores are much lower than the IQ's warrant, the principal would do well to look into the instruction which the class is getting. The alert principal who observes regularly in classrooms is rarely surprised at test results, for she is in touch with classroom instruction. When children are falling behind in their work because of poor teaching, the informed principal can take steps to remedy the situation. The test data give the principal objective evidence of these deficiencies as a basis for in-service work with the teacher. Of course, in evaluating the efficiency of a teacher, a principal should always consider pupil difficulties which are beyond the control of the school.

There are two points which the principal should keep in mind in interpreting test results. First, *a test score means nothing in itself.* Alfred scored grade 5.3 in reading; is that good or bad? The class average on the same test was grade 4.9. How satisfactory is this? Scores must be related to many other aspects of growth: the intelligence quotient, the children's background, their health, study habits, attendance, and personal adjustment. Teachers are inclined to praise pupils who score above average on standardized tests, when actually the score may be the result of high IQ rather than of effort. Teachers may get impatient with children who score low on tests, but a little study might reveal a lack of interest on the part of the home, or long absence during the preceding year. Again, a test score is meaningless in itself. It needs to be interpreted in the light of many other factors influencing the child and the class. The teacher is only one of these influences, though of course an important one.

Still more important, *the test should not become the course of study.* Teachers have a habit of identifying themselves with their class. If the class does poorly on a test, then the teacher wants to help them do better the next time. "Teaching the test" is what the teacher may be tempted to do to bring up the class scores. The wise principal can prevent most of this by her attitude toward standardized tests. First, she will, like the teacher, be aware that many factors need to be considered. As stated above, a test score means nothing in itself. Next, the principal and the teacher will consider the items tested. Should the pupils have been expected to know them? Were they in the course of study? Most importantly, the principal has, through her regular visits to the classroom, seen the kind of instruction which the children were receiving. The test score is valuable, but only as one index of learning. The objectives of the school are many; only a few of them can be measured by standardized tests. The tests show achievement in very limited areas. The school's objectives, on the other hand, should be the long-range goals of the teachers and the pupils. Overemphasis on test results can encourage the teacher to "teach the test," and thereby make the test content, and not the true objectives, the course of study in practice.

MEASURING OTHER ASPECTS OF PUPIL PROGRESS

The many and varied objectives of parochial school education require a variety of evaluative devices. The intellectual objectives are most easily measured, and have been discussed in the preceding section. Equally important but more difficult to measure are the spiritual and social objectives of education. Even in these complex areas, however, some techniques have been developed which provide a great deal of helpful information. For measuring pupil development in spiritual and social areas, the more important devices include the following: personality tests, projective techniques, sociograms, rating scales, check lists, inventories, anecdotal records, observation, conferences, and interviews. In the discussion which follows, emphasis will be given to devices which should prove helpful to the parochial school principal.

SPIRITUAL AND MORAL GROWTH

The appraisal of supernatural, spiritual, and moral development is the most difficult of all evaluation. The child's confessor alone has full insight into development along these lines, although the teacher can note certain indications of development. The child's frequenting the sacraments, his overt attitudes and actions in the classroom, in church, and on the playground, his reactions in conferences and interviews, his responses on inventories — all these furnish some insight into spiritual and moral development. The teacher can do a real service to the individual child by training him in the regular examination of conscience. This examination is strictly personal, of course, and the teacher makes no attempt to oblige a child to discuss conscience matters with her. However, the teacher can develop with the class certain objective standards by which they can evaluate their own actions and intentions. From a religious point of view, as well as from the standpoint of mental hygiene, the examination of conscience and frequent confession are effective means of self-development and self-evaluation.

In-Service Activities. There are certain in-service activities that promote better insight into spiritual and moral standards, and consequently insight into evaluation of these standards. The principal can help the staff improve in detecting signs of spiritual and moral growth by having competent speakers address the faculty on this topic. The pastor can provide individual religious instruction for lay teachers whose background in religion is deficient. A staff member with special training might be asked to collect timely and informative articles dealing with moral and spiritual development in children. Lives of the saints for children are often written up in such a way as to provide measuring rods, as it were, for the children's self-evaluation of their own development. Evaluation of the parochial school's teaching of moral and spiritual values can often be done indirectly by noting the after-school observance of Catholic graduates. The results are sometimes gratifying, and at other times disappointing.

The principal is also in a position to discourage misinformed attempts to measure the devotional practices of children. A teacher may think that she can evaluate a child's spiritual progress by noting the number of times he comes to church, receives the sacraments, or says the rosary. Hence, a teacher may display an artistically arranged chart on which to graph certain religious practices. Canon law is explicit in forbidding any such recognition of a child's receiving Holy Communion.[5] Hence, charts to mark church attendance, reception of the sacraments, or other devotions are not in keep-

---

[5] Instruction Congregation of Sacraments, Dec. 8, 1938, translated in Bouscaren, *Canon Law Digest*, Vol. 2, p. 208 ff.

ing with the mind of the Church. A poster to encourage devotion to the Blessed Virgin may be effective; a chart on which to mark recitation of the rosary is hardly good. In this area, the teacher should try to stimulate devotion and reverence, but should be wary about trying to evaluate these qualities.

Research in Moral Conduct. Over the past thirty years, a number of interesting studies have been conducted in measuring moral conduct. The best known of these are the studies in honesty by Hartshorne and others.[6] When religious educators first come into contact with these scientific attempts to measure moral conduct, there is a great deal of enthusiasm. However, the enthusiasm is short-lived, for the reader soon realizes the limitations of research.

A few isolated and obvious actions, such as cheating during tests or attending church services, have been studied under limited conditions and with a small number of subjects. Because it is not possible to control all the factors involved, the studies report only very generalized findings. In studying the relationship between Sunday church attendance and attitudes in school, the research workers have not been able to rule out the influence of the home background. Likewise, writers have not shown how intelligence and motivation affect scores on tests of religious information. Studies have, however, provided insight into many sociological influences on moral conduct, and many effects of socioeconomic status on teachers' attitude toward their students.[7] Research in moral conduct, interesting though it may be, offers slight help to parochial school teachers in their everyday evaluation of the spiritual and moral outcomes of their teaching.

The more one considers evaluation in supernatural and moral matters, the more difficult and delicate such evaluation is seen to be. Great caution and prudence are needed to respect the sacredness of these matters, while at the same time endeavoring to establish standards and to note signs of progress toward more perfect observance.

SOCIAL AND EMOTIONAL GROWTH

In recent years, there has been a great deal of emphasis on the personal and social adjustment of children. Experience has shown that difficulties in school may be due more to maladjustment than to lack of intelligence. The same has been true of follow-up studies of job placement; personal traits other than intelligence are usually the cause of lost jobs and unhappiness in adult life. The school shares with the family the responsibility of

---

[6] Hugh Hartshorne, M. A. May, and F. K. Shuttleworth, *Studies in the Organization of Character* (New York: The Macmillan Company, 1930).

[7] Leonard Carmichael, ed., *Manual of Child Psychology*, Second Edition (New York: John Wiley and Sons, Inc., 1954), pp. 781–832.

helping the child develop desirable personal and social attitudes and understandings that will enable him to adjust satisfactorily to himself and to the groups with which he associates.

A good school curriculum has as one of its major objectives the development of social and emotional maturity in pupils. The parochial school, as for example in the objectives set forth in the *Guiding Growth in Christian Social Living Curriculum*, aims at the development of personally and socially mature individuals as products of its instructional program. As in all other aspects of the curriculum, the objectives of social and emotional development need to be worked toward consistently by the staff. The faculty should ask itself: How can our teaching help pupils to develop emotionally and socially? What are we doing to see that these objectives are being carried out? How can we know how well we are accomplishing our objectives in the personal and social area? In other words, the three-point program is — objectives, methods and materials, and outcomes or evaluation. The bibliography lists a number of readable texts that discuss measurement of personal and social adjustment. The present discussion will be limited to a few techniques that can be used in the parochial school.

Standards of Social and Emotional Growth.   Evaluating social and emotional growth must be largely a matter of subjective judgment, but teachers can be helped toward establishing in their own minds certain developmental levels of growth. Many teachers have had college courses in child psychology, child growth and development, and child guidance. In these courses, certain reactions and activities were shown to be characteristic of definite stages in the personal and social development of children. Gesell,[8] one of the more readable authors in the field, has studied the same children over a period of years and has noted rates and stages of development in these important areas. The Ohio State University has prepared charts of longitudinal development in the various aspects of child growth.[9] Faculty meetings or committee work devoted to the study of these developmental patterns would be invaluable as a starting point in improved measurement in this area. Refreshing their minds, or perhaps meeting the concepts for the first time, teachers would broaden their outlook from emphasizing "conduct" and "effort" only, to noting many other indications of growth.

Pupil Report Cards.   More and more, there is a trend toward including on the pupil report card some evaluation of personal and social adjustment.

---

[8] Arnold Gesell and Francis L. Ilg, *The Child from Five to Ten* (New York: Harper and Brothers, 1946).

Arnold Gesell, Frances L. Ilg, and Louise Bates Ames, *Youth — The Years from Ten to Sixteen* (New York: Harper and Brothers, 1956).

[9] The Ohio State University, *How Children Develop*, "Adventures in Education," University School Series, No. 3, by the Faculty of the School (Columbus, Ohio: The Ohio State University, University School, 1946).

The newer reports provide space for the teacher to mark such personal and social traits as co-operation, courtesy, self-control, and work and study habits. Usually each of these qualities is described in a series of explanatory phrases, as:

CO-OPERATION
  Works well with other
  Shares responsibility for neatness of classroom
COURTESY
  Shows respect for teachers and other adults
  Practices common courtesies toward classmates
SELF-CONTROL
  Observes rules on the playground
  Obeys traffic directors
  Takes care of books and materials
WORK AND STUDY HABITS
  Follows directions
  Begins and completes work on time
  Makes wise use of time

Such descriptions of acceptable behavior help the teacher to evaluate the pupil somewhat objectively. Parents are also helped by such a reporting method, for improvement can be sought in specific ways. Pupils, too, can be aided in self-development when check lists are discussed with them regularly, at least before report cards are issued. In the upper grades, pupils enjoy measuring their success in the various behaviors noted, and they especially like to compare their self-ratings with the teacher's ratings. Students need to be trained in all of these qualities; the report card is one means of evaluating pupils in these areas of development.

Anecdotal Records. Teacher observation of pupil growth has been greatly sharpened through the use of anecdotal records. These records are a series of notes in which the teacher states exactly what a child did or said in concrete situations. Anecdotal records give incidents and reactions which a teacher considers important about a pupil's behavior. Anecdotal records may be brief jottings made on a form prepared for this purpose, such as given in Figure 36.

Anecdotal records should be brief, objective, spaced over a period of time, and filed in the pupil's folder. These records are invaluable in showing the typical behavior patterns of a child. Very important incidents can slip a teacher's mind unless recorded soon afterward. A teacher with a large class can perhaps plan to make these brief observations for a few children each week, so that all of the class will be included at regular intervals. Anecdotal records are especially effective when a teacher is emphasizing a particular

```
┌─────────────────────────────────────────────────────────────────────┐
│                                    Pupil's Name.....................  │
│        ANECDOTAL RECORD            Date ............................  │
│                                    Class ...........................  │
│                                                                       │
│     Directions:                                                       │
│     Enter statements which give a picture of what a child did or      │
│     said, but not how you feel about the child, or what you think     │
│     of his behavior.                                                  │
│     As:  "At the end of the arithmetic lessons, Jimmy scribbled on    │
│           his completed work-sheet when asked to hand it in."         │
│     Not: "At the end of the arithmetic lesson, Jimmy stubbornly       │
│           scribbled on his work-sheet in a temper."                   │
│                                                                       │
│     Incident                                                          │
│                                                                       │
│                                                                       │
│     Comment                                                           │
│                                                                       │
│                                                                       │
│                                                                       │
│                                    Teacher ........................   │
└─────────────────────────────────────────────────────────────────────┘
```

Figure 36.   Anecdotal Record Form for Classroom Use

trait in the personal and social area or is studying a child who seems maladjusted. When parents come for a conference with the teacher, these spaced, concrete indications of pupil behavior and reactions are helpful in directing the discussion along specific lines. Anecdotal records can profitably be used in making out pupil record cards, in entering evaluations on the cumulative record, and in recommending a child for special testing or treatment. These records furnish concrete data for evaluation of personal and social development of children.

Sociograms. Another device for measuring social development, or acceptance, is the sociogram. In this procedure, pupils are asked to write down the name of the child they prefer to work with, or play with, in a given setting. The procedure may also involve a first, second, and third choice of partner, and may even ask for the name of a pupil whom they would rather *not* work with in the project. If the teacher-pupil rapport is acceptable, the children ordinarily give the names of their choices, or rejections, without hesitation. Analysis of these choices furnishes the teacher with insight into the acceptance and rejection of pupils in her class. An analysis sheet for tabulating the responses might be made up somewhat as in Figure 37.

In the tabulation of choices, Mary C. receives 3 tallies, and Jack D. receives 2 tallies. None of the other children are chosen. Mary C. and Jack D. are undoubtedly the most popular gym partners in this small group.

Whom Would You Like to Choose as Your Partner During Gym Period?

Chosen → Chooser ↓	Ann B.	Mary C.	Jack D.	John E.	Harry F.
1. Ann B.		1			
2. Mary C.			1		
3. Jack D.		1			
4. John E.				1	
5. Harry F.		1			
Etc.					
Times Chosen	0	3	2	0	0

Code: 1 = Chosen

Figure 37.   Tabulating Pupil Choices

The sociogram below illustrates the choices of this group.

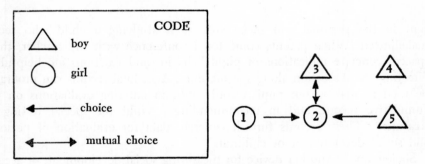

Figure 38.   A Simple Sociogram

Still further insight into group acceptance is given by considering the pupils who were positively rejected by members of the group. Not shown in the above chart, Ann B. was rejected by Mary C., Jack D., and Harry F. John E. was rejected only once — by Ann B; and Harry F. was rejected once — by John E. Thus, Mary C. is chosen three times and not rejected at all; Jack D. is chosen twice, and not rejected. John E. and Harry F. are each rejected once, while Ann B. is rejected by three of the group members. Ann B. seems to be considered very undesirable by this group as a gym partner.

In tabulating an entire class of pupils, there is opportunity to note still more complex variations in choices and rejections. The pupil most often chosen is called the "star," and the pupil on the fringe of the group is called the "isolate." There may be clusters of choices, indicating cliques, or two-way choices, indicating exclusive pairs. The sociogram thus reveals many acceptance patterns of which the teacher may not have been aware.

In interpreting the sociogram, however, the teacher must be careful about drawing unwarranted conclusions. The sociogram is only one measure of acceptance, and a narrow one at that, since the choices are based on a specific activity, such as games in gym. Also, children's preferences change rapidly, so that a valid sociogram might become unreliable in a few months. Still further, all relevant data should be included in a diagnosis of unpopularity, such as family background, newness in the classroom, health, temperament, and many other factors. The sociogram is an interesting device by which to measure limited aspects of pupil development. When supplemented by other pertinent data, the sociogram is useful in evaluating social acceptance by one's peers. The teacher can use the results of the sociogram to develop better attitudes and to help children work and play together.

Personality Tests. In addition to the foregoing means of evaluating personal-social growth, there are a few standardized personality tests of value to the elementary teacher. When administered, scored and interpreted by trained testing personnel, these personality tests or inventories provide principals and teachers with worthwhile insight into behavior and attitudes. However, the average classroom teacher, though experienced in giving other tests, should ordinarily not attempt to give personality tests. When pupils are obviously not adjusting to the classroom situation, it is advisable to refer such pupils to the local child guidance bureau — if one is available — for individual testing. In some cities, the public school board provides such services to parochial school pupils living within the local district. Some diocesan school boards have a testing center which administers personality tests upon request of parochial school principals. Personality tests have been developed to a point of great refinement, but their administration should ordinarily be delegated to trained psychometrists or psychologists.

In the area of emotional and social growth, then, the devices which seem to offer the most help to the classroom teacher are the following: in-service work in establishing developmental stages in growth, pupil report card evaluations, anecdotal records, sociograms, and professionally administered personality tests. Informed use of these techniques can do much to improve present methods of measuring personal-social growth.*

---

* Cf. books listed in "For the Principal's Professional Library," p. 388.

TEST PUBLISHERS

Publisher	Intelligence Test	Achievement Test
California Test Bureau 206 Bridge Street New Cumberland, Pa.	California Short-Form Test of Mental Maturity Calif. Test of Mental Maturity	California Achievement Test
Educational Testing Service Princeton, N. J.	....	Sequential Tests of Educational Progress
Houghton Mifflin Company 2500 Prairie Avenue Chicago 16, Ill.	Henmon-Nelson Lorge-Thorndike	Iowa Tests of Basic Skills
Personnel Press 188 Nassau Street Princeton, N. J.	Kuhlmann-Anderson	....
Scholastic Testing Service 3774 W. Devon Avenue Chicago 45, Ill.	....	Reading Achievement, Grades 4–8
Science Research Associates 57 W. Grand Avenue Chicago 10, Ill.	Otis Quick-Scoring Otis Self-Administering SRA Primary Mental Abilities	SRA Achievement Series
World Book Company 2126 Prairie Avenue Chicago 16, Ill.	Pintner General Ability: Verbal Series Terman-McNemar	Metropolitan Achievement Stanford Achievement

The readiness tests mentioned can be obtained as follows:

Gates Reading Readiness Test, from Bureau of Publications, Teachers College, Columbia University, New York

Lee-Clark Readiness Test, from the California Test Bureau (address above)

Metropolitan Readiness Test, from World Book Company (address above)

CHAPTER XIV

GRADES, RECORDS, AND REPORTS

Marking and grading are sources of much comment among parents and teachers. Some of this comment is unfavorable. Why? What can the principal do to overcome common weaknesses in marking and grading? Account for recent emphasis on adequate pupil records.

GRADES AND MARKS

THE grades that teachers put on pupils' papers and report cards are an important aspect not only of evaluation but also of public relations. Very often, the report card is the only contact which the parents have with the school. The effect of grades upon parents' attitudes and also upon pupil progress makes it necessary to develop a sound, consistent policy with regard to marks and grades.

DIFFERENCES IN GRADING PLANS

Grading systems vary widely in different schools. Some schools use only *Satisfactory — Unsatisfactory* ratings, trying to evaluate pupil progress in the light of the pupil's capacity. Fifth-grade Johnny, who has an IQ of 145 and scored at a tenth-grade level on the standardized reading test, is marked *Satisfactory* if his work shows high achievement. Johnny is intellectually gifted, so he is marked *Satisfactory* only if he does superior work. Timmy, on the other hand, is in the same grade, but scored 80 on the IQ test and at the third-grade level on the standardized reading test. Timmy is rated *Satisfactory* if he seems to be progressing as much as his limited ability will permit. Mary, however, scored in the average group on both tests, but her work has been careless; so, Mary is marked *Unsatisfactory*, though her per cent scores are higher than Timmy's. In systems that use this plan of marking, the idea is to stimulate bright pupils to their potential and at the same time to encourage slower pupils to do as well as they can. This system assumes that the classroom teacher can judge accurately just what every child's potential is, in each subject, and even in personal-social traits.

A variation of the above is a plan whereby three ratings are used: Superior, Satisfactory, and Unsatisfactory. The underlying philosophy is the same, but the high achiever is given more recognition. Sometimes Unsatisfactory means failure, but usually it seems to mean that more effort is needed. When a three-division breakdown is used, the system is approaching the letter system, using, however, only A, C, and F.

Many schools use a five-category rating plan, using letters, or descriptive phrases, or both. Such a plan is illustrated below.

TABLE XXIII. Five-Level Grading Plan

Letter	Grade Range	Description
A	90–100	Excellent
B	80– 89	Very Good
C	70– 79	Average
D	60– 69	Poor
F	Below 60	Failure

Some schools break this scheme down still further, by assigning seven or more ratings. In this plan, the teacher may use plus or minus signs. The basic idea underlying this plan is illustrated below

TABLE XXIV. Seven-Level Grading Plan

Level	Grade Range	Letter Equivalent
7	95–100	A
6	90– 94	B+ (A—)
5	80– 89	B
4	75– 79	C+ (B—)
3	70– 74	C
2	60– 69	D
1	Below 60	F

When teachers use both plus and minus signs, the grading plan may include as many as thirteen ratings.

There are schools that still use a percentage marking plan exclusively. Here, the teachers transfer from their record book the average percentage for the child in each subject. In arithmetic, Jane may average 61 per cent, in spelling 79 per cent, in English 71 per cent, and in religion 64 per cent. Her cousin in the same classroom may average twenty points higher in each subject. This grading plan assumes that the teacher has some objective way of actually assigning exact per cents in every subject. Also, the plan assumes that the teacher will transfer the percentages directly from her record book to the report card. Those experienced in this system find, however, that giving an exact percentage is impossible in many subjects, as for example, assigning a per cent of 63 to an English composition. Also, teachers find that they really can't transfer percentages exactly, for the marks would be too low. On a semester test, for instance, the entire class may get per cent grades that are very much lower than their usual report grades. Alice may have been averaging 86 per cent in arithmetic throughout the semester, and, on the midyear test, go down to 64 per cent. This is quite possible, even though Alice applied herself consistently and the teacher taught well. The weakness of per cent grades is that they assume the teacher can and will judge pupil achievement, precisely and coldly. Even with the most conscientious teachers, per cent grades are difficult to keep, and still more difficult to report to parents.

A few schools have tried to use a *Satisfactory-Unsatisfactory* rating in the primary grades, and then transfer to a letter grading plan in the fourth grade. Although this appealed to primary teachers, it was disturbing to parents. A child marked S for three years, and then suddenly marked D in fourth grade, finds the adjustment difficult. Schools that used S and U at the elementary level, and then transferred to a letter system in high school, created even more severe problems.

A study of grading systems, all of which have inherent weaknesses, seems to favor the seven-level rating presented above. This plan assigns the five letter grades, A, B, C, D, and F, and two plus or minus signs. It is true that this plan is also based on the idea that teachers can assign per cents to pupil achievement, but the range of per cents allows for a margin of error. This is the traditional system with which most parents are familiar. Involved marking systems that confuse parents really cannot be called "reports," because the ratings actually report nothing to the parents.

Although teachers will never like to mark "nice" children D, or even C, present-day school organization seems to make a letter-grading plan necessary. The teacher's desire to reward children who try can be satisfied in either of two ways: first, by marking their *Effort* high and commenting favorably to parents on the child's co-operativeness, and second, by indicating that a child can do better in a given subject. One school directs teachers to draw a circle around a letter grade that does not represent the child's best effort. This calls the parents' attention to the need for greater effort in that subject. Teachers really can't shield the child from knowing that other children are brighter than he, and that others are putting forth more effort. Even in the first grade, children know who reads best, who writes best, and who misbehaves. Nobody but the teacher is deceived by the names of the reading groups; children know whether the "bluebirds" are the best group or the poorest group. The same is true of letter grades. Most children know how well they have achieved. Though letter grades are not perfect, still they reflect the values of the present educational system as well as any plan yet devised. Since the majority of parochial schools use the letter-grading system, A, B, C, D, and F, the discussion which follows will be based on this plan.

IN-SERVICE WORK ON GRADING

As with all other matters of school policy, the Sister Principal plays a dominant role in the grading system used in her school. In some dioceses, there is a diocesan-wide system of grading and reporting. If so, the principal can use her background in this area to interpret diocesan policy and to carry it out in her school. Where there is no diocesan grading and reporting system, the work of the principal is more difficult. She must then devise a workable plan for the school. Whether the principal is to implement the diocesan plan of grading, or to develop a system for her school, there is considerable in-service work to be done with teachers.

First, the principal should help teachers broaden their concept of school grades. Perhaps a series of faculty meetings could be devoted to reports and discussions on various aspects of grading. The principal can take an active part in these discussions, as for example, by presenting the following material on the normal curve and grading. And the principal will need to correct faulty grading practices. The matter of grades and marks should be subject to continuous evaluation, just as any other aspect of the school program. A healthy attitude of inquiry and interest will do a great deal to make grades and marks serve the dual purpose of helping children make better progress and helping parents interpret school grades.

THE NORMAL CURVE AND SCHOOL GRADES

Using the Curve as a Guide. A device which the principal may find helpful is to discuss with the staff the ideas behind "grading on the curve." In Chapter XIII, the table from Terman and Merrill showed the percentage in each category, from "Very Superior" down to "Mentally Defective." Although these percentages do not directly apply to an ordinary classroom, still they may be used as guides in marking. Figure 39 shows how the

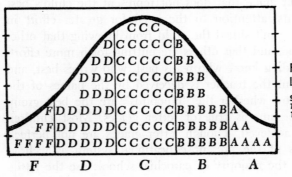

Figure 39. Assigning Letter Grades

Source: Herschel T. Manuel, *Taking a Test* (New York: World Book Company, 1956), p. 13. Used with permission.

normal curve may be used to illustrate the principles underlying "grading on the curve." In Figure 39, it is assumed that about 38 per cent of the class will normally fall into the C group, about 24 per cent in each of the B and D groups, and about 7 per cent in each of the A and F groups.

In Figure 39, the percentages cited above are written in as letter grades. Thus, the 7 per cent of the class receiving A's are shown as seven A's in the upper end of the curve. The 24 children receiving B's are shown as 24 B's in the curve, and so on. In most classes, the average child should get a C; the 38 C's presented graphically in the highest part of the curve emphasize the "normal" pattern of grade distribution. Figure 39 shows the balance in the letter grades assigned to the various groups according to their achievement.

It is somewhat easier to visualize the normal curve as being divided into the following pattern: A and F — 5 per cent; B and D — 20 per cent; C — 50 per cent. The figure below shows the possible variations in assigning letter grades according to the normal curve.

Figure 40.   Several Plans for Assigning Letter Grades to Pupils

Letter Marks →	F	D	C	B	A
Per Cent of Class →	5–8%	20–25%	34–50%	20–25%	5–8%

Source: Harry A. Greene, Albert N. Jorgensen, and J. Raymond Gerberich, *Measurement and Evaluation in the Elementary School* (New York: Longmans, Green and Co., 1942), p. 595. Used with permission.

These distributions will not apply to every group of children, as will be pointed out later. However, at the initial stage of the discussion, the principal can proceed to apply the normal curve pattern to report card averages. For a quarterly report card period, a class of 41 pupils had the averages reported in Table XXV for arithmetic quizzes and tests. An ideal distribution is given in this table, in order to illustrate more vividly how the normal curve can be applied to grading.

When the arithmetic averages are ranked in order, as in Table XXV, teachers can see that the scores can rather easily be grouped into the five-letter grading system, A to F. Also, the A's and the F's stand out from the B's and D's. The beginning teacher especially can be helped by thus visualizing the relationship between D's and F's. New teachers often think of 70 per cent as the cutoff point; all below 70 per cent are considered failures. Actually, this is not so. Even when grading systems state that below 70 per cent is failure, teachers sometimes add to the scores to save too many pupils from getting F's. In most instances, it is safe to say that there should be as many A's as F's. By arranging scores in descending order, as in Table XXV, teachers can see the logic of assigning letter marks

TABLE XXV. Assigning Letter Grades From Averages in Arithmetic

Average for Nine Weeks	Number of Pupils (N = 41)	Letter Marks
97	1	
96		
95	2	A = 7%
94		
93		
92	1	
91	1	
90		
89	2	
88	1	
87		B = 24%
86	1	
85		
84	1	
83	2	
82		
81	1	
80		
79	2	
78	3	
77	2	
76	2	
75	1	C = 38%
74	1	
73	2	
72		
71	1	
70	1	
69	2	
68	2	
67	1	
66	2	
65	1	D = 24%
64	1	
63	1	
62		
61		
60		
59	1	F = 7%*
58	1	
57	1	
Range 97–57	N = 41	100%

* Some of these pupils may be assigned S (Satisfactory) if their IQ is very low.
See the discussion of S grades later in this chapter.

according to the normal curve. Most teachers will be helped by such a visualization.

Table XXV can be used to get across the idea that the *distribution* of scores is more important than the scores themselves. In another quarterly period, the arithmetic averages might be considerably higher; perhaps the lowest score would be in the 60's, and the middle scores would be in the 80's. No matter what the range is, the teacher can be helped by using the normal curve pattern as a guide in assigning letter grades. The teacher can also be helped to see that the kind of tests she gives has a great deal to do with the scores which children receive. When teachers improve their tests, then the pupils' averages will not vary so much from time to time.

Summarizing Class Averages. A logical next step is to summarize the averages in Table XXV so that the teacher may use them in preparing her grades. Table XXVI presents this summary.

TABLE XXVI. Summary of 41 Pupils' Averages in Arithmetic

Average	Tally	Frequency	Per Cent	Letter Mark
95–100	111	3	7	A
80– 94	THL THL	10	24	B
70– 79	THL THL THL	15	38	C
60– 69	THL THL	10	24	D
Below 60	111	3	7	F*

* The S (Satisfactory) grade may be assigned instead of F, if the pupil has a very low IQ. See the discussion of S grades later in this chapter.

In Table XXVI, the averages in the left-hand column summarize the arithmetic averages given in Table XXV. When summarized in a frequency distribution, the tallies roughly correspond to a normal curve pattern. In the right-hand columns are the letter grades and the per cent of the group falling into each category. The letters A and F are each assigned to 7 per cent of the group, or to 3 pupils. B and D are each assigned to 24 per cent of the group, or to 10 pupils. C is assigned to 38 per cent to the group, or to 15 pupils. Table XXVI was planned as an idealized distribution; a class would rarely be divided so evenly. However, the table illustrates the parallel between letter-grades and the normal curve pattern. The pattern can be applied to any range of percentages used in a diocese.

Relating the IQ to Averages in Arithmetic. It should be emphasized that the letter marks discussed here assume that a given class has a normal distribution of intelligence quotients. The principal can point out that in the case of an unusually slow group, or an unusually bright group, the above percentages will vary. For example, in Table XXVI, the 15 pupils in the C group probably have IQ's between 90 and 110, the average range. The three pupils with A's are likely to have high IQ's, and the three with F's low IQ's. However, if the class is well above average, so that there are more pupils in the A group, there may be no F's assigned at all. Likewise, in an unusually slow group, there might be only one A, or no A's, and perhaps 15 D's, instead of only 10. The intelligence quotient can be used to help the teacher decide the brightness of the class on the whole. Intelligence test scores are not perfect, either; errors creep into these scores as well as into teachers' grades. But the IQ should be used, at least as a check on the teacher's impressions.

At the beginning of the year, it would be well for the teacher to use the IQ scores as a check on her letter grades. The teacher can use the class sheet which summarizes the results of the last intelligence test which her class took. This frequency distribution of IQ's can be placed side by side with teacher's proposed grades for the report card period. Figure 41 presents a form which may be used for this purpose.

In Figure 41, the range and frequency of IQ's are listed in the columns to the left. The data from Table XXVI are given again in the tabulation of arithmetic averages and the per cent receiving certain letter grades. Figure 35 is an idealized distribution; IQ's and achievement will never match perfectly in any class. The pupils' effort, their absence and illness, the kind of teaching they received, the kinds of homes they come from — all of these enter into report card grades, and also into the IQ score. Figure 41 is not intended as a mold for assigning grades; it is rather a suggestion for helping the teacher to consider many factors when assigning grades. Grades can sometimes be assigned capriciously by teachers; and grades sometimes cannot be justified by marks the child has received. Figure 41 can be used as one means for improving the grading system in a school.

THE "HALO EFFECT"

Especially in subjects that are difficult to grade, such as English and social studies, teachers may need to be warned against the "halo effect" in their grading. Teachers' marks are definitely colored by factors other than achievement. For example, teachers tend to mark girls higher than boys, even when test scores are identical. Also, teachers typically give better marks to pupils from higher socioeconomic homes. Teachers represent a middle-class culture, though they may have come from the lower classes themselves. Hence, teachers are known to favor middle-class values. The neat, polite, well-dressed, obedient, "co-operative" child almost invariably receives higher grades than the pupil who scores similarly on tests but who comes from a lower-class background. When teachers resent the dress, attitudes, and manners of lower-class pupils, they may really be trying to forget their own lower-class associations.

Especially in a parochial school should teachers be on guard against this

Figure 41. Proposed Report Card Grades

Teacher ....

Grade .... Room Number ....

Date ...... for I, II, III, IV Report Card (circle)

Number in Class ....

| IQ's | | | | | | | | | Letters — |
Range	Frequency	Letter Marks	Rel.	Arith.	Spelling	English	Rdg.	Soc. St.	Per Cents
125+	2	A		3					A = 7
105–124	9	B		10					B = 24
95– 104	17	C		15					C = 38
75– 94	9	D		10					D = 24
Below 74	4	F		3					F = 7
Total	41	—	41	41	41	41	41	41	—

Rel.	Arith.	Spelling	English	Rdg.	Soc. St.

↑ ↑

Comments

Use these spaces to comment on variations in the subject grades.

"halo effect." Since teachers are human, they are bound to be somewhat biased, even in their seemingly objective marks and grades. Unconscious discrimination can be brought to the surface, and counteracted to a degree by emphasis on objectivity in grading.

DEVELOPING SCHOOL POLICIES ON GRADING

There are two divergent attitudes that the principal may need to counteract in the matter of assigning letter grades. There are some teachers who believe that their class is the brightest, the best behaved, and the most studious in the building. These teachers carry over this attitude into grading, for their pupils receive grades very much higher than their IQ's or past performance would warrant. On the other hand, there are teachers who revel in the fact that their courses are "stiff," and that anyone who gets an A must be a near-genius. These teachers pride themselves on the high percentage of F's they assign, as indicative of the fine quality of their instruction and the poor preparation of pupils coming into their class. Both of these extreme attitudes may be found in a staff at the same time. These teachers may need to be dealt with individually in order to bring their grading closer to that of the staff as a whole.

In order to promote good grading policies, the principal should make sure, early in the year, that all of the faculty are acquainted with the details of grading as used in the school. The principal, through the advisers, will need to devote time to helping new teachers understand the grading procedures to be followed. Before the first report card is to be issued, it might be good practice to request that teachers submit to the principal a proposed distribution of grades in each subject, or in crucial subjects, and a distribution of IQ scores. Standard forms such as Figure 41 will help to reduce the time which teachers must spend in this tabulation. Frequently, when teachers can "see" the comparison between their proposed grades and the actual IQ scores, they are convinced that they need to examine the basis for their grading. In some schools, report cards are routinely placed on the principal's desk several days before issuance, so that any discrepancies in grading can be corrected. Concrete devices such as these are more effective than the hopeful admonition to "grade carefully."

PUPIL PERSONNEL RECORDS

Present conditions in this country make an adequate and accurate pupil record system more imperative than ever before. The broadened scope of the educational program has created the need for more detailed records. The high rate of pupil transfer likewise places a premium on good pupil records, so that the receiving school can make use of pertinent background data as soon as the new pupil is enrolled. Elementary school records are also being used more frequently by high school guidance personnel, so that the child's high school program will be better adapted to his capacities and achievements.

The day of the single 3 by 5 inch pupil record has gone forever. Much more information now is needed, and used, than ever before. Schools in general have tried to adapt their record system to pupil needs, but there is still some uncertainty as to how many, and how detailed, pupil personnel records should be.

A principal who is using the required diocesan record forms may feel that there is too much detail, or that there isn't enough. In a diocese where there are no system-wide records, the principal may be using forms which she or her predecessor developed. In either case there should be criteria for judging how satisfactory the records are. Thus, where records are inadequate, the principal can supplement the records with additional information as needed.

CHARACTERISTICS OF A GOOD RECORD SYSTEM

Records Should Reflect School's Philosophy. As stated earlier, one must first determine what the school is attempting to do, and only then can a just appraisal be made of its success. This same principle applies to pupil records. The records should reflect the school's philosophy and objectives. Each of the school's purposes is important enough to figure in the records which are kept of the child's development. Some of the school's objectives are quite difficult to achieve, and difficult also to evaluate. However, records should give a picture of the all-over purposes of the school and the way the child has succeeded in attaining them.

The objectives of the school may be stated in various ways. Perhaps the listing given by the Catholic University of America evaluative criteria is as clear and practical as any. The school should try to promote in its pupils physical fitness, economic competence, social responsibility, intellectual and cultural growth, and moral and spiritual perfection. A true picture of the parochial school program, then, should include an evaluation in each of these five areas. In the past, pupil records often overemphasized the intellectual aspect of the child's growth. Some of the current records overemphasize the social aspect of growth. A balanced record endeavors to show the child's progress in all the essential aspects of educational development. A good record system is based on sound criteria — the school's objectives, and is comprehensive, or all-inclusive.

Records Should Not Be Too Time-Consuming to Maintain. From the above, it would seem that many and very minute records should be kept of pupil progress. Immediately there arises the practical objection that such records would require too much time — the teacher's time, the principal's, and even the school clerk's. Hence, very detailed records of all

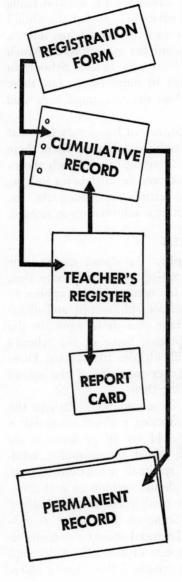

PUPIL PERSONNEL RECORDS

Registration Form

Background information on the pupil is assembled in conference with the parents at time of registration.

Cumulative Classroom Record

Basic data are transferred from the Registration Form to the Cumulative Classroom Record. Current data are added periodically, usually once or twice a year. The Cumulative Record accompanies the child from grade to grade, and is filed with the child's teacher.

Teacher's Register

Identifying data are copied in the Teacher's Register from the Cumulative Classroom Record. Daily attendance and achievement records are kept in the Register and transferred back to the Cumulative Record.

Report Card

Record of attendance and grades are transferred from the Teacher's Register to the Report Card.

Permanent Record

The Permanent Record Folder contains the Permanent Record Card, an exact duplicate of the Cumulative Classroom Record. Significant data are transferred from the Cumulative Record to the Permanent Record once a year. The individual folder for every child also contains supplemental data, such as the health record, test profiles, correspondence, teachers' comments, and confidential information. The Permanent Record is kept indefinitely in the office file.

Figure 42. Pupil Personnel Records
How the Basic Pupil Records Interrelate in Transfer of Data

aspects of the school program would be impractical because of the time element involved.

An efficient record system should include, then, forms which can be maintained with a reasonable expenditure of time. All aspects of the school curriculum should be evaluated, even if only in a modified way; but extensive records cannot be expected of the typical elementary school. In practice, this means that written evaluation of moral and spiritual growth, for example, will be limited to the sacramental record and to a few traits which can be objectively measured. In the area of economic and social development, teachers can be encouraged to keep anecdotal records and check lists, but these too will usually not be extensive. Records of physical fitness are rather complete in schools having regular medical service; otherwise, such records will be superficial. The intellectual traits are most easily measured, and often make up a large part of the pupil records. The discussion which follows will offer further suggestions concerning the amount of detail needed in adequate pupil records. (See the discussion of evaluating social, emotional, moral traits in the preceding chapter.)

KINDS OF PUPIL PERSONNEL RECORDS

Surveys of public and parochial schools have shown that certain basic records are kept by most schools. The law in some states requires that specified forms or kinds of information be kept on file. Whether or not state law affects the child accounting system, pupil personnel records usually include the following: registration form, cumulative record, permanent record, teacher's register, and report card. Because of the similarity in the kinds of records maintained in many dioceses, the forms developed by the Diocese of Youngstown are used as illustrations in this discussion.

Figure 42 illustrates the five common record forms, and their interrelationships. The registration form relates closely to the family background. The cumulative record, kept in the classroom, furnishes the teacher with needed information on pupil progress. The teacher's register, or record of attendance and scholarship, is an administrative record, required by some state laws, or at least by school officials. The report card is the teacher's contact with the home regarding the pupil's progress. The permanent record folder is the complete picture of pupil development while in the school; the permanent record duplicates the cumulative record and also adds supplementary information of interest.

Registration Form. When the child comes to the school to register for admittance, the parents supply complete information on the child's experience that is pertinent to the school program. This registration form is supplied by some dioceses; in other places, the individual school duplicates

Elementary Schools REGISTRATION FORM Diocese of Youngstown

Birth.. Name....................................... Family

Year   Month   Date   City   State   First   Second

Father's Name...................................... Birthplace................. Religion.................. Deceased ( )
                                                                                                          Separated ( )
                                                                                                          Remarried ( )

Mother's Maiden Name.............................. Birthplace................. Religion.................. Deceased ( )
                      First   Family   Separated ( )
                                                                                                          Remarried ( )

Father's Occupation.................. Place........ Mother's Occupation.................. Place.........

Guardian's Name...................... Birthplace.......... Guardian's Occupation........... Place.......

Remarks (if any).. Boy........ Girl........ Race.........

Date Entering.................. From what School................ Grade Entering..............
                                or Kindergarten   Name   City   State

Sacrament Record:

Baptism (Certificate Received)	First Communion	Confirmation
Date		
Church		
City, State		

HOME ADDRESS

Present Address.. Telephone.................
                    Street   City

Date of Immunization: { 1st.
Small Pox........ Diphtheria........ Typhoid Tetanus........ Pertussis........ Polio { 2nd.
                                                            (Whooping Cough)   { 3rd.

Physician to be contacted in case of need   Registration taken by..............

Name.......................................   School.............................

Address....................................   Date...............................

Phone......................................

Figure 43. A Sample Registration Form

its own registration blank. On this form should be included all information required for the classroom cumulative record, such as the following items:

1. Name — first, middle, last
2. Birthplace — country, state, city; Date — year, month, day
3. Sex
4. Race
5. Parents — father's name, birthplace, religion
   mother's maiden name, birthplace, religion
   Status of home — separation, or divorce
   Father's and mother's occupation — place of work, address of work, and telephone there
   (same information for guardian, if necessary)
6. Date entered this school; from what school; grade there
7. Date withdrawn from this school; transferred to; reason
8. Sacramental record:
   Date of: Baptism, First Communion, Confirmation
   Church, city, state; certificates received
9. Innoculations and date
10. Name of physician to be contacted if necessary
11. Information on transportation, school lunch, and fees, as needed by the school

The registration form supplies the basic data for the cumulative record card and the teacher's register (attendance and scholarship book). The registration blank for the Diocese of Youngstown provides the above information in a form for easy transferring of data to these other records.

Cumulative Classroom Record. The cumulative record, also called the teacher's record, classroom record, or desk card, is considered the most valuable of the pupil personnel records. This record may be a sheet, a card, or a folder, on which are entered important facts concerning the child's development. The cumulative record is begun when the child enters the school, and is based on the registration form. In addition to the basic data transferred from the registration form, the cumulative record contains a record of the child's progress in academic subjects as well as in personality and character, a record of intelligence and achievement tests, a sacramental record, and other pertinent data regarding his development. The cumulative record ideally is in the possession of the child's teacher, and goes along with him from grade to grade, from school to school, and even to high school.

The cumulative record is usually kept up to date by the classroom teacher, for whose information it is designed. This record furnishes the teacher with a complete educational history of the child for guidance purposes. When standardized tests are given, it is the classroom teacher who usually enters the test results. The cumulative record often contains a copy of the pupil's report card averages for each year. Because of its availability to the classroom

Elementary Schools

CUMULATIVE CLASSROOM RECORD

Diocese of Youngstown

				Name		
Birth *	Year	Month	Date	City	State	First	Second	Family

FAMILY RECORD

Father's Name _____ Birthplace _____ Religion _____ Deceased ( ) Separated ( )

Mother's Maiden Name _____ Birthplace _____ Religion _____ Deceased ( ) Separated ( )

Father's Occupation _____ Place _____ Mother's Occupation _____ Place

Guardian's Name _____ Birthplace _____ Guardian's Occupation _____ Place

Remarks _____ Boy _____ Girl _____ Race _____

Date Entered _____ From What School _____ Name _____ City _____ State _____ Grade

Date Withdrawn _____ Transferred to _____ School _____ City _____ State _____ Grade

** SACRAMENT RECORD

Baptism (Certificate Received _____)	First Communion	Confirmation

HOME ADDRESS

Date *	
Church	
City, State	

1. _____ Telephone _____ 3. _____ Telephone

2. _____ Telephone _____ 4. _____ Telephone

PROGRESS THROUGH SCHOOL

Grade	Age Sept. 1 (Yrs. – months)†	* Date Entered	Withdrawn	SCHOOL Name	City - State	TEACHER

* Record all dates 1960-9-27   †7–5=7 years and 5 months (born in April)   ** To be filled in when sacraments are received.

Figure 44A. Sample of Cumulative Record (front)

NAME

Family   First

RECORD OF MARKS

Year's Average - - June

GRADE	GRADE
Religion	Religious habits
Reading ∧	Is reverent at prayer
Reading aloud ∧	Behaves satisfactorily
Comprehension ∧	Practices courtesy
Phonics (Primary)	Study Habits
English	Begins, completes work on time
Spelling ∧	Makes an effort to improve
Weekly lesson ∧	Does required home assignments
In all written work ∧	Social Habits
Arithmetic ∧	Gets along well with others
Computation ∧	Keeps desk and materials neat
Problem solving ∧	Is careful of personal appearance
Geography ∧	Observes safety rules
History	
Civics	Days absent
Handwriting	Times late
Art	Reading level
Music	
Science	

∧ Each is averaged separately; e.g. Spelling has 3 averages.

Grade Placement at Time of Testing

Date of Testing	Grade Placement .0 .1 .2 .3 .4 .5 .6 .7 .8 .9	Year's Average - - June
Sept. 1- Sept. 15		
Sept. 16- Oct. 15		
Oct. 16- Nov. 15		
Nov. 16- Dec. 15		
Dec. 16- Jan. 15		
Jan. 16- Feb. 15		
Feb. 16- Mar. 15		
Mar. 16- Apr. 15		
Apr. 16- May 15		
May 16- June 15		

INTELLIGENCE TESTS

Date *	Test §	Level§	Form	Score	C. A.	M. A.	I. Q.

ACHIEVEMENT TESTS

Date *	Present** Grade	Test	Level§	Form	Score	Grade Equiv. †	%-ile Rank
		Metropolitan Readiness					

(Note - enter only averages for Reading Tests not Paragraphs and Vocabulary separately.)

A circle around a letter means that the child can do better in that subject.

S means satisfactory for this child; used for pupils following a below-grade program.

U means unsatisfactory for below-grade pupils; indicates lack of application.

On Permanent and Classroom Records, the year's average is entered in June. This average includes the six grades on the report card - two for semester tests and four for daily achievement.

An X indicates that improvement is needed. No X means that progress is satisfactory.
The X's are averaged thus: No X—A; 1 X—B; 2 or 3 X—C; 4 X—D.
On the Permanent and Class Records, these averages are entered in June.

* Record all dates 1960-9-27
** Give grade and month as 4.5—fifth month of Grade 6
† Pupil's grade score on the standard test, as 4.5—October 20 of Grade 6 (See chart at top of card)
§ Level as Primary, Elementary, etc. Copy from the test itself.

Scholastic Progress Code

A Excellent	96 - 100
B + Very Good	90 - 95
B Good	88 - 89
C + High average	78 - 87
C Average	70 - 74
D Poor	60 - 69
F Failure	Below 60

Character Code

Figure 44B. Sample of Cumulative Record (reverse)

DIOCESE OF YOUNGSTOWN

PROGRESS REPORT OF

Grades 4 - 8

TO PARENTS AND GUARDIANS:

This is the report of the conduct, effort, and scholastic progress of your child while in our care.

We are proud to share with you the privilege of helping your child grow spiritually, intellectually, and physically. Without full and effective cooperation from you, especially in training the child in all good habits, the school can hardly succeed.

You are earnestly requested to examine this report carefully, sign and return it promptly.

REV. JAMES W. MALONE
Superintendent of Schools

School _____, Ohio

Grade _____ Year 19 ____ to 19 ____

_____
TEACHER

_____
PASTOR

PARENT-TEACHER CONFERENCE

	1 Period	2 Period	3 Period
Conference requested by TEACHER			
PARENT			

Either parent or teacher may request a conference to discuss the child's progress. In the blank above, suggest a convenient date. The other party will confirm the appointment by letter or by telephone.

PARENT'S COMMENTS

FIRST REPORT _____

_____
PARENT'S SIGNATURE

SECOND REPORT _____

_____
PARENT'S SIGNATURE

THIRD REPORT _____

_____
PARENT'S SIGNATURE

PROMOTION RECORD

Next September, your child will be in the _____ GRADE

_____
PRINCIPAL

DATE _____

Figure 45A.   Sample Report Card (outside)

Name _____

CHARACTER DEVELOPMENT

Report Periods 1 2 3 4

RELIGIOUS HABITS

Is reverent at prayer

Behaves satisfactorily

Practices courtesy

STUDY HABITS

Begins and completes work on time

Makes an effort to improve

Does required home assignments

SOCIAL HABITS

Gets along well with others

Keeps desk and materials neat

Is careful of personal appearance

Observes safety rules

No **X** means that progress is satisfactory.

An **X** means that improvement is needed.

TIME LOST	Days Absent	Times late

SCHOLASTIC PROGRESS CODE

A — Excellent	95 — 100	C — Average	70 — 74
B+ — Very Good	90 — 94	D — Poor	60 — 69
B — Good	80 — 89	F — Failure	below 60
C+ — High Average	75 — 79		

SCHOLASTIC PROGRESS REPORT PERIOD 1 2 Exam 3 4 Exam

RELIGION

READING

Reading aloud

Comprehension

ENGLISH

SPELLING

Weekly lesson

In all written work

ARITHMETIC

Computation

Problem Solving

GEOGRAPHY

HISTORY

CIVICS

HANDWRITING

ART

MUSIC

SCIENCE

A circle around a letter means that the child **can do better** in that subject.

S means satisfactory for this child; used for pupils following a below-grade program.

U means unsatisfactory for below-grade pupils; indicates lack of application.

Figure 45B. Sample Report Card (inside)

teacher, the cumulative record should be the most used and most helpful of the pupil personnel records.

In some systems, an exact duplicate of the cumulative record is kept in the principal's office. Thus, the child's educational history is available to the teacher for guidance through the cumulative record, and also available to the principal for administrative use through the permanent record. A copy of the cumulative record in use in the diocese of Youngstown is given on pages 380–381 (Fig. 44). This record is kept in an indexed classroom record notebook in the teacher's desk or file.

Teacher's Register.   The record book in which attendance and sometimes report card grades are kept is called by various names, such as teacher's register, attendance register, or attendance and scholarship record. Some states require that a record of attendance be kept while the child is in the school, and that it be filed for a specified number of years after his withdrawal. In public schools, the attendance record is obligatory because of apportionment of funds for the school program. In parochial schools, accurate attendance keeping is also important, even where not required by state law, because of the welfare of the students.

The teacher's register depends upon the cumulative record for the child's address and other background data. From the teacher's register, the record of attendance, and sometimes the record of scholarship and character, are transferred to the cumulative record. The register and cumulative record are thus interdependent in a functional record system.

Report Card.   Although there is continuing emphasis on parent conferences and letters to the home, the report card is the most popular means of informing the home of pupil progress. Even where parent conferences and letters are used in a school system, the pupil report card often is an objective record used to summarize certain aspects of the pupil's development. The report card developed by the Diocese of Youngstown incorporates many features of current diocesan forms — size, arrangement, division into subject grades and personal-social ratings, and provision for comments by parent and teacher. Like many of the newer cards, the one illustrated also provides a space for recording promotion to the next higher grade, and breaks down certain subjects into easily analyzed components (Fig. 45).

The Report Card in Public Relations.   The report card is the only part of the pupil accounting system which parents see. The report card may also be the only record which pastors regularly examine. The report card, then, has a public relations aspect which should not be overlooked. At a faculty meeting early in the year, it would be well to develop with the staff a unified approach to the reporting system. The pastor would not only enjoy being present at this session, but would also have much to contribute as to the values and pitfalls of report cards. In many schools, the pastor or his assistant priests distribute report cards to the students. The pastor's comments on pupil progress assume importance in the minds of both pupils and parents. Therefore, both teachers and pastors should have the same attitude toward what to report, and how to report as regards pupil development.

Reducing Clerical Work. Another important feature of a good report card is that it keeps the teacher's clerical work to a minimum. Detailed letters to the parent might be a superior way of reporting; likewise, regularly scheduled and carefully planned parent conferences have much in their favor. But these methods are seriously handicapped by limitations in the teacher's ability to write effective reporting letters, and by limitations in teacher time for adequate parent conferences. Furthermore, the best report card as far as comprehensiveness is concerned might be an impossible report card because of the time required to fill it out. Therefore, a good report card keeps the teacher's work down to a minimum consistent with adequate reporting.

In the card used by the Diocese of Youngstown, and other similar cards, the reporting of personal-social traits attempts to do this. An X is marked after certain traits in which improvement is needed. At the end of the year, these X's are averaged into letter grades. Thus, time-consuming reporting in this area is reduced. In the marking of unsatisfactory achievement in any subject, the teacher merely encircles the letter grade, thus indicating to the parents that the child can do better in that subject. Children who are incapable of doing the work of the grade are marked only S for Satisfactory and U for Unsatisfactory. S and U grades are given only to IQ's below 70, on the Stanford-Binet, when possible. The S grade is given only to the lowest 3 per cent of the total school or class enrollment and then only to children who are retarded mentally. Before S or U grades are given to any child, the teacher, principal, and parent should confer on the child's limitations. The decision that a child will be marked S or U reduces the teacher's problems in grading, and provides an acceptable way of marking very slow pupils.

A final time-saving feature of current report cards is that they are issued only four, or even three, times a year. This cuts down the teacher's clerical work to two thirds, or even half of what it is when report cards are issued six times a year. When supplementary reporting forms, such as requests to confer with parents, are used discriminatingly, report cards issued four times a year have been found acceptable by both teachers and parents.

The report card, though it is only one of the pupil personnel records, receives more criticism than records not available to the public. A carefully worked out report card, representing pupil, parent, teacher, and pastor cooperation, is well worth the time taken to develop it.

Permanent Record. The last record of major importance in pupil personnel systems is the permanent record, also called the principal's record or the office card. By whatever title it is known, the permanent record serves as an educational history, permanently and centrally maintained by the school, for each child who has ever been in attendance there. The permanent record is for administrative use, is filed in or near the principal's office, and is ideally kept up to date by the principal's secretary. In schools which have only this permanent record, and not the cumulative classroom record, the permanent record should be made available to teachers for pupil guidance. Central filing in the principal's office may limit the use which teachers make of the permanent record. Rather typically, it seems, parochial schools keep a dual record system. The complete permanent record for each pupil is centralized in the principal's office, while a duplicate of the most important information is kept by the classroom teacher.

Using the Diocese of Youngstown forms again as typical, the permanent record card is the same size as the cumulative record, and contains exactly the same information as the cumulative record. The only differences between the two records are: (1) the cumulative record is punched for insertion in the classroom record notebook while the permanent record is filed in the individual pupil folder in the office; and (2) the cumulative record is buff, while the permanent record is green.

The pupil's permanent record can best be kept in an individual folder for each pupil. In some dioceses, this folder is imprinted with the permanent record, and data are written right on the folder itself. In most places, however, the folder is a blank manila folder, and the permanent record card is placed inside. In this folder are also placed other significant data on each pupil: test booklets or test profiles, important correspondence, reports on special tests given, such as individual intelligence or personality tests, records of guidance, work experience, and noteworthy achievement or problems. In some schools, the health record is also kept in the pupil's folder, though perhaps this record would be more accessible if filed in the clinic. The individual folder for the pupil should be maintained throughout the duration of his parochial schooling and then continued in the inactive file after graduation or withdrawal. While the pupil is in the school, the file is usually kept according to grade level, then alphabetically under grade. The inactive file of withdrawn pupils is usually kept alphabetically throughout, boys' and girls' folders together. There is a further discussion of record filing in Chapter XVI, which deals with the school office.

MAINTAINING AND HANDLING PUPIL RECORDS

Providing Clerical Help. Pupil personnel records should help teachers guide pupils and should also provide data for administrative planning. That they may serve these two purposes most efficiently, pupil personnel records should not be entirely maintained by teachers. Spending too much time on records means that less time is available for class preparation, and records are certainly meant to assist effective teaching, not detract from it. Therefore, a good working plan would be to have all records initially set up by capable clerical workers.

An office clerk can type the background information on cumulative and permanent records, prepare office folders for the permanent record, type identifying data on report cards, and file data in the permanent record folder. Each year, or each semester, the pupils' grades can be entered by the teacher on her own cumulative classroom record; but it is best to have data transferred from the cumulative to the permanent record by competent clerical workers. In this way, the teacher benefits directly from her work in entering data on the cumulative classroom record, while the principal uses clerical assistance to process administrative data.

Safeguarding Confidential Information. Great care must be exercised in handling pupil records. Data of this kind are to be kept in strictest confidence. Hence, these records should be available only to teachers and to other responsible persons designated by the principal. It is not democracy to open wide to every interested inquirer the information accumulated by the school for pupil guidance. It has been proved in court that the school is obliged to make pupil records available only to designated persons. Hence, in maintaining pupil records, the principal must be sure that contents are kept confidential. The particular difficulty here usually lies with volunteer or part-time clerical help, and student help. Certain home background data, or perhaps even test results, have a fascinating appeal to the curious. A word dropped here and there about some parishioner's home life, or the intelligence of the children, exposes the school to censure. Pupil personnel records are so important that part of the budget should be set aside for competent, responsible clerical help to process the records. Teachers usually know, but should be reminded at least each September, that the ethics of their profession demands their maintaining complete silence about confidential data, except when requested by the principal or other qualified person.

One way to safeguard highly confidential personal information is to enter it on a supplementary sheet, and not record it right on the record form. This sheet should be marked confidential, and should remain in the pupil's individual folder in the principal's office.

Insuring Accuracy of Records. Another point to be observed in maintaining pupil records is the need for accuracy. Ordinarily, the classroom teacher is responsible for entering the year's grades and test results on the cumulative classroom record. Each entry should be re-checked by the teacher, or if possible, two teachers should check each other's entries. Errors of this kind are not only possible, but probable, so re-checking should be a matter of routine. Also, when data from the cumulative record are transferred to the permanent record, re-checking is again necessary. One helpful way to assist teachers and clerks to be more accurate is to provide written directions for entering data on record forms. The principal should be sure that all staff members follow this form. Likewise, the principal should set up a time schedule for entering and transferring pupil data. In this way, errors will not be made because a record is requested unexpectedly and must be made out in a hurry.

Using Pupil Records. Every effort should be made to utilize pupil personnel records fully. Teachers should be aided in interpreting records; cumulative records should be transferred from grade to grade with the pupil, wherever possible; cumulative records should also accompany the pupil to high school. By providing at least a minimum of competent clerical help, and by assisting teachers in interpreting data, the principal will be able to utilize pupil personnel records to promote better guidance for children.

FOR THE PRINCIPAL'S PROFESSIONAL LIBRARY

Books

Fitzgerald, James A., and Fitzgerald, Patricia G., "Improving Instruction Through Testing," *Methods and Curricula in Elementary Education*, pp. 525–566 (Milwaukee: The Bruce Publishing Company, 1955), 591 pp., $5.50.
———— "Evaluation and Appraisal," *ibid.*, pp. 484–525
Jordan, A. M., *Measurement in Education: An Introduction* (New York: McGraw-Hill Book Company, 1953), 533 pp., $5.25.
Thomas, R. Murray, *Judging Student Progress* (New York: Longmans, Green and Company, 1954), 421 pp., $4.50.
    There are numerous other good books on evaluation. The few given here were selected because they are simple, readable, and practical.

Pamphlets

Jennings, Helen Hall, *Sociometry in Group Relations*, rev. ed. (Washington, D. C.: The American Council on Education, 1959), 105 pp., $1.50.
    Helpful in using *sociograms* to promote better understanding of children and thus to help them adjust better.
Lefever, D. Welty, Naslund, Robert A., and Thorpe, Louis P., *Measuring Pupil Achievement*, "Practical Ideas in Education Series" (Chicago: Science Research Associates, 1957), 46 pp., 60 cents.
    Readable overview of achievement testing for teachers and principals.
Ojemann, Ralph H., *Personality Adjustment of Individual Children*, "What Research Says to the Teacher," No. 5, Department of Classroom Teachers, American Educational Research Association (Washington, D. C.: National

Education Association, 1954), 32 pp., 25 cents.

Furnishes suggestions for teaching with a view toward helping children satisfy their basic needs.

Rothney, John W. M., *Evaluating and Reporting Pupil Progress*, "What Reseach Says to the Teacher," No. 7, Department of Classroom Teachers, American Educational Research Association (Washington, D. C.: National Education Association, 1955), 32 pp., 25 cents.

Stresses achievement tests and informal measures of personal-social development.

Wandt, Edwin, and Brown, Gerald W., *Essentials of Educational Evaluation* (New York: Henry Holt and Company, 1957), 117 pp., $1.60.

Excellent background material for the principal on the kinds and uses of tests, formal and informal.

Wrightstone, J. Wayne, *What Tests Can Tell Us About Children*, "Better Living Booklets" (Chicago: Science Research Associates, 1954), 47 pp., 60 cents.

Highly readable discussion of tests, with particular emphasis on understanding the varied abilities of each child.

CHAPTER XV

SPECIAL SERVICES FOR CHILDREN

*"The purpose of the school is to teach the 3 R's."
What is the relation of this statement to pupil
guidance? To pupil health and safety? To other
pupil services? What is the principal's function in
the area of special services for children?*

THE curriculum of the modern school includes much more than the
three R's, and in fact, much more than all the subjects taught. The curriculum includes many other experiences and services which contribute to
the all-round development of every child. Sometimes these services are
called "special," or "facilitating," or "auxiliary." By whatever name they
are known, such services endeavor to consider all of the objectives of the
school program and the total welfare of the child. Of the many services
now provided, the following will be discussed as they affect the principal's
role of leadership: pupil guidance, the health and safety program, food
service, school transportation, and library services.

PUPIL GUIDANCE

A "guidance program" may be much talked-of at the high school level.
There may be guidance counselors, and group guidance, and educational
and vocational planning. Many high schools have one or more persons
devoted to the various aspects of student guidance. However, in the elementary schools, special guidance services are not so common. Larger systems
may employ guidance personnel for grade schools, but mostly on a sharing
basis; the counselor may spend half a day a week in each of the elementary
schools of the system. Smaller systems often have no staff member assigned
as a full-time guidance worker.

The word *guidance* itself causes some difficulties. Doesn't a good teacher
"guide" pupils in the regular course of her work? Doesn't a "guidance
counselor" suggest that teachers aren't doing a good job? Does our school
have *that* many problems?

It is true that a good teacher does guide pupils all through the day. In Chapter VIII, guidance was pointed out as an essential function of the good teacher. In a certain sense, teachers all through the years have been guiding pupils effectively. Many former students go back to visit a teacher to express appreciation for her personal help during troublous days.

Teachers, however, are supposed to do more than merely guide children; they must also instruct them. Perhaps the relationship between *guidance* and *teaching* can be seen clearly in the following quotation:

> The teacher is acting in his guidance capacity when he attempts to learn about the various social, emotional, physical and intellectual factors in the personality of a child which make him what he is, and when he uses this growing background of understanding to adjust both the content and the methods of his teaching to harmonize with the child's level of readiness. He is performing his role as instructor when, through understanding each pupil, he finds the particular ways in which the child's interest may be kindled and his co-operation gained for learning the things which society demands. Thus the teacher who guides as he teaches has a greater chance of finding a congenial reception for that which he is attempting to teach. Because such a teacher appreciates each pupil as a human being and knows something of his thoughts and feelings and of the problems he is struggling to resolve, the chances are that each child will actually learn better the academic work which we typically associate with the instructional program.[1]

Ideally, then, every teacher is guiding children continuously. Guidance is not just something "applied" to a problem child, but a built-in quality of good teaching. When the teacher is aware of her role as guide and counselor, and is skilled in this role, then guidance in the grade school is mostly of a preventive nature. Alert to all of the developmental needs of children, the teacher conducts her classes so that all children have satisfying and purposeful experiences. Guidance at the elementary level includes helping all children to progress at their normal rate in acquiring the skills and abilities outlined in the course of study. Grouping for reading is just one of the ways in which the teacher takes care of individual differences. Individual and group remedial instruction also is part of good teaching, and is guidance of a preventive nature. A good school program presupposes that the teacher will not restrict her efforts to the three R's, but will enrich the program in many ways. Music, art, science, projects, health and safety education — all of these supply basic needs and give children, even slow and maladjusted children, a chance to be happy and successful. A heavy academic program, without enriching experiences in the arts and recreation, is bound to discourage all but the pupils with

---

[1] Camilla M. Low, *Guidance in the Curriculum*, 1955 Yearbook of the Association for Supervision and Curriculum Development (Washington, D. C.: The Association, 1955), p. 218. Used with permission.

high verbal IQ's. Good guidance in teaching provides a well-rounded program, and thus prevents many problems from developing.

However, more is needed than the teacher's knowledge of children and her ability to adapt her teaching to their needs. Some of the problems of childhood are not apparent to the teacher; some of the needed services cannot be rendered by the teacher. Over and above the guidance which every good teacher gives, there is need for outside assistance by the principal and special personnel. The aims of the guidance program are not ambitious; the machinery can be kept quite simple. Every principal, however, as part of good administration, should co-ordinate and supplement the efforts of the classroom teacher.

There are five ways in which the principal can improve pupil guidance in her school:

1. Maintain adequate pupil personnel records
2. Help teachers to develop a broader understanding of guidance and greater skill in guiding children
3. Provide the equipment, materials, and setting needed for good guidance
4. Utilize the special guidance services available to the school
5. Establish constructive home and school relations

THE ROLE OF PUPIL RECORDS IN GUIDANCE

As discussed in Chapter XIV, pupil records should include data related to each of the major objectives of the Catholic school curriculum: physical, economic, social, intellectual, and moral. The cumulative folder should ideally contain test results, correspondence, anecdotal records, health data, profiles, sociograms, information on out-of-school experience, and other data which shed light on the child's development. And again ideally, these records should be carefully and frequently studied by the classroom teacher.

One of the first steps in improving pupil guidance is to assemble complete records, and — get them used by teachers. Immediately, the problem of "no time" comes up. Especially when classes are large, compiling pupil records can be a burdensome job. And after the data are transferred, there is scarcely any time left to use the data! Clerical help has been mentioned often as a needed service to teachers. Clerical help is basic to improved guidance, for it frees teachers from clerical routines and gives them time for more professional work. For example, after intelligence tests are given, it can easily take the classroom teacher most of her study time for a few weeks to score the tests and record the results. Then, she must concentrate on class preparation, for she has let this slip in her effort to finish the tests. If the teacher could spend this ten hours or so in *studying the test results and in devising ways of adjusting her teaching* in the light of test results, how much more profitable the tests would be for children! In order to know what can be done for individual children, the teacher *must* study the records. The principal can assist the teacher by providing at least some clerical help in scoring tests and in recording data.

Pupil records will be useful only if they are accessible. As previously stated, some school systems have a duplicate pupil record which the teacher keeps in the classroom. This record is available for ready reference when the teacher needs to study a child more fully. An individual folder, in such systems, may be kept in the school office and can be consulted when additional information is needed. However, sometimes pupil records are kept in a room that is hard to reach, or in a locked room. Pupil records are confidential, and every effort should be made to see that the records are safeguarded. But they should also be easily available for teacher use.

The principal's attitude toward pupil records will have much to do with the way teachers regard these records. The principal needs to study the records before her classroom visits; the results of each group test should be summarized, so that the average of the group, and the spread of ability, can readily be seen. The principal's personal interest in the data for individual children will encourage teachers to use the files more analytically. The principal can help the teachers interpret data to parents and to the pupils themselves. Most of all, the principal can assist teachers in using data to the advantage of the individual child. Consistent use of pupil records is fundamental to good guidance; the principal can promote wider and more informed use of pupil records.

IN-SERVICE WORK IN GUIDANCE

The idea of helping children appeals to teachers. The faculty meetings for a whole year might profitably and enjoyably be spent in helping teachers improve their skill in guidance. Perhaps the simplest approach would be the "child development point of view." Most teachers have had a course in child development, but quite often the material did not "come to life" for them. If the principal has considerable background in this area, she might lead the first discussion herself. Or she might prefer to invite a speaker who knows the field well, but not too well. The "expert" often frightens or bores classroom teachers. After a good start with an outside speaker, other faculty meetings might be handled by the teachers themselves.

The range of topics is almost as broad as the whole of teaching. It is important for teachers to know more about the child's basic needs, the influence of the home, the relationship of intelligence to success in school, and teacher-pupil relationships. Topics which teachers might explore with profit are:

What makes poor readers?
Why do children play truant?

What do temper tantrums tell?
How can the grade school prevent high school dropouts?
What help can sociograms give?
Can dull children be happy in school?
Why do teachers dislike some children?
How can we counsel children more effectively?
Can we do more for the gifted child in our classroom?
How can we bring parents into our program?
Can religion play a more active part in pupils' lives?

All of these topics, and many more, come within the area of guidance. Guidance seeks to help children to understand themselves, to make wise plans and choices, to solve their personal problems, and to develop their potential. In order to guide children better, teachers need first of all a broader understanding of the child's nature — the "child development point of view," as mentioned earlier.

The principal's in-service program could well concentrate on guidance throughout an entire year. The curriculum is involved: what adjustments need to be made for gifted and retarded pupils? Teaching methods are involved: how to make learning a more satisfying experience for children? Discipline is involved: are teachers asking — why did he do that, as well as what did he do? The aim of such investigations is not to become too permissive, to let down on discipline. Controls are needed, reasonable controls; self-control needs to be developed. Through in-service work, teachers can be helped to guide children toward effective solutions to their problems, and toward more reasoned behavior.

THE SETTING FOR GOOD GUIDANCE

Among the conditions which promote good guidance, two are especially necessary: happy interpersonal relations and adequate equipment and materials. When the staff members get along together, teachers are better disposed toward their classes. When the teacher is happy in her work, she is likely to provide a secure and happy classroom for her pupils. The teacher's mental health is all-important in the pupils' adjustment. The principal can do much to promote good staff relations and better mental health. Chapter IV presented some of the factors in good interpersonal relations and mental hygiene. A good setting for guidance is also facilitated by sound administrative policies, as outlined in Chapters V, VI, and VII. A principal needs to read an occasional book on human relations if she is to appraise her own problems and her staff's problems realistically. The principal provides the constructive, happy atmosphere which promotes an accepting and positive attitude toward children.

The principal also contributes to guidance by providing the equipment and materials needed for a good curricular and extracurricular program. The pastor, it is true, signs the checks for unusual expenditures, but it is the principal who points out the need. What equipment should be added to make the school a happier and better place for children? Playground equipment, record players, bookcases, tables and chairs for reading corners, a slide projector, a public-address system, drinking fountains? Equipment and furnishings contribute to the ease with which the children do their work, and also contribute to pupil and teacher morale. In an environment that brings out the best in children, a guidance program has a good chance of being effective.

Instructional materials also contribute to improved guidance. For the principal's in-service program, for example, books, pamphlets, and mimeographed sheets will be needed. For an improved curriculum, teachers need varied library books, maps, globes, filmstrips, art materials and exhibits. A drab classroom, without variety in materials, makes for uninteresting experiences; uninterested children are likely to become "problem" children.

Effective use of equipment and materials seems to be infectious in a school. Mrs. Adams arranges a clever bulletin board display on the solar system, and immediately Miss Evans' bulletin board is alive with butterfly mounts. The children in third grade are doing an art lesson in rhythmic response to music; very soon the fourth grade class is pointing with pride to their jungle on the sand table. The principal again is the key figure in providing incentives for a better use of equipment and materials. Good guidance revolves about children happily engaged in activities that are satisfying and purposeful. The "child development point of view" makes both teacher and child happier in their work.

SPECIAL GUIDANCE PERSONNEL

Even in a good situation, there will be children who cannot be adequately taken care of by the school's facilities and personnel. Intelligence may be the crux of the maladjustment — too much or too little for the normal classroom. Physical handicaps in vision, hearing, or motor control may make special services necessary. Emotional maladjustment may require the help of a specialist. The psychiatrist, the speech correctionist, the social worker, and other special personnel may be needed.

Ordinarily, the classroom teacher is not fully informed of services available. It is part of the principal's job to keep in touch with the children so as to detect symptoms that may require outside help. In some places, the public school system includes the parochial schools in such services. Some dioceses have staff members who serve the schools as remedial reading instructors, speech therapists, and psychologists. The local Child Guidance Center may be a resource in some instances. The principal should be on the alert to note early symptoms of maladjustment and try to secure therapy to prevent the problem from becoming acute. The principal should plan to utilize guidance specialists wherever possible.

Besides outside help, the school can well use a special guidance person on the regular staff. Teacher shortages may make a full-time guidance counselor out of the question, but the principal can use her ingenuity in getting part-time help. The principal may be able to hire a trained person to serve as school consultant on a part-time basis. A qualified parishioner may be available, though this is not likely. However, right within her staff, the principal can help to develop the competence needed. It would be good if the Mother Superior would assign one Sister from each school to do special work in guidance during summer sessions. Even twelve credits would make a good start. A Sister thus trained might be freed one half day a week to take over some of the guidance responsibilities in the school. A more adequate pupil record system might be her project for the first year. Faculty meetings and committee work on aspects of guidance might be her emphasis the second year. Remedial work in various subjects might interest the faculty another year. A staff member who has a wholesome and healthy disposition and a real interest in children can do a great deal in guidance, even though she does not have a broad background in the field.

This Sister might be called the Guidance Assistant, and might be a member of a Faculty Advisory Committee which includes several such assistants. In a large staff, there might be a Safety Assistant, a Library Assistant, a Remedial Reading Assistant, an Audio-Visual Aids Assistant, and others needed in the particular school. "Assistant" might be better accepted than "counselor" or "director," and less pretentious. When the faculty understand the role of this worker, and they do not feel "threatened" because of her work, the Guidance Assistant can improve greatly the services needed by children.

HOME-SCHOOL RELATIONS AND GUIDANCE

The school cannot do an effective job of guidance alone; good working relations with parents are essential. The principal, again, is the chief promoter of constructive contacts with parents. Parent-teacher conferences are helpful to both parents and teachers; the principal can provide direction in improving such conferences. The teacher should guard, however, against thinking of the conference as a way of using therapy on the parent. The conferences should be a two-way learning process, and not just parent-guidance. Interpreting the school program to parents helps them to understand what the school is trying to do and how they can work along with the aims of the school. A good parents' handbook and parents' bulletins help to develop a co-operative spirit between home and school. Home visits furnish valuable insight into the way the child acts in the school situation. The standards in the home, the pressures exerted, the affection and security provided — these assist the teacher in getting the child to set realistic goals and to work consistently toward achieving them.

Schools have too long told parents, in effect, "You give the child plenty of rest, and good food, and time for home study. Then send him to school and I'll teach him." Working separately, parents and teachers can accomplish something, it is true; but working together, they can more than double their effectiveness. Warm, wholesome, constructive parent-teacher relations are basic to sound pupil guidance.

HEALTH AND SAFETY PROGRAM

TV advertisers have capitalized on America's interest in health. There is an increasing demand for TV-advertised medicines, vacations, housing, clothing, and food — anything that has "health" appeal. "The good life" is one of the most attractive of goals, and physical well-being looms large as part of the good life. School administrators, too, have become ever more aware of "physical fitness" as a valid objective of the curriculum.

Propaganda has no doubt stimulated some of the interest in health services, but the basic reasons are deep and sound. Experience has shown that children who are not well cannot profit fully from the school program. Also, an undesirable school environment limits the benefits which children can derive. Some homes have been negligent in their duty, and children's health has suffered as a result. However, even in good situations, the school can enhance the training received in the home, and thus enable children to develop and maintain a "sound mind in a sound body."

Like other schools, the parochial school has as one of its major objectives to promote the physical fitness of its pupils. The Sister Principal, then, has as an administrative duty to provide for an adequate health and safety program in her school. In co-operation with the pastor, certain aspects of the program can be arranged. The staff is directly concerned with instruction, of course, and personnel are needed to carry out the specialized services. The principal's duty has three aspects:

1. To provide for a safe and healthful school environment
2. To see that the health curriculum is sound and adequate
3. To secure specialized health services as needed

A SAFE AND HEALTHFUL SCHOOL ENVIRONMENT

Periodic Inspection. The principal's schedule presented in Chapter V sets aside a definite time each day for inspecting the building and the grounds, and every aspect of the school program. This daily "spot checking" is essential in maintaining a safe and healthful environment. On the playground, the principal notes the kinds of activities engaged in, the condition of playground equipment, the amount of supervision, the parking of bicycles, and the sanitary condition of the grounds. In the school, the principal checks fire and safety hazards: the custodian's workroom, the containers for disposal of refuse, locked doors and blocked exits, and desks too close to entrances. When the periodic fire inspection is made, the principal and pastor should offer immediate co-operation in improving conditions that might be even remotely dangerous to children. Also important to health are the heating and ventilation of classrooms, the lighting, the color and condition of wall paint in classrooms, adequacy and cleanliness of the lavatories, and accommodations for hanging up the children's wraps. The periodic inspection by the principal reveals trouble spots in building arrangements, supervision of children, health, and sanitary conditions. Carefully made inspections are basic to promoting health and safety.

Adequate Supervision. In the interests of children, the principal should provide adult supervision from the time the children enter the school grounds in the morning till they leave for home. In some schools this supervision is taken care of entirely by the teachers. This may be the simplest administrative measure, but teacher health must also be considered. It lowers the teacher's vitality, and her morale, to be constantly responsible for children almost eight hours a day. A school day can be this long for teachers, especially where there are school buses. Volunteer workers can take over much of this supervision, especially on the playground and in the lunchroom. With the many laborsaving devices in the typical home, mothers can often be free several hours a week for this service. The pastor and principal can plan a program for selecting, training, and directing the work of such volunteers. Training for playground supervision would include directions for appropriate games for each grade level, help in reducing disorderly behavior, and competence in rendering first aid.

Cafeteria supervision also promotes a more healthful environment for children. When lines move quickly, the children relax, enjoy their meal and profit more from it. Adult supervision is needed to see that food is not wasted and that proper table manners are observed. The principal has a duty to see that adult supervision is available to promote these worthwhile objectives of the school lunch program.

Attractive Grounds and Building. A clean, sanitary, and attractive school plant promotes pupil health, both physically and mentally. Adequate custodial service is essential. In co-operation with the pastor, the custodian can be directed to follow a good schedule in maintaining the plant — cleaning, dusting, repairing, and keeping adequate supplies in lavatories.

Many schools use pupil committees to help plan for beautifying the grounds, hall bulletin boards, and the classrooms. This is not to exploit children to do the work of adults, but rather enlist children's interest in school improvement. Various "weeks" emphasize such aspects as paper-free grounds, respecting lawns and gardens, and neatness in the cafeteria. Part of the training of children can be in sharing responsibility for the attractiveness of the school plant.

The color of paint, planters, inviting bulletin boards, cheerful classroom reading corners, attractive exhibits — all of these contribute to a wholesome environment which promotes better learning through better mental health.

AN ADEQUATE HEALTH CURRICULUM

The principal should supply the teachers with a text or course of study which specifies the expected health learnings, from the first through the eighth grade. Usually instruction in the following aspects is considered minimum: personal hygiene, nutrition, disease, teeth, mental health, exercise, rest and sleep, family living, alcohol, tobacco and narcotics, and safety. Many states have carefully planned the sequence of these learnings and have provided excellent bibliographies and audio-visual materials. The parochial school can well benefit from these instructional materials, even though strict adherence to the state program may not be obligatory.

Improving Health Instructions. It is well known that health instruction does not always carry over to the pupil's daily life. A study of food values, for example, may not help children to select proper foods in the cafeteria, or eat the foods selected. A unit on disease may not dispose children to stay home when ill. In order to achieve the best results from the health program, the principal should plan for spaced in-service work with the faculty. An occasional faculty meeting might profitably be devoted to better understanding of the value of health instruction and ways of improving pupil health. A physician and school nurse might discuss the importance of teacher observation in detecting illness, promoting better mental health in the classroom, care of children with chronic illnesses, and better use of pupil health records.

In-service work with the faculty might also include presenting free and inexpensive materials for teaching health. The American Red Cross, the Dairy Council, the U. S. Office of Education and large insurance companies have a wealth of appealing and practical instructional materials. A teacher committee would enjoy studying these materials and preparing kits of pamphlets and posters for each grade level. Physical education as part of health instruction is another topic which would promote active interest on the part of the staff. Even where space and facilities are limited, ingenious teachers carry on a balanced program of physical education and recreation. The principal's role is to provide a good curriculum guide to health teaching, to stimulate faculty interest, to provide effective instructional materials, and to co-ordinate the teaching of health throughout the school.

Improving Instruction in Safety. More and more material is being packed into the elementary school curriculum. How can teachers keep on adding subjects without increasing pupil and teacher pressures? Can't parents be expected to assume the responsibility for teaching their child safe habits?

The principal will no doubt sympathize with the amount of material the teacher is required to teach, but safety education is not the one thing that can safely be left out. These figures compiled by the National Safety Council may shock the teacher out of her complacency:

> Accidents kill 6500 elementary school children each year. Accidents kill 2 out of 5 school age children who die. In an average year, accidents kill 3 times as many children as cancer, the next most important cause of death among elementary school children.[2]

Added to the above figures are the still higher numbers of nonfatal accidents in which children are involved each year. The welfare of both the child and the community demand more teaching of safety, not less, and more effective teaching of safety.

Usually, instruction in safety is part of the course of study in health or science. Certainly, the basic material given there should be meaningfully presented. However, several devices can be used to improve the effectiveness of safety instruction. The principal may first of all broaden her own background in what a good elementary curriculum should include. Publications of the National Safety Council and the National Commission on Safety Education provide information on such important topics as the School Safety Patrol, bicycle safety, home accidents, fire safety education, school bus safety, and playground safety. Particularly helpful in improving school safety instruction is the use of the Standard Student Accident Reports of the National Safety Council. These forms help the principal analyze unsafe conditions in the school and point up the need for specific safety lessons. The report forms also help the National Safety Council to plan its own program of bulletins and posters as accident reports show the need. Many parochial schools have been placed on the National School Safety Honor Roll because of their work in developing safety consciousness among the pupils. Projects in school and home safety, student panels, and the Civics Club may all be used to teach children how to live more safely. Regular fire drills and instruction in fire safety should be planned as an essential part of the safety program. A complete and balanced safety

---

[2] National Safety Council, *A Lot to Live For* (Chicago: National Safety Council, 1959), p. 1. Used with permission.

program is necessary if the school is to achieve its objective of physical fitness for all pupils according to their capacity.

SPECIALIZED PERSONNEL IN HEALTH SERVICES

As a good administrator, the principal will endeavor to make full use of health personnel available to the school. Physicians, dentists, and nurses are becoming much more common in elementary schools today. In some cities, the local board of health provides certain health services to children, such as Salk vaccine inoculations. In other cities, broad health services are provided to all children regardless of the school they attend. There are localities also, where the individual parochial school must rely upon volunteer help from the medical profession. Whatever the local situation, the principal's duty is to work with the pastor to provide at least the minimum health services.

Children should have routine screening tests of vision and hearing, administered by trained personnel. Medical and dental examinations are likewise needed both to remedy deficiencies and to maintain good health. Teachers can be helped to observe the health needs of children more closely, and to refer to specialists any child who seems to be in need of attention. Many organizations are eager to help children whose parents are financially unable to provide glasses or other assistance.

In addition to enlisting the needed health specialists, the principal has the further job of seeing that health records are complete and accurate, and used to promote better health. Clerical help is needed for this, and also in-service work with the staff. The parochial school health program should reflect the school's earnest and intelligent planning for good health for every child.

FOOD SERVICE

"You can't teach a hungry child," teachers have known for many years. Kindhearted teachers have been adept at providing little "extras" for hungry pupils. Teachers at times have even set up kitchens to serve hot soup or cocoa or stew to families known to be undernourished. These attempts have had good effects; children learned better because they had better food, and also because the kindness improved their whole attitude toward the business of learning. Schools have grown larger, and these well-meant ventures have been replaced by a more scientific, but just as kindly, approach to the matter of feeding children. Food authorities have found that it isn't just the poor child who may be undernourished. Children from privileged homes may also suffer from inadequate diet because of poor planning or improper eating habits. Realizing the importance of proper food intake for good learning, school cafeterias have assumed the responsibility for large-scale food service. The National School Lunch Program and the National School Milk Program now make wholesome lunches and milk possible for millions of school children daily.

The importance of a good diet to general well-being and also to learning has caused the Federal Government to invest large sums of money in subsidizing the lunch and milk programs. During the 1955–56 school year alone, the government invested a total of 181 million dollars in cash and commodities to encourage better food service in schools.[3] In addition to this, the government invested another 61 million dollars during 1956–57 to encourage the drinking of milk through lowered prices on milk.[4] This money has been distributed to both public and parochial schools, either through the State agency or through the Agricultural Marketing Service in states whose constitutions forbid dispensing funds to nonpublic schools. This financial assistance has been a strong impetus toward setting up lunch and milk programs in keeping with government standards. The clerical work involved has been more than repaid in the improved nutritional status of children.

Although many teachers and parents realize the value of hot, nutritious lunches, occasionally there is some opposition. Children don't like the foods served; the meals may be Type A and may supply one third of the daily nutritional requirements, but the children prefer a candy bar. Supervising the lunchroom is burdensome to teachers; large groups of children require more disciplining, and the whole process takes up more of the teachers' noon hour. The cafeteria is drab and crowded and uninviting. Children's manners leave much to be desired. Keeping competent cafeteria workers is difficult, and a great deal of time must be spent in bookkeeping.

The principal's role of leadership is clearly defined for her. There are a number of ways in which she can promote better nutrition and at the same time improve attitudes toward the lunch hour.

1. The physical welfare of children is a responsibility shared by the school and the home. The pastor and the principal can work together to improve the present lunch program, or to inaugurate a program. Teaching is easier, and more effective, when children eat better.

2. The pastor and principal can work together to improve conditions during the lunch hour. Children may not understand why, but sometimes they do not feel like eating in the cafeteria. The cafeteria workers may not be sanitary; the room may be drab and uninviting; the food may be unattractively served; there may not be enough adult supervision to insure

---

[3] Albert R. Munse and Edna D. Booher, *Federal Funds for Education, 1956–57 and 1957–58*, Bulletin 1959, No. 2, U. S. Department of Health, Education, and Welfare (Washington, D. C.: U. S. Government Printing Office, 1959), p. 87.

[4] *Ibid.*, p. 89.

good order; there may be too much rushing to get finished and out to play. Close co-operation of the pastor, the principal, the faculty, and parents can improve all of these undesirable conditions.

3. The principal has a job of in-service work with both faculty and pupils. The health course may contain units on good eating habits, but very often these units do not change children's eating habits. Faculty meetings devoted to nutrition, or pamphlets, posters, and projects related to nutrition, or pupil activity in promoting better nutrition — all of these may be needed to make the daily health instruction carry over to practice. Selling candy in the school would be abandoned; time would be allowed for children to wash before eating; the lunch period would discourage rapid eating; orderly procedures for serving would be established; the practice of good table manners would be stimulated; the faculty would take an active interest in the children's food habits. Many writers bemoan the fact that the lunch period may have very little educational value. Well-planned in-service work can tone up the noon period and improve the children's nutritional status as well.

As with other aspects of the school program, the noon hour may be improved by seeing what other schools are doing. Sister Principals can exchange visits to other parochial and public schools to get ideas for improved service. National School Lunch personnel are often available to make suggestions for better lunches, equipment, and planning. The principal should be alert to new ideas concerning nutrition and food service, in order to promote to the fullest the physical well-being of the pupils.

TRANSPORTATION SERVICE[5]

Parochial school principals in large cities are seldom faced with a severe school bus problem. Most city children live near enough to the school to walk, or city buses and parents provide transportation. In the suburbs, however, and in smaller cities and rural areas, the school bus may loom as the Number One problem of the school day. Finance is a problem: how to raise the funds needed to provide safe and adequate transportation? Time is a problem, though related to finance: how to shorten the time children must spend en route? Behavior is another problem: how to improve the student's responsibility for safe, orderly, courteous conduct. Personnel is a problem: how to man the buses with qualified, reliable drivers.

---

[5] While it is true that some parochial schools depend upon buses hired from private individuals or companies, most parochial schools with a large attendance area endeavor to provide their own school buses. The discussion which follows, therefore, centers upon the school-owned bus. Much of the material applies, of course, to any type of situation in which children ride buses to and from school.

The principal and pastor need to co-operate in the matter of bus transportation. The pastor is responsible for the financial aspects of school transportation, and for staffing the growing fleet of parochial school buses. The principal, teachers, and parents share the responsibility for educating children to their duties as bus passengers. And children have increased responsibility, with age, for co-operating in the school bus program. The principal, however, is a key figure in transportation, for she is the educational leader of the school. It is generally agreed that whatever contributes to the educational program is part of the curriculum. And, when school buses are needed to bring the children to the school experiences, then transportation is a part of the curriculum. Though the principal may feel that she cannot add another duty, still in her role of administrator all that affects pupil learning is her business. Even where she has only indirect influence, as in matters of finance, the competent principal can do much to improve the conditions surrounding pupil transportation.

The principal's chief responsibility in school transportation is to provide for adequate safety education. Children sometimes shrug off safety admonitions as the "same old thing." Yet the high rate of children's accidents shows that more and not less safety education is needed. As a first step, the principal and staff need to plan for systematic teaching of the basic rules of safe traveling. The health course probably includes some directions, but the data sheet prepared by the National Safety Council really contains the needed information in simple and clear form. "Educating Pupil Passengers in School Bus Safety" will help the principal and teachers to make their instructions more meaningful.[6] Experience with bus passengers, and discussions with the drivers will add specific details that apply to the individual school.

What are some of the unsafe practices now seen on school buses? Arms out of the windows, children standing — even when the bus is not crowded, boisterous play, noisy talking and shouting, disregard for the driver's orders, dismounting before the bus comes to a complete stop, carelessness in mounting and dismounting — these are common disorders where safety education is not effective. The school aims to develop good character, not just for the classroom, but for out-of-school life as well. When passengers exhibit the undesirable actions noted above, the school cannot claim to be developing character. Each specific detail of bus safety needs to be taught, re-taught as needed, and put into practice. It is the principal's responsibility to make sure that the teaching carries over into practice in actual bus situations.

What are some of the means at the principal's disposal? Besides the

---

[6] National Safety Council, "School Bus Safety — Educating Pupil Passengers," Safety Education Data Sheet, No. 63 (Chicago: National Safety Council, 1954).

safety instructions themselves, the principal can make effective use of the eighth-grade Civics Club as a Student Safety Council. At the regular meetings, the topic of bus safety can be discussed by classroom representatives, standards set for bus conduct, and a method of enforcement decided upon. A school bus patrol is another helpful measure. Two older boys who live near the end of the line and are outstanding for responsibility can be assigned to each bus. The entire group of boys thus assigned make up the school bus patrol. This group may have special insignia, may have meetings, may give talks to the classes, and in general raise the tone of behavior on the bus, and while loading and unloading. A whole-staff meeting is an indispensable method of advancing bus safety. The pastor, principal, teachers, and bus drivers should meet before school opens, and during the year as needed. Together they can plan bus routes, set standards for bus behavior, plan for safe loading and unloading, and periodically review the progress of their program. The School Safety Accident Report Form has already been mentioned as an excellent safety device. Accidents on the way to and from school are reported on these forms, and a good picture can be obtained of weaknesses in the program. The annual School Safety Poster Contest, sponsored by the American Automobile Association, can be used to highlight the dangers of unsafe bus conduct.

The principal has a grave responsibility as regards the safety instruction of the pupils. She must be ingenious in finding ways and materials to inject new life into this instruction. Bus safety is an excellent means of developing qualities of leadership and responsibility in children. It goes without saying that orderly bus passengers are good public relations for the school. Many people who never enter a parochial school see the children on the buses. The opinions thus formed attract or repel. The public relations aspect of the school bus should not be forgotten when planning for improved bus service.

The principal can also assist in improving the efficiency of the bus service. A study might perhaps be made of the present service. This would include a map of the route, showing bus stops, a schedule of the time when each stop is made, a record of the time required to make each trip, and a record of the time which individual pupils spend on the bus, morning and afternoon. Since the pastor hires the bus driver, recommendations would logically be made to the pastor. No plan is ever perfect, and certainly not a bus routing plan, since changes are constantly being made. Both the pastor and the bus drivers appreciate suggestions to make the bus routing more economical and efficient. Long waits at bus stops and weary rides to and from school can nearly always be remedied through co-operative planning. Such planning is basic to improved bus service, and hence improved pupil learning.

State law regarding licensing of drivers must of course be met. However, in some states, these laws are not stringent enough to protect children adequately. Very often the principal learns about the bus driver's qualifications from the children, and the pastor may not hear any unfavorable comments. The principal promotes safety when she keeps in touch with the drivers' work and also acquaints the pastor with unsatisfactory performance.

School bus transportation is a considerable item in the budget. In public schools, five cents of every school dollar is paid for transportation.[7] In parochial schools, the service is just as expensive, and must usually be borne entirely by the congregation. Bus service can no longer be regarded as an "extra"; it is part of a good school curriculum. The expense of operating an adequate and safe bus service is more than repaid in the good effects upon children. Jointly, the pastor and the principal promote better public relations and better pupil learning when the school bus program is part of the total education which the school provides for its pupils.

LIBRARY SERVICE

"Literate Catholics" are needed in every occupation on the American scene. This does not mean merely Catholics with a high school diploma, or even a college diploma. "Literate Catholics" are those who know *how* to read, and who *read* widely. Where is the Catholic intellectual? Which is more prominent in Catholic homes — the television set or the family library? How many Catholic students frequent the library regularly? In how many classrooms do the children's eyes light up at the prospect of reading "their very own books"? Is the library service peripheral, or basic to Catholic education?

It may be objected that America as a nation does not value books highly. Library statistics show that there is an increase in circulation, and a greater variety in reading tastes than ever before. But librarians also lament that even popular books could have much wider circulation, and that the more scholarly books — well, the cost of cataloguing them seems hardly justified. Teachers may say, "It's the home. Too much rush, not enough family life, too much television, too crowded quarters." Parents may say, "I never see him reading a book for a book report. Don't they want children to read books any more?" If there is one way in the school program where home and school co-operation really shows, it is in library services. Parents want children to read; teachers do, too. Working together on improved library services is tremendously satisfying for parents, teachers, children, and of course for the pastor and the principal.

---

[7] Glenn Featherston, "Pupil Transportation, the Next Ten Years," *Nation's Schools*, LXII (Aug., 1958), pp. 33–37.

The principal may be a little weary of hearing, "Like everything else in the school, this service depends for its effectiveness upon the leadership of the principal." The teaching principal especially may feel frustrated when she considers how much she would like to do, and how little she is doing. However, good planning and wise delegation will result in vastly improved services. In planning for better library services, the principal will need to concentrate on three areas: books, in-service growth, and home-school co-operation. Each of these is essential in getting children to read more and better books, and thus develop the habit of reading.

BOOKS ARE NEEDED

Children who have an ample supply of books read. There is no difficulty in getting children to read under ideal circumstances. But the problem is: how to get closer to the ideal in providing books for children. The *school library* may seem like the answer. A spacious, well-equipped, competently administered school library, just like the pictures in library magazines — how ardently to be desired! A full-time, trained librarian who likes children and who knows how to guide their reading is a reality in some places, but is becoming more rare, unfortunately. Even in public schools, supported by tax funds, only 59 per cent of the elementary pupils had centralized school library services in 1953–54.[8] The percentage may have increased since that time, but when one looks around, one notes that many new public elementary schools are being built without libraries. Many elementary schools, both public and parochial, do have a library; but even where this is true the book collection and the librarian's service may be less than desired. This is not to belittle school libraries; on the contrary, there is probably no substitute for the right kind of library, and the right kind of service, in the elementary school. Habits are formed early; high school is really too late to begin to cultivate the "library habit." In practice, however, most schools cannot just "fold their hands and wait" for a dream library to come true. The children are here, now, and the present is the time to do something constructive about helping them in their reading.

The *classroom library* has been possible in many places. For one thing, schools are getting more crowded, and a large room adequate for library service may be out of the question. A good collection of books in each classroom may be a workable solution. Usually it is possible to have some shelves built in to accommodate a classroom collection. Librarians recommend from three to five books, carefully selected, per pupil. These books

[8] *Statistics of Public Libraries*, 1953–54, Biennial Survey of Education in the United States, 1952–54, Chapter Six, text prepared by Nora E. Beust and Emery M. Foster, U. S. Department of Health, Education, and Welfare, Office of Education (Washington, D. C.: U. S. Government Printing Office, 1957), p. 24.

should be chosen from a good list, such as *A Basic Book Collection for Elementary Grades*, and *A Basic Book Collection for Junior High Schools*, both compiled by the American Library Association.[9] A usable list for Catholic schools is that prepared at the Catholic University of America, "Two Hundred Books for the Catholic Elementary School."[10] The selections should be carefully based upon the amount of money available, the course of study for the grade, the range of reading ability in the grade, and the interests of both bright and slow children, and of boys and girls.

In a Catholic school, a certain percentage of the budget should be allocated to good religious books. There will never be funds enough to buy religious books indiscriminately, so a trained librarian should help to select religious books according to appeal, illustrations, and literary value. The Cleveland Public Library has rendered valuable assistance in book selection. Special lists are regularly prepared as a community service. An up-to-date mimeographed list of good Catholic books is available for teacher use. Many school and public libraries have drawn upon these lists in setting up collections and in guiding pupil reading. Similar services are no doubt available in other large libraries that have outstanding children's departments.

The classroom library can be used to develop a taste for reading and to train pupils in library skills. The classroom collection needs to be supplemented, of course, by material from a larger library, particularly in reference books.

The *public library* is an excellent source of books for children. Even when the school has its own library, and perhaps classroom libraries, too, the local public library has a wealth of resources that should be more widely used. Classroom loans of twenty books or more is a welcome supplement to the school's collection. Then there is the trained librarian, eager to bring the world of books closer to children. The public librarian is usually available for school visits and talks to classes on various topics. Too, this librarian is often available for conducted tours of the library facilities, and also for instruction in the use of the library. Children's librarians are as a group thrilled to serve individuals and schools. Long years in the children's room seem to increase their enthusiasm for children and books. The librarian can be of much more service to schools than she now is, provided the schools become informed of services available, and then exert

---

[9] *A Basic Book Collection for Elementary Grades*, compiled by Miriam Snow Mathes with consultants (Chicago: American Library Association, 1960).

A Basic Book Collection for Junior High Schools, compiled by Margaret V. Spengler with consultants, 3rd ed. (Chicago: American Library Association, 1960).

[10] Richard J. Hurley, *Your Library — How to Organize an Elementary School Library*, prepared for the Commission on American Citizenship (Washington, D. C.: The Catholic University of America Press, 1956).

every effort to benefit by these services. It takes a little effort to engineer a class group to the library once a month or so, but there is no substitute for actual experience in the library. The school bus can be utilized for this curricular activity, the parents' permission of course having been received in writing.

The *bookmobile* is a practical extension of service from the main library. Bookmobiles often service the outlying schools, public and parochial, providing a valuable supplement to the school and classroom library. Most outlying parochial schools welcome the bookmobile, and are eager to promote interest in the books thus provided. Even with bookmobile service, however, improved planning can utilize the resources even more fully than at present.

Families can sometimes be encouraged to begin a *home library*. In larger families, and in poorer families, there may not be money for buying children's books. But usually the parents can plan ahead to buy one good book for birthdays and for Christmas. When parents are guided in the purchase of books, this home library can be the beginning of a child's lifelong love for his "very own" books. Parents can also be urged to accompany their children to the library regularly. When convinced of the value of such experience, fathers have been known to devote their "day off" each week to taking their children to the library for books. The school can encourage reading, and some good effects will be evident. But the home instills and strengthens the more lasting attitudes and habits. Reading in the home means books in the home. The school should do all that it can to promote an interest in home libraries.

The above ways of supplying books can be used in varying degrees by all imaginative principals. Certainly, books are needed, carefully selected and varied, if children are to develop a genuine love of reading.

IN-SERVICE GROWTH IS NEEDED

Perhaps the first ingredient of an in-service program is a reawakening of enthusiasm for children's books. Sometimes a college instructor in children's literature can present to the faculty some of the newer books, and discuss trends in books for children. A faculty committee might present a panel discussion on outstanding authors or illustrators of children's books. A Book Fair of newly purchased books arouses keen interest. Book jackets, colorfully displayed, invite requests for the books described. The enthusiasm is infectious; the principal must plan, of course, but she need not work hard to arouse enthusiasm. Most teachers want to encourage reading, and need only a little stimulus to become more reading-conscious.

There are other aspects of a program designed to inspire familiarity with books. The first may seem too obvious to mention, but the day-to-day reading instruction is a first requisite to wider library reading. Through her classroom observations, the principal also sees clever ideas for stimulating reading, such as charts, clubs, reading corners, book talks, and dramatizations. Sharing these ideas with other faculty members is an excellent in-service technique. Teachers welcome ideas that "work"; suggestions for such as these are quickly put into practice. One faculty meeting or more each year can also be effectively used to promote wider and more discriminating reading. As mentioned previously, the librarian from the local public library may be available for a talk to the faculty, or for an in-service visit to the library. In such a visit, the librarian might show the teachers how instruction given at the library can be made part of the regular classroom activity.

A definite need is for a comprehensive view of library skills in the language arts program. Children, especially in the upper grades, tire of the usual English lesson, and are dissatisfied with the routine reading classes. Most schools need a planned program of library skills, or reading-study skills, as they are sometimes called. Such a program takes into account the greater maturity of the students, and their need for independent work with books. The American Library Association has an excellent pamphlet in this area, *Integrating Library Instruction with Classroom Teaching at Plainview Junior High School.*[10] Such an approach would be a "shot in the arm" to the language arts program. Children can be trained gradually to learn how to use books, how to do research, how to prepare reports and papers. It is too late to wait until the twelfth grade to expose students to the term paper. All of the basic skills can be introduced, a little at a time, beginning with the intermediate grades. Gifted children are especially receptive to research work, though all pupils should develop study skills according to their capacity. This kind of approach might require some departmentalized teaching, at least for a few years while the program was being initiated. To use books, one must know them well. Systematic instruction in the use of books and libraries can be one aspect of a worthwhile in-service program for teachers.

For a good in-service program, teacher materials are needed. A well-stocked teacher's shelf, with duplicates of the best works, is a beginning. Posters, pamphlets, files of magazine clippings — these will be developed in time through concentrated effort of the principal and staff. The principal supplies the impetus and the materials, and co-ordinates the efforts of the staff. The results are always rewarding, in terms of both pupil and teacher growth.

---

[10] Elsa Berner, *Integrating Library Instruction with Classroom Teaching at Plainview Junior High School* (Chicago: American Library Association, 1958).

HOME-SCHOOL CO-OPERATION IS NEEDED

The role of the parents in stimulating wider reading has been mentioned incidentally. A planned program of home-school co-operation is needed, however, in order to provide for lasting results. A Home and School Association meeting can well be devoted to the topic of library reading. Exhibits of good books, charts, and book lists promote parents' interest. Several teachers might give demonstrations on how children use encyclopedias, dictionaries, and almanacs in their regular classroom work. Children might also give brief book talks to parents of children in the grade. Such book talks might be through mock television programs or dramatizations. Emphasis should of course be on the learning activity, and not on dramatic production. Teachers can encourage reading at home by allowing pupils to take favorite books home to read to parents. A love of books is basic to wider reading of books. The teacher's enthusiasm stimulates the children, who in turn interest parents in what the school is doing to promote wider reading. Home and school co-operation is not achieved once for all; there is need for continued attention to books and their effects on pupil learning and satisfaction.

Mothers also can be of practical help to the school in promoting wider reading. In today's homes, when the youngest child starts to school, mothers usually have some time to spare. This is especially true in the suburbs, where there are few working mothers. The school library, or the classroom library, can profitably use the services of a Mothers' Library Club. After being trained in their duties, mothers can take turns doing various work for the library. Typing book cards, pasting in book pockets, numbering books, checking out books and checking them in, making reading posters and charts, and keeping a record of the circulation of each book — all of these are jobs which contribute to a good library. Mothers are happy to help the school promote wider reading in these ways.

Of course there is the problem of finance. Parochial school libraries are usually possible only through added contributions from parishioners. Only occasionally does a city or county library system provide completely adequate service. So, there is need of funds, and someone must raise them. The first impulse may be to have the Home and School Association begin a money-making drive for books. However, strictly speaking, the Home and School Association is not formed to raise money. Its purposes, as outlined in Chapter XII, are threefold: spiritual formation, educational information, and implementing the spiritual direction and information received at meetings. This third objective — often called simply "action" — does not necessarily mean money-raising activities; it means acting upon all worthy suggestions given at meetings. So, the problem arises — Who should raise funds for the school library? In some parishes, the library has been included in the regular church collections and "drives." Another organization has at times taken on this special activity; the Knights of Columbus and the Booster Club particularly have been interested in expanding the school library. Although the school library is a worthy cause, the Home and School Association should restrict its effort to its own specific activities; money-raising diverts the members' attention from the purposes of the organization.

The elementary school is really the place where good reading habits are developed. Library services are needed in order to cultivate interest and good taste. To have adult Catholics who read widely and discriminately, the parochial school needs to expand its library services and to motivate home reading more effectively. Again, in this crucial area, it is the Sister Principal who must provide the leadership.

FOR THE PRINCIPAL'S PROFESSIONAL LIBRARY

GUIDANCE

Books

American Association for Supervision and Curriculum Development, a Department of the National Education Association, *Guidance in the Curriculum*, 1955 Yearbook (Washington, D. C.: National Education Association, 1955), 231 pp., $3.75.
> A readable and interesting account of good guidance practices in action. Many practical suggestions.

American Council on Education, *Helping Teachers Understand Children* (Washington, D. C.: American Council on Education, 1945), $3.50.
> Suggestions for solving "behavior problems" through teacher guidance.

Johnston, Edgar G., Peters, Mildred, and Evraiff, William, *The Role of the Teacher in Guidance* (Englewood Cliffs, N. J.: Prentice-Hall, Inc., 1959), 276 pp., $4.95.
> Teachers would probably be interested in watching the teachers in the book deal effectively with children's needs. Easy reading.

Redl, Fritz, and Wattenberg, William W., *Mental Hygiene in Teaching* (New York: Harcourt, Brace and Company, 1951), 454 pp., $4.75.
> Vivid case materials showing how teacher personality affects pupil adjustment. Readable and practical.

Shuster, Albert H., and Wetzler, Wilson F., *Leadership in Elementary School Administration and Supervision* (Boston: Houghton Mifflin Company, 1958).
> A broad view of the principal's role in providing guidance services for the school.

Wiles, Kimball, *Teaching for Better Schools*, 2nd ed. (Englewood Cliffs, N. J.: Prentice-Hall, Inc., 1959), 341 pp., $5.95.
> Presents the role of the good teacher as a guide and counselor of children. "Quality teaching" depicted in an attractive way.

Pamphlets

Lewis, Gertrude M., *Educating Children in Grades Four, Five, and Six*, Bulletin 1958, No. 3, U. S. Department of Health, Education, and Welfare, Office of Education (Washington, D. C.: Government Printing Office, 1958), 215 pp., $1.
———— *Educating Children in Grades Seven and Eight*, Bulletin 1954, No. 14, U. S. Department of Health, Education, and Welfare, Office of Education (Washington, D. C.: Government Printing Office, 1954), 99 pp., 35 cents.
These two inexpensive booklets show how a good school program and facilities help teachers guide pupils effectively.
Sheviakov, George V., and Redl, Fritz, *Discipline for Today's Children and Youth*, new rev. ed. by Sybil K. Richardson, Association for Supervision and Curriculum Development (Washington, D. C.: National Education Association, 1956), 64 pp., $1.

LIBRARY SERVICE

Arbuthnot, May Hill, Clark, Margaret Mary, Horrocks, Edna M., Long, Harriet G., *Children's Books Too Good to Miss*, 2nd rev. ed. (Cleveland: Western Reserve University Press, 1959), 40 pp., $1.25.
A Basic Book Collection for Elementary Grades, compiled by Miriam Snow Mathes with consultants, 7th ed. (Chicago: American Library Association, 1960), 144 pp., $2.
A Basic Book Collection for Junior High Schools, compiled by Margaret V. Spengler with consultants, 3rd ed. (Chicago: American Library Association, 1960), 144 pp., $2.
Hurley, Richard J., *Your Library* — *How to Organize an Elementary School Library*, prepared for the Commission on American Citizenship (Washington, D. C.: The Catholic University of America Press, 1956), 57 pp., $1.
Standards for School Library Programs, American Association of School Librarians, a division of the American Library Association (Chicago: American Library Association, 1960), 152 pp., with *Discussion Guide*, $3.
The above books are basic references for the principal interested in organizing a good elementary library.

HEALTH AND SAFETY PROGRAM

Books

Two of the newer books which give specific helps in presenting health instruction are the following:
Smith, Helen N., and Wolverton, Mary E., *Health Education in the Elementary School* (New York: The Ronald Press Company, 1959), 315 pp.
Some practical suggestions for improving health and safety instruction can be found in Hicks, William V., and Jameson, Marshall C., *The Elementary School Principal at Work* (Englewood Cliffs, N. J.: Prentice-Hall, Inc., 1957), pp. 148–171.
Willgoose, Carl E., *Health Education in the Elementary School* (Philadelphia: W. B. Saunders Company, 1959), 450 pp., $5.25.

Pamphlets

NcNeely, Simon A., and Schneider, Elsa, *Physical Education in the School Child's Day*, U. S. Department of Health, Education, and Welfare, Office of Education, Bulletin 1950, No. 14 (Washington, D. C.: U. S. Government Printing Office, 1957), 94 pp., 35 cents.

———— *Teachers Contribute to Child Health*, U. S. Department of Health, Education, and Welfare, Office of Education, Bulletin 1951, No. 8 (Washington, D. C.: U. S. Government Printing Office, 1957), 44 pp., 20 cents.

Free, Inexpensive Teaching Materials, 10th ed. (Nashville, Tenn.: George Peabody College, 1960), 252 pp., $1.50.

> Excellent source for locating valuable pamphlets and other visual aids to enrich health instruction as well as other areas of the curriculum.

The National Safety Council, 425 N. Michigan Avenue, Chicago, has a wide variety of effective safety leaflets, at 6 cents each. Some of the most helpful titles are the following:

Bicycles, Bicycle Safety — Performance and Skill Tests, Desirable Experiences in Elementary Safety Education, A Lot to Live For (statistics on causes of children's deaths), Perfection-Plus for Emergency Evacuation Drills, School Safety Patrol — Policies and Practices, This They Believe (common misconceptions about safety).

To and From School, Your Fire Safety Education Program May Be Inadequate, What's Your Safety I.Q.?

The National Safety Council also provides posters and lesson plans at a minimum charge. Many local Safety Councils supply these materials free to schools. The American Automobile Association also distributes worthwhile safety materials for schools.

The principal will also be interested in the materials produced by the National Commission on Safety Education, a department of the National Education Association. Their book list contains many pertinent and inexpensive pamphlets on safety education.

The American Red Cross supplies many free and inexpensive materials for the teaching of health and safety.

CHAPTER XVI

CLERICAL WORK — PLUS

*Who does most of the clerical work in elementary
schools of which you know? Why? What can the
principal do about this situation?*

WHAT is the school office for? Typing? Record keeping? Reports? Yes,
the efficient office handles these routine clerical tasks. In fact, where there
is no secretary, the principal herself may be doing most of these clerical
jobs. However, the concept of the school office is changing. Even where
the principal is a full-time teacher, the office has taken on a "new look"
and a new meaning.

The first offices were usually called the "principal's office," and were
looked upon as a little strange. Teachers after all were supposed to teach
children, so a principal with "time off" usually felt obliged to take into
her office miscellaneous jobs like duplicating worksheets, typing announcements, and counting supplies and money. In fact, the title "free principal"
shows the attitude toward the principal who wasn't devoting all of her
time to teaching. Her office reflected the uncertainty of architects, teachers,
parents, and herself about what the principal's essential duties should be.
The office looked a little ill at ease about not being put to better use.

Of recent years, there is a growing trend toward a "school office," rather
than a "principal's office." The emphasis is upon the *services* which the
office should render, rather than upon the clerical work that is done there.
These services are to the staff, to the pupils, and to persons outside the
school. The office as a service center has become a popular concept.

If the office is actually to be a service center, then the Sister Principal
is the one who makes it so. What kind of services is the office providing
right now? What services *should* be provided in order to achieve the
objectives of Catholic education? How can present services be improved?
The answers to these questions involve the principal's whole philosophy
of education and of administration. What was once a drab little room,
off the beaten path, now becomes the hub of school services. This cannot
be otherwise in a school that has a professionally minded principal, whether

she is a full-time supervising principal or a full-time classroom teacher. It is true whether the school has an elaborate modern office suite or very inadequate office space. The professionally minded principal works consistently toward developing and improving the services rendered.

As with any change, improvements must be made thoughtfully and gradually. Four aspects seem fundamental to improvement: the principal's time in the office, the idea of expanded services, clerical help, and the school files. Many of the problems of the principal center about these four topics.

THE PRINCIPAL'S TIME IN THE OFFICE

In Chapter V, the principal was asked, "What did you do today? What else did you hope to get done?" The answers to these questions were used to show how the principal might distribute her time more wisely among her major duties. Similar questions might be asked in studying the matter of office services. "How much time did you spend in the office today? What did you do with this time?"

HOW MUCH TIME IN THE OFFICE?

Again referring to Chapter V, one notes in the tables there that an efficient principal plans her weekly and daily schedule well in advance. She uses as a guide the recommended time allotment given in Table I of Chapter V. This table is repeated below for purposes of convenience:

TABLE XXVII.   Hours Per Week Ideally Given to the Principal's Duties

Duty	Supervising Principal	Teaching Principal
Supervision	23	8
Administration	13	6
School-Community Relations	5	2
Clerical Work	5	2
Miscellaneous	4	2
Total Hours Per Week	50	20

Source of data: Chapter V, Table I, p. 84.

At first glance, it seems that clerical work alone would keep the Sister Principal in her office. However, each of the other duties also necessitates some time in the office. For example, as a supervisor the principal plans for classroom observation, holds conferences with the teacher observed, and follows up the conference by preparing materials and by keeping a written record of the observation and conference. So, supervision requires some time in the office. Administration also requires some time behind the desk.

Handling pupil transfers, directing the school clerk, budgeting, holding administrative conferences, writing administrative bulletins — all of these are part of good administration, and take place in the school office. School-community relations include discussions with parents and other interested persons, preparation of parent bulletins and handbooks, analysis of community conditions, and releasing school news to the press, and to radio and television stations. Much of this work is done in the school office. Miscellaneous jobs likewise can invade the office, as for example when the principal handles lost and found articles, does office housekeeping, and takes care of "routine" emergencies.

From the above, it is obvious that the principal does many things besides clerical work in the office. That is what causes the difficulty. It is so easy to be occupied with miscellaneous odd jobs, "puttering," actually, when the time might be much more profitably used. From Table XXVII, it is clear that a supervising principal might spend twenty-five hours a week in the school office, doing essentially supervisory and administrative duties. But, and this is the crux of the matter, the *supervising principal should allot no more than five hours a week to strictly clerical work and no more than four hours a week to miscellaneous jobs. The teaching principal should allow only two hours a week for clerical work and two hours for miscellaneous chores.* When the principal is in the office, it should be for essential duties — supervision, administration, and public relations. Principals often have said that they feel like "glorified clerks." But they need not feel that way *if* they allocate their time wisely and arrange for subprofessional help as needed.

How much time should the principal spend in the office? She should spend there enough time to discharge adequately her most important functions. She should not, however, be chained to her desk. The principal must be in touch with all aspects of the school program in order to administer services well and to improve instruction. Time in the office, yes, as it is needed to promote these two aims. The rest of the time, the principal should be in active circulation, noting, planning, conferring, observing, directing, and communicating. The office is not an ivory tower, nor can it ever become one in a well-conducted school. Nor is the office merely for "paper work." The professionally minded principal uses the office to further all of the aims of the school program.

HOW TO USE TIME WISELY?

Budgeting time is necessary if the principal is not going to let herself be caught on a merry-go-round of petty happenings. A pipe is leaking, the Red Cross worker has come for the favors, a child has been sent in for misbehavior, the projector's lamp has burned out, a salesman is opening his brief case, an irate parent is on the phone — and it is only 9:15! What can one do? Budget one's time. The merry-go-round will go round indefinitely. The principal must get off, and stay off, by preparing a thoughtful time budget. "Administrivia" is a term that has been coined for this preoccupation with the petty details of a school day. Not that a budget will automatically prevent all such trivia from happening in the future. No, such occurrences are normal in every school, but a time budget will enable the principal to spend her efforts on improving the school, rather than on breathlessly trying to keep up.

Chapter V gives some pointers on a good allocation of time for each of the major duties. These pointers can be applied specifically to the school office. In order to use her time to best advantage, the principal should —

1. Arrange an administrative calendar for the year, planned as far in advance as possible. The dates for the opening and closing of the school year, for holidays, for tests, for church functions, for drives and campaigns, for inoculations, for civic activities, for graduation — all of these and the many other events of importance should be put on a large calendar. This administrative calendar lets the faculty see what is coming this month and this week. The calendar also reminds the principal of needed planning for each event. There need be no breathless last-minute preparations when the principal plans well in advance by means of an administrative calendar.

2. Make a weekly and daily schedule of duties. Chapter V gave specific suggestions for making a good schedule. A copy of this schedule should be on the principal's desk. A posted schedule should show the faculty the points that concern them, as visits the principal will make to their rooms, faculty meetings, conferences, Home and School meetings, and other important events. This schedule should not be completely rigid, but should provide for minor changes as needed. A schedule is basic to good use of time.

3. Schedule time for office appointments each week. This time should be arranged for the convenience of teachers, parents, and others who need to confer with the principal. When the staff and others know that the principal has arranged a specific time each day, or several times a week, for them to talk over school matters with her, there will be far fewer emergencies and interruptions. Long-range planning will also be more effective.

4. Spend time planning at the end of each day. This is particularly needed by teaching principals. This planning will enable the principal to foresee the work of the next day, and to provide for the needs of staff and pupils either personally or through delegation.

5. Learn to delegate work that can be done by others. Teachers can be chairmen for drives and activities. Volunteer workers can do much of the routine office work. The office clerk, if there is one, can take on many tasks now performed by principals. Delegation, as outlined in Chapter IV, is basic to good administration. No principal can function effectively unless she delegates work wisely.

6. Look around in other school offices. How do these principals manage?

Which of their ideas can you use in your own work? Principals are usually amazed to learn that other schools have worked out forms, schedules, routines that would help other principals. There could be much more sharing of good ideas on clerical work.

7. Get ideas from the staff. Twenty heads are better than one, but the principal may be so taken up with "administrivia" that she doesn't draw upon the help her staff could give. The school planning committee may profitably spend a meeting or two in arranging short cuts that the principal herself might never have thought of. The staff's ideas are important, but the help they can give in carrying out the ideas is more important still. As mentioned before, administration should be a "constellation of experts," not just a solo performance by the principal.

The principal needs to spend a certain amount of time in the office in order to administer the school well. The above points will help her to utilize her time better in promoting the aims of the school program.

THE IDEA OF EXPANDED OFFICE SERVICES

One can tell the philosophy of the school by noting the activities that go on in the school office. When the principal has a narrow concept of the school's purposes, then the office is concerned only with such mechanics as giving teachers their supplies, filling out reports, and counting money. A modern school program, however, requires vastly expanded office services. Some of these services are of a clerical nature, such as those involved in providing detailed and complete pupil personnel records. But many of the services are broader in scope.

To a certain extent, the pastor determines the kind of services available. Certainly, the pastor invests parish money in equipment and supplies, in maintenance and improvement, and in clerical salaries. However, the principal also has an important role; it is she who interprets the need to the pastor and thereby secures the services, both in personnel and in equipment. The principal also determines how fully available personnel and materials will be utilized. Adequate services depend upon the pastor's provisions, in the first place, but also upon the principal's wise use of facilities, and her ingenuity in improvising where necessary.

In a good situation, the school office provides many services to the principal, the staff, the pupils, and the public.

SERVICES TO THE PRINCIPAL

A good school office first of all takes the burden of clerical work away from the principal. Even in a four-room school, the principal is responsible for many reports and records, for ordering and distributing supplies, and for budgeting and bookkeeping. And, in the smaller schools, the principal is likely to be a full-time teacher as well as administrator. A good office clerk is essential, though in small schools a part-time worker usually is sufficient.

A good school office provides adequate work space and facilities for the principal to do her work conveniently. The minimum in equipment would be a well-constructed desk and secretarial chair, typewriter, vertical file, work organizer, telephone, bookcase for professional books, and several chairs for conferences. Duplicating equipment is also essential, and where the office consists of only one room, this equipment is kept where the principal can use it conveniently. Equipment should be in good working condition and of good quality; stationery and filing supplies should also be plentiful and of good quality. Timesaving equipment and good supplies are essential if the principal is to do her work quickly and efficiently. The appearance of the office also contributes to efficiency. A harmonious paint job doesn't cost any more than a drab shade, but studies show higher morale, and hence greater production, when surroundings are pleasant and cheerful. Cleanliness is also indispensable to a good working situation. Custodial service which keeps floors clean, windows washed, and furniture repaired contributes greatly to the amount and quality of the work the principal can do in her office.

Now these services to the principal are for a single purpose — to relieve her of subprofessional jobs so that she can be a supervisor and administrator. The principal's schedule should show that she is actually visiting classes, holding conferences, preparing instructional materials, evaluating teaching, and promoting the in-service growth of her staff as well as her own professional growth. The principal freed from clerical tasks should also be able to point to greater pupil progress as a result. Public relations in the school should be on a high level of effectiveness. Giving the principal more clerical help and better working conditions is not done because of pity for the "poor principal." These improved services are made possible so that she can conserve her energy for the larger aspects of her job. The acid test is — where are the signs of improvement in the staff, the pupils, and the school? Better office conditions help the principal to show unmistakable signs of progress in each of these areas.

SERVICES TO THE STAFF

Some time ago, a teacher didn't go to the office unless she was "sent for." Today, a functionally designed office has as one of its chief aims to serve the needs of the staff. First, there are the instructional materials and supplies which teachers need; the efficient office is the center for *distributing requisitioned materials*. The teachers also *need to be informed* of coming activities and events. The office bulletin board displays timely notices; the teacher's individual mailboxes also serve to supply teachers with interesting current material and bulletins. Even in a school having clerical help, teachers need to type and run off material for their classes. An efficient office, or a room in the office suite, provides *duplicating equipment*, paper, masters, and fluid, storage shelves, tables for sorting and stacking, staplers, punches, wrapping paper, and paper cutter. When this equipment is adequate and kept in good condition, teachers are more interested in providing "extras" for their pupils.

Teachers are also helped when the office assumes responsibility for *collecting money*. Some of the small, voluntary collections, such as Red Cross, can be taken care of by the classroom teacher. But larger amounts should be collected centrally. Fees for book rental, money for lunches, school bus, and school uniforms would be better collected by an aide or clerk trained for that purpose. Collecting money is a chief source of dissatisfaction among teachers. The school office should provide a uniform plan for receipts, bookkeeping, and collecting larger sums of money. This is a service welcomed by teachers.

The good school office provides some *clerical assistance* to teachers. No office can supply enough clerks to help all teachers do everything in the clerical line, but a good office does provide some help. The idea underlying clerical help to teachers is this: when teachers are relieved of some clerical work, they can devote more time to preparation for teaching, and they can also share some administrative responsibilities. Teachers cannot possibly do all of the classroom clerical work, and also prepare interesting materials, and work on in-service committees. Professional time should be conserved for professional work. Hence, the good school office provides at least a limited amount of help to teachers. Test scoring is a welcome and needed service; so is help in transferring data from classroom records to permanent records; typing pupil records can be taken over at least in part by office workers, paid or volunteer. Perhaps once a week or so, a teacher might want to ditto a little exercise for her class; getting it typed and run off contributes to morale, and to good teaching. Clerical service to teachers needs to be carefully outlined and necessary limits imposed. A definite amount of help, even if only an hour a week per teacher, makes for satisfaction and better work.

An even more fundamental service which the good office renders is to promote the *professional development of the staff*. Conferences are essential to professional growth. The adequate office has a space set apart where conferences can be held in quiet and privacy, without interruptions and ringing bells. The space should be large enough to accommodate a group of teachers discussing professional matters. For a profitable discussion, educational materials are also needed. The office, or one room of the office, may well serve as the teacher's professional library. Teachers may frequent the library informally, or in organized groups. A varied and stimulating collection of professional books and magazines will almost certainly be in demand among good teachers. A teacher-librarian can do much both to select worthwhile materials and to create a demand for them.

To be a real service center, the office should actually supply real needs of the staff. To find out how to improve services to the staff, the alert principal will ask questions of those most concerned — the staff. What services now provided help you in your work? What other services could be provided with only a slight increase in expense? How could teachers make better use of office services? If the staff isn't used to democratic procedures, perhaps a question box will invite answers to these inquiries. Most teachers, however, when they know the principal really wants suggestions, will come through with down-to-earth and practical ideas for improving services and faculty use of services.

SERVICES TO PUPILS

The good school office also provides many services to children. The so-called "special services" are channeled through the office, such services as school bus and cafeteria service, health and safety services, and guidance services. In the office are located pupil personnel records used as background for interpreting pupil needs to parents, nurses, attendance officers, social workers, and juvenile court officers. Pupil records are also made available by the office for the convenient use of teachers. The health clinic is located near the office in the newer buildings, because of the principal's role in co-ordinating health services. Conferences with pupils are held in the office, for disciplinary as well as for other adjustment problems. Contacts with parents are also channeled through the office. In order to provide an adequate and well-balanced program for children, the school office plays a prominent role in all of these respects. In fact, all of the services which the office renders are in the last analysis for children. The school, and all of its facilities, are planned to provide an all-round education for its pupils.

SERVICES TO THE PUBLIC

An efficient school office serves the public in many ways. Prompt and gracious attention to telephone calls and visitors, clear and well-typed letters, timely news releases, accurate, complete records and reports — these are just a few of the ways the school office serves the public. A definite and courteous procedure for dealing with salesmen is also part of the service which a good school office renders. The parochial schools are financed by parish collections, and not taxes; still, the school office has a duty to supply information and to handle public relations competently. The school office has an important role in public relations, as will be discussed in the next section.

CLERICAL HELP

The school clerk is a rather recent addition to the elementary school staff. Many schools, public and parochial, still have no paid clerical help in the school office. However, in view of the expanded services of a modern school, the office clerk is fast being recognized as indispensable to a good program.

FULL OR PART TIME?

A large school is likely to have a school clerk, but even the smallest school needs some clerical help. Particularly when the principal is also responsible for a class does she need this kind of assistance. Chapter V presented some suggested norms for the amount of clerical help needed. Below 400 enrollment, the school will need from ten to twenty hours of office help weekly; above 400 enrollment, one clerk, full-time, and about 800 enrollment, two full-time clerks. To have an efficient school, the pastor will be wise to hire good help for the school office.

In a very poor parish, it may not be possible to pay a salary to a full-time office clerk. Then a part-time worker can be hired, and the rest of the clerical work can be done by volunteer workers. For example, if a clerk can be hired only for the mornings, then various other clerical jobs may be done by aides, on a part-time basis. Aides can collect cafeteria money and keep records of the money, take up absentee slips and make a report of absence, type letters and records, count out and distribute supplies to teachers, and use the duplicating machine. Directing part-time workers requires more of the principal's time, but it is better than having the principal and teachers use their professional time in subprofessional routines.

WHAT ABOUT SALARY?

Parochial schools have learned that good lay teachers can be obtained only if the salary is adequate. As discussed in Chapter VI, many lay teachers have found adequate a salary which is 80 per cent of the local public school salary. A similar norm might perhaps be applied to clerical salaries in parish schools. If in the local public schools the clerks are paid $1.50 an hour, or $60 a week, for forty weeks a year, then the local parochial school might get reasonably good service by offering a salary of $1.20 an hour, or $48 a week. The public school clerk would receive $2,400 a year for working forty weeks; the parochial school clerk would receive $1,920 for a forty-week year.

However, the above salary would not appeal to anyone who was self-supporting or who had dependents. At $1,920 a year, the pastor could expect to get only a married woman whose husband was making an adequate salary. It is usually not good to think of hiring for the school office a retired office worker. School office work can be strenuous, and older people have difficulty adjusting to the constant demands made upon them. Usually, when the salary is good (better than 80 per cent of the public school salary) the office clerk is more likely to stay. The training of a clerk is very time-consuming for the principal; hence, the pastor should try to pay a salary that will attract and keep an above-average person.

WHAT DOES A CLERK DO?

Occasionally, one goes into an office and finds the clerk reading a book or paging through a magazine. Immediately, the question comes to mind: "Is she really needed here?" Or, the clerk puts down a candy bar to take care of a phone call that is obviously an "interruption." Again, the thought comes: "Does she have enough to do?" And then there are the stories, some of them true, of office workers who take forty-five-minute "coffee breaks" morning and afternoon.

It is too bad that some clerks have given such impressions. A good clerk in a well-organized office has so much to do that a forty-hour week isn't long enough. The following outline gives some of the typical duties of a good clerk in a good office:

1. **Duties As Receptionist.** Too many principals forget that the school clerk contacts more people than any other staff member does. The clerk's voice is "the school" to persons outside; her manner and appearance leave a favorable or poor impression with the visitor. Because of her importance in public relations, the clerk should be trained to serve parents and the public pleasantly, graciously, and efficiently. Correct telephone technique is essential; the local telephone company will gladly furnish a book of good procedures. Courteous routines for dealing with visitors enhance the school's services. A clerk who is informed on school policies and activities can save the principal's time by supplying needed information.

Even though callers never meet the principal or a teacher, they will be impressed with the school just because of the secretary's manner of dealing with them. A little point that helps secretaries deal graciously with callers is to remind them that everyone should be received as if he were a Very Important Person. Office clerks sometimes "brush off" a poorly dressed caller, or one with no "manners." The father in his factory clothes may not be as charmingly received as the president of the Home and School Association. Each caller deserves considerate attention, no matter what his clothes are like, or his accent, or his name. Especially in Catholic schools, there should be no discrimination because of these accidentals.

2. Typing, Duplicating, and Filing. The clerk should produce clear, neat, and attractive letters and copy. All letters from the principal should be typed by the clerk, and read and signed by the principal. Letters from the teachers to parents should also be typed by the clerk, and read by the principal before they leave the office. Letters from the school loom very large in the eyes of the parents and the public. Every letter and bulletin should be representative of fine clerical work. The school files will be discussed at some length in the next section, but it is well here to consider filing as one of the clerk's essential jobs. Neatness and accuracy are basic to good filing, just as they are to quality correspondence.

3. Orders and Requisitions. Under the principal's direction, the clerk should keep on hand and distribute the supplies which teachers need for their work. A standard requisition form is good practice. The clerk can duplicate copies of the form to be used when teachers are requesting supplies. These requisition blanks enable the principal to plan carefully for future expenses; requisition blanks also help the clerk to distribute supplies quickly and efficiently. The clerk can take care of all incoming deliveries — books, supplies, and materials. She can also take charge of the storeroom; inventory supplies on hand, notify the principal when supplies are low, and shelve incoming supplies. To make for good order, the principal can arrange a set time for receiving and filing requisitions, and acquaint the staff with these routines. Particularly essential is the clerk's role in distributing audio-visual equipment and supplies, checking back the material when returned, and seeing that the equipment is kept in working order.

4. Office Records and Reports. As mentioned in the discussion of services to the staff, the clerk should maintain office records neatly, legibly, and accurately. She should be able to locate records and process them as required. The school clerk should also be able to compile many of the reports due at the Diocesan School Office and the State Department of Education. The principal can help improve the clerk's efficiency by writing out directions for filing and handling records. By saving these direction sheets over a period of time, the principal has the beginning of an office manual to use in orienting new personnel.

5. Collections and Bookkeeping. The teacher's work is greatly facilitated when money is collected, counted, and recorded in the school office. Sometimes it is best to have the classroom teacher receive the money in a labeled envelope, and then send the unopened envelopes to the office clerk. The clerk can keep separate records for each class, and send receipts, in envelopes, back to the classroom teacher for distribution. When money is recorded centrally, the principal always knows the financial status of the school account. According to parish policy, bills can be sent from the office to parents who are in arrears.

Another aspect of school bookkeeping is writing checks for materials received, filing invoices, and keeping books on expenditures. Budgeting is far from satisfactory even in public schools, where accounting for funds is a legal requirement. Budgeting in parochial schools can be improved, if accurate records are kept of disbursements and receipts. For example, the Sister Principal spends only the amount of money she has, whether from parish collections entirely or from parish funds supplemented by book rental fees and money-raising activities. Budgeting will not, of course, result in greatly increased funds for operation. However, budgeting will allow for systematic improvement in certain areas each year. For one year, a certain amount of money might be allocated to supplementing the classroom libraries, over and beyond the state minimum requirements. Another year, the budget might allow for emphasis upon improved audio-visual aids. This kind of preplanning is possible only if the school office has good bookkeeping. Thus, a seemingly clerical task actually affects the educational program.

School clerks also perform many other duties, such as registering new pupils, guiding visitors to rooms, helping substitute teachers with routines, and handling various emergencies that come up in the course of a normal day. A study of clerical help convinces one that the average school could profitably use much more clerical help than is now provided. And, of course, better use of clerical help can improve the school program still more. The school in which there is adequate clerical help, wisely used, is likely to be a superior school.

OFFICE FILING

Most elementary schools of any size can be expected to have at least one four-drawer vertical file, with lock. But principals, especially teaching principals, usually have never had time to make that file as beautiful inside as outside. Then, too, principals are trained teachers, not file clerks, so "filing" always seems mysterious. Perhaps a few suggestions are in order both to simplify the principal's problem, and to provide better service to the staff and students. Of the many technicalities of filing, three may be selected as particularly needed in the elementary school: setting up headings for the school file, getting the file in working order, and keeping the system up to date.

SETTING UP HEADINGS FOR THE SCHOOL FILE

Every time the principal opens the mail, she gets her desk cluttered with many kinds of interesting and semi-interesting booklets, bills, samples, and notices. That advertisement for stand-up letters, plastic, three-inch — that would be good to save for the Home and School Open House, coming soon. Those bills, especially the ones with the hands stamped on them, simply have to be saved; but the top drawer of the desk is already filled, and the urgent bills might be forgotten there. Every item seems to pose a special problem. While she is trying to clear her desk, the principal is probably wishing there were a simpler way. There is, but the time to provide a simpler way is now, *before* Saturday's mail brings fresh problems.

The big decision to make is this: Where shall I put this material so that I can find it when I need it? This question involves setting up headings for filing. Now most principals have already worked out some headings for their own files. The first and most obvious one is based on the *date* of the material — this year, last year, this week, next week, Christmas. Then there could be a division according to the pupils and the Diocesan School Office. Many other such headings suggest themselves, but the trouble is that a perfectly good heading can be forgotten by the time one goes to look for the material. "How did I file it? I know I put it in this drawer, but I can't seem to find it." Practically everyone who has ever filed anything has had this desperate feeling. "It *has* to be here, but I can't find it." St. Anthony has earned a prominent place over many educational files, and he has done admirably. Even after the principal has perfected her system considerably, she will still need his assistance, but he can probably take a well-earned rest most of the time.

Headings for filing need to be *logical*, and they need to be *written down* or they will be forgotten. The National Association of Educational Secretaries has developed a good filing system for public school offices. The classifications need to be modified somewhat for use in parochial schools.[1] The principal is asked to read through the following subject classifications to see how the materials now in her file may fit under one or other of the headings given below.

HEADING FOR OFFICE FILE

ADMINISTRATION   1*
*1 Diocese (Archdiocese)
   Bulletins
   Calendar of Reports

Correspondence
Handbook
Reports to
Local Public School District

---

[1] The headings developed here have been based to a certain extent on the following publication: National Association of Educational Secretaries, *File It Right* (Washington, D. C.: National Education Association, 1953), pp. 20–23. This material has been used with the permission of the National Education Association.

* Each subject classification has its own number. The folders following the classification guide all carry this same number. Numbering the folders speeds up filing, and helps to check on folders inaccurately filed. The guide is numbered to the *right*; the folders are numbered to the *left*. See the accompanying illustration of a well-arranged file drawer (Figure 48).

1 State Department of Education
  Bulletins
  Certification laws
  Handbook
  Reports to

BUSINESS AFFAIRS   2

2 Bookkeeping
  Budget
  Cash receipts
  Checks, canceled
  Invoices, paid
  Invoices, unpaid
  Petty cash account
2 Bookstore
2 Equipment and supplies
2 Fees
2 Inventories
2 Insurance
2 Orders
2 Requisitions, pending
2 Requisitions filled

CALENDARS AND SCHEDULES   3

3 Audio-visual aids schedule
3 Bell schedule
3 Cafeteria schedule
3 Confraternity of Christian Doctrine
    Calendar
3 Custodian's cleaning schedule
3 Diocesan school calendar
3 Home and School meeting schedule
3 Library schedule
3 Nurse's schedule
3 Patrol Boy schedule
3 Principal's schedule
3 Religious instruction by priests
    (schedule)
3 Supervisor's schedule
3 Teachers' daily programs
3 Test schedules
3 Transportation, bus schedules

CATALOGS   4

4 Audio-visual
4 Books
4 Equipment and supplies
4 Miscellaneous
4 Religious articles
4 Tests

EVENTS AND PROGRAMS   5

5 Assemblies
5 Ceremonies
  Christmas
  Confirmation
  Dedication
  First Holy Communion

  First Mass
  Forty Hours
  Holy Week
  May procession
5 Contests
  Spelling Bee
5 Drives and campaigns
  Community Chest
  Diocesan Newspaper Drive
5 Exhibits
  Art Exhibit
  Science fair
5 Holiday observance
5 Special observances
  American Education Week
  Business-Education-Industry
  Open House — Home and School
  Pastor's Feast

FORMS USED IN SCHOOL   6
  (two copies of each form)
6 Diocesan forms will include report
    cards, transfer cards, registration
    blanks, etc.
6 School-made forms will include req-
    uisitions, receipts, etc.

GOVERNMENT, U. S., State, Local   7

7 Civilian Defense
7 Federal Lunch Program
7 Federal Milk Program
7 Fire regulations (or, under *Safety*)
7 Flag, regulations for display
7 Laws, as Child Labor

INSTRUCTIONAL PROGRAM   8

8 Audio-visual program
8 Books, required
8 Books, supplementary
8 Curriculum areas
  Bulletins
  Courses of study
  Materials
8 In-service program
  Advisory program
  Committees
  Faculty meetings
8 Student teaching and observation
8 Summer school
8 Teaching methods and ideas

MOTHER HOUSE   9

9 Bulletins
9 Correspondence
9 Events and programs
9 Faculty meetings (minutes)
9 Handbook

GETTING THE FILE IN WORKING ORDER

First, take ten dollars. It costs just about that to make a good start with the right kind of filing materials. To set up the Subject Classifications given above, the principal will need the following materials:

Filing guides — 16 letter-size index guides, one-third cut, 8 in first position, and 8 in second position, blank metal tab, strong pressboard, priced at about 30 cents each. (Angled tabs are easier to read.)

File folders — 200 letter-size manila folders, double fold at top, one-third cut, third position, priced at about $2.50 a hundred

Gummed labels — one box of 250; Oxford R444 will fit best, priced at about 35 cents a box

These materials will be sufficient to set up a filing system for everything but pupil records.

And now for the steps in the process of setting up the file in good working order.

Step One. For each Subject Classification in capital letters, type in clear black type each of the sixteen headings, beginning with ADMINISTRA-

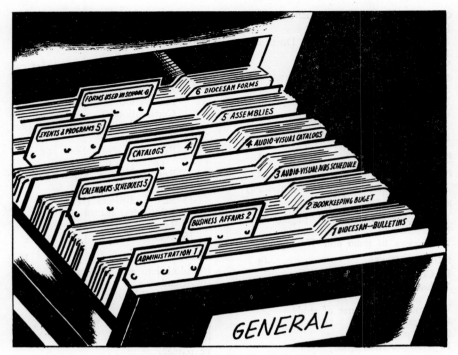

Figure 46.   File drawer — administration

TION, and ending with STUDENTS. Insert one heading in each of the sixteen blank metal tab guides. Arrange the guides in alphabetical order and stand them upright in the empty file drawer. There is bound to be a glow of satisfaction, for the file already looks promising.

Step Two.   Begin with ADMINISTRATION, and type a gummed label for each of the ten subheadings. The labels will read: *Diocese — Bulletins, Diocese — Calendar of Reports, Diocese — Correspondence, Diocese — Handbook,* and so on. *Local Public School District* will have a gummed label, and the state department folders will be typed like the diocesan folders. Some principals prefer to give the name of the state, as *Ohio State Dept. — Bulletins.* These ten gummed labels can then be pasted on the double-fold manila folders and placed in the file. Already, ADMINISTRATION looks much more important than before. At this stage, the principal may be thinking that there are some other headings that belong under ADMINISTRATION, but if she is patient, she will see how these logically can be placed under some of the other classifications.

Step Three.   Locate all the material that belongs in these ten folders, no matter what the date. Even if the bulletin or announcement came from the diocese three years ago, for now just put it into the folder labeled *Diocese — Bulletins*. As time goes on, and the principal has time to refine the system, she will be adding new folders, *dated*, for example, *Diocese — Bulletins, 1961–62*. Locating the file material that belongs in these folders may take a little time, for the teachers may have some of it, the principal may have the State Standards at the convent or may have loaned it to the pastor, and so on. The important thing is to get the feeling of what belongs in the section on ADMINISTRATION.

Step Four. BUSINESS AFFAIRS, the second subject classification, can be prepared for the file in the same manner, except that finances always cause the most trouble — shortages of money and also of invoices and records. The principal should spend just enough time on BUSINESS AFFAIRS to file the material she can readily locate, and then go on to each of the other subject classifications.

As the principal works through each heading and subheading, she will find herself adding topics peculiar to her own diocese, city, and school. And, as the principal uses the system, she will be thinking in terms of subject classifications and subheadings, and will almost automatically be making new folders. At first, it may seem like a waste of money and time to make a folder which may house only one record, as for example, under CALEN-DARS AND SCHEDULES, the folder for *Diocesan School Calendar*, or for *Custodian's Cleaning Schedule*. In the long run, however, time is saved when a single important record is filed for easy reference.

Step Five. Type out the Subject Classifications given on the preceding pages, with the subheadings, and place this sheet in a folder in front of the guide marked ADMINISTRATION. This folder should be marked *Filing Classifications*. It will save time to have all of these headings typed out on paper, so that the principal can quickly go through the Subject Classifications list to determine what folder should contain the material. This list should be kept in this folder routinely. The principal can add new headings when the need arises, and at the end of the year cancel out any headings that proved to be unnecessary. A single list will be invaluable for efficient use of the classifications.

Step Six. The Subject Classifications STAFF and STUDENTS will require more time than the other headings. In fact, it will probably take all year to get these two classifications in good working order. For example, under STAFF, for the folder marked *Teachers — Addresses*, this information might be quickly assembled just by having each teacher write out the information on an index card and submit it to the principal. However, the folder *Teachers — Policies* will take time to fill. If the school has a handbook, the sections of the handbook which apply might be included here. Or, through the year, the staff might develop teacher personnel policies. However, the folder will not be an easy one to use. Likewise, *Teachers — Welfare* will take time to develop, for this folder should ideally include information on sick leave, retirement benefits, Social Security, and the like. Also, under *Teachers — Personal Data*, the principal will have an individual folder for each teacher, religious and lay. The entries listed in the Subject Classification are ones that a complete record system should include. However, this information is difficult to assemble, so this section of the file may be incomplete for a while.

The Subject Classification STUDENTS also will require time, effort, and money beyond the original ten dollars. *Students — Records* will require, not a folder, but perhaps several file drawers. The best practice seems to be to separate current records from records of students who have left the school, because of graduation or any other reason. The file drawer below illustrates good practice for current student records:

In the drawer marked *Student Records* (Figure 47), each grade is assigned the same kind of pressboard guide as given to each Subject Classification. Each student has an individual folder, containing the permanent record, test data, and similar important records. (See Chapter XIV.) When there is more than one section of a grade, another set of guides

Figure 47. File drawer — student records

can be inserted in the center position of the drawer; these guides might be marked with the teacher's name or the room number. Each classroom, or the entire grade, is alphabetized boys and girls together after the guide marking the grade number.

In the drawer marked *Student Records — Inactive*, all records are filed alphabetically, boys and girls together, regardless of date of leaving the school.

If money permits, a set of alphabetic guides is best for inactive records — metal tab, 50-division, or 100-division. If finances do not permit, then sheets of cardboard may be cut the size of a guide, and gummed labels may be marked with the letters of the alphabet. Inactive records must be kept indefinitely, so the principal should budget money for standard guides as soon as possible.

These suggestions will have to be modified according to the needs of the school system. For example, where the student does not have an individual folder, then heavy folders should be bought to house the permanent records for students according to grades. Health records also may require special filing, depending upon local regulations. The above plan will apply to many, if not most, parochial schools.

Students — Testing will also require more than a folder. It is sometimes advisable to file together in a folder the summary of test results for each class. For example, the results of the intelligence test given to selected classes in the fall may be filed in a folder marked *Students — Intelligence Test, Oct., 1961*. Also, the principal will need extra tests for pupils who enter the school after the test has been given to the whole group. These tests can be filed after a guide marked TESTS — INTELLIGENCE, or TESTS — ACHIEVEMENT, or TESTS — DIOCESAN, JAN., 1962. Tests can be kept in labeled folders, after these guides, so the principal can readily locate the needed tests for individual pupils.

As pointed out, *Students — Records* will require one or more file drawers. The headings mentioned earlier — beginning with *Administration* and ending with *Staff* will require at least one drawer. This drawer will look very much like Figures 46 and 47.

Setting up a filing system for a school requires a great deal of initial effort. However, principals who have developed satisfactory filing systems feel that their effort was more than repaid in the greater efficiency of their office and the greater usefulness of the materials.

KEEPING THE FILE IN WORKING ORDER

When all the guides are marked, the folders labeled, and the materials inserted, the principal has made a good start. Certainly, with concentration, she can now locate everything she has put into the file. That is quite an accomplishment. However, if a filing system is not well maintained, it is worse perhaps than no filing system at all. The humorous definition of filing can indeed be true: "A file is a place where you lose things systematically." The principal needs to follow through at least a few minimum procedures in order to keep her file at peak efficiency.

Only One Person Should File.   For a while, the principal may have to do all the filing herself, in order to be sure that all the headings are consistently interpreted. Important papers can be lost by someone who puts the paper in the folder before, or just behind, the right one. All papers should be filed with the top going in the same direction. Also, by doing the filing herself at least for a while, the principal will become doubly familiar with the material being filed; hence, she can locate it more quickly, and will use it oftener, because she knows where it is and what it is.

A Definite Time Should Be Set Aside for Filing.   Filing weekly may be often enough in the elementary school. Perhaps Saturday morning may be the best time, when there will be fewer interruptions from children and staff. Filing will take about half an hour in most cases, at least after all the folders have been put in order. "Material to-be-filed" should not be allowed to accumulate, for the most recent items are usually the most important.

"Material To-Be-Filed" Should Be Kept in One Place.   Practically everything that will eventually find its way to the file comes in the mail. So, handling the mail is crucial. A work organizer, or tray with several tiers, is indispensable in keeping incoming papers intact for processing and filing. The mail should be delivered to a tray, or box, opened and sorted at the same desk, if possible, and also filed temporarily in an organizer on the same desk. This will eliminate the predicament of the busy principal who opens mail "en route," and then cannot locate the forms which must be filled out and returned immediately. If the organizer, or tiered tray, has several compartments, perhaps the principal may label them "Urgent," "Staff," and "Second Class," "Catalogues," etc. Then, as the mail is opened, or as other papers come to the principal's desk, they may be sorted there to await filing day. "Material to-be-filed" should never be put into desk drawers. or brief cases, or horrors! pockets. If the principal can work out the above plan, she can always be assured that the material is either in the work organizer, or in its proper place in the file.

"Out" Cards Should Be Used for Material Removed From the File. When a teacher asks to see the procedure for handling Community Chest collections, for example, the principal expects to remember who borrowed the information sheet. However, with the hundreds of things that come up in a day, the principal will probably forget who took out the sheet. In fact, the teacher may also forget; teachers are busy, too. As a safeguard of filed material, an "out" card or sheet should be filled out whenever *anyone* borrows *anything* from the file, be it a student record or a catalog. One can buy "out" cards at an office supply store, but they can also be made inexpensively. The forms usually ask for the following information: name of person, date, heading of folder, brief description of the material borrowed, and the expected date of return. "Out" cards are usually taller than the guides, so they call attention to the fact that material has been removed. Anyone who takes filed material out of the file should conscientiously record the above information.

Recent Papers Should Be Filed in Front. Since the principal will usually be looking for the most recent material, these papers should be filed in the front of each folder. An occasional check is needed, to re-sort papers into chronological order.

Folders and File Drawers Should Not Be Crowded. When a folder contains thirty or forty papers, it is time to start a new folder. At that point, one should probably date the new folder, as *MOTHER HOUSE, Bulletins, 1961–62.* Sometimes it may be good to divide the material in a folder, perhaps *Teaching Methods — Drills,* and *Teaching Methods — Motivations.* File drawers should not be packed tight, but should allow room for filing and removing material quickly and easily. Inactive student records become cumbersome; transfer boxes are relatively inexpensive and can be used for storing very old records, out of the office, but in a safe place.

The Filing System Should Be Modified and Expanded As Needed. As new activities and services are added, and old ones dropped, the filing classifications can be adjusted. Likewise, as the system becomes more familiar, the principal may want to change the wording on some of the labels. Very old notices can be destroyed; in fact, some dioceses specify how long records and bulletins are to be retained in the school. The file should reflect the status of operations in the school; the file should show growth, not only in the number of drawers needed, but also in the refinement of subject classifications.

One Should File All Information Prepared for School Procedures, Processions, Programs, and the Like. This year, the Sisters found a very interesting little play for the pastor's feast day. With adaptations, the play suited the occasion perfectly. If the revised version is filed under EVENTS AND PROGRAMS — *Pastor's Feast,* then the material can be located quickly when another school wants to borrow it. Likewise, the procedure for First Holy Communion was especially smooth this year, although the class was large. By all means, the Sister in charge should write out exactly how she planned the occasion. Her directions should be filed under *Ceremonies — First Holy Communion.* Next year, these directions will be welcome when practices begin for this important occasion. When an event is over, everyone feels that the routines will be remembered for "the next time," but usually the most helpful ideas are forgotten. A great deal of time may be spent in copying the music for a hymn or song not in the standard books; but this time is almost wasted unless the copy is filed where it can be located easily in the future. Someone said that the secret to efficient management is to "File, file, file, and keep on filing." Certainly, information and suggestions developed by the staff deserve to be saved for future use. Accurate filing preserves important material for future reference.

The Files Should Be Accessible to Those Who Need Them. In the newest schools, there are several rooms in the office suite, and the students' records can easily be filed where teachers have access to them. Even in the older buildings, however, student records can be housed so that teachers have a minimum of difficulty in using them. Certainly, records are kept because they furnish useful information. An important function of a good filing system is to make this information available to qualified persons. On the other hand, the files contain confidential information which should not be open to the staff. Teacher records, for example, should not be kept where a casual observer might peruse them. Sometimes confidential matter can be safeguarded by placing it in a separate file, or by providing a special lock on one drawer of the file. Ordinarily, the staff need to use only the students' records, and not other filed material unless removed from the file by the principal.

A sound filing system, carefully planned and maintained, will be a satisfaction to the principal and a service to both staff and students. A trained school clerk can assume the responsibility for filing, under the direction of a principal who is thoroughly familiar with the system and the contents of the file.

FOR THE PRINCIPAL'S PROFESSIONAL LIBRARY

Books

There are helpful discussions of the school office in the following books. The principal may prefer to borrow them from the library rather than buy them, if her budget for professional books is limited.

Elsbree, Willard S., and McNally, Harold J., *Elementary School Administration and Supervision*, 2nd ed. (New York: American Book Company, 1959), pp. 449–543.

Otto, Henry J., *Elementary-School Organization and Administration*, 3rd ed. (New York: Appleton-Century-Crofts, Inc., 1954), pp. 588–611.

Shuster, Albert H., and Wetzler, Wilson F., *Leadership in Elementary School Administration and Supervision* (Boston: Houghton Mifflin Company, 1958), pp. 379–401.

Pamphlets

The National Association of Educational Secretaries, a Department of the National Education Association, has three excellent booklets for *school offices:*
Blueprint for Action, a Handbook of Handbooks, 1955, 48 pp., $1.50.
File It Right, 1953, 73 pp., $1.50.
Plan Your Work, and Do It!, 1959, 40 pp., $1.50.
Down-to-earth suggestions for improving school office routines. Order from the NEA, 1201 Sixteenth Street, N.W., Washington, D. C.

CHAPTER XVII

THE SCHOOL PLANT
W. W. Theisen, Ph.D.*

> What should a principal know about problems
> concerning the school plant? Why? What diffi-
> culties arise when a principal has inadequate knowl-
> edge about the school plant? What are the relative
> responsibilities of the pastor and the principal in
> matters pertaining to the school plant?

THE purpose of this chapter is to point out some of the relationships
between the school plant and the curriculum opportunities that accrue to
the children as a result of adequate physical facilities. It is intended to
reach not only principals and teachers who must use the facilities of the
school from day to day, but also parish or diocesan representatives who
may be responsible for important decisions in connection with the construction, operation, and maintenance of the school building. It seeks to
point out some of the important considerations in the way of teaching
opportunities, serviceability, and cost that should be observed, whenever a
new building is contemplated or an older structure is to be enlarged or
remodeled. Whenever a building project is under consideration, principals
and teachers should be in a position to make recommendations as to the
educational features to be provided. All concerned need to have a clear
understanding of the bearing that the physical accommodations should
have upon the learning of the children.

INTRODUCTION

The importance of physical environment in which children learn can
scarcely be overestimated. The educational program of today encompasses
far more than mere rote learning characteristic of the "little red schoolhouse"
of bygone days, to which some unthinking individuals would have us return.

---

* Professor of Education, Marquette University.

Those who would have us do so have little appreciation of the vast social changes that have occurred and with which the schools of the future must reckon.

In the days before the automobile, instruction in traffic safety, for example, offered no problem. Today it is a recognized responsibility of the school. Then, too, wide-open spaces provided ample play area and the subject of adequately sized playgrounds received little consideration in planning school buildings. The present-day distractions presented by commercial entertainment were largely absent. Life as a whole was relatively simple. We were largely a nation with the characteristics of a rural rather than an urban economy.

Personal, social, religious, and other character-building experiences were gained largely within the family circle and its immediate environment. Parents were concerned primarily with family responsibilities. Fewer fathers than now spent the day far from home, and mothers were rarely employed outside the home. As a result of the changes in family living, many of the values formerly offered by the home have been lost and the responsibilities thrust upon the school and the church. Children were sheltered both day and night. They were not supervised by a baby sitter, or, as often occurs now if a bit older, cast adrift with the price of admission in hand to some form of commercial entertainment, while the parents spend their leisure hours in recreational activities far from home. With this shortening of the work day, the school of today is expected to step into the breach by providing preparation for leisure for both children and adults.

With increasing realization of the importance of physical and mental health, the school again has been saddled with additional responsibilities. Adequate playgrounds, gymnasiums, periodic medical and dental examinations, and the control of communicable diseases are considered essential to the physical well-being of the child, for which the school should make provision. Methods of teaching are expected to be adjusted to the mental health needs of the child. This is an entirely new concept among the school's responsibilities which has developed within the past generation.

Present-day philosophy of education accepts a far greater responsibility for the rearing of the whole child than did the educational philosophy of "little-red-schoolhouse" days. It is concerned with his physical and mental health, his safety, his social, emotional, moral, and religious development, as well as his mastery of the so-called fundamentals. It is concerned with the development of his attitudes, his ideals, and his talents as a potential contributor to society.

The school today is vitally concerned with the child's development as a responsible citizen in our democracy. This, too, has resulted in changes in methods of teaching. The older authoritarian forms of control have been modified in many instances by the need for training in democratic procedures. Moreover, it is concerned with a longer period of schooling for the child. Society through legal enactments has extended the period of required school attendance to an age where dropouts before the completion of the eighth grade are becoming rare.

With the longer period of schooling has come an understanding of the wide differences among children. Where children of lesser ability often dropped from school before they had completed the fifth grade, they now are required to remain in school. This in turn has forced upon the elementary school the need for modifying its curriculum content and its methods of teaching.

This situation has provided additional stimulus to the greater development and use of audio-visual aids, since the slow learning child is known to profit greatly from their use. It has increased the need for books and library services. Present-day construction of school buildings calls for provisions for necessary installation to permit their use, servicing, and storage. Efforts to provide more adequately for individual differences have led also to the incorporation of industrial arts and home economics and greater emphasis upon fine arts in the upper elementary years, with accompanying equipment and space requirements. The more recent emphasis upon science is likewise having an impact upon building space, particularly in the form of storage requirements and space for experimental and observational activities.

In bygone days children learned much by doing outside of school. Many of the opportunities that then existed have disappeared with the development of cities, modern conveniences, and packaged goods. Developments in the field of the psychology of learning have had a marked impact upon methods of teaching. We realize more clearly, too, that learning involves more than mastery of a set of facts, valuable as they may be as isolated bits of information. If knowledge is to serve the individual, opportunities need to be provided for the child to apply the acquired facts in a functional way.

This has led to a greater emphasis upon activities which afford learning situations, both within the classroom and within the school. If activities are to be carried out properly, consideration must be given to space requirements. The modern kindergarten, in which much of the learning results from doing, affords a good illustration of need for more space than was considered necessary when kindergartens were first introduced. Crowded classrooms with practically all available space occupied by fixed seats are not conducive to activity teaching. Whether added space is allowed in planning each classroom, as is attempted in the so-called "self-contained classroom," or special areas within the building are designed for activity use, the result is a larger building than was formerly required for the same number of children. Like Daniel Boone, children need "elbow room," if they are to have opportunities to apply their factual learning, whether in arithmetic, the language arts, the social studies, the fine arts, or other areas.

A very important objective is to develop the ability to do reflective thinking with the facts in hand. The child needs experience in assembling facts, in analyzing them, and in evaluating and organizing them for their bearing upon problems and issues to be solved.

New schools today are concerned with the effect of the environment upon the child's attitude toward school and toward learning. The school building with an aesthetic appearance, both outwardly and inwardly, and in a rich setting for learning is more likely to appeal to the child as a place where he finds happiness and desires to be than does one with a drab and unattractive appearance.

The foregoing discussion of the impact of social changes and improved understanding of factors that condition learning, together with readjustments in our educational philosophy, should serve to impress the school planner that the most important consideration in planning a school building is the curriculum to be offered. The planner must also anticipate the possibility of future changes in curriculum offerings. A well-built school may be expected to serve the larger part of a century. During that period of time numerous changes are likely to occur both in what is taught and how it is taught. For this reason consideration should be given to the matter of flexibility. The internal structure should be designed so that changes can be made at minimum cost. In modern structures, bearing walls between classrooms are generally avoided, and service systems are installed with regard to the possibility of future changes.

DETERMINING THE NEED

Factors which lead to the construction of new schools are: (1) overcrowding of present schools; (2) parishes now without schools; (3) obsolescence; and (4) destruction by fire or other causes. No new schools should be undertaken without a careful study of the surrounding conditions likely to affect the number of children to be accommodated. Long-range planning is essential to orderly schoolhouse construction. Parishes and dioceses as well as public schools should be looking ahead to their possible needs several years in advance.

Among matters to be observed over a period of years are population, school census and birth-rate trends, and land-usage studies. A census of Catholic homes and Catholic children to be served should be made and reviewed at intervals of two to five years, to note trends. Should the rate of increase continue, what will be the probable number of children to be accommodated at a given date in the future?

Studies of land usage within a parish will serve as a further guide to the probable number of children to be served in the future. How much of the territory is already built up? What are the zoning regulations? What areas are available for residential development in terms of single and multi-family units?

Other items of information needed are conditions in neighboring parochial and public schools. What plans do they have for the future? To what extent are they overcrowded or not filled? What are the possibilities of assigning some of the children to a neighboring parish? Could certain grades, such as a kindergarten or a primary grade, be sent to an adjoining public school without endangering the religious instruction of the children? In the city of Milwaukee, for example, few parish schools operate kindergartens, with the result that parents of children of this age send them to a neighboring public school until they are ready to enter the first grade. This results in a substantial reduction in the total cost of a new building.

Another important bit of information needed is the number of elementary school children of each age group to be accommodated. If a given residential area is populated largely by young families with several children not yet in school or in the lower grades, there is grave danger that the picture of need may become distorted. While the school may be overcrowded, we must remember that in the normal course of events many children will have completed their stay in the elementary school and have moved on to high school. As families mature and remain residents of the parish, there will be fewer elementary school children to be housed from a given number of families. It is advisable, therefore, to distinguish between the probable maximum, or "peak," enrollment to be housed and the normal or stabilized load to be expected. In the event of a substantial difference between the anticipated "peak" load and the expected, stabilized load the size of the permanent building should be modified accordingly. In such cases the preferred practice is to build the permanent structure of sufficient size to house the stabilized load and to provide for the excess in "peak" load times through temporary structures.

SITE SELECTION

The site chosen for a school will have an important bearing upon the functioning of the school and upon public relations. Ideally it should meet several criteria. Among these are: (1) central location; (2) accessiblity without requiring children to travel long distances or to make long detours because of lakes, rivers, rail lines, heavily traveled highways, deep ravines or mountainous hills to be crossed; (3) freedom from objectionable surroundings; (4) soil well drained and its condition suitable for placing a building without settling or requiring expensive excavation because of rock outcropping; (5) scenic surroundings, or affording a beautiful outlook; (6) adjoining or near a park or recreational area; (7) size adequate for future as well as immediate needs; (8) price reasonable; and (9) satisfactory to the parish members and to church authorities. Proximity to the parish church, present or future, is a vital consideration, for obvious reasons.

It is seldom if ever that a site satisfies all of the criteria, particularly if it is intended for enlarging a site adjoining an older parish church, or if the selection was delayed until the decision to begin the erection of a school was reached. Whenever possible the site should be selected by those responsible, in accordance with a long-range plan for the territory, and several years in advance of actual construction. If site selection is delayed, choice parcels are likely to be sold for other purposes, or will prove much more expensive.

THE TYPE OF BUILDING

Such matters as the general type of building, the number of stories, its general shape and its location on the site will need to be decided in consultation with the architect, after weighing the factors involved. Architects commonly furnish their clients with a preliminary sketch of the building, in order that the latter may have a better understanding of the proposed appearance of the building when completed.

Whether to build a single or a multistory structure should be decided upon the basis of a number of factors. These include appearance, safety, impact upon play areas, ease of administration, plant operation and maintenance, and cost. Recent trends are strongly in favor of single story buildings, but these require larger sites. The factor of fire or earthquake safety in buildings of two or more stories as compared with single story buildings is in the favor of the latter. A widely spread single story building sometimes presents a somewhat larger problem of administration and supervision, and may present heating difficulties in extremely cold weather. Single story buildings are not necessarily more costly, on a square foot or cubic foot basis, for the reason that footings and walls may be of lighter construction than when bearing the weight of additional stories. The single story building has the advantage of affording greater use of daylight lighting through the admission of natural light from the ceiling. It permits greater flexibility in classroom shape because the distance from windowed walls is no longer a controlling factor in room depth.

WHAT TO INCLUDE IN THE ELEMENTARY SCHOOL BUILDING

CLASSROOMS

The first consideration in deciding what to include in an elementary school is the number of classrooms needed to house the expected enrollment. A decision will need to be made as to the size of classes desired. While research evidence as to the most desirable size of class is not conclusive, perhaps the most commonly accepted practice is approximately 35. Teachers can do a better job of providing for individual differences with small numbers. However desirable small classes may be, few schools can afford to have small classes, because of the additional cost involved both in construction and in teacher salaries.

Before specifying the size of classrooms to be provided, consideration should be given to the teaching procedures to be followed, and as to whether all teaching is to be done within the classroom or whether special rooms shall be provided for instruction in such subjects as art, music, industrial arts, home economics, and science. As indicated earlier, present-day methods include a variety of activities for which some additional space is needed. An alcove at the rear or side of the room, for work projects requiring more floor or table space than is afforded by the individual pupil desk, will usually prove sufficient. If movable desks or tables are used rather than fixed seats, the entire room may be used at times for group and special activities. Flexibility within the classroom adds greatly to ways in which floor space may be used.

Display Facilities

Modern classrooms have less chalkboard and more bulletin board space than classrooms of earlier days. This is due to changes in methods of teaching. Teachers have fewer occasions to send large numbers of children to the board at a time; they make much more use of illustrative materials. One-half inch cork strips with sliding hooks over chalkboards for attaching charts and maps or other materials, a recessed metal picture molding, and exhibit cases for displaying pupil materials are keenly appreciated by most teachers. A cork board surface above the chalkboard and extending the length of the chalkboard is sometimes provided, but should not be used on walls on which paintings are to be hung. A section of pegboard, or a combination bulletin and pegboard, is another desirable piece of display equipment.

Furniture and Equipment

Ample provision should be made for filing and storage of materials needed by pupils and teachers. These materials include such items as books, magazines, clippings, charts, collections of specimens, maps, papers of various kinds, pictures, and other visual aid materials. Working surfaces in the form of shelves and tables where children may plan and work while using these materials are very desirable. Tables for reading and group activities, and for demonstrations, as in science or other areas, are very much needed.

Storage space requirements in classrooms depend somewhat upon the central storage provisions of the building, and the ease with which materials desired for use at a given time may be obtained. To provide storage space in classrooms for materials rarely used is expensive and wasteful.

Storage cases or cupboards may be built in or movable. Present practice favors movable units in modular lengths of approximately four feet, thus making them readily interchangeable. They should be durable but of lightweight construction. In some cases, as in primary grades, they are put on rollers and made to fit into wall niches not occupied by heating units or under window-high shelves, when not needed elsewhere in the room.

Shelving in cases or cupboards should be adjustable. Filing cases for the teachers should be movable and of standard dimensions. Many prefer a desk-high filing case which can be placed alongside the teacher's desk. Space is needed also for storing the teachers' wraps, especially if lay teachers are employed. The need for storing small items of play equipment, such as balls and bats, should not be overlooked. All furniture finishes should be nongloss and light.

In addition to a standard teacher's desk, most teachers will have use for an additional table. A reading table of suitable height is highly desirable in primary grades. Self-contained classrooms in which activity programs are followed should have available one or more workbenches and tools.

Classroom Seating

Seating in modern classrooms is movable, in order to lend flexibility and thus facilitate the use of the room for various types of activities. Movable seating, whether of the table and chair or combination desk and seat type, makes any desired rearrangement possible within a few moments. Varied sizes are preferable to adjustable seats, for several reasons. In practice adjustments are seldom made. If made frequently, the life span of the seat is likely to be reduced. Besides, they cost more. Care should be exercised to choose seats that are not only comfortable but contribute to posture and are well constructed. Bids should be taken in such a way as to permit the selection of the best seat for the purpose, even though the cost per unit may be somewhat higher. So-called "cheap" sets are likely to prove very expensive when length of service is considered. The colors should be light and the finish dull to prevent glare. Sizes of seats and tables required for children of various heights are provided by reputable manufacturers and dealers.

KINDERGARTENS

Unless children of kindergarten age attend public schools, rooms designed for the purpose should be included in parochial schools. The number required will depend upon the relationship of the expected kindergarten enrollment to the school's total enrollment, the ages of the children to be admitted, and whether the children will attend all day or only one-half days as customary. In a normal six grade school of 350 pupils, one kindergarten room will be sufficient, if the kindergarten is limited to one year and children attend only half days.

A modern kindergarten should have a minimum of 1000 square feet of floor area exclusive of facilities for storage provision for wraps and space for toilet rooms, of which there should be one for boys and one for girls.

Storage space is needed to accommodate the types of supplies used, which often include oversized papers and paper on a large roller. An enclosure of approximately 40 square feet in area with a Dutch-door opening and adjustable shelving with cupboards below will be sufficient. Wall cupboards, at window-ledge height and movable, are desirable for materials in daily use by the children. Teachers usually desire a wall chalkboard not less than 10 ft. long, with the remaining wall space up to the top of the chalkboard covered with display boards, often divided between cork and pegboard. Where wall surface permits, a section of cork board extended to within a short distance of the floor is desirable.

CLOTHING STORAGE

Various means have been used for storing pupils' wraps, including corridor recesses, corridor lockers, separate cloakrooms, wardrobes within the classroom, movable and fixed coat racks, and others. Factors to be considered include such matters as safety, cleanliness, convenience, control, cost, space utilization, and ages of the children. Present trends in a number of communities is in the direction of corridor recesses, with hook strips and a hat and bookshelf above, especially for rooms above the kindergarten and primary grades. Where theft is not a problem such recessed storage has proved very satisfactory, and avoids not only the cost of lockers but the noise element of slamming doors. Wardrobes inside the classroom have several disadvantages, especially in northern climates where winter snows are carried in on overshoes and melt on the classroom floor. Perhaps a more serious objection is the fact that inside wardrobes of whatever type take up valuable wall space needed for chalkboards, bulletin boards, and materials cases. Where efforts have been made to fasten bulletin or chalkboards to the front of the wardrobe the results have often been unsatisfactory. Cloakrooms at the end of classrooms, common at one time, are expensive in terms of space use, but are still often provided for the little children of kindergarten and primary levels.

CENTERS FOR SPECIAL SUBJECTS AND CLASSES

In eight-grade elementary schools, industrial arts and home economics are frequently taught to seventh- and eighth-grade classes, as is done in junior high schools. These subjects require much specialized equipment and storage space with rooms especially designed for the purpose. The number enrolled in these subjects and grades in one school is seldom sufficient to warrant a special room for each of these activities. Unless the rooms are made to serve children from other schools, in addition to their own, they will be occupied only a few periods per week. If necessary administrative arrangements are made, one school in an area can be made to serve as a center for instruction in either of these subjects. Such an arrangement has long been in operation in Milwaukee, where pupils from parochial schools spend a few hours each week in a public school industrial arts or home-economics center. This avoids the necessity of providing special rooms for these activities.

Most schools are faced with the problem of providing for handicapped children. The handicapped occur in a variety of forms: physical, mental, emotional, and social. To the extent that their needs cannot be adequately met in the regular classroom, special facilities will often be needed. Since the number of those in any one school attendance area having a particular handicap is small, good practice favors the establishment of centers for the different types of handicapped children. The deaf and hard of hearing may be transported to one center equipped with audio aids of various kinds and staffed with teachers schooled in the education of the deaf and near deaf. The number in such classes is usually less than ten and may be adequately quartered in a room of approximately one half the size of a classroom. Another center may be organized to accommodate the mentally handicapped. The aim is usually to have a sufficient number in a fairly narrow range of mental ages to make some forms of group instruction possible. Such classes seldom exceed 15 to 20 in number. Special equipment for carrying on handicraft activities will be necessary unless provided elsewhere in the building. Furniture adapted to the sizes of the children and adequate storage space for the wide range of materials used by such classes is essential. For a more complete treatment of provisions for the handicapped the reader is referred to a publication of the National Council on Schoolhouse Construction, *Elementary School Plant Planning*.

THE LIBRARY

A library is deemed an essential in a modern school and is preferable to sizable individual classroom libraries. It should be centrally located and should serve not only for books and other printed materials, but also as a source of visual-aid materials. A small room adjoining the library is desirable for storage of maps and projection equipment. The library should not be less than one classroom in size. In some cases the room is designed so that it may be used as an emergency classroom.

Library shelving should be adjustable to accommodate books of different sizes. A magazine rack and a small bulletin board add to the usefulness of the library. Cupboard space for books and magazines awaiting rebinding, standard filing drawers for miscellaneous materials and pictures, and a small card file should be provided. Seating facilities should provide accommodations for group conferences as well as for class instruction. A sink and a small work space are highly desirable. Electrical outlets for audio-visual use are essential. A storage room for surplus texts and sets of supplementary books out of use should be provided elsewhere in the building but should not occupy more valuable space in the library.

LARGE GROUP ROOMS

In designing an elementary school the educator and the architect are faced with the problem of providing space for activities requiring more than a classroom. Such activities as physical education and recreation, lunch service, and those involving large audiences require more space.

The number of such rooms required and their sizes will depend upon the program to be offered, the anticipated enrollment of the school, and the expected attendance at various functions. Present trends are in favor of maximum use of such spaces. Whenever possible such rooms are made to serve several purposes.

To provide separate rooms for auditorium activities, physical education, and lunch service is costly if the areas are used only a few hours during the day or the week. For this reason, school planners often endeavor to have such rooms serve several purposes. In schools of 500 or less one room designed for many possible uses is frequently provided. The floor in such cases is necessarily level, with either a portable or a permanent stage, a kitchen alcove, and storage space for equipment. In small schools a room

40 by 80 feet, exclusive of a kitchen alcove and storage space, is usually sufficient. This will provide a playing or seating floor approximately 60 feet in length with the remainder for a permanent stage if desired. If it is planned to use a temporary stage the total length may be reduced. In a larger school the width may be increased.

If a permanent stage is provided it should be raised 36 to 38 inches above its floor level to permit proper viewing by the audiences. This will also permit storage of seats underneath whenever the main floor must be cleared.

Curtains and drapes for elementary schools are usually simple and mounted on tracks to facilitate arranging or drawing. As a safety precaution they should be flame-treated. Provision for overhead flood lighting, for spot lighting, and signaling should be made. A suspended screen for picture showing is essential.

To minimize the cost in small schools, a portable stage with riser approaches is sometimes used, the several sections of which may be folded. Storage space will be needed not only for stage parts but for chairs and other portable equipment. Suspended curtains need to be so installed that they may be pulled aside when not in use.

THE ASSEMBLY ROOM OR AUDITORIUM

A practice common in large elementary schools is to provide a separate assembly room or auditorium with a sloping floor, and in such cases fixed seats. Present practice appears to favor a room having a maximum capacity of 300–400. Experience has indicated that only on rare occasions is a larger auditorium in an elementary school filled to capacity. Moreover it is seldom that an elementary school program provides suitable listening or viewing material for all grades. Provisions for silent and sound projection are essential. The location of the room on the ground floor should be such as to provide easy access from a corridor or exit into a corridor or the outside, without the necessity of a special foyer. The number, location, and size of exit doors is usually prescribed by state or local codes.

In deciding whether to rely upon a many-purpose room, or to provide more than one room to meet the purposes mentioned above, consideration should be given to the probable schedule requirements of each, particularly during the winter season in northern climates, when activities in physical education are conducted largely indoors. If the facilities are to be used for evening adult activities of different kinds, care in dovetailing schedules will be necessary.

MULTIPURPOSE ROOMS

In the absence of a relatively large room serving several purposes, as already discussed, or to supplement it, some schools include a smaller multipurpose room which serves to accommodate smaller group activities requiring more than a classroom. Such a room may serve as an indoor playroom, an auxiliary gymnasium, for dramatic presentations, as a meeting room for parents, or for other all-school purposes. If two or more classrooms in unit size, it may be subdivided in emergencies and used for classroom purposes.

If a multifold type of partition and movable furniture are used, with adequate provision for storage, such a room can serve for evening events, even though used for classroom purposes during the day. If funds for a larger multipurpose room as described above are lacking, or the school's enrollment is relatively small, the smaller multipurpose room may be made to serve various purposes, until larger quarters of this type are required and means of financing can be found.

PHYSICAL EDUCATION FACILITIES

A room 40 by 60 and having a ceiling height of 16 to 20 feet will be adequate for most indoor physical education activities conducted in a six-grade elementary school housing 600 or less. If the school is a relatively large one and includes seventh and eighth grade pupils, a room large enough to be divided into separate sections for boys and girls should be considered. In this case, or if it is to be used for gymnasium activities for evening adult groups, showers and dressing room facilities are desirable. Both sections may be used simultaneously by lower grade classes.

LUNCHROOM USE

In a several-purpose room the size and arrangement of the kitchen alcove for lunchroom use will depend not only upon the children to be served but also upon other factors. The architect should be informed as to whether it is intended also for adult use, and whether or not the food is to be prepared at the school or brought in from an outside or central kitchen serving several schools. In either event, provision should be made for receiving and for storing certain foods, even if only on a temporary basis. If the food is prepared at the school, refrigeration as well as equipment for food processing, cooking, dish washing, and dish storage will be needed. Provision should also be made for a cool room for vegetable storage. If food is prepared outside of the school there will still be need for keeping food warm, refrigeration, dish washing, and dish storage. In planning this portion of the building the advice of a person experienced in food service is indispensable.

The seating of a lunchroom that is used for physical activities presents a problem in making it ready for immediate use after the lunch period.

For this reason many schools are equipped with tables and attached chairs or benches that fold into the wall. In other cases collapsible tables that may be speedily wheeled away by the custodian may be used. Unless otherwise conveniently near, lavatory and clothing change facilities should be installed for lunchroom employees. Hand washing and drinking facilities for children should be conveniently located with reference to the lunchroom.

HEALTH SUITE

A health suite, where the school doctor and nurse or the school dentist can function properly and for pupils who become ill, is an essential. A room approximately 22 to 24 feet in length and 18 to 20 feet in width is considered adequate by some health authorities. A 20 foot length is desired for eye testing in preference to the use of expensive equipment required for shorter distances. There should be a sink with an ordinary nonspring faucet. A section of approximately 100 square feet should be designed as a rest room, with space for cots which may be removed when the room is desired for clinical examinations as often occurs at certain seasons. The suite should be equipped with a toilet, a built-in medicine cabinet, and a number of electrical outlets. The suite should be located in a quiet section, preferably adjoining the office suite or nearby. In planning a health suite school officials will find it advisable to consult local health authorities before directing the architect to design the suite.

THE OFFICE SUITE

The office suite should be located near the main entrance. Persons having business at the school can then approach the principal's office without disturbing school activities in other parts of the building. Teachers, too, find it convenient for picking up keys and mail or filing reports upon entering or leaving the building. The over-all space requirements of a satisfactory suite in an elementary school of ordinary size will approximate one classroom, exclusive of health and special service facilities. Minimum needs include: an inner office for the principal with lavatory and cloak storage space; a clerk's office and work space; a public waiting room; and a supply storage room. The waiting room should be separated from the clerk's room by an information counter with standard record filing and storage space beneath. A key rack, a bulletin board, and mailboxes for teachers are other essentials. There should be space for duplicating materials and equipment in the space allotted to the clerk, or nearby.

Adjoining the office or nearby, there should be a small room for conferences or use by attendance, supervisory, welfare, or other staff personnel serving the school on a part-time basis.

The principal's office should be accessible from the waiting room and the clerk's office and should have an exit door leading directly to the corridor. Entrance doors should have the upper portion of mottled glass, preferably with a narrow vision strip centered or along the edges.

CORRIDORS, ENTRANCES, EXITS, AND STAIRWAYS

Minimum requirements in the number and sizes of corridors, entrances, exits, and stairways are commonly regulated by code, as are maximum distances that children may be expected to travel to reach an exit. Exit doors are invariably equipped with release bars, and often marked by a red exit light. These are matters of safety to be observed strictly. Rigid rules prohibiting anyone from locking exits so that children cannot open them by pressing upon the door bar should be rigidly enforced. Exits should be free of all obstructions and pockets. At least one exit should open directly onto the playground.

Unless carefully planned, corridors and stairways can be a source of waste in construction and may lead to traffic congestion. In climates requiring enclosed corridors, they should be double loaded; i.e., with rooms on both sides. In a well-planned building, not more than 20 per cent of the total floor area is occupied by stairways and corridors.

Main corridors in elementary schools are usually 10 to 12 feet wide, while secondary corridors are commonly 8 to 10 feet wide, depending somewhat upon whether clothing is stored in the corridor or not. Corridor walls of cement block, glazed brick, or of glazed tile to a height of approximately six feet require little maintenance. Colors should be light, and adequate lighting, either artificial or natural, should be provided. Corridors should be equipped with bulletin boards and lighted exhibit cases, flush with the wall and located at convenient places. Locker spaces should be ventilated.

Large foyer type entrances, often desired by architects, are wasteful of space and serve little useful purpose other than decorative. If entrances are located in line with corridor intersections there should be little occasion for a lobby.

STAIRWAYS

Every stairway should lead directly to an exit. There should be no stair wells or winding stairs. Waste space is frequently to be seen in open spaces between stairway sections. Stair treads should not be less than 10 inches wide, and risers not more than 6½ inches high. Stairways from one floor to the next should be in two sections or runs and should have a width of 44 to 48 inches as a minimum. All surfaces should be nonslip and of very hard, wear-resistant material. To facilitate cleaning, the edges or surfaces where treads and risers meet should be curved. If ramps are used the pitch should not exceed one in ten and the surface should be slightly abrasive to prevent slipping. Guard rails should be provided on stairways where any danger exists that pupils may fall or be pushed over. Ends of handrails should be turned into and secured to the wall. Fire codes frequently require that stairways be enclosed with fire doors and fire resistive walls and ceilings. Glass openings must be of wire-glass in metal frames.

DRINKING, WASHING, AND TOILET FACILITIES

It is highly desirable that an adequate number of corridor drinking fountains be provided at heights suitable to the children who use them, to avoid long waiting lines in warm weather. If bubblers are provided in individual rooms the number in corridors may be reduced. Current practice favors a sink within each classroom as a source of water supply and for hand washing or cleaning purposes. The floor area around the sink should be of material not easily damaged by drip water.

Separate toilets for each classroom, recommended by some, are more easily supervised than general toilets, but do not eliminate the need for general toilets required in connection with after-school and summer playground and adult use. Classroom lavatories tend to be expensive in space consumption, as well as cost, and do not always work out satisfactorily.

OUTDOOR PHYSICAL EDUCATION AND RECREATION FACILITIES

As indicated under the treatment of sites, efforts should be made to secure a site large enough to meet all needs for play areas, both present and future. Separate areas should be designated for use by various age groups. Separate areas should also be provided for boys and girls, particularly above the primary grades. A school location adjoining a park is much to be desired because of the many opportunities for outdoor activities.

In general, playground areas should be hard surfaced in most climates. Dust, sand, or mud are highly undesirable from the standpoint of health and cleanliness. Hard topped surfaces, as well as any other form of surface, should be kept free of stones and bits of glass or metal. The area should be well drained and free from pockets where water may accumulate and freeze as in northern climates.

Differences of view prevail with reference to playground apparatus, for safety and sanitary reasons, and also because of the limiting effect on the uses to which the area occupied by fixed apparatus can be put. Climbing apparatus such as "jungle gyms" and other pieces that expose children to the danger of falling most often meet with objection. Such pieces of apparatus as horizontal bars, ladders, swings, and slides are considered less dangerous. Because of the problems of sanitation involved, sandboxes are frowned upon.

SPACE CONDITIONING

LIGHTING

Two rather widely differing practices prevail with reference to lighting. One makes use of large glass areas in classrooms and corridor walls to admit a maximum of daylight. In single story buildings, top, or dome, lighting is also used. In such cases steps are usually taken to prevent direct sunlight from striking the children. This is accomplished by such means as jib wall projections, baffles, overhangs, louvers, and tinted glass, or through the use of ordinary shades. To provide for audio-visual aid use, darkening shades of some form are also provided.

Those who favor the other practice of lighting would make greater use of artificial lighting with often only a vision strip for admitting daylight into the classroom. They find it easier to provide for picture projection. Ceilings can be lower but electrical consumption will be higher. Those contemplating a new school should plan to visit a number of modern schools of each type before final plans are developed.

Plans for modern school lighting center around the concept of brightness balance, which has as its objective comfortable lighting of adequate intensity. Lighting comfort increases as the brightness in the field surrounding the visual task approaches the brightness of the task, regardless of the type of activity in which the pupil is engaged. Adults are aware of the discomfort that occurs when reading directly under an intense light, while the surrounding surface darkens rapidly as they move from the center of the light cone. This occurs with certain types of lamp shades. Present practice favors a condition wherein the surrounding field is not less than one-third as bright as the task. Similarly, the adjoining surfaces should not be excessively brighter than that of the task. When these conditions are met, either by daylight or electric lighting, there should be little discomfort or glare. In general, comfort considerations should receive preference over high intensity.

Lighting systems should be designed to supplement day lighting and to provide adequate lighting for night use. To afford lighting comfort under varying conditions of daylight, some form of shading, as already indicated, is needed to reduce both direct and reflected sunlight. Light, even from north exposures, may be discomforting if reflected from white cumulus clouds.

For classroom purposes today, fluorescent lighting is more often installed in preference to incandescent lighting. In spaces not requiring high intensities, the latter type is probably in more common use. In modern construction lighting fixtures are frequently embedded in or flush with the ceiling, or shielded in "egg crates" or by baffles running crosswise of the room. This tends to prevent light shining directly into the eyes of pupils and also to increase eye comfort by reducing brightness differences between the light source and the surrounding field. White ceilings are favored above others because they aid in diffusing the light and in reducing brightness differences.

In many older classrooms originally equipped with incandescent lighting, fluorescent lights are now being installed. This can usually be done without increasing the load carrying potential of the original wiring. Current consumption in fluorescent lighting is usually less, but tube replacements are more expensive than light bulb replacements. Because of the expense involved in converting from incandescent to fluorescent lighting, it may be necessary to change only a few rooms at a time. If so, a list of priorities should be established. Lighting may often be greatly improved by washing or repainting ceilings and walls and by prompt replacement of worn bulbs and tubes.

HEATING AND VENTILATING

The purpose of any heating and ventilating system, as is also true of any cooling system, is to provide body comfort. To be comfortable our bodies require that the air in which we live not only be within certain temperature limits, but that it have the proper humidity and rate of movement. A room temperature of 70–72 degrees may be comfortable or uncomfortable, depending upon the relative humidity and the rate of air movement. Thermostatic controls are usually set at constant temperatures and necessary adjustments are made to maintain the proper humidity and rate of air flow. Air movement during the heating season should not be less than 5 feet per minute and not more than 20 feet during the cooling season. To operate the heating and ventilating system in such a way as to provide the proper combination of these factors is the problem of the school engineer, who should receive the benefit of whatever instruction is needed.

In conditioning air for school use, provision for dust removal is necessary for health reasons. Three methods are commonly employed. These are: filtering, used especially in unit ventilators, spray washing, and electric precipitation. Fresh air intakes should be located at points least likely to contribute to air pollution or to be affected by strong prevailing winds.

Heating and ventilating systems in schools range from simple stoves with window ventilation to modern combination heating and ventilating units in each classroom. Systems include heating by transmitting warm air, hot water or steam radiation, and combinations of these. Warm air systems vary from those which depend solely upon a jacketed furnace and gravity for air movement, as found in small schools of an older generation, to much more elaborate systems with a central fan and individual ducts for delivering clean, tempered air to each room. In some buildings the air, or a part of it, is recirculated as a means of saving fuel.

Older schools are frequently equipped with a dual or split system, using both warm air and some form of radiation. Either hot water or steam may be used to provide heat for radiation, but general practice appears to favor hot water, which may be furnished through low pressure boilers. Radiation may be from the familiar type of radiator placed under windows and elsewhere, heating pipes along the wall or embedded in the floor or ceiling, and the combination heating and ventilating units.

In dual systems, heat supplied by radiation is used to provide the initial heating of the space, as in the early morning. The fans supplying tempered air are not turned on until shortly before occupancy and then for both ventilating and heating purposes. In extremely cold weather both parts of the dual system may operate throughout the day. Fans are usually stopped soon after the day's activities cease. They are turned on occasionally during the heat of the summer for purposes of drying and removing odors.

Necessary outlays for heating and ventilating vary with climatic conditions. Schools in northern climates must expect to spend more for these purposes than those in milder climates. Initial outlays are affected also by available fuels. Schools in regions where natural gas is plentiful may need to spend relatively little on heating plants. This is also true of schools heated by oil or electricity. The type of fuel chosen will often depend upon the ultimate cost of one, as compared with others, over a period of years, as well as the assured availability of the fuel used. Gas, oil, and electric firing methods require less space for installation and less labor than does coal but are not necessarily cheaper. Ultimately the cost will depend upon the relative cost of the different fuels. Whatever the type of heating employed, it should be adequate to meet the needs of comfort in extremes of weather.

HEATING ECONOMIES

Proper operation and maintenance are highly important to heating economy, whatever the system used. A small investment in published material on the subject for use by school engineers or janitors may yield large returns, not only in heating economies, but in helping them to keep the heating plant in first class condition. Heating economies depend upon the condition of the heating plant and its operation, the quality of the fuel used, and the construction and condition of the building itself.

Heat loss from buildings varies with the materials used in its construction. In buildings with large glass wall areas losses are greater in cold weather and heat absorption is greater in warm weather than in other types of construction. Losses and gains are larger in buildings with longer perimeters per total volume than in more compact buildings. Buildings without well insulated basements or attic ceilings and roofs suffer greater heat losses in cold weather than those which are properly insulated. Some maintain that heat loss by the structure itself may be responsible, in some cases, for as much as 20 per cent of the total heat requirements. A substantial saving in fuel as well as an increase in comfort can often be brought about in old buildings by the simple expedient of calking and weather stripping windows and exit doors or insulating attic spaces.

Among causes of heat waste other than from leakage are: imperfect combustion of the fuel, loss by radiation from noninsulated flues and piping or from the boiler or the furnace itself. Excessive building temperatures either while school is in session or at other times is another cause. Poor combustion in the furnace may be due to various causes, including insufficient air, a poor mixture of air and gases, too low furnace temperature, and insufficient time for proper combustion.

Whether coal, gas, or oil is used as fuel, purchases should be made on the basis of standard specifications. Suggested standards are frequently available from governmental purchasing agencies. Some grades of coal, for example, contain excessive amounts of noncombustible material and water. Shale costs money but produces no appreciable heat. Iron pyrite (a yellow mineral), if present, may lead to spontaneous combustion in coalbins. The latter should be frequently checked. When the season's coal is delivered, a sample should be taken from each truckload for testing. Failure to receive a proper return on coal purchases may be the result of poor coal or faulty methods of firing. Boiler tubes need to be cleaned weekly to remove accumulated soot, which acts as an insulating substance. Boilers need also to be inspected periodically for safety reasons. No person should be permitted to operate a heating plant without having been properly schooled in methods of operation and care.

Another important factor in heating economy and comfort is the use of automatic devices for controlling room temperatures. These can be set at any given temperature desired for day or night. Temperature may be controlled by zones or by individual rooms. This is particularly desirable for evening use when only a few rooms or the assembly hall may be occupied, or for administrative offices during winter vacation periods.

SOUND CONTROL

Great strides have been made in the past few decades in reduction of objectionable noises through the use of materials on ceiling and wall especially prepared to absorb excessive sound. All are familiar with the effect that annoying and distracting sounds have upon the comfort of the learner, especially because of the difficulty of hearing what is being said. The problem is one of controlling undesirable sounds and amplifying the desirable ones.

In planning a new school the site should be chosen with the thought of placing the school at a suitable distance from objectionable noise producing activities, as in the case of heavily traveled roads or streets. Within the building, consideration should be given to the location of rooms designed to house loud, noise-producing activities. While the sound volume emanating from these activities may be reduced through proper acoustical treatment, they should not be located near the library, or regular classrooms and spaces to be used for consultation, counseling, interviewing or testing. Corridors, lunchrooms, auditoriums, and gymnasiums, as well as heating and ventilating flues and machines whose noises are frequently transmitted to other parts of the building, should receive special consideration in the matter of noise control. Classrooms, too, especially in old buildings, frequently need treatment to reduce undesirable sound reverberation and to facilitate hearing.

Sound reverberation most often occurs when walls, floors, and ceilings are not only hard surfaced but are parallel or perpendicular to one another. Sound waves are reflected from one of two parallel surfaces to the other. In modern construction of an auditorium, for example, the sidewalls not only taper inward from the rear to the front, but often are designed to have rounded sections rather than continuous parallel flat walls. Ceilings not only slope but may be shaped as a series of waves. Curving surfaces cause some waves to be deflected instead of traveling back and forth as they do between parallel surfaces. Drapes, carpets, cork and linoleum materials absorb sound waves and thus serve to reduce reverberation.

Many elementary schools are now equipped with sound amplification facilities. Sound amplification of assembly or auditorium programs is highly desirable. If proper wiring is installed and speakers provided, radio programs may be brought into classrooms from the outside, or broadcast from the school office or studio. Announcements to all rooms may be made simultaneously. Wiring for possible reception of television programs is also highly desirable. In constructing new schools, some necessary conduits may be installed immediately for future televising of programs originating in the school.

MINIMIZING OPERATION AND MAINTENANCE COSTS

The term *operation* as applied to a school building refers to custodial services, such as are involved in cleaning and heating the building, regulating temperatures and humidity, checking water and light service, and all the materials consumed in connection therewith. Fuel, electricity, and water used represent operating charges.

The term *maintenance* commonly refers to those activities, including the materials used, that are designed to restore a structure or its equipment to a satisfactory condition, or to prevent further deterioration. It commonly refers to repairs such as replacing a broken window or installing new grates in a furnace. The term is sometimes used in connection with minor improvements, such as replacing a worn piece of equipment with one that is superior to the original.

The need for maintenance expenditures may arise from several causes. One of these is careless or incompetent operation of the plant, as in the case of a boiler ruined for lack of water. More frequently maintenance needs result from the action of the elements — rain, hail, freezing, and wind. Others may result from fire, overheating, smoke, shrinkage of improperly cured timbers, rotting, and settling. Still others result from the action of termites and rodents. Ordinary wear and tear and rough usage are other contributors to maintenance needs. Very often heating and ventilating, lighting, or plumbing facilities were designed years ago, when standards of performance were much lower. To bring these services up to present-day standards may require sizable expenditures. The task of the designer, the builder, the administrator, and the service personnel is to perform their respective functions in such ways as to minimize expenditures for maintenance. The job of the maintenance crew is to forestall the need for major repairs and to overcome the effects of damages as promptly as possible.

The need for repairs or replacements at any given time depends very much upon the quality of the materials used in the original construction, the care with which the specifications were written, the quality of the workmanship, and the care since received. If high standards were lacking, either in materials or services performed, any seeming economies to be gained from the use of "cheap" materials are likely to be lost, because of resulting higher maintenance costs.

Maintenance costs can often be kept relatively low not only by using durable materials in the original construction but also by making repairs promptly, as in the case of roof leaks, cracks in plaster or walls, and deterioration of mortar between bricks. Metal and wood surfaces in need of paint should receive immediate care. Holes or cuttings made in walls or elsewhere for admitting service lines should be promptly rectified.

Use of a very hard and washable type of plaster on stairway walls or below the wainscot in classrooms and corridors will reduce maintenance costs. In new structures glazed tile is often used along stairways, and brick or tile in corridors and entrances to a height of six feet or more. Tile wainscots are sometimes used in classrooms. Tile finish is preferred on locker and shower room walls and in toilet rooms. In recent years concrete block construction has often been used, particularly in corridor and classroom walls, or other places where moisture absorption is not a problem. It is less expensive than some other kinds of wall construction but requires painting for good appearance.

FLOORS AND FLOOR MAINTENANCE

Among materials used today in floors, in addition to wood, are asphalt, ceramic, rubber, and vinyl tiles; concrete; cork; linoleum; and terrazzo. Each has certain merits. In fire resistant buildings these materials are commonly laid over a cement base. Present trends are strongly in favor of tiles in classrooms, with linoleum, rubber, or cork preferred in libraries, and terrazzo, tile, linoleum, or concrete in corridors. For long service, resilience, and appearance no type of classroom flooring has proved more satisfactory over the years than maple flooring when properly laid and cared for. For best results it requires cleaning, sealing, waxing, and buffing. Water should be used sparingly. Occasionally a wood floor may require sanding but, if not abused, this should not be necessary more frequently than at 10 to 15 year intervals. Oil on wood floors should be avoided from the standpoint of safety, sanitation, appearance, and light absorption.

A substantial saving in floor maintenance can be made if floors are properly treated from the outset. Correcting past mistakes is time-consuming and expensive. Certain precautions should be observed. A new or a newly sanded wood floor should be cleaned without water, then sealed, buffed and a second coat of seal applied. The floor is then ready for waxing, but wax should never be applied before sealing. The use of cleaning and soap powders should be avoided. Instead, a neutral liquid cleaner should be used. This applies not only to wood but to all types of floors.

Cork and linoleum floors are resilient, and with proper care require little maintenance. Water should be used sparingly and surfaces should be waxed after cleaning, but solvent or spirit waxes should be avoided.

Present trends strongly favor the use of vinyl tile because of its high durability. The cost varies with the percentage of vinyl used in connection with other materials. Vinyl is more resistant to greases and abrasives than other tiles. Asphalt tile serves best if combined with vinyl, which adds flexibility and durability. Rubber tile, while highly resilient, requires careful treatment. Soaps of all kinds are injurious to rubber as are oils and greases. For this reason rubber tile should not be used in kitchens. Cleaners and polishes containing these ingredients as well as solvent waxes should be avoided. Water wax may be used and buffed with a fine grade of steel wool to preserve appearance. Mild abrasives should be used sparingly. Alcohol may be used on spots which are only solvent in alcohol.

Concrete, if properly laid, is very durable but difficult to keep clean; it requires thorough scrubbing and rinsing. A diluted floor seal should be used. Terrazzo, used frequently in entrances and corridors, is highly resistant to wear but requires good care as the substance, made of marble chips and cement, is porous. If harsh cleaning agents, acids and alkalies are used, they penetrate the pores and lead to deterioration. An excellent cleaning job can be done by mopping with a soap solution, then shaking a mildly abrasive powder on the wet floors and machine-scrubbing with steel wool, rinsing, and mopping with clean mops. Water wax may then be used but care must be exercised to avoid a slippery condition.

PAINTING AND COLORS

Exterior wood and metal surfaces require frequent painting to prevent deterioration. Metal paints may now be had that are highly resistant to rust. Wood surfaces need two well brushed coats of paint in addition to a filler coat. While interior surfaces require less frequent painting, they will usually require cleaning or washing within a period of four to five years under normal conditions. In areas of excessive smoke, washing may be required more frequently. Since paint often deteriorates after one or two washings, some school buildings are alternately washed and painted. Colors should be selected only after careful study of the color combinations most appropriate for various exposures. Except for ceilings, uniform colors in all classrooms and on all its walls or in all corridors should be avoided.

Ceilings painted a flat white, when clean, should reflect 85 per cent of the light. Cases have been known where painting a drab ceiling a flat white has improved the lighting at seats farthest from the window side by nearly 100 per cent. Proper choice of paint or tile colors will serve not only to improve light conditions, but will add greatly to the attractiveness of an interior, and also to the feeling of comfort. Warm colors such as yellows and tans are frequently used in rooms receiving little or no sunlight. Light pastel shades of green, blue, and aquamarines tend to have a pleasing effect, especially in rooms that receive sunlight. To avoid glare, flat paints should always be used above eye level. Other factors which contribute to classroom lighting are: floors in natural wood color, or light shades of tan in composition floors; light finishes on furniture and cabinets; and chalkboards and bulletin boards of light color. If blackboards are used, some means of covering them with lighter colored material will contribute to the lighting condition of the room.

BREAKAGE

No small amount of maintenance trouble arises from excessive use of glass in wall construction common today. The greatest amount of breakage in many communities results from sheer vandalism. Large amounts of glass surface, as in curtain-wall and glass-block construction, while admitting generous amounts of sunlight, provide inviting targets for prospective vandals. Breakage resulting accidentally from batted and thrown balls or other causes may be reduced if windows facing play areas are screened. Gymnasium lights should also be screened. If full length glass doors are used in corridors, entrances or elsewhere, the presence of the glass should be indicated by a distinctive color stripe across the door. This will reduce the chances of persons walking directly into the glass.

PRINCIPLES OF ECONOMY

Throughout this chapter suggestions have been made on economies in site selection, building construction, maintenance, and operation. Much more could be added on this very important topic. Because of space limitation, however, the reader is referred to a publication of the National Council on Schoolhouse Construction entitled 13 Principles of Economy in School Plant Planning and Construction.

SELECTION OF THE ARCHITECT

A very important decision to be made in connection with the building of a school is the choice of the architect. In fact, the architect becomes a key person in any such undertaking. For this reason high standards should be set for his selection. Preferably he or his firm should have specialized in school buildings. Experience in building commercial or industrial structures does not necessarily qualify him as a good school architect, even though his reputation as a designer in other fields may be excellent. Unless he has a good understanding of the many details that enter into the planning of a school building, he will need continual and excessive, time-consuming guidance in matters affecting the functioning of the building as a school.

Among other important considerations in selecting an architect or an architectural firm are the following. (1) What engineering service can be provided to insure that the building will be structurally safe and sound? (2) Will the necessary inspection service be provided? There should be no loopholes for shoddy workmanship or deliberate omissions of items called for in the plans and specifications. (3) What is the size of the architectural staff and the capacity for turning out high grade plans and specifications within a reasonable length of time? A period of two months or more is usually required after the architect has been furnished with the educational specifications, and the preliminary sketches have been approved. The time required will vary somewhat with the size of the building. (4) What is the architect's reputation for building within the original estimate of the cost? Should the building cost 25–50 per cent more than the preliminary estimates, as sometimes happens, a parish may find itself in financial difficulty. (5) Is the architect open-minded to suggestions from the educational authorities, in connection with the preparation of plans; i.e., is he willing to correct obvious faults in design and to accept suggestions for improvement in his proposed design of the various features of the building? (6) Does he have an adequate financial rating?

Before the final choice is made, those responsible should visit other schools which the architect has designed and should consult with the local authorities as to their satisfaction with the work done by the architect. In case actual visitation is impractical, the plans and specifications used should be studied, preferably under the guidance of an educational consultant familiar with school building problems.

PREPARATION OF EDUCATIONAL SPECIFICATIONS

No architect can be expected to design the kind of building desired unless he is furnished with a set of educational requirements in considerable detail. Such matters as the number of rooms of each kind to be included, their locations, arrangements, and size, the amount and location of the chalk and bulletin boards in each, the provision for clothing storage, built-in equipment, if any, the provisions for various services to be made, and any other provisions desired, should be indicated in considerable detail. Unless the local school authorities have had recent experience in preparing the list of educational needs, they will do well to visit other recently constructed schools or engage an educational consultant to assist and guide them in this undertaking.

ARCHITECTURAL PLANS AND SPECIFICATIONS

Upon receipt of the educational requirements the architect usually proceeds to draw preliminary floor plans and sketches, so that the school authorities may judge as to its suitability from the standpoint of function, location, and appearance. These sketches require very careful examination and study. If changes are necessary, this is the time to indicate the particular items that will require altering before working drawings are prepared or contracts awarded. After making the changes indicated, a revised set of preliminary plans should be submitted by the architect. The process should be repeated, if necessary, until the plans are entirely satisfactory to and approved by the school authorities.

Unless the school authorities are experienced in the field of school buildings, they may find it advisable to bring in consultants at various stages of the planning. Plans and specifications for a cafeteria or a gymnasium, for example, should be carefully scrutinized by persons proficient to advise the architect on many details in these areas. This principle applies to all aspects of the building. A good architect is usually highly appreciative of such assistance, in order that together he and the school authorities may best meet the needs of the community. A detailed set of completed plans may involve fifty or more sheets of drawings, while the specifications may cover several hundred pages of typewritten material. The plans and specifications must cover every bit of material and every detail of construction used in the construction or the remodeling of a building. In good planning, no aspect of the building is left to the judgment of the contractors. The detailed plans and specifications indicate to the architect, contractors, and the inspector, as well as to owners, just what is to be done and how.

BIDS AND CONTRACTS

As plans and specifications are completed and approved, provisions will need to be made for the taking of bids and the awarding of contracts. In fact, preliminary steps to discover competent bidders should be taken well in advance. Steps should be taken to avoid bidding by incompetent would-be contractors. Those guilty of shoddy performances, poor workmanship, failure to follow specifications, using materials of an inferior grade, inability to complete projects undertaken, or to meet payrolls in the past should be eliminated at the outset. Reliance is usually placed upon the architect for recommending approval or disapproval of a would-be bidder's qualifications. The practice of requiring contractors to establish their qualifications in advance is not only conducive to better original construction but serves to minimize later maintenance. It also serves to reduce the possibilities of legal entanglements likely to result if a contract is awarded to an incompetent bidder.

Some school systems follow a practice of taking separate bids on various portions of the total project, such as excavation and concrete work, carpentry, masonry work, heating and ventilating, electrical work, artificial lighting, glazing, painting, plastering, plumbing, tile work, sheet metal work and others. If the sum of the low bids for each of the separate divisions is lower than the bid of any general contractor, separate contracts are usually awarded to the low bidders in each division. This serves to pinpoint the responsibility for each aspect of the job. Should a general contractor's bid be lower than the combined low bids for the various divisions, he may be required to indicate the various qualified subcontractors to whom he expects to assign the various divisions of the work to be performed.

A common practice is to require that bidders accompany their bid with a certified check or bond equal to a fixed percentage of the estimated cost of the work to be done. This may represent as much as 15 per cent or more of the estimated cost. When a contract is awarded, bonds and checks submitted by unsuccessful bidders are promptly returned, while those of the successful bidder are retained as a guarantee that the work will be done in accordance with the plans and specifications.

Payments are commonly made on the basis of the architect's estimate of the percentage of the work completed at a given date, and evidence that workmen have been paid and materials paid for. To withhold all payments until the work is completed results in a severe hardship on the contractor, who is then required to have a much larger bank account or credit rating. If so, he will of necessity submit a higher bid than would otherwise be the case. The effect will be to increase the total cost of the building.

SOME SELECTED REFERENCES

Books

American Association of School Administrators.
    American School Buildings, Twenty-seventh Yearbook (Washington, D. C., 1949).
    Common Sense in School Lighting (Washington, D. C., 1956).
    Planning America's School Buildings (Washington, D. C., 1960).
American Association of School Administrators and National School Public Relations Association, *How Much Should a School Cost?* (Washington, D. C., 1957).
American Society of Heating and Air Conditioning Engineers, *Heating, Ventilating, Air-Conditioning Guide* (New York, 1958).
Caudill, William W., *Toward Better School Design* (New York: F. W. Dodge Corp., 1954).
Englehardt, N. L.; Englehardt, N. L. Jr.; and Leggett, Stanton, *Planning Elementary School Buildings* (New York: F. W. Dodge Corp., 1953).
Herrick, John H., McLeary, Ralph D., Clapp, Wilfred F., and Bogner, Walter F., *From School Program to School Plant* (New York: Henry Holt & Co., 1956).

MacConnell, James D., *Planning for School Buildings* (New York: Prentice-Hall, Inc., 1957).

McLeary, R. D., *Guide for Evaluating School Buildings*, New England School Development Council (Cambridge, Mass., 1949).

McQuade, Walter, *Schoolhouse* (New York: Simon and Schuster, 1959).

National Council on Schoolhouse Construction, *Guide for Planning School Plants*, 1958. *Elementary School Plant Planning*, 1958.

13 *Principles of Economy in School Plant Planning and Construction* (Nashville, Tenn.: George Peabody College, 1955).

National Fire Protective Association, *Building Exit Codes* (Boston, 1952).

mentary School Buildings (Washington, D. C., 1959).

National Fire Protective Association, *Building Exit Codes* (Boston, 1952).

Perkins, Lawrence B., *Work Place for Learning* (New York: Reinhold Publishing Corp., 1957).

Strevell, W. H., and Burke, Arvid J., *Administration of the School Building Program* (New York: McGraw-Hill, 1959).

Sumption, Merle R., and Landes, Jack L., *Planning Functional School Buildings* (New York: Harper & Bros., 1957).

Taylor, J. L., *Planning and Designing the Multipurpose Room in Elementary Schools*, Office of Education Special Publication No. 3 (Washington, D. C.: Govt. Printing Office, 1954).

Viles, N. E., *School Buildings: Remodelling, Rehabilitation, Modernization and Repairs*, U. S. Office of Education, 1950, No. 17 (Washington, D. C.: Gov't. Printing Office, 1954).

Periodicals

The American School Board Journal (Milwaukee, Wis.: The Bruce Publishing Company).

Catholic Management Journal (Milwaukee, Wis.: The Bruce Publishing Company).

Catholic Property Administration (Greenwich, Conn.: The Administration Publishing Co.).

The Nation's Schools (Chicago, Ill.: 919 N. Michigan Avenue).

Overview (New York: 470 Park Avenue, South, Zone 16).

School Management (Greenwich, Conn.: School Management Magazines, Inc.).

CHAPTER XVIII

THE PRINCIPAL STUDIES HERSELF
John P. Treacy, Ph.D.

AN OFT-QUOTED statement in the field of administration is that the principal should exemplify in her own work the same educational principles she expects to see exemplified in the work of her teachers. For example, the principal wants her teachers to plan their work carefully; then, the principal should plan her work carefully. The principal expects the teachers to base their teaching on carefully thought out objectives; then, the principal should see that her work reflects a careful study of objectives — and so on for other educational principles.

In general, principals probably do "practice what they preach" fairly well. A possible exception is in the area of self-evaluation and self-improvement. As indicated in previous chapters, the in-service growth of teachers is assumed if they are to keep professionally alert. This growth should begin with an honest self-appraisal by the teachers. But is it also assumed that there should be in-service growth of the principal? Should not she regularly and honestly analyze her professional assets and liabilities and make whatever changes seem to be indicated?

If a principal does not analyze rigorously her professional activities, there probably are some good reasons. Perhaps she is overloaded with work — many principals are. Perhaps immediate problems of her teachers distract her from long range thinking regarding herself. Perhaps her being relatively more capable and mature than those about her keeps her from even considering her own professional growth. Whatever the reasons, a principal who does not systematically take stock of her professional assets and liabilities, and does not plan a program of self-improvement based on this analysis, is missing an opportunity for greater service to her school, and for the personal satisfaction that comes from knowing that one is growing professionally.

If a principal is to evaluate herself, she must do it according to certain criteria, certain standards, certain points against which she may compare herself. The check lists presented in Chapter V, by which a principal may analyze her effectiveness in various aspects of her job, are excellent. They are, however, too detailed for use in making a general evaluation of a principal's professional status. Therefore, more comprehensive questions are presented here, against which a principal may compare her own qualities, concepts, and procedures. It is suggested that occasionally the Sister Principal might appraise herself in terms of such criteria, and take whatever steps are indicated by this analysis.

Some of these questions for self-evaluation may seem to apply to the school as a whole rather than to the principal. The assumption here is that the principal, at least partially, is responsible for what goes on in her school, and should look upon any strength or weakness here as being related to her own effectiveness.

Rate yourself "A" for "superior"; "B" for "very satisfactory"; "C" for "satisfactory"; "D" for "not satisfactory"; "E" for "unsatisfactory"; and "O" for "does not apply." If you have rated yourself low in some area, jot down reasons why this situation exists, and how you plan to improve it.

MY PHILOSOPHY OF EDUCATION

Have I a sound philosophy of education upon which to base all teaching and administration? Do I encourage the study of educational philosophy among my teachers? Do I make available suitable reading materials in this area? Do I alert teachers to common dangers in contemporary philosophy of education? Do I do a reasonable amount of reading which would expand my vision regarding Catholic education in general, and administration and supervision in particular? Do I relate all of my work as a principal to sound objectives of education? Do I encourage my teachers to think of the basic issues and principles behind what they do in the classroom?
My self-evaluation:

MY UNDERSTANDING OF CHILDREN

Is education in our school built upon a sound concept of the nature of the child? Do teachers and I continuously strive to understand children better, at all ages? Do we help parents to understand children?
My self-evaluation:

MY RELATIONSHIPS WITH OTHERS IN CATHOLIC EDUCATION

Do I have a clear picture of where the Catholic elementary principal fits into the diocesan organization? Do I understand my relationship to our pupils, to my teachers, to my pastor, to my Mother Superior, to our supervisors, to my Diocesan Superintendent, to our Diocesan Board, to the

Bishop? If conflicts arise in these relationships, do I resolve the differences by going through the right channels?
My self-evaluation:

MY CONCEPT OF THE PRINCIPALSHIP AS A PROFESSION

Do I have clear ideas regarding what a principal's basic functions are? Have I analyzed the principal's work into logical groups of activities? Do I think of my job as principal merely in terms of keeping the school running smoothly? Or in terms of the vast possibilities for educational leadership which I have? Do I strive to achieve a more professional interpretation of the principal's function? Do I associate myself with professional organizations and activities designed to improve the status of the elementary principal?
My self-evaluation:

MY PLANNING

Do I adequately plan my work as principal? Do I have long-range and short-range plans? Where the work of staff members is involved, do I enlist their co-operation in setting up policies, plans, and procedures? Do I realize that one of the best means of developing interest in an activity is to allow teachers to participate in its planning? Do I appreciate the contribution which my staff members can make to over-all plans for our school?
My self-evaluation:

MY DISTRIBUTION OF TIME

Do I distribute my time wisely among the various aspects of my work: teaching, supervision, administration, clerical work, etc.? Or, do I allow time to be absorbed by immediate routine problems, some of which could be avoided or delegated to others? Do I have a time schedule which is respected by pupils, teachers, parents, and by me?
My self-evaluation:

CLERICAL DUTIES

Do clerical duties occupy too much of my time? If so, have I taken adequate steps to relieve the situation? Is my office so arranged as to facilitate efficiency in clerical work?
My self-evaluation:

LAY TEACHERS IN OUR SCHOOL

Do I accept the fact that lay teachers are becoming an essential part of Catholic elementary education? Does my school have defensible policies and procedures regarding such matters as recruitment, salary, tenure, sick leave,

and retirement plans? Are lay faculty members regarded as essential members of our staff or as outsiders "filling in" during an emergency?
My self-evaluation:

RAISING TEACHING STANDARDS

Do I have a clear concept of the teacher's role? Of what good teaching is? Do I help my teachers to establish sound criteria of teaching success? Do I create a professional atmosphere which is conducive to improvement in teaching? Do I analyze individual staff members for ways in which their teaching may be improved? Do I try to help staff members to overcome weaknesses which may be interfering with their optimum effectiveness? Do I study individual staff members for special strengths, and try to give opportunities in the school program for the expression of these strengths? Have I, with the co-operation of my teachers, planned definite activities and approaches for the improvement of our teaching? Do I do all in my power to surround the staff with working conditions which are conducive to teaching effectiveness?
My self-evaluation:

THE SCHOOL AND THE COMMUNITY

Do I help my teachers to look upon each parish and each school community as unique? Do I assume adequate leadership in ascertaining significant information regarding the parish? Does our teaching reflect a recognition of the unique characteristics of our local community?
My self-evaluation:

SCHOOL-COMMUNITY RELATIONS

Am I "public relations minded"? Do I realize that there is only so much a school can do unless it has the backing of parents and other adults? Do our public relations activities just "happen," or is there a planned program for acquainting adults in the community with the work of the school, and for enlisting co-operation? Do I show adequate leadership in making the school a part of the community, rather than an isolated institution within it? Do I clearly communicate policies and procedures to pupils, teachers, parents, and others? Do I frequently check on how well ideas have been communicated?
My self-evaluation:

PUPIL EVALUATION

Is there in our school a long-range plan for appraising pupils? For evaluating achievement? Have we an in-service plan for acquainting teachers with the fundamentals of measurement? Has our evaluation program a nice

balance between teacher made and standardized tests? Do we strive to measure *all* of the objectives of education, even though some educational outcomes are difficult to measure objectively? Are test results used? If not, do I try to have them used?
My self-evaluation:

GRADES AND REPORTS

Is our marking system based on all of the objectives of Catholic education, or just on the academic aspects? Does it relate pupil's progress to the pupil's ability to learn? Does it show a pupil's progress toward goals, as well as where he is now? Do parents understand our marking system?
My self-evaluation:

PUPIL RECORDS

Do our records contain the information needed by teachers and others for effective teaching and guidance of each pupil? Are our records so arranged as to give a longitudinal picture of pupil progress? Do our records require a minimum of time? Have I a plan for overcoming any weaknesses our records may have?
My self-evaluation:

SPECIAL SERVICES

Does our school do its part in meeting *all* pupil needs (academic, health, emotional, spiritual, etc.)? Are there definite procedures for meeting the less tangible pupil needs? Are parents helped to see the respective responsibilities of the home and the school in these matters?
My self-evaluation:

THE SCHOOL PLANT

Have I taken advantage of opportunities to know what school building standards should be? Do I know how my building rates in terms of accepted standards? Do I make the best use of the facilities I have? Do I acquaint the responsible authorities with the limitations of our school? Is building maintenance looked upon as something anyone can do, or as something for which special training is needed? If a new school building is contemplated, have I considered the preliminary plans for their educational suitability?
My self-evaluation:

MY OWN PROFESSIONAL GROWTH

Do I realize the possibilities and need for my own professional growth? Do I have a plan for this growth — through self-evaluation, professional reading, attendance at meetings, conferences with others, and the like? Do

I keep abreast of the Sister-Formation movement, and co-operate in actualizing the objectives of this group? Does my school have a professional library which contains references on the most promising movements in education in general, and in Catholic education in particular?
My self-evaluation:

INDEX

Absence, teacher, 129 ff; teacher, causes of, 130

Achievement tests, 345 ff; formal, 348 ff; informal, 346 ff

Administration, effective, guidelines for, 56 ff; functions of theory in, 57 ff; guidelines for principal, 60 ff; phases of, 60; principal's duties in, 81; present weaknesses in elementary, 5; self-evaluation checklist, 96 f; theory of, 56 ff

Administrative duties, versus clerical work, 100 f

Administrative leadership, effects of, 8

Administrative planning, basis of, 61 f; importance of, 61; pitfalls in, 64; of principal, 63 ff

Adviser, Sister, 255 ff

Advisory personnel, in diocesan school system, 46 ff

Advisory program, for new teachers, 253 ff

Agenda, for faculty meetings, 214

Aides, teacher, 164 ff

Archdiocesan, see Diocesan

Architect, school, 462 f

Aristotle, on man's quasi infinite powers, 13; on need for doing, 14

Assembly rooms, 449

Auditorium, 449

Augustine, St., man's end, 19

Authority, delegation of, 69 f, 89 f; line of, in diocesan school system, 28 f; position of principal, 42

Baltimore, Third Plenary Council of, decree for establishing Catholic schools, 6, 25

Basic instruction, adequate, 20 f

Being, and knowing, 18 f

Bids and contracts, 464 f

Bishop, head of diocesan school system, 29 f; relationship to Mother Superior, 35; relationship to pastor, 38; relationship to superintendent, 30 f

Board of Education, see Diocesan School Advisory Board; Diocesan superintendent

Browne, Rev. Henry J., principal-pastor relationships, 6 f

Building, school, see School building

Bulletins, faculty, 170 f; parents', 327; of principal, and faculty meeting, 216

Bus, school, 403 ff

Cafeteria, and health program, 401 ff; school, 450 f

Catholic education, basic problem in, 3

Catholics, "borderline," 298; "fallen away," 298 f; "ideal," 298; "ordinary," 298; and religious practice, 295 ff

Catholic schools, function of, 25; reasons for, 25; see also Parochial school

Catholic school system, growth of, 25

"Charts," and spiritual growth, 357

Child, dignity of, 10 f; principal agent in learning, 19

Christian Education of Youth, 186

Classroom observation, 219 ff; difficulties of, 219; need for, 219 f; principal's preparation for, 220 ff; principal's procedure during, 225 f; principal's record of, 226 ff; principal's schedule for, 222 f; results of, 221; teachers' reactions to, 218 f; teaching principal and, 222 ff

Classrooms, 444 ff

Class size, problems of, 172 ff

Clerical work, 100 f; of the principal, 81; versus administration, 100 f; see also Filing; School files; School office

Clerical workers, guide for hiring, 87; need for, 87 f; tasks assigned to, 88

Clerk, school, 423 ff

Clothing storage, 446 f

Communication, devices for principal, 72; effective, 72 f; three kinds of, 72 ff

Community, definition of, 278 ff; learning about, 280 ff; and parish school, 277 ff; religious, and the diocese, 34 ff

Community-relations program, 310 ff; see also School-community relations

Community supervisor, personality of, 52 f; representative of Mother Superior, 52; role of, 51 ff

Competency, guidance as a teacher competency, 197 ff; teachers', 191 ff; see also Teacher competency

Conference, group, 228 ff; individual, 230 f; in orientation program, 257 f; with parents, 328 ff

Confraternity of Christian Doctrine, 303

Construction, school, 441 f

Contracts (teacher), annual, 134; continuing, 134 f; elements of a good, 138; lay

473